Eleventh Edition

Psychology
Applied *to* Work®

An Introduction
to Industrial and
Organizational
Psychology

Paul M. Muchinsky
Satoris S. Culbertson

Hypergraphic Press

Hypergraphic Press

Psychology Applied to Work®: An Introduction to Industrial and Organizational Psychology, **Eleventh Edition**

Paul M. Muchinsky   Satoris S. Culbertson

Production Service: Newgen—Austin
Compositor: Newgen—Austin
Interior Design: Newgen—Austin
Interior Design Image: Shutterstock

Cover Design: Michael Lane
Cover Image: Shutterstock
Printer: Signature Book Printing
Indexer: Wendy Allex

Hypergraphic Press, Inc.
P.O. Box 743
Summerfield, NC 27358

For permission to use material from this text, submit a request to *info@hypergraphicpress.com.*

Printed in the United States of America
1 2 3 4 5 6 21 20 19 18 17 16

Library of Congress Control Number: 2014951899

ISBN: 978-0-974-93450-1

To the Next Muchinsky Generation
Hillary, Eric, Nathan, Michael, Ellie, and Daphne

To My Boys
Matthew and Ryan Culbertson

About the Authors

Paul M. Muchinsky was born and raised in Connecticut. He received his B.A. degree in psychology from Gettysburg College, his M.S. degree in psychology from Kansas State University, and his Ph.D. degree in industrial/organizational psychology from Purdue University. He was a faculty member of Iowa State University for twenty years. In 1993 he was appointed the Joseph M. Bryan Distinguished Professor of Business at The University of North Carolina at Greensboro. In 2004 Dr. Muchinsky was the inaugural recipient of the Distinguished Teaching Contribution Award from the Society for Industrial and Organizational Psychology for his outstanding educational contributions to the field. In 2008 Dr. Muchinsky was awarded the honorary Doctor of Science (D.Sc.) degree from Gettysburg College. He is a Fellow of four divisions of the American Psychological Association: the Society for Industrial and Organizational Psychology; the Society for the Teaching of Psychology; the Society of Consulting Psychology; and the Society of Counseling Psychology. He is a Diplomate of the American Board of Professional Psychology (in industrial/organizational psychology). Many of the cases and examples of concepts presented in this book come directly from his professional experiences. When not engaged as an I/O psychologist, Dr. Muchinsky fantasizes about playing baseball for the New York Yankees. He can be reached at pmuchinsky@hypergraphicpress.com.

Satoris "Tori" Culbertson was born and raised in the Midwest, the proud daughter of two enlisted members of the United States Air Force. She earned her B.S. degree in psychology and public relations from the University of Central Missouri, her M.S. degree in industrial and organizational (I/O) psychology from Missouri State University, and her Ph.D. in I/O psychology from Texas A&M University. At the end of her graduate studies, she worked as a consultant in the Chicago branch of a global leadership solutions consulting firm. She then transitioned back into academia, working for a year at the University of Wisconsin - River Falls before joining the faculty in the Department of Psychological Sciences at Kansas State University. There she received the College of Arts and Sciences William L. Stamey Teaching Award in 2012. She is currently in the Department of Management in the College of Business Administration at Kansas State University. Her main research interests include the employment interview, performance appraisal and feedback, work-family issues, and judgment and decision making, areas in which she has authored and coauthored numerous journal articles and chapters in edited volumes. Dr. Culbertson is an active member of the Society for Industrial and Organizational Psychology. When not engaged in I/O psychology, Dr. Culbertson enjoys spending time with her husband, Jimmy, and two children, Matthew and Ryan (often relating non-I/O psychology topics to I/O psychology, much to their dismay). Tori can be reached at sculbertson@hypergraphicpress.com.

Brief Contents

Contents

Chapter 8   ## Organizations and Organizational Change   **237**

Chapter 9   ## Teams and Teamwork   **272**

Chapter 10   ## Affect, Attitudes, and Behavior at Work   **302**

Preface

About 35 years ago I decided to write a textbook on I/O psychology. My goal was to write a book that was high in quality but written for readers who were new to the field. I was told my goal was unattainable: only upper level books were of high quality. I was determined to prove I could do it. The title of the book, *Psychology Applied to Work*®, was selected because that is what I/O psychology is—psychology applied to work. I wanted the book to have a research basis. The book would be the story of I/O psychology as told through the many voices of people who contributed to it. But in addition, I wanted the book to bring I/O psychology to life. I included a special feature called *Field Notes* that animated the research findings. Over the years I added two additional features, *Cross-Cultural I/O Psychology* and *I/O Psychology and the Economy*. Each feature was added to capture the continuously changing nature of work. Three and one-half decades, ten editions, and multiple foreign language translations later, I am delighted that my book has been read by hundreds of thousands of students. In January 2014 the U.S. Department of Labor rated I/O psychology as being the fastest growing occupation over the next twenty years. I hope my book has contributed to the growing awareness of I/O psychology's value to society.

I/O psychology is growing so rapidly I felt it would now take two authors to chronicle all the current advancements in the field. I wanted a co-author who possessed the same passion for I/O psychology and both the skill and commitment to its narration. I was privileged to have Dr. Satoris Culbertson of Kansas State University join me in presenting the 11th edition of *Psychology Applied to Work*®. Tori brings a depth of knowledge of the field and keen insight into writing. Together we crafted this edition, although the long-standing *Field Notes* remain my own.

Paul M. Muchinsky

I discovered and fell in love with I/O psychology my last semester of college. I stumbled upon a course that filled a gap in my schedule. The appeal of I/O psychology for me was and continues to be the direct application that it has for individuals in their lives. Furthermore, I find the fact that every topic has relevance for so many people across the globe both exciting and energizing. It is for these reasons that I am thrilled to be joining Paul in telling the story of I/O psychology. My hope is that, by partnering with Paul on the 11th edition of *Psychology Applied to Work*®, I can generate some of the same enthusiasm that I have for the field to others.

In this latest edition, I have added a new feature called *Social Media and I/O Psychology* that discusses the role of social media within the workplace. Social media have revolutionized the ways in which people communicate with one another. As information from a multitude of sources is more readily available, there are clear implications for the world of work. These features explore some of the ways in which various topics within I/O psychology have been impacted by the advent of social media. My hope is that curiosity becomes piqued and discussions ensue, not only with regard to this new feature but for the content within this 11th edition as a whole.

Satoris S. Culbertson

The chapter-by-chapter revisions for the 11th edition include the following:

- **Chapter 1.** A new major section on humanitarian work psychology. The U.S. Department of Labor report listing I/O psychology as the fastest growing occupation in the United States over the next twenty years. Updates in the timeline of major world events and I/O psychology, the growth in I/O psychology, and salaries paid in the field.

- **Chapter 2.** New major sections on data mining, organizational neuroscience, and determining causality in research. Significant updates on qualitative research and meta-analysis.

- **Chapter 3.** Updates on work analysis, counterproductive work behavior, emotional labor, and adaptive behavior.

- **Chapter 4.** New sections on faking in personality assessment, the dark triad personality, and testing in retrospect. Updates on high-stakes testing, situational judgment tests, and assessment centers.

- **Chapter 5.** New major section on organizational strategy and staffing. Significant new material on affirmative action, adverse impact, diversity, and the diversity-validity dilemma. Updates on EEOC statistics on unfair discrimination by protected group status, recruitment, and validity generalization.

- **Chapter 6.** New major sections on assessing training needs and active learning approaches. New material on self-regulatory training. Significant updates on diversity training and mentoring.

- **Chapter 7.** New major sections on the performance management process, purposes of performance management systems, and reactions to performance management systems. Significant new material on giving and seeking feedback as well as typical reactions to feedback. Updates on rater errors and biases, relative and absolute rating systems, and rater training and motivation.

- **Chapter 8.** Major new section on person-organization fit. Significant new material on organizational culture, vertical versus horizontal downsizing, corporate volunteerism, and other manifestations of corporate social responsibility.

- **Chapter 9.** New major sections on the defining characteristics of work teams and the team life cycle. Significant new material on the processes within teams that permit them to function smoothly and efficiently, including transition, action, and interpersonal processes.

- **Chapter 10.** Major new section on the role of affect, moods, and emotions in the workplace. Significant updates on work commitment and employee engagement. New material on the honeymoon-hangover effect relating to job satisfaction. Updates on workplace bullying and organizational politics.

- **Chapter 11.** Major new sections on workplace stress and the stigma of dirty work. Significant new material on psychological capital, work-family enrichment, and work-family interventions. Updates on work-family conflict, alcohol and drug abuse in the workplace, and the psychological effects of unemployment.

- **Chapter 12**. New major section on the impact of time on work motivation. New sections on four theories of motivation: biological-based, flow, self-determination, and equity theories. Updates to goal-setting theory and the synthesis of work motivation theories.

- **Chapter 13**. New major sections on the dark side of leadership and leadership in teams. New sections on the contingency approach to leadership, full-range leadership theory, authentic leadership, and servant leadership. Significant updates to leader-member exchange theory.

- **Chapter 14**. Major new section on the future of labor unions. Significant new material on the formation of a union, public sector strikes, the cost/value of unionized labor, commitment to the collective bargaining process, and psychology and labor relations.

We have four special features in every chapter: *Field Notes, Cross-Cultural I/O Psychology, I/O Psychology and the Economy*, and *Social Media and I/O Psychology*. The *Social Media and I/O Psychology* section is new to this edition. Some of the other features have been changed or updated since the previous edition. Collectively they offer exciting new insights into how the field of I/O psychology is evolving in response to social changes. We believe you will be very satisfied with the recency, comprehensiveness, and readability of this edition of *Psychology Applied to Work*®. We welcome your feedback.

We both are indebted to several people for their support in our writing this book. I (PMM) would like to thank three people in particular. I am extremely grateful to the Mom half of the Mom-and-Pop company that is Hypergraphic Press, Inc., Lynn Southard. Lynn brings order to chaos, much of which I create. Lynn has typed six of the previous editions of *Psychology Applied to Work*®. Her skill with a computer is equaled by her attention to detail. Mary Sue Hawkins taught me about hind legs and the need for two mules to always pull in the same direction. I am especially grateful for her daughter. Finally, to my lovely wife, Kay, who is as beautiful inside as outside. You love me on days when the words flow and on days when they don't. I love you, too.

I (SSC) would like to thank my parents and grandmother — Richard and Renee Youngcourt and Mary Bruneau — for crafting me into the person I am today. Every day I find myself saying and doing things that are clear indicators that I'm turning into each one of you. And I'm now mature and smart enough to embrace it rather than run from it. I am also grateful to my graduate school advisors — Bob Jones, Bob Pritchard, and Stephanie Payne — whose guidance helped me not only be a better scholar, but a better person. For that, I'll be forever thankful. Last but certainly not least, I'm thankful for my husband, Jimmy Culbertson, for reminding me what is really important in life. You'll never know how much your unparalleled love and support has meant to me. I love you, and I owe you a steak dinner.

Ancillaries for Instructors and Students

For Instructors

Instructor's Manual with Test Bank.   The *Instructor's Manual with Test Bank* is electronically downloadable and is available to every registered instructor. It includes case studies, chapter outlines, learning objectives, test items (true/false, multiple choice, short answer, and essay), instructional tips, and web links. PowerPoint slides are provided for each chapter that summarize the main points of the text, the content of which can be modified for individual instructor customization. The instructor should register online at www.PsychologyAppliedtoWork.com to access the *Instructor's Manual with Test Bank*.

For Students

Student Study Guide.   The *Student Study Guide* is electronically downloadable and is available at no cost to students. Its purpose is to provide additional assistance in understanding industrial/organizational psychology. The free *Student Study Guide* can be accessed at www.PsychologyAppliedtoWork.com.

The Historical Background of I/O Psychology

Learning Objectives

- Explain how I/O psychology relates to the profession of psychology as a whole.
- Be able to identify the major fields of I/O psychology.
- Understand how and why psychologists are licensed.
- Learn the history of I/O psychology, including major people, events, and eras.
- Give the reasons for cross-cultural interest in I/O psychology.
- Understand the basis of humanitarian work psychology.

Psychology is defined as the scientific study of thinking and behavior. It is a science because psychologists use the same rigorous methods of research found in other areas of scientific investigation. Some of their research is more biological in nature (such as the effects of brain lesions on a rat's food consumption); other research is more social in nature (such as identifying the factors that lead to bystander apathy). Because psychology covers such a broad spectrum of content areas, it is difficult to have a clear and accurate image of what a psychologist does. Many people think that every psychologist "is a shrink," "has a black couch," "likes to discover what makes people tick," and so on. In fact, these descriptions usually refer to the specialty of clinical psychology—the diagnosis and treatment of mental illness or abnormal behavior. Most psychologists do not treat mental disorders, nor do they practice psychotherapy. In reality, psychologists are a very diversified lot with many specialized interests.

Many psychologists are united professionally through membership in the American Psychological Association (APA), founded in 1892. As of 2014, the APA had more than 130,000 members. The broad diversity of interests among psychologists is reflected by the fact that the APA has 54 divisions representing special-interest subgroups. There are not really so many different specialty areas of psychology, just many fields in which the same basic psychological principles are applied. Although some APA members have no divisional affiliation, others belong to more than one. The APA publishes many journals—vehicles through which psychologists can communicate their research findings to other scholars. The APA also holds regional and national conventions, sets standards for graduate training in certain areas of psychology (that is, clinical, counseling, and school), develops and enforces a code of professional ethics, and helps psychologists find employment. In 1988, the Association for Psychological Science (APS) was founded in part because the membership and emphasis of the APA had shifted significantly toward the healthcare practice areas of psychology. The purpose of the APS is to advance the discipline of psychology primarily from a scientific perspective. Most of its members are academic psychologists.

Industrial/Organizational Psychology

Society for Industrial and Organizational Psychology (SIOP) The professional organization that represents I/O psychologists in the United States.

One of the specialty areas of psychology is industrial/organizational (I/O) psychology (represented by Division 14 of the APA, the **Society for Industrial and Organizational Psychology**, or **SIOP**). In 2014, SIOP had about 8,000 professional members (approximately 50% male and 50% female). The percentage of women entering the field has greatly accelerated over the past decade. SIOP is the primary professional organization for I/O psychologists in the United States. SIOP's website, *www.siop.org*, provides information about careers in I/O psychology. In other countries what we call *I/O psychology* has other names. In the United Kingdom it is often referred to as *occupational psychology*, in many European countries as *work and organizational psychology*, and in South Africa *industrial psychology*. Over the past decade there has been a large upsurge in the globalization of interest in I/O psychology. Kraut (2010) reported that international membership in SIOP has doubled since the year 2000, and is now up to 15%. Professional organizations of I/O psychologists around the world include the *European Association of Work and Organizational Psychology*, the *Japanese Association of Industrial/Organizational Psychology*, and in Australia the *College of Organisational*

Psychology. As society has witnessed the globalization of business, I/O psychology has also been recognized as a valuable resource throughout the world. Of the 20 fastest growing jobs between 2012–2022, the U.S. Department of Labor (2014) ranked I/O psychology first, with a projected growth rate of 53%. SIOP has entered into an alliance with other international I/O organizations as a way to achieve a stronger voice on matters of mutual professional interest (Griffith & Wang, 2010). It is widely accepted that the profession is now in the "Global I/O" era.

Approximately 6% of all psychologists work in the I/O area. Our relatively small representation in the total population of psychologists probably explains why some people are unaware of the I/O area. As noted by Campbell (2007), the various applications of psychology are often directed toward enhancing the welfare of an individual or an institution (as a school or business organization). Clinical psychology, for example, is directed toward enhancing the lives of individuals. I/O psychology strives to enhance both the institution and the individual, but the image of the field is often portrayed as more aligned with institutional welfare.

Until most recently, I/O psychology has long grappled with its image. The general public is not as aware of I/O psychology as, for example, clinical psychology. Various efforts have been made to understand why I/O psychology has a low level of recognition. Payne and Pariyothorn (2007) reported that every year approximately 1.5 million students in the United States enroll in an introductory psychology course. Although students presumably learn about the various areas of psychology in an introductory course, many I/O psychologists believe their area does not get much notice or coverage. Along these lines, Culbertson (2011) reported that only 49% of instructors who taught General Psychology courses reported covering I/O psychology in their classes, and only 16% covered I/O psychology as its own section. Much of psychology is organized around processes (such as sensation and cognition) and explanatory concepts (such as intelligence and personality), not major life activities, like work (Vinchur & Koppes, 2011). Thus there is the perception that I/O psychology is dissimilar to traditional academic psychology. Zickar and Gibby (2007) also commented on how I/O psychology is misperceived, in part because it is associated with ideas about psychology that don't reflect I/O psychology's focus. "One I/O psychologist complained that the mere mention of 'psychology' often evokes images of Freud, couches, and psychoanalysis, not to mention sex therapy" (p. 76). After decades of professional obscurity (especially compared to the healthcare areas of psychology), I/O psychology is currently experiencing growth in visibility and recognized value.

I/O psychology
An area of scientific study and professional practice that addresses psychological concepts and principles in the work world.

As a specialty area, **I/O psychology** has a more restricted definition than psychology as a whole. Many years ago Blum and Naylor (1968) defined it as, "simply the application or extension of psychological facts and principles to the problems concerning human beings operating within the context of business and industry" (p. 4). In broad terms, the I/O psychologist is concerned with behavior in work situations. There are two-sides of I/O psychology: science and practice. I/O psychology is a legitimate field of scientific inquiry, concerned with advancing knowledge about people at work. As in any area of science, I/O psychologists pose questions to guide their investigation and then use scientific methods to obtain answers. Psychologists try to form the results of studies into meaningful patterns that will be useful in explaining behavior and to replicate findings to make generalizations about behavior. In this respect, I/O psychology is an academic discipline. Hulin (2014) commented, "Work psychology has been too long treated as the redheaded stepchild of psychology; we should welcome it into the intellectual research family as a full-time member . . . Work is a core activity of most individuals, and studying it is not simply for the purpose of applications that improve production" (p. 15).

The other side of I/O psychology—the professional side—is concerned with the application of knowledge to solve real problems in the world of work. I/O psychologists can use research findings to hire better employees, reduce absenteeism, improve communication, increase job satisfaction, and solve countless problems in the workplace. Most I/O psychologists feel a sense of kinship with both sides: science and practice. Accordingly, the education of I/O psychologists is founded on the **scientist–practitioner model**, which trains them in both scientific inquiry and practical application. Ployhart (2014) described a scientist-practitioner as "someone who tries to understand real-world phenomena using all of the tools of science, most notably by applying scientific theories and the scientific method" (p. 259).

As I/O psychologists, we are pleased that the results of our research can be put to some practical use. But, by the same token, we are more than technicians—people who go through the motions of finding solutions to problems without knowing why they "work" and what their consequences will be. I/O psychology is more than just a tool for business leaders to use to make their companies more efficient. So the I/O psychologist has a dual existence. Well-trained I/O psychologists realize that an effective application of knowledge can come only from sound knowledge, and they can therefore both contribute to knowledge and apply it.

I/O psychologists work in four main employment settings: universities, consulting firms, business, and government, with universities and consulting firms being the primary employers. Across these four areas, I/O psychologists are unevenly split in their scientist–practitioner orientation. Universities employ more scientists; consulting firms employ more practitioners; business and government have a good mix of both. As of 2012 the annual average income for M.S. graduates in I/O psychology was approximately $84,000, whereas Ph.D. graduates in I/O psychology earned approximately $124,000 (Khanna et al., 2013). However, these annual salaries are heavily influenced by whether the I/O psychologist is employed primarily as an academic or a practitioner. Some members of our profession who work in consulting firms earn more than $1 million annually.

Scientist-practitioner model
A model or framework for education in an academic discipline based on understanding the scientific principles and findings evidenced in the discipline and how they provide the basis for the professional practice.

Fields of I/O Psychology

Like psychology in general, I/O psychology is a diversified science with several subspecialties. The professional activities of I/O psychologists can be grouped into five general fields.

Selection and Placement.   I/O psychologists who work in this field are concerned with developing assessment methods for the selection, placement, and promotion of employees. They are involved in studying jobs and determining to what degree tests can predict performance in those jobs. They are also concerned with the placement of employees and identifying those jobs that are most compatible with an individual's skills and interests.

Training and Development.   This field is concerned with identifying employee skills that need to be enhanced to improve job performance. The areas of training include technical skills enhancement (e.g., computer operations), managerial development programs, and training of all employees to work together effectively. I/O psychologists who work in this field must design ways to determine whether training and development programs have been successful.

Performance Management.   Performance management is the process of enhancing the contributions of the workforce to facilitate attaining the overall goals of the organization. Performance management involves designing ways to assess employee work behavior and provide helpful feedback to improve performance. I/O psychologists in this field are concerned with the accuracy and value of the assessments made of individuals and work teams.

Organizational Effectiveness.   This is the broadest area of professional activity for I/O psychologists. It is concerned with maintaining or improving the quality of the workforce, but also the quality of relationships with customers and suppliers the organization needs for its continued success. Issues pertaining to motivation, leadership, and helping the organization adapt to continuous change are often of central importance.

Quality of Work Life.   I/O psychologists who work in this field are concerned with factors that contribute to a healthy and productive workforce. They may be involved in finding ways to make the conduct of work (i.e., when and where it is performed) more compatible with the personal or family needs of employees. A high-quality work life contributes to greater productivity of the organization and to the emotional health of the individual.

In summary, psychology as a discipline is composed of many specialty areas, one of which is I/O psychology. And I/O psychology consists of several subspecialties. Thus I/O psychology is not really a single discipline; it is a mix of subspecialties bonded together by a concern for people at work. Each of the subspecialties of I/O psychology will be explored to various degrees in this book.

Licensing of Psychologists

Licensure
The process by which a professional practice is regulated by law to ensure quality standards are met to protect the public.

What makes a psychologist a psychologist? What prevents people with no psychological training from passing themselves off as psychologists? One way professions offer high-quality service to the public is by regulating their own membership. Selective admission into the profession helps protect the public against quacks and charlatans who can cause great damage not only to their clients, but also to the profession they allegedly represent.

The practice of professional psychology is regulated by law in every state. A law that regulates both the title and practice of psychology is called a *licensing law*. **Licensure** limits those qualified to practice psychology as defined by state law. Each state has its own standards for licensure, and these are governed by regulatory boards.

The major functions of any professional board are to determine the standards for admission into the profession and to discipline its members when professional standards are violated. Typically, licensure involves education, experience, examination, and administrative requirements. A doctoral degree in psychology from an approved program is usually required as well as one or two years of supervised experience. Applicants must also pass an objective, written examination covering many areas of psychology, although the majority of questions pertain to the healthcare (i.e., clinical and counseling) areas of psychology. Specialty examinations (for example, in I/O psychology) usually are not given. Currently, psychologists must pass a uniform national examination to obtain a license. Finally, the applicant must meet citizenship and residency requirements and be of good moral character.

The licensure of I/O psychologists is controversial. The original purpose of licensure in psychology was to protect the public in the healthcare areas of psychology. Because I/O psychologists are not healthcare providers, the need for licensure to protect the public is not so pressing (Howard & Lowman, 1985). Also, some I/O psychologists object to the heavy emphasis placed on clinical and counseling psychology in the licensure process. Most states regard I/O psychologists as they do other types of applied psychologists who offer services to the public and require them to be licensed. A few states regard I/O psychologists as having a sufficiently different mandate to exempt them from requiring licensure. The issue of licensing remains an ongoing professional concern for I/O psychologists (Macey, 2002).

The History of I/O Psychology

It is always difficult to write *the* history of anything; there are different perspectives with different emphases. It is also a challenge to divide the historical evolution of a discipline into units of time. In some cases, time itself is a convenient watershed (decades or centuries); in others, major events serve as landmarks. In the case of I/O psychology, the two world wars were major catalysts for changing the discipline. This historical overview will show how the field of I/O psychology came to be what it is and how some key individuals and events helped shape it.[1]

The Early Years (1900–1916)

In its beginnings, what we know today as I/O psychology didn't even have a name; it was a merging of two forces that gathered momentum before 1900. One force was the pragmatic nature of some basic psychological research. Most psychologists at this time were strictly scientific and deliberately avoided studying problems that strayed outside the boundaries of pure research. However, the psychologist W. L. Bryan published a paper (Bryan & Harter, 1897) about how professional telegraphers develop skill in sending and receiving Morse code. A few years later in 1903, Bryan's (1904) presidential address to the American Psychological Association touched on having psychologists study "concrete activities and functions as they appear in everyday life" (p. 80). Bryan did not advocate studying problems found in industry per se, but he emphasized

---

[1]A more detailed treatment of the history of I/O psychology can be found in the book by Koppes (2007).

examining real skills as a base upon which to develop scientific psychology. Bryan is not considered the father of I/O psychology, but rather a precursor.[2]

The second major force in the evolution of the discipline came from the desire of industrial engineers to improve efficiency. They were concerned mainly with the economics of manufacturing and thus the productivity of industrial employees. Industrial engineers developed "time and motion" studies to prescribe the most efficient body motions per unit of time to perform a particular work task. For example, by arranging parts to be assembled in a certain pattern, a worker could affix a nut to a bolt every 6 seconds, or 10 per minute.

The merging of psychology with applied interests and concern for increasing industrial efficiency was the impetus for the emergence of I/O psychology. Koppes (2002) observed that in the late 19th century American society was undergoing rapid changes and developments because of industrialization, immigration, a high birthrate, education, and urban growth. A drive for social reform prevailed, Americans were ready for the useful, and society looked toward science for practical solutions. These societal demands forced psychologists to popularize their science and demonstrate the value of psychology in solving problems and helping society. As eloquently stated by Koppes and Pickren (2007), "The prevailing generation wanted to make the American society a better and safer place to live and work. Society turned to science for practical solutions to everyday problems. Improving the quality of work was part of a broad-based social effort to improve the quality of life" (p. 10). I/O psychology took its place upon the social stage to help achieve this result. By 1910 "industrial psychology" (the "organizational" appendage did not become official until over 60 years later) was a legitimate specialty area of psychology.

Four individuals stand out as the founding figures of I/O psychology in the United States. They worked independently of one another, and their major contributions deserve a brief review.

Archives of the History of American Psychology at the University of Akron

Walter Dill Scott

Walter Dill Scott.   Scott, a psychologist, was persuaded to give a talk to some Chicago business leaders on the need for applying psychology to advertising. His talk was well received and led to the publication of two books: *The Theory of Advertising* (1903) and *The Psychology of Advertising* (1908). The first book dealt with suggestion and argument as means of influencing people. The second book was aimed at improving human efficiency with such tactics as imitation, competition, loyalty, and concentration. By 1911 Scott had expanded his areas of interest and published two more books: *Influencing Men in Business* and *Increasing Human Efficiency in Business*. During World War I, Scott was instrumental in the application of personnel procedures in the army. Landy (1997) described Scott as the consummate scientist–practitioner who was highly respected in both spheres of professional activity. Scott had a substantial influence on increasing public awareness and the credibility of industrial psychology.

[2]The term *industrial psychology* was apparently used for the first time in Bryan's 1904 article. Ironically, it appeared in print only as a typographical error. Bryan was quoting a sentence he had written five years earlier (Bryan & Harter, 1899), in which he spoke of the need for more research in individual psychology. Instead, Bryan wrote "industrial" psychology and did not catch his mistake.

Frederick W. Taylor

Frederick W. Taylor.   Taylor was an engineer by profession. His formal schooling was limited, but through experience and self-training in engineering he went on to obtain many patents. As he worked himself up through one company as a worker, supervisor, and finally plant manager, Taylor realized the value of redesigning work to achieve both higher output for the company and a higher wage for the worker. His best-known work is his book *The Principles of Scientific Management* (1911). Van De Water (1997) reported these principles as: (1) science over rule of thumb, (2) scientific selection and training, (3) cooperation over individualism, and (4) equal division of work best suited to management and employees. In perhaps the most famous example of his methods, Taylor showed that workers who handled heavy iron ingots (pig iron) could be more productive if they had work rests. Training employees when to work and when to rest increased average worker productivity from 12.5 to 47.0 tons moved per day (with less reported fatigue), which resulted in increased wages for them. The company also drastically increased efficiency by reducing costs from 9.2 cents to 3.9 cents per ton.

As a consequence of this method, it was charged that Taylor inhumanely exploited workers for a higher wage and that great numbers of workers would be unemployed because fewer were needed. Because unemployment was rampant at this time, the attacks on Taylor were virulent. His methods were eventually investigated by the Interstate Commerce Commission (ICC) and the U.S. House of Representatives. Taylor replied that increased efficiency led to greater, not less, prosperity and that workers not hired for one job would be placed in another that would better suit their potential. The arguments were never really resolved; World War I broke out and the controversy faded.

Lillian Moller Gilbreth

Lillian Moller Gilbreth.   Koppes (1997) reported that Lillian Gilbreth was one of several female psychologists who made substantial contributions in the early era of I/O psychology. Along with her husband, Frank, she pioneered industrial management techniques that are still used. Her husband was more concerned with the technical aspects of worker efficiency, while she was more concerned with the human aspects of time management. Lillian Gilbreth was among the first to recognize the effects of stress and fatigue on workers. Koppes noted that Gilbreth made a historic speech at a meeting of industrial engineers in 1908. She was asked for her opinion because she was the only woman at the meeting. According to Yost (1943), Gilbreth

. . . rose to her feet and remarked that the human being, of course, was the most important element in industry, and that it seemed to her this element had not been receiving the attention it warranted. The engineer's scientific training, she said, was all for the handling of inanimate objects. She called attention to the fact that psychology was fast becoming a science and that it had much to offer that was being ignored by management engineers. The plea in her impromptu remarks was for the new profession of scientific management to open its eyes to the necessary place psychology had in any program industrial engineers worked out. (Koppes, 1997, p. 511)

The mother of 12 children, Gilbreth combined a career and family and was called by a leading publication, "a genius in the art of living." Two of her children wrote a book about her life, *Cheaper by the Dozen*, which was made into a motion picture in 1950 and remade in 2003.

Archives of the History of American Psychology at the University of Akron

Hugo Münsterberg

Hugo Münsterberg. Münsterberg was a German psychologist with traditional academic training. The noted American psychologist William James invited Münsterberg to Harvard University, where he applied his experimental methods to a variety of problems, including perception and attention. He was a popular figure in American education, a gifted public speaker, and a personal friend of President Theodore Roosevelt. Benjamin (2006) stated, "Münsterberg's personality made him a natural for the role of scientific expert. . . . He was authoritarian in manner; he promoted the application of psychology. Indeed, he would argue that the contributions of psychological science were necessary for success in business and in everyday life" (p. 420). Münsterberg was interested in applying traditional psychological methods to practical industrial problems. His book, *Psychology and Industrial Efficiency* (1913), was divided into three parts: selecting workers, designing work, and using psychology in sales. One of Münsterberg's most renowned studies involved determining what makes a safe trolley car operator. He systematically studied all aspects of the job, developed an ingenious laboratory simulation of a trolley car, and concluded that a good operator could comprehend simultaneously all of the influences that bear on the car's progress. Some writers consider Münsterberg *the* founder of industrial psychology. Landy (1992) reported that many prominent I/O psychologists throughout the 20th century can trace their professional roots back to Münsterberg. Münsterberg's influence in the history of the field is well evidenced by the coterie of I/O psychologists who were guided by his teachings.

Salgado et al. (2010) recently reported that Münsterberg has been falsely credited as the founder of scientific employee selection. The authors identified several psychologists in Europe whose research pre-dated Münsterberg's work by a decade. Accordingly, Salgado et al. asserted that the origin of scientific employee selection was in Europe, not North America. However, there appears to be no leading figure among those early psychologists in Europe who had the galvanizing effect on industrial psychology that Münsterberg had in the United States.

When World War I broke out in Europe, Münsterberg supported the German cause. He was ostracized for his allegiance, and the emotional strain probably contributed to his death in 1916. Only the U.S. involvement in the war gave some unity to the profession. The primary emphasis of the early work in I/O psychology was on the economic gains that could be accrued by applying the ideas and methods of psychology to problems in business and industry. Business leaders began to employ psychologists, and some psychologists entered applied research. However, World War I caused a shift in the direction of industrial psychological research. Figure 1-1 shows a running timeline from 1900 to the present of major events in I/O psychology and major events in world history.

World War I (1917–1918)

World War I was a potent impetus to psychology's rise to respectability. Psychologists believed they could provide a valuable service to the nation, and some saw the war as a means of accelerating the profession's progress. Robert Yerkes was the psychologist most instrumental in involving psychology in the war. As president of the APA, he maneuvered the profession into assignments in the war effort. The APA made many proposals, including ways of screening recruits for mental deficiency and of assigning selected recruits to jobs in the army. Committees of psychologists investigated soldier motivation and morale, psychological problems of physical incapacity, and discipline. Yerkes continued to press his point that psychology could be of great help to the United States in wartime.

The army, in turn, was somewhat skeptical of the psychologists' claims. It eventually approved only a modest number of proposals, mostly those involving the assessment of recruits. Yerkes and other psychologists reviewed a series of general intelligence tests and eventually developed one that they called the **Army Alpha**. When they discovered that 30% of the recruits were illiterate, they developed the **Army Beta**, a special test for those who couldn't read English. Many military recruits in WWI were foreign-born and had limited capacity to read and write English. The Army Beta was used to assess such recruits, and contained information presented in the form of pictures and graphics (Salas, DeRouin et al., 2007). Meanwhile, Walter Dill Scott was conducting research on the best placement of soldiers in the army. He classified and placed enlisted soldiers, conducted performance ratings of officers, and developed and prepared job duties and qualifications for more than 500 jobs.

Plans for testing recruits proceeded at a slow pace. The army built special testing sites at its camps and ordered all officers, officer candidates, and newly drafted recruits to be tested. Both the Army Alpha and Army Beta group intelligence tests were used, as were a few individual tests. The final order authorizing the testing program came from the Adjutant General's office in August 1918. However, the war ended just three months later, and testing was terminated just as it was finally organized and authorized. As a result, the intelligence testing program didn't contribute as much to the war as Yerkes had hoped. Even though 1,726,000 individuals were ultimately tested in the program, actual use of the results was minimal.

Although psychology's impact on the war effort was not substantial, the very process of giving psychologists so much recognition and authority was a great impetus to the profession. Psychologists were regarded as capable of making valuable contributions to society and of adding to a company's (and in war, a nation's) prosperity. Also in 1917 the oldest and most representative journal in the field of I/O psychology—the *Journal of Applied Psychology*—began publication. Some of the articles in the first volume were "Practical Relations Between Psychology and the War" by G. S. Hall, "Mentality Testing of College Students" by W. V. Bingham, and "The Moron As a War Problem" by F. Mateer. The first article published in the *Journal of Applied Psychology* not only summarized the prevailing state of industrial psychology at the time, but also addressed the science-versus-practice issue that still faces I/O psychologists today.

> The past few years have witnessed an unprecedented interest in the extension of the application of psychology to various fields of human activity. . . . But perhaps the most strikingly original endeavor to utilize the methods and the results of psychologi-

Army Alpha
An intelligence test developed during World War I by I/O psychologists for the selection and placement of military personnel.

Army Beta
A nonverbal intelligence test developed during World War I by I/O psychologists to assess illiterate recruits.

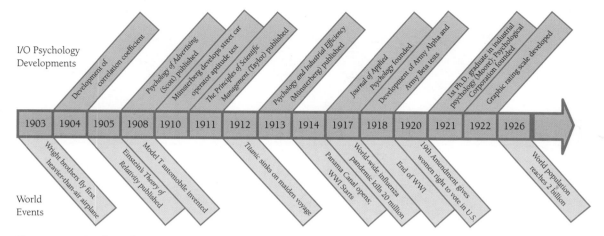

Figure 1-1 *Timeline of major I/O psychology developments and world events*

cal investigation has been in the realm of business. This movement began with the psychology of advertising. . . . Thence the attention of the applied psychologist turned to the more comprehensive and fundamental problem of vocational selection—the question, namely, of making a detailed inventory of the equipment of mental qualities possessed by a given individual, of discovering what qualities are essential to successful achievement in a given vocation, and thus of directing the individual to the vocational niche which he is best fitted to fill. . . . Every psychologist who besides being a "pure scientist" also cherishes the hope that in addition to throwing light upon the problems of his science, his findings may also contribute their quota to the sum-total of human happiness; and it must appeal to every human being who is interested in increasing human efficiency and human happiness by the more direct method of decreasing the number of cases where a square peg is condemned to a life of fruitless endeavor to fit itself comfortably into a round hole. (Hall et al., 1917, pp. 5–6)

After the war, there was a boom in the number of psychological consulting firms and research bureaus. The birth of these agencies ushered in the next era in I/O psychology.

Between the Wars (1919–1940)

Applied psychology emerged from World War I as a recognized discipline. Society was beginning to realize that industrial psychology could solve practical problems. Following the war, several psychological research bureaus came into full bloom. The Bureau of Salesmanship Research was developed by Walter Bingham at the Carnegie Institute of Technology. There was little precedent for this kind of cooperation between college and industry. The bureau intended to use psychological research techniques to solve problems that had never been examined scientifically. Twenty-seven companies cooperated with Bingham, each contributing $500 annually to finance applied psychological research. One of the early products of the bureau was the book *Aids in Selecting Salesmen*. For several years the bureau concentrated on the selection, classification, and development of clerical and executive personnel as well as salespeople.

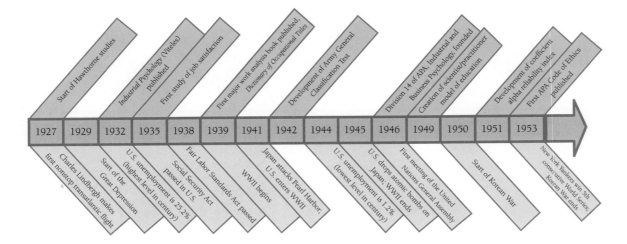

Another influential organization during the period was the Psychological Corporation, founded by James Cattell in 1921. Cattell formed it as a business corporation and asked psychologists to buy stock in it. The purpose of the Psychological Corporation was to advance psychology and promote its usefulness to industry. The corporation also served as a clearinghouse for information. To protect against quacks and charlatans, who were becoming increasingly prevalent, it provided companies with reference checks on prospective psychologists. Unlike many agencies that began at the time, the Psychological Corporation has remained in business. Over the years it has changed its early mission, and today it is one of the country's largest publishers of psychological tests.

In 1924 a series of experiments began at the Hawthorne Works of the Western Electric Company (see Figure 1-2). Although initially they seemed to be of minor scientific significance, they became classics in industrial psychology. In the opinion of many writers, the **Hawthorne studies** "represent the most significant research program undertaken to show the enormous complexity of the problem of production in relation to efficiency" (Blum & Naylor, 1968, p. 306).

Hawthorne studies
A series of research studies that began in the late 1920s at the Western Electric Company and ultimately refocused the interests of I/O psychologists on how work behavior manifests itself in an organizational context.

Figure 1-2   *Badge worn by visitors to the Hawthorne Works of the Western Electric Company*

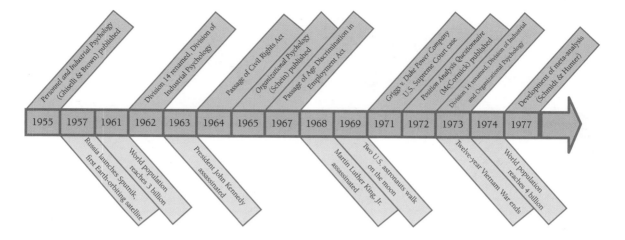

The Hawthorne studies were a joint venture between Western Electric and several researchers from Harvard University (none of whom were industrial psychologists by training). The original study attempted to find the relationship between lighting and efficiency. The researchers installed various sets of lights in workrooms where electrical equipment was being produced. In some cases the light was intense; in other cases it was reduced to the equivalent of moonlight. Much to the researchers' surprise, productivity seemed to have no relationship to the level of illumination. The workers' productivity increased whether the illumination was decreased, increased, or held constant. The results of the study were so bizarre the researchers hypothesized that some other factors must be responsible for the increased productivity.

The precise reason for the change in behavior (for example, the novelty of the situation, special attention, or prestige from being selected for study) was not clear. Sometimes behavior change is due to just a change in the environment (for example, the presence of the researchers) and not to the effect of some experimentally manipulated variable (for example, the amount of illumination). This finding is so important to researchers that it is known within the field of psychology as the *Hawthorne effect.*

The Hawthorne studies also revealed the existence of informal employee work groups and their controls on production. They also learned the importance of employee attitudes, the value of having a sympathetic and understanding supervisor, and the need to treat workers as people instead of merely human capital. Their revelation of the complexity of human behavior opened new vistas for industrial psychology, which for nearly 40 years had been dominated by the goal of improving company efficiency. Today the Hawthorne studies, though regarded by some psychologists as having been based on flawed research methods, are considered by many to be the single most influential event in the formation of industrial psychology. They also showed that researchers sometimes obtain totally unexpected results. Because the investigators were not tied to any one explanation, their studies took them into areas never before studied by industrial psychology and raised questions that otherwise might never have been asked. Industrial psychology was never the same again.

In 1932 Morris Viteles wrote a classic textbook that advanced the field of industrial psychology beyond personnel selection to also include motivation, job satisfaction,

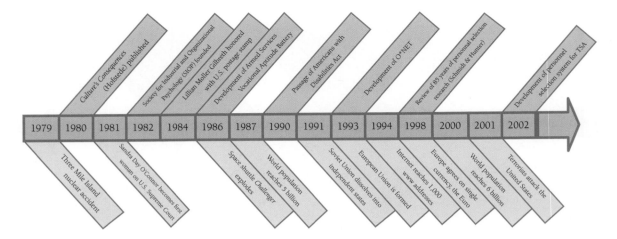

and leadership (Viteles, 1932). His book had a profound influence on educational programs in industrial psychology. Mills (2012) noted that Viteles worked both as a professor and in industry, and was an exemplar of the scientist-practitioner.

This era in industrial psychology ended with the coincidental conclusion of the Hawthorne studies and the outbreak of World War II. Industrial psychologists were now faced with an immense task: helping to mobilize a nation for a global war.

World War II (1941–1945)

When the United States entered World War II, industrial psychologists were more prepared for their role in the war effort than they had been in 1917. By this time, psychologists had studied the problems of employee selection and placement and had refined their techniques considerably.

Walter Bingham chaired the advisory committee on classification of military personnel that had been formed in response to the army's need for classification and training. Unlike in World War I, this time the army approached the psychologists first. One of the committee's earliest assignments was to develop a test that could sort new recruits into five categories based on their ability to learn the duties and responsibilities of a soldier. The test that was finally developed was the **Army General Classification Test (AGCT)**, a benchmark in the history of group testing. Harrell (1992), in reflecting on his own involvement in developing the AGCT 50 years earlier, reported that 12 million soldiers were classified into military jobs on the basis of the test. The committee also worked on other projects, such as methods of selecting people for officer training, trade proficiency tests, and supplemental aptitude tests.

Psychologists also worked on the development and use of situational stress tests, a project undertaken by the U.S. Office of Strategic Services (OSS) (Murray & MacKinnon, 1946). The purpose of this testing program was to assess candidates for assignment to military intelligence units. During a three-day session of extremely intensive testing and observation, the candidates lived together in small groups under almost continuous observation by the assessment staff. Specially constructed situational tests, many modeled after techniques developed in the German and British armies, were used to assess candidates in nontraditional ways. One test, for example, involved

Army General Classification Test (AGCT)
A test developed during World War II by I/O psychologists for the selection and placement of military personnel.

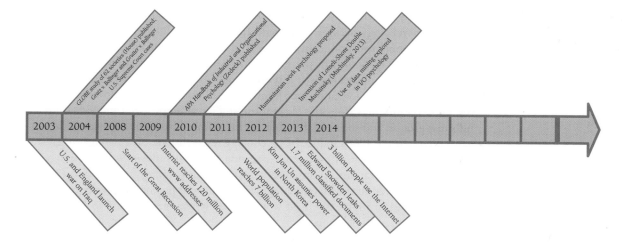

constructing a 5-foot cube from a collection of wooden poles, pegs, and blocks. It was impossible for one person to assemble the cube in the allotted time, so two "helpers" were provided. These were actually psychologists who played prearranged roles. One helper acted very passive and contributed little; the other obstructed work by making impractical suggestions and ridiculing and criticizing the candidate. Of course, no candidate could complete the project with this kind of "help." The real purpose of the test was not to see whether the candidates could construct the cube but to assess their emotional and interpersonal reactions to stress and frustration.

Throughout the war, industrial psychology was also being used in civilian life. The use of employment tests in industry increased greatly. Because the nation needed a productive workforce, psychologists were called on to help reduce employee absenteeism. Industry discovered that many of the techniques of industrial psychologists were useful, especially in the areas of selection, training, and machine design, and industrial leaders were particularly interested in the applications of social psychology. New methods of measuring soldier attitude and morale could also be used in industry. In short, the techniques developed during the war could be applied to business and industry in peacetime. World War II was a springboard for refining industrial psychological techniques and honing the skills of applied psychologists.

Each of the two world wars had a major effect on industrial psychology but in a somewhat different way. World War I helped form the profession and give it social acceptance. World War II helped develop and refine it. The next era in the history of I/O psychology saw the discipline evolve into subspecialties and attain higher levels of academic and scientific rigor.

Toward Specialization (1946–1963)

In this era industrial psychology evolved into a legitimate field of scientific inquiry, having already been accepted as a professional practice. More colleges and universities began to offer courses in "industrial psychology," and graduate degrees (both M.S. and Ph.D.) were soon given. The Division of Industrial Psychology of the APA was created in 1946. Benjamin (1997) reported that earlier I/O psychologists had less professional identity, being represented in the family of "applied psychologists."

As in any evolving discipline, subspecialties of interest began to crystallize and industrial psychology became splintered. That part of industrial psychology specializing in personnel selection, classification, and training became identified as "personnel psychology." Sometime in the 1950s, interest grew in the study of organizations. Long the province of sociologists, this area caught the interest of psychologists. Elton Mayo was a founder of what became known as the human relations movement. Drawing upon the findings from the Hawthorne studies, it emphasized individual needs, informal groups, and social relationships as the primary bases for behavior within organizations. In the 1960s industrial psychology research took on a stronger organizational flavor. Investigators gave more attention to social influences that impinge on behavior in organizations. Terms such as *organizational change* and *organization development* appeared in the literature regularly. Industrial psychology began to address a broader range of topics (the field would officially change its name to "industrial/ organizational" psychology in 1973). Classic textbooks of the 1950s, such as *Personnel and Industrial Psychology* by Ghiselli and Brown (1955), gave way in title (as well as in substance) to books with more of an organizational thrust. Traditional academic boundaries between disciplines began to blur in this postwar period. This melding of disciplines was healthy because it decreased the use of narrow, parochial attempts to address complex areas of research.

Government Intervention (1964–1993)

In the late 1950s and early 1960s, the nation was swept up in what became known as the "civil rights movement." As a nation, the United States became more sensitized to the plight of minorities who had systematically been denied equal opportunities to various sectors of life, including housing, education, and employment. In 1964 Congress passed the Civil Rights Act, a far-reaching piece of legislation designed to reduce unfair discrimination against minorities. One component of the Civil Rights Act, Title VII, addressed the issue of discrimination in employment. The significance of the law to I/O psychologists is explained as follows: for years I/O psychologists were given a relatively free rein to develop a wide variety of psychological assessment devices (that is, tests, interviews, and so on) to make employment decisions. The result of these employment decisions was the disproportionately small representation of minorities (most notably Blacks and women) in the workplace, particularly in positions above lower-level jobs. Because historically these decisions seemed to result in discrimination against minorities, Title VII authorized the government to monitor and remedy discriminatory employment practices.

By 1978 the government had drafted a uniform set of employment guidelines to which employers were bound. Companies were legally mandated to demonstrate that their employment tests did not uniformly discriminate against any minority group. In addition, the new government standards were not limited to just paper-and-pencil tests or the personnel function of selection; they addressed all devices (interviews, tests, application blanks) used to make all types of personnel decisions (selection, placement, promotion, discharge, and so on).

The discipline of I/O psychology now had to serve two ultimate authorities. The first authority is what all disciplines must serve—namely, to perform high-quality work, be it conducting scientific research or providing services to clients. The second authority added was government scrutiny and evaluation. I/O psychologists now had to accept the consequences of being legally accountable for their actions. As professionals, I/O psychologists would continue to evaluate themselves, but government policies and agencies would also judge their actions. In 1990 President George H. W. Bush signed into law the Americans with Disabilities Act and in 1991 an updated version of the Civil Rights Act. Both acts were designed to remedy further inequities in the workplace. In 1993 President William Jefferson Clinton signed into law the Family and Medical Leave Act which grants workers up to 12 weeks of unpaid leave from work to attend to family and medical issues.

I/O psychology also made a major contribution to the military during this era. Campbell and Knapp (2010) described the efforts of I/O psychologists to develop a test for the selection and classification of military personnel. This massive research project involved many psychologists and took twelve years to complete. Called "Project A," it involved developing the **Armed Services Vocational Aptitude Battery (ASVAB)**. Every year the ASVAB is administered to between 300,000 and 400,000 people; of that number, 120,000 to 140,000 individuals are selected to join the military. The selected personnel are then assigned to the many military jobs within the various branches of the Armed Services. Project A represents one of the finest contributions of I/O psychology; it fulfilled a pressing practical need through the application of scientific knowledge.

Armed Services Vocational Aptitude Battery (ASVAB)
A test developed in the 1980s by I/O psychologists for the selection and placement of military personnel.

The Information Age (1994–Present)

In the early 1980s the personal computer provided individuals with access to a technology previously limited to large businesses. By the early 1990s the Internet enabled individuals and businesses throughout the world to be connected electronically. Although several years might be identified as the start of the Information Age, we have selected 1994 in part because that is the year the total number of Internet sites first surpassed 1,000. In one decade that number grew to exceed 45 million (Zakon, 2004). Ten years later it was estimated that three billion people use the Internet (Internetworldstats, 2014). A major shift has occurred in the way society functions, primarily revolving around the explosion in available information and how that information changes our lives. Kapp and O'Driscoll (2010) reported that if all the people on Facebook were a nation, it would be the third most populous nation in the world. Social media sites Facebook, LinkedIn, and Twitter have revolutionized how members of society interact with each other, and made information the primary medium of social exchange. To further understand the power of social media, we include in each chapter a highlighted section entitled "Social Media and I/O Psychology" (see Social Media and I/O Psychology: *Web 2.0 and the World of Work*). Amazon, Google, and eBay are highly successful companies that were created on the basis of the need for people to harness information and use it to their advantage. Kapp and O'Driscoll explained the current era: "We are witnessing the acceleration of the co-evolution of society and technology. In a socio-technical system like the one we are in, information is the currency, individuals are the transport mechanism, interaction is the transfer mechanism, and insight is the value-added outcome" (p. 5). The critical theme of the current era is that change, dramatic change, is upon us, and both organizations and employees must find ways to adapt to this rapidly changing world.

Social Media and I/O Psychology: *Web 2.0 and the World of Work*

For many readers of this book, it might be hard to imagine a world without the Internet. In 1998, Ron Nief and Tom McBride created the Beloit College Mindset List, which pointed out interesting facts about incoming college freshmen at the time. The list was meant to prepare college professors for the incoming students and help them understand and better appreciate their world view. The list has become an annual tradition, and in 2011, the list noted that the incoming class that year (the class that would be graduating in 2015) had never known a world without the Internet. More specifically, it noted that for these individuals, most of them born in 1993, "there has always been an Internet ramp onto the information highway" (www.beloit.edu/mindset/previouslists/2015/).

The Internet as we know it today has evolved considerably. Richards (2012) noted that in its original form, known as Web 1.0, the Internet was fairly static, with a small number of individuals posting information for others to view. It has since evolved to Web 2.0, with a focus on social interaction and the ability for everybody to not only consume the information that is posted, but contribute to its manufacturing. Richards noted that this shift from Web 1.0 to Web 2.0 is reflected in "the rise of blogs and micro-blogging, social networking sites, virtual worlds, peer-to-peer file sharing sites and wikis" (p. 24).

With the advent of social media, the world of work as we know it has changed, and is continuing to change. Whereas, according to Richards, the Internet was once an "elite tool requiring specialist knowledge" (p. 36), it is now easily accessible and capable of leading to socially organized behavior, facilitating employee-led discourses and knowledge sharing, and influencing union strategy. The line between one's work life and personal life has become increasingly blurred, creating unique boundary issues and raising potential legal and ethical concerns that were unheard of in previous decades. While it is unclear what the future has in store, it appears that the level of connectedness of individuals will only increase. As such, organizations and employees alike must consider social media's immediate and long-term impact on them to facilitate positive, rather than negative, outcomes.

Murphy (1999) described how the turbulent changes faced by organizations (such as the need to change products or services frequently in response to changing market conditions) have led to the need for frequent changes in workers' responsibilities, tasks, and work relationships. Organizations that once held rigid specifications for what employees are supposed to do in their job find it difficult to compete in an environment that must be responsive to change. Organizations are more likely to hire generalists (i.e., people who are intelligent, ambitious, and willing to adjust to the demands of change) rather than specialists (i.e., people hired to perform a single job with pre-established responsibilities). Electronic communication (like the Internet) has revolutionized business and customer-oriented service. The concept of "e-business" entails networks of suppliers, distributors, and customers who make products and render services by exchanging information online (Pearlman & Barney, 2000). Additionally, there is greater urgency to deliver products and services quickly. In decades past the typical standards for judging organizations were the quality and quantity of their products and services. In the Information Age, we add a new critical standard: speed of delivery.

The very language of work is being challenged. A "job" is the traditional unit around which work is organized and the means by which individuals are linked to organizations. As individuals we desire a sense of social identity about the job we hold. In the Information Age, tasks and duties are constantly changing, as are the skills needed to perform them. As such, a "job" as a useful and meaningful way to describe work performed is starting to erode.

Cappelli and Keller (2013) described the many variations of jobs in modern society in addition to full-time regular employees. There are part-time workers (20 hours/week) and on-call workers (as needed). Also there are temporary workers (hired by an employment agency who are assigned to a particular company) and independent contractors (individuals who are not employees and thus receive no benefits). Additionally, some employees rotate across different locations of the same company as needed (e.g., a teller working in multiple branches of a bank).

With the innovations of telecommuting (doing work at home and communicating it electronically to the office), virtual work teams and offices, and wireless communications, work is no longer a physical place. Furthermore, integrated work is now performed in different continents at the speed of electronic transmission. For example, assume a patient goes to see a doctor. The doctor speaks into a handheld voice recorder,

Reprinted with permission from *www.CartoonStock.com*

describing the patient's condition and treatment. By the close of business that day, the verbal account of the visit to the doctor is sent electronically halfway around the world (which at that time is the start of the workday). The verbal account is rendered into a transcription format by typists and then electronically returned to the doctor by the next business day. The transcribing work is sent overseas because of much cheaper labor costs there, perhaps as much as 80% lower than wages paid to U.S. workers. The transcription is downloaded via a printer in the doctor's office and placed in the patient's file. As has been said regarding the irrelevance of national boundaries to the conduct of work, "geography is history." Information plays such a big role in the conduct of work today that many organizations have entire units or departments devoted to "IT"—information technology. The head of that unit often holds the title of "CIO"—chief information officer. Hesketh (2001) suggested that the objective of vocational psychology, which historically was devoted to helping people identify vocations suitable for them, should shift its emphasis to help workers cope with the stress caused by radical and rapid changes in the workplace.

By any reasonable standard, the past two decades have witnessed a dramatic shift in how work is performed and where it is performed, if not a change in the meaning of the concept of work. Among the leading skills workers must possess today to remain competitive in the workplace is the willingness and capacity to effectively deal with change. These changes affect the very substance of I/O psychology.

Overview

The history of I/O psychology is rich and diverse. The field was born at the confluence of several forces, developed and grew through global conflict, and was woven into the societal fabric of which it is a part. Our history is relatively brief and our members are not great in number, but we believe I/O psychologists have contributed greatly to both economic and personal welfare. Our history is marked by a continuous interweaving of scientific and professional contributions. At certain points in our history, particularly during wars, the practice of I/O psychology has been at the vanguard of our professional efforts (see Field Note: *I/O Psychology and 9/11/01*).

At other times, our scientific advances have been more noteworthy. As stated earlier in this chapter, however, the science and practice of I/O psychology can never be too far apart. Katzell and Austin (1992) quoted a memorable statement by Morris Viteles, one of the early pioneers of our field, who aptly summarized the two domains of I/O psychology: "If it isn't scientific, it's not good practice, and if it isn't practical, it's not good science" (p. 826). Likewise, Farr and Tesluk (1997) cited a comment by the first president of Division 14, Bruce Moore, on the duality of the science and practice of I/O psychology: "The extreme applied practitioner is in danger of narrow, myopic thinking, but the extreme pure scientist is in danger of being isolated from facts" (p. 484).

Today I/O psychology is multidisciplinary in both its content and its methods of inquiry. On reflection, it was the same at the turn of the 20th century—a confluence of interest in advertising research, industrial efficiency, and mental testing. In a sense, the evolution of I/O psychology is the chronicle of mushrooming interests along certain common dimensions as molded by a few seismic events. As we enter what some call the "global era" of civilization, where national and cultural boundaries are less

Field Note: *I/O Psychology and 9/11/01*

I/O psychologists have long contributed to our nation's welfare. We have made some of our most enduring contributions during times of national crisis, as witnessed by our roles in World War I and II. So too did we contribute following the terrorist attacks on September 11, 2001. On November 19, 2001, President George W. Bush signed into law the Aviation and Transportation Security Act, which, among other things, established a new Transportation Security Administration (TSA). The law was designed to create a secure air travel system while ensuring freedom of movement for people and commerce. The TSA was faced with a Herculean task. It had to establish effective selection standards to hire airport security screening personnel, design new procedures to screen passengers and luggage, and do so in a matter of months. Several I/O psychologists played key roles in implementing this new program that was of extreme national urgency. The new TSA security screeners were to be a highly-skilled workforce, meeting specific standards at date of hire and throughout their career (e.g., annual certifications), and they were to be provided ongoing training and development. Kolmstetter (2003) described the development of a day-long assessment of applicants for the job of security screener. The tests included assessments of English proficiency (e.g., reading, writing, listening), personality (e.g., integrity, positive work ethic, customer service orientation), and technical aptitudes (e.g., visual observation of X-ray images). The assessment also included a structured job interview, a physical abilities test (e.g., lifting and searching luggage), and a medical evaluation. The candidates who were hired were taught the job duties of each of five primary screening jobs, and they rotated their job assignments throughout each work shift.

Approximately 1,300 screeners were hired by March 2002. By November 2002 the TSA had processed more than 1.8 million applications, tested about 340,000 candidates, and hired about 50,000 screeners. These screeners were deployed at the nation's 429 commercial airports. Women made up 38% of the screeners, and ethnic minorities made up 44%. The size of the total TSA workforce (58,000) exceeds that of the FBI, Customs Service, and Secret Service combined. Through the skill, diligence, and commitment of a handful of people (many of whom were I/O psychologists), in record time, a large vitally important federal agency was created and staffed to meet a national mandate. As I/O psychologists, we are proud of what our colleagues were able to contribute to ensuring our nation's safety.

On the tenth anniversary of 9/11, Silver (2011) summarized the role of psychology in dealing with terrorism: "Only in retrospect can we clearly see how the attacks of 9/11 have shifted the direction of our country . . . Terrorists seek to create disruption by instilling fear and anxiety that leads to wide-ranging social, political, psychological, and economic consequences. Thus psychologists have much to contribute to an analysis of that day and its short- and long-term effects on both individuals and society at large" (p. 427).

I/O Psychology and the Economy: *Economic Expansion and Contraction*

When the economy is moving in a positive direction, there is *expansion* in business. New organizations are created and existing organizations grow. Business expansion entails the creation of new jobs and the need for people to fill them. Productivity increases and unemployment decreases. Organizations spend more money to facilitate the expansion, including purchasing more supplies, equipment, advertising, etc., as well as the added payroll costs of newly hired workers. There is more work to perform during an expansion, including work for I/O psychologists.

When the economy is moving in a negative direction, there is *contraction* in business. Organizations sell less (because there is less demand for their products or services) and buy less (because they have reduced sales revenue). Organizations need fewer employees when there is less demand for the products or services they offer. Therefore, when the economy is contracting, the level of unemployment increases.

Economists are interested in many indices, but three are of major importance: the amount of domestic productivity, the amount of consumer spending, and the level of unemployment. Over a two-quarter (i.e., six months) period, when domestic productivity declines, consumer spending declines, and unemployment increases, the economy is said to be in a *recession*. Throughout history, national economies have fallen into recessionary periods, and then they typically rebound and enter periods of expansion. Between 2008 and 2009, for six quarters, there was a recession in the United States (as well as much of the world). The magnitude of the contraction was so great it was called the "Great Recession."

We are no longer in a recession, but the hoped-for level of expansion has not been great. That is, national productivity and consumer spending are increasing, but not by a large amount. Unemployment has decreased, but it is still at an economically unhealthy level. Descriptions of the current economy include "sluggish" and "not fully recovered." In short, while we are not as economically imperiled as during the Great Recession, our economy is also not robust.

Two other issues should be noted. First, economic indicators reflect the past, not necessarily the future. That is, we know we are in an economic recession only after it has already occurred. Second, economic indices are also computed by area and industry. As such, the national economy may not be in a recession, but individual states or industries might be.

confining, I/O psychology has also expanded its domains of interest and involvement. Entrance into the global era has compelled I/O psychology to become more knowledgeable of cultures other than those typified by Western civilization. We have learned that there are broad cultural differences in the importance placed on work in life.

Since I/O psychology is directed toward the work world, there is a strong linkage between prevailing economic conditions and the substance of I/O psychology. To further understand this relationship, each chapter includes a highlighted section entitled "I/O Psychology and the Economy" that explains how economic conditions influence a topic presented in the chapter (see I/O Psychology and the Economy: *Economic Expansion and Contraction*).

Cross-Cultural I/O Psychology

Cross-cultural psychology
An area of research that examines the degree to which psychological concepts and findings generalize to people in other cultures and societies.

Cross-cultural psychology studies "similarities and differences in individual psychological and social functioning in various cultures and ethnic groups" (Kagitcibasi & Berry, 1989, p. 494). When extended to I/O psychology, the investigation pertains to the work context. The globalization of business has compelled I/O psychology to examine how its theories and practices apply in cultures other than North America and Western Europe. The increased interest in cross-cultural I/O psychology stems from greater cultural diversity in the workforce, U.S. companies doing business overseas, partnerships or joint ventures between companies from different countries, and the development of new electronic means of communication that render geographic boundaries between nations meaningless. Smith et al. (2001) posed the basic question, "Does I/O psychology contain an established body of well-researched knowledge, which organizations would be best advised to draw upon wherever their operation is located?" (p. 148). As a scientific discipline, I/O psychology is examining to what degrees and in what ways cultural differences influence the work world.

The amount of time people spend engaged in work varies greatly across cultures. Brett and Stroh (2003) reported that American workers work 137 hours per year more than Japanese workers and 499 hours per year more than French workers. The official workweek in France is 35 hours (compared to 40 in the United States), and Europeans at all job levels typically take four to six weeks of vacation per year. Further research reveals that U.S. managers work 50–70 hours per week. It has been proposed that American work hours are related to the American culture and that other cultures do not share this value. Is it correct to describe workers in cultures that work less than Americans as "lazy"? No, just as it is not correct to describe American workers as "compulsive." Work hours are a reflection of the values each culture has for the role that work plays in life. It is these types of cross-cultural differences that must be addressed in the melding of workers and work-related practices across different nations.

As this book will reveal, the full range of topics that I/O psychologists address is influenced by cross-cultural differences. Topics include preferences for how to select employees, the degree to which workers compete versus cooperate with each other, and preferred styles of leadership, among many others. The issue of cross-cultural I/O psychology is so salient that beginning with the next chapter a highlighted section is presented on cross-cultural issues pertaining to a topic within the chapter. As Aycan and Kanungo (2001) aptly summarized, "In our business dealings we will encounter people of different nations across real and virtual borders. In this world order understanding the impact of culture on various aspects of organizations and their practices will become more critical than ever to increase synergy, productivity and welfare of the workforce within and across countries" (p. 385).

Humanitarian Work Psychology

Since its inception over a century ago, I/O psychology has been regarded as an agent for helping organizations to be more effective. Indeed, I/O psychologists who work as practitioners are hired by organizations to achieve that very result. An examination of the organizations that are staffed with I/O psychologists reveals that these organizations are often large, in the private sector (i.e., non-government), and measure their effectiveness by such financial indices as sales volume, profit level, and market share. While this generalization does not extend to all I/O practitioners, there is a plausible basis for how our profession is perceived.

Recently there has been a call for I/O psychology to become more heavily involved in additional types of organizations whose actions are guided by values not reflected in financial indices. More specifically, the call has emerged from within the discipline for I/O psychology to expand its focus to help the world become a better place by using the knowledge and skills we have developed. The name for this new direction for I/O psychology is **humanitarian work psychology** (Carr et al., 2012).

When we read or hear the word "humanitarian," it is often followed by the word "aid" or "relief." It typically refers to the giving of resources (e.g., food, clothing, shelter) to people who have an urgent need for them, as following an earthquake or flood. In the case of humanitarian work psychology, it is directing the resources of I/O psychology (what we know and can do) to relieving global poverty, promoting social justice in organizations, protecting the rights of workers, and so on (Reichman & Berry, 2012). The need for humanitarian work psychology is the recognition of the long-standing ills afflicting the global population. It is consistent with the Ethical Principles of Psychologists and Code of Conduct (APA, 2002): to promote good for mankind.

All people need to earn a decent wage to live. It is argued that humanitarian work psychology demands I/O psychology assume a more vigorous role in increasing the standard of living for all people. That is, in addition to addressing the needs of individuals and organizations, we should also be addressing the needs of nations and societies (Gloss & Thompson, 2013). Accordingly, I/O psychology should expand its mission simply because it is the morally right thing to do. Lefkowitz (2012) argued that "any kind of reputable organization can and ought to be *humanistic* in nature, even if its core objectives are not per se humanitarian (italics in original, p. 104).

Humanitarian work psychology
The practice of I/O psychology directed to the societal goal of improving employment for all mankind.

The Mandate of I/O Psychology

I/O psychology is confronted with a daunting task—to increase the fit between the workforce and the workplace at a time when the composition of both is rapidly changing. Today's workforce is unlike any other in our history. More people are seeking employment than ever before, and they have higher levels of education. There are more women entering the workforce seeking full-time careers, more dual-income couples, and more individuals whose native language is not English. Likewise, the nature of work is changing. There are increasing numbers of jobs in service industries, and jobs that require computer literacy and proficiency with electronic communication. Societal changes also influence employment, as evidenced by the continuing problems of drug abuse and violence in the workplace. On an even larger scale, climate change is beginning to alter how organizations operate. I/O psychologists can contribute to helping people cope with these changes in their work lives. Huffman et al. (2009) described how I/O psychology can facilitate organizational responses to climate change, as for example, the need to recruit and hire employees who can contribute to an organization's "eco-friendly" business practices. This topic is discussed in greater detail in Chapter 8.

As a profession, we find ourselves on the threshold of some areas where we have little prior experience. We find the mandate of I/O psychology to be very challenging, with the unending variety of issues we address being a great source of stimulation. Although some disciplines rarely change their content, I/O psychology most certainly is not the "same old stuff." We can think of few other fields of work that are as critical to human welfare as I/O psychology. We spend more of our lifetimes engaged in working than in any other activity. Thus I/O psychology is devoted to understanding our major mission in life. When you have finished reading this book, you should have a much better understanding of human behavior in the workplace. Perhaps some of you will be stimulated enough to continue your work in I/O psychology. It is a most challenging, rewarding, and useful profession.

Chapter Summary

- Industrial/organizational (I/O) psychology is one area of specialization within the broad profession of psychology.
- I/O psychologists generally function in one of two roles: scientists or practitioners.
- I/O psychology is practiced and studied throughout the world.
- The discipline of I/O psychology comprises several subfields.
- The history of I/O psychology is best represented by seven eras, the most recent being the Information Age (1994–present).
- Business is now conducted on a global scale, which presents many professional opportunities for I/O psychologists.
- Humanitarian work psychology proposes I/O psychology should also be directed toward achieving societal good.
- The mandate of I/O psychology is to increase the fit between the workforce and the workplace when the composition of both is rapidly changing. As work assumes a more central role in our lives, the need for I/O psychology to balance work and family issues continues to grow.

Research Methods in I/O Psychology

Chapter Outline

Learning Objectives

- Understand the empirical research cycle.
- Know the relative advantages and disadvantages of the laboratory experiment, quasi-experiment, questionnaire, and observation research methods.
- Understand meta-analysis and data mining.
- Understand the purpose of organizational neuroscience.
- Understand the value of qualitative research.
- Understand the concept of correlation and its interpretation.
- Understand the limitations of assessing causality.
- Have an awareness and appreciation of the ethical issues associated with I/O psychological research.
- Understand the difference between academic-based and practitioner-based research.

Research
A formal process by which knowledge is produced and understood.

Generalizability
The extent to which conclusions drawn from one research study spread or apply to a larger population.

We all have hunches or beliefs about the nature of human behavior. Some of us believe that red-haired people are temperamental, dynamic leaders are big and tall, blue-collar workers prefer beer to wine, the only reason people work is to make money, and the like. The list is endless. Which of these beliefs are true? The only way to find out is to conduct **research**, the systematic study of phenomena according to scientific principles. Much of this chapter is devoted to a discussion of research methods used in I/O psychology. Understanding the research process helps people solve practical problems, apply the results of studies reported by others, and assess the accuracy of claims made about new practices, equipment, and so on.

I/O psychologists are continually faced with a host of practical problems. Knowledge of research methods makes us better able to find useful solutions to problems rather than merely stumble across them by chance. An understanding of research methods also helps us apply the results of studies reported by others. Some factors promote the generalizability of research findings; others retard it. **Generalizability** is defined as the degree to which the conclusions based on one research sample are applicable to another, often larger, population. People often assert the superiority of some new technique or method; a knowledge of research methods helps us determine which ones are truly valuable. It has been suggested that science has three goals: description, prediction, and explanation. The descriptive function is like taking a photograph—a picture of a state of events. Researchers may describe levels of productivity, numbers of employees who quit during the year, average levels of job satisfaction, and so on. The second function is prediction. Researchers try to predict which employees will be productive, which ones are likely to quit, and which ones will be dissatisfied. This information is then used to select applicants who will be better employees. The explanatory function is the most difficult to unravel; it is a statement of *why* events occur as they do. It tries to find causes: why production is at a certain level, why employees quit, why they are dissatisfied, and so forth.

This chapter will give you some insight into the research process in I/O psychology. The process begins with a statement of the problem and ends with the conclusions drawn from the research. This chapter should help you become a knowledgeable consumer of I/O psychological research.

The Empirical Research Process

Figure 2-1 shows the steps that scientists take in conducting empirical research. The research process is basically a five-step procedure with an important feedback factor; that is, the results of the fifth step influence the first step in future research studies. First, the research process begins with a statement of the problem: what question or problem needs to be answered? Second, how do you design a study to answer the question? Third, how do you measure the variables and collect the necessary data? Fourth, how do you apply statistical procedures to analyze the data? (In other words, how do you make some sense out of all the information collected?) Finally, how do you draw conclusions from analyzing the data? Let's look at each of these steps in more detail.

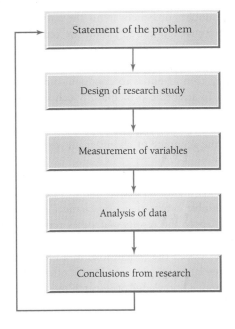

Figure 2-1   *The empirical research cycle*

Statement of the Problem

Theory
A statement that proposes to explain relationships among phenomena of interest.

Inductive method
A research process in which conclusions are drawn about a general class of objects or people based on knowledge of a specific member of the class under investigation.

Deductive method
A research process in which conclusions are drawn about a specific member of a class of objects or people based on knowledge of the general class under investigation.

Questions that initiate research don't arise out of thin air. They are based on existing knowledge—your own and others' experiences with the problem, personal intuition or insight, or a theory. A **theory** is a statement that proposes to explain relationships among phenomena—for example, a theory of why individuals are attracted to each other. As researchers conduct their studies, they become more familiar with the problem and may expand the scope of their questions. One person's research may stimulate similar research by someone else; thus researchers often benefit from their colleagues' studies. After conducting much research on a topic, researchers may propose a theory about why the behavior occurs. The sequence that starts with data and culminates in theory is the **inductive method** of science. The opposite sequence is the **deductive method**, in which a researcher first forms a theory (perhaps by intuition or by studying previous research) and then tests the theory by collecting data. If the theory is accurate, the data will support it; if it is inaccurate, they will not.

The value of theory in science is that it integrates and summarizes large amounts of information and provides a framework for the research. Campbell (1990) noted, however, that as a scientific discipline, psychology is much more difficult to investigate than physics or chemistry. People are far too variable, both across individuals and from day to day within one person, to be defined by a single formula or equation. "The situation is not the same in physics or chemistry. A molecule of water has the same formula no matter where in the universe it might be" (p. 46). Psychology has no equivalent of universal natural laws, such as Newton's three laws of motion. The following quotes illustrate three different yet valid views on theory:

- "There is nothing quite so practical as a good theory."—Kurt Lewin, noted social psychologist

- "Research designed with respect to theory is likely to be wasteful."—B. F. Skinner, noted experimental psychologist
- "Theory, like mist on eyeglasses, obscures facts."—Charlie Chan, noted fictional detective

Lewin's statement is often cited in psychology. Its essence is that a theory is useful for conducting research. A theory synthesizes information, organizes it into logical components, and directs the researcher's efforts in future studies. But Skinner believes that too much effort is spent on "proving" theories; that is, the theory is master of the research. Skinner thinks that most theories eventually fall out of favor and that productive research does not require a theory. His position is an extreme case of empiricism. Charlie Chan thinks that researchers become too committed to proving their theories and become blinded to information that doesn't conform to the theory they want to believe. A good researcher doesn't let the theory obscure the facts. Rather than thinking of theories as "right" or "wrong," we try to think of them in terms of their usefulness. A useful theory gives meaning to the problem; it helps the subject matter make more sense. Theorizing or theory development is an on-going process. A theory is proposed, then tested with empirical data, which in turn may result in the theory being fine-tuned or sharpened in focus. Theories are not "born" fully intact with unquestioned adherence, but are the objects of scientific scrutiny and evaluation. Some theories may receive extensive empirical support and confirmation, while others may repeatedly be disconfirmed and ultimately dismissed by scientists. Vancouver (2005) expressed the process of theory development as follows:

> Clearly, any theory should go through rigorous testing under a cloud of skepticism. This is what we do as scientists . . . Any theory that is still the focus of research is a work in progress. We do not know what it might explain or fail to explain. We do not know what past, present, or future revisions will make it better or worse. (pp. 49–50)

Campbell believes that theories are only a means to an end and thus have no inherent value. He stated that theories should "help us develop better research questions, provide more useful interpretation of data, or guide the future investment of research resources" (pp. 66–67). A theory is an important way to specify research questions, but it is only one way to formulate a research problem. Other methods can also result in high-quality research. This is especially true in a pragmatic area like I/O psychology, where some research problems come from everyday work experiences. If 50% of a company's workforce quit every year, one doesn't need a theory to realize that this could be a serious problem. However, a theory of turnover can help explain why the turnover is occurring.

Design of the Research Study

Research design
A plan for conducting scientific research for the purpose of learning about a phenomenon of interest.

A **research design** is a plan for conducting a study. A researcher can use many strategies; the choice of method depends on the nature of the problem being studied as well as on cost and feasibility. Research strategies may be compared along several dimensions, but two are most important: (1) the naturalness of the research setting and (2) the investigator's degree of control over the study. No one strategy is the best under all conditions; there are always tradeoffs. These two dimensions affect both the

Social Media and I/O Psychology: *Getting Past the WEIRD Participants*

As a specialization, I/O psychology is subject to many of the same criticisms of the broader profession of psychology. One such criticism involves the samples of participants that have typically been used to answer empirical questions. According to Henrich et al. (2010), most behavioral scientists, including psychologists, have relied to a large extent on what they call "WEIRD" people. WEIRD stands for Western, Educated, Industrialized, Rich, and Democratic, and reflects the societies from which participants are usually drawn. They argue that researchers often mistakenly believe that the results from their studies that use these participants will generalize to individuals in other societies. Unfortunately, they note that WEIRD participants are often the exception to the rule, and quite different from the rest of the world. As a result, it would appear that more diverse samples are needed to obtain a better understanding of various phenomena.

Research within I/O psychology is equally guilty in many ways of limiting the types of people who have been studied. Until recently, it has been difficult to obtain data from diverse samples (i.e., non-WEIRD samples), particularly when the researchers themselves may be WEIRD. Social media offer a new avenue for conducting research, revealing opportunities to broaden participant pools and create more heterogeneous samples. Gregori and Baltar (2013) note that social network sites such as Facebook have the ability to "facilitate access to the 'hard to involve' population" as well as "expand sample size and the scope of the study" (p. 134). Similarly, Bhutta (2012) noted that Facebook allows researchers to reach more people in a shorter amount of time than they would otherwise. She pointed out that the average Facebook user is connected to friends with whom they have strong friendships, as well as individuals with which they are weakly tied, including acquaintances and even strangers. She noted that these "weak ties are the bridges between small clusters of close friends, linking us together to form an elaborate web of social relationships" (p. 80). By recruiting participants through Facebook by posting recruitment messages on group pages and encouraging snowball sampling (in which a request to participate is sent to one person, who forwards it to a second person, who then forwards it to a third person, and so forth), researchers are better able to ensure a more diverse, potentially non-WEIRD sample.

Another tool that has become increasingly popular as a means for data collection is Amazon's Mechanical Turk (MTurk). MTurk is a website that allows researchers to recruit people from a large, global, diverse pool of individuals and provide compensation to them for their participation in an online study. According to Buhrmester et al. (2011), the individuals who participate in the studies on MTurk appear to be motivated to participate for the sake of enjoyment. In addition, they found that MTurk participants are "more demographically diverse than standard Internet samples and significantly more diverse than typical American college samples" (p. 4). I/O psychologists have begun to rely on samples drawn from MTurk. For example, Phillips et al. (2014) recruited individuals from MTurk to examine how people reacted to a recruitment message regarding a job's travel requirements.

In short, limiting ourselves to WEIRD samples that are not as reflective of the world's population as we might think is problematic for the science and practice of psychology as a whole, I/O psychology included. The use of social media to reach and recruit more diverse samples may be the key to obtaining a better understanding of workplace issues.

Internal validity
The degree to which the relationships evidenced among variables in a particular research study are accurate or true.

External validity
The degree to which the relationships evidenced among variables in a particular research study are generalizable or accurate in other contexts.

internal and external validity of the research. **Internal validity** is the degree to which the relationships evidenced among variables in a particular research study are accurate or true. **External validity** is the extent to which findings from a research study are relevant to individuals and settings beyond those specifically examined in the study. External validity is synonymous with generalizability, and is a function not only of the realism of the research design, but also the types of people used as participants (see Social Media and I/O Psychology: *Getting Past the WEIRD Participants*). If a study lacks internal validity, it can have no external validity.

Naturalness of the Research Setting.   In some research strategies, the problem can be studied in the environment in which it naturally occurs. This is desirable because we don't want the research strategy to destroy or distort the phenomenon under study. Some research strategies appear phony because they study the problem in unnatural ways. In contrast, for example, the Hawthorne studies were conducted in the plant with actual employees performing their normal jobs. Some studies do not need to be conducted in a natural environment, however, because the behavior under investigation is assumed to be independent of the setting. For example, a study to test whether people react faster to red or green lights could be conducted as appropriately in a laboratory as in a natural field setting.

Degree of Control.   In some research strategies, the researcher has a high degree of control over the conduct of the study. In others, very little control is possible. In the Hawthorne studies, the researchers could control the exact amount of lighting in the work area by installing (or removing) lights, although it turned out that factors other than lighting affected the workers' performance. Suppose you want to study the relationship between people's ages and their attitudes toward I/O psychology. You are particularly interested in comparing the attitudes of people over age 40 with those under 40. You develop a questionnaire that asks their opinions about I/O psychology (is it interesting, difficult to understand, and so on) and distribute it to your classmates. It turns out that every person in the class is under 40. Now you have no information on the over-40 group, so you can't answer your research question. This is an example of a low degree of control (you cannot control the age of the people in your class). Low control is particularly endemic to the questionnaire research method.

Primary research methods
A class of research methods that generates new information on a particular research question.

Primary Research Methods

Laboratory experiment
A type of research method in which the investigator manipulates independent variables and assigns subjects to experimental and control conditions.

This section is a discussion of four primary research methods used in I/O psychology. A **primary research method** provides an original or principal source of data that bears on a particular research question. No one method is perfect; that is, none offers a high degree of both naturalism and control. Each method will be described with a highly illustrative study that exemplifies the strengths and weaknesses of each method.

Laboratory Experiment

Laboratory experiments are conducted in contrived settings as opposed to naturally occurring organizational settings. Stone–Romero (2011) referred to a laboratory as a "special purpose setting" because the laboratory was created for the explicit purpose of conducting research. In a laboratory, the researcher has a high degree of control over the conduct of the study, especially over those conditions associated with the observations of behavior. The experimenter designs the study to test how certain aspects of an actual environment affect behavior. The laboratory setting must mirror certain dimensions of the natural environment where the behavior normally occurs. A well-designed laboratory experiment will have some of the conditions found in the natural environment but will omit those that would never be present. Furthermore, in a laboratory experiment, the researcher randomly assigns the study participants to the various treatment conditions, which enhances control and facilitates drawing causal inferences.

Streufert et al. (1992) conducted a laboratory experiment on the effects of alcohol intoxication on visual-motor performance. A sample of adult men participated for two days; one day they consumed alcohol and the other day they consumed mineral water (disguised with a mild ethanol spray to provide the odor of alcohol). The mineral water served as a control condition against which to compare alcohol intoxication. The alcohol dosage was designed to produce breath alcohol levels of either .05 or .10. Visual-motor performance was measured on a task similar to a video game. The researchers studied several aspects of performance, including risk taking and errors. They compared performance under alcohol intoxication with performance under the control condition for each person. The results showed that error rates were dramatically higher under conditions of alcohol consumption. Serious performance deterioration was found even at the lower (.05) intoxication level. Under the effects of alcohol, some individuals exhibited greater cautiousness (i.e., slower reaction time) to the visual-motor task, trading off speed of response for fewer errors. The researchers regarded errors in the task to be equivalent to an air traffic controller's failure to ward off aircraft that have come too close to each other. Additionally, although reduced speed of response may decrease errors, it also may prevent engaging in needed defense maneuvers.

This study illustrates the defining characteristics of a laboratory experiment. By controlling for other factors, the researchers were able to determine the causal link between alcohol consumption and performance on a visual-motor task. They could also control the dosage of alcohol to produce precise breath alcohol levels of .05 or .10, typical levels of intoxication associated with drinking alcohol in naturalistic settings. Nevertheless, one can question the generalizability of the skills needed to perform the selected visual-motor task to real jobs. Some jobs, such as a surgeon, require even greater concentration and coordination. In such a case, the magnitude of the "errors" caused by alcohol intoxication would be greater. Other jobs, such as a manual laborer, have fewer visual-motor skill requirements, in which case the errors would be less. In short, the findings from the study pertain to the effects of alcohol on visual-motor performance, not the total spectrum of skills needed for performance across many jobs. Nevertheless, the laboratory experiment is a classic research method for addressing highly specific research questions, and the results from such experiments can often be interpreted with a high degree of clarity.

Quasi-experiment
A type of research method for conducting studies in field situations where the researcher may be able to manipulate some independent variables.

Quasi-Experiment

Quasi is defined as "seemingly but not actually;" therefore, a **quasi-experiment** resembles an experiment but actually provides less control over the variables under investigation. A quasi-experiment is a research strategy in which independent variables are manipulated in a field setting (that is, the people in the study do not perceive the setting as having been created to conduct the research). Stone-Romero referred to a field context for conducting research as a "non-special purpose setting" because the location in which the research is conducted was originally created for other purposes. As in a laboratory experiment, the researcher tests the effects of a few variables on the subjects' behavior. But there is also less control. In a laboratory experiment, all the variables are manipulated at the researcher's discretion and can be included or excluded according to the design of the study.

In a quasi-experiment, however, variables that occur in the field setting are also part of the investigation. Although they add to the richness and realism of the study, they also lessen the researcher's control. Furthermore, random assignment of study participants is often not possible in a field setting, which leads to less generalizable conclusions by the researcher (Shadish, 2002).

Latham and Kinne (1974) conducted a classic study that clearly demonstrates the quasi-experiment as a research method. It examined how a one-day training program on goal setting affected the job performance of pulpwood workers. The subjects in the study were 20 pulpwood logging crews. Their behavior was observed as they performed their normal job duties harvesting lumber in a forest. The experimenters split the subjects into two groups of ten crews each. They matched the two groups on a number of factors so that they were equal in terms of ability and experience. One group was given a one-day course on how to set production goals—that is, how many cords of wood to harvest per hour. The other group was not given any special instructions and worked in the usual way. The experimenters then monitored the job performance of the wood crews over the next three months. Results showed that the crews who were trained to set production goals for themselves harvested significantly more wood than the other crews. The study supported the use of goal setting in an industrial context.

The major strength of this study in terms of demonstrating the quasi-experiment method is that the context was real. Actual workers were used in the context of their everyday jobs. The setting was a forest, not a laboratory where the crews would have been pretending. Although the study's design was not complex enough to rule out competing explanations for the observed behavior, it did allow the researchers to conclude that the goal-setting technique probably caused the increase in job performance. This study also illustrates some weaknesses of the quasi-experiment method. Some workers who were supposed to participate in the goal-setting group decided not to. This forced the researchers to redesign part of the study. Also, few I/O psychologists are able to influence a company to change its work operations for research purposes. (In fact, one of the authors of this study was employed by the lumber company, which undoubtedly had some effect on the company's willingness to participate.)

Questionnaire

Questionnaire
A type of research method in which subjects respond to written questions posed by the investigator.

Questionnaires rely on individuals' self-reports as the basis for obtaining information. They are classified as a "non-experimental" research method because no independent variables are controlled in the study. They can be constructed to match the reading ability level of the individuals being surveyed. Questionnaires are a means of maintaining the anonymity of respondents if the subject matter being covered is sensitive. The non-experimental research method is most frequently used in I/O psychology (Stone-Romero, 2011). Murphy et al. (1991) used the questionnaire method to ascertain the acceptability of employee drug testing. The authors asked two samples of individuals (college-aged students and older, nontraditional students) to indicate the degree to which they view testing for illicit drug use as justified in each of 35 jobs (such as salesperson, surgeon, mechanic, and airline pilot). The students rated each job on a 7-point scale from low to high acceptance of drug testing. The jobs were carefully selected to represent different types of skills and temperaments needed for their successful conduct as well as physical conditions under which the jobs are performed. The results indicated that the degree to which different jobs involved danger to the worker, coworkers, or the public was most strongly related to the acceptability of employee drug testing. The authors concluded that it would be relatively easy to justify drug testing for some jobs, whereas substantial efforts may be necessary to overcome resistance to drug testing for other jobs. Furthermore, the responses by both sets of students were virtually the same; that is, the attitudes of college-aged students were the same as those of older individuals (average age of 35). However, the results also revealed a high degree of variability in attitudes toward drug testing among members of both groups. Some individuals were in favor of drug testing across all jobs, whereas other individuals were opposed to drug testing for any job.

Despite the popularity of this research method in I/O psychology, it suffers from several practical limitations. Some people are not willing to complete a questionnaire and return it to the researcher. Roth and BeVier (1998) reported that a 50% return rate is considered adequate in survey research, yet the return rate of mailed questionnaires

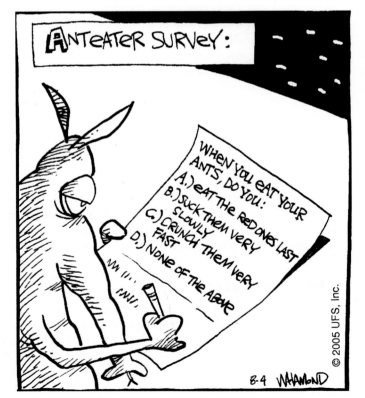

Reality Check: © United Feature Syndicate, Inc.

Cross-Cultural I/O Psychology: *Cross-Cultural Research*

As noted in Chapter 1, the era of global interdependence is upon us. Nations and cultures can no longer operate in isolation. I/O psychologists need to understand to what degree our knowledge is universal versus culture-specific. Gelfand et al. (2002) discussed how cross-cultural research can aid I/O psychologists in understanding work-related behavior around the world. Concepts developed in Western cultures by I/O psychologists might not be the same in other cultures. Even the process of participating in research varies across cultures. In the United States, the questionnaire method is a very popular approach to conducting research. This method is consistent with U.S. cultural values such as individualism, freedom of speech as a basic human right, and the comfort and willingness to express one's opinion. However, these values are not universal. In one study, despite the researcher's instructions to work independently, Russian participants worked collectively to complete the questionnaire. As a group, they read the questions aloud, decided upon a group answer, and all circled the same response. These participants found the individual questionnaire research method to be inconsistent with their own cultural experiences and values, and therefore they modified the instructions to achieve group consensus. Gelfand et al. discussed additional cross-cultural issues in research, including the equivalence of concepts translated from one language to another, the acceptability of the researcher to the participants before truthful responses are given, and the willingness of participants to use the extreme ends of a rating scale (e.g., very satisfied or very dissatisfied) in responding. Both Brutus et al. (2010) and Shen et al. (2011) concluded that many I/O psychological research findings are potentially biased by their heavy reliance on English-speaking samples. There is unknown generalizability of research findings to other cultures.

is often less than 50%. For example, in the Murphy et al. (1991) study, the return rate of questionnaires mailed to the homes of the nontraditional students was 31%. Such a low response rate raises the question of how representative or unbiased the responses are for the group as a whole. Indeed, Rogelberg et al. (2000) found that nonrespondents to an organizational survey exhibited more negative attitudes about various aspects of their work than did respondents to the survey. The researchers were able to ascertain the attitudes of both groups by means of interviews. Their findings cast doubt on the generalizability of the answers from respondents of some surveys to the larger population in question. More positively, Stanton (1998) found that responses to a survey using the Internet contained fewer incomplete or missing answers than responses to the same survey administered via the mail. The author supported using the Internet as an efficient means of collecting survey data. Church (2001) reported very small differences in the quality of data collected by various survey methods and suggested that researchers choose the method based on ease of administration.

Another issue is the truthfulness of the responses given by respondents to questions asked. Research indicates questions that are perceived to be sensitive or threatening are more likely to produce distorted responses than benign questions. For example, Tourangeau and Yan (2007) reported that as many as 70% of the people who tested positive for drug use in a urine analysis denied on a questionnaire having recently taken any illicit drugs.

Despite their limitations, questionnaires are used extensively in I/O psychology to address a broad range of research questions (see Cross-Cultural I/O Psychology: *Cross-Cultural Research*).

Observation

Observation is a method that can be used when the research is examining overt behaviors. In natural field settings, behavior may be observed over extended periods of time and then recorded and categorized. As a research method, observation is not used very frequently in I/O psychology, primarily because it requires substantial amounts of time and energy. Komaki (1986) sought to identify the behaviors that differentiate effective and ineffective work supervisors. She had observers record the behaviors of 24 managers: 12 previously had been judged as effective in motivating others and 12 judged as relatively ineffective. Approximately twenty 30-minute observations were made of each manager's behavior over a seven-month period (232 hours of observation in total). The managers were observed as they conducted their normal day-to-day job duties. The observer stood out of sight but within hearing distance of the manager and used a specially designed form for recording and coding the observations. Komaki found the primary behavior that differentiated the effective and ineffective managers was the frequency with which they monitored their employees' performance. Compared with ineffective managers, effective managers spent more time sampling their employees' work. The findings were interpreted as underscoring the importance of monitoring critical behaviors in producing effective supervisors. However, this conclusion requires corroborating empirical evidence because the two groups of managers were merely observed with no attempt to control for other variables that might account for the results.

Observation is often a useful method for generating ideas that can be tested further with other research methods. The observation method is rich in providing data from environments where the behavior in question occurs. But how successful can observers be in acting like "flies on the wall," observing behavior but not influencing it? In the Komaki study, the managers were aware that they were being observed. Given this, to what degree did the managers modify their conduct to project socially desirable behaviors (e.g., monitoring of their subordinates)? Perhaps effective managers are more sensitive to social cues than ineffective managers and thus are better able to be perceived in a positive fashion. Note that we are dealing with interpretations of the behavior (the "why"), not merely the behavior itself (the "what"). It has been suggested that acceptance and trust of the observers by the study participants are critical to the success of this research method. Stanton and Rogelberg (2002) suggested that the Internet may become a fruitful mechanism for conducting observational research through the use of webcams and smartcards.

Table 2-1 compares the four primary research methods on two major dimensions: researcher control and realism. No method rates high on both factors. There is always

Table 2-1 *Comparison of primary research strategies*

	Laboratory Experiment	Quasi-Experiment	Questionnaire	Observation
Control (potential for testing causal relationships)	High	Moderate	Low	Low
Realism (naturalness of setting)	Low	High	Moderate	High

a tradeoff; a researcher may sacrifice realism for control or vice versa, depending on the study's objectives. Dudley-Meislahn et al. (2013) stated that researchers need to identify the knowledge they seek to measure and then determine if a particular method will be useful in doing so. A well-trained I/O psychologist knows the advantages and disadvantages of each method.

Secondary Research Methods

Meta-analysis

Secondary research methods
A class of research methods that examines existing information from research studies that used primary methods.

Meta-analysis
A quantitative secondary research method for summarizing and integrating the findings from original empirical research studies.

While a primary research method gathers or generates new information on a particular research question, a secondary research method looks at existing information from studies that used primary methods. One particular secondary research method, meta-analysis (Hunter & Schmidt, 1990; Rosenthal, 1991), is being used with increasing frequency in I/O psychology. Meta-analysis is a statistical procedure designed to combine the results of many individual, independently conducted empirical studies into a single result or outcome. The logic behind meta-analysis is that we can arrive at a more accurate conclusion regarding a particular research topic if we combine or aggregate the results of many studies that address the topic, instead of relying on the findings of a single study. The result of a meta-analysis is often referred to as an "estimate of the true relationship" among the variables examined because we believe such a result is a better approximation of the "truth" than would be found in any one study. A typical meta-analysis might combine the results from perhaps 25 or more individual empirical studies. As such, a meta-analysis is sometimes referred to as "a study of studies." Although the nature of the statistical equations performed in meta-analysis is beyond the scope of this book, they often entail adjusting for characteristics of a research study (for example, the quality of the measurements used in the study and the sample size) that are known to influence the study's results. Cohn and Becker (2003) explained how a meta-analysis increases the likelihood of achieving more accurate conclusions than could be reached in an individual study by reducing errors of measurement.

Despite the apparent objectivity of this method, the researcher must make a number of subjective decisions in conducting a meta-analysis. For example, one decision involves determining which empirical studies to include. Every known study ever conducted on the topic could be included or only those studies that meet some criteria of empirical quality or rigor. The latter approach can be justified on the grounds that the results of a meta-analysis are only as good as the quality of the original studies used. The indiscriminate inclusion of low-quality empirical studies lowers the quality of the conclusion reached. The findings derived from poorly conducted primary research studies cannot be elevated in quality by conducting a meta-analysis of them. Another issue is referred to as the "file drawer effect." Research studies that yield negative or nonsupportive results are not published (and thus not made widely available to other researchers) as often as studies that have supportive findings. The nonpublished studies are "filed away" by researchers, resulting in published studies being biased in the direction of positive outcomes. Thus a meta-analysis of published studies could lead to a distorted conclusion because of the relative absence of (unpublished) studies reporting negative results. McDaniel et al. (2006) found evidence of the file drawer effect among meta-analyses published by professional test vendors. By selectively excluding those studies that reported negative results for their tests, the findings from a meta-analysis are inevitably biased in an upward direction. However, the field is divided on the magnitude of the file drawer effect in meta-analysis (i.e., Dalton et al., 2012; Ferguson & Brannick, 2012).

Additionally, Ostroff and Harrison (1999) noted that original research studies on a similar topic sometimes differ in the **level of analysis** used by the researchers. For example, one original study may have examined the individual attitudes of employees in a work team, whereas another original study may have examined the attitudes of different teams working with each other. It would not be appropriate to meta-analyze the findings from these two studies because the level (or unit) of analysis in the first study was the individual, but in the second study it was the work team. Ostroff and Harrison argued that researchers must be careful meta-analyzing findings from original studies that focused on different topics.

Despite the difficulty in making some of these decisions, meta-analysis is a popular research procedure in I/O psychology. Refinements and theoretical extensions in meta-analytic techniques attest to the sustained interest in this method across the areas of psychology. Schmidt and Oh (2013) proposed a "second order" meta-analysis. It is a meta-analysis of a number of statistically independent and methodologically comparable meta-analyses that examine the same empirical relationships, but now expanded to different contexts (as across cultures or nations). For example, many original research studies have examined the relationship between job attitudes and leadership. Meta-analyses have been conducted on these studies based on U.S. samples. If meta-analyses were conducted using samples from various other countries, a second order meta-analysis would reveal the degree to which national differences influence the findings.

As an illustration of the value of meta-analysis, many companies have sponsored smoking cessation programs for their employees to promote health and reduce medical costs. Viswesvaran and Schmidt (1992) meta-analyzed the results from 633 studies of smoking cessation involving more than 70,000 individual smokers. They found that 18.6% of smokers quit after participation in a cessation program, but the results differed by type of program. Instructional programs were found to be twice as effective as drug-based programs. The results of this meta-analysis can be of considerable practical value in assisting organizations to develop effective smoking cessation programs for their employees. Many of the scientific findings reported in this book are based upon meta-analysis. Schmidt and Hunter (2001) concluded, "It is hard to overemphasize the importance of [meta-analysis] in advancing cumulative knowledge in psychology" (p. 66).

Data Mining

Data mining (also known as "big data") has been used to study consumer shopping decisions. Every time a supermarket scanner beeps, a new piece of information enters a database about shopping patterns. A single supermarket in just one day may sell 250,000 items. Data mining might reveal consistent patterns in items purchased both across and within shoppers. For example, laundry products are purchased by a broad spectrum of shoppers, while bottled water may more likely be purchased by people who also buy fresh vegetables. Other sources of big data are the various branches of

Level of analysis
The unit or level (individuals, teams, organizations, nations, etc.) that is the object of the researchers' interest and about which conclusions are drawn from the research.

Data mining
An emerging secondary research method in I/O psychology that looks for patterns of association among the measured items in very large data sets.

the U.S. government that record data on employment, crime, education, and so on. George et al. (2014) stated the value of data mining is not the number of individuals in a data set but the amount of information per individual that can be analyzed.

Stanton (2013) described the various stages of data mining in a survey conducted by the U.S. Department of Labor on 98,000 employed adults. The survey assessed how people spend their time performing work, commuting, childcare activities, etc. The goal of the research was to ascertain what demographic and background variables accounted for the relative time spent in work versus non-work activities. First, the data had to be prepared for analysis. In this study, 38,000 individuals were deleted from the analysis because of excessive missing data on key variables and other statistical issues. Next, the data set was made more manageable by reducing the original survey items from 134 to 39, focusing on the variables of greatest interest to the researcher. Third, the data were analyzed using statistical software programs that use mathematical algorithms, or rules, for determining patterns of associations among the variables. Finally, the data were interpreted to answer the questions posed by the researcher. In this study the results revealed there were six distinctive profiles of time use in work and non-work activities evidenced among the 60,000 people included in the study.

It is too early to judge whether data mining will become a frequently used secondary research method in I/O psychology. In the formative years of meta-analysis, its use was minimal and it attracted considerable criticism. Today meta-analysis is widely accepted and is a frequently used research method. Perhaps in time data mining will receive comparable acceptability in I/O psychology.

However, there are three research issues about data mining that are distinctive compared to other research methods in I/O psychology. First, most concepts examined in I/O psychology cover a wide range of possible scale values, from high to low, as a person's level of job performance or verbal ability. In data mining the variables are simply recorded as yes or no, as whether a particular product was purchased, or whether a person was over age 40. In the study by Stanton, there were originally 139 variables, each measured either yes or no. A typical I/O psychological research study measures far fewer variables, but with most variables assuming a range of scale values.

Second, the traditional statistical index used in I/O psychological research is the correlation coefficient. Data mining also uses the correlation coefficient, but can involve other statistical indices not traditionally used in I/O psychology. One such example is an *affinity index*, a statistic that is based on the probability of two (or more) items being paired together. For example, consumer research reveals that people who purchase beer are also likely to purchase pretzels. This type of research finding (while informative) is not conventional in I/O psychology.

Finally, it is currently fashionable in I/O psychological research to test theories. In the study by Stanton, which was a demonstration of how data mining has potential value in I/O psychology, no theory was tested. Consistent with conventional practice, the data were "sifted through" looking for meaningful patterns. Future data mining research may involve testing theory, but at this nascent stage of development, its conduct is decidedly exploratory in nature.

As a final issue, it should be noted that in the survey by the U.S. Department of Labor, none of the participants were identified by name. The same is true of purchases at a supermarket. However, when personally identifiable information (PII) as the person's name, birth date, address, etc., are included in a data set, there are strict privacy regulations that must be followed by researchers. The liability for handling PII and its security rests with the organization (Reynolds, 2010). The U.S. Department of Commerce identified seven principles outlining the "safe harbor" of personal information, including access, security, and enforcement (U.S. Safe Harbor Framework, 2014). Over 3,000 organizations in the United States and the European Union abide by these principles. With the advent of data mining, ethical issues for conducting data analyses are of paramount importance in psychological research (Wasserman, 2013).

Organizational Neuroscience

Neuroscience is the scientific study of the brain. Over the past 20 years research in various scientific disciplines has begun to examine neural activity associated with decision making and attitude formation in various areas of life. The underlying scientific process of studying neural activity is the same across disciplines, but different terms are used to reference it. When applied to studying styles of decision making (as in making investments), it is called "neuroeconomics." When applied to how people respond to advertising, it is called "neuromarketing" (Becker & Cropanzano, 2010). In I/O psychology it is called **organizational neuroscience**. A more generic term for its broad applicability is "social cognitive neuroscience."

Organizational neuroscience
The scientific study of neural activity as evidenced in organizational attitudes and behavior.

Adis and Thompson (2013) made the attention-getting statement, "I/O psychology has been a brainless science" (p. 405). The statement is literally true. I/O psychology has not considered neural activity as part of understanding psychology applied to work. Only quite recently has I/O psychology, along with other scientific disciplines, begun to study behavior from the perspective of neuroscience.

The field of neuroscience is devoted to studying human behavior at its most fundamental basis—the physiological level. Three major techniques of studying the brain are the following (Adis & Thompson):

- Structural magnetic resonance imaging (MRI) for identifying the structure of the brain;
- Functional magnetic resonance imaging (fMRI) for identifying the process of brain activity; and
- Electroencephalography (EEG) for recording the brain's electrical output.

Each technique is used for a different purpose. Researchers interested in studying creativity, for example, have used MRI to reveal that different parts of the brain are activated in performing novel tasks versus routine tasks. EEG assessments are useful in measuring reaction time to stimuli. We have a faster reaction time to the color red than any other color, which is the basis for why stop lights and warning lights are red. However, it is fMRI that appears to hold the most promise for I/O psychology. As stated by Adis and Thompson, "the 'functional' in functional MRI means this measurement approach examines the brain in action" (p. 413). It is hypothesized that differences in leadership may be attributable to varying patterns of neural activity, as might personality differences. However, as Lee et al. (2012) stated, an fMRI reveals what parts of the brain are activated in sequence by exposure to a stimulus; an fMRI does not prove cause.

Becker and Cropanzano refer to organizational neuroscience as an "emerging discipline" (p. 1055). In all likelihood the techniques of neuroscience will not soon render the traditional research methods of I/O psychology obsolete. The cost of neuroscience instruments is extremely high, especially compared to traditional I/O psychological research methods. For example, the cost of an MRI is approximately $1,000,000, and each brain scan costs approximately $3,000 (Burghart & Finn, 2011). Additionally, it takes a highly-skilled technician to interpret MRI data. Nevertheless, it would be exciting for the field of I/O psychology to have a neurological assessment be part of a personnel selection system for high level jobs. Its greatest value may be in eliminating candidates for employment who, if hired, would produce grave harm to people. A discussion of dysfunctional personality in organizations is presented in Chapter 4.

Qualitative Research

Qualitative research
A class of research methods in which the investigator takes an active role in interacting with the subjects he or she wishes to study.

In recent years there has been an increase in interest among some disciplines in what is called **qualitative research**. Qualitative research is not new. As Locke and Golden-Biddle (2002) noted, its origins are from the ancient Greeks who desired to document the course of human history. Gephart (2013) described qualitative research simply as "doing research with words" (p. 265). Qualitative research involves new ways of understanding research questions and how these ways influence the conclusions we reach about the topic under investigation. Qualitative research (compared with traditional research methods) requires the investigator to become more personally immersed in the entire research process, as opposed to being just a detached, objective investigator. For example, Harms and Lester (2012) described a study of U.S. military officers in combat in Iraq. The authors presented the following account of a researcher who was studying an officer:

> In one particular case, I interviewed a lieutenant that I got to know very well. And 10 days after I interviewed him, he was killed in an ambush. And I have the last recording of this young officer's voice. I was in Afghanistan when I was told he was killed, and I downloaded the recording, put it on a thumb drive, wrote a letter to his mother, and sent it to her. Nothing you learn in graduate school prepares you for a situation like that. (p. 18)

Maxwell (1998) stated that qualitative research often begins by examining why the investigator is interested in conducting the research in the first place. He proposed three kinds of purposes for conducting a scientific study: personal, practical, and research. Personal purposes are those that motivate *you* to conduct a study; they can include a desire to change some existing situation or simply to advance your career as a researcher. Such personal purposes often overlap with the practical and research purposes. It is critical that you be aware of your personal purposes and how they may shape your research. Maxwell advised researchers to be fully cognizant of the multiple purposes for doing a study, and of how these purposes can interact to influence the conclusions we reach in our research.

Wanberg et al. (2012) conducted a qualitative study on the long-term impact of unemployment. The sample consisted of 72 men who had successful careers in such areas as finance, marketing, operations, and sales. They held professional positions, and their average last salary was $136,000 per year. They lost their jobs during the

Great Recession and were seeking new employment. The authors developed a set of questions that became the basis of a lengthy telephone interview. Each interview was tape-recorded and transcribed, with each interview averaging 10 single-spaced pages in length. The authors spent many hours analyzing the transcriptions. Here are two verbatim comments from the interviews:

> Networking has pretty well gone down the tubes because it seems like everyone is in the same boat right now, among my colleagues, everyone. The companies we all work for, there are no openings. They're all just hanging on by their fingernails just trying to survive. (p. 890)

> It's hard. (Laughs.) It's really, really hard. It's so hard that some days you think you want to die . . . People who you never think would contemplate suicide are contemplating suicide because they feel like they're in a vortex of a black hole where the option is going and working at Whole Foods or moving back in with their families and feeling like they're a failure. (p. 903)

Through an analysis of the comments, the authors identified more specific knowledge on the psychological effects of long-term unemployment. They learned about how repeated rejection leads to a sense of depersonalization and has a negative impact on families. The value of qualitative research was clearly evidenced through the powerful evocative words of the individuals in the study.

The essence of qualitative research is to recognize the number of different ways we can reach an understanding of a phenomenon. We can learn through watching, listening, and in some cases participating in the phenomena we seek to understand. Madill and Gough (2008) noted there are many ways of knowing and coming to understand issues in life. They asserted that psychology embraces pluralism—there are different ways of living the human experience—and the ways we come to understand it should be pluralistic as well. By example, in this book we use field notes along with empirical research findings to facilitate an understanding of issues in I/O psychology. Kidd (2002) offered this assessment of qualitative research: "It is a better way of getting at meaning, at how people construe their experiences and what those experiences mean to them. That's often difficult to capture statistically or with quantitative methods" (p. 132). One qualitative research approach is **ethnography** which Fetterman (1998) portrayed as the art and science of describing a group or culture. The description may be of any group, such as a work group or an organization. An ethnographer details the routine daily lives of people in the group, focusing on the more predictable patterns of behavior. Ethnographers try to keep an open mind about the group they are studying. Preconceived notions about how members of the group behave and what they think can severely bias the research findings. It is difficult, if not impossible, however, for a researcher to enter into a line of inquiry without having some existing problem or theory in mind. Ethnographers believe that both the group member's perspective and the external researcher's perspective of what is happening can be melded to yield an insightful portrayal of the group. The insider's view is called the **emic** perspective, whereas the external view is the **etic** perspective. Because a group has multiple members, there are multiple emic views of how group insiders think and behave in the different ways they do. Most ethnographers begin their research process from the emic perspective and then try to understand their data from the external or etic perspective.

Ethnography
A research method that utilizes field observations to study a society's culture.

Emic
An approach to researching phenomena that emphasizes knowledge derived from the participants' awareness and understanding of their own culture. Often contrasted with etic.

Etic
An approach to researching phenomena that emphasizes knowledge derived from the perspective of a detached objective investigator in understanding a culture. Often contrasted with emic.

High-quality ethnographic research requires both perspectives: an insightful and sensitive interpretation of group processes combined with data collection techniques.

Rennie (2012) noted that while qualitative research is being looked upon more favorably, it is still rarely used in comparison to the more traditional quantitative research. Meta-analysis would be an example. It is also true that there are clearer standards of quality for quantitative research (e.g., large sample sizes, control groups in experimental research, etc.) than for qualitative research (Cassell & Symon, 2011). However, I/O psychology appears to be increasingly more accepting of qualitative methods to facilitate our understanding of organizational issues. In the final analysis, there is no need to choose between qualitative and traditional research methods; rather, both approaches can help us understand topics of interest. Lee et al. (2011) concluded, "Qualitative research provides a different and enriching window for observing behavioral phenomenon and can be invaluable for providing a different perspective on topics that are in need of some innovation and creative new thinking" (p. 82).

Measurement and Analysis

Variable
An object of study whose measurement can take on two or more values.

Quantitative variables
Objects of study that inherently have numerical values associated with them, such as weight.

Categorical variables
Objects of study that do not inherently have numerical values associated with them, as gender. Often contrasted with quantitative variables.

Independent variable
A variable that can be manipulated to influence the values of the dependent variable.

Dependent variable
A variable whose values are influenced by the independent variable.

Measurement of Variables

After developing a study design, the researcher must carry it out and measure the variables of interest. A **variable** is represented by a symbol that can assume a range of numerical values. **Quantitative variables** (age, time) are those that are inherently numerical (21 years or 16 minutes). **Categorical variables** (gender, race) are not inherently numerical, but they can be "coded" to have numerical meaning: female = 0, male = 1; or White = 0, Black = 1, Hispanic = 2, Asian = 3; and so forth. For research purposes, it doesn't matter what numerical values are assigned to the categorical variables because they merely identify these variables for measurement purposes.

Variables Used in I/O Psychological Research.   The term *variable* is often used in conjunction with other terms in I/O psychological research. Four such terms that will be used throughout this book are *independent, dependent, predictor*, and *criterion*. Independent and dependent variables are associated in particular with experimental research strategies. **Independent variables** are those that are manipulated or controlled by the researcher. They are chosen by the experimenter, set or manipulated to occur at a certain level, and then examined to assess their effect on some other variable. In the laboratory experiment by Streufert et al. (1992), the independent variable was the level of alcohol intoxication. In the quasi-experiment by Latham and Kinne (1974), the independent variable was the one-day training program on goal setting.

Experiments assess the effects of independent variables on the dependent variable. The **dependent variable** is most often the object of the researcher's interest. It is usually some aspect of behavior (or, in some cases, attitudes). In the Streufert et al. study, the dependent variable was the subjects' performance on a visual-motor task. In the Latham and Kinne study, the dependent variable was the number of cords of wood harvested by the lumber crews.

The same variable can be selected as the dependent or the independent variable depending on the goals of the study. Figure 2-2 shows how a variable (employee

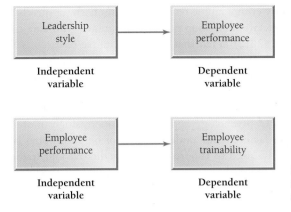

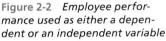

Figure 2-2 *Employee performance used as either a dependent or an independent variable*

performance) can be either dependent or independent. In the former case, the researcher wants to study the effect of various leadership styles (independent variable) on employee performance (dependent variable). The researcher might select two leadership styles (a stern taskmaster approach versus a relaxed, easygoing one) and then assess their effects on job performance. In the latter case, the researcher wants to know what effect employee performance (independent variable) has on the ability to be trained (dependent variable). The employees are divided into "high-performer" and "low-performer" groups. Both groups then attend a training program to assess whether the high performers learn faster than the low performers. Note that variables are never inherently independent or dependent. Whether they are one or the other is up to the researcher.

Predictor and criterion variables are often used in I/O psychology. When scores on one variable are used to predict scores on a second, the variables are called **predictor** and **criterion** variables, respectively. For example, a student's high school grade point average might be used to predict his or her college grade point average. Thus, high school grades are the predictor variable; college grades are the criterion variable. As a rule, criterion variables are the focal point of a study. Predictor variables may or may not be successful in predicting what we want to know (the criterion). Predictor variables are similar to independent variables; criterion variables are similar to dependent variables. The distinction between the two is a function of the research strategy. Independent and dependent variables are used in the context of experimentation. Predictor and criterion variables are used in any research where the goal is to determine the status of subjects on one variable (the criterion) as a function of their status on another variable (the predictor). Independent variables are associated with making causal inferences; predictor variables are not.

Predictor variable
A variable used to predict or forecast a criterion variable.

Criterion variable
A variable that is a primary object of a research study; it is forecasted by a predictor variable.

The Correlation Coefficient

Vinchur and Bryan (2012) noted the empirical foundation of most I/O psychological knowledge is based on data analytical methods developed over 100 years ago by such statisticians as Karl Pearson and Charles Spearman. While increasingly more complex analytical methods evolved over the years, I/O psychology still relies heavily on the statistical techniques developed in the early years of the field's history. I/O psychological research often deals with the relationship between two (or more) variables. In particular, we are usually interested in the extent that we can understand one variable (the criterion variable) on the basis of our knowledge about another (the predictor variable). A statistical procedure useful in determining this relationship is called the correlation coefficient, as developed by Pearson and Spearman. A **correlation coefficient** reflects the degree of linear relationship between two variables, which we shall refer to as X and Y. The symbol for a correlation coefficient is r, and its range is from -1.00 to $+1.00$. A correlation coefficient tells two things about the relationship between two variables: the direction of the relationship and its magnitude.

The direction of a relationship is either positive or negative. A positive relationship means that as one variable increases in magnitude, so does the other. An example of a positive correlation is between height and weight. As a rule, the taller a person is, the more he or she weighs; increasing height is associated with increasing weight. A negative relationship means that as one variable increases in magnitude, the other gets smaller. An example of a negative correlation is between production workers' efficiency and scrap rate. The more efficient workers are, the less scrap is left. The less efficient they are, the more scrap is left.

The magnitude of the correlation is an index of the strength of the relationship. Large correlations indicate greater strength than small correlations. A correlation of .80 indicates a very strong relationship between the variables, whereas a correlation of .10 indicates a very weak relationship. Magnitude and direction are independent; a correlation of $-.80$ is just as strong as one of $+.80$.

It is instructive to consider why the correlation coefficient became important to the field of I/O psychology. Zickar and Gibby (2007) identified an emphasis on quantification and correlational analysis as one of the enduring themes throughout the history of I/O psychology. I/O psychologists have long believed that better decisions (for example, as in personnel selection) can be made on the basis of a statistical analysis of the relationship between how well people perform on an employment test and how well they perform on the job. Such quantification leads to more confidence and soundness of the resulting selection decision than impressionistic or "gut feel" approaches. The quantitative approach provides an empirically-based justification for why we do what we do (e.g., use employment tests to assess job applicants). The correlation coefficient is the most frequently used method in I/O psychology for revealing the statistical relationship between two variables.

Figure 2-3 to Figure 2-6 are graphic portrayals of correlation coefficients. The first step in illustrating a correlation is to plot all pairs of variables in the study. For a sample of 100 people, record the height and weight of each person. Then plot the pair of data points (height and weight) for each person. The stronger the relationship between the two variables, the tighter is the spread of data points around the line of best fit that runs through the scatterplot.

Figure 2-3 shows a scatterplot for two variables that have a high positive correlation. Notice that the line of best fit through the data points slants in the positive direction, and most of the data points are packed tightly around the line. Figure 2-4 shows a scatterplot for two variables that have a high negative correlation. Again, notice that the data points are packed tightly around the line, but in this case, the line slants in the negative direction. Figure 2-5 shows a scatterplot for two variables that have a low positive correlation. Although the line slants in the positive direction, the data points in the scatterplot are spread out quite widely around the line of best fit. Finally, Figure 2-6

Correlation coefficient
A statistical index that reflects the degree of relationship between two variables.

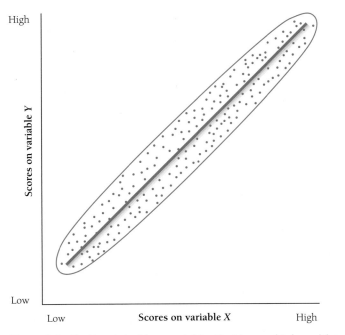

Figure 2-3   *Scatterplot of two variables that have a high positive correlation*

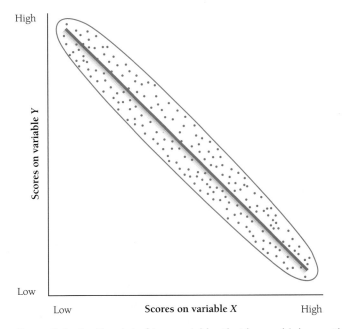

Figure 2-4   *Scatterplot of two variables that have a high negative correlation*

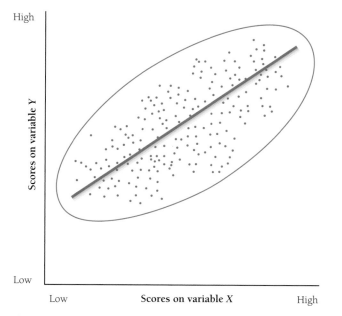

Figure 2-5 *Scatterplot of two variables that have a low positive correlation*

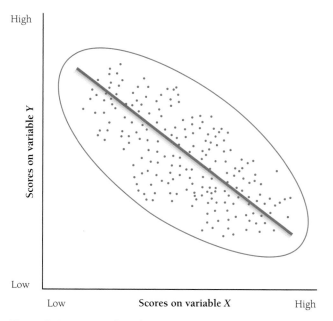

Figure 2-6 *Scatterplot of two variables that have a low negative correlation*

shows a scatterplot for two variables that have a low negative correlation. The line of best fit slants in the negative direction, and the data points are not packed tightly around the line.

The stronger the correlation between two variables (either positive or negative), the more accurately we can predict one variable from the other. The statistical formula used to compute a correlation will not be presented in this book because it is available in statistics books and it will not be necessary for you, as you read this book, to compute any correlations. However, it is important that you know what a correlation is and how to interpret one. The only way to derive the exact numerical value of a correlation is to apply the statistical formula. Although the eyeball-inspection method of looking at a scatterplot gives you some idea of what the correlation is, research has shown that people are generally not very good at inferring the magnitude of correlations by using this method.

Determining Causality

Perhaps the most laudable goal of any field of scientific inquiry is the determination of causality. A complete understanding of any phenomenon is based upon knowing causal determinants. Rarely in the behavioral sciences do we achieve this result. For example, many years of extensive research led to the conclusion that cigarette smoking causes cancer. That research finding became the basis of powerfully worded warnings placed on packs of cigarettes. While cigarette smoking is the leading cause of lung cancer, the relationship between the two is not immutable. That is, there are some people who smoke but who do not develop lung cancer. There are also some people who develop lung cancer but never smoked. However, this causal relationship is a basis for laws and organizational policies. For example, cigarettes are heavily taxed, smoking is prohibited in many public places, and smokers can be denied insurance.

What do we know about causal relationships in I/O psychology? By its very nature I/O psychology is concerned about understanding behavior in a context (the workplace) where many factors are simultaneously exerting influence on individuals. They include transient moods, personality attributes, tolerance for stress, family issues, economic conditions, and many more. In short, our work lives exist in a complex and ever-changing context. As Hanges and Wang (2012) noted, there are so many "moving parts" operating at one time it is extraordinarily difficult to disentangle "what causes what" to occur. Causality can be determined in a laboratory experiment where a single variable can be isolated, and other possible determinants of behavior are removed in the experiment. In such a controlled environment, and only in such an environment, can causality be determined. Unfortunately for I/O psychology, the very behavior we wish to understand invariably cannot be removed from the uncontrolled context in which it occurs.

Lilienfeld (2012) commented that the inability to understand causal relationships contributes to the public perception that psychology is not as valuable to society as chemistry or physics. Our inability to make precise predictions about a particular individual's behavior can be the source of public frustration. For example, when an individual commits a violent crime, it is common to have some people ask, "Why couldn't we have predicted (and prevented) this behavior?" Lilienfeld stated this is the equivalent of asking a physicist to predict the fall of a single snowflake.

I/O psychological research is heavily based on the concept of correlation. While some I/O psychological research is based on the experimental method, most is based on the correlational method. A correlation coefficient does not permit any inferences to be made about causality—that is, whether one variable *caused* the other to occur. Even though a causal relationship may exist between two variables, just computing a correlation will not reveal this fact.

Suppose you wish to compute the correlation between the amount of alcohol consumed in a town and the number of people who attend church there. You collect data on each of these variables in many towns in your area. The correlation coefficient turns out to be .85. On the basis of this high correlation, you conclude that because people drink all week, they go to church to repent (alcohol consumption causes church attendance). Your friends take the opposite point of view. They say that because people have to sit cramped together on hard wooden pews, after church they "unwind" by drinking (church attendance causes alcohol consumption). Who is correct? On the basis of the existing data, no one is correct because causality cannot be inferred from a single correlation coefficient. Proof of causality must await experimental research. In fact, the causal basis of this correlation is undoubtedly neither of the opinions offered. The various towns in the study have different populations, which produces a systematic relationship between these two variables along with many others, such as the number of people who eat out in restaurants or attend movies. Just the computation of a correlation in this example does not even determine whether the churchgoers are the drinkers. The effect of a third variable on the two variables being correlated can cloud our ability to understand the relationship between the variables in purely correlational research.

There are some researchers who believe that based on recent statistical advances, it is possible to infer causality from data collected with non-experimental research methods. Critics contend the causes of human behavior are too complex to be unraveled by statistical calculations. Stone-Romero, citing a statistician, summarized this skeptical perspective: "Causal inferences from correlational (i.e., non-experimental) data in the absence of controlled experiments are at best a form of statistical fantasy" (p. 61). Determining causality in I/O psychological research has been referenced as the "Holy Grail" (Hanges & Wang, p. 79). Our capacity to only understand the (statistical) association among factors, but not their causal relationship, retards our ability to implement policies in the workplace that are "proven" to determine behavior (Jaffe et al., 2012). Most of the research findings discussed in this book are based on correlational analyses.

As stated previously, non-experimental research methods (e.g., questionnaires) are most frequently used in I/O psychology. Given the limitations of drawing causal inferences from data derived from non-experimental methods, most I/O psychologists are extremely reluctant to assert definitive relationships among variables examined in their research. Correlations reveal statistical associations among variables; correlations do not reveal causal relationships.

Conclusions from Research

After analyzing the data, the researcher draws conclusions. A conclusion may be that alcohol intoxication impairs certain skills more than others, or jobs that require skills more adversely impaired by alcohol consumption warrant more restrictive standards than other jobs. Latham and Kinne's study concluded that goal setting increased the rate of wood harvesting. So a company might decide to implement the goal-setting procedure throughout the firm. Generally, it is unwise to implement any major changes based on the results of only one study. As a rule, we prefer to know the results from several studies. We want to be as certain as possible that any organizational changes are grounded in repeatable, generalizable results.

Sometimes the conclusions drawn from a study modify beliefs about a problem. Note in Figure 2-1 that a feedback loop extends from "Conclusions from research" to "Statement of the problem." The findings from one study influence the research problems in future studies. Theories may be altered if empirical research fails to confirm some of the hypotheses put forth. One of the most critical issues in conducting research is the quality of the generalizations that can be drawn from the conclusions. A number of factors determine the boundary conditions for generalizing the conclusions from a research study to a broader population or setting. One factor is the representativeness of individuals who serve as the research subjects. Much research is conducted in university settings, and university students often serve as subjects in research studies because they are an available sample. It has been a matter of great debate within the entire field of psychology whether the conclusions reached from studying college students generalize to a larger and more diverse population. There is no simple answer to this question: it depends greatly on the research topic under consideration. Asking typical college students to describe their vocational aspirations is highly appropriate. Asking typical college students to describe how they will spend their retirement years, 50 years from now, would have limited scientific value. Because I/O psychology is concerned with the world of work, and thus the population of concern to us is the adult working population, we are generally cautious in attempting to generalize findings based on studies of college students.

Research is a cumulative process. Researchers build on one another's work in formulating new research questions. They communicate their results by publishing articles in journals. A competent researcher must keep up to date in his or her area of expertise to avoid repeating someone else's study. The conclusions drawn from research can affect many aspects of our lives. Research is a vital part of industry; it is the basis for changes in products and services. Research can be a truly exciting activity, although it may seem tedious if you approach it from the perspective of only testing stuffy theories, using sterile statistics, and inevitably reaching dry conclusions. Daft (1983) suggested that research is a craft, and a researcher, like an artist or craftsperson, has to pull together a wide variety of human experiences to produce a superior product. Being a researcher is more like unraveling a mystery than following a cookbook. However, research is not flash-in-the-pan thrill seeking; it involves perseverance, mental discipline, and patience. There is no substitute for hard work. We can recall many times when we anxiously anticipated seeing statistical analyses that would foretell the results of a lengthy research study. This sense of anticipation is the fun of doing research—and research, in the spirit of Daft's view of researchers being craftspersons, is a craft we try to pass on to our students. Klahr and Simon (1999) believe researchers from all scientific disciplines, though differing in the methods used in their respective disciplines, are all basically problem solvers. They invoke research methods to solve problems and answer questions of interest to them. Researchers are driven by a sense of curiosity, like that of a child. Klahr and Simon added: "Perhaps this is why childlike characteristics, such as the propensity to wonder, are so often attributed to creative scientists and artists" (p. 540). Grant et al. (2011) reported Einstein once quipped, "If we knew what we were doing, it wouldn't be called research, would it?" (p. 444).

McCall and Bobko (1990) noted the importance of serendipity in scientific research. *Serendipity* refers to a chance occurrence or happening. "The history of science is filled with chance discoveries. [For example] a contaminated culture eventually led [Alexander] Fleming to learn about and recognize the properties of penicillin" (p. 384). Rather than discarding the culture because it was contaminated, Fleming sought to understand how it had become so. The lesson is that we should allow room for lucky accidents and unexpected observations to occur and be prepared to pursue them.

Ethical Issues in Research

The American Psychological Association (2010) has a code of ethics that must be honored by all APA members who conduct research. The code of ethics was created to protect the rights of research participants and to avoid the possibility of unqualified people conducting research. It is the responsibility of the researcher to balance ethical accountability and the technical demands of scientific research practices. It is not at all unusual for psychologists to face ethical conflicts in the conduct of their work, including research.

As stated by Aguinis and Henle (2002), participants in psychological research are granted five rights that are specified in the code of ethics:

1. **Right to informed consent**. Participants have the right to know the purpose of the research, the right to decline or withdraw participation at any time without negative consequences, and the right to be informed of any risks associated with their participation in the research. This right is perhaps the most fundamental because most research aims to meet the needs of the researcher, not the participants.

2. **Right to privacy**. Researchers must respect the participants' right to limit the amount of information they reveal about themselves. How much information the participants might be required to reveal and the sensitivity of this information may offset their willingness to participate.

3. **Right to confidentiality**. Confidentiality involves decisions about who will have access to research data, how records will be maintained, and whether participants will be anonymous. Participants should have the right to decide to whom they will reveal personal information. By guaranteeing participants' confidentiality, researchers may be able to obtain more honest responses.

4. **Right to protection from deception**. Deception refers to a researcher intentionally misleading a participant about the real purpose of the research. Examples are withholding information and producing fake beliefs and assumptions. Deception is sometimes used by researchers in the belief that it is critical to understanding the phenomenon of interest. Researchers who wish to use deception must demonstrate to an institutional review board that the value of the research outweighs the harm imposed on participants and that the phenomenon cannot be studied in any other way. It has been argued that deception does not respect par-

ticipants' rights, dignity, and freedom to decline participation and may result in participants being suspicious of psychological research. In short, deception can be used in research, but participants are assured that it is used only as a last resort.

5. **Right to debriefing**. After the study is completed, debriefing must take place to answer participants' questions about the research, to remove any harmful effects brought on by the study, and to leave participants with a sense of dignity. Debriefing should include information about how the current study adds to knowledge of the topic, how the results of the study might be applied, and the importance of this type of research.

Researchers who violate these rights, particularly in studies that involve physical or psychological risks, are subject to professional censure and possible litigation. Aguinis and Henle also noted that many countries have developed codes of ethics regarding research. Although nations differ in the breadth of research issues covered, every country emphasizes the well-being and dignity of research participants in their ethics code by addressing informed consent, deception, protection from harm, and confidentiality.

The researcher is faced with additional problems when the participants are employees of companies. Even when managers authorize research, it can cause problems in an organizational context. Employees who are naive about the purpose of research are often suspicious when asked to participate. They wonder how they were "picked" for inclusion in the study and whether they will be asked difficult questions. Some people even think a psychologist can read their minds and thus discover all sorts of private thoughts. Research projects that arouse emotional responses may place managers in an uncomfortable interpersonal situation.

There are additional problems associated with conducting research with employees. Most problems involve role conflict, the dilemma of being trained to be a good researcher yet having to comply with both company and professional standards. For example, consider a role-conflict problem we faced in doing research with industrial employees. We used a questionnaire to assess the employees' opinions and morale. Management had commissioned the study. As part of the research design, all employees were told that their responses would be anonymous. One survey response revealed the existence of employee theft. Although we did not know the identity of the employee, with the information given and a little help from management, that person could have been identified. Were we to violate our promise and turn over the information to management? Should we tell management that some theft had occurred but we had no way to find out who had done it (which would not have been true)? Or were we to ignore what we knew and fail to tell management about a serious problem in the company? In this case, we informed the company of the theft, but we refused to supply any information about the personal identity of the thief. This was an uneasy compromise between serving the needs of our client and maintaining the confidentiality of the information source (see Field Note 1: *An Ethical Dilemma*).

Furthermore, ethical issues in psychology are not limited to the conduct of research. Adherence to the code of ethics also applies to such issues as conflict of interest, plagiarizing, and the treatment of clients. Following the terrorist attacks of 9/11, the APA began to examine the ethical implications of psychologists' role in interrogating suspected terrorists (Behnke & Moorehead-Slaughter, 2012). For applied psychologists

Field Note 1: *An Ethical Dilemma*

Many ethical problems do not have clear-cut solutions. Here is one I ran into. I was trying to identify some psychological tests that would be useful in selecting future salespeople for a company. As part of my research, I administered the tests to all the employees in the sales department. With the company's consent, I assured the employees that the test results would be confidential. I explained that my purpose in giving the tests was to test the tests—that is, to assess the value of the tests—and that no one in the company would ever use the test results to evaluate the employees. In fact, no one in the company would even know the test scores. The results of my research were highly successful. I was able to identify which tests were useful in selecting potentially successful salespeople. A few weeks later the same company's management approached me and said they now wanted to look into the value of using psychological tests to promote salespeople to the next higher job in the department, sales manager. In fact, they were so impressed with the test results for selecting new salespeople that they wanted to assess the value of these very same tests for identifying good sales managers. And since I had already given the tests to their salespeople and had the scores, all I would have to do is turn over the scores to the company, and they would determine whether there was any relationship between the scores and promotability to sales manager.

I said I couldn't turn over the test results because that would violate my statement that the results were confidential and that no one in the company *would* ever know how well the employees did on the tests. I offered two alternatives. One was to readminister the same tests to the employees under a different set of test conditions—namely, that the company *would* see the test results and, in fact, the results could be used to make promotion decisions. The second alternative was for me (not the company) to determine the value of these tests to make promotion decisions. In that way I would maintain the confidentiality of the test scores. Management totally rejected the first alternative, saying it made no sense to readminister the same tests to the same people. I already had the test results, so why go back and get them a second time? The second alternative was also not approved. They said I was deliberately creating a need for the company to pay me for a second consulting project when they were perfectly capable of doing the work, with no outside help and at no extra cost. They said, in effect, I was holding the test results "hostage" when I would not release them.

In my opinion, the company's management was asking me to compromise my professional integrity by using the test results in a way that violated the agreement under which the tests were originally administered. The issue was never really resolved. The company soon faced some major sales problems caused by competitors and lost interest in the idea of using psychological tests for identifying sales managers. The management is still angry about my decision, asserting that I am assuming ownership of "their" test results. I have not been asked to do any more consulting work for them, but it is also quite possible that they would no longer have needed my services even if I had turned the test results over.

there can be conflict between national security related needs and the ethical obligations to all individuals, including suspected terrorists, not to inflict harm. Lefkowitz (2003) noted that I/O psychology is sometimes portrayed (incorrectly) as being a value-free science. This view is advanced by those who believe the field is entirely objective, despite our service to the highly competitive world of business. Reynolds (2008) observed we become aware of the importance of ethics more typically through the actions that violate it. It is unethical behavior that gets reported, not ethical behavior. Reynolds identified differences among people regarding ethical sensitivity; individuals must be sensitive to ethical issues before they can behave ethically. The ethical conduct of psychologists is critical for maintaining the integrity of our profession.

Academic-Based and Practitioner-Based Research

Within some professions (such as medicine), there is a close relationship between those individuals who conduct scientific studies (i.e., medical researchers) and those individuals who are practitioners (i.e., physicians). The medical researchers may, for example, develop and test new pharmaceutical products. If the results of their research are positive, the new drug treatments will be manufactured by a pharmaceutical company. In turn, product representatives of the company will call upon physicians to inform them of the availability of the new drug treatment. Lastly, physicians can prescribe the new medications to patients for treating their illnesses. In short, medicine has an established and accepted procedure for advancing research products from "lab to life." Pfeffer (2007) reported there has been a 50% reduction in death rates from heart disease over the past several decades because physicians have implemented the findings from medical research.

I/O psychologists who study work aspire to have their research findings used by managers in running organizations. However, unlike medicine, there is not a strong connection between I/O psychological research findings and the management of organizations. The difference between scientific research findings on organizations and their management versus how organizations are actually managed is called the **scientist-practitioner gap**. The scientist-practitioner gap is regarded as evidence that either managers are unaware of I/O psychological findings, or that academic researchers study topics with little relevance to day-to-day organizational issues. Several reasons have been proposed to explain why the gap exists. Hambrick (2007) noted that academic researchers have over-emphasized the importance of theory in determining what constitutes useful research. While theory may guide scientific research, how organizations run is not guided by theory. Organizations are run by leaders who make decisions in the best interests of maintaining and improving the organization. Hambrick stated if the behavior of organizational leaders happens to conform to some academic theory, the theory is not a cause of their behavior, just a corollary. Suddaby et al. (2011) argued that the scientist-practitioner gap is the product of not having theories that are developed specifically to explain workplace behavior. The vast majority of psychological theories attempt to explain human behavior (e.g., motivation), and these are tested for their applicability in the workplace (e.g., work motivation). The authors proposed developing theories around typical workplace issues and problems.

Cascio (2007) observed that unlike medicine, management is not a profession.

Scientist-practitioner gap The difference between scientific research findings on organizations and their management versus how organizations are actually managed.

Managers are not licensed (like physicians) and they are not required to keep abreast of scientific advances in their field. Additionally, there is the problem of how managers would learn about scientific research findings in I/O psychology. Most scientific writing is very technical, typically written for an academic readership, not business managers. Lawler (2007) acknowledged the lack of publications that serve to "translate" complex scientific findings into more readily understandable terms that could be understood by non-scientists (i.e., managers). There is also no equivalent for managers of "product representatives" who keep physicians informed of recent medical treatments. Lawler added, "Even where research results are known, and have clear implications for practice, they may not impact practice because they run counter to what practitioners prefer to do or believe is right (when it comes to people, everyone is an expert!)" (p. 1033). Cascio and Aguinis (2008) examined 45 years of published research in I/O psychology and determined that academic research has only a modest effect on management practices. They concluded that if I/O academic scientists want their research findings put into practice by managers, the scientists will have to change their approach to research (i.e., what they study and how they study it).

While academic-based research may have only a modest impact in some areas of management practice, many I/O psychologists in non-academic roles also conduct research. Some of the finest research contributions of I/O psychology attained such a legacy precisely because they did have a very large impact on practice. From a historical perspective, examples include the Army General Classification Test (AGCT) and the Armed Services Vocational Aptitude Battery (ASVAB). Currently, many large consulting firms have their own research divisions, as do large organizations that employ I/O psychologists (see I/O Psychology and the Economy: *How the Economy Influences Research*). Research conducted in these settings is often more focused on addressing particular organizational problems than is research conducted by academic scientists. There are also legitimate differences in the types of research findings that are of interest to scientists and practitioners. Recall from earlier in the chapter that the statistical index most commonly used by I/O researchers is the correlation coefficient. Bazerman (2005) considers correlational research findings to be *descriptive* ("what is the statistical relationship between X and Y"), while managers prefer findings that are *prescriptive* in nature ("if X occurs, do Y"). For example, a scientist would be interested in knowing if there is a relationship between employee job performance and voluntary turnover (i.e., are good or poor employees more likely to quit their jobs). A manager, on the other hand, would be more interested in learning how to prevent his or her top-performing employees from quitting. Each of these lines of inquiry is important, but each represents a different research question. The former seeks to understand a relationship between two variables, while the latter seeks knowledge as a basis to take action (see Field Note 2: *Win the Battle but Lose the War*). As Rynes (2012) observed, science is heavily quantitative, while practitioners prefer verbal explanations for phenomena. In a similar view, Brandon (2011) described the challenge of "translating" complex research findings into actionable management policies.

In conclusion, academic scientists and practitioners who work in business and for consulting firms are often engaged in the conduct of I/O psychological research. While the objectives of academic-based and practitioner-based research are different, they both require knowledge of the research methods and issues related to interpreting research findings that were presented in this chapter.

I/O Psychology and the Economy: *How the Economy Influences Research*

The state of the economy dictates the level of business activity. Many I/O psychologists who work for consulting firms and in other practitioner settings conduct research designed directly to assist their clients or their employer's business needs. The exact nature of the research is heavily influenced by large scale economic considerations.

When the economy is expanding, business is in a growth mode, and more financial resources are provided to develop the human resources needed for work. Under these conditions, I/O psychologists may be asked to develop new ways to recruit and select employees, create new training programs, and so on. The general theme to their activity is to make sure the workforce keeps pace with growing business opportunities available to the organization. When economic times are good, resources are plentiful, and there is often a general sense of excitement associated with prosperity.

However, when the economy is contracting, business activity slows, fewer people are needed to perform work, and there is often very little discretionary spending by organizations. Research performed by I/O psychologists under these economic conditions is considerably different than in prosperous times. First, the direction of the research follows the general edict of cutting back on expenses. I/O psychologists may be asked to develop less expensive ways to recruit and select employees, find ways to consolidate different training programs, develop methods by which employees can learn to perform other jobs, etc. Alternatively, following the adage that "time is money," the research may be directed toward reducing the amount of time it takes, for example, to learn new job skills. The overall theme of the research is to find ways to "do it cheaper or do it faster."

Second, in cutting back on expenses, money spent on research is often among the first items to be reduced in an organization's budget. Research may be conducted on a smaller scale, or in extreme cases, not at all. Unless the I/O psychologists can perform other work within the organization besides research, they may be laid off as part of the overall cost-savings actions.

Third, many organizations recognize the value of what I/O psychology can provide to improve their welfare. However, the recognition of this value does not necessarily mean that they have to hire an I/O psychologist as an employee. Instead, the organization may turn to a consulting firm to, in effect, "rent" the I/O psychological expertise needed to solve their problems. Unless the organization has a continuous large-scale need for I/O psychologists, it may be cheaper for the organization to use the (temporary) services of a consultant. Proportionately more I/O psychologists today work for consulting firms (relative to business) than they did twenty years ago. Likewise, proportionately more consulting firms today have their own research function within the firm. The I/O psychologists in the firm who function as researchers develop new products (e.g., a new method of leadership development) that are, in turn, marketed to clients by the I/O psychologists who function as consultants.

No organization is immune from economic influence. You might think that research conducted by dedicated scientists might be "above the fray" when it comes to dealing with changing economic conditions. However, such is not the case. Economic conditions influence the nature and scope of research conducted by I/O psychologists working in business and for consulting firms.

Field Note 2: *Win the Battle but Lose the War*

Industry-based research is always embedded in a larger context; that is, it is conducted for a specific reason. Sometimes the research is successful, sometimes it isn't, and sometimes you can win the battle but lose the war. A client of mine gave promotional tests—tests that current employees take to be advanced to higher positions in the company at higher rates of pay. These tests were important to the employees because only through the tests could they be promoted. The company administered an attitude survey and discovered that many employees did not like the tests. They said many test questions were outdated, some questions had no correct answers, and most questions were poorly worded. As a result of these "bad" questions, employees were failing the tests and not getting promoted. I was hired to update and improve the promotional tests (there were 75 of them). Using the full complement of psychological research procedures, I analyzed every question on every test, eliminated the poor questions, developed new questions, and in general "cleaned up" each of the tests. By every known standard, the tests were now of very high quality.

Both the company's management and I felt confident the employees would be delighted with these revised tests. We were wrong. In the next attitude survey administered by the company, the employees still thought poorly of the (new) tests, but their reasons were different from before. Now they complained that the tests were too technical and required too much expertise to pass. The employees failed the new tests with the same frequency they had failed the old tests and were just as unhappy. In fact, they may have been even more unhappy; their expectations about the tests had been elevated because the company had hired me to revise them. I felt I had done as good a job in revising the tests as I possibly could have, but in the final analysis I didn't really solve the company's problem. I was hired to revise the tests, but what management really wanted was to have the employees be satisfied with the tests, which didn't occur.

Chapter Summary

- Research is a means by which I/O psychologists understand issues associated with people at work.
- The four primary research methods used by I/O psychologists are experiments, quasi-experiments, questionnaires, and observation.
- The four primary research methods differ in their extent of control (potential for testing causal relationships) and realism (naturalness of the research setting).
- I/O psychologists measure variables of interest and apply statistical analyses to understand the relationships among the variables.
- Meta-analysis is a secondary research method that is useful in integrating findings from previously conducted studies.
- Data mining is a secondary research method that is relatively new to I/O psychology.

- Organizational neuroscience is an emerging scientific method in I/O psychology.
- Qualitative research findings add richness and detail to our understanding of phenomena.
- All psychological research is guided by a code of ethics that protects the rights of research participants.
- Research is conducted in both academic (university) and applied (organizational) settings, but usually for different purposes.
- As a profession, I/O psychology has a broad base of knowledge derived from both academic and applied research.
- There are cross-cultural differences in both people's willingness to serve as research participants and their responses.

3

Criteria: Standards for Decision Making

Chapter Outline

Learning Objectives

- Understand the distinction between conceptual and actual criteria.
- Understand the meaning of criterion deficiency, relevance, and contamination.
- Explain the purpose of work analysis and the various methods of conducting one.
- Explain the nine major criteria of job performance examined by I/O psychologists.
- Understand the concept of dynamic criteria.

Criteria
Standards used to help make evaluative judgments.

Each time you evaluate someone or something, you use criteria. **Criteria** (the plural of *criterion*) are best defined as evaluative standards; they are used as reference points in making judgments. We may not be consciously aware of the criteria that affect our judgments, but they do exist. We use different criteria to evaluate different kinds of objects or people; that is, we use different standards to determine what makes a good (or bad) movie, dinner, ball game, friend, spouse, or teacher. In the context of I/O psychology, criteria are most important for defining the "goodness" of employees, programs, and units in the organization as well as the organization itself.

When you and some of your associates disagree in your evaluations of something, what is the cause? Chances are good the disagreement is caused by one of two types of criterion-related problems. For example, take the case of rating Professor Jones as a teacher. One student thinks he is a good teacher; another disagrees. The first student defines "goodness in teaching" as (1) preparedness, (2) course relevance, and (3) clarity of instruction. In the eyes of the first student, Jones scores very high on these criteria and receives a positive evaluation. The second student defines "goodness" as (1) enthusiasm, (2) capacity to inspire students, and (3) ability to relate to students on a personal basis. This student scores Jones low on these criteria and thus gives him a negative evaluation. Why the disagreement? Because the two students have different criteria for defining goodness in teaching.

Disagreements over the proper criteria to use in decision making are common. Values and tastes also dictate people's choice of criteria. For someone with limited funds, a good car may be one that gets high gas mileage. But for a wealthy person, the main criterion may be physical comfort. Not all disagreements are caused by using different criteria, however. Suppose that both students in our teaching example define goodness in teaching as preparedness, course relevance, and clarity of instruction. The first student thinks Professor Jones is well-prepared, teaches a relevant course, and gives clear instruction. But the second student thinks he is ill-prepared, teaches an irrelevant course, and gives unclear instruction. Both students are using the same evaluative standards, but they do not reach the same judgment. The difference of opinion in this case is due to discrepancies in the meanings attached to Professor Jones's behavior. These discrepancies may result from perceptual biases, different expectations, or varying operational definitions associated with criteria. Thus, even people who use the same standards in making judgments do not always reach the same conclusion (see Social Media and I/O Psychology: *Criteria for "5 Star" Organizations*).

Austin and Villanova (1992) traced the history of criterion measurement in I/O psychology over the past 75 years. Today's conceptual problems associated with accurate criterion representation and measurement are not all that different from those faced at the birth of I/O psychology. Furthermore, the profession of I/O psychology does not have a monopoly on criterion-related issues and problems. They occur in all walks of life, ranging from the criteria used to judge interpersonal relationships (communication, trust, and respect, for example) to the welfare of nations (literacy rates, per capita income, and infant mortality rates, for example). Since many important decisions are made on the basis of criteria, it is difficult to overstate their significance in the decision-making process. Because criteria are used to render a wide range of judgments, we define them as the evaluative standards by which objects, individuals, procedures, or collectivities are assessed for the purpose of ascertaining their quality. Criterion issues have major significance in the field of I/O psychology.

Social Media and I/O Psychology: *Criteria for "5 Star" Organizations*

A defining feature of social media is that individuals are able to create and share information, ideas, and opinions with others. We use social media sites as platforms to express ourselves, obtain information on a variety of topics, and to solicit feedback from others on a multitude of matters. When seeking advice from others on social media, however, it is important to remember that individuals have different conceptualizations of what is important. Searching for a lunch box for my son, for example, I found one on Amazon.com that had customer reviews ranging from 1 star to 5 stars. Digging into the content of the reviews, I discovered that many of the 5 star reviewers commented on how "cute" and durable the lunch box was. The 1 star reviewers were commenting on the lack of insulation (food apparently didn't stay cold long) and the size (hard to fit a juice box in with a sandwich without squishing the sandwich). Clearly the reviewers had different ideas of what constitutes a "good" lunch box.

Individuals are not just seeking information about products. They are also using input from others to make decisions regarding their employment. Glassdoor.com, for example, is a site where current and former employees can anonymously post reviews about an organization's compensation and benefits, culture and values, and career opportunities that others (such as prospective employees) can use when making employment decisions (such as whether to apply for or accept a job with a certain company). Glassdoor verifies that the reviews come from actual employees but keeps the authors of posts anonymous. In addition, they do not edit or alter content within reviews that are posted. In this way, it is believed that the reviews can be trusted as being the reviewers' true feelings, not being overly positive out of fear of repercussions from management. Looking at reviews, however, it is again clear that people have different criteria they use to form opinions about an organization. The pros and cons for organizations vary considerably depending on the reviewer. One reviewer may give a 5-star rating based on benefits and salary while another does so based on leadership and office culture. The usefulness of any rating depends upon our knowledge of the criteria used by the reviewer in making the rating.

Conceptual Versus Actual Criteria

Psychologists have not always thought that criteria are of prime importance. Before World War II, they were inclined to believe that "criteria were either given of God or just to be found lying about" (Jenkins, 1946, p. 93). Unfortunately, this is not so. We must carefully consider what is meant by a "successful" worker, student, parent, and so forth. We cannot plunge headlong into measuring success, goodness, or quality until we have a fairly good idea of what (in theory, at least) we are looking for.

Conceptual criterion
The theoretical standard that researchers seek to understand.

A good beginning point is the notion of a conceptual criterion. The **conceptual criterion** is a theoretical construct, an abstract idea that can never actually be measured. It is an ideal set of factors that constitute a successful person (or object or collectivity) as conceived in the psychologist's mind. Let's say we want to define a successful college student. We might start off with intellectual growth; that is, capable students should experience more intellectual growth than less capable students. Another dimension might be emotional growth. A college education should help students clarify their own values and beliefs, and this should add to their emotional development and stability. Finally, we might say that a good college student should want to have some voice in civic activities, be a "good citizen," and contribute to the well-being of his or her community. As an educated person, the good college student will assume an active role in helping to make society a better place in which to live. We might call this dimension a citizenship factor.

Thus these three factors become the conceptual criteria for defining a "good college student." We could apply this same process to defining a "good worker," "good parent," or "good organization." However, because conceptual criteria are theoretical abstractions, we have to find some way to turn them into measurable, real factors. That is, we have to obtain **actual criteria** to serve as measures of the conceptual criteria that we would prefer to (but cannot) assess. The decision is then which variables to select as the actual criteria.

A psychologist might choose grade point average as a measure of intellectual growth. Of course, a high grade point average is not equivalent to intellectual growth, but it probably reflects some degree of growth. To measure emotional growth, a psychologist might ask a student's adviser to judge how much the student has matured over his or her college career. Again, maturation is not exactly the same as emotional growth, but it is probably an easier concept to grasp and evaluate than the more abstract notion of emotional growth. Finally, as a measure of citizenship, a psychologist might count the number of volunteer organizations (student government, charitable clubs, and so on) the student has joined over his or her college career. It could be argued that the sheer number (quantity) of joined organizations does not reflect the quality of participation in these activities, and that "good citizenship" is more appropriately defined by quality rather than quantity of participation. Nevertheless, because of the difficulties inherent in measuring quality of participation, plus the fact that one cannot speak of quality unless there is some quantity, the psychologist decides to use this measure. Table 3-1 shows the conceptual criteria and the actual criteria of success for a college student.

How do we define a "good" college student in theory? With the conceptual criteria as the evaluative standards, a good college student should display a high degree of intellectual and emotional growth and should be a responsible citizen in the community. How do we operationalize a good college student in practice? Using the actual criteria as the evaluative standards, we say a good college student has earned high grades, is judged by an academic adviser to be emotionally mature, and has joined many volunteer organizations throughout his or her college career. In a review of the relationship between the two sets of criteria (conceptual and actual), remember that the goal is to

Actual criteria
The operational or actual standards that researchers measure or assess. Often contrasted with conceptual criteria.

Table 3-1 *Conceptual and actual criteria for a successful college student*

Conceptual Criteria	Actual Criteria
Intellectual growth	Grade point average
Emotional growth	Adviser rating of emotional maturity
Citizenship	Number of volunteer organizations joined in college

obtain a reasonable estimate of the conceptual criterion by selecting one or more actual criteria that we think are appropriate.

Criterion Deficiency, Relevance, and Contamination

Criterion deficiency
The part of the conceptual criterion that is not measured by the actual criterion.

Criterion relevance
The degree of overlap or similarity between the actual criterion and the conceptual criterion.

Criterion contamination
The part of the actual criterion that is unrelated to the conceptual criterion.

We can express the relationship between conceptual and actual criteria in terms of three concepts: deficiency, relevance, and contamination. Figure 3-1 shows the overlap between conceptual and actual criteria. The circles represent the contents of each type of criterion. Because the conceptual criterion is a theoretical abstraction, we can never know exactly how much overlap occurs. The actual criteria selected are never totally equivalent to the conceptual criteria we have in mind, so there is always a certain amount (though unspecified) of deficiency, relevance, and contamination.

Criterion deficiency is the degree to which the actual criteria fail to overlap the conceptual criteria; that is, how lacking the actual criteria are in representing the conceptual ones. There is always some degree of deficiency in the actual criteria. By careful selection of the actual criteria, we can reduce (but never eliminate) criterion deficiency. Conversely, criteria that are selected because they are simply expedient, without much thought given to their match to conceptual criteria, are grossly deficient. **Criterion relevance** is the degree to which the actual criteria and the conceptual criteria coincide. The greater the match between the conceptual and the actual criteria, the greater the criterion relevance. Again, because the conceptual criteria are theoretical abstractions, we cannot know the exact amount of relevance.

Criterion contamination is that part of the actual criteria that is unrelated to the conceptual criteria. It is the extent to which the actual criteria measure something other than the conceptual criteria. Contamination consists of two parts. One part, called *bias*, is the extent to which the actual criteria systematically or consistently

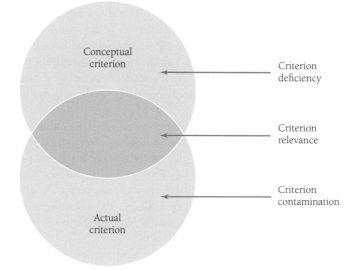

Figure 3-1   *Criterion deficiency, relevance, and contamination*

measure something other than the conceptual criteria. The second part, called *error*, is the extent to which the actual criteria are not related to anything at all.

Both contamination and deficiency are undesirable in the actual criterion, and together they distort the conceptual criterion. Criterion contamination distorts the actual criterion because certain factors are included that don't belong (that is, they are not present in the conceptual criterion). Criterion deficiency distorts the actual criterion because certain important dimensions of the conceptual criterion are not included in the actual criterion.

Let us consider criterion deficiency and contamination in the example of setting criteria for a good college student. How might the actual criteria we chose be deficient in representing the conceptual criteria? Students typically begin a class with differing amounts of prior knowledge of the subject matter. One student may know nothing of the material, while another student may be very familiar with it. At the end of the term, the former student might have grown more intellectually than the latter student, but the latter student might get a higher grade in the course. By using the grade point average as our criterion, we would (falsely) conclude that the latter student grew more intellectually. So the relationship between good grades and intellectual growth is not perfect (that is, it is deficient). A rating of emotional maturity by an academic adviser might be deficient because the adviser is not an ideal judge. He or she might have only a limited perspective of the student. Finally, it is not enough to just count how many volunteer groups a student belongs to. Quality of participation is as important as (if not more important than) quantity.

How might these actual criteria be contaminated? If some academic majors are more difficult than others, then grades are a contaminated measure of intellectual growth; students in "easy" majors will be judged to have experienced more intellectual growth than students in difficult majors. This is a bias between earned grade point averages and the difficulty of the student's academic major. The source of the bias affects the actual criterion (grades) but not the conceptual criterion (intellectual growth). A rating of emotional maturity by the student's adviser could be contaminated by the student's grades. The adviser might believe that students with high grades have greater emotional maturity than students with low grades. Thus the grade point average might bias an adviser's rating even though it probably has no relationship to the conceptual criterion of emotional growth. Finally, counting the number of organizations a student joins might be contaminated by the student's popularity. Students who join many organizations may simply be more popular rather than better citizens (which is what we want to measure).

If we know that these criterion measures are contaminated, why would we use them? In fact, when a researcher identifies a certain form of contamination, its influence can be controlled through experimental or statistical procedures. The real problem is anticipating the presence of contaminating factors. Komaki (1998) noted that a problem with some criteria is that they are not under the direct control of the person being evaluated. For example, two salespeople may differ in their overall sales volumes because they have different-sized sales territories, not because one is a better salesperson than the other.

Psychologists have spent a great deal of time trying to discover new and better ways to measure actual criteria. They have used various analytical and computational procedures to get more precise assessments. Over fifty years ago Wallace (1965) recommended that rather than dwelling on finding new ways to measure actual criteria, psychologists should spend more time choosing actual criteria that will be adequate measures of the conceptual criteria they really seek to understand. The adequacy of the actual criterion as a measure of the conceptual criterion is always a matter of professional judgment—no equation or formula will determine it. As Wherry (1957) said in a classic statement, "If we are measuring the wrong thing, it will not help us to measure it better" (p. 5).

Work Analysis

Work analysis
A formal procedure by which the content of work is defined in terms of activities performed and attributes needed to perform the work.

The topic of work in society—what work is required and who should do it—can be traced back to Socrates in the 5th century BC (Primoff & Fine, 1988). However, the formal analysis of work began at the start of the 20th century. Two of the founding figures of I/O psychology were instrumental in developing the concept of work analysis as a means to increase industrial efficiency. Frederick Taylor advocated **work analysis** as a cornerstone of the principles of scientific management. Lillian Moller Gilbreth and her husband used time-and-motion studies to identify units or segments of work in performing a job, which they called a "Therblig" ("Therblig" is "Gilbreth" spelled backwards, almost). For many years I/O psychology referred to work analysis as "job analysis." Only recently (e.g., Morgeson & Dierdorff, 2011; Pearlman & Sanchez, 2010) has the field of I/O psychology preferred to use the term "work analysis." While jobs are often at the heart of work analysis, the psychological meaning of a job (i.e., a standardized set of tasks requiring specific skills for their conduct) is eroding because of the continuously changing nature of the modern work world. As expressed by Sanchez and Levine (2001), "Although static 'jobs' maybe a thing of the past, studying work processes and assignments continues to be the foundation of any human resource system today and in the foreseeable future" (p. 86).

I/O psychologists must often identify the criteria of effective work performance. These criteria then become the basis for hiring people (choosing them according to their ability to meet performance criteria), training them (to perform work tasks that are important), and paying them (high levels of performance warrant higher pay). Work analysis is a useful procedure in identifying the criteria or performance dimensions of a job; it is conducted by a work analyst. Pearlman and Sanchez referred to work analysis as "any systematic process for gathering, documenting, and analyzing information about: (a) the content of the work performed by people in organizations (e.g., tasks, responsibilities, or work outputs), (b) the worker attributes related to its performance (often referred to as knowledge, skills, abilities, and other personal characteristics), or (c) the context in which work is performed (including physical and psychological conditions in the immediate work environment and the broader organizational and external environment)" (p. 73).

This basic information is used to make many personnel decisions. Its use is mandated by legal requirements, and estimated annual costs for work analyses can exceed $1,000,000 for large organizations. Wilson (2007) offered an insightful statement about the role that work analysis serves within I/O psychology. "The field of [work] analysis is especially important because it is the precursor to many other areas of I/O psychology. [Work] analysis often serves as a first step that cannot be ignored even though the investigator's primary interests may be in other areas" (p. 219). Wilson's statement that work analysis is a "first step that cannot be ignored" is most accurate. Using the peg-and-hole analogy written over 90 years ago as presented in Chapter 1, work analysis serves to define or describe the "shape of the hole." Failing to conduct a work analysis leaves us in the perilous position of trying to fit a given peg into a hole of unknown size or shape. Thus work analysis is often regarded as a required first step in many areas of I/O psychology for practical, theoretical, and legal reasons. Levine and Sanchez (2012) added, "The [work] analysis should successfully capture the job's underlying constructs that are critical in such areas as selecting, compensating, training, or evaluating the performance of employees, but a successful analysis does not automatically guarantee that the programs developed as a result of the analysis will be successful" (p. 129). That is, a professionally crafted work analysis does not obviate the need to put equal emphasis into the practical uses (e.g., selection, training) of work analysis (Gutman & Dunleavy, 2012).

Sources of Work Information

Subject matter expert (SME)
A person knowledgeable about a topic who can serve as a qualified information source.

The most critical issue in work analysis is the accuracy and completeness of the information. There are three major sources of work information, and each source is a **subject matter expert (SME)**. The qualifications for being an SME are not precise, but a minimum condition is that the person has direct, up-to-date experience with the work for a long enough time to be familiar with all of its tasks.

The most common source of information is a *job incumbent*—that is, the holder of a job. The use of job incumbents as SMEs is predicated upon their implicit understanding of their own jobs. Landy and Vasey (1991) believe that the sampling method used to select SMEs is very important. They found that experienced job incumbents provide the most valuable job information. Given the rapid changes in work caused by changing technology, Sanchez (2000) questioned whether job incumbents are necessarily qualified to serve as SMEs. New jobs, jobs that don't currently exist in an organization and for which there are no incumbents, also have to be analyzed. Sanchez proposed the use of statistical methods to forecast employee characteristics needed in the future as technology shifts the way work is conducted. A second source of information is the *supervisor* of the job incumbent. Supervisors play a major role in determining what job incumbents do on their jobs, and thus they are a credible source of information. Although supervisors may describe jobs somewhat more objectively than incumbents, incumbents and supervisors can have legitimate differences of opinion. It has been our experience that most differences occur not in what is accomplished in a job, but in the critical attributes needed to perform the job. The third source of job information is a trained *work analyst*. Work analysts are used as SMEs when comparisons are needed across many jobs. Because of their familiarity with work analytic methods, analysts often provide the most consistent across-job ratings. Work analyst expertise lies not in the subject matter of various jobs per se, but in their ability to understand similarities and differences across jobs in terms of work activities performed and human attributes needed.

In general, incumbents and supervisors are the best sources of descriptive job information, whereas work analysts are best qualified to comprehend the relationships among a set of jobs. The most desirable strategy in understanding a job is to collect

Task
The lowest level of analysis in the study of work; a basic component of work (such as typing for a secretary).

Position
A set of tasks performed by a single employee. For example, the position of a secretary is often represented by the tasks of typing, filing, and scheduling.

Job
A set of similar positions in an organization.

Job family
A grouping of similar jobs in an organization.

Task-oriented procedure
A procedure or set of operations in work analysis designed to identify important or frequently performed tasks as a means of understanding the work performed.

information from as many qualified sources as possible, as opposed to relying exclusively on one source.

Work Analytic Procedures

The purpose of work analysis is to explain the activities that are performed on the job and the human attributes needed to perform the job. A clear understanding of work analysis requires knowledge of four work-related concepts, as shown in Figure 3-2. At the lowest level of aggregation are tasks. **Tasks** are the basic units of work that are directed toward meeting specific work objectives. A **position** is a set of tasks performed by a single employee. There are usually as many positions in an organization as there are employees. However, many positions may be similar to one another. In such a case, similar positions are grouped or aggregated to form a **job**. An example is the job of secretary; another job is that of receptionist. Similar jobs may be further aggregated based on general similarity of content to form a **job family**—in this case, the clerical job family.

It is possible to understand work from either a task-oriented or a worker-oriented perspective. Both procedures are used in conducting work analyses.

Task-Oriented Procedures.   A **task-oriented procedure** seeks to understand work by examining the tasks performed, usually in terms of *what* is accomplished. Task-oriented procedures focus on *activities* involved in performing work. The procedure begins with a consideration of work duties, responsibilities, or functions. Williams and Crafts (1997) defined a duty as "a major part of the work that an incumbent performs, comprised of a series of tasks, which together accomplish a job objective" (p. 57). Tasks thus become the basic unit of analysis for understanding work using task-oriented procedures. The work analyst develops a series of *task statements*, which are concise expressions of tasks performed. Examples are "splice high-voltage cables," "order materials and supplies," and "grade tests." Task statements should not be written in too general terminology, nor should they be written in very detailed language. They should reflect

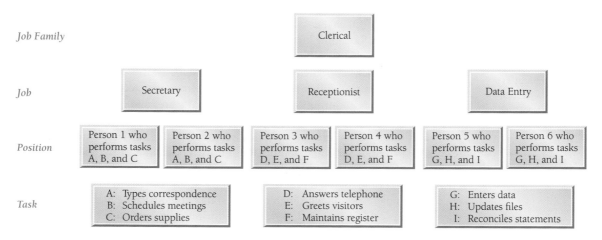

Figure 3-2 *Relationships among tasks, positions, jobs, and job families*

a discrete unit of work with appropriate specificity. Clifford (1994) estimated that the number of tasks required to describe most jobs typically is between 300 and 500.

Following the development of task statements, SMEs (most often incumbents) are asked to rate the task statements on a series of scales. The scales reflect important dimensions that facilitate understanding the job. Among the common scales used to rate task statements are frequency, importance, difficulty, and consequences of error. For example, the frequency scale would indicate whether a particular task was performed *rarely* (as once or twice per year) to *very often* (several times per day). Based on an analysis of the ratings, we acquire an understanding of a job in terms of the rated frequency, importance, difficulty, and other dimensions of the tasks that make up the job.

A classic example of a task-oriented method of work analysis is **Functional Job Analysis (FJA)**, developed by Fine and Cronshaw (1999). FJA obtains two types of task information: (1) *what a worker does*—the procedures and processes engaged in by a worker as a task is performed, and (2) *how a task is performed*—the physical, mental, and interpersonal involvement of the worker with the task. These types of information are used to identify what a worker does and the results of those job behaviors. Perhaps the most notable characteristic of FJA is that tasks are rated along three dimensions: People, Data, and Things. When a task requires involvement with People, the worker needs interpersonal resources (sensitivity, compassion, etc.). When a task requires involvement with Data, the worker needs mental resources (knowledge, reasoning, etc.). When a task is defined primarily in relation to Things, the worker needs physical resources (strength, coordination, etc.). Each of these three dimensions (People, Data, Things) is presented in a hierarchy ranging from high to low. Thus, for example, a given job may be defined as requiring a medium level of People, a high level of Data, and a low level of Things. FJA has been used to analyze jobs in many sectors of society but most frequently in the federal government. The method is regarded as one of the major systematic approaches to the study of work.

Functional Job Analysis (FJA)
A method of work analysis that describes the content of jobs in terms of People, Data, and Things.

Worker-Oriented Procedures.

A **worker-oriented procedure** seeks to understand work by examining the human *attributes* needed to perform it successfully. The human attributes are classified into four categories: knowledge (K), skills (S), abilities (A), and other (O) characteristics. *Knowledge* is specific types of information people need to perform a job. Some knowledge is required of workers before they can be hired to perform a job, whereas other knowledge may be acquired on the job. *Skills* are defined as the proficiencies needed to perform a task. Skills are usually enhanced through practice—for example, skill at typing and skill at driving an automobile. *Abilities* are defined as relatively enduring attributes that generally are stable over time. Examples are cognitive ability, physical ability, and spatial ability. However, when considered over a lifetime, some abilities (e.g., physical stamina) decline at a faster rate than others (e.g., verbal ability). Skills and abilities are confused often and easily, and the distinction is not always clear. It is useful to think of skills as cultivations of innate abilities. Generally speaking, high levels of (innate) ability can be cultivated into high skill levels. For example, a person with high musical ability could become highly proficient in playing a musical instrument. Low levels of (innate) ability preclude the development of high skill levels. *Other* characteristics are all other personal attributes, most often personality factors (e.g., remaining calm in emergency situations) or capacities (e.g.,

Worker-oriented procedure
A procedure or set of operations in work analysis designed to identify important or frequently utilized human attributes as a means of understanding the work performed.

withstanding extreme temperatures). Foster et al. (2012) noted that because personality measures are being increasingly used for personnel selection in a wide range of jobs (especially customer-service jobs), more emphasis should be placed on requisite personality attributes in work analysis. Collectively these four types of attributes, referred to as **KSAOs**, reflect an approach to understanding work by analyzing the human attributes needed to perform them.

KSAOs
An abbreviation for "knowledge, skills, abilities, and other" characteristics. Often used in the context of work analysis.

Like task statements, KSAO statements are written to serve as a means of understanding the human attributes needed to perform a job. They are written in standard format, using the wording "Knowledge of," "Skill in," or "Ability to." Examples are "Knowledge of city building codes," "Skill in operating a pneumatic drill," and "Ability to lift a 50-pound object over your head." The KSAO statements are also rated by SMEs, reflecting whether they are of *little importance* on the job, up to being *critically important*. Similar to analyzing the ratings of task statements, the ratings of KSAO statements are analyzed to provide an understanding of a job based on the human attributes needed to successfully perform the job.

Linkage analysis
A technique in work analysis that establishes the connection between the tasks performed and the human attributes needed to perform them.

Other analytic procedures can be followed to gain greater understanding of a job. A **linkage analysis** unites the two basic types of work analytic information: task-oriented (i.e., work activities) and worker-oriented (i.e., human attributes). A linkage analysis examines the relationship between KSAOs and tasks performed. The results of this analysis reveal which particular KSAOs are linked to the performance of many important and frequently performed tasks. Those KSAOs that are linked to the performance of tasks critical to the job become the basis of the employee selection test. A linkage analysis is also useful in establishing the relationship between each item on an employment test and the KSAOs needed for successful job performance (Doverspike & Arthur, 2012). Thus, if a high degree of mechanical ability is needed to perform a job, the linkage of test items that assess mechanical ability and job performance is strong and direct.

While incumbents are typically regarded as the most credible source for information about the jobs they perform, the linkage analysis that ties KSAOs to tasks performed has been found more reliable when provided by work analysts than incumbents (Baranowski & Anderson, 2006). One possible explanation for this finding involves an "inferential leap" in making the attribute-to-activity link. Suppose a task activity is typing and the human attribute under consideration by raters is finger dexterity. The link between finger dexterity and typing is direct, thus the inferential leap in judgment is small. However, consider the task activity of calling people on the telephone to sell a product (i.e., the job of a telemarketer) and the attribute under consideration is the personality dimension of sociability. In this case the inferential leap (i.e., you have to be highly sociable to speak with people on the telephone to convince them to buy something) is large. Telemarketers perform their job by reading scripts on a computer screen. The script tells them what to say, and in most cases, how to respond to hesitation or reluctance by the prospective customer. Having a sociable personality probably wouldn't lower job performance, but sociability might not be the only reason for successful performance as a telemarketer. Telemarketer success could be the result of a highly sociable personality, or being very determined, or being verbally persuasive to overcome customer resistance. Some jobs can be structured so as to allow for idiosyncratic styles in behavior and thus there can be different reasons for successful job performance. In a study by Lievens et al. (2010), the highest incumbent agreement was for jobs involving use of equipment. The implication is that there are *not* different ways one can successfully operate equipment. Jobs that permit wide variation in *how* they are performed make it more difficult to reach consensus in identifying which critical KSAOs are needed to be successful.

How to Collect Work Analytic Information

Some written material, such as task summaries and training manuals, may exist for a particular job. A work analyst should read this written material as a logical first step in conducting a formal work analysis. Then the work analyst is prepared to collect more extensive information about the job to be analyzed.

Procedures for Collecting Information. Three procedures are typically followed: the interview, direct observation, and a questionnaire. In the first procedure, the *interview*, the work analyst asks SMEs questions about the nature of their work. SMEs may be interviewed individually, in small groups, or through a series of panel discussions. The work analyst tries to gain an understanding of the tasks performed on the job and the KSAOs needed to perform them. The individuals selected to be interviewed are regarded as SMEs, people qualified to render informed judgments about their work. Desirable characteristics in SMEs include strong verbal ability, a good memory, and cooperativeness. Also, if SMEs are suspicious of the motives behind a work analysis, they are inclined to magnify the importance or difficulty of their abilities as a self-protective tactic (see Field Note 1: *A Memorable Lesson*).

The second method is called *direct observation*: employees are observed as they perform their jobs. Observers try to be unobtrusive, observing the jobs but not getting in the workers' way. Observers generally do not talk to the employees because it interferes with the conduct of work. They sometimes use cameras or videotape equipment to facilitate the observation. Direct observation is an excellent method for appreciating and understanding the adverse conditions (such as noise or heat) under which some jobs are performed; however, it is a poor method for understanding *why* certain behaviors occur on the job.

The third procedure for collecting work information is a structured *questionnaire* or inventory. The analyst uses a commercially available questionnaire that organizes existing knowledge about work information into a taxonomy. A **taxonomy** is a classification scheme useful in organizing information—in this case, information about jobs. The information collected about a particular job is compared with an existing database of job information derived from other jobs previously analyzed with the questionnaire. Peterson and Jeanneret (1997) referred to this procedure as being *deductive* because the work analyst can deduce an understanding of a job from a preexisting framework for analyzing jobs. Alternatively, the interview and direct observation procedures are *inductive* because the work analyst has to rely on newly created information about the job being analyzed. Because work analysts are often interested in understanding more than one job, the structured inventory is a very useful way to examine the relationships among a set of jobs. Most of the recent professional advances in work analysis within the field of I/O psychology have occurred with deductive procedures.

Taxonomic Information. There are several sources of taxonomic information for work analysis. One is the **Position Analysis Questionnaire (PAQ)** (McCormick &

Taxonomy
A classification of objects designed to enhance understanding of the objects being classified.

Position Analysis Questionnaire (PAQ)
A method of work analysis that assesses the content of jobs on the basis of approximately 200 items in the questionnaire.

Field Note 1: *A Memorable Lesson*

When interviewing employees about their jobs, work analysts should explain what they are doing and why they are doing it. If they do not fully explain their role, employees may feel threatened, fearing the analysts may somehow jeopardize their position by giving a negative evaluation of their performance, lowering their wages, firing them, and so on. Although work analysts do not have the power to do these things, some employees assume the worst. When employees feel threatened, they usually magnify the importance or difficulty of their contributions to the organization in an attempt to protect themselves. Therefore, to ensure accurate and honest responses, all work analysts should go out of their way to allay any possible suspicions or fears. I learned the importance of this point early in my career. One of my first work analyses focused on the job of a sewer cleaner. I had arranged to interview three sewer cleaners about their work. However, I had neglected to provide much advance notice about myself, why I would be talking to them, or what I was trying to do. I simply arrived at the worksite, introduced myself, and told the sewer cleaners that I wanted to talk to them about their jobs. Smelling trouble, the sewer cleaners proceeded to give me a memorable lesson on the importance of first establishing a nonthreatening atmosphere. One sewer cleaner turned to me and said, "Let me tell you what happens if we don't do our job. If we don't clean out the sewers of stuff like tree limbs, rusted hubcaps, and old tires, the sewers get clogged up. If they get clogged up, the sewage won't flow. If the sewage won't flow, it backs up. People will have sewage backed up into the basements of their homes. Manhole covers will pop open, flooding the streets with sewage. Sewage will eventually cover the highways, airport runways, and train tracks. People will be trapped in their homes surrounded by sewage. The entire city will be covered with sewage, with nobody being able to get in or out of the city. And that's what happens if we don't do our job of cleaning the sewers." Sadder but wiser, I learned the importance of not giving employees any reason to overstate their case.

Jeanneret, 1988), which consists of 195 statements used to describe the human attributes needed to perform a job. The statements are organized into six major categories: information input, mental processes, work output, relationships with other persons, job context, and other requirements. Some sample statements from the Relationships with Other Persons category are shown in Figure 3-3. From a database of thousands of similar positions that have been previously analyzed with the PAQ, the work analyst can come to understand the focal job.

A second source of taxonomic information is the research of Fleishman and his associates in developing a taxonomy of human abilities needed to perform tasks (Fleishman & Quaintance, 1984). Fleishman identified 52 abilities required in the conduct of a broad spectrum of tasks. Examples of these abilities are oral expression, arm–hand steadiness, multilimb coordination, reaction time, selective attention, and night vision. Fleishman calibrated the amount of each ability needed to perform tasks.

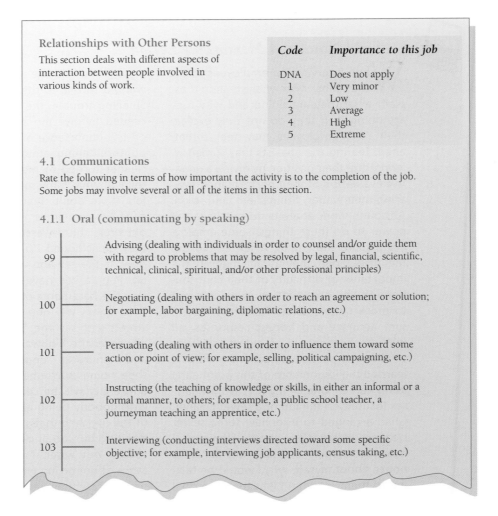

Relationships with Other Persons
This section deals with different aspects of interaction between people involved in various kinds of work.

Code	Importance to this job
DNA	Does not apply
1	Very minor
2	Low
3	Average
4	High
5	Extreme

4.1 Communications
Rate the following in terms of how important the activity is to the completion of the job. Some jobs may involve several or all of the items in this section.

4.1.1 Oral (communicating by speaking)

99 — Advising (dealing with individuals in order to counsel and/or guide them with regard to problems that may be resolved by legal, financial, scientific, technical, clinical, spiritual, and/or other professional principles)

100 — Negotiating (dealing with others in order to reach an agreement or solution; for example, labor bargaining, diplomatic relations, etc.)

101 — Persuading (dealing with others in order to influence them toward some action or point of view; for example, selling, political campaigning, etc.)

102 — Instructing (the teaching of knowledge or skills, in either an informal or a formal manner, to others; for example, a public school teacher, a journeyman teaching an apprentice, etc.)

103 — Interviewing (conducting interviews directed toward some specific objective; for example, interviewing job applicants, census taking, etc.)

Figure 3-3   *Sample items from the PAQ*

For example, with a scale of 1 (low) to 7 (high), the following amounts of *arm–hand steadiness* are needed to perform these tasks:

Cut facets in diamonds	6.32
Thread a needle	4.14
Light a cigarette	1.71

Fleishman's method permits jobs to be described in terms of required abilities and levels of those abilities needed to perform tasks.

The third source of taxonomic information available for work analysis is the U.S. Department of Labor. The **Occupational Information Network (O*NET)** is a national database of worker attributes and job characteristics. Based on analyses of thousands of jobs, massive compilations of information provide users with broad job and occupational assessments. It contains information about KSAOs, interests, general

Occupational Information Network (O*NET)
An online computer-based source of information about jobs.

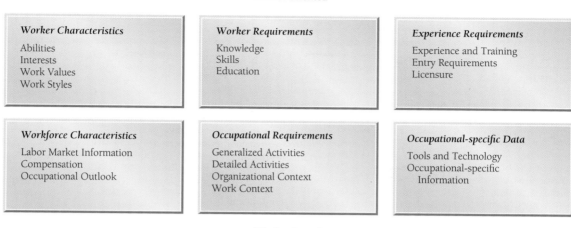

Worker-oriented

Worker Characteristics
Abilities
Interests
Work Values
Work Styles

Worker Requirements
Knowledge
Skills
Education

Experience Requirements
Experience and Training
Entry Requirements
Licensure

Workforce Characteristics
Labor Market Information
Compensation
Occupational Outlook

Occupational Requirements
Generalized Activities
Detailed Activities
Organizational Context
Work Context

Occupational-specific Data
Tools and Technology
Occupational-specific
   Information

Work-oriented

Figure 3-4   *Content model for the Occupational Information Network*

work activities, and work contexts. The database provides the essential foundation for facilitating career counseling, education, employment, and training activities. Additional information about O*NET can be found at *www.onetcenter.org*. A related database exists in Europe (The International Standard of Occupational Classifications and EurOccupations).

Figure 3-4 shows the conceptual model upon which O*NET is based. There are six domains of descriptive information: three worker-oriented and three work-oriented. The worker-oriented domains include information about worker characteristics (stable attributes of people pertaining to their abilities, interests, values, and personality), worker requirements (characteristics of people that can be enhanced through education, as knowledge and skills), and experience requirements (as entry requirements and the need for licensure). The work-oriented domains include information about workforce characteristics (such as compensation levels), occupational requirements (such as activities performed and the context in which work is performed) and occupation-specific data (such as tools and technology). As stated by Morgeson and Dierdorff (2011), the content model of O*NET "represents a comprehensive way to conceptualize virtually all of the types of work-related data that are of interest to both individuals and organizations" (p. 15). The authors recommended O*NET be used as a starting point for work analysis, as it provides a broad-based assessment of approximately 900 occupations. Depending upon the specific need for more customized work analytic information, organization-specific data can then be collected to augment O*NET results.

For example, consider Table 3-2. It shows the most important work styles (or personality factors) for childcare workers as rated by expert occupational analysts on a scale from 0–100. The table identifies the work style, provides a definition, and presents its O*NET importance rating. If a childcare agency believed these results did not accurately describe the personality factors needed for successful performance in their particular agency, the findings could be modified or adjusted as needed. It is unlikely the findings would require substantial modification, but perhaps another personality

Table 3-2   *Most important work styles for childcare workers*

Title of O*NET Work Style	Definition of O*NET Work Style	O*NET Importance Rating
Dependability	Job requires being reliable, responsible, and dependable and fulfilling obligations.	92
Self-control	Job requires maintaining composure, keeping emotions in check, controlling anger, and avoiding aggressive behavior, even in very difficult situations.	89
Concern for others	Job requires being sensitive to others' needs and feelings and being understanding and helpful to others on the job.	86
Integrity	Job requires being honest and ethical.	86
Cooperation	Job requires being pleasant with others on the job and displaying a good-natured, cooperative attitude.	82
Stress tolerance	Job requires accepting criticism and dealing calmly and effectively with high-stress situations.	81
Social orientation	Job requires preferring to work with others rather than alone, and being personally connected with others on the job.	78

factor (as persistence) might also be regarded as critically important. The significance of the findings is that job candidates would be assessed on the identified personality factors as part of the personnel selection process for childcare workers (see Cross-Cultural I/O Psychology: *Work Analysis and Individualism*).

Jeanneret et al. (2004) described an application of O*NET to assist individuals who lost their jobs to become re-employed. The process involves several phases. Individuals search for new occupations based on their self-reported interests, abilities, and skills. The first phase allows individuals to take online self-assessments to identify occupations that fit with their work values and/or interests. The next phase identifies potential occupations based on selected criteria such as abilities, interests, general work activities, and work values. The third phase determines other occupations that are the best relative match to the individual's values and skills.

O*NET is continuously being revised in response to the ongoing changes in the work world. Levine and Oswald (2012) reported that online recruitment companies found the O*NET system of classifying jobs to be useful in matching people with work. For example, Monster.com uses the O*NET system to organize more than 60 million resumes of people seeking employment or re-employment. O*NET is held in very high professional esteem. Peterson and Sager (2010) regard it as "a milestone of I/O psychology's achievements" (p. 906).

Cross-Cultural I/O Psychology: *Work Analysis and Individualism*

As described, work analytic data have many uses. They include identifying specific standards of job performance, matching different human attributes to the performance of different tasks, providing a rational basis to differentiate unacceptable from acceptable job performance, etc. You should be struck with the high level of precision in work analytic data: attribute ratings reported to the second decimal place, the specification of hundreds of different tasks performed in a position, and so on. Work analysis is a manifestation of the Western cultural value of individualism that emphasizes competition (including in the workplace), setting specified performance goals, individual achievement, and the allocation of rewards (pay raises, promotions) based on goal attainment. As such, work analysis provides a logical framework upon which to execute personnel decisions within such a culture.

However, work analysis is not universal. In fact, its uses can be *contrary* to the values of other cultures. Many non-Western cultures emphasize commonality, unity, and cohesion among people. Specifying precise standards of performance invites the inevitable consequences for employees meeting and not meeting them. Identifying different attributes needed across jobs does not address the common attributes needed by employees across all jobs. Cultural values that promote solidarity and unity are not served by methods that accentuate differences in people pertaining to attributes needed and tasks performed. Giving differential rewards does not promote within-group cohesion. Individualism intentionally produces winners and losers, those in and those out, those who get more and those who get less.

Work analysis is highly consistent with a cultural value that seeks differences. Work analysis cannot be exported and adapted to a culture that seeks to avoid the very outcomes the method was ultimately designed to produce.

Managerial Work Analysis

With an emphasis on work activities that are performed on the job, traditional work analytic methods are typically well-suited to traditional blue-collar and clerical jobs. In such jobs the work performed is evidenced by overt behaviors, such as hammering, welding, splicing wires, typing, and filing. These behaviors are observable, and the product of the work (e.g., a typed letter) flows directly from the skill (e.g., typing). In managerial-level jobs the link between the KSAOs and the work output is not nearly so direct. Managerial work involves such factors as planning, decision making, and forecasting, mainly cognitive skills, which are not so readily observable. As such, it is often more difficult to conduct an accurate work analysis for managerial-level jobs because of the greater inferential leap between the work performed and the KSAOs.

Several work analytic methods have been developed to assist in the understanding of managerial jobs. Mitchell and McCormick (1990) developed the *Professional and Managerial Position Questionnaire*, which examines work along the dimensions of complexity, organizational impact, and level of responsibility. Raymark et al. (1997) developed the *Personality-Related Position Requirements Form*, which analyzes work on the basis of the personality factors needed to perform them. Some of the personality dimensions measured are general leadership, interest in negotiation, sensitivity to interest of others, thoroughness and attention to details, and desire to generate ideas. These personality dimensions are based on previous research that links them to managerial-level work activities. As a rule, however, the level of precision and accuracy of managerial work analyses are not as high as those for clerical jobs because the attributes measured are more abstract.

Uses of Work Analytic Information

Work analytic information produces the criteria needed for a wide range of applications in I/O psychology, as the ensuing chapters will show. It is instructive to consider its uses.

First, an analysis of KSAOs reveals those attributes that are needed for successful job performance, including those needed upon entry into the job. The identification of these attributes provides an empirical basis to determine what personnel selection tests should assess. Thus, rather than selection tests being based on hunches or assumptions, work analytic information offers a rational approach to test selection. This topic will be described in Chapter 4. Second, work analytic information provides a basis to organize different positions into a job and different jobs into a job family. Such groupings provide a basis for determining levels of compensation, because one basis of compensation is the value of the attributes needed to perform the work. Third, work analytic information helps determine the content of training needed to perform the job. The tasks identified as most frequently performed or most important become the primary content of training. This topic will be discussed in Chapter 6. Finally, work analytic information provides one basis to conduct performance evaluations. A work analysis reveals the tasks most critical to job success, so the performance evaluation is directed at assessing how well the employee performs those tasks. This topic will be discussed in Chapter 7. In addition to these uses of work analytic information, the information can be used in vocational counseling, offering insight into the KSAOs needed to perform successfully in various occupations.

Work analysis offers additional value to organizations. The Americans with Disabilities Act requires employers to make adjustments for accommodating people with disabilities. As Brannick and Levine (2002) described, work analysis can help ascertain what is a "reasonable accommodation" versus an "undue hardship" for the employer. Although what is "reasonable" is a matter of opinion, employers can provide flexible work schedules and wheelchair ramps for workers with disabilities to facilitate the conduct of their jobs. Additionally, work teams have increased in frequency of use as the means by which many organizations accomplish their objectives (work teams are the subject of Chapter 9). Work teams involve the coordinated activity of several individuals, often with different skill sets, to achieve an outcome of higher quality or greater speed than could be achieved by a single employee. Brannick et al. (2007) discussed how the analysis of work performed by teams is more complex than the analysis of work performed by individuals. The selection of a new team member may involve consideration of more factors than the selection of an individual to perform a single job.

Evaluating Work Analytic Methods

Research comparing various methods of work analysis has revealed the methods are differentially effective and practical depending on the purposes for which they may be used. No one method was consistently best across the board. We believe that a well-trained work analyst can draw accurate inferences and conclusions using any one of several questionnaire methods. The converse is also true. No method can ensure accurate results when used by someone who is inexperienced with work analysis. A related opinion was reached by Harvey and Lozada-Larsen (1988), who concluded that the most accurate work analysis ratings are provided by raters who are highly knowledgeable about the job. Morgeson and Campion (1997) outlined a series of potential inaccuracies in work analytic information caused by such factors as biases in how work analysts process information about the jobs they are analyzing, and loss of motivation among SMEs who are less than enthusiastic about participating in work analyses. Morgeson and Campion believe the chances for inaccuracies are considerably lower in task-oriented work analysis. That is, the ratings of observable and discrete tasks are less subject to error than the ratings of some abstract KSAOs. Dierdorff and Morgeson (2009) concluded that most incumbents do not think of how they perform their jobs in the way work analysts think about work. Incumbents more typically describe their jobs in terms of activities or tasks performed, not the KSAOs needed to perform the work. The link between KSAOs and task activities can be particularly difficult for incumbents to rate when the work allows for stylistic differences in behavior, thus leading to subjectivity in judgment. Sackett and Laczo (2003) summarized the prevailing professional status of work analysis:

> [Work] analysis is an information-gathering tool to aid researchers in deciding what to do next. It always reflects subjective judgment. With careful choices in decisions about information to collect and how to collect it, one will obtain reliable and useful information. . . . The use of sound professional judgment in [work] analysis decisions is the best that can be expected. (pp. 34–35)

Competency Modeling

Competency modeling
A process for determining the human characteristics (i.e., competencies) needed to perform successfully within an organization.

A recent trend in establishing the desired attributes of employees is called **competency modeling**. A *competency* is a characteristic or quality of people that a company wants its employees to manifest. In traditional work analytic terms, a competency is a critical KSAO. *Modeling* refers to identifying the array or profile of competencies that an organization desires in its employees. Experts (e.g., Schippmann, 1999; Schippmann et al., 2000) agree that work analysis and competency modeling share some similarities in their approaches. Work analysis examines both the work that gets performed and the human attributes needed to perform the work, whereas competency modeling does not consider the work performed. The two approaches differ in the level of generalizability of the information across jobs within an organization, the method by which the attributes are derived, and the degree of acceptance within the organization for the identified attributes. First, work analysis tends to identify specific and different KSAOs that distinguish jobs within an organization. For example, one set of KSAOs would be identified for a secretary, while another set of KSAOs would be identified for a manager. In contrast, competencies are generally identified to apply to employees in all jobs within an organization or perhaps a few special differentiations among groups of jobs, as for senior executives. These competencies tend to be far more universal and abstract than KSAOs, and as such are often called the "core competencies" of an organization. Here are some examples of competencies for employees:

- Exhibiting the highest level of professional integrity at all times;
- Being sensitive and respectful of the dignity of all employees;
- Staying current with the latest technological advances within your area;
- Placing the success of the organization above your personal individual success.

As can be inferred from this profile or "model," such competencies are applicable to a broad range of jobs and are specifically designed to be as inclusive as possible. KSAOs are designed to be more exclusive, differentiating one job from another. As Schippmann et al. stated, "Although [work] analysis can at times take a broad focus (e.g., when conducting job family research), the descriptor items serving as a basis for the grouping typically represent a level of granularity that is far more detailed than is achieved by most competency modeling efforts" (p. 727).

Second, KSAOs are identified by work analysts using technical methods designed to elicit specific job information. As such, the entire work analysis project is often perceived by employees to be arcane. In contrast, competency modeling is likely to include review sessions and group meetings of many employees to ensure that the competencies capture the language and spirit that are important to the organization. As a result, employees readily identify with and relate to the resulting competencies, an outcome rarely achieved in work analysis.

Third, competency modeling tries to link personal qualities of employees to the larger overall mission of the organization. The goal is to identify those characteristics that tap into an employee's willingness to perform certain activities or to "fit in" with the work culture of the organization (Schippmann et al.). We will discuss the important topic of an organization's culture in Chapter 8. Work analysis, on the other hand, does not try to capture or include organizational-level issues of vision and values. Traditional work analysis does not have the "populist appeal" of competency modeling by members of the organization.

Although competency modeling does not have the same rigor or precision found in work analysis, it does enjoy approval and adoption by many organizations. For example, Campion et al. (2011) identified the best professional uses of competencies. They reported one leading company "recommended choosing only those competencies that would contribute to job and organizational performance, distinguish high performers, and would be directly used in the management of employees (i.e., selection, promotion, retention, and development)" (p. 248). It is believed the future might see a blurring of borders as the competency modeling and work analysis approaches evolve over time.

Job Performance Criteria

Bartram (2005) cogently stated the importance of first understanding criteria before we undertake the development of psychological assessments designed to predict the criteria.

Perhaps we have been preoccupied for too long with the wonderful personality questionnaires and ability tests we have constructed to measure all sorts of aspects of human potential. In so doing, we may have lost sight of why it is important to measure these characteristics. As a consequence, [I/O] practitioners have often had difficulty explaining to their clients the value of what we have to offer. We need to realize that this inability may be due in no small part to our failure to address the issues that actually concern clients: performance at work and the outcome of that performance. (p. 1200)

What criteria are used to evaluate job performance? No single universal criterion is applicable across all jobs. The criteria for success in a certain job depend on how that job contributes to the overall success of the organization. Nevertheless, there is enough commonality across jobs that some typical criteria have been identified. You may think of these criteria as the conventional standards by which employees are judged on the job. However, successful performance may be defined by additional criteria as well. The criteria we study and seek to understand are an implied statement of what we think is important.

Job performance criteria may be objective or subjective. **Objective performance criteria** are taken from organizational records and supposedly do not involve any subjective evaluation. **Subjective performance criteria** are judgmental evaluations of a person's performance (such as a supervisor might render). Although objective criteria may involve no subjective judgment, some degree of assessment must be applied to give them meaning. Just knowing that an employee produced 18 units a day is not informative; this output must be compared with what other workers produce. If the average is 10 units a day, 18 units clearly represent "good" performance. If the average is 25 units a day, 18 units is not good.

Nine Major Job Performance Criteria

Production.   Using units of production as a criterion is most common in manufacturing jobs. If an organization has only one type of job, then setting production criteria is easy. But most companies have many types of production jobs, so productivity must be compared fairly. That is, if average productivity in one job is 6 units a day and in another job it is 300 units a day, then productivities must be equated to adjust for these differences. Statistical procedures are usually used for this. Other factors can diminish the value of production as a criterion of performance. In an assembly-line job, the speed of the line determines how many units are produced per day. Increasing the speed of the line increases production. Furthermore, everyone working on the line has the same level of production. In a case like this, units of production are determined by factors outside of the individual worker, so errors that are under the worker's control may be the criterion of job performance. Errors are not fair criteria if they are more likely in some jobs than others. Due to automation and work simplification, some jobs are almost "goof-proof." Then error-free work has nothing to do with the human factor.

Sales.   Sales volume is a common performance criterion for wholesale and retail sales jobs. People working in sales jobs are often paid on a commission basis; that is, a

---

Objective performance criteria A set of factors used to assess job performance that are (relatively) factual in character.

Subjective performance criteria A set of factors used to assess job performance that are the product of someone's (e.g., supervisor, peer, customer) judgment of these factors.

percentage of total sales figure. For example, a real estate salesperson may receive 8% commission on the sale of a house. If a house sells for $200,000, a $16,000 commission is paid.

Sales volume is a highly objective criterion, but it can be contaminated by factors other than the performance of the salesperson. Salespeople are typically assigned to territories or geographic locations. As described by Hausknecht and Langevin (2010), these territories can differ in market potential (e.g., population, socioeconomic status), prevailing economic conditions, and company infrastructure (i.e., if the company services what it sells). There can also be differences among salespeople regarding travel time in between accounts, and the proclivity to sell to existing customers versus generating new sales business. If there are these types of differences across salespeople, there are statistical adjustments that can be made to more fairly compare sales volume as a criterion of job performance (McManus & Brown, 1995). Ideally, any differences in sales performance are then due to the ability of the salespeople.

Tenure or Turnover.   Length of service (or tenure) is a very popular criterion in I/O psychological research. Turnover is typically calculated on an annual basis as a percentage of the company's workforce. For example, if a company has 200 employees and an annual turnover rate of 4%, eight employees leave the company per year. Turnover not only has a theoretical appeal but also is a practical concern. Most employers want to hire people who will stay with the company. Hom et al. (2012) reported employees stay with an employer for many reasons, including the enjoyment and meaning they derive from their work, the lack of other employment opportunities, and to accommodate a spouse and/or children. For obvious practical reasons, employers usually don't want to hire chronic job-hoppers. The costs of recruiting, selecting, and training new hires can be extremely high. However, some industries (as fast food) have extraordinarily high turnover rates, in the range of 200%-300% per year. While such massive turnover rates would cripple most industries, the cost associated with hiring and training workers for fast food jobs is minimal. Turnover is a valuable and useful criterion because it measures employment stability, and also has relevance at the national level. The greater the degree of job loss (without re-employment), the higher is the rate of unemployment (see I/O Psychology and the Economy: *Unemployment*). Campion (1991) suggested that many factors should be considered in the measurement of turnover. One is *voluntariness* (whether the employee was fired, quit to take another job with better promotional opportunities, or quit because of some source of dissatisfaction). Another factor is *functionality* (whether the employee was performing

I/O Psychology and the Economy: *Unemployment*

The national unemployment rate is interpreted as a criterion of the state of the general economy. Virtually all industrialized nations compute their level of unemployment. When unemployment is low, there are many jobs to be filled, and individuals have the luxury of being selective in which jobs they take. When unemployment is high, there are many people out of work, and individuals can be far less selective about which job they will accept. In short, the level of unemployment can be thought of as a general index of the amount of competition people face in finding a job.

Since the level of unemployment attracts so much attention in the media, it is instructive to describe how the national level of unemployment is calculated. In the United States responsibility for assessing the unemployment rate is assigned to the Census Bureau, under the auspices of the Bureau of Labor Statistics, a division of the U.S. Department of Labor. Every month 60,000 households covering 3,000 counties representing all 50 states are contacted. The sample of 60,000 households is considered to be sufficiently large as to yield accurate information that can be generalized to the national population. The specific households that are contacted are generally not the same each month. The monthly survey of households is referred to as the Current Population Survey, and the results are released to the public on the first Friday of each month.

The Bureau of Labor Statistics considers the national labor force to be all individuals who are age 16 and older who either have a job or are holding a job. The unemployment rate represents the percentage of the labor force that is unemployed. To be officially counted as unemployed, an individual must: (a) be unemployed, and (b) have been actively looking for work over the previous four weeks. Actively looking for work includes sending out resumes, placing or answering notifications about jobs, contacting employment agencies, and talking to friends or relatives about possible employment. However, the following types of people are *not* classified as being unemployed:

- Individuals who are unemployed but have not sought work over the previous four weeks. Such people include those who have given up on the prospects of finding a job. These individuals are referred to as "discouraged" workers.
- Individuals who want full-time employment but currently are getting by through performing "odd jobs." They accept work in whatever capacity it can be found, often on a hit-or-miss basis, with each assignment typically lasting a brief time.
- Individuals who are employed in full-time jobs, but the jobs require knowledge and skills far below what the individuals possess, and at a level of compensation below what they are capable of earning. These individuals are referred to as "underemployed" workers by economists, and "overqualified" workers by I/O psychologists.

Since the start of the 20th century, the highest level of unemployment in the United States was 25%, witnessed during the Great Depression of the 1930s. At no time in history has there ever been 0% unemployment. According to the International Labor Organization, an agency of the United Nations, the current level of unemployment in the U.S. is 6.1%, as compared with, for example, Canada (7.1%), China (4.6%), France (10.5%), Mexico (5.0%), and Spain (26.7%). The rates change monthly, and all nations do not compute their levels of

I/O Psychology and the Economy: *Unemployment* (continued)

unemployment the same way. In many countries unemployment rates are also computed by region, by industry, and by worker age.

Care must be exercised in the interpretation of criterion measures and the inferences drawn from them. A 6.1% level of unemployment should not be interpreted to mean 93.9% of the labor force is stable and fully employed. Records are not kept on the percentage of discouraged workers, those individuals who work sporadically, and those who are underemployed. Additionally, there are no definitive records on people who are concurrently working at multiple jobs to meet their financial needs. As with many criterion measures, the overall picture is often more complicated than it initially appears.

the job effectively or ineffectively). Williams and Livingstone (1994) meta-analyzed studies that examined the relationship between turnover and performance, and concluded that poor performers were more likely to voluntarily quit their jobs than were good performers.

Absenteeism.   Absence from work, like turnover, is an index of employee stability. Although some employee turnover is good for organizations, unexcused employee absenteeism invariably has bad consequences. Excused absenteeism (e.g., personal vacation time) is generally not a problem because it is sanctioned and must be approved by the organization. Rhodes and Steers (1990) and Martocchio and Harrison (1993) reviewed many studies on why people are absent from work. Absence appears to be the product of many factors, including family conflicts, job dissatisfaction, alcohol and drug abuse, and personality. However, as Johns (1994) noted, employees are likely to give self-serving justifications for their absence. For example, being absent from work to care for a sick child is more socially acceptable than acknowledging deviant behavior such as drug use. Accordingly, self-reports of why employees are absent can be highly inaccurate. Absenteeism is a pervasive problem in industry; it costs employers billions of dollars a year in decreased efficiency and increased benefit payments (for example, sick leave) and payroll costs. Absenteeism has social, individual, and organizational causes, and it affects individuals, companies, and even entire industrial societies.

Accidents.   Accidents are sometimes used as a criterion of job performance, although this measure has a number of limitations. Tetrick et al. (2010) reported that 80% of accidents are a result of human error. First, accidents are used as a criterion mainly for blue-collar jobs. (Although white-collar workers can be injured at work, the frequency of such accidents is small.) Thus accidents are a measure of job performance for only a limited sample of employees. Second, accidents are difficult to predict, and there is little stability or consistency across individuals in their occurrence (Senders & Moray, 1991). Third, accidents can be measured in many ways: number of accidents per hours worked, miles driven, trips taken, and so on. Different conclusions can be drawn depending on how accident statistics are calculated. Fourth, accidents are not synonymous with injuries. Accidents can result in property damage ranging from minor to catastrophic with no personal injury. Personal injuries ranging from minor to fatal can result from accidents. Employers do not want to hire people who, for whatever reason, will have job-related accidents. But in the total picture of job performance, accidents are not used as a criterion as often as production, turnover, or absence.

Theft.   Employee theft is a major problem for organizations. Harris et al. (2012) reported in a study of hundreds of U.S. companies, 54% said they expected their own employees to steal company funds, equipment, or merchandise over the next year. Estimates of the annual cost of employee theft are highly variable, ranging from $50 billion to $200 billion per year. Avery et al. (2012) reported losses from employee theft per year exceeded losses from customer shoplifting. From an I/O psychologist's perspective, the goal is to hire people who are unlikely to steal from the company, just as it is desirable to hire people who have a low probability of incurring accidents. The problem with theft as a criterion is that we know very little about the individual identity of employees who do steal. Greenberg and Scott (1996) asserted that some employees resort to theft as a means of off-setting perceived unfairness in how their employer treats them. Figure 3-5 shows a program one retail company uses to curtail theft by its own employees. For a cash award, employees are provided an opportunity to report coworkers who are stealing from the company.

A drawback in using theft as a job performance criterion is that only a small percentage of employees are ever caught stealing. The occurrence of theft often has to be deduced on the basis of shortages calculated from company inventories of supplies and products. In addition, many companies will not divulge any information about theft to outside individuals. Although companies often share information on such criteria as absenteeism and turnover, theft records are too sensitive to reveal. Despite these limitations, I/O psychologists regard theft as an index of employment suitability, and we will probably see much more research on theft in the years ahead (see Field Note 2: *Theft of Waste*).

Counterproductive work behavior
A broad range of employee behaviors that are harmful to other employees or the organization.

Counterproductive Work Behavior.   **Counterproductive work behavior** (also called deviant work behavior) includes a broad range of employee actions that are harmful for the organization. Rotundo and Spector (2010) defined them as "intentional behavior by employees that harms or intends to harm organizations and people in organizations, including employees and customers/clients" (p. 489). Theft is an example of counterproductive behavior, but it was discussed as a separate criterion because of its extreme criticality for many organizations. Berry, Ones, and Sackett (2007) proposed a two-part classification of deviance: interpersonal and organizational. Interpersonal counterproductive behavior is targeted toward other individuals, and is represented by gossip, bullying, threats of violence, and theft from coworkers. Organizational counterproductive behavior is targeted against the organization as a whole, and includes intentionally working slowly, damaging company property, and disclosing confidential information. A common thread running through all of these counterproductive behaviors is intentionality; that is, the employee deliberately engages in them. Wu and LeBreton (2011) proposed that counterproductive work behaviors are committed by individuals who have aberrant personalities. Several personality assessments have been specifically designed to identify such people (the topic of integrity testing is discussed in Chapter 4). From a personnel selection standpoint, the goal of the organization is to screen out applicants who are predicted to engage in these behaviors. In contrast to attributes that are used to "select in" applicants because they reflect positive or desir-

---

SILENT WITNESS INCENTIVE AWARD PROGRAM

The Silent Witness Incentive Award Program provides every associate the opportunity to share in substantial cash awards and at the same time help reduce our losses caused by dishonest associates.

CASH AWARDS
$100.00 to $1,000.00

HOW YOU CAN PARTICIPATE

When somebody causes an intentional loss to our company, each associate pays for it. If you observe or become aware of another associate causing loss to our company, you should report it immediately. Your Loss Prevention Department investigates all types of shortage including the theft of Cash, Merchandise, Underrings, and all types of Credit Card Fraud.

MAIL-IN INFORMATION

1. Associate's name involved? _____

2. Where does associate work?   Store _____ Dept. _____

3. What is associate doing?   a) taking money   b) taking merchandise _____
   c) under-ringing merchandise   d) credit card fraud _____

4. How much has been stolen? $_____

5. Is there anything else you wish to add? _____

_____

_____

_____

Figure 3-5 *Incentive award method for reporting employee theft*

Emotional labor
The requirement in some jobs that employees express emotions to customers or clients that are associated with enhanced performance in the job.

able work behaviors, counterproductive work behaviors reflect criteria used to "screen out" applicants who are predicted to exhibit them on the job. Counterproductive work behavior is discussed in greater detail in Chapter 10.

Emotional Labor.   The term **emotional labor** (as opposed to emotional behavior, for example) was selected deliberately to connote toil, or a sense of onerous duty on the part of the employee whose job requires it. Most jobs calling for the employee to exhibit emotions "appropriate" for the context are positive in nature. Examples of such

Field Note 2: *Theft of Waste*

Many organizations experience problems of theft by employees. Thefts include office supplies used in work, such as staplers and tape dispensers, as well as items that are intended for sale to customers. Sometimes cash is stolen. What all these items have in common is that they are assets or resources of the company. I once had an experience with a company where the biggest concern was not the theft of resources, but the theft of waste! The company printed U.S. postage stamps. The worth of each stamp was the value printed on the stamp—usually the cost of 1 ounce of first-class postage, currently 49¢. Although there was some concern that employees would steal the postage stamps for their personal use, the bigger concern was the theft of misprints or errors. Printing errors occur when a stamp

is printed off-center or, in extreme cases, when the printing on the stamp is correct but the image is inverted. One 49¢ stamp printed with an inverted image may be worth thousands of dollars to philatelists (stamp collectors). In the printing of postage stamps, errors occur as they do in all other types of printing. In this case, however, the errors have very high market value. To reduce the possibility of theft of misprints that were scheduled to be destroyed, the company had three elaborate and extensive sets of search and security procedures for anyone leaving the company. Somewhat paradoxically, there was no security for people entering the building. All the security procedures involved people leaving the building, as they were searched for the theft of highly valuable waste or scrap.

emotions include warmth, caring, and gratitude. Employees who must exhibit these emotions are trained to engage in *display rules*. Display rules are specific behavioral acts that reflect the underlying emotions customers expect. Examples include smiling, voice inflection, and eye contact. These display rules and corresponding emotions are typically found in the service industry, and are generally referenced as "service with a smile" (Grandey et al., 2005). However, research by Groth et al. (2009) revealed customers can "decode" displays of emotions by employees. Customers prefer authentic emotional displays, not phoniness (i.e., those that appear contrived for the purpose of manipulation). An example would be employees who always smile irrespective of the nature of the customer/employee interaction.

The recognition of how behaviors reflect emotions has rapidly grown in I/O psychology. The Disney Corporation has built theme parks where employees interacting with customers is of paramount importance. Customers (i.e., theme park attendees) are referred to as "guests" and employees are called "cast members." The following is from a Disney training manual on how all employees should treat customers (Pugh et al., 2013):

> Make eye contact and smile . . . Looking a guest in the eye and smiling is a positive interaction. Smile! We are famous for our courtesy and friendliness. Display appropriate body language . . . Don't lean. Smile and look happy . . . Don't be preoccupied . . . Have a pleasant look on your face. Thank every guest . . . Do it with sincerity and a smile. (p. 199)

As Groth et al. (2013) noted, these positive emotional displays result in satisfied customers becoming repeat customers, and who in turn recommend the experience to others.

Customer service employees can also be the recipients of emotional displays by the people they serve. For example, Côté et al. (2013) reported that customers seeking to return a purchase appeal to the emotions of regret and perhaps pity for making an impulsive purchase. Even call center employees who neither give nor receive face-to-face emotional displays with customers must be adept at handling customer complaints over the phone. Some call centers use computerized emotion detector systems to analyze emotions based on voice pitch, tone, cadence, and word usage. The intent of the system is to alert supervisors to highly disgruntled customers that drain the emotional capacity of employees in dealing with such extreme cases. The supervisors can intervene in the call, sparing the employee, and being more responsive to the irate customer (van Jaarsveld & Poster, 2013).

Not all required emotions need be positive. For jobs such as security personnel and bill collectors, the desired emotions would include aggressiveness, suspicion, and skepticism. The corresponding display rules would include a stern tone of voice, facial scowling, and arms crossed against the chest to indicate a defensive posture (Beal et al., 2006). Trougakos et al. (2011) identified a third type of emotional display, that of being neither positive nor negative, but appearing unemotional. The need for this type of emotional display is found in law enforcement where "keeping your cool and not getting emotional or showing emotion while dealing with others can be the difference between life and death" (p. 350).

Rupp and Spencer (2006) noted that display rules can be considered a form of social acting, and differentiated surface from deep acting. One major difference between the two is the length of time the "actor" (the employee) must engage in the behavior. A food server at a restaurant, for example, may only have to exhibit a warm, cheerful, and attentive demeanor for a few minutes at a time while taking orders and also when delivering the food to the table. Conversely, a funeral director would be required to exhibit the emotions of shared grief, compassion, and empathy for several hours in succession with the relatives of the deceased. Rupp and Spencer proposed that the surface acting exhibited by the food server may be more stressful because of the intermittent chronicity associated with having to exhibit the display rules (e.g., alternating "on/off" interactions of short duration with many customers). Conversely, the deep acting exhibited by the funeral director may require the employee to regulate his or her own internal emotions. The duration of the interaction (several hours per funeral) may require deeper immersion in the emotion to sustain the requisite behaviors. As such, deep acting may induce less stress in employees because the emotions are internalized by the employee, which is not required in surface acting. In summary, employees who must project certain emotions through display rules as part of their jobs may not allow their own personal emotional states to interfere with the emotional front they must exhibit for their customers.

Adaptive and Citizenship Behavior.   This final criterion is somewhat contrary to the theme of this section—criteria of *job* performance—because its focus can extend beyond the job. Adaptive and citizenship behaviors reflect the importance of employees contributing to the welfare of the *organization* in ways that transcend their specific jobs.

Adaptive behavior
A range of behaviors that enable employees to increase their capacity to cope with organizational change.

The emergence of **adaptive behavior** as being important derived from the continuous pressures placed on organizations over the past 35 years (as discussed in Chapter 1), and the need for employees to adapt their own behavior to these changing work duties. As stated by Dorsey et al. (2010), "Because of the highly dynamic and changing nature of modern work environments, demand is high for employees with various types and levels of versatility, flexibility, and adaptability" (p. 463). Huang et al. (2014) conducted a meta-analysis on personality factors associated with adaptive work behavior, and found emotional stability and ambition to be most strongly predictive of it. The essence of adaptive behavior is for people to be aware of changing conditions in their work environment, and to adjust their own behavior in a manner to become more effective. Examples include changing work conditions due to new customer demands and new technology systems to which employees must be responsive. Furthermore, the employees must accept the need to continuously adapt their behavior without displays of resistance or complaint. Pulakos et al. (2012) attribute technology and globalization to increasing the work pace of organizations, with the most valued employees being those who can best adapt to the ever-changing conditions.

Citizenship behavior
Employee behavior that transcends job performance and is directed to the overall welfare of the organization.

In addition to employees being holders of a job, they can also be regarded as "citizens" of the organization. **Citizenship behavior** refers to those aspects of employee performance that transcend performing tasks on a job. They address contributions made by the employee for the betterment of the organization. As such, employees who make these behavioral contributions are regarded as "good citizens" of the organization. Citizenship behaviors are represented in two broad dimensions: personal support and organizational support. Personal support involves doing little things that help other employees perform their jobs more effectively. Examples include helping others by offering ideas and suggestions about their work, and being courteous and considerate in relations with coworkers. Organizational support refers to exhibiting loyalty to the organization through publically endorsing its mission and goals, and being a good "ambassador" of the organization by promoting its achievements. Employees who exhibit citizenship behavior are typically regarded most favorably by organizations. Bolino et al. (2013) noted that unmarried employees may be expected by organizations to engage in more citizenship behaviors under the assumption they have more time to devote to non-job activities compared to their married colleagues. Rynes et al. (2002) ascertained from a survey of human resource managers that the degree to which a candidate was judged to be a "good fit" with the organization (not just the job) was becoming increasingly important in making personnel selection decisions. In fact, there is evidence that positive citizenship behaviors can carry more weight than successful task performance in supervisory assessments of overall work performance. The topic of citizenship behaviors is discussed in greater detail in Chapter 10.

Summary of Job Performance Criteria.   A consideration of the nine major job performance criteria reveals marked differences not only in what they measure but also in how they are measured. They differ along an objective/subjective continuum. Some criteria are highly objective, meaning they can be measured with a high degree of accuracy. Examples are units of production, days absent, and dollar sales volume. There are few disagreements about the final tally because the units, days, or dollars are merely counted. Nevertheless, there could be disagreements about the interpretation or meaning of these objectively counted numbers. Other criteria are less objective. Theft, for example, is not the same as being caught stealing. Based on company records of merchandise, an organization might know that employee theft has occurred but not know who did it. As was noted, although employee theft is a major problem, relatively few employees are ever caught stealing. The broader criterion of counterproductive work behavior includes dimensions that are particularly subjective. For example, we all probably waste some time on the job, but only at some point is it considered "deviant." Likewise, there is probably a fine line between being "outspoken" (it is good to express your feelings and opinions) and "argumentative" (it is bad to be negative and resist progress). Customer service behavior is a highly subjective criterion. An employee's customer service performance is strictly a product of other people's perceptions, and there may be as many judgments of that behavior as there are customers. Likewise, how adaptive we are at work and the degree to which we are regarded as good organizational citizens are judgments typically made by others. How we perceive ourselves and how others perceive us within an organizational context can be quite different. Chapter 7 will examine sources of agreement and disagreement in assessing job performance.

From this discussion, it is clear that no single measure of job performance is totally adequate. Each criterion may have merit, but each can also suffer from weakness along other dimensions. For instance, few people would say that an employee's absence has no bearing on overall job performance, but no one would say that absence is a complete measure of job performance. Absence, like production, is only one piece of the broader picture. Don't be discouraged that no one criterion meets all our standards. It is precisely because job performance is multidimensional (and each single dimension is a fallible index of overall performance) that we are compelled to include many relevant aspects of work in establishing criteria. Furthermore, every job performance criterion suffers from some degree of deficiency and contamination.

Dynamic Performance Criteria

Dynamic performance criteria
Aspects of job performance that change (increase or decrease) over time.

The concept of **dynamic performance criteria** applies to job performance criteria that change over time. It is significant because job performance is sometimes not stable or consistent over time, and this dynamic quality of criteria adds to the complexity of making personnel decisions. Steele-Johnson et al. (2000) identified three potential reasons for systematic changes in job performance over time. First, employees might change the way they perform tasks as a result of repeatedly conducting them. Second, the knowledge and ability requirements needed to perform the task might change because of changing work technologies. Third, the knowledge and skills of the employees might change as a result of additional training.

Consider Figure 3-6, which shows the levels of three job performance criteria—productivity, absence, and accidents—over an eight-year period. The time period represents a person's eight-year performance record on a job. Notice that the pattern of behavior for the three criteria differ over time. The individual's level of accidents is stable over time, so accidents are a stable (not dynamic) performance criterion. A very different pattern emerges for the other two criteria. The individual's level of productivity increases over the years, more gradually in the early years and then more dramatically in the later years. Absence, on the other hand, follows the opposite pattern. The employee's absence was greatest in the first year of employment and progressively declined over time. Absence and productivity are dynamic performance criteria. When

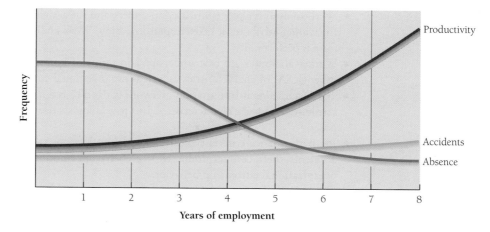

Figure 3-6 *Performance variations in three criteria over an eight-year period*

a job applicant is considered for employment, the organization attempts to predict how well that person will perform on the job. A hire/no hire decision is then made on the basis of this prediction. If job performance criteria are static (like accidents in Figure 3-6), the prediction is more accurate because of the stability of the behavior. If job performance criteria are dynamic, however, a critical new element is added to the decision, *time*. It may be that initially productivity would not be very impressive, but over time the employee's performance would rise to and then surpass a satisfactory level. Dynamic performance criteria are equivalent to "hitting a moving target," as the level of the behavior being predicted is continuously changing. Furthermore, the pattern of change may be different *across* individuals. That is, for some people productivity may start off low and then get progressively higher, whereas for others the pattern may be the reverse.

Sturmin (2007) proposed that dynamic performance criteria can be explained by a learning curve. Work productivity improves based on the accumulation of experience, and employees exhibit different rates of learning-by-doing. Conversely, individuals with a relatively flat learning curve will be much slower, in comparison, to exhibit performance improvements in their jobs. Sonnentag and Frese (2012) refer to learning curves as "performance trajectories" that can elevate due to knowledge acquisition or skill development, or decline due to fatigue or stress. From an empirical perspective, our ability to understand and predict learning curves can only be achieved by studying employee behavior over an extended time period. In practice, however, most research on employee behavior has tended to be cross-sectional (i.e., at one point in time).

Chapter Summary

- Criteria are evaluative standards that serve as reference points in making judgments.
- The two levels of criteria are conceptual (what we would like to measure if we could) and actual (what we do measure). All actual criteria are flawed measures of conceptual criteria.

- Work analysis is a procedure used to understand the activities performed in a job and the worker attributes it takes to perform a job. Work analysis establishes the criteria for job performance.
- Worker attributes are best understood in terms of knowledge, skills, abilities, and other (KSAOs) characteristics as well as organizational competencies.
- The Occupational Information Network (O*NET) is a national database of worker attributes and work characteristics. I/O psychologists use it for a wide range of purposes.
- Job performance criteria typically include production, sales, turnover, absenteeism, accidents, theft, counterproductive work behavior, emotional labor, and adaptive and organizational citizenship behavior.
- The magnitude of job performance criterion measurements can change over time for workers, decreasing the accuracy of long-term predictions of job performance.

4 Predictors: Psychological Assessments

Learning Objectives

- Identify the major types of reliability and what they measure.

- Understand the major manifestations of validity and what they measure.

- Know the major types of psychological tests categorized by content.

- Explain the role of psychological testing in making assessments of people, including ethical issues and predictive accuracy.

- Explain non-test predictors such as interviews, assessment centers, physical ability testing, work samples, biographical information, and letters of recommendation.

- Understand the controversial methods of assessment.

A predictor is any variable used to forecast a criterion. In weather prediction, barometric pressure is used to forecast rainfall. In medical prediction, body temperature is used to predict (or diagnose) illness. In I/O psychology, we seek predictors of job performance criteria as indexed by productivity, absenteeism, turnover, and so forth. Although we do not use tea leaves and astrological signs as fortune-tellers do, I/O psychologists have explored a multitude of devices as potential predictors of job performance criteria. This chapter will review the variables traditionally used, examine their success, and discuss some professional problems inherent in their application.

Assessing the Quality of Predictors

Psychometric
Literally, the measurement ("metric") of properties of the mind (from the Greek word "psyche"). The standards used to measure the quality of psychological assessments.

Reliability
A standard for evaluating tests that refers to the consistency, stability, or equivalence of test scores. Often contrasted with validity.

Test–retest reliability
A type of reliability that reveals the stability of test scores upon repeated applications of the test.

Equivalent-form reliability
A type of reliability that reveals the equivalence of test scores between two versions or forms of the test.

All predictor variables, like other measuring devices, can be assessed in terms of their quality or goodness. We can think of several features of a good measuring device. We would like it to be consistent and accurate; that is, it should repeatedly yield precise measurements. In psychology we judge the goodness of our measuring devices by two **psychometric** criteria: reliability and validity. If a predictor is not both reliable and valid, it is useless.

Reliability

Reliability refers to the consistency, stability, or equivalence of a measure. A measure should yield the same estimate on repeated use if the measured trait has not changed. Even though that estimate may be inaccurate, a reliable measure will always be consistent. Three major types of reliability are used in psychology to assess the consistency or stability of the measuring device, and a fourth assessment of reliability is often used in I/O psychology.

Test–Retest Reliability.   **Test–retest reliability** is perhaps the simplest assessment of a measuring device's reliability. We measure something at two different times and compare the scores. We can give an intelligence test to the same group of people at two different times and then correlate the two sets of scores. This correlation is called a *coefficient of stability* because it reflects the stability of the test over time. If the test is reliable, those who scored high the first time will also score high the second time, and vice versa. If the test is unreliable, the scores will "bounce around" in such a way that there is no similarity in individuals' scores between the two trials.

When we say a test (or any measure) is *reliable*, how high should the coefficient of stability be? The answer is the higher the better. A test cannot be too reliable. As a rule, reliability coefficients around .70 are professionally acceptable. Furthermore, the length of time between administrations of the test must be considered in the interpretation of a test's test–retest reliability. Generally the shorter the time interval between administrations (e.g., one week vs. six months), the higher will be the test–retest reliability coefficient.

Equivalent-Form Reliability.   A second type of reliability is parallel or **equivalent-form reliability**. Here a psychologist develops two forms of a test to measure the same attribute and gives both forms to the same group of people. The psychologist then correlates the two scores for each person. The resulting correlation, called a *coefficient of equivalence*, reflects the extent to which the two forms are equivalent measures of the same concept. Of the three major types of reliability, this type is the least popular because it is usually challenging to come up with one good test, let alone two. Many tests do not have a "parallel form." Furthermore, research (e.g., Clause et al., 1998) reveals it is by no means easy to construct two tests whose scores have similar meanings and statistical properties such that they are truly parallel or equivalent measures. However, in intelligence and achievement testing (to be discussed shortly), equivalent forms of the same test are sometimes available. If the resulting coefficient of equivalence is high, the tests are equivalent and reliable measures of the same concept. If it is low, they are not.

Internal-consistency reliability
A type of reliability that reveals the homogeneity of the items comprising a test.

Internal-Consistency Reliability.   The third major assessment is the **internal-consistency reliability** of the test—the extent to which it has homogeneous content. Two types of internal-consistency reliability are typically computed. One is called split-half reliability. Here a test is given to a group of people, but in scoring the test (though not administering it), the researcher divides the items in half, into odd- and even-numbered items. Each person thus gets two sets of scores (one for each half), which are correlated. If the test is internally consistent, there should be a high degree of similarity in the responses (that is, right or wrong) to the odd- and even-numbered items. All other things being equal, the longer a test, the greater its reliability.

A second technique for assessing internal-consistency reliability is to compute one of two coefficients: Cronbach's alpha or Kuder-Richardson 20 (KR20). Both procedures are similar though not statistically identical. Conceptually, each test item is treated as a minitest. Thus a 100-item test consists of 100 minitests. The response to each item is correlated with the response to every other item. A matrix of inter-item correlations is formed whose average is related to the homogeneity of the test. If the test is homogeneous (the item content is similar), it will have a high internal-consistency reliability coefficient. If the test is heterogeneous (the items cover a wide variety of concepts), it is not internally consistent and the resulting coefficient will be low. Internal-consistency reliability is frequently used to assess a test's homogeneity of content in I/O psychology.

Inter-rater reliability
A type of reliability that reveals the degree of agreement among the assessments provided by two or more raters.

Inter-Rater Reliability.   When assessments are made on the basis of raters' judgments, it is possible for the raters to disagree in their evaluations. Two different raters may observe the same behavior yet evaluate it differently. The degree of correspondence between judgments or scores assigned by different raters is most commonly referred to as **inter-rater reliability**, although it has also been called *conspect reliability*. In some situations raters must exercise judgment in arriving at a score. Two examples are multiple raters analyzing a job and multiple interviewers evaluating job candidates. The score or rating depends not only on the job or candidate but also on the persons doing the rating. The raters' characteristics may lead to distortions or errors in their judgments. Estimation of inter-rater reliability is usually expressed as a correlation and reflects the degree of agreement among the ratings. Evidence of high inter-rater reliability establishes a basis to conclude that the behavior was reliably observed, and in turn we conclude that such observations are accurate. Inter-rater reliability is frequently assessed to judge the degree of agreement across subject matter experts in work analysis.

In summary, the four types of reliability are assessed for different reasons. They are not interchangeable.

Validity

Reliability refers to consistency and stability of measurement; validity refers to accuracy. A valid measure is one that yields "correct" estimates of what is being assessed. However, another factor also distinguishes validity from reliability. Reliability is inherent in a measuring device, but validity depends on the use of a test. **Validity** is the test's appropriateness for predicting or drawing inferences about criteria. A given test may be highly valid for predicting employee productivity but totally invalid for predicting employee absenteeism. In other words, it would be appropriate to draw inferences about employee productivity from the test but inappropriate to draw inferences about absenteeism. There are several manifestations of validity, and they all involve determining the appropriateness of a measure (test) for drawing inferences.

The word *validity* is often associated with two other words: *validation* and *validate*. Validation is the empirical process of determining the degree to which test scores are statistically related to criterion scores. To "validate a test" means to establish the degree to which it predicts one or more criteria. The results of a validation process may be to conclude a test is unrelated to a criterion of interest. The process of validating a test does not assure or guarantee any particular empirical outcome.

The word *valid* has a different meaning in everyday life compared to its use in psychology. We can speak of having a "valid" driver's license—either the driver's license is valid or not. This "either/or" thinking does not apply to the psychological meaning of the word "valid." Rather than either/or, the accuracy of a psychological test to predict a criterion can range from "not valid" to "highly valid." Arrayed along a *continuum* of validity, psychologists must decide if a test manifests enough validity to warrant its use. However, it is overly simplistic to think of tests as either being valid or not.

The words validate and validation also have other meanings in everyday life. Consider Figure 4-1. It shows a badge worn by a salesperson in a retail store in the city of

Validity
A standard for evaluating tests that refers to the accuracy or appropriateness of drawing inferences from test scores. Often contrasted with reliability.

Figure 4-1   *Badge worn by a salesperson referencing "validate" and "validation"*

Palo Alto (CA). The badge states, "We Validate" and parking is "Free with Validation." If a customer made a purchase in a store, the customer's parking ticket would be stamped by the salesperson ("We Validate"), and the customer would not have to pay a parking fee ("Free with Validation"). In the parlance of everyday language, *validate* is a mechanical act (in this case using a rubber stamp), and the validation of the parking ticket results in free parking for the customer. The end result would be either the customer had a valid parking ticket or not. In psychology, tests are validated through carefully developed scientific methods, and the outcome of the validation process could yield a wide range of conclusions about the validity of the tests.

Validity has been a controversial topic within the field of psychology (Newton & Shaw, 2013). For many years psychologists believed there were "types" of validity, just as there are types of reliability (test–retest, internal consistency, etc.). Now psychologists have come to believe there is but a single or unitary conception of validity. Psychologists are involved in the formulation, measurement, and interpretation of constructs. A *construct* is a theoretical concept we propose to explain aspects of behavior. Examples of constructs in I/O psychology are intelligence, motivation, mechanical comprehension, and leadership. Because constructs are abstractions (ideas), we must have real, tangible ways to assess them; that is, we need an actual measure of the proposed construct. Thus a paper-and-pencil test of intelligence is one way to measure the psychological construct of intelligence. The degree to which an actual measure (i.e., a test of intelligence) is an accurate and faithful representation of its underlying construct (i.e., the construct of intelligence) is **construct validity**.

Construct validity
The degree to which a test is an accurate and faithful measure of the construct it purports to measure.

Construct Validity.   In studying construct validity, psychologists seek to ascertain the linkage between what the test measures and the theoretical construct. Let us assume we wish to understand the construct of intelligence, and to do so we develop a paper-and-pencil test that we believe assesses that construct. To establish the construct validity of our test, we want to compare scores on our test with known measures of intelligence, such as verbal, numerical, and problem-solving ability. If our test is a faithful assessment of intelligence, then the scores on our test should converge with these other known measures of intelligence. More technically, there should be a high correlation between the scores from our new test of intelligence and the existing measures of intelligence. These correlation coefficients are referred to as *convergent validity coefficients* because they reflect the degree to which these scores converge (or come together) in assessing a common concept, intelligence.

Likewise, scores on our test should *not* be related to concepts that we know are *not* related to intelligence, such as physical strength, eye color, and gender. That is, scores on our test should diverge (or be separate) from these concepts that are unrelated to intelligence. More technically, there should be very low correlations between the scores from our new test of intelligence and these concepts. These correlation coefficients are referred to as *divergent validity coefficients* because they reflect the degree to which these scores diverge from each other in assessing unrelated concepts. Other statistical procedures may also be used to establish the construct validity of a test.

After collecting and evaluating much information about the test, we accumulate a body of evidence supporting the notion that the test measures a psychological construct. Then we say that the test manifests a high degree of construct validity. Tests that manifest a high degree of construct validity are among the most widely respected and frequently used assessment instruments in I/O psychology.

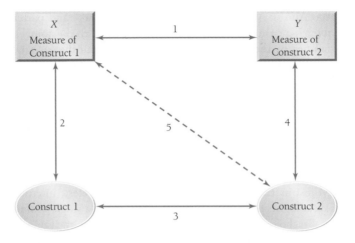

Figure 4-2   *Inferential linkages in construct validation*

Adapted by permission from "Validity of Personnel Decisions: A Conceptual Analysis of the Inferential and Evidential Bases," by J. F. Binning and G. V. Barrett, 1989, *Journal of Applied Psychology, 74*, p. 480. Copyright © 1989 American Psychological Association.

Binning and Barrett (1989) described construct validation as the process of demonstrating evidence for five linkages or inferences, as illustrated in Figure 4-2. Figure 4-2 shows two empirical measures and two constructs. *X* is a measure of construct 1, such as a test of intelligence purports to measure the psychological construct of intelligence. *Y* is a measure of construct 2, such as a supervisor's assessment of an employee's performance purports to measure the construct of job performance. Linkage 1 is the only one that can be tested directly because it is the only inference involving two variables that are directly measured (*X* and *Y*). In assessing the construct validity of *X* and *Y*, one would be most interested in assessing linkages 2 and 4, respectively. That is, we would want to know that the empirical measures of *X* and *Y* are faithful and accurate assessments of the constructs (1 and 2) they purport to measure. Because our empirical measures are never perfect indicators of the constructs we seek to understand, Edwards and Bagozzi (2000) believe researchers should devote more attention to assessing linkages 2 and 4. For the purpose of constructing theories of job performance, one would be interested in linkage 3, the relationship between the two constructs. Finally, Binning and Barrett noted that in personnel selection, we are interested in linkage 5; that is, the inference between an employment test score and the domain of performance on the job. Thus the process of construct validation involves examining the linkages among multiple concepts of interest to us. We always operate at the empirical level (*X* and *Y*), yet we wish to draw inferences at the conceptual level (constructs 1 and 2). Construct validation is the continuous process of verifying the accuracy of an inference among concepts for the purpose of furthering our ability to understand those concepts, and the confidence we have in the inferences made is directly related to the strength of the evidence collected (Schmitt et al., 2010).

Criterion-related validity
The degree to which a test forecasts or is statistically related to a criterion.

Criterion-Related Validity.   One manifestation of construct validity is the **criterion-related validity** of a test. As its name suggests, criterion-related validity refers to how much a predictor relates to a criterion. It is a frequently used and important manifestation of validity in I/O psychology. The two major variations of criterion-related validity are concurrent and predictive. Concurrent validity is used to diagnose the existing status of some criterion, whereas predictive validity is used to forecast future status. The primary distinction is the time interval between collecting the predictor and criterion data.

In measuring *concurrent* criterion-related validity, we are concerned with how well a predictor can predict a criterion at the same time, or concurrently. Examples abound. We may wish to predict a student's grade point average on the basis of a test score, so we collect data on the grade point averages of many students, and then we administer a predictor test. If the predictor test is a valid measure of grades, there will be a high correlation between test scores and grades. We can use the same method in a work setting. We can predict a worker's level of productivity (the criterion) on the basis of a test (the predictor). We collect productivity data on a current group of workers, administer a test, and then correlate their test scores with their productivity records. If the test is of value, then we can draw an inference about a worker's productivity on the basis of the test score. In measurements of concurrent validity, there is no time interval between collecting the predictor and criterion data. The two variables are assessed concurrently, which is how the method gets its name. Thus the purpose of assessing concurrent criterion-related validity is so the test can be used with the knowledge that it is predictive of the criterion.

In measuring *predictive* criterion-related validity, we collect predictor information and use it to forecast future criterion performance. A college might use a student's high school class rank to predict the criterion of overall college grade point average four years later. A company could use a test to predict whether job applicants will complete a six-month training program. Figure 4-3 graphically illustrates concurrent and predictive criterion-related validity.

The logic of criterion-related validity is straightforward. We determine whether there is a relationship between predictor scores and criterion scores based on a sample of employees for whom we have both sets of scores. If there is a relationship, we use scores on those predictor variables to select applicants on whom there are no criterion scores. Then we can predict the applicant's future (and thus unknown) criterion performance

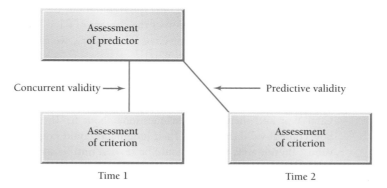

Figure 4-3 *Portrayal of concurrent and predictive criterion-related validity*

Validity coefficient
A statistical index
(often expressed as a
correlation coefficient)
that reveals the degree
of association between
two variables. Often
used in the context of
prediction.

from their known test scores based on the relationship established through criterion-related validity. When predictor scores are correlated with criterion data, the resulting correlation is called a **validity coefficient**. Whereas an acceptable reliability coefficient is in the .70–.80 range, the desired range for a validity coefficient is .30–.40. Validity coefficients less than .30 are not uncommon, but those greater than .50 are rare. Just as a predictor cannot be too reliable, it also cannot be too valid. The greater the correlation between the predictor and the criterion, the more we know about the criterion on the basis of the predictor. By squaring the correlation coefficient (r), we can calculate how much variance in the criterion we can account for by using the predictor. For example, if a predictor correlates .40 with a criterion, we can explain 16% (r^2) of the variance in the criterion by knowing the predictor. This particular level of predictability (16%) would be considered satisfactory by most psychologists, given all the possible causes of performance variation. A correlation of 1.0 indicates perfect prediction (and complete knowledge). However, as Lubinski and Dawis (1992) noted, tests with moderate validity coefficients are not necessarily flawed or inadequate. The results attest to the complexity of human behavior. Our behavior is influenced by factors not measured by tests, such as motivation and luck. We should thus have realistic expectations regarding the validity of our tests.

Some criteria are difficult to predict no matter what predictors are used; other criteria are fairly predictable. Similarly, some predictors are consistently valid and are thus used often. Other predictors do not seem to be of much predictive value no matter what the criteria are, and thus they fall out of use. Usually, however, certain predictors are valid for predicting only certain criteria. Later in this chapter there will be a review of the predictors typically used in I/O psychology and an examination of how accurate they are in predicting criteria.

Content validity
The degree to which
subject matter experts
agree that the items in a
test are a representative
sample of the domain
of knowledge the test
purports to measure.

Content Validity.   Another manifestation of construct validity is **content validity**. Content validity is the degree to which a predictor covers a representative sample of the behavior being assessed. It is limited mainly to psychological tests but may also extend to interviews or other predictors. Historically, content validity was most relevant in achievement testing. Achievement tests are designed to indicate how well a person has mastered a specific area of knowledge. To be "content valid," an achievement test on Civil War history, for example, must contain a representative sample or mix of test items covering the domain of Civil War history, such as battles, military and political figures, and so on. A test with only questions about the dates of famous battles would not be a balanced representation of the content of Civil War history. If a person scores high on a content-valid test of Civil War history, we can infer that he or she is very knowledgeable about the Civil War.

How do we assess content validity? Unlike criterion-related validity, we do not compute a correlation coefficient. Content validity is assessed by subject matter experts in the field the test covers. Civil War historians would first define the domain of the Civil War and then write test questions about it. These experts would then decide how content valid the test is. Their judgments could range from "not at all" to "highly valid." Presumably, the test would be revised until it showed a high degree of content validity.

Face validity
The appearance that
items in a test are
appropriate for the
intended use of the test
by the individuals who
take the test.

A similar type of validity based on people's judgments is called **face validity**. This is concerned with the appearance of the test items: do they look appropriate for such a test? Estimates of content validity are made by test developers; estimates of face validity are made by test takers. It is possible for a test to be content valid but not face valid, and vice versa. In such a case, the test developers and test takers would disagree over the relevance or appropriateness of the items for the domain being assessed. Within the field of psychology, content validity is thought to be of greater significance or importance than face validity. However, the face validity of a test can greatly affect how individuals perceive the test to be an appropriate, legitimate means of assessing them for some important decision (such as a job offer). Individuals are more likely to bring legal challenges against companies for using tests that are not face valid. Thus issues of content validity are generally more relevant for the science of I/O psychology, whereas issues of face validity are generally more relevant for the practice of I/O psychology.

Once used mainly for academic achievement testing, it is also relevant for employment testing. There is a strong and obvious link between the process of work analysis (discussed in Chapter 3) and the concept of content validation. The logic of content validity is if a test measures knowledge associated with a particular job, the content of that test is related to the content of that job, and therefore the test is a useful predictor of job performance. An example would be a test that measures knowledge of street locations for the job of taxi driver. The problem with this logic is there is no demonstrated empirical link between test performance and job performance (i.e., the former predicts the latter). Establishing such a link is the result of assessing the criterion-related validity of a test. There is certainly no harm in having employment tests where the content of the test corresponds to the job. But the mere similarity of content between the two offers no insights about the likely job performance of the selected candidates, which is the fundamental rationale of why assessments of job candidates are made. Murphy et al. (2009) reported that content-matched tests did not result in higher criterion-related validity coefficients than did tests that did not match the content of the job. In fact, it is possible for a test to have a high degree of content match with a job but manifest no criterion-related validity. Murphy (2009) summarized the prevailing opinion among I/O psychologists as follows: "content validation is useful for many things, but validity isn't one of them" (p. 453). The word "validity" has special significance for psychologists, as it addresses the meaning and accuracy of the inferences we make about people. As such, when the content of an employment test corresponds to the content of a job, most I/O psychologists would prefer to describe the "content representativeness" of the test rather than its "content validity." The distinction may be subtle but its importance is substantial.

Predictor Development

The goal of psychological assessment is to know something about the individual being assessed for the purpose of making an inference about that person. In I/O psychology the inference to be made often pertains to whether the individual is likely to perform well in a job. What the "something" is that we seek to know is a construct we believe is important to success on the job. That "something" could be the individual's intelligence, ambition, interpersonal skills, ability to cope with frustration, willingness to learn new concepts or procedures, and so on. How do we assess these characteristics of individuals? I/O psychologists have developed a broad array of predictor measures designed to help us make decisions (i.e., hire or not hire) about individuals. A discussion of these predictor measures is presented in the rest of this chapter. For the most part, these predictor measures can be classified along two dimensions.

The first dimension is whether the predictor seeks to measure directly the underlying psychological construct in question (e.g., mechanical comprehension), or whether it seeks to measure a sample of the same behavior to be exhibited on the job. For example, let us assume we want to assess individuals to determine whether they are suitable for the job of a mechanic. On the basis of a work analysis we know the job of mechanic requires the individual to be proficient with tools and equipment and with diagnosing mechanical problems. We could elect to assess mechanical ability with a paper-and-pencil test of mechanical comprehension. Such a test would reveal to what degree the individual possesses mechanical knowledge, but it would not assess proficiency in the use of tools (i.e., because it is a paper-and-pencil test). Alternatively, we could present the individual with a mechanical object in a state of disrepair and say, "This appears to be broken. Figure out what is wrong with it and then fix it." The individual's behavior in diagnosing and repairing the object would be observed and rated by knowledgeable individuals (i.e., SMEs). This latter type of assessment is called "behavioral sampling" because it samples the types of behavior exhibited on the job (in this case, diagnosing and repairing mechanical objects). This particular assessment would measure the individual's proficiency with tools used in diagnosis and repair; however, it is limited to only one particular malfunctioning mechanical object. The assessment lacks the breadth of coverage of a paper-and-pencil test. Furthermore, the behavioral sampling method of assessment measures whether the individual can perform the diagnosis and repair at this time, but not whether he or she could learn to do so with proper training. These types of issues and others will be presented in the discussion of predictor methods.

A second distinction among predictors is whether they seek to measure something about the individual currently or something about the individual in the past. A job interview is a current measure of a person's characteristics because the interviewer assesses voice quality, interpersonal demeanor, and poise. An assessment of these factors would be used to predict whether the individual will succeed in a job. Alternatively, a predictor measure could assess whether the individual exhibited these behaviors in the past, not concurrently. An example would be a letter of recommendation solicited from a former employer who supervised the individual in a previous job. Here the intent is to make a prediction about future behavior (in the new job) on the basis of past behavior (in the old job). Thus predictor measures are used to make inferences about future behavior on the basis of current or past behavior. Some predictor measures can be developed that measure both past and current behaviors. The job interview is one example. The interviewer can assess the individual's behavior in the interview as it is happening and can also ask questions about the individual's previous work history.

Not all predictor measures fall neatly into either the construct/behavioral sampling categories or the assessment of past/present characteristics of individuals. However, this classification approach is a reasonable way to understand the varieties of predictor measures and their respective intents. In all cases predictor measures are designed to forecast future behavior. They differ in the approaches they take in making these predictions. The degree to which these approaches differ in reliability, validity, fairness, social acceptability, legal defensibility, time, and cost has been the subject of extensive research in I/O psychology.

The Purpose of Testing

A test is one way to learn about a person's knowledge, skills, abilities, and personality. As such, it is a source of information about people. Many other methods can be used as a source of information, including speaking with them directly, asking other people about them, considering their past behavior, and so on. It is important to keep in mind the difference between methods of assessment versus the human attributes we seek to assess. There is no one method that is superior for measuring all human attributes. Simply put, depending upon the particular attribute, some assessment methods are better than others. Each of these methods is a predictor of subsequent behavior in the workplace. In this first section on predictors, the focus is on tests.

The practice of psychological testing includes both tests and surveys. Surveys are also called questionnaires and inventories. Tests have right/wrong answers while surveys do not. Pearlman (2009) differentiated three types of testing in organizations based upon the potential consequences of the assessment. *Low-stakes* testing refers to results that help the individual but have no bearing on the employee's status within the organization. An example would be a survey about preference for meeting times. In *moderate-stakes* testing the results might influence the employee's status in the organization. An example would be a survey about willingness to participate in training programs. In *high-stakes* testing there is a direct consequence to the individual, as being hired by the organization or being promoted within it. The higher the stakes, the greater is the pressure on the organization for the test to provide an accurate and fair assessment of the individual. Likewise, the greater is the pressure on the individual to perform well for achieving the desired outcome.

Test Content

Tests can be classified according to their content. This section will discuss the major types of constructs assessed by tests relevant to employment. Also presented will be information on how valid the various types of tests have been in personnel selection as documented from their use in the psychological literature.

Intelligence

Intelligence or cognitive ability is the most heavily researched construct in all of psychology. Interest in the assessment of intelligence began more than 100 years ago. Despite the length of time the construct of intelligence has been assessed, however, there remains no singular or standard means to assess it. Furthermore, recent research suggests intelligence is even more complex than we have believed.

What is generally agreed upon regarding intelligence? Intelligence traditionally has been conceptualized as having a singular, primary basis. This concept is known as *general mental ability* and is symbolized by g. By assessing g, we gain an understanding

g
The symbol for "general mental ability," which has been found to be predictive of success in most jobs.

of a person's general level of intellectual capability. Tests that measure *g* have been found to be predictive of performance across a wide range of occupations (e.g., Ree et al., 1994). The criterion-related validity of *g* is impressive, often in the range of .40–.50. Many researchers believe it is the single most diagnostic predictor of future job performance. Simply put, if we could know only one attribute of a job candidate upon which to base a prediction, we would want an assessment of intelligence. General intelligence is regarded to be a ubiquitous predictor of a wide variety of performance criteria, prompting Brand (1987) to observe: "*g* is to psychology what carbon is to chemistry" (p. 257). Reeve and Hakel (2002) summarized the prevailing scientific status of general mental ability: "A wealth of data has confirmed that there is virtually no circumstance, no life outcome, no criterion for which even minimal cognitive functioning is required in which *g* is not at least moderately predictive of individual differences . . ." (p. 49).

Although research clearly supports the validity of general intelligence as a predictor, some researchers believe that conceptualizing intelligence merely as *g* encourages oversimplification of the inherent complexity of intelligence. Murphy (1996) asserted that intelligence is not a unitary phenomenon, and other dimensions of intelligence are also worthy of our consideration. Ackerman (1992), for example, reported superior predictive power of multiple abilities over general intelligence in complex information processing tasks, as in the job of air traffic controller. Ackerman and Kanfer (1993) developed a useful selection test for air traffic controllers based in large part on the assessment of spatial ability. From an I/O psychology perspective, therefore, the controversy regarding the assessment of intelligence rests primarily on the adequacy of measuring general intelligence (*g*) only or assessing multiple cognitive abilities in forecasting job behavior. The current body of research seems to indicate that in most cases measuring the *g* factor of intelligence offers superior predictive accuracy in forecasting success in most jobs.

As Daniel (1997) stated, our means of assessing intelligence (i.e., a test) are heavily guided by how we view what we are trying to assess (see Field Note 1: *What is Intelligence?*). *Academic* intelligence represents what intelligence tests typically measure, such as fluency with words and numbers. Table 4-1 shows two sample test questions from a typical intelligence test. *Practical* intelligence is needed to be competent in the everyday world and is not highly related to academic intelligence. *Creative* intelligence pertains to the ability to produce work that is both novel (i.e., original or unexpected) and appropriate (i.e., useful). A view of intelligence dominated by academic intelligence will lead us to assess that particular kind to the relative exclusion of practical and creative intelligence. Hedlund and Sternberg (2000) asserted that the contemporary world of business seeks employees who are adaptable to highly changing conditions. Real-life problems tend to be ill-defined, ambiguous, and dynamic, and such problems

Table 4-1 *Sample test questions from a typical intelligence test*

1. What number is missing in this series?
   3–8–14–21–29–(?)
2. SHOVEL is to DITCHDIGGER as SCALPEL is to:
   (a) knife   (b) sharp   (c) butcher   (d) surgeon   (e) cut

Field Note 1: *What is Intelligence?*

The construct of intelligence is highly complex, perhaps more complex than researchers have realized. Theorists have long debated whether intelligence is a unitary concept or whether there are various forms of intelligence, such as verbal and quantitative. Tests of intelligence are designed and interpreted based on these theoretical formulations. The questions on traditional tests of intelligence have a correct answer and only one correct answer. Examples include the answers to questions about mathematics and vocabulary. However, research suggests that there are other manifestations of intelligence. Many problems in life do not have any correct answer; other problems may have more than one correct answer. Furthermore, in real life, solutions to problems are not so much correct and incorrect as they are "feasible" and "acceptable." Examples include dealing with interpersonal problems at the individual level and with global problems at the national level. It takes intelligence to solve such problems, but these types of questions do not appear on typical tests of intelligence. There is an adage that "young people are smart and old people are wise." Perhaps wisdom is a form of intelligence that is derived through many years of successfully dealing with problems that lack single correct solutions. Psychologists refer to knowledge that helps solve practical problems as procedural or tacit knowledge. Indeed, Sternberg and Horvath (1999) described how tacit knowledge contributes to success in a broad array of occupations, such as law, military command, medicine, and teaching. As Marchant and Robinson (1999) stated on the subject of legal expertise, all lawyers are knowledgeable of the law. That is what they are taught in law school. But the truly successful lawyers understand how to interpret the law and the dynamics of the entire legal system. The capacity to derive feasible and acceptable solutions to complex problems that do not have any correct answer is, as current research supports, a legitimate form of intelligence.

do not match the types of problems on which intelligence traditionally has been assessed. Hedlund and Sternberg believe the concept of practical intelligence is intended to complement, rather than to contradict, the narrower views of *g*-based theories of intelligence.

As can be inferred from the foregoing discussion, the construct of intelligence is highly complex. Scherbaum et al. (2012) stated we need a better understanding of general cognitive ability. As jobs are becoming increasingly more complex, perhaps *g* will be increasingly more predictive of job performance over an entire career. From an I/O psychology perspective, we are concerned with the degree to which cognitive ability forecasts job performance. Murphy summarized the prevailing conclusion: "Research on the validity of measures of cognitive ability as predictors of job performance represents one of the 'success stories' in I/O psychology" (p. 6). While other abilities and attributes are also necessary for different jobs, "I/O psychologists generally agree that cognitive ability tests are valid and fair, that they provide useful information, although perhaps not complete information about the construct of general cognitive ability" (Murphy et al., 2003, p. 670).

Mechanical Aptitude

Mechanical aptitude tests require a person to recognize which mechanical principle is suggested by a test item. The underlying concepts measured by these items include sound and heat conductance, velocity, gravity, and force. One of the more popular tests of mechanical reasoning is the Bennett Test of Mechanical Comprehension (Bennett, 1980). The test is a series of pictures that illustrate various mechanical concepts and principles. Other tests of mechanical comprehension have also been developed.

Muchinsky (2004) reported that tests of mechanical ability are highly predictive of performance in manufacturing/production jobs. However, women traditionally perform worse than men on tests of mechanical ability. Recent attempts to include test questions pertaining to kitchen implements and other topics about which women may be more familiar (e.g., high-heel shoes) have reduced, but not eliminated, the male/female score differential (Wiesen, 1999).

Personality

Unlike the previously cited tests, which have objective answers, personality inventories do not have right or wrong answers. Test takers answer how much they agree with certain statements (e.g., "People who work hard get ahead"). In personality inventories similar types of questions typically comprise a scale, which reflects a person's introversion, dominance, confidence, and so on. Items are scored according to a predetermined key such that responding one way or another to an item results in a higher or lower score on a particular scale. Although there are no right/wrong answers to personality questions, employers have clear preferences for candidates who have high scores on selected personality scales. The basic rationale is that successful employees possess a particular personality structure, and scales reflective of that structure become the basis for selecting new employees.

Personality assessment is one of the fastest growing areas in personnel selection. The five-factor model of personality has received the most empirical support. It is often referred to as the **Big 5 personality theory**. These are the five personality factors:

Big 5 personality theory
A theory that defines personality in terms of five major factors: emotional stability, extraversion, openness to experience, agreeableness, and conscientiousness. Also called the "Five Factor" theory of personality.

- **Emotional stability**—the tendency to be calm, even-tempered, and emotionally balanced
- **Extraversion**—the tendency to be sociable, assertive, active, talkative, energetic, and outgoing
- **Openness to experience**—the disposition to be curious, imaginative, and unconventional
- **Agreeableness**—the disposition to be cooperative, helpful, and easy to get along with others
- **Conscientiousness**—the disposition to be purposeful, determined, organized, and controlled.

Extensive empirical support for its validity was provided by McCrae and Costa (1987) and Hogan (1991). Personality inventories have also been developed based upon this theory—for example, the NEO-PI (P. T. Costa, 1996) and the Hogan Personality Inventory (Hogan & Hogan, 1992). Barrick and Mount (1991) concluded from a meta-analysis that extraversion is a valid predictor of performance in occupations that involve social interactions, such as managers and salespeople. Tokar et al. (1998) revealed that personality is linked to many aspects of work behavior, including job performance, career progression, and vocational interests. Conscientiousness shows the most consistently high correlations with job performance criteria for all occupations and across different cultures (Salgado, 1997). The five personality factors are considered a durable framework for understanding personality structure among people of many nations, and they have prompted McCrae and Costa (1997) to refer to their pattern of interrelationships as a "human universal." Furthermore, such personality measures provide *incremental* predictive validity beyond measures of intelligence (Judge et al., 1999).

On a conceptual level intelligence and personality have typically been viewed as separate constructs. Intelligence traditionally has reflected the "can do" dimension of an individual; namely, the person "can do" the work because he or she is judged to possess an adequate level of cognitive ability. Personality traditionally has reflected the "will do" dimension of an individual; namely, the person "will do" the work because he or she is judged to possess the demeanor to do so. Kehoe (2002) explained how intelligence and personality can both be predictive of job performance, each in its own way. Assume a personality test and a test of g both correlate equally with job performance. The employees selected by each of these tests will not be the same. "The 'personality' employees might achieve their overall performance by being relatively more dependable, persistent, attentive, helpful, and so on. The 'cognitive' employees might achieve their overall performance by being relatively more accurate, faster, effective problem solvers, and the like" (pp. 103–104). Hofstee (2001) proposed the existence of a "p factor" (a general personality factor reflecting the ability to cope), which is parallel to the g factor in intelligence. Further research may lead to a melding of these two constructs, which have typically been viewed as distinct.

The diagnosis and treatment of personality disorders is the traditional domain of clinical psychology. Individuals with extreme personality disorders are not capable of sustaining employment. However, individuals with less severe personality disorders can and do enter the workplace (Wille et al., 2013). There are three personality disorders which collectively are called the **dark triad** (O'Boyle et al., 2012).

The first is *Machiavellianism*. It is named after a book written about 500 years ago by Niccolo Machiavelli, an Italian nobleman. The focus of the book is about acquiring and using political power. The foundation of Machiavellianism is having a dark and cynical interpretation of human nature. The goal in life is to get your way by manipulating other people. No actions or tactics are deemed inappropriate if they lead to attaining what you want.

The second is *narcissism*. It is named after a mythical Greek figure, Narcissus, who was infatuated with his own physical attractiveness. People afflicted with narcissism exhibit a high degree of self-importance. They simultaneously desire to be in control of other people and be admired by them. Relentlessly self-promoting and unaffected by criticism, they exude subtle arrogance.

The third member of the dark triad is *psychopathy*. Derived from Ancient Greek terms, *pathos* is suffering, and *psycho* referring to properties of the mind. Psychopaths are sometimes portrayed in the popular media as being deranged killers. However, psychopaths are not inherently violent. They are characterized by lacking any concern

Dark triad
A cluster of three personality disorders associated with counterproductive work behavior: Machiavellianism, narcissism, and psychopathy.

for others. They may come across as glib, but they are emotionally shallow. Exhibiting a sense of charisma, others may be drawn to them without being aware of the basis of attraction.

Only in recent years have I/O psychologists examined the dark triad in the workplace. Scores on assessments of the dark triad have been found predictive of counterproductive work behavior (as discussed in Chapter 3). Paradoxically, some organizations may initially reward employees who exhibit dark triad behaviors because of their relentless pursuit of self-advancement. In such cases organizations place more emphasis on the employees having reached certain performance criteria (e.g., sales volume), while being less concerned about the harm inflicted on others in the process. Babiak and Hare (2006) described such individuals as "snakes in suits." The authors explained how psychopaths can work their way into leadership roles and thus are positioned to cause immeasurable harm within the organization because of their destructive personalities. "Some companies quite innocently recruit individuals with psychopathic tendencies, because some hiring managers may mistakenly attribute leadership labels to what are, in actuality, psychopathic behaviors. For example, taking charge, making decisions, and getting others to do what you want are classic features of leadership and management, yet they can also be well-packaged forms of coercion, domination, and manipulation" (p. *xi*).

As implied by Babiak and Hare, people with dark triad personality disorders can be easily confused with others who have healthy personalities. The dark triad attributes are subtle and only manifest themselves to others over time. Guenole (2014) stated the goal of personality assessment for these types of people is to screen them out of any future consideration for employment. Individuals exhibiting dark triad attributes are also skilled at their concealment, even in times of formal scrutiny.

Faking in Personality Assessment

A long-standing concern with using personality inventories for personnel selection is that job applicants might not give truthful responses. Rather, applicants may fake their responses to give what they believe are socially desirable responses. Morgeson et al. (2007) concluded that **faking** (or response distortion) on personality inventories is unavoidable because job candidates will necessarily try to project highly positive images of themselves to hiring organizations. The capacity and desire of people to present themselves in a positive way when relating to others is called "impression management." Barrick and Mount (2012) stated, "The responses to the personality inventory capture the impression the individual chooses to present, which mirrors what most people do in everyday interactions with others" (p. 240). The distinction between subtle impression management and blatant response distortion is the fine line that differentiates describing yourself in a positive manner versus faking. There are many facets to the broad issue of response distortion by job candidates in the process of being evaluated for employment. McGrath et al. (2010) presented the scope of the issue as follows: (a) across people (we all do it to some degree); (b) some people do it frequently; (c) some people do it in certain circumstances; and (d) some people do it more intensely than others. More specifically, Berry and Sackett (2009) posited that response distortion is higher when competition is high, and when the purpose of the test is relatively transparent (or when applicants are told what the test measures). Komar et al. (2008) used computer simulation to estimate the effect of faking on the validity of

Faking
The behavior of job applicants to falsify or fake their responses to items on personality inventories to create a favorable impression.

conscientiousness as a predictor of job performance. The greatest reductions in validity were due to the proportion of people who gave faked responses in the applicant pool (a few vs. many) and the magnitude of the faking (a little vs. a lot).

McFarland (2013) observed that the structure of personality inventory questions may paradoxically encourage faking. Personality inventories do not permit candidates to qualify or explain their answers. A question such as, "I typically work hard at everything I do," requires a singular answer in a personality inventory. There is no opportunity, for example, for candidates to explain that they work hard on the job but not in recreational activities. To avoid the impression that they do not work hard on the job, their answer (e.g., "true" or "strongly agree") implies they work hard at everything in life, a most dubious response, likely to be interpreted as faking.

I/O psychologists are not in agreement regarding the frequency and extensiveness of response distortion in personality testing. Furthermore, there is no agreement as to what actions organizations should take in response to applicant faking. Three options have been proposed. Personality tests can be designed to include specific questions that reveal response distortion. The first option is to eliminate from further employment consideration those candidates who give faked responses. Of practical concern with this option is the degree to which faking would result in elimination of candidates (i.e., a few or many). The second option is to use statistical corrections on the test scores, essentially re-scoring the test. Of practical concern with this option is the magnitude of the re-scoring for candidates with faked responses. How much should their test scores be lowered because of detected faking? The third option does not involve specific questions on the test designed to detect faking, but rather the organization strongly warns the candidates against giving faked responses. Of practical concern with this option is candidates may perceive few negative consequences for faking versus the potential benefit of being hired (Oswald & Hough, 2011). Fan et al. (2012) developed a warning to candidates taking an online personality assessment. The warning indicated their responses were exhibiting a pattern similar to people who faked responses. The authors believed the best way to deal with faking is during the assessment process, not after it already occurred. Landers et al. (2011) asserted that if there are no serious consequences to faking (e.g., candidates who fake responses will no longer be considered for employment), it will likely continue. Griffith and Robie (2013) concluded there is no professionally accepted remedy to faking. The decision to make a job offer is often the product of multiple assessments, some of which cannot be faked (e.g., ability tests and verification of educational attainment) and some that can be faked (e.g., personality inventories and interviews).

In summation, research has shown that assessments of personality add to our capacity to predict job performance over and above assessments of cognitive ability and work experience. From a practical perspective the problem is to find ways to measure personality without candidates distorting their responses (Hough & Dilchert, 2010). Recent research has attempted to do so. Despite the problems encountered with faking on personality inventories, the construct of personality is not irrelevant in the workplace (Murphy et al., 2013). As Murphy commented, "I have more faith in the constructs than in the measures . . . If you want to know about someone's personality just ask his or her coworkers" (Morgeson et al., 2007, p. 719). Two studies examined the validity of observer ratings of personality compared to self-report personality measures in predicting the criterion of overall job performance. Oh et al. (2011) obtained superior validity coefficients with observer ratings of personality compared to scores on

Social Media and I/O Psychology: *Assessing Personality via Facebook*

What can you tell about someone from their Facebook page? Some people are quite open about themselves online, sharing their political views, their opinions on recent news topics, details about their family events, and even what they may have eaten for dinner. Others are more private, perhaps using Facebook as a means to know what is going on with others rather than post anything about themselves. From status updates, somebody may appear easily riled, whereas another person may seem to be consistently positive about the world and its events. Indeed, it would seem that you may be able to discover one's personality from how they present themselves on Facebook.

This is indeed what researchers have discovered. Researchers have found that the number of friends people have, how often they post, and what they post about are related to their self-reported personality. For example, various studies have shown that the number of friends and how frequently they post status updates is positively related to extraversion. Further evidence has suggested that individuals high on narcissism and psychopathy tend to post updates that are more negative (vs. positive) in nature. Furthermore, individuals who are higher on openness to experience tend to have more friends of the opposite sex. Researchers have even discovered some differences between individuals who use Facebook versus those who choose not to use Facebook.

It would seem that individuals can portray themselves in any way they wish online. The ability to invent and reinvent one's own image online is extraordinarily easy. Individuals can describe themselves in flattering terms on dating sites, highlight certain skills (whether true or not) on LinkedIn for employers to see, or portray their lives as more exciting on Facebook. Nevertheless, it may be that regardless of how you think you're presenting yourself, the number of posts and content of them may limit your ability to fake your personality. Some of the research in this area, for example, has looked beyond the specific things said in status updates and instead looked at the structure of sentences to reveal differences in personality. Thus, whereas there are some clear issues that must be considered when using information obtained from social media sites when hiring employees (such as invasion of privacy issues, which may impact how applicants view an organization), there is reason to believe that Facebook and other social networking sites may be one avenue for obtaining indirect information on an individual's personality.

a personality inventory for each of the Big 5 factors. The validity of observer ratings of conscientiousness was the highest, .32. While Oh et al. used observer ratings from peers, Connelly and Ones (2010) recommended that people qualified to rate someone's personality could be family members, friends, and roommates. In addition, there is evidence that personality may be gleaned from how people present themselves online (see Social Media and I/O Psychology: *Assessing Personality via Facebook*). As such, perhaps the vexing problem of applicant faking on personality inventories can be allayed by using a different source of personality assessment. However, as empirically appealing as observer ratings may be, there could be logistical issues associated with obtaining them for making personnel selection decisions in an employment context.

Integrity

The prevalence of personality assessment in personnel selection is also demonstrated by the development and growing use of honesty or integrity tests. **Integrity tests** are designed to identify job applicants who will not steal from their employer or otherwise engage in deviant behavior on the job. These tests are paper-and-pencil tests and generally fall into one of two types (Sackett & Wanek, 1996). In the first type, an *overt integrity test*, the job applicant clearly understands that the intent of the test is to assess integrity. The test typically has two sections: one deals with attitudes toward theft and other forms of dishonesty (namely, beliefs about the frequency and extent of employee theft, punitiveness toward theft, perceived ease of theft, and endorsement of common rationalizations about theft), and a second section deals with admissions of theft and other illegal activities (such as dollar amounts stolen in the past year, drug use, and gambling). There is some evidence (Cunningham et al., 1994) that the responses to such tests are distorted by the applicants' desire to create a favorable impression. Alliger et al. (1995) found that the questions in integrity tests are value-laden and transparent (e.g., "Are you a productive person?"), which makes it easy for applicants to distort their responses to affect the desired result. Berry, Sackett, and Wiemann (2007) concluded that respondents appear able to fake an integrity test when instructed to do so. This conclusion was reached by comparing the scores of people who were instructed to "respond honestly" and also to "respond as a job applicant who wanted to fake good to beat the test." The second type of test, called a *personality-based measure*, makes no reference to theft. These tests contain conventional personality assessment items that have been found to be predictive of theft. Because this type of test does not contain obvious references to theft, it is less likely to offend job applicants.

Research findings have shown that integrity tests are valid. Collins and Schmidt (1993) conducted a study of incarcerated offenders convicted of white-collar crimes, such as embezzlement and fraud. Compared with a control sample of employees in upper-level positions of authority, offenders had greater tendencies toward irresponsibility, lack of dependability, and disregard of rules and social norms. In a meta-analytic review, Van Iddekinge et al. (2013) found that integrity tests predicted counterproductive work behavior criteria more accurately than job performance or turnover. This finding is supportive of why integrity testing was developed.

Situational Judgment

Advances are being made in the format of test questions. Traditional multiple-choice test questions have one correct answer. Given this characteristic, test questions have to be written such that there is indeed a correct answer to the question, and only one correct answer (Haladyna, 1999). In real life, however, many problems and questions don't have a single correct answer. Rather, an array of answers is possible, some more plausible or appropriate than others. There is a growing interest in designing tests that require the test taker to rate a series of answers (all correct to some degree) in terms of their overall suitability for resolving a problem. One name given to this type of assessment is **situational judgment test** (McDaniel et al., 2001). An example of a situational judgment test (SJT) question is presented in Table 4-2. Research on this type of test reveals that it measures a construct similar to intelligence, but not the same as

Table 4-2   *Sample question from a situational judgment test*

> You are a leader of a manufacturing team that works with heavy machinery. One of your production operators tells you that one machine in the work area is suddenly malfunctioning and may endanger the welfare of your work team. Rank order the following possible courses of action to effectively address this problem, from most desirable to least desirable.
>
> 1. Call a meeting of your team members to discuss the problem.
> 2. Report the problem to the Director of Safety.
> 3. Shut off the machine immediately.
> 4. Individually ask other production operators about problems with their machines.
> 5. Evacuate your team from the production facility.

the traditional conception of *g*. SJTs reflect the theoretical rationale of practical intelligence discussed earlier in the chapter.

The preferred rank ordering of possible responses to a situation is determined by incumbents who serve as subject matter experts in the design of the SJTs. Furthermore, the situation-based questions are often derived from the incumbents' work experiences. Ployhart and MacKenzie (2011) proposed that SJTs could serve to reinforce the status quo within an organization, because the highest scoring job applicants would be those whose values and perceptions regarding how to respond to problem situations were most similar to those of incumbents.

McDaniel et al. (2007) concluded that SJTs are a valuable means of assessing personnel because they provide incremental validity beyond cognitive and personality measures combined. Christian et al. (2010) reported SJTs could be presented in paper-and-pencil and video-based formats, and both provided useful assessments of candidates. Indeed, Lievens and Sackett (2012) developed a video SJT administered to first-year medical students. The video depicted vignettes showing interactions between physicians and patients. The medical students had to rate the appropriateness of four responses to handling the interactions. The scores on the SJT predicted performance as a medical intern seven years later and job performance as a physician nine years later.

SJTs represent a type of assessment that is designed to measure an attribute other than cognitive ability. Personality inventories would represent another example. The fact that these types of assessments have been found to add to the prediction of job performance criteria above and beyond cognitive ability does not mean they are unrelated to *g*. Bobko and Roth (2012) noted that *g* is indirectly measured in both personality inventories and SJTs. That is, it takes cognitive ability to read and interpret multiple choice questions on a personality inventory. Likewise, it is difficult to believe that exercising good judgment (the "J" in SJT) is not cognitively based. In short, not only is cognitive ability ubiquitous in life's activities, it is a component of assessments expressly designed to measure attributes other than *g*.

Computerized Adaptive Testing

One of the major advances in psychological testing is called **computerized adaptive testing (CAT)**, or "tailored testing" (Wainer, 2000). Here is how it works: CAT is an automated test administration system that uses a computer. The test items appear

Computerized adaptive testing (CAT)
A form of assessment using a computer in which the questions have been precalibrated in terms of difficulty, and the examinee's response (i.e., right or wrong) to one question determines the selection of the next question.

on the video display screen, and the examinee answers using the keyboard. Each test question presented is prompted by the response to the preceding question. The first question given to the examinee is of medium difficulty. If the answer given is correct, the second question selected from the item bank of questions has been precalibrated to be slightly more difficult. If the answer given to that question is wrong, the third question selected by the computer is somewhat easier. And so on.

The purpose of CAT is to get as close a match as possible between the question difficulty level and the examinee's demonstrated ability level. In fact, by the careful calibration of question difficulty, one can infer ability level on the basis of the difficulty level of the questions answered correctly. CAT systems are based on complex mathematical models. Proponents believe that tests can be shorter (because of higher precision of measurement) and less expensive and have greater security than traditional paper-and-pencil tests. The military is the largest user of CAT systems, testing thousands of examinees monthly. Tonidandel et al. (2002) reported that two-thirds of all military recruits were assessed via a CAT version of the ASVAB. In an example of CAT used in the private sector, Overton et al. (1997) found their CAT system achieved greater test security than traditional paper-and-pencil tests. Additionally, traditional academic tests like the Scholastic Aptitude Test (SAT) and the Graduate Record Exam (GRE) are available for applicants using an online CAT system. An added benefit is that the results of the test are available to the applicant immediately upon completion of the test.

Testing on the Internet

In recent years the biggest change in psychological testing is in the way tests are administered and scored. Psychological assessment is moving inexorably from paper-and-pencil testing to online computer testing. As Thompson et al. (2003) described, the movement "from paper to pixels" is affecting all phases of assessment. As a society we are growing more comfortable with computer-based services in life and that includes psychological assessment. Naglieri et al. (2004) described how the Internet offers a faster and cheaper means of testing. Test publishers can download new tests to secure testing sites in a matter of moments. Updating a test is also much easier because there is no need to print new tests, answer keys, or manuals.

Nevertheless, computer-based testing produces potential problems as well. One is test security and whether test content can be compromised. A second issue pertains to proctoring. With unproctored web-based testing, the applicant completes the test from any location with Internet access and without direct supervision of a test administrator. With proctored web-based testing, the applicant must complete the test in the presence of a test administrator, usually at a company-sponsored location. Ployhart et al. (2003) reported that many organizations will accept the results from only proctored web-based testing. As increasingly more testing is done online, our profession will have to respond to a new range of issues associated with this means of assessment. The growing use of Internet testing has prompted researchers to compare Internet tests to traditional paper-and-pencil tests. Tippins et al. (2006) stated that one of the goals of Internet testing is to reduce the time between candidate assessment and the personnel selection decision. As such, a candidate can take a test on the Internet at any time, and in so doing, the test taking would not be proctored by a test administrator. The authors raised serious questions about unproctored Internet testing, including whether the candidate had others assist in answering the questions. Because of potential security issues, Scott and Lezotte (2012) recommended that unproctored Internet testing not be used for high-stakes testing (see I/O Psychology and the Economy: *The Power of the Internet*).

Potosky and Bobko (2004) examined many practical differences between Internet and paper-and-pencil testing. For example, in a paper-and-pencil test the candidates flip through the pages and answer questions in whatever order they wish. "Flipping the pages" in a paper-and-pencil test is replaced with "scrolling up and down" in an Internet test, which can take more time. Furthermore, some computer-based tests do not allow the next set of questions to be presented until all of the first set have been answered. Thus, paper-and-pencil tests are generally more conducive to "skipping around" the questions than are Internet tests. The authors believe this difference can influence the scores on the two types of tests, with possible implications for selection decisions based on these test scores.

Testing in Retrospect

Society has tended to imbue psychological tests with some arcane mystical powers, which, as the evidence reviewed in this chapter indicates, is totally unwarranted. There is nothing mysterious about psychological tests; they are merely tools to help us make better decisions than we could make without them. The psychological testing profession has a large number of critics. Furthermore, as noted by Sackett et al. (2008), "Testing is one aspect of the field of psychology with which virtually the entire public comes into contact" (p. 215). Many people have decried the "tyranny of testing"—the fact that critical decisions (as entrance into a college or professional school) that affect an entire lifetime are based on a single test. Testing has its place in our repertoire of diagnostic instruments; tests should help us meet our needs and not be the master of our decisions. This is sound advice that psychologists have long advocated. However, it is advice that both the developers and users of psychological tests have occasionally ignored or forgotten. It is also the case that many people don't like to be tested, find the process intimidating or anxiety-producing, and worry about what use will be made of their test results. Furthermore, when organizations receive more applications for employment or admission than they have openings, decisions have to be made about who will be hired/admitted and who will be rejected.

Test results are often used to help make selection decisions. The desire to throw tests out by those individuals who didn't get what they wanted (i.e., to be hired or admitted) and to replace them with some other (and often less valid) method of assessment serves no purpose other than to acknowledge that everyone can't be satisfied with the outcome of selection decisions. Abandoning tests is the equivalent of wanting to "shoot the messenger" because the message is displeasing. Alternatively stated, "Tests may be legitimately criticized, but they deserve criticism for their defects, not for doing their job" (Gottfredson, 2009, p. 14). We cannot seriously hope to abolish testing in society because the alternative to testing is not testing at all. What we can strive to accomplish is to make testing highly accurate and fair to all parties concerned.

I/O Psychology and the Economy: *The Power of the Internet*

People who reached adulthood in the Information Age may have a difficult time imagining life before the invention of the Internet. It is beyond the scope of this book to examine how the Internet changed many areas of life. But how the Internet changed the field of I/O psychology with regard to assessment and personnel selection is worth knowing. Not surprisingly, its origins have a strong economic basis.

The Internet became available to the general population in the early 1990s. It was a time of economic prosperity. It was an era of job growth, particularly in areas involving new technology. Employers needed to identify bright people who could rapidly learn new job skills, and to hire these people despite heavy competition from other organizations for talent acquisition. The Internet emerged as a business solution to a business problem: the need to make rapid assessments of candidates to facilitate rapid hiring decisions.

The prevailing business mentality of the era was one where organizations placed increased emphasis on their "core business functions," and placed relatively less emphasis (especially financial resources) on non-core activities. Personnel assessment and staffing are not core business functions. They are performed only for the purpose of getting talented people into jobs within the organization to perform needed work. As such the Internet became a faster and cheaper means of providing the organization with a stream of vital human resources. In short, assessment and staffing are but a means to an end, and the Internet offered an extremely efficient means.

After the invention of the Internet, society was faced with a "digital divide." While the capacity to go "online" was technically possible, many organizations were reluctant to develop their own websites because they didn't recognize its capacity to enhance business. Likewise, many individuals did not feel particularly comfortable in using a computer to do that which had long been accomplished by making a phone call or writing a letter. Younger people were more technologically savvy and accepting of the Internet than their older counterparts. The "digital divide" was the split between those individuals and organizations that recognized and accepted the power of the Internet and those who didn't. However, the sheer force of the Internet was so great that it pulled vast segments of society into its wake. As cited in Chapter 1, the number of people who use the Internet grew to three billion in less than 20 years. Companies and individuals that were reluctant to accept the Internet were faced with a clear choice: either become part of it or get left behind. As much as "going online" is today a social reflex, just twenty-five years ago the entire concept didn't even exist.

Due to technological advances as the Internet, the economic playing field has become more level. Small companies can use the Internet to enhance their business just as readily as large corporations. The use of the Internet for administering employment tests is still in its infancy. Most assuredly there are potential problems with Internet-based assessment not found with paper-and-pencil assessment. The driving force behind Internet-based assessment is the same as why organizations and individuals use the Internet for other reasons. What remains to be seen is the rate of adoption by organizations in using the Internet for making a wide range of personnel assessments. As long as the economic benefits outweigh the costs, Internet-based assessment will likely follow the trend of Internet usage in other aspects of life for both organizations and individuals.

Getting a job offer in a highly competitive market can be dependent on a test score. As such, there are inducements to cheat on employment tests. Bartram and Burke (2013) reported an increased frequency at attempts to cheat on employment tests, especially unproctored Internet testing. Foster (2013) noted there are different forms of cheating including crib sheets, fake IDs, and bribing test proctors. Because employment testing has high-stakes consequences, there is a growing market for companies that offer a "competitive advantage" to job candidates. Foster described individuals who take tests for the purpose of recalling questions. The memorized questions are then sold to online companies who in turn sell them to the public as a form of "test preparation." Foster referred to these "braindump sites" as a form of institutionalized cheating.

What we have learned about psychological tests from an I/O perspective is that some tests are useful in forecasting job success and others are not. As an entire class of predictors, psychological tests have been moderately predictive of job performance. Yet some authors believe that, all things considered, psychological tests have outperformed all other types of predictors across the full spectrum of jobs. Single-validity coefficients greater than .50 are as unusual today as they were in the early years of testing. Because each single method of assessment has limited predictive capacity, it is common practice to use multiple methods in making predictions. The logic of using multiple methods to predict criteria is that each method offers incremental predictive accuracy of the criterion we seek to understand (Arthur & Villado, 2008). Although test validity coefficients are not as high as we would like, it is unfair to condemn tests as useless. Also, keep in mind that validity coefficients are a function of both the predictor and the criterion. A poorly defined and deficient criterion will produce low validity coefficients no matter what the predictor is like. Because of the limited predictive power of tests, psy-

"Let's put it this way—if you can find a village without an idiot, you've got yourself a job."

chologists have had to look elsewhere for forecasters of job performance. The balance of this chapter will examine other predictors that psychologists have investigated.

Interviews

The employment interview is the most commonly used method of personnel selection. It is universally used across different jobs, organizations, and cultures. Barrick et al. (2010) described an employment interview as a social exchange between the interviewer and candidate. "The interview, at its core, is an agenda-driven social exchange between strangers. One important objective for the interviewer is to judge the candidate's qualifications for the job. In contrast, the candidate's primary objective is to get a job" (p. 1171). As such, various social factors can influence the outcome of the interview, quite apart from the objective qualifications of the candidate. Examples include the degree of similarity between the interviewer and candidate (in terms of gender, race, and attitudes), nonverbal behavior (smiling, head nodding, hand gestures), and verbal cues (pitch, speech rate, pauses, and amplitude variability). Because of these additional sources of variance in the outcome of the interview (hire or reject), interviews are a more dynamic means of assessment than traditional testing (e.g., a test of general mental ability). Thus information derived from a work analysis should be the primary basis for the questions posed in an interview. Because interviews are used so often in employment decisions, they have attracted considerable research interest among I/O psychologists.

Degree of Structure

Unstructured interview
A format for the job interview in which the questions are different across all candidates. Often contrasted with the structured interview.

Structured interview
A format for the job interview in which the questions are consistent across all candidates. Often contrasted with the unstructured interview.

Interviews can be classified along a continuum of structure, where *structure* refers to the amount of procedural variability. In a highly **unstructured interview**, the interviewer may ask each candidate different questions. For example, one candidate may be asked to describe previous jobs held and duties performed, whereas another applicant may be asked to describe career goals and interests. In a highly **structured interview**, the interviewer asks standard questions of all job candidates (Levashina et al., 2014). Whatever the focus of the questions (e.g., past work experiences or future career goals), they are posed to all candidates in a similar fashion. It is not unusual for the interviewer to use a standardized rating scale to assess the answers given by each candidate. In reality, however, interviewer ratings of a candidate's responses to questions always involve some degree of subjectivity. Thus, no matter how structured the interview, the interviewer does exert some influence on the judgment of the candidate. Most employment interviews fall somewhere along the continuum between highly unstructured and highly structured. Research results indicate a higher validity for the structured interview than for the unstructured type. Huffcutt et al. (2001) determined that the predictor constructs most often assessed by interviewers of candidates were personality factors (conscientiousness, agreeableness, etc.) and applied social skills (interpersonal relations, team focus, etc.). However, highly unstructured and highly structured interviews do not tend to measure the same constructs. In particular, highly unstructured interviews often focus more on constructs such as general intelligence, education, work experience, and interests, whereas highly structured interviews often focus more on constructs such as job knowledge, interpersonal and social skills, and problem solving.

Maurer and Solamon (2006) reported that candidates can be successfully coached to perform well in an employment interview. Impression management is the process of creating a desired impression or effect on individuals we are trying to influence. As described by Barrick et al. (2009), in social interactions (as the interview) we try to craft a positive image of ourselves (i.e., what we think others are looking for in us) for the purpose of increasing the likelihood that we will get what we want. Astute job candidates often rehearse specific tactics of impression management in preparation for the interview. The outcome of the interview often tilts the final selection decision among otherwise equally qualified finalists in favor of one candidate (who performed well in the interview), or against another candidate (who performed poorly in the interview).

In an interview the formal questions are typically preceded by informal rapport-building comments where the goal of the interviewer is to put the candidate at ease by engaging in "small talk." During this brief exchange, interviewers develop perceptions of candidates through such factors as smiling, manner of dress, manner of speech, and firmness of handshake. This small talk phase may be limited to only the first two-three minutes of the interview. Although very brief in duration, how candidates come across to the interviewer have been found to be predictive of internship offers and performance on the formal questions in the interview (Barrick et al., 2010). Candidates can be trained in how to manage interviewer impressions of them from the moment the two parties meet. However, as Dipboye et al. (2012) commented, interviewers are also trained in how candidates try to impress them. "Impression management backfires if the attempt is too strident or comes across as blatantly manipulative. For example, attempts to convey competence through self-promotion that end up conveying arrogance . . . The most effective impression management occurs in the form of a conversation that flows back and forth in an effortless fashion rather than as a staged or forced presentation" (p. 342).

As previously noted, the employment interview is the single most widely used method of personnel selection. In fact, in some cultures, it is used almost exclusively. It may be tempting to conclude the interview, given its frequency of use, is the most valid means of making personnel selection decisions. Such is not the case, however. The validity of the interview is less than tests of general mental ability. Huffcutt and Culbertson (2011) offered the following observation regarding our reliance on the interview in making selection decisions:

> As a practical matter, the interview is not needed because critical KSAOs usually can be assessed by other means and often done so more accurately. It would appear that there is a basic human need to want personal contact with others before placing them in a position of importance even if they have a proven track record, a tendency from which personnel managers and others involved in organizational selection do not appear to be exempt. It is almost as if a part of the human make up does not trust objective information completely, even if it is accurate: mere facts do not supersede an underlying desire for personal verification. (p.185)

Situational interview
A type of job interview in which candidates are presented with a hypothetical problem and asked how they would respond to it.

Situational Interviews

Situational interviews present the applicant with a situation and ask for a description of the actions he or she would take in that situation. Situational interviews focus on hypothetical, future-oriented contexts in which the applicants are asked how

Low	*Medium*	*High*
Responses showed limited awareness of possible problem issues likely to be confronted. Responses were relatively simplistic, without much apparent thought given to the situation.	Responses suggested considerable awareness of possible issues likely to be confronted. Responses were based on a reasonable consideration of the issues present in the situation.	Responses indicated a high level of awareness of possible issues likely to be confronted. Responses were based on extensive and thoughtful consideration of the issues present in the situation.
1	2 3 4	5

Figure 4-4   *Example of rating scale for scoring a situational interview*

they would respond if they were confronted with these problems. Pulakos and Schmitt (1995) offered the following example of a situational interview question:

> "Suppose you were working with an employee who you knew greatly disliked performing a particular job task. You were in a situation where you needed this task completed, and this employee was the only one available to assist you. What would you do to motivate the employee to perform the task?" (p. 292)

A candidate's response to such a question is typically scored on the type of scale shown in Figure 4-4. The interviewer has to use his or her best judgment to evaluate the candidate's response because the question clearly has no one correct answer. Thus the situational judgment interview is the oral counterpart of the written situational judgment test. Each candidate responds to several such situational questions, and the answers to each question might be evaluated on different dimensions, such as "Taking Initiative" and "Problem Diagnosis." McDaniel et al. (1994) estimated the criterion-related validity of the situational interview to predict job performance to be .39. This level of predictive accuracy is less than that for tests of general mental ability (see Cross-Cultural I/O Psychology: *Cross-Cultural Preferences in Assessing Job Applicants*).

Work Samples and Situational Exercises

Work Samples

Work samples
A type of personnel selection test in which the candidate demonstrates proficiency on a task representative of the work performed in the job.

Motowidlo et al. (1997) classified **work samples** as "high-fidelity simulations," where *fidelity* refers to the level of realism in the assessment. A literal description of a work sample is that the candidate is asked to perform a representative sample of the work done on the job, such as using a word processor, driving a forklift, or drafting a blueprint.

A classic example of a work sample was reported by Campion (1972), who wanted to develop a predictor of job success for mechanics. Using work analytic techniques, he learned that the mechanic's job was defined by success in the use of tools, accuracy of work, and overall mechanical ability. He then designed tasks that would show an applicant's performance in these three areas. Through the cooperation of job incumbents, he designed a work sample that involved such typical tasks as installing pulleys and repairing gearboxes. The steps necessary to perform these tasks correctly were identified

Cross-Cultural I/O Psychology: *Cross-Cultural Preferences in Assessing Job Applicants*

Responding to growing interest in cross-cultural I/O psychology, several studies have examined differences across nations in the predictors used to forecast job performance. There are differences *within* countries (i.e., not all companies in a given nation use the same predictors) as well as substantial differences across nations. Newell and Tansley (2001) reported the following differences:

- Situational tests and assessment centers are used more often in the United Kingdom, Germany, and the Netherlands than in France and Belgium, and assessment centers are not used at all in Spain.
- There is a greater use of tests in France and Belgium than in the United Kingdom and Germany.
- There is somewhat greater use of letters of recommendation by British companies compared with France, Germany, and Belgium.
- In Greece selection methods are primitive and simple compared with methods used in other European countries.
- Drug testing and integrity testing are popular in the United States, but they are rarely used elsewhere.
- In China selection decisions rely heavily on personal and economic information and little emphasis is placed on assessing whether the candidate has the competencies to perform the job.
- Italian companies make little use of any method except the interview.

Newell and Tansley believe that the increasing globalization of business will help diffuse knowledge about our best (valid) predictors, which will reduce the variability in how selection decisions are made across nations. However, if the different selection methods used in these countries are part of their national cultures, then their differential use will continue.

and given numerical values according to their appropriateness (for example, 10 points for aligning a motor with a dial indicator, 1 point for aligning it by feeling the motor, 0 points for just looking at the motor). Campion used a concurrent criterion-related validity design, and each mechanic in the shop took the work sample. Their scores were correlated with the criterion of supervisor ratings of their job performance. The validity of the work sample was excellent: it had a coefficient of .66 with use of tools, .42 with accuracy of work, and .46 with overall mechanical ability. Campion showed that there was a substantial relationship between how well mechanics performed on the work sample and how well they performed on the job. In general, work samples are among the most valid means of personnel selection.

But work samples do have limitations (Callinan & Robertson, 2000). First, they are effective primarily in blue-collar jobs that involve either the mechanical trades (for example, mechanics, carpenters, and electricians) or the manipulation of objects. They are not very effective when the job involves working with people rather than things. Second, work samples assess what a person can do; they don't assess potential. They seem best suited to evaluating experienced workers rather than trainees. Finally, work samples are time-consuming and costly to administer. Because they are individual tests, they require extensive supervision and monitoring. Few work samples are designed to be completed in less than one hour. If there are 100 applicants to fill 5 jobs, it would not be worthwhile to give a work sample to all applicants. Perhaps the applicant pool can be reduced with some other selection instrument (for example, a review of previous work history). Yet, despite their limitations, work samples are useful in personnel selection.

Situational Exercises

Situational exercise
A method of assessment in which examinees are presented with a problem and asked how they would respond to it.

Situational exercises are roughly the white-collar counterpart of work samples; that is, they are used mainly to select people for managerial and professional jobs. Unlike work samples, which are designed to be replicas of the job, situational exercises mirror only part of the job. Accordingly, Motowidlo et al. referred to them as "low-fidelity simulations" because they present applicants with only a description of the work problem and require them to describe how they would deal with it. Situational exercises involve a family of tests that assess problem-solving ability. Two examples are the In-Basket Test and the Leaderless Group Discussion. The In-Basket Test has applicants sort through an in-basket of things to do. The contents are carefully designed letters, memos, brief reports, and the like that require the applicant's immediate attention and response. The applicant goes through the contents of the basket and takes the appropriate action to solve the problems presented, such as making a phone call, sending an email, or calling a meeting. Observers score the applicant on such factors as productivity (how much work got done) and problem-solving effectiveness (versatility in resolving problems). The In-Basket Test is predictive of the job performance of managers and executives, a traditionally difficult group of employees to select. But a major problem with the test is that it takes up to three hours and, like a work sample, is an individual test. If there are many applicants, too much time is needed to administer the test. Schippmann et al. (1990) reported the typical validity coefficient for the In-Basket Test is approximately .25.

In a Leaderless Group Discussion (LGD), a group of applicants (normally, two to eight) engage in a job-related discussion in which no spokesperson or group leader has been named. Raters observe and assess each applicant on such factors as individual prominence, group goal facilitation, and sociability. Scores on these factors are then used as the basis for hiring. The reliability of the LGD increases with the number of people in the group. The typical validity coefficient is in the .15–.35 range.

Although neither the In-Basket Test nor the LGD has the validity of a typical work sample, remember that the criterion of success for a manager is usually more difficult to define. The lower validities in the selection of managerial personnel are as attributable to problems with the criterion and its proper articulation as anything else. As Lievens and Patterson (2011) noted, although high-fidelity simulations (like work samples) are often highly valid, they are also time-consuming to administer and costly to develop. However, the converse is also undesirable; a selection method that is inexpensive but also has little predictive accuracy. The authors recommended low-fidelity simulations as a reasonable compromise between the twin goals of high validity and low cost.

Assessment Centers

Assessment centers involve evaluating job candidates, typically for managerial-level jobs, using several methods and raters. Highhouse and Nolan (2012) reported that the use of assessment centers could be traced back about 100 years to the testing of German and British military officers in WWI. However, their use as an accepted means of assessing candidates in business and industry began in the 1960s by researchers at AT&T who were interested in studying the lives of managers over the full span of their careers. **Assessment centers** are a group-oriented, standardized series of activities that provide a basis for judgments or predictions of human behaviors believed or known to be relevant to work performed in an organizational setting. Because assessment center assessments are expensive, they have been used mainly by large organizations; however, consulting firms also offer assessment center appraisals for smaller companies. Here are five characteristics of the assessment center approach:

Assessment center
A technique for assessing job candidates using a series of structured, group-oriented exercises that are evaluated by raters.

1. Those individuals selected to attend the center (the assessees) are usually management-level personnel that the company wants to evaluate for possible selection, promotion, or training. Thus assessment centers can be used to assess both job applicants for hire and current employees for possible advancement.

2. Assessees are evaluated in groups of 10 to 20. They may be divided into smaller groups for various exercises, but the basic strategy is to appraise individuals against the performance of others in the group.

3. Several raters (the assessors) do the evaluation. They work in teams and collectively or individually recommend personnel action (for example, selection, promotion). Assessors may be psychologists, but usually they are company employees unfamiliar with the assessees. They are often trained in how to appraise performance. The training may last from several hours to a few days.

4. Assessors evaluate the assessees on a number of performance dimensions judged relevant for managerial jobs. These dimensions typically include leadership, decision making, practical judgment, and interpersonal relations skills.

5. A wide variety of performance appraisal methods or exercises are used. Many involve group exercises—for example, leaderless group discussions in which leaders "emerge" through their degree of participation in the exercise. Other methods include oral presentations, written case studies, role plays, in-baskets, and interviews. Typically each exercise is used to provide an evaluation of multiple performance dimensions, but it is rare to use each exercise to evaluate every performance dimension (Arthur & Day, 2011). The assessment typically takes one to several days; it is the most extensive assessment developed by I/O psychologists.

Klimoski and Strickland (1977) proposed a source of bias in assessment center evaluation. They contended that assessment center evaluations are predictive because both assessors and company supervisors hold common stereotypes of the effective employee. Assessors give higher evaluations to those who "look" like good management talent, and supervisors give higher evaluations to those who "look" like good "company" people. If the two sets of stereotypes are held in common, then (biased) assessment center evaluations correlate with (biased) job performance evaluations. The danger is that organizations may hire and promote those who fit the image of the successful employee. As Lievens and Klimoski (2001) stated, "Assessors do not judge assessees exclusively on the basis of the prescribed dimensions but also take into account the fit of the applicants into the culture of the organization" (p. 259). The long-term result is an organization staffed with people who are mirror images of one another. Opportunity is greatly limited for creative people who "don't fit the mold" but who might be effective if given the chance.

Assessment centers provide a complex assessment of job candidates. While the major source of variance in ratings is ideally due to differences among the candidates (or assessees), research has shown that variance in assessment center ratings is also attributable to assessors, the exercises (e.g., leaderless group discussion, interview) used in the evaluations, and the dimensions of behavior (e.g., motivation, problem-solving ability) being rated (Putka & Hoffman, 2013). It is also a matter of theoretical debate whether there *should* be high agreement across different exercises designed to measure the same dimension of behavior (Speer et al., 2014). The lack of agreement can be reflective of the psychological complexity of the behavior being assessed. There is also the possibility that virtual assessment centers can be created. In lieu of face-to-face interactions between assessors and assessees, the assessees could be situated in different locations and would participate through web-cams (Porah & Porah, 2012). Given that assessment centers are the most expensive form of personnel evaluation, and there is growing concern about their overall predictive value (Kuncel & Sackett, 2014), perhaps techniques of virtual assessment would provide better cost/benefit value.

Physical Abilities Testing

Psychological assessment has long focused on cognitive abilities and personality characteristics. However, research (e.g., Fleishman & Quaintance, 1984) has also examined the assessment of physical abilities, and in particular how these physical abilities relate to performance in some jobs. As stated by Gebhardt and Baker (2010), increases in productivity and reductions in lost work time and injuries can be achieved through physical ability testing in jobs that are physically demanding. Fleishman and Quaintance (pp. 463–464) presented the set of abilities relevant to work performance. Here are some critical physical abilities:

- **Static strength**—"the ability to use muscle force to lift, push, pull, or carry objects"
- **Explosive strength**—"the ability to use short bursts of muscle force to propel oneself or an object"
- **Gross body coordination**—"the ability to coordinate the movement of the arms, legs, and torso in activities where the whole body is in motion"
- **Stamina**—"the ability of the lungs and circulatory (blood) systems of the body to perform efficiently over time."

A common research finding (e.g., Courtright et al., 2013) is that men exhibit greater static and explosive strength than women. A physical ability test may be one component of an assessment process that includes other attributes, as intellect and personality. The results of a work analysis should determine how much importance the physical ability test has in the overall assessment of candidates. Baker and Gebhardt (2012) proposed that if a job permits employees to perform a wide variety of tasks, it may be possible to assign women to those tasks that involve less static and explosive strength. Furthermore, physical ability tests are used to determine who enters a job, not who can keep it. With the advent of new technologies in law enforcement, for example, tasers make physical strength less important in subduing a criminal suspect.

In general the research on physical abilities reveals they are related to successful job performance in physically demanding jobs, such as firefighters, police officers, and construction workers. However, physical ability testing represents an unusual challenge from an assessment perspective. Imagine, for example, a manual labor job requires repeatedly lifting a 25-pound object (e.g., a bag of cement), and carrying it a distance of 40 feet every two minutes. The primary physical demand of the job is neither the weight (25 lbs.) nor the distance (40 feet), but the endurance required to do so 30 times per hour, 240 times per day. If the selection tests consisted of lifting a 25-pound object and carrying it a distance of 40 feet, not only could the vast majority of people do so (one time), such a test would fail to assess the critical physical ability, endurance (reflecting performance over time). One of the requisite characteristics of an effective selection test is its reasonableness in terms of time, especially for the job in question. The job of manual laborer would not warrant extensive assessment time. The assessment challenge with some physical abilities is to make accurate predictions about the sustained job behavior from a relatively brief sample of similar behavior exhibited in the selection test.

Biographical Information

Biographical information
A method of assessing individuals in which information pertaining to past activities, interests, and behaviors in their lives is considered.

The theory of using biographical information as a method of personnel selection is based on our development as individuals. Our lives represent a series of experiences, events, and choices that define our development. Past and current events shape our behavior patterns, attitudes, and values. Because there is consistency in our behaviors, attitudes, and values, an assessment of these factors from our past experiences should be predictive of such experiences in the future. **Biographical information** assesses constructs that shape our behavior, such as sociability and ambition. To the extent that these constructs are predictive of future job performance, through biographical information (or biodata) we assess previous life experiences that were manifestations of these constructs.

Biographical information is frequently recorded on an application blank. The application blank, in turn, can be used as a selection device on the basis of the information presented. The questions asked on the application blank are predictive of job performance criteria. Mael (1991) recommended that all biographical questions pertain to historical events in the person's life, as opposed to questions about behavioral intentions or presumed behavior in a hypothetical situation. Table 4-3 lists 16 dimensions of biographical information and an example item for each dimension, as reported by Schoenfeldt (1999).

Biographical questions should not be invasive. Invasiveness addresses whether the respondent will consider the item content to be an invasion of his or her privacy. As Nickels (1994) noted, asking questions about certain types of life experiences that are generally regarded as private matters (e.g., religious beliefs) is off limits for assessment. Mael et al. (1996) reported two types of biodata questions that are regarded as intrusive: a question that refers to an event that could have been explained away if the applicant had the chance to do so, and a question with a response that does not reflect the type of person the respondent has since become. Questions that are perceived to invade privacy invite litigation against the hiring organization by job applicants (see Field Note 2: *Inappropriate Question?*).

To what extent do individuals distort their responses to create a more socially

Table 4-3 *Sixteen biographical information dimensions*

Dimension	Example Item
Dealing with people	
1. Sociability	Volunteer with service groups
2. Agreeableness/cooperation	Argue a lot compared with others
3. Tolerant	Response to people breaking rules
4. Good impression	What a person wears is important
Outlook	
5. Calmness	Often in a hurry
6. Resistance to stress	Time to recover from disappointments
7. Optimism	Think there is some good in everyone
Responsibility/dependability	
8. Responsibility	Supervision in previous jobs
9. Concentration	Importance of quiet surroundings at work
10. Work ethic	Percent of spending money earned in high school
Other	
11. Satisfaction with life	How happy in general
12. Need for achievement	Ranking in previous job
13. Parental influence	Mother worked outside home when young
14. Educational history	Grades in math
15. Job history	Likes/dislikes in previous job
16. Demographic	Number in family

Adapted with permission from "From Dustbowl Empiricism to Rational Constructs in Biographical Data," by L. F. Schoenfeldt, 1999, *Human Resource Management Review, 9,* pp. 147–167. Copyright © 1999.

desirable impression? Research (Becker & Colquitt, 1992; Kluger et al., 1991) revealed that faking does occur in responses to certain types of questions. The questions most likely to be faked in a socially desirable direction are those that are difficult to verify for accuracy and have the appearance of being highly relevant to the job. Levashina et al. (2012) discovered when given the chance to elaborate on their answers to biodata items, candidates gave more elaboration to non-verifiable items than verifiable items. The authors believed requiring elaboration decreased the likelihood of faking.

Using biographical information is a logically defensible strategy in personnel selection. Mumford and Stokes (1992) portrayed biographical information as revealing consistent patterns of behavior that are interwoven throughout our lives. By assessing what applicants have done, we can gain considerable insight into what they will do.

Letters of Recommendation

One of the most commonly used and least valid of all predictors is the letter of recommendation. Letters of recommendation and reference checks are as widespread in personnel selection as the interview and the application blank. Unfortunately, they often lack comparable validity. Letters of recommendation are usually written on behalf of an applicant by a current employer, professional associate, or personal friend. The respondent rates the applicant on such dimensions as leadership ability and com-

Field Note 2: *Inappropriate Question?*

Biographical items sometimes lack content validity and face validity for the job in question even though they manifest empirical criterion-related validity. The seeming irrelevance of biographical questions is always a concern in personnel selection. Here is a case in point. A city had developed a biographical inventory that was to be used along with some psychological tests to evaluate police officers for promotion to police detectives. All the questions in the biographical inventory were predictive of job performance as a detective, as determined by a criterion-related validity study. One of the questions on the inventory was: "Did you have sexual intercourse for the first time before the age of 16?" Some police officers who took this promotional exam and failed it sued the city for asking such a question in an employment test, a question so obviously lacking face validity. The officers said the question had absolutely no relevance to the conduct of a detective's job, and furthermore it was an invasion of their privacy. They had been denied a detective's job because of a totally inappropriate question, and therefore they wanted the entire test results thrown out. The case was heard at the district court. The judge ruled in favor of the officers, saying that the question totally lacked content validity and was an invasion of their privacy. Therefore the officers should be reconsidered for promotion to detective. The city appealed the verdict to the state supreme court. The supreme court reversed the lower court ruling and allowed the test results to stand, meaning the officers would not get promoted. The state supreme court based its decision on the grounds that the answer to that question did correlate with job performance as a detective. From a practical and legal standpoint, it is advisable to avoid asking such invasive questions in the first place, even though in this case a lengthy legal battle ultimately resulted in a decision favorable to the city.

munication skills. The responses are then used as a basis for hiring. The typical validity coefficient for letters of recommendation is estimated to be .13.

Letters of recommendation are one of the least accurate forecasters of job performance. One of the biggest problems with letters of recommendation is their restricted range. As you might expect, almost all letters of recommendation are positive. Most often, the applicants themselves choose who will write the letters, so it isn't surprising that they pick people who will make them look good. Because of this restriction (that is, almost all applicants are described positively), the lack of predictive ability of the letter of recommendation is not unexpected. Because the vast majority of letters of recommendation have a uniform tone, recipients of the letters can become highly sensitized to "reading between the lines" in forming evaluations of the candidates. The recipients not only form opinions of candidates about what is contained in the letters, but also what is *not* discussed or mentioned by the letter writer. Madera et al. (2009) reported subtle gender differences consistent with traditional sex roles in the letters of recommendation written on behalf of male and female candidates applying for the job of a university professor.

Drug Testing

Drug testing
A method of assessment typically based on an analysis of urine that is used to detect illicit drug use by the candidate.

Drug testing is the popular term for efforts to detect *substance abuse*, the use of illegal drugs and the improper and illegal use of prescription and over-the-counter medications, alcohol, and other chemical compounds. Substance abuse is a major global problem that has far-reaching societal, moral, and economic consequences. The role that I/O psychology plays in this vast and complex picture is to detect substance abuse in the workplace. Employees who engage in substance abuse jeopardize not only their own welfare but also potentially the welfare of fellow employees and other individuals. I/O psychologists are involved in screening out substance abusers among both job applicants and current employees. Unlike other forms of assessment used by I/O psychologists that involve estimates of cognitive or motor abilities, drug testing embraces chemical assessments. The method of assessment is typically based on a urine sample (hair samples can also be used). The rationale is that the test will reveal the presence of drugs in a person's urine. Therefore a sample of urine is treated with chemicals that will indicate the presence of drugs if they have been ingested by the person. There are two basic types of assessments. A screening test assesses the potential presence of a wide variety of chemicals. A confirmation test on the same sample identifies the presence of chemicals suggested by the initial screening test. I/O psychologists are not directly involved with these tests because they are performed in chemical laboratories by individuals with special technical training. The profession of I/O psychology does become involved in drug testing because it assesses suitability for employment, with concomitant concerns about the reliability, validity, legality, and cost of these tests.

Normand et al. (1990) conducted a study on the effects of drug testing and reported sobering results. A total of 5,465 job applicants were tested for the use of illicit drugs. After 1.3 years of employment, employees who tested positive for illicit drugs had an absenteeism rate 59.3% higher than employees who tested negative. The involuntary turnover rate (namely, employees who were fired) was 47% higher among drug users than nonusers. The estimated cost savings of screening out drug users in reducing absenteeism and turnover for one cohort of new employees was $52,750,000. This figure does not reflect the compounded savings derived by cohorts of new employees added each year the drug-testing program is in existence. As can be seen, drug testing is an exceedingly complex and controversial issue. Although the analysis of urine is beyond the purview of I/O psychology, making decisions about an applicant's suitability for employment is not. I/O psychology has been drawn into a complicated web of issues that affects all of society. Our profession must now address problems unimaginable a century ago.

Controversial Methods of Assessment

This final section is reserved for two controversial methods of assessing job applicants.

Polygraphy or Lie Detection

A **polygraph** is an instrument that measures responses of the autonomic nervous system—physiological reactions of the body such as heart rate and perspiration. In theory

Polygraph
An instrument that assesses responses of an individual's central nervous system (heart rate, breathing, perspiration, etc.) that supposedly indicate giving false responses to questions.

these autonomic responses will "give you away" when you are telling a lie. The polygraph is attached to the body with electronic sensors for detecting the physiological reactions. Polygraphs are used more to evaluate people charged with criminal activity in a *post hoc* fashion (for example, after a theft within a company has occurred) than to select people for a job, although it is used in the latter capacity as well.

Is polygraphy foolproof? No. People can appear to be innocent of any wrongdoing according to the polygraph but in fact be guilty of misconduct. Research conducted by the Federal Bureau of Investigation (Podlesny & Truslow, 1993) based on a crime simulation reported that the polygraph correctly identified 84.7% of the guilty group and 94.7% of the innocent group. Countermeasures are anything that a person might do in an effort to defeat or distort a polygraph examination. It is unknown how effective countermeasures are because funding for research on countermeasures is limited to the Department of Defense Polygraph Institute and all findings from such research are classified (Honts & Amato, 2002). In 1988 President Ronald Reagan signed into law a bill banning the widespread use of polygraphs for pre-employment screening by private-sector employers. However, as Honts (1991) reported, polygraph use by the federal government continues to grow. It is used extensively in the hiring process of government agencies involved in national security as well as in law enforcement. The U.S. Joint Security Commission offered the following summation of the polygraph as a method of personnel selection. "Despite the controversy, after carefully weighing the pros and cons, the Commission concludes that with appropriate standardization, increased oversight, and training to prevent abuses, the polygraph program should be retained. In the Central Intelligence Agency and the National Security Agency, the polygraph has evolved to become the single most important aspect of their employment and personnel security programs" (Krapohl, 2002, p. 232).

Tests of Emotional Intelligence

Recently I/O psychology has begun to address what has historically been regarded as the "soft" side of individual differences, including moods, feelings, and emotions. For many years the relevance of these constructs to the world of work were denied. They were regarded as transient disturbances to the linkages between abilities (e.g., intelligence) and performance. However, we are beginning to realize that moods, feelings, and emotions play a significant role in the workplace, just as they do in life in general. The concept of **emotional intelligence** was initially proposed by Salovey and Mayer (1990).

Emotional intelligence
A construct that reflects a person's capacity to manage emotional responses in social situations.

It is proposed that individuals differ in how they deal with their emotions, and those who effectively manage their emotions are said to be "emotionally intelligent." Some theorists believe that emotions are within the domain of intelligence, rather than viewing "emotion" and "intelligence" as independent or contradictory.

Perrewé and Spector (2002) stated, "Few constructs in psychology have generated as much controversy as emotional intelligence. Exaggerated claims of its importance and relevance for both life and career success have made many researchers skeptical about its value as a topic of scientific research" (p. 42). Much of the controversy surrounds the construct meaning of emotional intelligence. Emotional intelligence was originally proposed as ability. It referred to the capacity to process information about emotions and to use this information as a basis of influence in one's thinking and be-havior (Mayer et al., 2008). Some researchers interpreted emotional intelligence more as a dimension of personality and how it influenced emotional health, particularly as it relates to social adaptiveness (Lievens & Chan, 2010). Joseph and Newman (2010) conducted a meta-analysis of studies examining the criterion-related validity of emo-tional intelligence. The results confirmed that emotional intelligence is positively cor-related with performance for high emotional labor jobs. A few commercially available tests (e.g., Mayer et al., 2002) of emotional intelligence have been developed, but in general assessments of emotional intelligence are not widely used in making personnel selection decisions.

Overview and Evaluation of Predictors

Personnel selection methods can be evaluated by many standards. We have identified four major standards that are useful in organizing all the information we have gath-ered about predictors.

1. *Validity* refers to the ability of the predictor to forecast criterion perfor-mance accurately. Many authorities argue that validity is the predominant evalu-ative standard in judging selection methods; however, the relevance of the other three standards is also substantial.

2. *Fairness* refers to the ability of the predictor to render unbiased predic-tions of job success across applicants in various subgroups of gender, race, age, and so on. The issue of fairness will be discussed in greater detail in Chapter 5.

3. *Applicability* refers to whether the selection method can be applied across the full range of jobs. Some predictors have wide applicability in that they appear well suited for a diverse range of jobs; other methods have particular limitations that affect their applicability.

4. The final standard is the *cost* of implementing the method. The various personnel selection methods differ markedly in their cost, which has a direct bear-ing on their overall value.

Table 4-4 presents 12 personnel selection methods apprised on each of the four evaluative standards. Each standard is partitioned into three levels: low, moderate, and high. This classification scheme is admittedly oversimplified, and in some cases the evaluation of a selection method did not readily lend itself to a uniform rating. Nevertheless, this method is useful in providing a broad-brush view of many person-nel selection methods.

Average validity coefficients in the .00–.20, .21–.40, and over .40 ranges were la-beled low, moderate, and high, respectively. Selection methods that have many, some, and few problems of fairness were labeled low, moderate, and high, respectively. The applicability standard, the most difficult one to appraise on a single dimension, was classified according to the ease of using the method in terms of feasibility and general-izability across jobs. Finally, direct cost estimates were made for each selection method. Methods estimated as costing less than $50 per applicant were labeled low; $51–$100,

Table 4-4   *Assessment of 12 personnel selection methods along four evaluative standards*

Selection Method	Evaluative Standards			
	Validity	**Fairness**	**Applicability**	**Cost**
Intelligence tests	High	Moderate	High	Low
Mechanical aptitude tests	Moderate	Moderate	Low	Low
Personality inventories	Low	High	Moderate	Moderate
Physical ability tests	High	Moderate	Low	Low
Situational judgment tests	Moderate	Moderate	High	Low
Interviews	Moderate	Moderate	High	Moderate
Assessment centers	High	High	Low	High
Work samples	High	High	Low	High
Situational exercises	Moderate	(Unknown)	Low	Moderate
Biographical information	Moderate	Moderate	High	Low
Letters of recommendation	Low	(Unknown)	High	Low
Drug tests	Moderate	High	Moderate	Moderate

moderate; and more than $100, high. The ideal personnel selection method would be high in validity, fairness, and applicability, and low in cost. Inspection of Table 4-4 reveals that no method has an ideal profile. The 12 methods produce a series of tradeoffs among validity, fairness, applicability, and cost. This shouldn't be surprising; if there were one uniformly ideal personnel selection method, there probably would be little need to consider 11 others.

In terms of validity, the best methods are intelligence tests, work samples, assessment centers, and physical abilities tests. However, each of these methods is limited by problems with fairness, applicability, or cost. Ironically, the worst selection method in terms of validity, letters of recommendation, is one of the most frequently used. This method is characterized by high applicability and low cost, which no doubt accounts for its popularity.

Fairness refers to the likelihood that the method will have differential predictive accuracy according to membership in any group, such as sex or race. Although the issue of fairness has generated a great deal of controversy, no method is classified in Table 4-4 as having low fairness. Insufficient information is available on two of the methods (situational exercises and letters of recommendation) to render an evaluation of their fairness, but it seems unlikely they would be judged as grossly unfair. Although several methods have exhibited some fairness problems (thus warranting caution in their use), the problems are not so severe as to reject any method as a biased means of selecting personnel.

The applicability dimension was the most difficult to assess, and evaluation of this dimension is most subject to qualification. For example, work samples are characterized by low applicability because they are limited to only certain types of jobs (that is, jobs that involve the mechanical manipulation of objects). However, this limitation appears to be more than offset by the method's high validity and fairness. Simply put, the problem with this method is its feasibility for only a selected range of jobs. In contrast, other methods have high applicability (such as the interview) and qualify as an almost universal means of selection.

The cost dimension is perhaps the most arbitrary. Selection methods may have indirect or hidden costs—costs that were not included in their evaluation but perhaps could have been. The break points in the classification scheme are also subjective. For example, we considered a $60-per-applicant cost to be moderate; others might say it is low or high. These issues notwithstanding, one can see a full range of cost estimates in Table 4-4. Some methods do not cost much (for example, letters of recommendation), but they do not appear to be worth much either.

This chapter has examined the major types of predictors used in personnel selection. These predictors have been validated against a number of different criteria for a variety of occupational groups. Some predictors have been used more extensively than others. Furthermore, certain predictors have historically shown more validity than others. The ideal predictor would be an accurate forecaster of the criterion, equally applicable across different groups of people, and not too lengthy or costly to administer. But predictors rarely meet all these standards in practice. Furthermore their frequency of use varies across nations.

This chapter has described the diversity of methods that organizations use to predict whether an individual will succeed on the job. All of the methods involve candidates being administered assessments (test, interview, work sample, etc.), receiving scores on those assessments, and then employers deciding whether a candidate's score profile meets the organization's standards for selection. However, there is another way that suitability for employment can be judged—an examination of work experience (Quiñones et al., 1995). The logic of this selection method is captured by a quotation from the philosopher Orison Swett Marden:

> Every experience in life, everything with which we have come in contact in life, is a chisel which has been cutting away at our life statue, molding, modifying, shaping it. We are part of all we have met. Everything we have seen, heard, felt, or thought has had its hand in molding us, shaping us. (p. 485)

Levine et al. (2004) proposed three dimensions to judgments of job-related experience. *Personal attributes* are affected by exposure to work-related settings and activities. The *perceived outcome of experience* is the meaning we attach to our experiences, the perceived changes in our attributes we derive from them. Finally, *aspects of experience judged relevant and important* are determined from the perspective of the evaluation of the experience. Hiring organizations attempt to understand how past experiences of candidates will be translated into future job performance. As with all personnel selection methods, assessments of education and experience must meet federal standards for test fairness. Buster et al. (2005) developed a content valid process for assessing education- and experience-based minimum qualifications approved by federal courts.

As Tesluk and Jacobs (1998) stated, I/O psychology is just beginning to understand the linkage between work experience and future job behavior. Our discipline has to learn about candidates who, for example, have rich and lengthy work experience yet score poorly on some form of psychological assessment. Currently we have no professionally established and accepted system for equating or even comparing assessment results with work experience.

Although the methods used to select employees vary across cultures, what is constant is the need for all organizations to make good personnel decisions. This process is the subject of the next chapter.

Chapter Summary

- Psychological assessments are methods (such as a test, interview, or letter of recommendation) used to predict a criterion.
- High-quality predictors must manifest two psychometric standards: reliability and validity.
- Psychological tests and inventories have been used to predict relevant workplace criteria for more than 100 years.
- Psychological assessment is a big business. There are many publishers of psychological tests used to assess candidates' suitability for employment.
- The most commonly used predictors are tests of general mental ability, personality inventories, aptitude tests, work samples, interviews, and letters of recommendation.
- I/O psychologists are concerned about job applicants faking their responses in the following methods of assessment: personality inventories, integrity tests, interviews, and biographical data.
- Predictors can be evaluated in terms of their validity (accuracy), fairness, cost, and applicability.
- Online testing is a major trend in psychological assessment.
- Controversial methods of prediction include polygraphy and tests of emotional intelligence.
- There are broad cross-cultural differences in the acceptability of predictors used to evaluate job candidates. The interview is the most universally accepted method.

Personnel Decisions

Chapter Outline

Learning Objectives

- Explain the social and legal context for personnel decisions.

- Describe the process of personnel recruitment and affirmative action.

- Understand how organizational strategy influences personnel decisions.

- Explain the concept and significance of validity generalization.

- Describe the selection of employees and the process of assessing job applicants.

- Identify issues pertaining to the determination of the passing score.

- Explain the concept and significance of test utility related to organizational efficiency.

- Describe the personnel functions of placement and classification.

The Social Context for Personnel Decisions

I/O psychologists have historically contributed to the process of making personnel decisions by developing assessment instruments, conducting validational research on the boundaries of a test's usability, and explaining the consequences of how the instrument is used (e.g., the implications of determining the passing score). Members of an organization are also involved in making personnel decisions, including professionals in human resources, managers of the prospective employees, and in some cases coworkers of the prospective employees. Furthermore, personnel decisions are influenced by organizational values, such as an organization's preference for hiring only applicants who possess superior credentials. Additionally, organizations operate within the social or cultural context in which they are embedded. These larger-scale forces have a direct bearing on who gets hired and who doesn't. For example, hiring only the very best applicants will create a chronically unemployed segment of society. Not every applicant can be the "best," yet all people benefit from employment. Unemployment results in a host of serious ills for individuals and society as a whole, a topic we will discuss in Chapter 11.

There are also cultural differences in what makes for a desirable employee. Many Western cultures consider the hiring of family members of employees to be undesirable. The term **nepotism** refers to showing favoritism in the hiring of family members (Jones, 2012). In the United States nepotism is usually viewed negatively because it results in unequal opportunity among job applicants, which is anathema to our cultural values. In some non-Western cultures, however, nepotism in hiring is viewed positively. The logic is that a family member is a known commodity who can be trusted to be loyal, unlike an anonymous applicant. Why *not* give preferential treatment to candidates who are associated by birth or marriage with members of the hiring organization? Personnel decisions are always embedded in a larger organizational and social context. They do not "stand apart" in a vacuum unrelated to the larger social system.

The first documented personnel selection test in recorded history is reported in the Bible (Judges 12:4–6). Two warring tribes differed in their ability to pronounce a word—*shibboleth.* The members of one tribe could not utter the "sh" sound, and pronounced the word as "sibboleth." The inability to pronounce the word indicated the person was a member of the opposing tribe. Today one meaning of *shibboleth* is a test that is used to make a major personnel decision (those tribesmen who could not pronounce the word were executed).

Guion (1998a) developed a schematic representation of the forces that affect personnel decisions, as shown in Figure 5-1. At the top of the diagram is the organization, which reflects that all personnel decisions are designed to serve the needs of the organization. I/O psychology draws heavily upon scientific theory (e.g., the concept of validity) to conduct research and develop assessment instruments. The instruments are used to assess candidates and help reach a decision about those candidates. The boxes in Figure 5-1 represent the traditional areas of activity among I/O psychologists in making personnel decisions. However, there is another important concept shown in the diagram that typically does not draw as much attention among I/O psychologists. It is the social and cultural context in which the total organization exists. The end product of the personnel selection process is to offer employment to some candidates

Nepotism
An approach to personnel staffing whereby family members receive preferential treatment because of birth or marriage.

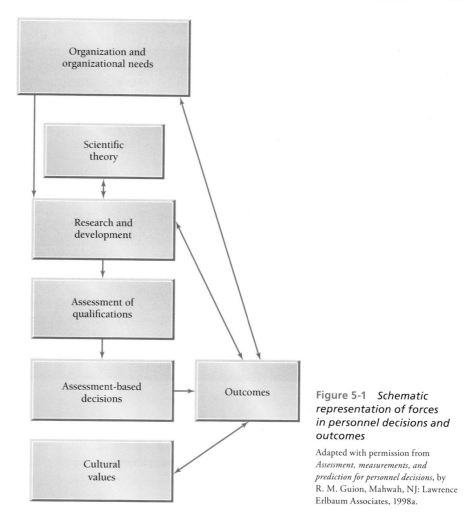

Figure 5-1 *Schematic representation of forces in personnel decisions and outcomes*

Adapted with permission from *Assessment, measurements, and prediction for personnel decisions*, by R. M. Guion, Mahwah, NJ: Lawrence Erlbaum Associates, 1998a.

and deny it to others. Some issues that affect this outcome transcend the scientific and technical.

The science of personnel selection is sometimes dismissed because it does not reflect the way hiring occurs "in the real world." There is truth to the assertion that some organizations make hiring decisions without regard to the forces presented in Figure 5-1. Guion (1998b) noted that the way some organizations hire people tends to be more intuitive, nonquantitative, often not based on validated, empirically-derived factors. As described by Highhouse (2008), despite the demonstrated empirical validity of psychological tests, some managers are reluctant to use them in making personnel selection decisions. Instead, they rely on their own hunches or intuition in deciding who to hire. Improvements in selection decisions are not achieved by replacing scientific evidence with hunches. This chapter will discuss the science and practice of making personnel decisions with the full realization that some organizations' practices are only loosely linked to science.

Cross-Cultural I/O Psychology: *Preferences in Ideal Job Candidates*

Nyfield and Baron (2000) described trends in selection practices around the world. Universalist cultures follow what they see as universal codes of practice and rules. They favor rational arguments. Particularist cultures put more emphasis on relationships and are willing to bend the rules in making selection decisions. They consider the particular relationship between the parties to be more important than a set of rules or procedures. The United States, Canada, and Australia are universalist cultures, whereas France, Greece, and Italy are much more particularist. Particularist countries rely more extensively on the interview, which is regarded as an open-ended conversation between two individuals. Attempts to structure and formalize the interview are likely to be resisted. Countries also differ in their general preference for a calm, neutral style of interacting versus a strongly emotional one. In a neutral approach more emphasis is placed on the candidate's intellectual skills, whereas in an emotional culture the interviewer's emotional response to the candidate has more influence than what the candidate can actually do. The Japanese and Chinese are renowned for their neutral, reserved approach, whereas southern European and South American countries are more emotional. To an emotional interviewer, a calm, rational presentation by the candidate might be interpreted as dullness or lack of interest. Concentrating on the facts of an experience might be seen as a failure to understand the emotional impact of the experience. The reverse can also be true. To a neutral interviewer, an emotional candidate might seem overly excitable and undependable. The interviewer might be frustrated by the difficulty of understanding the facts of a particular experience. As Nyfield and Baron concluded, there may be similarities in cross-cultural methods of selection, but there can be strong cultural differences in the desired performance of the candidate.

There are also cross-cultural differences in personnel selection (see Cross-Cultural I/O Psychology: *Preferences in Ideal Job Candidates*). The means of matching people and work are the subject of cultural lore since antiquity. Salgado (2000) recounted the following tale from long ago:

> A farmer did not know what profession he should choose for his son. One day, in order to orient himself, he gave a Bible, an apple, and a coin to the boy. The farmer thought:
>
> If the boy eats the apple, he will be a gardener; if he reads the Bible, he will serve to be an ecclesiastic; and if he puts the money in his pocket, he will be a merchant. Some time later, the farmer found the boy seated on the Bible, with the money in his pocket, and eating the apple. "Aha," said the farmer, "A clever boy. He has the makings of a politician." (p. 191)

It can also be the case that for some people the attraction to a job is so strong that rather than "the person finding the job, the job finds the person." This strong sense of attraction between person and job is identified as a "calling," named after the attraction members of the clergy report as to why they entered religious work. A calling often implies a sense of destiny about the vocational choice. Dobrow (2013) described a calling as "a consuming, meaningful passion" toward a particular activity. Dobrow and Tosti-Kharas (2011) reported that people who view their work as particularly meaningful go through a process of "searching for" and then "finding" their calling.

A calling is regarded more as a cause of job choice rather than as a consequence of the other factors. A calling provides both a sense of clarity and personal mission to the individual. While a calling conceivably could occur in any vocation, it seems most evident in jobs that have pro-social intentions (i.e., making the world a better place) and jobs involving artistic expression.

The Legal Context for Personnel Decisions

Civil Rights Act of 1964

For the first 60 years or so of I/O psychology, there was virtually no connection between psychologists and the legal community. Psychological tests were developed, administered, and interpreted by psychologists, and as a profession psychologists governed themselves. However, during the late 1950s and early 1960s, the United States was swept up in the civil rights movement. At that time civil rights concerned primarily the conditions under which Blacks lived and worked in this country. Blacks were denied access to colleges, restaurants, and jobs—in short, their civil rights were denied. Under the administration of President John F. Kennedy and President Lyndon Johnson steps were taken to change this aspect of American society. In 1964 the Civil Rights Act, a major piece of federal legislation aimed at reducing discrimination in all walks of life, was passed. As noted by Zedeck (2010), discrimination has a legal basis and is fundamentally not a psychological concept. The section of the law most relevant to I/O psychology is Title VII, which pertains to employment discrimination. In essence, this was the message: Blacks were grossly underemployed throughout the country in both private- and public-sector jobs, particularly in jobs above the lower levels of organizations. To reduce discrimination in employment (one of the mandates of the Civil Rights Act), the federal government began to intervene in employment decisions; in essence, it would monitor the entire procedure to ensure fairness in selection. Thus personnel decisions became deeply embedded within a legal context in the 1960s. As Guion (1998a) asserted, previously the federal government had regulated *things* (e.g., food and drugs), but with this Act it regulated *behavior*. The Civil Rights Act was expanded to cover other groups of people as well. In fact, five groups were identified for protection: race, sex, religion, color, and national origin[1]. People of all races, both sexes, all religions, etc., are afforded equal protection. They are referred to as the **protected groups**. The Civil Rights Act includes all personnel functions—training, promotion, retention, and performance appraisal—in addition to selection. Furthermore, any methods (tests, interviews, assessment centers, etc.) used for making personnel decisions are subject to the same legal standards.

Title VII specifies several unlawful employment practices, including the following:

- Employers may not fail or refuse to hire, or discharge, anyone on the basis of their status in one of the five protected groups.

Protected group
A designation for members of society who are granted legal status by virtue of a demographic characteristic, such as race, sex, national origin, color, religion, age, and disability.

---

[1] Some scholars believe adding sex to the list of legally protected groups was a joke offered as a means to decrease the likelihood the Civil Rights Act would be voted into law. Other scholars believe its inclusion was sincere in addressing the legal rights of women. The interested reader is encouraged to examine both sides of this issue (Highhouse, 2011).

- Employers may not separate or classify employees or applicants so as to deprive anyone of employment opportunities on the basis of any of the five protected groups.

- Employment advertising or training opportunities may not indicate preferences for any group, as witnessed, for example, in separate classified advertisements for "Help Wanted—Men" and "Help Wanted—Women."

In 1967 the Age Discrimination in Employment Act (ADEA) was passed, which extends to people aged 40 and over the same legal protection granted to the five protected groups under the Civil Rights Act. As such, age (40 years and over) became the sixth protected group.

Americans with Disabilities Act

In 1990 the Americans with Disabilities Act (ADA) was signed into law by President George H. W. Bush. It was followed by its successor, the ADA Amendments Act in 2008. The ADA is the most important piece of legislation ever enacted for persons with disabilities (O'Keeffe, 1994), with disability becoming the seventh protected group. A *disability* is defined by the ADA as "a physical or mental impairment that substantially limits one or more (of the) major life activities; a record of such impairment; or being regarded as having such an impairment." A major life activity is seeing, hearing, walking, learning, breathing, and working. An employment test that screens out an individual with a disability must be job-related and consistent with business necessity. The law states that employers must provide persons with disabilities *reasonable accommodation* in being evaluated for employment and in the conduct of their jobs. Employers are required to modify or accommodate their business practices in a reasonable fashion to meet the needs of persons with disabilities. This can include providing elevators or ramps for access to buildings for those who cannot walk, or providing readers for those who have dyslexia or are blind. The fundamental premise of the law is that individuals with disabilities can effectively contribute to the workforce, and they cannot be discriminated against in employment decisions because of their disabilities. If a reasonable accommodation on the employer's part is needed to meld these individuals into the workforce, it is so prescribed by the ADA. Santuzzi et al. (2014) discussed how the law extends to employees with invisible disabilities, such as Attention Deficit Hyperactivity Disorder (ADHD) and psychological disorders, such as Post Traumatic Stress Disorder (PTSD). The challenge to employers under the ADA is that they must choose solutions that accommodate an applicant's disability yet still permit a valid assessment of that applicant's qualifications for the job.

In 2001 the U.S. Supreme Court ruled on the case of *Martin v. PGA Tour*. Martin was a professional golfer who suffered from a physical disability in his right leg that restricted his ability to walk a golf course. He asked the PGA of America for permission to ride a golf cart during tour competition. The PGA refused on the grounds that riding in a cart would give Martin an unfair advantage over other golfers who are compelled by PGA rules to walk the course. Martin sued the PGA for the right to use a golf cart under the ADA, claiming that his riding in a cart was a reasonable accommodation the PGA could make in his pursuit of earning a living as a golfer. Furthermore, Martin contended it would not be an "undue burden" (or hardship) on the PGA to allow Martin to ride. The U.S. Supreme Court ruled in favor of Martin, saying that making shots was an essential job function but walking between shots was not.

In summary, discrimination laws are passed on the perceived need to remedy problems affecting certain groups in society[2]. The groups so identified are called "protected groups" on the basis of them having protection provided by a law. Currently there are seven protected groups covered by federal discrimination laws. As Steiner (2012) noted, other nations have provided legal protection for additional groups including sexual orientation, union membership, political party, and marital status. Additionally, there are different laws at the state level pertaining to protected group membership in employment discrimination. Colella et al. (2012) reported that 21 states have laws prohibiting discrimination based on sexual orientation. In 2010 President Barrack Obama signed a law removing all restrictions on lesbian, gay, bisexual, and transgender (LGBT) individuals serving in the military (Estrada, 2012). The passage of additional federal laws on employment discrimination will depend on societal pressure and the political resolve for such legislation.

Adverse Impact

Through the Civil Rights Act unfair discrimination may be charged under two legal theories. One is **adverse impact** (also called *disparate impact*), in which discrimination affects various groups (vis-à-vis the protected groups) differently. Evidence that one group (e.g., women) as a whole are less likely to be hired compared to other members of the group (e.g., men) is evidence of discrimination against those group members. The second theory is **disparate treatment**, which refers to evidence that a member of a protected group is treated differently from other individuals in the employment process. All job applicants should receive the same treatment with regard to employment. By example, a certain job might require a moderate amount of physical effort. Because men (on average) have greater physical strength and endurance than women (on average), the employer assumes men are more suitable for this job than women. However, so as not to preclude women from being considered for the job, the employer requires female applicants, but not male applicants, to be administered a test of physical strength as part of the assessment process. Such an assessment process would be deemed a clear case of disparate treatment as the female and male applicants for the same job are treated differently. Singling out some applicants or employees for different employment procedures constitutes disparate treatment.

Of the two legal bases of discrimination, adverse impact has garnered greater attention among I/O psychologists. Adverse impact exists when employment procedures result in a differential effect between protected minority and majority group members. A simple rule of thumb was created to operationalize the concept of adverse impact: the "80%" (or "⅘ths") rule. The rule states that adverse impact occurs if the selection ratio (that is, the number of people hired divided by the number of people who apply) for any group of applicants is less than 80% of the selection ratio for another group.

Adverse impact
A type of unfair discrimination in which the result of using a particular personnel selection method has a negative effect on protected group members compared with majority group members. Often contrasted with disparate treatment.

Disparate treatment
A type of unfair discrimination in which protected group members are afforded differential employment procedures compared to members of other groups. Often contrasted with adverse impact.

---

[2] The word "discriminate" is neutral in meaning. It means to differentiate. The purpose of administering employment tests is to discriminate (differentiate) candidates who are more likely to perform well on the job from those who are less likely to do so. Employment laws were enacted to prohibit *unfair* discrimination — rejecting candidates on the basis of a protected group membership (e.g., race, sex, age, etc.). Over the years of using the word in an employment context, society has gotten linguistically lazy, usually dropping the word "unfair" from the term "unfair discrimination." In contemporary language, "discrimination" has become verbal shorthand for "unfair discrimination." Being consistent with common usage, the term "discrimination" is used in this book to mean "unfair discrimination."

Suppose 100 Whites apply for a job and 20 are selected. The selection ratio is thus 20/100, or .20. By multiplying .20 by 80%, we get .16. If fewer than 16% of Black applicants (for example) are hired, the selection test is deemed to produce adverse impact. So if 50 Blacks apply for the job and if at least 8 (50 × .16) Blacks are not selected, then the test produces adverse impact.

If adverse impact is found to exist, the organization faces two alternatives. One is to demonstrate that the test *is* a valid predictor of job performance. The second alternative is to use a different test that has no adverse impact (but may also be less valid than a test that does manifest adverse impact). As Pyburn et al. (2008) indicated, using less valid measures to reduce adverse impact violates no laws but doing so comes at the cost of not having the organization be staffed with the most qualified applicants. If adverse impact does not result from using the selection method, then the organization is not required to validate it. Obviously, however, it is a sound business decision to validate any selection method at any time. A company would always want to know whether its selection method is identifying the best candidates for hire. As Gutman (2004) noted, multiple legal interpretations of adverse impact can be inferred from court rulings. There are other methods of assessing adverse impact in addition to the 80% rule. What they all have in common, however, is their intent of determining whether a disproportionately large percentage of one group of applicants is rejected for employment compared with another group.

As part of the Civil Rights Act, the Equal Employment Opportunity Commission (EEOC) was established to investigate charges of prohibited employment practices and to use conciliation and persuasion to eliminate prohibited practices. The EEOC subsequently produced the *Uniform Guidelines on Employee Selection Procedures* for organizations to follow in making employment decisions. When there is a conclusion of "just cause" to believe charges of employment discrimination are true, the EEOC can file suit in court. If the organization cannot be persuaded to change its employment practices, then the issue is brought before the court for adjudication. Organizations that lose such cases are obligated to pay financial damages to the victims of their employment practices. The financial awards in these cases can be class-action settlements (the individual who is suing represents a class of similar people), back-pay settlements (the organization has to pay a portion of what victims would have earned had they been hired), or both. The courts have granted multi-million-dollar awards in single cases. However, not everyone who fails an employment test automatically gets his or her day in court. A lawsuit must be predicated on just cause, and the two parties can reach an agreement without resorting to litigation.

Table 5-1 shows 2013 statistics from the EEOC on the number of employment discrimination cases filed in the United States involving alleged adverse impact against the seven protected groups, as well as cases involving alleged disparate treatment (e.g., retaliation). As can be seen in the table, the three protected groups with the greatest frequencies are race, sex, and disability, respectively. Of all the employment discrimination cases filed in 2013, 80% allege adverse impact and 20% allege disparate treatment. Lindsey et al. (2013) argue that the number of cases represented in Table 5-1 (over 150,000 cases in one year) attests that after 50 years following passage of the Civil Rights Act, we have not eliminated employment discrimination. More pointedly, Offerman and Basford (2014) concluded: "Unfortunately, decades of effort in the United States directed at increasing equal employment opportunity and eliminating

Table 5-1   *EEOC statistics on employment discrimination (2013)*

Legal Theory			
Adverse Impact			
Protected Group	**Law**	**# Cases**	**%**
Race	CRA	32,727	26.3%
Sex	CRA	27,343	22.0%
National Origin	CRA	10,467	8.5%
Religion	CRA	3,658	2.9%
Color	CRA	3,100	2.6%
Age	ADEA	21,157	17.0%
Disability	ADA	25,744	20.7%
	Total	124,196	80.0%
Legal Theory	**Law**	**# Cases**	**%**
Disparate Treatment	CRA	31,084	20.0%

CRA = Civil Rights Act (1964); ADEA = Age Discrimination in Employment Act; ADA = Americans with Disabilities Act

prejudice and discrimination have not been met with declines in reports of workplace discrimination. According to the EEOC, the number of charges filed over the past ten years is actually on the rise" (p. 231). Additional information about the EEOC can be found at *www.eeoc.gov*.

The *Uniform Guidelines on Employee Selection Procedures* were published in 1978. The *Guidelines* reflected the prevailing state of scientific knowledge at that time about test validation. Now almost 40 years old, Banks and McDaniel (2012) argue they are outdated and should either be abolished or revised because they are based upon scientific knowledge about validity that has since been refuted. McDaniel et al. (2011) asserted the *Guidelines* are now actually a detriment to attaining the employment outcomes they were intended to achieve. Sharf (2011) believes the *Guidelines* are not a scientific document. Therefore, it is questionable whether new research advances in the science of validation will inspire a revision of them. Sharf stated the *Guidelines* are a tool of political advocacy; that is, a document designed to effectuate the intent of the Civil Rights Act. At the core of the issue is whether as a nation we desire equal opportunity (i.e., members of every protected group will receive equal consideration to enter all jobs) or equal employment (i.e., members of every protected group will be represented in all jobs). This distinction is based on values and cannot be resolved by scientific evidence.

In conclusion, issues of employment discrimination are complex. There are no simple answers or easy solutions to resolving these problems. As Bobko and Roth (2010) aptly summarized, I/O psychologists are not members of the legal community, and thus we are not positioned to solve legal problems. However, I/O psychologists can help the legal system understand how psychological issues (such as test reliability, validity, passing scores, etc.) associated with selection tests can influence employment discrimination.

FRANK AND ERNEST   by Bob Thaves

HOW CAN A WOMAN BE SUING US FOR SEX DISCRIMINATION?... WE'VE NEVER EVEN HAD ONE WORK HERE!

THAVES

Frank & Ernest: © Thaves/Dist. by Newspaper Enterprise Association, Inc. Reprinted with permission.

Diversity

Diversity
A goal of staffing whereby demographic differences in society are reflected in the workforce.

The word **diversity** is frequently cited in both popular and scientific literatures. The word diversity derives from "diverse" meaning *different*. In the realm of personnel selection, diversity represents one goal of organizational staffing.

The logical basis of diversity as a staffing goal is that society is composed of many types of people. People differ in many ways, including the demographic variables of sex, race, ethnicity, and age (among others). While people in society can differ in many ways, in reality we also have much in common. One common denominator is that most of us have to work for a living. We need money to live, and we earn money through employment. As such, the need to earn a living is "the great equalizer" that unites all people.

Some societies exhibit more diversity than others, particularly by race and ethnicity. Personnel selection in organizations is a matter of making choices; more specifically, who is selected for employment and who is rejected. A large amount of psychological research has indicated that people generally prefer environments that are predictable and understandable to them. Their preferences are guided by familiarity, which is a product of previous exposure or experience. With regard to personnel selection, if our choices are guided by feeling more comfortable with the familiar, organizations would be driven to select new employees who are similar to current employees. As such, organizations would tend to clone themselves. If the selected employees are judged to be qualified, what is wrong with staffing an organization with members of the entire same demographic group (such as men)? The answer is, in part, that members of other groups can be equally qualified to perform the job (in this case, women), but because they are different compared to the status quo, they are rejected for employment. Employment laws have been enacted that prohibit selection decisions on the basis of the very factors that constitute why we are different from each other—sex, race, ethnicity, etc. The right to be judged fairly (i.e., without regard to one's demographic membership) is established by law. Therefore, to the extent that job candidates from various demographic groups are qualified, there should be proportional representation of them in the workforce. An organization that is staffed by a diverse range of employees is mirroring the society of which it is a part. Organizations must have valid reasons for why they select (and reject) job candidates. In short, most of us need jobs to support ourselves, and organizations are providers of employment opportunities. To the extent candidates from different demographic groups are qualified to perform the work, organizations should be staffed with a diverse range of employees.

Diversity is typically measured by calculating the percentage of each of the seven groups protected by federal law in the composition of an organization's workforce (Ryan & Powers, 2012). Diversity is another term for the statistical concept of variance or dispersion. In the context of workplace diversity, there is a fundamental paradox. On the one hand, organizations strive to *reduce* variance in employee job performance. That is, organizations want all their employees performing at the same high level. Indeed, the intent of recruitment, selection, training, and performance management is to achieve better (and more similar) levels of job performance in all employees across the organization. On the other hand, the intent of diversity in the workplace is to achieve that uniform high performance through different identifiable groups of people as found in society. The ultimate goal is to achieve low variance in job performance (i.e., everyone is performing very well) by having high variance in the demographic groups comprising the workforce (Ostroff & Fulmer, 2014). Roberson (2012) advocates the development of new ways to measure differences across people other than legally protected group status. There can obviously be differences across people *within* a group. It is a fallacy to assume that all members of a particular group (Asians, for example) have the same skills, values, opinions, etc. There can be as much variance in the attributes of members within a group as between groups. Such is the need to find additional ways to measure diversity.

As mentioned previously, organizations are keenly aware that diversity is an index of being a socially responsible employer. Organizations differ in the extent to which they successfully pursue diversity initiatives, and they differ in the extent to which they make public statements about their efforts. Jonsen and Ozbilgin (2014) developed a taxonomy that summarized these differences across organizations, as shown in Figure 5-2. "Reality" is whether organizations achieve a diverse workforce, and "Rhetoric" is whether they talk actively about their efforts.

The upper left quadrant ("Walk the talk") represents organizations that achieve diversity in reality in addition to verbally promoting their efforts in doing so. The

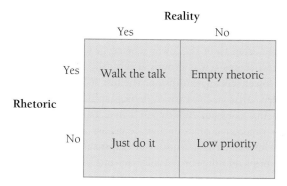

Figure 5-2 *Typology of organizational diversity initiatives*

Adapted from "Models of Global Diversity Management," by K. Jonsen and M. Ozbilgin, in *Diversity at work: The practice of inclusion* (2014). Reprinted by permission from Jossey-Bass.

lower right quadrant ("Low priority") represents organizations that neither achieve nor talk about their diversity efforts. The upper right quadrant ("Empty rhetoric") reflects organizations that talk about their diversity efforts, but in reality their workforce is not diverse. The lower left quadrant ("Just do it") refers to organizations that do not publicly discuss or promote their diversity achievements, but in reality have created a diverse workforce. Jonsen and Ozbilgin believe there should be alignment or consistency between what an organization does and what it says. If diversity is not an enacted value of the company, it should not be proclaimed as one. However, if diversity is central to the company's identity, it is appropriate to communicate it.

Finally, Winters (2014) argues it is more valuable to focus on *inclusion* than diversity. Winters offers this distinction: "Diversity is the mix. Inclusion is making the mix work" (p. 206). Diversity is easy to measure, as computed by dividing the members of a particular group by the size of the total workforce, resulting in a percentage. Inclusion is more difficult to achieve and measure. Inclusion involves people from all groups feeling they contribute to the whole organization while still retaining their own identities. By analogy, each of the 50 states has its own name and identity, but each is included in a national identity, the United States. Inclusion generates a feeling of being an authentic insider who is both trusted and respected for contributions made. Inclusion advances the concept of diversity by going beyond nominal representation to feelings of self-worth. As Winters noted, while the goals of inclusion are most laudable, they are difficult to achieve in practice.

The Diversity-Validity Dilemma

The diversity goal of staffing is challenged when it is asserted that the members of various demographic groups are *not* (on average) equally qualified to perform work. In some jobs this assertion is patently evident. For example, construction jobs and manual labor often require heavy lifting, explosive strength, and physical endurance. Men (on average) have larger muscles in their arms, legs, and back, compared to women (on average). As such, men are more likely than women to be judged qualified to perform physically demanding work. The alleged lack of comparability in qualifications across demographic groups becomes more difficult to establish when the job requires something other than overt physical strength. When suitability for employment is determined by tests of knowledge, mental ability, or personality, group differences in test scores can result in differential rates of hiring, with the higher scoring groups being selected more often than the lower scoring groups. The explanation for the difference in average test scores across groups is typically either that the tests are flawed (biased against the lower scoring groups), or the test scores are simply exhibiting what there is to be revealed. That is, the various demographic groups in society are *not* equal in the attributes being assessed. As discussed in Chapter 4, the one attribute that has been found most predictive of performance across a wide array of jobs is general mental ability (g). However, a vast amount of empirical research has revealed that the various protected groups do not score equally on tests of general mental ability.

One strategy to eliminate group differences in assessment results is to make statistical adjustments to the test scores. In 1991 President George H. W. Bush signed into law an amendment to the Civil Rights Act that prohibited test score adjustments as a means of equalizing group differences. Specifically, the amended Civil Rights Act stated that it shall be an unlawful practice for an employer "in connection with the selection or referral of applicants or candidates for employment or promotion to adjust the scores of, use different cutoffs for, or otherwise alter the results of employment related tests on the basis of race, color, religion, sex, or national origin."

The second goal of staffing is to select the most qualified applicants—those who have the highest probability of contributing to the success of the organization. The term for the desire to maximize the twin goals of staffing—hiring those applicants who have the highest probability of success and achieving a fully diverse workforce—is the **diversity-validity dilemma**. It is a dilemma because individuals from all the groups that populate society do not score equally on personnel selection tests. Therefore, members of certain groups are more likely to be selected than others. As stated by Schmitt and Quinn (2010), "the dilemma then is how best to balance organizational concerns with the maximization of expected levels of performance against the individual, social, and organizational desire for a diverse workforce/student body and equitable treatment of members of different racial/ethnic groups" (p. 426). These two goals are embedded not only in a social context but also in a legal one. Laws have been passed to help achieve social goals, and personnel selection decisions are held to these legal standards. The population of the United States is a melting pot or amalgam of a broad range of racial, ethnic, and religious groups. As a nation we want that diversity reflected in our workforce. The constant tension in our society regarding personnel selection revolves around meeting these two goals—selecting qualified applicants and achieving diversification in the workforce. Sackett et al. (2001) described "high-stakes testing" which reflects that important decisions in life (e.g., admission into a school or job) often depend on the results of a test. Caught in the bind of using valid tests to make hiring decisions that produce adverse impact, some institutions have sought to use less valid tests that produce less adverse impact. However, doing so weakens the institution's commitment to selecting the most qualified applicants. Sackett et al. believe that the massive amount of research findings on psychological assessment reveals that it is not possible to simultaneously maximize the twin goals of having a highly diversified workforce (or student population) in selecting the most qualified applicants.

Nevertheless, various types of strategies have been examined to reduce the tradeoff between validity and diversity. Such strategies include the use of alternative modes of assessment besides paper-and-pencil tests, increasing time limits on testing, coaching to reduce test anxiety, and retesting. Arthur and Woehr (2013) stated that switching assessment methods (as from a test to an interview) of the same construct rarely reduces sub-group differences in scores. It is possible to find methods that produce no sub-group differences in scores (as by flipping a coin), but what that method measures (i.e., randomness) is not related to job performance. Wee et al. (2014) tried to reduce adverse impact but retain validity by breaking down the overall construct of g into specific subtests (as one test of verbal ability, a second test of numerical ability, and so on). Then they differentially weighted the sub-tests with the goal of reducing adverse impact. Their approach led to an increase of 8% in job offers to minority candidates compared to a unitary assessment of g.

De Corte et al. (2011) used a complex mathematical model for personnel selection that simultaneously sought to maximize validity and diversity. The results yielded the conclusion that it was not possible to maximize both. The most valid predictor produced adverse impact, and predictors that maximized diversity had diminished validity.

Diversity-validity dilemma
The paradox of organizations being unable to simultaneously hire the most qualified applicants and members of the full range of demographic groups that populate society.

The authors concluded that a trade-off between the twin goals of validity and diversity is required, as the exclusive pursuit of one will not achieve the second. Finally, Hausknecht et al. (2007) examined what effect retesting has on cognitive ability test scores. They concluded that retesting does improve scores, especially when accompanied by coaching and when the same form of the test was administered in both occasions. Schleicher et al. (2010) estimated the degree to which improvement in scores through retesting would alter the outcome of the selection decision. The authors reported that the improved scores candidates received in being retested would result in a different selection outcome (from fail to pass) for about 20% of the candidates. Van Iddekinge, Morgeson et al. (2011) posited that improvements in scores upon retesting were due to less anxiety about the assessment plus greater motivation to perform at a higher level.

As can be inferred, our professional inability to simultaneously achieve the twin goals of validity and diversity is a source of frustration for I/O psychologists. Eradicating employment discrimination as a societal goal is a noble objective. But if our societal goal is to eradicate adverse impact in test scores, doing so will require nullifying empirically established differences between certain groups on certain attributes (e.g., that men have greater upper-body strength than do women).

Most of our efforts have been directed at the predictor side of the equation: trying different selection methods that assess the same construct, differentially weighting test scores, etc. Less research has been directed toward the criterion side of the equation. Perhaps some jobs allow for different behavioral styles in performing tasks. That is, there may be more than one way to successfully perform a job. Each way or behavioral style can be effective, as the job permits such variability in how tasks are performed. Furthermore, assume each behavioral style is characterized by a different set of human attributes. If the different sets of attributes are distributed across the various protected groups, members of one group may be successful by possessing one set of attributes, while members of another group may be successful by possessing another set of attributes. While focusing on the criterion side instead of the predictor side is potentially fruitful, in reality it is unknown how many jobs can be performed successfully using multiple styles. Furthermore, if general mental ability is required no matter what style is used, we would once again find ourselves facing the vexing diversity-validity dilemma.

Major Court Cases

A trial court applies the facts of a given case to the relevant law. If a case is appealed, a higher court (or appellate court) can issue a written opinion that becomes *case law* (or "precedent"). Several landmark decisions rendered by the U.S. Supreme Court have shaped the interpretation of the Civil Rights Act. In *Griggs v. Duke Power Company*, the Court ruled in 1971 that individuals who bring suit against a company do not have to prove that the company's employment test is unfair; rather, the company has to prove that its test is fair. Thus the burden of proving the fairness of the test rests with the employer. This finding is referred to as "Griggs' Burden." One effect of the Griggs case was to curtail the use of employment tests in the 1970s by organizations in making selection decisions for fear they would invite charges of illegal discrimination. In *Albemarle v. Moody*, the Court ruled that the EEOC's Guidelines have the "deference of law," even though they were issued by an administrative agency and not written by Congress and signed by the President. In *Bakke v. University of California*, the Court ruled that Whites can be the victims of discrimination as well as Blacks. Bakke (a White man) sued the University of California on the grounds that his race had been a factor in his being denied admission to its medical school. The Court ruled in Bakke's favor and required the University of California to admit Bakke to the medical school. This case was heralded as a classic case of "reverse discrimination," which technically is incorrect. First, the name connotes that Whites cannot be discriminated against, which is not true. Second, reversal of the process of discrimination results in nondiscrimination.

The legality of affirmative action was challenged in *United Steelworkers v. Weber*. Weber, a White male, worked for Kaiser Aluminum and Chemical, and was a member of the United Steelworkers of America labor union. The company had a policy of using seniority to admit Whites and Blacks into a supervisory training program on a one-to-one basis. Weber argued that even though he had more seniority than the Black workers who were admitted into the training program, he was not. Weber's position was that race was used as a selection factor, a violation of the Civil Rights Act. It was the position of the company and the union that they were using affirmative action to remedy past employment discrimination against Blacks. The Supreme Court ruled against Weber, claiming affirmative action plans are lawful as a temporary remedy to correct for racial imbalance in the workforce. A badge worn by supporters of affirmative action in this case is shows in Figure 5-3. In *Watson v. Fort Worth Bank & Trust*, the Court ruled that the *cost* of alternative selection procedures must be considered in making decisions about selection methods. Previously, cost had not been a concern of the courts or the EEOC. In *Wards Cove Packing Company v. Atonio*, the U.S. Supreme Court modified both the applicant's and employer's responsibilities in employment litigation pertaining to such issues as burden of proof. Literally thousands of cases have been adjudicated in the district, appellate, state supreme courts, and U.S. Supreme Court on employment law issues. These six cases (all from the U.S. Supreme Court) represent a very small sampling.

A consideration of these court cases might lead one to the conclusion that employment testing is a risky business strategy and that the prudent employer should abandon

Figure 5-3   *Badge worn by supporters of affirmative action*

testing in making personnel decisions. However, that is not the case at all. Sharf and Jones (2000) stated:

> The use of demonstrably job-related employment tests is a winning strategy for minimizing the risk of employment litigation. Forty-plus percent of employment decisions in the private sector are based on the results of employment tests. Litigation challenging employment test use, however, occurs in less than one-half of 1 percent of all discrimination claims. So the tides have turned from the post-Griggs days, when employers abandoned the casual use of employment tests. Legally defensible employment testing is now one of the safest harbors offering shelter from the howling gales of class-action EEO litigation. (p. 314)

Zickar and Gibby (2007) summarized how federal employment laws came to influence I/O psychology:

> The Civil Rights Act of 1964 and successive U.S. Supreme Court decisions expressively forbid using hiring devices that resulted in adverse impact against several protected classes . . . unless the test was shown to be valid for the particular personnel decision for which it was being used. Although these rulings frightened employers from using employment tests (for fear of being sued), these rulings highlighted the importance of using well-developed selection testing practices. I/O psychologists quickly assumed the role of experts in deciding whether particular tests were biased in particular test usages. (p. 71)

After reviewing legal cases pertaining to employment discrimination, Gutman (2012) concluded:

> Court rulings can illustrate what employers do wrong, what they do right, or what employees fail to understand . . . The best solution for heading off complaints, and for limiting legal vulnerability, is to create policies that anticipate potential problems. The goal of these policies should be to inform employees of their rights, and managers and supervisors of their responsibilities. (p. 715)

Affirmative Action

Affirmative action
A social policy that advocates members of protected groups will be actively recruited and considered for selection in employment.

Affirmative action is a social policy aimed at reducing the effects of prior discrimination. It is not a requirement under the Civil Rights Act, although it is included in the EEOC guidelines. The original intent of affirmative action was aimed primarily at the recruitment of new employees—namely, that organizations would take positive (or affirmative) action to bring members of minority groups into the workforce that had previously been excluded.

Campbell (1996) described four goals of affirmative action:

1. **Correct present inequities**. If one group has "more than its fair share" of jobs or educational opportunities because of current discriminatory practices, then the goal is to remedy the inequity and eliminate the discriminating practices.

2. **Compensate past inequities**. Even if current practices are not discriminatory, a long history of past discrimination may put members of a minority group at a disadvantage.

3. **Provide role models**. Increasing the frequency of minority group mem-

bers acting as role models could potentially change the career expectations, educational planning, and job-seeking behavior of younger minority group members.

4. Promote diversity. Increasing the minority representation in a student body or workforce may increase the range of ideas, skills, or values that can be brought to bear on organizational problems and goals.

As straightforward as these goals may appear, there is great variability in the operational procedures used to pursue the goals. The most passive interpretation is to follow procedures that strictly pertain to recruitment, such as extensive advertising in sources most likely to reach minority group members. A stronger interpretation of the goals is *preferential selection*: organizations will select minority group members from the applicant pool if they are judged to have substantially equal qualifications with nonminority applicants. The most extreme interpretation is to set aside a specific number of job openings or promotions for members of specific protected groups. This is referred to as the *quota interpretation* of affirmative action: organizations will staff themselves with explicit percentages of employees representing the various protected groups, based on local or national norms, within a specific time frame. Quotas are legally imposed on organizations as a severe corrective measure for prolonged inequities in the composition of the workforce. Quotas are not the typical interpretation of affirmative action. There is a common belief that affirmative action involves the abandonment of merit as an employment principle. Rather than presuming that affirmative action compels organizations to hire employees with less merit, affirmative action programs should be regarded as an attempt to get qualified employees who are representative of their proportion in the relevant labor market.

Affirmative action has been hotly debated by proponents and critics. In particular, over the past 30 years the subject of affirmative action has been a major political issue (Crosby & VanDeVeer, 2000). Criticism of the quota interpretation in particular has been strident, claiming the strategy ignores merit or ability. Under a quota strategy it is alleged that the goal is merely "to get the numbers right." Proponents of affirmative action believe it is needed to offset the effects of years of past discrimination against specific protected groups. Several states have reversed their commitment to affirmative action in the admission of students into their universities. Preliminary evidence indicates the new admission policy has resulted in less representation of some minority groups in the student population.

Has affirmative action been effective in meeting national goals of prosperity in employment for all people? Some experts (e.g., Guion, 1998a; Heilman, 1996) questioned its overall effectiveness, asserting that unemployment rates are much higher and average incomes much lower now for some groups (particularly Blacks) than they were at the inception of affirmative action more than 40 years ago. Although there appears to be consensus that affirmative action has not produced its intended goals (Lindsey et al., 2013), there is considerable reluctance to discard it altogether. President William Jefferson Clinton stated the nation should "amend it, not end it." It is feared that its absence may produce outcomes more socially undesirable than have occurred with its presence, however flawed it might be. Dovidio and Gaertner (1996) asserted that affirmative action policies are beneficial in that they emphasize outcomes rather than intentions and they establish monitoring systems that ensure accountability.

Ward Connerly, founder and chairman of the American Civil Rights Institute, is an outspoken critic of racial and gender preferences in selection decisions. He contends that affirmative action creates the stigma of incompetence among beneficiaries of its practices. Connerly offered the following opinion on the perception of affirmative action by the general public (as reported in Evans, 2003): "Every day that I walk into class I have this feeling that people are wondering whether I'm there because I got in through affirmative action. The reality is the stigma exists. It exists, and they know it exists" (p. 121). Heilman et al. (1992) reported that individuals viewed as having been hired because of affirmative action were not believed to have had their qualifications given much weight in the hiring process. The stigma of incompetence was found to be fairly robust, and the authors questioned whether the stigma would dissipate in the face of disconfirming information about the individuals' presumed incompetence. Similar results have been reported by Heilman and Alcott (2001). Highhouse et al. (1999) found that subtle differences in the way jobs were advertised reflected a company's commitment to affirmative action and influenced the attitudes of Black engineers to pursue employment with the company. The authors concluded that minority applicants are sensitive to the manner in which a company projects its stance on minority recruitment and selection. Kravitz and Klineberg (2000) identified differences within minority group populations with regard to their support for affirmative action. Blacks were found to support affirmative action more strongly than Hispanics. White et al. (2008) concluded that a thorough explanation of the benefits of affirmative action by organizations can be effective in creating positive attitudes, as opposed to relying on passive acceptance of the supposed need for affirmative action.

In June 2003 the U.S. Supreme Court ruled on two major cases involving affirmative action. Both involved the admission of students into the University of Michigan. The first case, *Gratz v. Bollinger*, challenged the process used by the University of Michigan in admitting students into the undergraduate program. As an attempt to comply with the intent of affirmative action (increase minority representation), the University of Michigan assigned points to all the variables examined in the student's application, such as points for SAT scores, high school grade point average, extracurricular activities, and so on. For admission 100 points were needed (out of 150 possible points). The university automatically assigned 20 points (or one-fifth of the total needed for admission) if a candidate was an "under-represented minority race." The Supreme Court ruled against the university, deciding that giving points for membership in certain races was unconstitutional. The second case, *Grutter v. Bollinger*, challenged the process used by the University of Michigan in admitting students into the law school. The law school did consider race in making selection decisions but did not use any point system to evaluate candidates for admission. Race could be considered a "plus" in each candidate's file, yet the entire selection system was flexible enough to consider the particular qualifications of each candidate. The Supreme Court ruled in favor of the University of Michigan's law school admissions system. If we consider both cases in their totality, it appears the Supreme Court recognized the legitimate need to have a broad representation of all groups in those candidates selected for admission, but it opposed the general practice that creates two groups of candidates based exclusively on group membership (in the *Gratz* case, those candidates who did and did not get points on the basis of their race).

The two opposing rulings by the Supreme Court illustrate the complexity of the issues raised by affirmative action. On the one hand, we recognize that society will be better served by having all segments of our population enjoying the benefits of admission into school or employment. On the other hand, it is not fair or lawful to explicitly reward some applicants (and in effect, punish others) for their particular group membership. Perhaps more than any other country, the United States is populated by an amalgam of citizens who (with the exception of native American Indians) originally came to this country from someplace else. Given the extreme diversity of people from various racial, cultural, and religious backgrounds, conflicts over who gets to participate in social benefits (education and employment) are perhaps inevitable. Affirmative action is an attempt to recognize the paramount need for all segments of society to be fairly represented in receiving these benefits. Nevertheless, there is ambiguity and disagreement over how best to achieve these goals. As Gutman (2003) noted, it is plausible for a law school with 4,000 applicants to scrutinize all or most of the applicants. It is implausible for an undergraduate program with 50,000 applicants to do likewise.

A Model of Personnel Decisions

Figure 5-4 is a model that shows the sequence of factors associated with making personnel decisions. Several of these factors have been discussed in earlier chapters. The process of work analysis initiates the sequence and was described in Chapter 3. An analysis of the job and organization establishes the context in which the personnel decisions will be made. The results of these analyses provide information useful in determining the criteria of job performance (also discussed in Chapter 3) as well as provide insights into predictor constructs useful in forecasting job performance (as discussed in Chapter 4). The linkage between the predictors and criteria is the essence of validity—the determination of how well our predictors forecast job performance (discussed in Chapter 4). The Society for Industrial and Organizational Psychology has issued a set of principles for the validation and use of personnel selection procedures (SIOP, 2003). The *Principles* specify established scientific findings and generally accepted professional practices in the field of personnel selection. The *Principles* describe the choice, development, evaluation, and use of personnel selection procedures designed to measure constructs relating to work behavior with a focus on the accuracy of the inferences that underlie employment decisions. These *Principles* outline our responsibilities as I/O psychologists to assist in making accurate and fair personnel selection decisions. As Boutelle (2004) stated, "Based upon a set of test results, we are making judgments about people and their abilities and their suitability to perform specific jobs. These judgments have enormous impact upon people and their careers and we, as I/O psychologists, need to be very diligent in providing strong evidence supporting outcomes derived from test scores" (p. 21).

Organizational Strategy and Staffing

An organization's strategy refers to how it seeks to accomplish its goals. It is a topic that is heavily researched in business, but it has not been addressed in I/O psychology until most recently (Ployhart & Schneider, 2012; Hausknecht & Wright, 2012).

Just as individuals have financial budgets, so too do organizations. For most individuals, housing is the single largest expense item in their budget. Organizations,

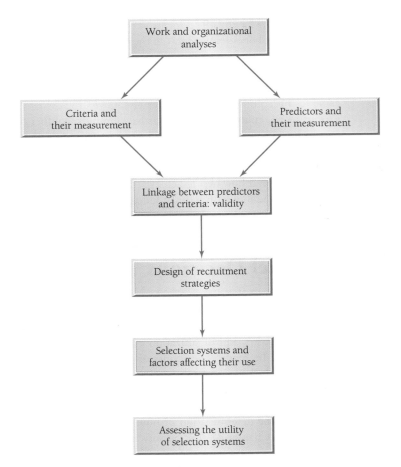

Figure 5-4 *Model of personnel decisions in organizations*

depending upon their strategy, differ in how much they spend on their human resources. For some organizations, human resources are the largest single expense item
in their budget. For other organizations, the cost of human resources is not their leading expenditure. The organization's strategy is the basis for how much it spends on its
human resources.

In the fast food industry, for example, customers desire to purchase inexpensive
food served quickly. There is a highly routinized system for customers to order their
food, pay for it, and have it served. The human component of the system (i.e., the
people who perform these tasks) are but a relatively minor component in meeting the
customer's needs. Jobs in the fast food industry require low levels of KSAOs. The tasks
are highly structured and require little training time. Most jobs in the fast food industry pay minimum wage. People who work in the fast food industry typically do so for
brief periods of time, such as after school, over the summer, or until they can find better jobs. There is a large supply of people who can perform the relatively simple tasks
in these jobs. It is rare to find a person who works in the fast food industry as a career

(with the possible exception of those individuals who work their way up into management positions). Turnover in the fast food industry is very high, about 300% per year, meaning the average employee works only about four months before leaving. The turnover rate is not a problem given the volume of people in the workforce who can replace departed workers. Accordingly, the recruitment process for these entry-level employees is not formalized and the selection process is cursory. The fast food industry uses this approach to recruitment and selection because it fits its strategy. Customers are attracted by inexpensive food served quickly, not who takes their orders or serves them. By keeping their human resource costs to a minimum, the fast food industry can keep the cost of their food low, a critical component of their strategy.

A very different organizational strategy is evidenced in the medical field. Medicine is devoted to preventing illnesses and the treatment of the people who become ill or injured. The organizational strategy in the field of medicine is the opposite of the fast food industry with regard to human resources. Rather than a cost to be minimized, the medical field regards human resources as an investment. It is precisely because of the high KSAOs needed to enter the field of medicine that qualified people are in low supply and high demand. The quality of human resources in the medical field is critical to achieving its goals. The amount of education and training required to be a physician is measured in years, not weeks or days. Once an individual enters the medical field, it typically becomes a lifetime career. Given the cost of recruitment, selection, and training, the medical field tries to minimize turnover. While a 300% annual turnover rate in the fast food industry is typically deemed acceptable, a 10% turnover rate in the medical field is typically deemed unacceptably high. As a result, the level of compensation paid for many jobs in the medical field is high. Aside from physicians, people trained in diagnostics and specialized care, for example, command high salaries. In short, human resources in the medical field (and other industries that depend upon highly skilled individuals) are regarded as an investment, not a cost to be minimized. If an organization's strategy is built upon the value of its human resources, the organization must invest heavily in the recruitment, selection, training, compensation, and management of its employees. As such, the quality of the employees become an asset of the organization (Ployhart, 2012), and the cost of their human resources is often the largest item in its budget.

While fast food and medicine represent contrasting organizational strategies involving the importance of human resources, many other organizations fall somewhere in between these two extremes. In such cases differential importance is placed on jobs within an organization. The banking industry would be a case in point. Customer service jobs, as tellers, require fewer KSAOs than financial investors. Accordingly, a bank would not invest heavily in the recruitment, selection, and training of people who hold the job of teller, as compared with people who are responsible for making major investment decisions.

Organizational strategies that depend heavily on the quality of their employees for success have given birth to new terms in the practice of I/O psychology. They were created to reflect the growing recognition of just how important people are for achieving an organization's goals, depending on its strategy. While "KSAO" is a conventional term used in I/O psychology to reflect human attributes, a new term is "talent." The processes of recruitment and selection result in the "acquisition" of new employees. Thus "talent acquisition" is a recent term in the practice of I/O psychology. Once a candidate becomes a new employee, "onboarding" begins. Onboarding (previously known as "organizational socialization") is the process that tries to ensure that new hires feel welcome in the organization and are prepared to fill their new position. Successful onboarding gives new employees the confidence and resources to more quickly make an impact in the organization. Onboarding helps bridge the gap between being hired and becoming a high-performing employee. However, it should be understood that these concepts are differentially relevant to organizations based on their position on the continuum between regarding employees as a cost to be minimized versus an investment to be carefully nurtured. Having high-quality employees is desirable for all organizations, but far more critical for the success of some than others.

Crook et al. (2011) conducted a meta-analysis of studies that examined the relationship between the quality of employees and the performance of the organization. The research question the authors sought to address was whether the quality of the employees related to the performance of the organization. To improve overall organizational performance, should companies attract, retain, and develop their human resources? The findings led to this conclusion: "Our results leave little doubt that to achieve high performance, firms need to acquire and nurture the best and brightest human capital available and keep these investments in the firm" (p. 453). In short, when the quality of employees is critical to the success of the organization, the employees should be carefully recruited and selected with equal effort applied to their retention.

Recruitment

Recruitment
The process by which individuals are solicited to apply for jobs.

The personnel function of **recruitment** is the process of attracting people to apply for a job. Organizations can select only from those candidates who apply. Attracting and keeping competent employees is critical to the success of most organizations. How organizations recruit new employees depends upon many factors. Among them are the skills required, how wide of a geographic area must be searched to find the needed personnel, the methods used by organizations to announce job vacancies, the messages organizations convey in their recruitment efforts to indicate they are an attractive employer, and the amount of money organizations are willing to commit to their recruitment budget. Over a century ago many companies could recruit needed personnel by simply hanging a hand-written notice in a storefront window, "Help Wanted." Individuals passing on the sidewalk who saw the sign, and were looking for work, became job candidates. Some small stores may still use this recruitment method, but today such an approach simply won't attract the caliber of talent that most organizations need for staffing (see Social Media and I/O Psychology: *Social Recruitment*). As the need for a potential applicant pool expands from passers-by on a sidewalk to a city, state, or nation, there are corresponding changes in not only where organizations look for talent but how they look. And as noted previously, the state of the economy will have a strong effect on how many people express interest in becoming employees.

Osicki and Kulkarni (2010) reported on the typical costs associated with recruitment. An organization can expect to pay approximately $1,000 to recruit an hourly wage worker, $7,000 to recruit a yearly salaried worker, and $23,000 to recruit an executive level employee. Different recruiting approaches are used depending upon the job level in question and may include paper media, radio and television, job fairs,

Social Media and I/O Psychology: *Social Recruitment*

The number of people who use social media sites daily is staggering. As such, it is only natural that when organizations have something that they want a lot of people to see, they're going to use social media to disseminate it. Job announcements are no different. According to a survey conducted in 2012 by Jobvite, the most common social media outlet for recruitment is LinkedIn, with 93% of companies using it for such activities. Organizations are also relying on word of mouth through Facebook to reach future employees. Capitalizing on the notion that employee referrals may lead to high-quality hires, roughly two-thirds of all recruiters are using the social media powerhouse to reach individuals who they may not reach otherwise. In fact, to encourage employees to help in this effort, many organizations are offering referral bonuses to employees who help secure a viable applicant. Twitter has also become a popular tool for organizations to use in their recruiting efforts, with 54% of recruiters using it to help in the search for talent. For example, Citigroup, Garmin, Warner Brothers, Starbucks, FedEx, and Hallmark are just a few of the companies that have tweeted about current and upcoming job openings, using the power of social media to connect with potential applicants.

Of course, the use of social media for recruiting purposes is not only beneficial for organizations. Applicants benefit too. For example, by following the right companies on Twitter, job seekers can get information about job openings as soon they become available, if not before. In addition, Jobvite's survey revealed that it took less overall time to hire when social media were utilized in recruitment efforts as compared to when social media were not used to recruit. Not only is this advantageous for organizations, but applicants also benefit as it means a person in need of a job may have a better chance of more quickly beginning work. In short, it would seem that updating that LinkedIn profile (and keeping it professional) may be a good first step in obtaining that dream job.

and online. There are companies called "search firms" that specialize in matching people with jobs, but they typically only serve clientele at the higher job levels. The fee charged by the search firm for a successful match might be 50% of the individual's annual salary. The importance of recruiting for organizations varies in direct proportion to the criticality of having talented employees for the organization's success. As stated by Osicki and Kulkarni, "If recruiting strategies don't help identify a sizeable and suitable pool of talent, even the most accurate selection process will be of little or no use" (p. 113).

But as Breaugh (2012) noted, larger applicant pools do not necessarily result in the selection of higher quality personnel. Increasing the number of unqualified applicants in the pool does not enhance the quality of those selected. Increasing the applicant pool with more qualified applicants permits the employer to be extremely selective, with the result being the selected candidates have a high probability of being successful on the job.

How organizations recruit employees can be regarded from one of three conceptual positions. In times of high unemployment, organizations seek new talent the way that miners prospect for gold nuggets. The organizations sift through candidates looking for a proverbial gold nugget, and if found, the nugget is selected. In times of low unemployment, the process works in reverse. Now candidates sift through organizations, looking for their own proverbial gold nugget—the ideal employer. However, these "prospecting" theories of recruiting are extreme positions. More often, recruiting is a middling position more aptly regarded as "mating," where both the organization and the individual try to ascertain whether they are a good match with each other. The mating approach to recruiting is a most reasonable way to understand the process of meeting the needs of both parties.

Just as in any mating process, both parties share information with each other, but with the intent of increasing their perceived attractiveness to each other. Candidates engage in impression management, offering information about themselves they think recruiters want to hear. Candidates try to distinguish themselves from their peers in whatever way they can (Bangerter et al., 2012). For example, candidates who did well academically may also emphasize participating in a range of extra-curricular activities. This is a form of social handicapping; implying to the organization they succeeded academically despite involvement in other activities that took time away from academics. However, the process also works in reverse. In attempts to impress candidates, organizations may accentuate their accomplishments in socially desirable activities as diversity and environmental responsibility (Jones et al., 2014). Griepentrog et al. (2012) stated organizations should manage the image of the company on a continuous basis as a means of attracting potential employees. Sponsoring college events, getting cited as a good place to work, and offering scholarships are indirect means of recruitment. Such activities can make selected organizations "employers of choice" as they "reap the benefits of investing resources to plant the early seeds of attachment" (p. 744).

Despite advances in the more sophisticated electronic-based approaches to recruiting, the old fashioned word-of-mouth source of candidates is still operative. Van Hoye and Lievins (2009) reported that positive information through word-of-mouth channels (i.e., friends, relatives, neighbors) was associated with perceptions of organizational attractiveness and behavioral outcomes (e.g., applying for a job). Onsite visits by candidates to the organization (as opposed to just a telephone contact, for example) signal to the candidates that the organization is serious about them and regards them to be important (Breaugh et al., 2008). The site visit not only provides information for both parties about each other, but also serves to affirm the value each holds for the other. However, as noted by Dineen and Soltis (2011), success in getting candidates interested in joining an organization (the purpose of recruiting) is not the same as actually getting new employees to join the organization (i.e., staffing the organization). Some organizations have a difficult time filling key jobs even in times of high unemployment and the most serious recruiting efforts.

Gilliland and Steiner (2012) noted that candidates form opinions of the fairness of methods used to evaluate them for selection into an organization. Schuler (1993) referred to the quality of a selection process that is acceptable to job candidates as "social validity," an extension of face validity discussed in Chapter 4. Selection methods that produced the highest ratings of fairness had these characteristics: 1) were job-related (seemingly relevant to the work performed in the job); 2) provided candidates with an opportunity to demonstrate their ability to perform the job; and 3) provided prompt feedback on their performance. McCarthy et al. (2013) identified a positive correlation between candidates' performance on a selection test and their opinion of its fairness.

Field Note 1: *The Left-Handed Dentist*

One of the more unusual personnel selection consulting projects I've worked on involved hiring a dentist. A dentist in my town had just experienced an unpleasant breakup with his partner. They disagreed on many major issues surrounding dentistry, including the relative importance of preventive dental maintenance versus treatment, pain management for patients, and so on. Their parting was not amicable. The dentist who remained solicited my help in getting a new partner. He described at great length the characteristics he was looking for in a new partner. Some related to certain dentistry skills, while others dealt with attitudinal or philosophical orientations toward dentistry. I didn't envision any major problems in picking a new partner because the desired characteristics seemed reasonable and I knew dental schools turned out many graduates each year (thus I would have a large applicant pool). Then came a curve ball I neither anticipated nor understood initially. The dentist said to me, "And, of course, my new partner must be left-handed." The dumb look on my face must have told the dentist I didn't quite catch the significance of left-handedness. The dentist

then explained to me something I had never realized despite all the years I have gone to dentists. Dental partners often share instruments in their practice, and there are both left-handed and right-handed dental instruments. The dentist was left-handed himself, so therefore his new partner would also have to be left-handed. I then asked the dentist what proportion of dentists were left-handed. He said he didn't know for sure, but knew it was a small percentage. Suddenly, my task had become much more difficult. It was one thing to find a new dentist who met the specifications for the job and who would like to set up a practice in a small Iowa town. It was another thing to have the size of the potential applicant pool greatly reduced by such a limiting factor as left-handedness. There is a technical term for left-handedness in this case: "bona fide occupational qualification" (BFOQ). For a qualification to be a BFOQ, it must be "reasonably necessary to the operation of that particular business or enterprise." Thus an employer could use left-handedness as a BFOQ in dentistry, but left-handedness would not be a BFOQ in accounting, for example.

Ployhart and Ryan (1998) found that job applicants held negative views of an organization for using what they considered unfair selection procedures, even when the applicants were offered jobs.

No one likes to be rejected, but organizations can provide thoughtful and considerate explanations as to why candidates were not accepted for hire (Truxillo & Bauer, 2011). Applicant reactions to assessment procedures are often vividly personal and highly emotional. Harris (2000) observed that it might be a wiser investment for organizations to explain to rejected candidates why they were denied employment in a way that reduces negative feelings and damage to self-esteem than to gird for potential litigation (see Field Note 1: *The Left-Handed Dentist*).

Personnel Selection

Personnel selection
The process of determining those applicants who are selected for hire versus those who are rejected.

Personnel selection is the process of identifying from the pool of recruited applicants those to whom a job will be offered. As long as there are fewer job openings than applicants, some applicants will be hired and some won't. Selection is the process of separating the selected from the rejected applicants. Ideally, the selected employees will be successful on the job and contribute to the welfare of the organization. Two major factors influence the quality of newly selected employees and the degree to which they can affect the organization: the validity of the predictor and the selection ratio.

Predictor Validity.   Figure 5-5 shows a predictor–criterion correlation of .80, which is reflected in the oval shape of the plot of the predictor and criterion scores. Along the predictor axis is a vertical line—the **predictor cutoff** —that separates accepted from rejected applicants. We can think of the predictor cutoff score as the passing score. People above the cutoff (or cutscore) are accepted for hire; those below it are rejected. Also, observe the three horizontal lines. The solid line, representing the criterion performance of the entire group, cuts the entire distribution of scores in half. The dotted line, representing the criterion performance of the rejected group, is below the performance of the total group. Finally, the dashed line, which is the average criterion performance of the accepted group, is above the performance of the total group. In a simple and straightforward sense, that is what a valid predictor does in personnel selection: it identifies the more capable people from the total pool.

Predictor cutoff
A score on a test that differentiates those who passed the test from those who failed; often equated with the passing score on a test.

A different picture emerges for a predictor that has no correlation with the criterion, as shown in Figure 5-6. Again, the predictor cutoff separates those accepted from

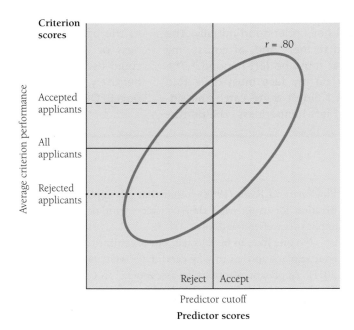

Figure 5-5 *Effect of a predictor with a high validity (r = .80) on test value*

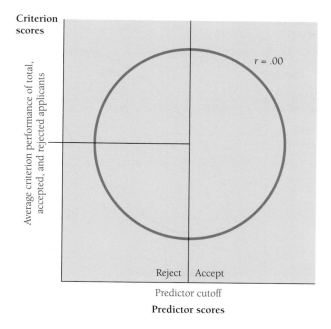

Criterion scores

Average criterion performance of total, accepted, and rejected applicants

$r = .00$

Reject | Accept

Predictor cutoff

Predictor scores

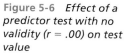

Figure 5-6 *Effect of a predictor test with no validity (r = .00) on test value*

those rejected. This time, however, the three horizontal lines are all superimposed; that is, the criterion performance of the accepted group is no better than that of the rejected group, and both are the same as the performance of the total group. The value of the predictor is measured by the difference between the average performance of the accepted group and the average performance of the total group. As can be seen, these two values are the same, so their difference equals zero. In other words, predictors that have no validity also have no value.

On the basis of this example, we see a direct relationship between a predictor's value and its validity: the greater the validity of the predictor, the greater its value as measured by the increase in average criterion performance for the accepted group over that for the total group.

Selection Ratio.   A second factor that determines the value of a predictor is the selection ratio (SR). The **selection ratio** is defined as the number of job openings (*n*) divided by the number of job applicants (*N*):

$$SR = \frac{n}{N}$$ [Formula 5-1]

Selection ratio
A numeric index ranging between 0 and 1.00 that reflects the selectivity of the hiring organization in filling jobs; the number of job openings divided by the number of job applicants.

When the SR is equal to 1.00 (there are as many openings as there are applicants) or greater (there are more openings than applicants), the use of any selection device has little meaning. The company can use any applicant who walks through the door. But most often, there are more applicants than openings (the SR is somewhere between 0 and 1.00) and the SR is meaningful for personnel selection.

The effect of the SR on a predictor's value can be seen in Figures 5-7 and 5-8. Let us assume we have a validity coefficient of .80 and the selection ratio is .75, meaning

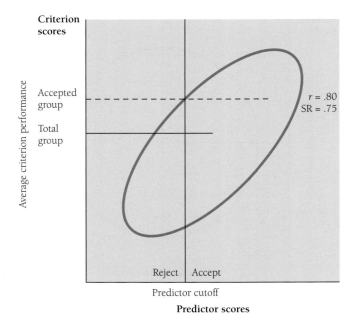

Figure 5-7   *Effect of a large selection ratio (SR = .75) on test value*

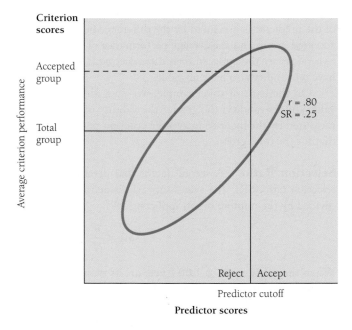

Figure 5-8   *Effect of a small selection ratio (SR = .25) on test value*

we will hire three out of every four applicants. Figure 5-7 shows the predictor–criterion relationship, the predictor cutoff that results in accepting the top 75% of all applicants, and the respective average criterion performances of the total group and the accepted group. If a company hires the top 75%, the average criterion performance of that group is greater than that of the total group (which is weighted down by the bottom 25% of the applicants). Again, value is measured by this difference between average criterion scores. Furthermore, when the bottom 25% is lopped off (the one applicant out of four who is not hired), the average criterion performance of the accepted group is greater than that of the total group.

In Figure 5-8 we have the same validity coefficient ($r = .80$), but this time the SR is .25; that is, out of every four applicants, we will hire only one. The figure shows the location of the predictor cutoff that results in hiring only the top 25% of all applicants and the average criterion performances of the total and accepted groups. The average criterion performance of the accepted group is not only above that of the total group as before, but the difference is also much greater. In other words, when only the top 25% are hired, their average criterion performance is greater than the performance of the top 75% of the applicants, and both of these values are greater than the average performance of the total group.

The relationship between the SR and the predictor's value should be clear: the smaller the SR, the greater the predictor's value. This should also make sense intuitively. The fussier we are in hiring people (that is, the smaller the selection ratio), the more likely it is that the people hired will have the quality we desire. A third factor (albeit of lesser significance) also affects the value of a predictor in improving the quality of the workforce. It is called the **base rate**, defined as the percentage of current employees who are performing their jobs successfully. If a company has a base rate of 99% (that is, 99 out of every 100 employees perform their jobs successfully), it is unlikely that any new selection method can improve upon this already near-ideal condition. If a company has a base rate of 100%, obviously no new selection system can improve upon a totally satisfactory workforce. The only "improvement" that might be attained with a new test is one that takes less time to administer or one that costs less (but still achieves the same degree of predictive accuracy).

Base rate
The percentage of current employees in a job who are judged to be performing their jobs satisfactorily.

Selection Decisions

As long as the predictor used for selection has less than perfect validity ($r = 1.00$), we will always make some errors in personnel selection. The object is, of course, to make as few mistakes as possible. With the aid of the scatterplot, we can examine where the mistakes occur in making selection decisions.

Part (a) of Figure 5-9 shows a predictor–criterion relationship of about .80, where the criterion scores have been separated by a **criterion cutoff**. The criterion cutoff is the point that separates successful (above) from unsuccessful (below) employees. Management decides what constitutes successful and unsuccessful performance. Part (b) shows the same predictor–criterion relationship, except this time the predictor scores have been separated by a predictor cutoff. The predictor cutoff is the point that separates accepted (right) from rejected (left) applicants. The score that constitutes passing the predictor test is determined by the selection ratio, cost factors, or occasionally

Criterion cutoff
A standard that separates successful from unsuccessful job performance.

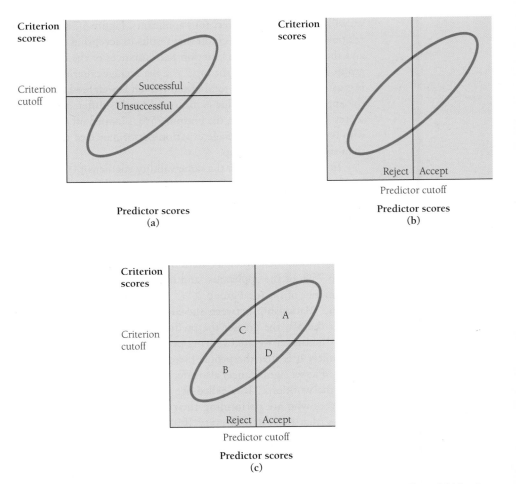

Figure 5-9   *Effect of establishing (a) criterion cutoff, (b) predictor cutoff, and (c) both cutoffs on a predictor–criterion scatterplot*

True positives
A term to describe individuals who were correctly selected for hire because they became successful employees.

True negatives
A term to describe individuals who were correctly rejected for employment as they would have been unsuccessful employees.

law[3]. Part (c) shows the predictor–criterion relationship intersected by both cutoffs. Each of the resulting four sections of the scatterplot is identified by a letter representing a different group of people:

   Section A: Applicants who are above the predictor cutoff and above the criterion cutoff are called **true positives**. These are the people we predict will succeed on the job because they passed the selection test, and who in fact turn out to be successful employees. This group represents a correct decision: we correctly decided to hire them.

   Section B: The people in this group are those we predicted would not succeed on the job because they failed the selection test and who, if hired anyway, would have performed unsatisfactorily. This group represents a correct decision: we correctly predicted they would not succeed on the job. These people are **true negatives**.

---

[3]In some public-sector organizations (for example, state governments), the passing score for a test is determined by law. Usually a passing score is set at 70% correct.

False negatives
A term to describe individuals who were incorrectly rejected for employment as they would have been successful employees.

False positives
A term to describe individuals who were incorrectly accepted for employment as they became unsuccessful employees.

Section C: People who failed the selection test (and are thus predicted not to succeed on the job) but who would have succeeded had they been given the chance are called **false negatives**. We have made a mistake in our decision-making process with these people. They would really turn out to be good employees, but we mistakenly decided they would not succeed. These are "the good ones we let get away."

Section D: The people who passed the selection test (and are thus predicted to succeed on the job) but perform unsatisfactorily after being hired are called **false positives**. We have also erred with these people. They are really ineffective employees who should not have been hired, but we mistakenly thought they would succeed. They are "the bad ones we let in."

Positive/negative refers to the result of passing/failing the selection test; true/false refers to the quality (good/bad) of our decision to hire the candidate. In personnel selection we want to minimize the false positives and false negatives.

If there is no difference between making false positive and false negative decisions (that is, letting a bad worker in is no worse than letting a good one get away), it does no good to "juggle" the predictor cutoff scores. By lowering the predictor cutoff in Figure 5-9 (moving the line to the left), we decrease the size of section C, the false negatives. But by reducing the number of false negatives, we increase the space in section D, the false positives. The converse holds for raising the predictor cutoff (moving the line to the right). Furthermore, classification errors (false positives and false negatives) are also influenced by extreme base rates. For example, when the behavior being predicted occurs very rarely (such as employees who will commit violent acts in the workplace), the differential likelihood of one type of error over the other is great (Martin & Terris, 1991). However, cutoff scores cannot be established solely for the purpose of minimizing false positives or false negatives. For example, if the base rate of employees committing violence in the workplace is 1%, by selecting all candidates we would be correct 99% of the time. When violence occurs in the workplace, we derive no comfort from the fact that "only one" employee out of many was a perpetrator. Cascio et al. (1988) indicated that there must be some rational relationship between the cutoff score and the purpose of the test. Issues pertaining to the cutoff score will be discussed in the next section.

Better personnel decisions are made on the basis of more than one piece of information. Combining two or more predictors often improves the predictability of the criterion. The combined relationship between two or more predictors and the criterion is referred to as a **multiple correlation**, symbolized as R. The only conceptual difference between r and R is that the range of R is from 0 to 1.00, whereas r ranges from -1.00 to 1.00. When R is squared, the resulting R^2 value represents the total amount of variance in the criterion that can be explained by two or more predictors. The increase in predictive accuracy resulting from using two or more predictors results in fewer selection mistakes (i.e., false negatives and false positives). That is why multiple predictors are used in making personnel selection decisions.

Multiple correlation
A statistical index used to indicate the degree of predictability (ranging from 0 to 1.00) in forecasting the criterion on the basis of two or more other variables.

For many years, employers were not indifferent between making false positive and false negative mistakes. Most employers preferred to let a good employee get away (in the belief that someone else who is good could be hired) rather than hire a bad worker. The cost of training, reduced efficiency, turnover, and so on made the false positive highly undesirable. Although most employers still want to avoid false positives, false negatives are also important. The applicant who fails the predictor test and sues the employer on the grounds of using unfair tests can be very expensive. If people do fail an employment test, employers want to be as sure as possible that they were not rejected because of unfair and discriminatory practices. Denying employment to a qualified applicant is unfortunate; denying employment to a qualified minority applicant can be both unfortunate and expensive. An organization can reduce both types of selection errors by increasing the validity of the predictor tests. The greater the validity of the predictors, the smaller the chance that people will be mistakenly classified. Additionally, economic factors can influence the amount of time and money that organizations are willing to invest in making personnel selection decisions (see I/O Psychology and the Economy: *How the Economy Influences Assessment and Selection*).

Personnel Selection from a Human Perspective

Amid all the statistical terms and graphs, it may be tempting to forget that personnel selection is, first and foremost, about people; real people with real lives, who apply for selection into real organizations. The word "personnel" means "people." In an attempt to humanize the statistical approach to personnel selection, consider Figure 5-10.

Figure 5-10 is similar to Figure 5-9, except it will be explained by reference to four individual people. The organization in question is a college. The criterion of successful performance in college is the student's grade point average. The criterion cutoff is 2.00 (a C average) with a maximum of 4.00. The predictor is a standardized test of verbal ability. The college has set the predictor cutoff at a score of 500 on the verbal ability test. Applicants who score 500 and above are admitted, and applicants who score below 500 are rejected. Figure 5-10 shows four data points. These "data points" are people, four high school students among the many who applied for college admission.

Two of the applicants have the same test score, a score of 400. We will call these two students "Pat" and "John," respectively. Because both Pat and John scored below the predictor cutoff of 500, both were denied admission into the college. However, if the college had admitted them anyway, without regard to their test score, two very different outcomes regarding their performance in college would have occurred. John's college grade point average would have been below the criterion cutoff, approximately 1.50. As such, the college would have made the correct decision to reject John for admission, because he would not have earned a sufficiently high grade point average to receive his degree. Using the terminology of personnel selection, John is a true negative. Conversely, Pat, who also scored 400 on the test, would in fact, have succeeded in college. Pat's college grade point average would have been approximately 2.50, well above the criterion cutoff of 2.00 needed to receive a degree. The college made a mistake in rejecting Pat. Pat would be termed a false negative. Why didn't the college "know" that Pat would have been successful in college, while John would have been unsuccessful? It wouldn't, and it couldn't. Based on an inspection of Figure 5-10, it is evident that far more applicants who scored 400 on the test would have been true negatives (the larger area) than false negatives (the smaller area). The college made the best use of the information available to it in attempting to make correct personnel selection decisions on Pat and John. In hindsight, the decision to reject John was correct, but the decision to reject Pat was incorrect.

I/O Psychology and the Economy: *How the Economy Influences Assessment and Selection*

When unemployment is low, high-quality job applicants can be in scarce supply. Jobs are plentiful and applicants can be very selective as to which offer of employment they will accept. Hiring organizations will typically try to impress applicants with why their company is a great place to work. Organizations are under time pressure to identify those applicants to whom they will extend job offers. The degree of attention given by the organization to applicants may be less than thorough. While organizations do not want to be rushed in making selection decisions, they can ill-afford to take a slow and deliberate approach to applicant assessment. A desirable applicant may well choose another employer that has already extended a job offer, rather than continue to wait for an organization to make a decision.

In times of high unemployment, hiring organizations face a different set of circumstances regarding the assessment of applicants. With many people out of work and perhaps even more wanting to get a better job than the one they currently hold, hiring organizations may be overwhelmed with the sheer number of job applicants. A job opening that might attract 20 applicants in times of moderate unemployment might attract 100 applicants in times of high unemployment. How does an organization respond to 100 individuals applying for one position vacancy? The answer is to use the various types of predictor measures in succession (i.e., in stages over time). The organization has the luxury of plenty of time to make its final decision. For example, the 100 applicants might first be screened in terms of their education and work experience, as presented on their resumes. Perhaps only the top 40 applicants advanced to the next round of assessment. The surviving 40 applicants might next be given a brief (e.g., 10-minute) telephone interview. Perhaps only the top 20 applicants proceed to the next stage of assessment, a test of intelligence or personality. Based on the results of that test, the top 10 finalists are each given a more lengthy (e.g., 45-minute) interview. Of those 10, perhaps the organization ranks the top 3 applicants in terms of desirability, and proceeds to make a contingent job offer to the top ranked applicant. The job offer is contingent upon passing yet another assessment, a drug test. If the applicant fails the drug test or declines the offer, the organization then proceeds to its second choice. The process is repeated until the position is filled.

Two major points should be recognized about assessing job applicants in times of high unemployment. First, organizations can elect to use several different types of selection methods in their assessment of applicants. In this example the organization used: (1) an evaluation of education and experience; (2) a brief telephone interview; (3) a psychological test; (4) a lengthy interview; and (5) a drug test. Second, the time it would take to conduct all these assessments is lengthy. The organization is allowed this time because there are so many individuals desirous of obtaining work, and time is not much of an issue. In contrast, during periods of low unemployment the time taken to assess applicants is critically important, and the entire assessment process must be handled most expeditiously. As you might imagine, organizations are more likely to make errors in selection decisions when they are rushed to do so.

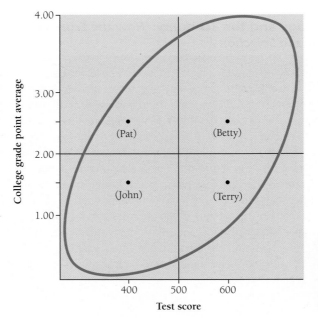

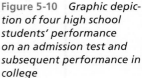

Figure 5-10 *Graphic depiction of four high school students' performance on an admission test and subsequent performance in college*

We now examine two other applicants who scored above the predictor cutoff, and accordingly, both were admitted into the college. Both of these applicants scored 600 on the test. These two "data points" are also people, who we will call "Terry" and "Betty." Despite having identical test scores, two very different outcomes occurred for them in college. Betty's college grade point average of approximately 2.50 was well above the criterion cutoff, and thus she received her degree from the college. As such, Betty would be termed a true positive, and the college made a correct decision to admit her. Terry, however, never earned a college grade point average needed to receive a degree. Terry's college grade point average (approximately 1.50) was below the criterion cutoff. The college made a mistake in admitting Terry. Terry would be termed a false positive. Why didn't the college "know" Betty would be successful and Terry would be unsuccessful? It wouldn't, and it couldn't. The logic for their selection is the same as the logic for Pat and John. More applicants who scored 600 on the test are true positives (the larger area) than false positives (the smaller area).

Four high school students applied to college. The college admitted two and rejected two. Of the two that were admitted, one (Betty) went on to get her degree. Of the two that were rejected, one (Pat) would have graduated if given the chance. The lives of John, Pat, Terry, and Betty were all affected by the high-stakes personnel selection decisions made by the college. Across all applicants, as evidenced in Figure 5-10, the college made more correct decisions (true positives and true negatives) than incorrect decisions (false positives and false negatives). Two of the incorrect decisions (Pat and Terry) were caused by the imperfect validity of the predictor test upon which selection decisions are made. Selection mistakes will always occur when predictor tests have imperfect validity, and no test has perfect validity. Thus personnel selection "errors," "mistakes," or "incorrect decisions" always occur. However, the number of incorrect decisions the college made is exceeded by the number of correct decisions that were made. As the validity of the selection process increases, the number of incorrect decisions is further reduced.

Because every predictor test has imperfect validity, the use of any single selection test will yield imperfect results. However, the validity of a personnel selection process can be increased by using multiple selection tests, with each one contributing to increased predictive accuracy. Just how good are we in predicting the criteria of interest to us? There is no one answer to this question, as it all depends upon the particular criterion in question. Consider Figure 5-11. The circle represents the variance in the criterion we are trying to predict. Assume the criterion is again success in earning a college degree. Five assessments have been found valid in predicting this criterion and are indicated by the shaded area of the circle. Each of the five predictors accounts for a "slice" or portion of the criterion variance. The five predictors are: 1) a standardized test of verbal ability; 2) a standardized test of numeric ability; 3) the student's high school grade point average; 4) a personal statement written by the student; and 5) letters of recommendation submitted on behalf of the student. The degree to which each assessment predicts academic success in college is shown by each of the respective slices of the circle. Assume the combined predictive capability of all five predictors results in a multiple correlation (R) of .70. The squared multiple correlation (R^2) would thus be .49. The unshaded portion of the circle is the amount of criterion variance that cannot be predicted. A question mark has been placed in this unshaded area to indicate it is that portion of the criterion variance that is unknown. The statistical term for the squared multiple correlation is the *coefficient of determination*, so named because it

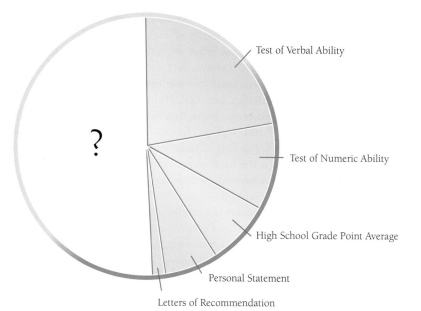

Figure 5-11 *Graphic depiction of the predictability of college grade point average using five assessment methods*

reflects the amount of criterion variance that can be determined from using the predictors. In this case, the coefficient of determination is .49, which can be interpreted as 49% of the criterion variance that can be predicted or explained. The statistical term for that portion of the criterion variance that cannot be predicted or explained is the *coefficient of non-determination*. It is computed by simply subtracting the coefficient of determination from 1.00. In this case,

$$1.00 - .49 = .51$$

which again is interpreted as a percentage, or 51%. We thus can predict 49% of what we want to know, and cannot predict 51% of what we want to know.

People unfamiliar with the science of personnel selection may make statements like, "I could flip a coin and have a 50% chance of making a correct personnel decision." However, a coin, used as a method of personnel selection, has no validity. That is, 0% of the criterion variance is predicted by whether the coin turns up heads or tails. The probability (p) of getting a head or tail on a coin flip must not be confused with the coefficient of determination (R^2). A probability of .50 associated with a coin flip is not indicative of a slightly more accurate personnel selection method than evidenced by a selection method that produces a coefficient of determination of .49. Personnel selection by coin flipping would produce random hiring decisions, the "worst case scenario" in staffing. The reason I/O psychologists have spent over 100 years developing valid personnel selection tests is to improve upon random hiring decisions. The more strongly performance on a selection test is associated with performance on the job, the more correct selection decisions will be made. Flipping coins produces as many incorrect selection decisions as correct ones. The history of personnel selection in I/O psychology has been directed at making more correct selection decisions than incorrect ones. Even with our best tests, incorrect personnel decisions are still made. But their frequency is far less than what would result from random selection.

A literal interpretation of Figure 5-11 is that there is slightly more (51%) that we can't predict than what we can predict (49%) about success in college. What is the reason for the unexplained variance? This has been the subject of debate since psychological assessments were invented over 100 years ago. There is no one reason for the unexplained variance. Human behavior is very complex, and thus difficult to predict. However, we know that success in any life activity is a function of the mix of the "can do" and "will do" factors. In this example the best predictors are ability (verbal and numeric) tests, classic "can do" factors. The absence of highly valid "will do" tests has been the bane of predicting human behavior. "Will do" tests would assess a personality factor such as ambition, and test questions that seek to measure ambition are prone to faking by applicants. The "will do" factor is a major determinant of successful performance; the problem is our limited capacity to measure it and understand it. Thus, some students might have the ability to succeed in college, but they lack the ambition necessary to achieve it. Some students do not earn the needed grade point average to graduate (they "flunk out"), while others lose their ambition for college before graduating (they "drop out"). Success in college can also be a function of a good match between the student's interests and abilities, and having the resources (typically time and money) needed to complete the degree requirements. In short, there are multiple reasons for the unexplained variance in the criterion of academic success in college. In an employment context, the overall level of predictability is often considerably less

($R^2 = .25$ would be more typical) than in an academic context. Van Iddekinge, Putka, and Campbell (2011) found vocational interests to be related to work criteria, contributing an additional 4%-8% in predicted criterion variance beyond cognitive and personality measures. However, like the assessment of personality, the assessment of vocational interests can be faked by job candidates trying to enhance their perceived fit with a job or organization.

We conclude with a final consideration of John, Pat, Terry, and Betty. Betty was admitted to the college and went on to earn her degree. John was denied admission, and would not have graduated even if he had been admitted. Pat would have graduated if given the opportunity. What Pat lacked in the "can do" factors would have been offset by Pat's level of ambition (the "will do" factor). Terry had sufficient ability to earn a college degree, but lacked the needed ambition to succeed. From an organizational perspective, applicants with lower ability are less likely to be selected, despite the organization's awareness that high ambition can overcome lesser ability. As such, organizations give more weight to ability measures than may be warranted, but they have no better way to make personnel selection decisions in a practical and efficient manner.

Validity Generalization

Validity generalization
A concept that reflects the degree to which a predictive relationship empirically established in one context spreads to other populations or contexts.

As noted by Outtz (2011), certain events in history have had an impact on personnel selection and conceptions of validity. The concept of validity generalization was developed shortly after the passage of federal legislation began to alter how I/O psychologists regarded validity evidence in support of personnel selection. The concept of **validity generalization** refers to a predictor's validity spreading or generalizing to other jobs or contexts beyond the one in which it was validated. For example, let us say that a test is found to be valid for hiring secretaries in a company. If that same test is found useful for hiring secretaries in another company, we say its validity has generalized. That same test could also be useful in selecting people for a different job, such as data entry. This is another case of the test's validity generalizing. Murphy (2003) stated, "Validity generalization represents a specialized application of meta-analysis . . . to draw inferences about the meaning of the cumulative body of research in a particular area" (p. 3). Schmitt and Landy (1993) graphically depicted the domains across which validity can generalize, as shown in Figure 5-12. Validity generalization has long been a goal of I/O psychologists because its implication would certainly make our jobs easier. However, the problem is that when we examined whether a test's validity would generalize across either companies or jobs, we often found that it did not; that is, the test's validity was specific to the situation in which it was originally validated. The implication, of course, was that we had to validate every test in every situation in which it was used. We could not assume that its validity would generalize.

Schmidt and Hunter (1978, 1980) supported validity generalization as a means of selecting personnel. They argued that the problem of situational specificity of test validity was based on psychologists' erroneous belief in the "law of small numbers;" the belief that whatever results hold for large samples will also hold for small samples. They thought this belief was incorrect—that small-sample results were highly unstable and gave highly variable test validities. Schmidt and Hunter believed that in most cases psychologists use small samples (40 to 50) to validate tests. Indeed, Salgado (1998)

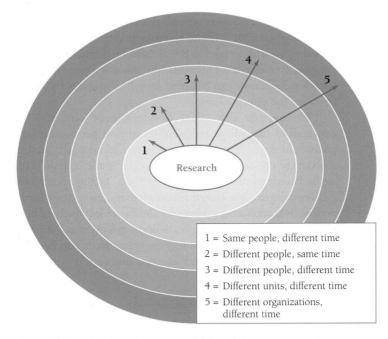

Figure 5-12   *The domains across which validity can generalize*

Source: From *Personnel selection in organizations*, by N. Schmitt and F. J. Landy. Copyright © 1993 John Wiley & Sons, Inc. Reprinted with permission of John Wiley & Sons, Inc.

reported the average sample size in typical criterion-related validity studies is too small to produce stable, generalizable conclusions, resulting in the (erroneous) conclusion that test validity is situation-specific. Schmidt and Hunter argued that if tests were validated in large samples, the results would generalize (not be situation-specific).

Validity generalization means that there is a single "true" relationship between a test and job performance, as for a secretary. Let us say that relationship has a correlation of .40 based on validity studies involving thousands of subjects each. In theory, we could generalize the validity of these findings from huge sample sizes to more typical employment situations with small samples. Organizations with immense sample sizes (such as the military or federal government) would validate certain tests; the rest of the business world would simply "borrow" these validities as a basis for using the tests for hiring. Alternatively, appropriately large samples can be created by pooling results from many smaller studies through meta-analysis.

In support of their position, Schmidt and Hunter (1978) presented data based on a sample of more than 10,000 individuals. The sample was drawn from the army. Data were reported on ten predictors that were used to forecast success in 35 jobs. The results indicated highly similar validity coefficients across different jobs, meaning that differences among jobs did not moderate predictor–criterion relationships. The researchers concluded that the effects of situational moderators disappear with appropriately large sample sizes. One psychological construct that is supposedly common for success in all jobs (and which accounts for validity generalizing or spreading) is general mental ability (g) and, in particular, the dimension of g relating to information processing.

Meta-analyses of the relationship between tests of cognitive ability and job performance have consistently yielded evidence that the validity of intelligence does indeed generalize across a wide variety of occupations. Schmidt and Hunter (1981) stated, "Professionally developed cognitive ability tests are valid predictors of performance on the job and in training for all jobs" (p. 1128). This conclusion increases our reliance on measures of g to forecast job performance. However, as Guion (1998a) observed, the validity generalization conclusion about cognitive ability does not indicate that all cognitive tests are *equally* valid predictors across all jobs, all criteria, or all circumstances. Although cognitive ability does predict job performance across many occupations, it is not comparably predictive in all cases. Even in lower-level jobs, however, cognitive ability still exhibits respectable levels of predictive validity. While I/O psychologists do not believe that a test's validity is unique to every situation, some question whether a test's validity is completely generalizable across different job applicants and organizations (James & McIntyre, 2010).

Muchinsky and Raines (2013) questioned whether validity generalization has been "overgeneralized" in the capacity of g to predict performance in certain occupations. Examples include the performing arts (musicians, singers, actors) and athletics, occupations rarely studied in I/O psychology. The reaction of the legal community to validity generalization has not been positive. Employers who are legally challenged to demonstrate the validity of their selection methods have not found the courts to be receptive to the theory of validity generalization (Biddle, 2008). As such, the legal defensibility of validity generalization is far more tenuous than its degree of scientific support. Hoffman and McPhail (1998) stated, "Sole reliance on validity generalization to support test use is probably premature" (p. 990). Newman et al. (2007) proposed a statistical method whereby the results from both local validation studies and validity generalization could be used to establish the validity of personnel selection systems that satisfy both legal requirements and business objectives. Those authors believe that the local validation study and the validity generalization concept both have something to offer.

Murphy (1997) concluded that the most important message of validity generalization research is that "validation studies based on small samples and unreliable measures are simply a bad idea" (p. 337). Such studies are more likely to mislead us into believing that validity varies greatly across situations. The impact of validity generalization research has been to improve the way researchers design validation studies. When research is designed improperly, the conclusions will most likely be erroneous. Guion (1998a) believes that validity generalization is one of the major methodological advances in personnel selection research in the past 35 years.

The paradoxical verdict on the validity generalization of g is based on the science versus practice of I/O psychology. At a scientific level, validity generalization has received much empirical support. At a practical level, validity generalization has *not* been deemed by the courts as an acceptable method of defending an organization against allegations of using discriminatory personnel selection procedures.

Determination of the Cutoff Score

Have you ever wondered how certain cutoff scores came to be? Why is 70% correct associated with passing a test (such as a driving test)? In educational institutions, why are the cutoffs of 90%, 80%, and 70% usually associated with the grades of A, B, and C, respectively? It has been reported that several thousand years ago a Chinese emperor decreed that 70% correct was needed to successfully pass a test. That 70% correct figure, or a relatively close approximation, has been used throughout history in a wide range of assessment contexts as a standard to guide pass/fail decisions. Although I/O psychologists are primarily limited to assessment decisions in employment contexts, we too have had to wrestle with issues pertaining to where to set the cutoff score and how to interpret differences in test scores (e.g., Strickler, 2000).

Cascio et al. (1988) addressed the legal, psychometric, and professional issues associated with setting cutoff scores. As they reported, there is a wide variation regarding the appropriate standards to use in evaluating the suitability of established cutoff scores. In general, a cutoff score should be set to be reasonable and consistent with the expectations of acceptable job proficiency in the workplace. As Zieky (2001) commented, "There are two types of errors of classification that are made when cutscores are used operationally. If the cutscore is set relatively high, people who deserve to pass will fail. If the cutscore is set relatively low, then people who deserve to fail will pass. It is important to realize that adjusting the cutscore up or down to reduce one type of error will automatically increase the other type of error. Setting a sensible cutscore requires a determination of which error is more harmful" (p. 46). Thus it would be sensible to set a high cutscore for airline pilots and a low cutscore for manual laborers.

There is no such thing as a single, uniform, correct cutoff score. Nor is there a single best method of setting cutoff scores for all situations. Cascio et al. (1988) made several suggestions regarding the setting of cutoff scores. Here are three:

- The process of setting a cutoff score should begin with a work analysis that identifies relative levels of proficiency on critical knowledge, skills, and abilities (KSAs).
- When possible, data on the actual relationship of test scores to criterion measures of job performance should be considered carefully.
- Cutoff scores should be set high enough to ensure that minimum standards of job performance are met.

In summarizing the process of determining a passing score, Ebel (1972) noted: "Anyone who expects to discover the 'real' passing score . . . is doomed to disappointment, for a 'real' passing score does not exist to be discovered. All any examining authority . . . can hope for, and all any of their examinees can ask, is that the basis for defining the passing score be defined clearly, and that the definition be as rational as possible" (p. 496).

Banding

A method of interpreting test scores such that scores of different magnitude in a numeric range or band (e.g., 90–95) are regarded as being equivalent.

Banding is an alternative method to setting cutoff scores (Murphy et al., 1995). The traditional approach to personnel selection is to rank applicants on the basis of their test scores and select the applicants with the highest scores. In test score banding, some differences in test scores are ignored, and individuals whose scores fall within the same band are selected on some basis other than the test score (such as sex or race), thereby eliminating or greatly reducing adverse impact. The width of the band is a function of the reliability of the test. Highly reliable tests produce relatively narrow bands, whereas less reliable tests produce wider test score bands. Thus a one point difference in test scores (e.g., a score of 90 vs. 89) is not judged to be of sufficient magnitude to reflect a meaningful difference in the applicants' respective abilities. One then extends this logic to a two-point difference in test scores, a three-point difference, and so on. Eventually, a certain magnitude of difference in test scores is determined to reflect a meaningful difference in ability. It is at this point where this band ends, and other bands may be formed from the distribution of test scores.

Arnold (2001) reported that one recent court ruling accepted the use of banding of test scores in employment selection, stating it is the equivalent of assigning letter grades in college. The court said, "Banding is best legitimized from the perspective that it aids in the interpretation of test data and is appropriate from a scientific and/or common sense perspective" (p. 153). The court decision also underscores the point raised by Ebel that there is no one professionally agreed upon method to determine passing scores on tests. Furthermore, sometimes selection decisions are made for reasons that have little to do with passing scores (see Field Note 2: *Dirty Politics*).

Test Utility and Organizational Efficiency

Utility
A concept reflecting the economic value (expressed in monetary terms) of making personnel decisions.

Many resources contribute to the success of an organization; employees are just one of them. Each resource must contribute to the organization's overall success. A basic question is how much the improved personnel selection techniques contribute to the overall profitability or efficiency. The **utility** of a test is literally its value—where "value" is measured in monetary or economic terms. Several studies have shown just how much utility a valid testing program can provide.

For example, Cascio and Fogli (2010) described a study of bank tellers that compared the job performance of tellers who scored at the 80th percentile on a selection test verses those who scored at the 20th percentile. Those tellers that scored at the 80th percentile on average served 1,791 customers per month, while those who scored at the 20th percentile served 945 customers per month. Quite clearly, better job performance follows from better test performance. However, measuring gains in job performance through the use of valid employment tests is not the same as measuring the monetary value that accrues to the organization from greater job performance. In the case of the bank tellers, the question is how much value does the bank accrue from having the tellers serve 846 (1,791 - 945) more customers per month?

I/O psychologists have long struggled with finding ways to demonstrate to organizational leaders the utility of hiring high quality workers (as identified through testing) in a manner that is understandable and credible (Winkler et al., 2010). Complex statistical analyses have estimated the utility of using valid selection methods to identify high-performing employees. The benefits can be millions of dollars per year, depending upon the number of employees hired and the value of the job to the organization. However, we have more confidence in estimating the utility gains for certain types of jobs than others. For example, we have more confidence in estimating the utility of hiring good production workers in a factory than good counselors in a social services agency (Yoo & Muchinsky, 1998). Furthermore, many business leaders find it difficult to accept and understand the results from complex statistical analyses. In short, I/O psychologists have had more success in demonstrating the gains in job performance from using valid selection methods than in translating gains in job performance into credible monetary indices.

Benchmarking
The process of comparing a company's products or procedures with those of the leading companies in an industry.

One method that is highly accepted among managers in getting organizations to adopt testing procedures is called benchmarking. **Benchmarking** is the process of comparing leading organizations in terms of their professional practices. Jayne and

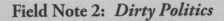

Field Note 2: *Dirty Politics*

This chapter is devoted to explaining how personnel decisions are made. Many factors have been identified and explained, but one has been left out. I've rarely seen it discussed in any book or article on personnel selection, but (unfortunately) it is sometimes a critical, if not deciding, factor. It is called politics. Consider this experience I had. I was hired for a very important consulting project: to pick the chief of police for a large city. The job has tremendous visibility, high influence, and great responsibility. I didn't want to "blow it" as the consultant. The city recruited applicants for the opening, and a total of 50 applicants met the minimum qualifications for consideration set by the city. I was handed the 50 applications and told to identify the best candidates in the applicant pool. My first step was to evaluate each candidate in terms of education and experience using a weighted application-blank procedure. That got the applicant pool down to 25. These 25 quarter-finalists then had to submit written answers to three essay test questions about how they would handle some difficult police problems. These answers were evaluated, and the 15 best applicants proceeded to the semi-finalist stage. Here the candidates took a series of personality inventories and intelligence tests. Based on those results, 10 finalists were selected and in turn were subjected to a lengthy oral interview. From all the assessment results, I rank ordered the 10 finalists and submitted the list to the city council, which had the judicial authority to approve the new chief of police. The candidate ranked first was from a different state; the candidate ranked second was the current assistant chief of police, the second in command.

The candidate ranked first was clearly the best person for the job, far and away better than anyone else. I thought the city council (composed of seven people) had an easy job: to approve the top candidate as the new chief of police. It is here that politics came in, and it got rather dirty. The assistant chief of police was a close friend of three city council members. They played cards together, as did their wives. From the very beginning, the three city council members had known the assistant chief of police would rank high in the selection process. In fact, nearly everyone had thought he would be the next chief of police. When I presented the city council with my list of the 10 candidates, things got very awkward: "Their man" was not first on the list. The press followed the selection process carefully because it was a hot news item. The media announced the rank order of the 10 finalists. The public's general reaction was to have the city council approve the candidate who had been ranked first. But the head of the city council was not about to sell out his old friend.

The head of the city council (one of the three friends) then made this startling announcement. Because every rookie cop on the force dreams about one day rising to be the chief, to award the chief's job to an "outsider" (that is, a candidate not native to the city) would destroy the morale of the police force and take away every rookie's dream forever. Therefore he was going to advise the city council to select as the next chief of police not the person ranked first (the outsider) but the person ranked second (the assistant chief, and his friend). This was the first time anyone had made any reference at all to the insider/outside distinction. It was a

Field Note 2: *Dirty Politics* (continued)

new hurdle imposed at the eleventh hour as a means of bumping the top-ranked candidate from the list. Some members of the community howled in protest at this announcement, as did the media, declaring it was a "fix" to install the council's personal choice. All the three city council members had to do was convince a fourth member to vote for the second-ranked person and he would be in. In a highly electrified meeting of the city council in a council chamber jam-packed with reporters and camera crews, the city council members publicly cast their votes. By a 4–3 vote, the number one ranked candidate (the outsider) was approved and became the new chief of police.

I would like to believe the four "yes" votes came from people who recognized the quality of the top candidate, but I know better. Politics being what it is, strange things can happen. They voted the way they did not simply because they supported the stronger candidate but because they wanted to even a score with the three council members against whom they had held a grudge from a previous political episode. In short, the right decision was made, but for the wrong reason.

I wish to emphasize that there was absolutely nothing in my graduate training to prepare me for this experience. The topic of "organizational politics" is discussed in Chapter 10. Politics is a driving force in all organizations at all levels. Given this fact, sometimes I wonder how I/O psychologists accomplish as much as they do.

Rauschenberger (2000) stated, "Executives are fascinated with comparing practices of their own firms with those of others. They provide decision makers with specific real-world examples that a proposed intervention works" (p. 140). In short, business leaders are often skeptical of the ability to assess the exact dollar value of using selection tests. However, if other leading companies in an industry are using tests, it becomes prudent to follow their practices.

Placement and Classification

The vast majority of research in I/O psychology is on selection, the process by which applicants are hired. Another personnel function (albeit less common) involves deciding which jobs people should be assigned to *after* they have been hired. This personnel function is called either placement or classification, depending on the basis for the assignment. In many cases selection and placement are not separate procedures. Usually people apply for particular jobs. If they are hired, they fill the jobs they were applying for. In some organizations (and at certain times in our nation's history), however, decisions about selection and placement have to be made separately.

Placement differs from classification on the basis of the number of predictors used to make the job assignment. **Placement** is allocating people to two or more groups (or jobs) on the basis of a single predictor score. Many middle school students are

Placement
The process of assigning individuals to jobs based on one test score.

Classification
The process of assigning individuals to jobs based on two or more test scores.

placed into math classes on the basis of a math aptitude test. **Classification** is allocating people to jobs on the basis of two or more valid predictor factors. For this reason, classification is more complex; however, it results in a better assignment of people to jobs than placement. Classification uses smaller selection ratios than placement, which accounts for its greater utility. The reason classification is not always used instead of placement is that it is often difficult to find two or more valid predictors to use in assigning people to jobs. The military has been the object of most classification research. Military recruits take a battery of different tests (including the ASVAB) covering such areas as intelligence, ability, and aptitude. On the basis of these scores, recruits are assigned to jobs in the infantry, medical corps, military intelligence, and so on. Other organizations that have to assign large numbers of employees to large numbers of jobs also use this procedure. Given this constraint, relatively few companies need to use classification procedures.

The problems and issues associated with staffing the military are even more complex than in the civilian sector. The U.S. military has to compete with other employers for talent. As reported by De Angelis and Segal (2012), staffing the military is guided not only by the need for meeting job requirements and diversity representation (by race and sex), but also with consideration of the candidates' vocational interests. The military currently has 1.4 million active duty and 800,000 reserve personnel; 20% are racial minorities and 15% are female. Given the volume of candidates assessed annually and the growing complexity of technical advances in weaponry, the military is highly dependent on sophisticated classification methods to meet its staffing needs (Rumsey, 2012). Furthermore, unlike the civilian sector of employment, the military does not hire people from outside the military (e.g., the civilian workforce) to fill middle or higher-level jobs. Jobs in the military must be filled by current military personnel, adding greatly to the critical need of assigning people to jobs for which they are highly suited.

Chapter Summary

- Personnel decisions are decisions made in organizations that affect people's work lives, such as selection, placement, and classification.
- All business organizations must make personnel decisions about their employees. Some organizations use less formal and scientifically-based methods than others.
- In the United States (and in most countries) personnel decisions are made within a strong legal context. Many laws protect the rights of individuals as employees.
- Affirmative action is a social policy designed to achieve a diverse and productive workforce. There is much controversy and social debate about the merits of affirmative action.
- Recruitment is the process by which individuals are encouraged to apply for work. The individuals selected for employment can be drawn only from those who have been recruited.
- Organizational strategy has a major influence on how human resources are managed.
- Validity generalization is the principle that the predictive capacity of a test generalizes or is applicable to a wide range of job applicants and employment contexts.

- Because our tests do not have perfect validity, errors or mistakes in hiring occur. We can falsely hire a poor employee or falsely reject someone who would have been a good employee. True positives and negatives and false positives and negatives are useful concepts to consider in selection decisions.
- It has been demonstrated that using valid personnel selection methods leads to large productivity gains for the hiring organization.
- Placement and classification decisions refer to assigning workers to those jobs for which they are best suited.

Chapter Outline

Learning Objectives

- Explain the relationship between learning and task performance.
- Describe the steps to assess training needs within an organization.
- Know the major methods of computer-based and non–computer-based training and their associated strengths and weaknesses.
- Identify approaches and benefits of active learning approaches.
- Describe the importance of diversity training, expatriate training, and sexual harassment training in the workplace.
- Describe the role of mentoring and executive coaching in management development.
- Explain how knowledge and skills from training are transferred back to the job.
- Explain the evaluation of training and development programs.

s we have discussed throughout this book, the work world is changing rapidly. The economic and social pressures brought to bear on organizations affect the conduct of work and make it necessary for employees to serve larger strategic business needs. A generation ago employees were hired primarily to fill jobs that had specified KSAOs and tasks to be performed. Emphasis was placed on selection, finding the "round peg (the person) for the round hole (the job)." Metaphorically speaking, today the shape of the hole is continuously changing, thereby weakening the meaning of a "job." One implication of this changing nature of work is that greater relative importance is placed on skill *enhancement*. Organizations need to hire intelligent workers who are willing to learn new skills, skills determined by external demands. For example, the skills may require increased technological sophistication, a greater emphasis on teamwork, the ability to deal with a diverse customer base, or any other issue related to the success of the organization. Simply put, organizations (and their employees) must continually learn new skills to adapt to a rapidly changing business world.

The title of this chapter is "Organizational Learning," which encompasses issues associated with the **training** and **development** of the workforce. Roughly speaking, training and development are both aimed at enhancing the KSAOs of employees, and differ only in their immediacy of use. That is, training is targeted at enhancing KSAOs needed for an immediate job or role whereas development refers to enhancing KSAOs for which there may not be an immediate purpose. Furthermore, there is an important difference between learning through formalized organization-based training and informal or unintentional learning. Informal or unintentional learning is the knowledge we acquire and use to better our lives simply by paying attention to our environment and adapting to it. Informal learning is described as self-guided and learner-directed (i.e., we desire to learn and choose to do so). Tannenbaum et al. (2010) estimated that formal training contributes only about 10% to our learning within organizations. The remainder of our learning is achieved informally. In a world where it has become vital for organizations to continuously learn and develop, the responsibility falls far more on the capacity and willingness of individuals to do so. As important and valuable as formal training programs may be, they are limited in their power to effectuate the developmental growth needed in the contemporary work world.

The importance of organizational learning is escalating at a dizzying pace. The job title of the person in the organization responsible for these activities is evolving from "Director of Training and Development" to "Chief Learning Officer" (Danielson & Wiggenhorn, 2003). Thus "learning" has ascended to the same level previously reserved for finance (Chief Financial Officer) and operations (Chief Operating Officer). Danielson and Wiggenhorn offered the following assessment of the importance of organizational learning:

> Today's progressive corporations have moved from treating learning as an obligatory cost factor to regarding it as a weapon in the battle for competitive advantage . . . The escalating level of investment corporations have made in learning, and the accompanying expectations of the investment's enhancing firm performance, have combined to create greater urgency in the search for models or tools for evaluating and improving transfer of learning. (p. 17)

In Chapter 1 we noted that the current era in the history of I/O psychology is called the Information Age, and is characterized by a transition to a knowledge-based

Training
The process through which the knowledge and skills of employees are enhanced for an immediate job or role.

Development
The process through which the knowledge and skills of employees are enhanced but for which there is no immediate use.

economy. We are awash in a sea of information in our lives, and how we convert this information to usable knowledge is the basis of our modern economy. Tannenbaum (2002) stated, "An increasing percentage of people in the workforce can be thought of as knowledge workers—they work with information and ideas or solve problems and carry out creative tasks" (p. 15). The U.S. Department of Labor estimated that today on average 50% of an employee's knowledge and skills become outdated every 30–60 *months*, compared with an estimated 12–15 *years* in the 1970s. Although not all work is changing as rapidly as work that is information-intensive, we have reached a point where the skills we bring to a job are dwarfed in comparison to the new skills we must acquire as part of "learning a living." Molloy and Noe (2010) portrayed the pre-Internet era as one where a career was chosen early in one's life by learning the knowledge required to gain admission into that career. In the post-Internet knowledge-based world, learning must occur continuously because individuals will likely have multiple careers over their years in the workforce. As stated by Molloy and Noe, "There is not a topic more critical to the study of successful careers than the issue of how people reinvent and redefine themselves, in ways that bring them psychological success" (p. 355).

Learning and Task Performance

Learning
The process by which change in knowledge or skills is acquired through education or experience.

Learning can be defined as the process of encoding, retaining, and using information. This view of learning prompted Howell and Cooke (1989) to refer to individuals as "human information processors." The specific procedures by which we process information for both short-term and long-term use has been the subject of extensive research in cognitive psychology (Weiss, 1990). This section will examine some useful findings from this body of research that facilitate our understanding of how learning affects the training and development process.

Declarative knowledge
A body of knowledge about facts and things.

Anderson (1985) suggested that skill acquisition be segmented into three phases: declarative knowledge, knowledge compilation, and procedural knowledge. **Declarative knowledge** is knowledge about facts and things. The declarative knowledge of skill acquisition involves memorizing and reasoning processes that allow the individual to attain a basic understanding of a task. During this phase the individual may observe demonstrations of the task and learn task-sequencing rules. Individuals must devote nearly all of their attention to understanding and performing the task. Performance in the declarative knowledge stage is slow and prone to error. Only after the person has acquired an adequate understanding of the task can he or she proceed to the second phase, the **knowledge compilation** phase.

Knowledge compilation
The body of knowledge acquired as a result of learning.

Procedural knowledge
A body of knowledge about how to use information to address issues and solve problems.

During this second stage of skill acquisition, individuals integrate the sequences of cognitive and motor processes required to perform the task. Various methods for simplifying or streamlining the task are tried and evaluated. Performance then becomes faster and more accurate than in the declarative knowledge phase. The attentional demands on the individual are reduced as the task objectives and procedures are moved from short-term to long-term memory.

Procedural knowledge is knowledge about how to perform various cognitive activities. This final phase of skill acquisition is reached when the individual has essentially automatized the skill and can perform the task efficiently with little attention (Kanfer & Ackerman, 1989). After considerable practice, the person can do the task with minimal impairment while devoting attention to other tasks. DuBois (2002) reported this procedural knowledge becomes second nature to expert performers, so that they report difficulty in describing what they know that others do not know.

Ackerman (1987) proposed that three major classes of abilities are critically important for performance in the three phases of skill acquisition. *General mental ability* (*g*) is posited to be the most important factor in acquiring declarative knowledge. When the individual first confronts a novel task, the attentional demands are high. As he or she begins to understand the demands of the task and develops a performance strategy, the attentional demands decrease and the importance of intellectual ability for task performance is lessened.

As the individual moves along the skill acquisition curve from declarative to procedural knowledge, *perceptual speed abilities* become important. The individual develops a basic understanding of how to perform the task but seeks a more efficient method for accomplishing the task with minimal attentional effort. Perceptual speed abilities seem most critical for processing information faster or more efficiently at this phase.

Finally, as individuals move to the final phase of skill acquisition, their performance is limited by their level of *psychomotor ability*. "Thus individual differences in final, skilled performance are not necessarily determined by the same abilities that affect the initial level of task performance or the speed of skill acquisition" (Kanfer & Ackerman, 1989, p. 664). Farrell and McDaniel (2001) found empirical support for this model of skill acquisition when examined in an applied setting. Therefore psychomotor abilities (such as coordination) determine the final level of task performance in the procedural knowledge phase.

It should be evident based on these research findings from cognitive psychology that there are complex relationships between individual abilities and phases of task performance. These findings offer an explanation of why some individuals may be quick to acquire minimal competency in a task but do not subsequently develop a high degree of task proficiency. Alternatively, other individuals may initially learn a task slowly but gradually develop a high level of task proficiency. These findings bear not only on why certain individuals learn at different rates of speed but also on how training and development processes have to be targeted to enhance selected individual abilities.

Several major studies have been conducted that reveal the process by which learning occurs and transfers to the job. Ford and Kraiger (1995) identified three distinguishing characteristics of people who are regarded as experts on a topic versus novices. The first is proceduralization and automaticity. *Proceduralization* refers to a set of conditional action rules: if Condition A exists, then Action B is needed. *Automaticity* refers to a state of rapid performance that requires little cognitive effort. Automaticity enables a person to accomplish a task without conscious monitoring and thus allows concurrent performance of additional tasks. Experts not only "know" things but also know when that knowledge is applicable and when it should not be used. Novices may be equally competent at recalling specific information, but experts are much better at relating that information in cause-and-effect sequences. The second characteristic is *mental models*, which is the way knowledge is organized. The mental models of experts are qualitatively better because they contain more diagnostic cues for detecting meaningful patterns in learning. Experts have more complex knowledge structures, resulting in faster solution times. The third characteristic is *meta-cognition*. Meta-cognition is an individual's knowledge of and control over his or her cognitions. Experts have a greater understanding of the demands of a task and their own capabilities. They are more likely to discontinue a problem-solving strategy that would ultimately prove to be unsuccessful.

According to Salas et al. (2012), "expertise is a product of deliberate practice over a prolonged period of time" (p. 356). One way of getting employees the knowledge and skills they need to gain expertise is through training programs and development opportunities within the workplace. The remainder of this chapter is related to these opportunities.

Assessing Training Needs

Training needs assessment
A systematic process of identifying and specifying training requirements. Consists of organizational, task, and person analyses.

Organizational analysis
Part of the training needs assessment in which the organization's strategic objectives and the availability of resources and support are identified.

Task analysis
Part of the training needs assessment in which the tasks that require training are identified.

Person analysis
Part of the training needs assessment in which the people who need training are identified.

It is important to understand what deficiencies exist in individual, team, and organizational performance prior to developing a training program. According to Surface (2012), a **training needs assessment** is a systematic process that helps identify and specify training requirements to determine specific learning objectives and to ascertain what training methods and techniques will be the most appropriate for reducing or eliminating any performance deficiencies. In short, a training needs assessment helps figure out whether, and to what extent, training is needed.

There are three stages to a training needs assessment. The first stage consists of **organizational analysis**. The goal in this stage is to identify the organization's primary strategic objectives and determine whether there are resources available to develop and conduct training and if management and employees will support its implementation. According to Salas et al. (2012), many training efforts fail due to barriers and constraints. An organizational analysis helps identify those barriers and amend them prior to training. Without proper resources for a training program, for example, there is little reason to expect it will be successful. On the other hand, organizations that demonstrate a willingness to invest in training programs can reap great rewards, both within and outside of the training programs. For example, Sung and Choi (2014) found that organizations that invested in internal training programs had significant increases in organizational innovation over the following two years.

The second stage is **task analysis**. The goal in this stage is to identify whether some tasks are consistently performed poorly and/or whether there are deficient KSAOs across the workforce. According to Arthur et al. (2003), task analysis identifies what individuals must know to perform their job effectively. In line with this, Salas et al. (2012) note that task analysis is used to develop clear and comprehensive training objectives. Information from a work analysis (as discussed in Chapter 3) is highly relevant here. The tasks and KSAOs identified from the work analysis help determine training objectives, particularly when there is evidence that performance is subpar. Such evidence can come from performance appraisals that indicate substandard performance or specific workplace incidents suggesting the need for training (such as accidents or noncompliance citations from external auditors). For example, receiving a low grade from a health inspector may suggest the need for training on the policies and procedures for the restaurant staff.

The final stage is **person analysis**, which has the goal of identifying which workers should be trained. As Salas et al. (2012) summarize, "person analysis ensures that the right people receive the right training" (p. 340). It may be the case that not all employees are performing poorly or have deficient KSAOs. In addition, not all training will be beneficial to all people within an organization. For example, a task analysis may reveal that the workforce is deficient in terms of its selling skills. However, not all employees need to be skilled at making sales. Thus, this stage seeks to identify which workers should be trained rather than wasting resources by including people in training that have no need for it.

According to Kraiger and Culbertson (2013), person analysis also seeks to identify "characteristics of learners that can shape the design and delivery of training (e.g., trainee aptitude or trainee motivation)" (p. 245). As Surface noted, not all performance deficiencies can be addressed through learning. Indeed, employees may know what they are supposed to do but lack the ability or motivation to do it—or do it properly. A training program on dunking a basketball would be a complete waste of time and money for the authors of this textbook, for example, as we readily admit our physical limitations in this regard.

Despite the advantages for conducting training needs assessments in terms of facilitating trainee motivation and ensuring efficient use of resources, it appears that in practice few training needs assessments are conducted prior to the design and delivery of training programs. Surface noted that sometimes it is obvious what the training requirements are, in which case needs assessments may be abbreviated or foregone entirely. Another reason that training may be done without a needs assessment is when the training is done to meet a legal or certification requirement. For example, the Equal Employment Opportunity Commission (EEOC) has noted that the best tactic for eliminating sexual harassment in the workplace is through prevention, and has advised organizations to clearly communicate that such harassment will not be tolerated. They further note that providing sexual harassment training (to be described later in this chapter) is one way of doing this. As such, many organizations require all employees to complete sexual harassment training regardless of their current understanding of the law or motivation to learn about such things.

Methods and Techniques of Training

Kraiger (2008) reported as theories of learning evolved over time, so did training methods proposed by I/O psychologists. Training methods used in the past tended to assume there was a certain amount or type of knowledge that employees needed to perform their jobs. The question became how best to impart that knowledge to the employee. Upon sufficient acquisition of this knowledge, the employee was deemed sufficiently qualified to perform the job. However, a contemporary view of learning is that it is not simply a case of knowledge acquisition (as achieved through having taken a course or attended a workshop). In most jobs there are multiple behavioral styles that can lead to successful job performance. In short, there is often more than one way to perform a job. According to Kraiger, what matters is whether the performance objectives of the job are fulfilled, with less emphasis placed on how the objectives were fulfilled. In this conception of learning, the role of training should be to encourage learning the various ways the performance objectives can be obtained.

In the Information Age knowledge needed to perform a job is not static. As stated by Kraiger, "the distinction between learning and job performance is becoming increasingly blurred" (p. 462). Salisbury (2009) echoed this perspective by describing the modern work world as one requiring "continuous immersion" in learning new information.

A wide array of training methods exist, including some that will not be described here. They differ in the breadth of skills they seek to enhance. As we will describe below, for example, some methods (such as behavioral modeling) have a narrow focus whereas others (such as business games) have a broader focus. The methods also differ in the types of skills they seek to enhance. Some (such as role playing) are designed primarily to enhance social interpersonal skills, whereas others (such as intelligent tutoring systems) tend to enhance cognitive skills. The biggest trend in training methods is the shift toward computer-based training, which we will first describe. We will then provide an overview of various non-computer-based training methods.

Computer-Based Training

Just as computers and the Internet have altered how work is performed, so too have they offered revolutionary ways of enhancing organizational learning. The power of modern communication technology is so great it is inducing psychologists to advance new theories of how learning occurs, as well as how knowledge influences behavior. The new approach to learning has been referenced as *e-learning* (Clark & Mayer, 2008). There is nothing particularly instructive about the computer, per se, as a medium for learning that makes it superior to reading a book. For example, the educational value of a book is not enhanced simply because it can be read on a computer screen. The conversion from paper to pixels does not enhance learning. Rather, what makes the computer such a powerful medium is its capacity to facilitate learning in ways that other media (such as a book) cannot do.

Computer-based training
A method of training that utilizes computer technology to enhance the acquisition of knowledge and skills.

According to Kraiger (2008) **computer-based training** is well-suited for the view that training should encourage learning the various ways that performance objectives can be obtained. Learning can occur through multiple channels, as audio and visual conferencing, threaded discussions, chat rooms, and file sharing. The versatility of web-based training is congruent with the versatility in behavioral styles that are exhibited in successful job performance. Instead of learning the "one way" to perform a job, computer-based learning can help individuals discover "which way" works best for them. Computer-based training is highly interactive, and the learner becomes an active contributor to what is learned.

Blanchard and Thacker (2004) presented a comprehensive description of various computer-based training methods. The social acceptance and adoption of electronic technology and computer networks witnessed since the birth of the Internet in the early 1990s created this general class of training methods.

Programmed instruction
The most basic computer-based training that provides for self-paced learning.

Programmed Instruction.   **Programmed instruction** is regarded as the basis from which all other computer-based training methods have been derived. It was developed as a manual training system long before the advent of the computer. It is a method of self-paced learning managed by both the trainee and the computer system. The basic framework of programmed instruction is as follows: information is presented to the trainee, a question is posed regarding the information, and depending on the trainee's response to the question, the program proceeds to the next question. If the trainee provides a correct answer, the trainee moves on to new information. If the answer is incorrect, the trainee is taken back to review the relevant information. This format allows trainees to move through the material at their own pace. Trainees who answer more questions correctly move rapidly through the material. Van Buren (2001) estimated that 80% of leading companies use programmed instruction in some form. In a study within an educational setting, Stanisavljevic and Djuric (2013) found that individuals presented information through programmed instruction learned more and demonstrated a higher quality of learning than individuals provided the same course content through lecturing. Martin et al. (2014) noted that programmed instruction "is flexible and allows for repeated practice, its consistent delivery means that the learning experience is standardized, and it also has the ability to offer multisensory features (color, sound, text, animation, graphics, and special effects)" (p. 27). Despite these advantages, however, they also note that it can cause frustration and lower motivation for people who aren't comfortable with technology and that it requires greater self-discipline than some other methods, as people may be able to easily cheat or skip parts of the training without others knowing.

Intelligent tutoring systems
A sophisticated type of computer-based training that uses artificial intelligence to customize learning to the individual.

Intelligent Tutoring Systems. Intelligent tutoring systems are more sophisticated than programmed instruction and use the concept of artificial intelligence to guide the instructional process. Based on the trainee's responses to questions posed, the system continuously modifies the level of instruction presented to the trainee. An intelligent tutoring system involves several components. The domain expertise is the set of knowledge to be learned. According to Blanchard and Thacker (2004), "The trainee model stores information about how the trainee is performing during training. As the trainee responds to items, the information is used to tutor the trainee. The training session manager is the component that interprets the trainee's responses and responds with either more information, helping the trainee further explore the topic, or guiding the trainee toward the correct answer" (pp. 246–247). Intelligent tutoring systems are also capable of varying the order and difficulty of the questions presented. The method differentiates itself from programmed instruction by its level of sophistication in tailoring the learning process to the pattern of trainee responses. According to Salas and Kozlowski (2010), intelligent tutoring systems "can provide organizations with powerful tools to deliver training in a robust, effective, and efficient way" (p. 473).

Interactive multimedia training
A type of computer-based training that combines visual and auditory information to create a realistic but non-threatening environment.

Interactive Multimedia Training. Interactive multimedia training is a more technologically sophisticated system than intelligent tutoring. As the term *multimedia* suggests, the training combines text, photos, graphics, videos, animation, and sound to achieve a rich simulation of a real-life situation. Cannon-Bowers and Bowers (2010) referred to interactive and virtual training methods as "synthetic learning environments." The method is "interactive" in that it allows the trainee to make decisions and then receive immediate feedback on the quality of the decisions. Interactive multimedia training provides an opportunity to learn skills in a nonthreatening environment, where the consequences of errors are not as serious as in a real-life setting. Blanchard and Thacker (2004) described an application of multimedia training in teaching medical students:

Active Learning Approaches

Learning can be approached passively or actively. According to Kraiger and Culbertson (2013), training programs that take an active learning approach "are those that facilitate knowledge acquisition by encouraging trainees to ask questions, explore, seek feedback, and reflect on potential results, thus emphasizing the trainee's role in his or her own development" (p. 250). Bell and Kozlowski (2010) note that active learning approaches differ from more traditional, passive approaches (such as lectures or videos) in two key ways. First, active approaches put the trainees in control of their own learning, whereas passive approaches make the trainees a mere recipient of information. With active approaches, individuals must take more responsibility for their learning, making such decisions as where to focus their attention, how to monitor their progress, and how to judge the effectiveness of their efforts. The second distinction between active and passive learning approaches is that active approaches are based on the assumption that learning occurs inductively, when individuals are able to manipulate their environment and arrive at conclusions on their own. Passive approaches, on the other hand, are based on the assumption that learning is deductive in nature, and that individuals obtain knowledge by having it provided to them by some external agent (such as a trainer or computer program). As Bell and Kozlowski note, with active learning approaches, "individuals explore and experiment with a task to infer the rules, principles, and strategies for effective performance" (p. 266). By actively engaging in the material, it is presumed that individuals will have a richer understanding of the important concepts and be able to more readily transfer them to the workplace, even to situations that they didn't encounter during training. Two specific active learning approaches will be discussed: error-management training and self-regulatory training.

Error-Management Training

One of life's great truths is that we learn from experience. In particular, making mistakes, and learning from those mistakes, is a very powerful form of learning. Yet there is a seeming paradox to making errors: while we learn from them, we are often punished for committing them. In school, low grades are assigned to students who make errors. In the workplace, employees can be disciplined, even fired, for making an error. As such, we learn to avoid making errors to prevent being punished. However, from a psychological perspective, errors enhance learning and could be a strategic component of training. This principle has led to **error-management training**, a concept where participants are explicitly encouraged to make errors and learn from them. Ellis et al. (2006) stated that people can learn from their mistakes and perform better in the future provided there is a careful review and explanation of what specific actions of the individual led to the mistake. Creating an organizational culture that does not take a punitive approach to errors was proposed by van Dyck et al. (2005). The authors believe that two factors are critical to this organizational culture: open communication about errors; and early detection and recovery from errors.

Error-management training has the potential to be a very useful approach to learning. However, two issues must be squarely addressed in its consideration. First, it represents an inversion of conventional thinking about what contributes to our perception of a top performer within a company. Instead of employees who are highly

Error-management training
A system of training in which employees are encouraged to make errors, and then learn from their mistakes.

FRANK & ERNEST: © Thaves / Dist. by United Feature syndicate, Inc.

regarded because "they rarely (if ever) make a mistake," the emphasis would switch to employees who "do make mistakes, and they have learned from their errors." The second issue is the practical reality that whatever mistakes are made must not inflict harm to the organization. As such, the "best" mistakes would be those that produce few or no negative consequences to the organization. Their learning value to the individual is high, they are generalizable across other situations, and they are acceptable to all parties with vested interests in the outcome. Accordingly, perhaps such errors would be more acceptable in training environments such as simulations and trial runs, where the potential negative consequences to the organization are artificially constrained. Keith and Frese (2008) concluded that error-management training is more useful when the goal of training is to learn skills that will generalize to many tasks, in contrast to learning a particular skill limited to performing one task.

In short, the fundamental premise of error-management training is sound: we learn from our mistakes. However, it is possible that despite the learning potential of mistakes to the individual, such employees may acquire the stigma of being "error-prone," while the error-avoidant employee may be regarded more favorably for assignments where the negative consequences of errors are potentially high. Furthermore, some employees are likely to respond better to error-management training. For example, Cullen et al. (2013) found that individuals who were highly conscientious and/or extraverted performed better in an error-management training program than individuals low on conscientiousness and/or extraversion. Thus, it appears that the active learning approach of error-management training may be beneficial, but may not be as appropriate or effective for all individuals.

Self-Regulatory Training

Self-regulatory training
A system of training in which employees are prompted to monitor and adjust their actions and reactions during training.

Self-regulation refers to processes that allow individuals to monitor their thoughts, moods, and behaviors over time and adjust them accordingly to meet task requirements. Prompting people to self-regulate their actions and reactions during training can make them more likely to stay on task and find solutions for themselves, which aids in transferring knowledge and skills to unique situations outside of the training. According to Bell and Kozlowski (2010), **self-regulatory training** has three general parts, as shown in Figure 6-1. The first involves *practice behaviors* during training. This involves having trainees actively engage in tasks to focus on skill improvement. The second part involves *self-monitoring*, or focusing their attention on how much progress they are making toward the training objectives. This part of the training is the cogni-

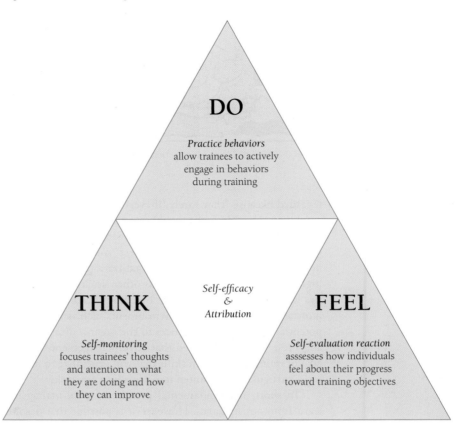

Figure 6-1   *Components of self-regulatory training*

tive component, requiring trainees to actively think about how they are doing and what they can do to improve their efforts. The third part is *self-evaluation reaction*, which involves the emotional responses that individuals may have for their progress.

Bell and Kozlowski further note that for self-regulatory training to be most effective, individuals should have high levels of confidence in their abilities to successfully complete the tasks (called **self-efficacy**), and they should make appropriate attributions for the cause of their performance. That is, if individuals attribute the reason for their success to luck or the reason for their failure to an unfriendly trainer, the likelihood of their self-regulatory processes being engaged and maintained over time will be lessened. This is because they are making external attributions for their successes and failures. Rather than credit or blame external factors for their performance, trainees should form causal attributions that make it clear that good performance was due to their diligence and poor performance was a result of inappropriate effort or task strategies.

The effects of self-regulatory training interventions have been promising. Sitzmann et al. (2009) found that individuals who engaged in self-regulation during training had higher declarative and procedural knowledge compared to those who were not prompted to self-regulate their thoughts and behaviors during training. Sitzmann and Ely (2010) found that prompting trainees to engage in self-regulation during training

Self-efficacy
The belief in one's capabilities and capacity to perform successfully.

led to more time spent on the task, which then led to the trainees learning more. We will revisit the topic of self-regulation in Chapter 12 when we discuss self-regulation theories of motivation.

Special Training Topics

Training topics can vary widely within organizations and are largely determined by the needs of the organization and its employees. Training can focus on specific knowledge that needs to be transmitted to various skills that must be learned. There are three topics that are widely covered through training within organizations. These include training on diversity, training to prepare individuals for overseas assignments, and training to prevent and deter sexual harassment.

Diversity Training

The workforce has become increasingly diverse. With advances in technology and increased globalization comes an era where the people with whom we interact, whether as colleagues, clients, or employers, are often not the same as us. Diversity involves both *surface-level* characteristics, such as demographic differences that are easily seen with the naked eye, and *deep-level* characteristics, such as personality and values that are unknown at first glance. Rather than to passively react to increases in diversity, organizations are advised to proactively manage it. Chrobot-Mason and Quiñones (2002) summarized the practical importance of diversity in the workplace:

> As the workplace continues to diversify, organizations will have to make a choice: either ignore this trend and continue business as usual or take steps to prepare for diversity. Ignoring demographic changes may cause such problems as an inability to attract and retain minority employees or a hostile work environment that increases risk of litigation. In contrast, organizations that work to change or create organizational practices and policies that support a diverse workforce may not only minimize exposure to discrimination lawsuits but also realize the benefits of the creativity and problem-solving capabilities that a diverse workforce can provide. (p. 151)

Diversity training
A method of training directed at improving interpersonal sensitivity and awareness of differences among employees.

The goal of **diversity training** is to reduce barriers, such as values, stereotypes, and managerial practices, that constrain employee contributions to organizational goals and personal development (Noe & Ford, 1992). According to Roberson et al. (2012), diversity training seeks to increase knowledge about diversity, improve trainees' attitudes regarding diversity, and help them develop skills addressing diversity. As Hayles (1996) summarized, diversity training involves "head (knowledge); hand (behaviors and skills); and heart (feelings and attitudes)" (p. 106).

To accomplish these objectives, many diversity training programs focus exclusively on diversity awareness. Roberson et al. note that increasing awareness involves three primary goals. The first is to increase trainee knowledge about issues. This could include providing information about the organization's stance on diversity, dispelling myths about various groups, providing facts about the changing demographics in society, and helping people understand how stereotypes and biases are formed. Chrobot-Mason and Quiñones (2002) note that these discussions can be emotionally charged and trigger reactance and defensiveness. As such, it is recommended that traditional classroom methods be used by experienced trainers.

The second goal of diversity awareness is to encourage trainees to consider how they categorize people and find common ground between themselves and others. The focus here is on weakening beliefs that some people are in an "in-group" whereas others are in an "out-group." Instead, trainees are encouraged to find similarities and focus on individual identities rather than group characteristics. Roberson et al. note that a common exercise used to make individuals rethink how they categorize others is the "Who am I?" exercise. In this activity, participants list and discuss how they view themselves. The idea is that participants may discover that their own self-identities are actually quite similar to how other seemingly different people view themselves.

Lastly, diversity awareness seeks to challenge individuals' knowledge about themselves and their own belief systems. The intent is to get people to understand their own attitudes and behaviors and to make people mindful of how they view and treat others. Roberson et al. noted that training methods that are meant to increase participants' self-knowledge are often confrontational in nature. For example, Pendry et al. (2007) described an exercise on social privilege in which participants are asked to line up on one side of a room and respond to a number of statements (e.g., "I attended a private school") by taking a pace forward if they concur (i.e., had the privilege). Typically, participants from the dominant racial group take many more paces forward than participants representing other ethnic or racial groups, "thereby providing a spatial demonstration of what happens in society" (p. 32). In addition to moving forward, participants may be asked to move backwards if the statement reflects a disadvantage. This exercise can also include privilege based on sex, sexual orientation, socioeconomic status, and other characteristics that are related to having a social advantage over others. Table 6-1 shows sample items from such an activity.

Table 6-1   *Sample items in a privilege walk exercise designed to increase diversity awareness*

Privilege Statements
1. If your family had health insurance, take one step forward.
2. If you have visible or invisible disabilities, take one step backward.
3. If you completed high school, take one step forward.
4. If you have ever felt unsafe walking alone at night, take one step backward.
5. If you were raised in a home that had libraries of both children's and adult's books, take one step forward.
6. If you took out loans for your education, take one step backward.
7. If you commonly see people of your race or ethnicity as heroes or heroines on television programs or in movies, take one step forward.
8. If you ever got a good paying job because of a friend or family member, take one step forward.
9. If you have been divorced or impacted by divorce, take one step backward.
10. If your parents completed college, take one step forward.

Roberson et al. (2012) noted that, in general, diversity programs are largely successful at increasing knowledge for participants, both in the short-term and the long-term. In addition, they appear to be successful at changing general attitudes toward diversity, but less effective in changing attitudes toward specific groups of people. Rynes and Rosen (1995) conducted a major survey of human resource professionals about diversity issues in their organizations. Organizations that had successfully adopted diversity programs had strong support from top management and placed a high priority on diversity relative to other competing organizational objectives. Diversity training success was also associated with mandatory attendance for all managers, long-term evaluation of training results, managerial rewards for increasing diversity, and a broad inclusionary definition of what is meant by "diversity" in the organization.

However, not all programs result in positive effects. There is evidence that diversity programs sometimes lead to defensiveness and an increase in negative behaviors (e.g., Sanchez & Medkik, 2004). Indeed, some critics believe that diversity training has been largely unsuccessful. Hemphill and Haines (1997) cited that Texaco paid a record settlement of $176 million in a racial discrimination suit, and the U.S. Army has been confronted with potential sexual harassment claims from more than 5,000 women. Both of these organizations had previously implemented diversity training. The authors believe organizations can do little to compel changes in how people feel about each other, but organizations should adopt a zero-tolerance policy for discrimination and harassment practices.

Expatriate Training

Expatriate
A person native to one country who serves a period of employment in another country.

The term **expatriate** refers to an employee who serves on an overseas assignment (typically for a defined time period, such as 2–5 years). The need for expatriate training has grown for two reasons. The first is the increase in the number of individuals so assigned, and the second is the relatively high failure rate of employees in such assignments. For example, according to Wildman et al. (2010), about one-third of expatriate managers terminate their international assignments prematurely. Even if the managers complete their assignments, their performance in that role may not be regarded as successful. The estimated annual cost of expatriate failures is approximately $2B.

It is not unusual for global organizations to desire their employees to sequentially assume multiple international assignments, resulting in a group of people who continuously move from one locale to another. Fan and Wanous (2008) refer to these individuals as "sojourners" (i.e., travelers). Regardless of the time spent travelling or number of assignments an individual is given, however, training may be needed to enhance an expatriates chances for success. As noted by Caligiuri and Hippler (2010), there is a difference between serving in an international assignment versus developing cross-cultural competence. Not all individuals have the capacity to develop cross-cultural skills from international assignments.

Not surprisingly, a key aspect of expatriate training is a focus on cross-cultural issues. Many programs serve as a means of educating individuals about what differences to expect in their target destination and how to cope with these differences. Individuals receive information on such topics as business customs, etiquette, and potential barriers to communication. By making people aware of such things as differences between expressions and gestures across cultures, the fear of the unknown is lessened and

of gender. The inherent complexity of "sexual harassment" as a manifestation of human behavior in the workplace leads to uncertainty as to what exactly organizations should do in their training initiatives designed to decrease the frequency of its occurrence.

Sexual harassment training frequently consists of teaching sensitivity to other people's values and preferences. It should not be assumed, for example, that people prefer to be touched (as on the hand or arm) when engaged in conversation. There are also broad cultural differences in the degree to which physical contact between people is regarded as acceptable. People differ in the degree to which verbal statements, including profanity, are considered offensive or inappropriate. Most sexual harassment training programs are designed to be fundamentally educational in nature. Participants are taught to recognize the manifestations of harassment and understand why victims are likely to find it offensive. However, some people engage in purposeful and intentional forms of sexual harassment. In these cases knowledge-based sexual harassment training will be ineffectual in decreasing its occurrence, and in its place the organization must seek to control its occurrence through sanctions (e.g., suspensions and terminations).

Recent research on sexual harassment has been extended to include the organizational context in which it occurs. For example, Gettman and Gelfand (2007) identified another organizational arena in which sexual harassment can occur. As we move to a more service-oriented economy, organizations place strong emphasis on employees being highly attentive to customer needs. However, employees in service jobs can also be targeted for sexual harassment by clients and customers; the people that the organization relies on for business. Thus the potential for sexual harassment for employees can transcend the traditional boundaries of an organization to include other individuals not directly under the organization's control. Furthermore, boundaries between work and non-work have become blurred as employees engage in workplace romances and technology cuts across areas. As such, sexual harassment issues are becoming more complex for organizations (see Social Media and I/O Psychology: *Workplace Romances, Social Media, and Sexual Harassment Concerns*).

Management Development Issues

Management development
The process by which individuals serving in management or leadership positions enhance their talents to better perform the job.

Management development is the process by which individuals learn to perform effectively in managerial roles. According to Kraiger and Culbertson (2013), management development is distinct from typical training programs in that "its learning objectives are typically knowledge, skills, and competencies for future (usually higher level) positions in the organization" (p. 254). Organizations are interested in management development in large part because they recognize its value as a strategy to improve organizational performance. Kotter (1988) argued the one factor that seems to distinguish excellent companies from others is the amount of time and energy spent in the planning, design, and execution of developmental activities. Tharenou (1997) reported that many managers seek continual advancement, not just until they reach a particular level in the organization. For them, successful development activities are particularly critical because they contribute greatly to what Tharenou called "career velocity." The literature on management development tends to focus on major issues or processes managers address as part of their professional maturation. In contrast, the literature on personnel training tends to be more concerned with specific methods or techniques of

Social Media and I/O Psychology: *Workplace Romances, Social Media, and Sexual Harassment Concerns*

Given the amount of time that people spend at work, it is not surprising that friendships are frequently formed between coworkers. As Mainiero and Jones (2013) observed, "Coworkers are likely to 'friend' each other on Facebook, 'connect' as colleagues on LinkedIn, and monitor each other's locations on Foursquare before a lunch meeting" (p. 187). Occasionally, these friendships may develop into something more romantic in nature. In a 2013 survey of over 3,000 U.S. workers, it was revealed that 38% of people have dated a coworker and 24% have dated someone higher up in the organizational ranks (CareerBuilder, 2013).

However, not all relationships last. What happens when members of failed romances stay connected through social media? A flirtatious post on a coworker's Facebook wall may have been welcomed during the relationship, but afterwards may be grounds for a sexual harassment claim if posted during work hours or from a work computer. Furthermore, even if the posts occur outside of business hours, they may be problematic. According to Mainiero and Jones, "new social media technologies have created situations where some employees complain that other employees have created a hostile work environment *outside* the office—through Facebook, LinkedIn, or Twitter—that affects their behavior *inside* the office" (italics in original, p. 190).

Given the potential for harassment claims, what is an organization to do? A survey conducted by the Society for Human Resource Management (SHRM, 2013) reported that 42% of organizations have a written or verbal policy addressing workplace romance. The idea of having policies regarding workplace romances is nothing new. Some have even proposed "love contracts" that members of a romantic relationship sign that affirms the relationship is consensual and won't affect their work. However, few human resource practitioners in the SHRM survey report using these and most deem them to be ineffectual. What is new is the intersection between workplace romances and social media use. As Mainiero and Jones noted, "Given the current digital and social media trends, the prevalence of workplace romance, and the risk that some romances may turn into harassment, corporations must update their sexual harassment policies to include all social media applications, regardless of who owns the device and whether or not such contacts take place inside or outside office boundaries" (p. 192).

Clearly, social media have blurred the lines between personal and professional lives, as have workplace romances. A lot remains to be seen regarding what will and won't work as deterrents to sexual harassment complaints that are borne out of failed romances and social media gaffes. Until then, individuals embarking on relationships with colleagues would be wise to keep things professional, even when they get personal.

training. However, the larger systemic issues of needs assessment, skill enhancement, and transfer are equally applicable to both training and development.

Whetten and Cameron (1991) identified critical management skills and linked them to successful performance on the job. Three *personal skills* were noted: developing self-awareness, managing stress, and solving problems creatively. Four *interpersonal skills* were also identified: communicating supportively, gaining power and influence, motivating others, and managing conflict. The authors pointed out that these skills overlap and managers must draw upon all of them to perform effectively in a managerial role. Yukl et al. (1990) developed a survey that assesses managerial practices based on these skills. Subordinates and peers describe how much a manager uses these practices and make recommendations on whether the manager's behavioral style should be modified. Managers compare this feedback with their own self-assessment of behavior. Ratings of the importance of these behaviors for the manager's job provide additional information for identifying relevant developmental activities. Lombardo and McCauley (1988) proposed that underutilization of selected managerial skills and practices contribute to *derailment*. Derailment occurs when a manager who has been judged to have the ability to go higher fails to live up to his or her full potential and is fired, demoted, or plateaued below the expected level of achievement.

Managerial skills are often difficult to train in traditional formats. As such, two special forms of training and development that are particularly salient for managerial development deserve discussion: mentoring and executive coaching.

Mentoring

Mentoring became an established means of developing managers starting around 1980. Mentoring can be regarded as one process that facilitates the transition between phases or stages of our lives, and mentoring can be provided by parents, teachers, or other people serving as role models who are sources of positive influence. Mentoring in an employment context is merely an extension of that concept (Eby, 2011).

Mentor
Typically a more senior or experienced person who helps to professionally develop a less experienced person (the protégé).

Protégé
Typically a more junior and less experienced person who is helped and developed in his or her career by a more experienced person (the mentor).

Mentors are more senior or experienced individuals who advise and shepherd new people (**protégés**) in the formative years of their careers. According to Eby (2012), mentors are typically at a higher position in an organization than their protégés. Nevertheless, peer mentoring in which a more experienced employee serves as a mentor to a less-seasoned colleague is common as well. Furthermore, mentoring can be informal, in which the relationship between mentor and protégé forms spontaneously and based on mutual attraction and shared interests, or it can be formal, in which the relationship is formed and dictated by the organization.

Kram (1985) noted that mentoring relationships typically progress through four phases. As depicted in Figure 6-3, the first phase is *relationship initiation*, which occurs as the two individuals are connected, whether formally or informally, and determine whether a mentoring relationship will be valuable. According to Eby (2012), this is "the 'make or break' phase of the mentoring relationship" (p. 616) in that some relationships never move beyond superficial interpersonal interactions. The second phase is *cultivation*, which is when the heart of mentoring occurs. At this stage, the mentor provides instruction, support, and advice to the protégé and in return the protégé demonstrates commitment and engagement to the process and admiration for the mentor. The mentor and protégé are seen as being in a mutually beneficial partnership at this point. The third phase is *separation*, when the protégé no longer needs the ongoing support of the mentor. Alternatively, separation may occur if the mentor–protégé relationship has not been successful or a breach in trust has occurred. The final phase of the mentoring relationship is *redefinition*. Here the mentor and the protégé decide what the future of their relationship holds. If the partnership was a success, they may continue their bond at a lower level or have more of a peer-like friendship. If the partnership ended on bad

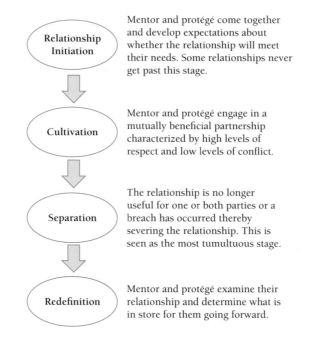

Relationship Initiation — Mentor and protégé come together and develop expectations about whether the relationship will meet their needs. Some relationships never get past this stage.

Cultivation — Mentor and protégé engage in a mutually beneficial partnership characterized by high levels of respect and low levels of conflict.

Separation — The relationship is no longer useful for one or both parties or a breach has occurred thereby severing the relationship. This is seen as the most tumultuous stage.

Redefinition — Mentor and protégé examine their relationship and determine what is in store for them going forward.

Figure 6-3   *The four phases of mentoring relationships*

terms, however, hostility and resentment may dictate that all ties are cut between the two parties.

Wanberg et al. (2003) developed a three-factor model of mentoring relationships. *Frequency* refers to the frequency of meetings between mentor and protégé, which influences the amount of time mentors and protégés spend together. *Scope* addresses the breadth of mentoring functions received by the protégé in tandem with the breadth of subjects addressed during the mentoring relationship. *Strength of influence* is the degree to which the protégé is influenced by the mentor. Some mentors offer only superficial ideas and suggestions to protégés. Allen et al. (2004) differentiated task-related from psychosocial mentoring of protégés. Mentoring behaviors such as sponsorships, exposure, visibility, and coaching are more directly related to enhancing task-related aspects of work that facilitate objective career success. Behaviors associated with psychosocial mentoring, such as role modeling, acceptance and confirmation, counseling, and friendship, are more highly related to satisfaction with the mentor than with career success (see Cross-Cultural I/O Psychology: *The Acceptability of Mentoring Across Cultures*).

As in most relationships, there are benefits and drawbacks for both protégés and mentors. The benefits for protégés are much clearer than are those for mentors. The nature of the relationship is based on the premise that the mentor can help the protégé in some way. Eby et al. (2013) noted that mentors provide both career-related and psychosocial support for protégés. Career-related support includes such things as increased visibility, protection from organizational politics, and career coaching. Psychosocial support includes a focus on increasing the protégé's self-esteem and self-efficacy. The amount of support may vary, however, by the sex of the mentor. A meta-analytic

Cross-Cultural I/O Psychology: *The Acceptability of Mentoring Across Cultures*

The acceptability of mentoring as a means of professional development varies across nations. One underlying factor that accounts for its acceptability is *power distance*. Power distance is based on human inequality, that people differ in prestige, wealth, and power. Power differentials are highly evident and formalized in boss–subordinate relationships. Part of the effectiveness of mentoring is that someone who *does* have more power, status, and expertise can use such resources to develop a protégé. Furthermore, the mentor is *willing* (if not desirous) to do so. In cultures that have a small power differential, mentoring is a more common means of professional development. Although the mentor has more formal power at work than does the protégé, the differential power is not used to distance the two parties from each other. In cultures that have a large power differential, the degree of inequality between the boss and subordinate is a defining characteristic of their relationship. For a boss to mentor a subordinate would, in effect, serve to lessen the distance between them.

Based on research by Hofstede (2001), countries with a small power distance are found in northern Europe (e.g., Austria, Denmark, England) and North America. Countries with a large power distance are more typically found in Asia (e.g., Malaysia, Philippines, Singapore) and South America (e.g., Guatemala, Panama, Mexico). A large power distance is not compatible with mentoring, particularly the psychosocial dimensions. Serving as a counselor, confidant, and friend lessens the inequality between the two parties. In cultures with a small power distance, mentoring is a manifestation of power (i.e., choosing to help someone when it is possible to do so). In cultures with a large power distance, not mentoring is a manifestation of power (i.e., asserting the inequality between the two parties).

study by O'Brien et al. (2010) revealed that protégés with female mentors received more psychosocial support than protégés with male mentors. In addition, as reported by Eby (2011), protégés have faster rates of promotion, higher motivation, and more positive interpersonal relations than peers who are not in mentoring relationships. For mentors, however, the benefits are primarily limited to greater personal satisfaction in their work lives. While there may be organizational recognition for mentoring efforts, this is not the norm, particularly for information mentoring relationships. The drawbacks for protégés can include being paired with a mentor who does not know how to be a good mentor, despite both parties desiring the mentor to have such skills. Mentors and protégés can have mismatched values, personalities, and work styles, and the negative consequences of the mismatch fall more heavily on the protégé. The drawbacks for mentors include protégés who are unwilling to learn, engage in breaches of trust, are jealous, and highly competitive (the mentor may be the immediate boss of the protégé, and may well be positioned to assume the mentor's job). In brief, although there are substantial drawbacks for both protégés and mentors from a failed relationship, both parties can reap great rewards when the relationship is seen as a mutually beneficial partnership.

Executive coaching
An individualized developmental process for business leaders provided by a trained professional (the coach).

Executive Coaching

Another means of developing managers is through **executive coaching**. While mentors are internal to the organization (i.e., typically a more senior colleague), coaches are external to the organization. Furthermore, as Salas et al. (2012) noted, "Unlike mentors, it is not vital for coaches to have expertise in the industry/arena in which the coachee works, as coaches tend to focus more on developing broader skill sets related to communication and leadership" (p. 356). Grant et al. (2010) reported 93% of U.S.-based global companies use coaching. As the name implies, it is directed toward top-level employees of an organization. Bono et al. (2009) referred to executive coaching as a tailored and individually-customized type of training. Two parties are involved: the coach and the person being coached. Coaching is more than counseling, although the two have similarities. Counseling involves intensive listening on the part of the therapist (who provides a supportive environment for the client), and often the client arrives at his or her own solutions to problems. In coaching, the coach also listens carefully and provides a supportive environment but then takes an active and direct role in preparing solutions and developing plans of action for the manager to follow.

According to Sperry (2013), executive coaches can be used to help individuals learn a new skill (skill coaching), to perform better in their present job (performance coaching), or prepare them for a future leadership role (development coaching). Thus, a fundamental tenet of coaching is learning. Peterson (2002, p. 173) offered the following types of skills that can be enhanced through coaching:

- Interpersonal skills, including relationship building, tact, sensitivity, assertiveness, conflict management, and influencing without authority;
- Communication, including listening skills, presentations, and speaking with impact;
- Certain cognitive skills, such as prioritizing, decision making, and strategic thinking;
- Leadership skills, including delegating, mentoring, and motivating others; and
- Self-management skills, including time management, emotion and anger management, and work–life balance.

Part of the value of coaching is that it is specifically geared to the person's problems and needs (see Field Note 1: *Low Skill, High Tech*). As a one-on-one activity, coaching has no general curriculum designed to appeal to a wide audience. Furthermore, there are no formal standards or requirements to be a coach—it is an unlicensed and unregulated activity. Whereas coaches can be a member of the International Coach Federation, for example, which has developed its own certification mechanism and code of ethics, in practice a coach needs only to be professionally credible to others. Coaching can be conducted in person, online, or over the phone.

Much of what is known about coaching is primarily from the perspective of the coach and the process of coaching. However, more recently attention is being given to the individuals being coached. Peterson (2011) described the development of a classification for participants in terms of their level of coachability. At the lowest level the participant is regarded as uncoachable; at the highest level the participant is committed to inner-directed lifelong learning. Participants low in coachability will probably not benefit from coaching in any form through any means. Participants high in coachability will continue to grow and develop throughout their lifetime, and a particular coach is but one source of growth in their lifelong development.

In a study of 428 coaches, Bono et al. (2009) found that the average hourly fee for coaches was $237. Given its high costs, it is logical to question whether the expense is worth it. Fortunately, there appears to be evidence that coaching is effective. In their meta-analysis, Theeboom et al. (2013) found that coaching resulted in substantial improvements in performance. In addition, they found that coaching was related

Field Note 1: *Low Skill, High Tech*

One of the principles of organizational learning is that *all* employees, including upper management, need to continuously develop new skills to compete in the ever-changing world of work. CEOs are also not immune from having to acquire new skills, but rank does have its privileges.

One company that I know purchased a highly sophisticated multimedia communication system. People around the world could now simultaneously both hear and see each other in a multi-site conference presentation. The system also had basic communication features, such as a speaker phone for telephone calls. Late one afternoon, the CEO and a company salesperson were meeting in the high-tech communication room. The company was located on the east coast, and a question came up about an important supplier on the west coast. The CEO wanted to show off his new communication system to the salesperson, who had not seen it before. The CEO turned on the system, hit a button that had the supplier's telephone number on speed-dial, and within seconds was talking to the supplier. The call lasted only a few minutes, whereupon the meeting ended. Both the CEO and salesperson left the room and went home for the day.

The next morning at 9:00 a.m., the CEO had scheduled a high-level staff meeting in the communication room. The purpose of the meeting was to discuss a highly confidential plan for the company to market more of its products on a global basis. If consensus was reached among the CEO's staff, other locations of the company around the world would join in the discussion. The CEO left strict word with his Administrative Assistant that the meeting was not to be interrupted.

Around 10:50 a.m. Eastern time, the CEO's office received an urgent telephone call. The caller said it was imperative to speak with the CEO. The Administrative Assistant dutifully said the CEO was not available. The caller again pressed the point the call was extremely urgent. The Administrative Assistant reiterated the CEO's unavailability, and added he was in an extremely important meeting and left instructions that he was not to be disturbed. The caller dryly stated he knew the CEO was in a meeting, and was discussing a confidential global marketing strategy. The Administrative Assistant said she was surprised the caller knew about the important meeting and its confidential agenda. The caller stated it would be difficult for him not to know, because when he arrived at his office a few minutes previously, he could hear every word spoken in the meeting over *his* high-tech communication system. The Administrative Assistant rushed to the communication room, whispered something to the CEO, who in turn asked aloud, "Does anyone here know how to turn this thing off?" The CEO had neglected to shut the system off from his late afternoon phone call from the day before. The caller was the supplier on the west coast who had just arrived at work at 7:50 a.m. Pacific time to discover he was unintentionally eavesdropping on a customer's confidential meeting. The global marketing idea had absolutely no relevance to the supplier, but to other parties it could have greatly compromised the company's position. The CEO took full responsibility for the unauthorized broadcast of the meeting. However, rather than learning how to operate the communication system, he promised he would never again attempt to use it on his own.

to greater well-being, greater ability to cope with present and future job demands, and more positive attitudes about work. Lastly, they found that coaching was related to the setting and attainment of goals.

Transfer of Training

Transfer of training
The application of knowledge and skills learned in training back to the job.

A successful training program doesn't end when the training program ceases. Instead, the hope is that individuals will transfer what they have learned within training back to the job itself. Beier and Kanfer (2010) identified that this **transfer of training** is greatly facilitated by the individual's motivation to sustain the new behaviors. Motivation is enhanced when the organization has a culture that supports continuous learning, and there are organizational consequences associated with having succeeded or failed in training. Some employees leave training with new skills and with strong intentions to apply those skills to their job, but limitations in the post-training environment interfere with the actual transfer of training (see Field Note 2: *The Willingness to be Trained*). As Machin (2002) stated, "When training does not transfer it is likely that employees will perceive training to be a waste of their time and employers will continue to question the benefit of their investment in it" (p. 263). Baldwin et al. (2009) noted that behavioral change occurs over time, and sometimes the change takes longer than expected. The authors regard transfer of training as a transitioning process that passes through three phases. The first is letting go of old behaviors that are to be replaced with something new, and the second is the in-between time when the old is gone but the new is not yet in place. The third and final phase is when the new behaviors make sense and the individual uses them in a productive manner. It is at the end of this third phase when the transfer of training is complete.

Holton and Baldwin (2003) proposed that training can transfer across different "distances" through two phases, with six key events representing points along the progression from cognitive learning to broad performance applications, as shown in Figure 6-4. Baldwin and Ford (1988) noted the distinction between *generalization*,

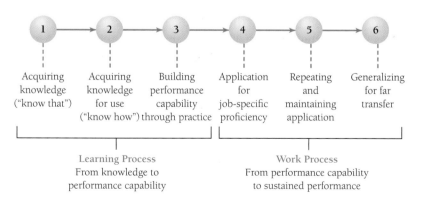

Figure 6-4 *Conceptual model of how training transfers from knowledge acquisition to sustained performance*

Source: From "Making Transfer Happen: An Active Perspective on Learning Transfer Systems," by E. F. Holton and T. T. Baldwin, in E. F. Holton and T. T. Baldwin (Eds.), *Improving learning transfer in organizations* (San Francisco: Jossey-Bass, 2003). This material is used by permission of John Wiley & Sons, Inc.

Field Note 2: *The Willingness to Be Trained*

When I was in graduate school, I helped a professor with a study of the coal mining industry. Many on-the-job accidents occurred in coal mines, and our assignment was to develop a safety training program to reduce them. My personal assignment was to observe and interview the coal miners about their work. While down in the mines, I noticed that the miners engaged in dangerous behaviors, such as not wearing their hard hats, leaving off their masks (which filtered out coal dust), and smoking in the mine (where an open flame could trigger an explosion). In addition to being unsafe, some of these behaviors were blatant violations of safety rules.

After the miners finished their work shifts, I interviewed them about their jobs. I was particularly interested in why they did such hazardous things. Since our goal was to develop a training program to reduce accidents, I felt that eliminating these unsafe behaviors was an obvious place to start. So I asked them why they didn't wear safety equipment at times. I did not expect their answer. Many said they believed there was no relationship between what they did in the mine and what happened to them. They felt their lives were in the hands of luck, fate, or God, and it did not really matter how they conducted themselves. They all seemed to have personal anecdotes about other miners who were extremely safety conscious (that is, always wore all the safety equipment and were exceedingly cautious people in general) yet suffered serious injuries or death in accidents through no fault of their own, such as a cave-in. In short, the miners were highly fatalistic. They believed that if "your number was up," you would get hurt or killed, and there was nothing you could do about it. Although a hard hat was a fine thing to wear, it would not do much good if five tons of rock fell on you. Therefore many miners were not interested in engaging in safe behavior because their behavior did not matter one way or another.

This experience taught me many lessons about training. The major one is that if people are not motivated to be trained, to learn some new behaviors, it is pointless to try. As every teacher can tell you, if students do not want to learn or just do not care, there is nothing you can do to force them to learn. Many of the coal miners simply did not want to learn new behaviors because in their minds their lives and welfare were determined by factors beyond their control. Trainers are like chefs: they can prepare the finest meals, but they cannot make you eat if you are not hungry.

the extent to which trained skills and behaviors are exhibited in the transfer setting, and *maintenance*, the length of time that trained skills and behaviors continue to be used on the job. They believe that supervisory support is a major environmental factor that can affect the transfer process. In the post-training environment, supervisor support includes reinforcement, modeling of trained behaviors, and goal-setting activities. Another factor that can influence transfer is the extent to which the post-training environment provides opportunities for trainees to apply what they have learned.

Ford et al. (1991) studied technical trainees after they completed training and found significant differences in opportunities to apply the training and wide variations in the lengths of time before trainees first performed the tasks for which they had been trained. Tracey et al. (1995) concluded that post-training knowledge and behavior are more likely to perseverate in organizations that have strong social support systems. Specifically, transfer of training is enhanced in organizations that have a culture that recognizes the importance of continuous learning.

Evaluation Criteria of Training Programs

Reaction criteria
A standard for judging the effectiveness of training that refers to the reactions or feelings of individuals about the training they received.

As is the case with any assessment or evaluation, some measure of performance must be obtained. Measures of performance refer to criteria, and the criteria used to evaluate training are just as important as those used in personnel selection. Relevance, reliability, and freedom from bias are all important considerations. One distinction between criteria used in personnel selection and criteria used to evaluate training is that training criteria are more varied and are used to evaluate multiple aspects of a training program.

The most common means of evaluating training is Kirkpatrick's (1976) classic typology, which reflects four levels of training criteria that increase in complexity: reaction, learning, behavior, and results. **Reaction criteria** refer primarily to the participants' reaction to the training program. These criteria measure impressions and opinions about the training; for example, did they believe it was useful or added to their knowledge? Reaction criteria are treated as a measure of the face validity of the training program. Sitzmann et al. (2008) concluded that most of the reactions of trainees to training depend on the instructional content, but reactions are also based on the level of anxiety associated with training and pre-training motivation. According to Salas et al. (2012), whereas most evaluations assess trainee reactions, complete evaluation goes beyond these reactionary assessments.

Learning criteria
A standard for judging the effectiveness of training that refers to the amount of new knowledge and skills acquired through training.

Learning criteria refer to what knowledge has been acquired, skills improved, or attitudes changed as a result of training. Three measures can be taken. The first is immediate knowledge learned or skills acquired, which is often assessed at the conclusion of the training. The second is knowledge retention, where evaluators assess (as through a test) what has been learned at a later time. The third measure is a behavioral/skill demonstration. This measure is more than a score on a knowledge test, as perhaps a demonstration in a role-playing exercise or a simulation that is a behavioral manifestation of the knowledge, attitudes, or skills obtained or changed in training. Collectively, reaction and learning criteria are called *internal criteria*; that is, they refer to assessments internal to the training program itself.

Behavioral criteria
A standard for judging the effectiveness of training that refers to changes in performance that are exhibited on the job as a result of training.

Behavioral criteria refer to actual changes in performance once the employee is back on the job. These criteria are most clearly reflected in the concept of transfer of training. These criteria address such questions as to what extent the desired changes in the job behaviors of the trainee are realized by the training program. If the goal of the training program is to increase production, then the behavioral criterion assesses output before and after training. Other behavioral criteria are absenteeism, scrap rate, accidents, and grievances. All of these are objective criteria; they can be measured easily and have relatively clear meaning, as discussed in Chapter 3. But if the goal of the training program is to increase managers' sensitivity toward people with disabilities, then "increased sensitivity" has to be translated into some objective behavioral criteria. Note that scores on learning criteria and on behavioral criteria do not always correspond to a high degree. Some people who perform well in training do not transfer their new knowledge or skills back to the job. This is particularly true for training programs aimed at changing attitudes or feelings.

Results criteria
A standard for judging the effectiveness of training that refers to the economic value that accrues to the organization as a function of the new behaviors exhibited on the job.

Results criteria relate to the economic value of the training program to the company. Van Iddekinge et al. (2009) described the effects of a two-week training program in the fast-food industry. The profitability of each location (unit) was measured over multiple times for one year. The authors concluded that training enhanced customer service performance which leads to increased unit profitability. However, it is usually neither easy nor obvious to demonstrate the degree to which training enhances the overall goals of the organization. Brown and Sitzmann (2011) offered the following observation: "Those who evaluate training are placed in the challenging role of collecting time-consuming data requested by managers even though such data may be insufficient (or even counterproductive) to actually convincing them of the value of training" (p. 492). Furthermore, there can be hidden costs to even the most successful training programs.

Collectively, behavioral and results criteria are called *external criteria*; they are evaluations external to the training program itself. Consideration of these four criteria sometimes produces different conclusions about the effectiveness of training than a judgment reached by just one or two criteria. For example, Warr et al. (1999) found that reaction criteria were more strongly related to learning criteria than to subsequent job behavior criteria.

In a major meta-analytic review of the effectiveness of training in organizations, Arthur et al. (2003) concluded that organizational training exerted a moderate effect on reaction, learning, behavior, and results criteria. Although there were differences in various types of training, on the whole organizational training is moderately effective in enhancing performance outcomes. Training programs that produce a large effect are relatively scarce.

The success of any training and development system is intimately tied to the culture of the organization (see I/O Psychology and the Economy: *How the Economy Influences Staffing*). The organization sets the tone for the relative importance and need placed on enhancing the skills of its employees. Training and development activities are a mirror of the organization's deeper values. Smith et al. (1997) spoke to the need for *alignment* between the organization's culture and training initiatives. For example, a traditional authoritarian organization may not be supportive of individuals who attempt to take risks and try out new strategies. Mistakes and errors may be viewed as actions to be avoided rather than as opportunities from which to learn and develop. Kraiger and Jung (1997) described the importance of linking training objectives to training evaluation criteria. Given the subtleties of how we learn, what we learn, and the duration of our learning, methods of assessing learning must be appropriately refined. Learning is the foundation of training and development, and organizational learning is the foundation for organizational growth.

$ £ ¥ € I/O Psychology and the Economy: *How the Economy Influences Staffing*

There are two classic ways to staff organizations. The first is the selection approach. Organizations select individuals because they possess the needed knowledge and skills to perform the job. Individuals obtain the knowledge/skills through education prior to joining the organization. Examples include typists having gone to a secretarial school or electricians having gone to a vocational school. Ready to "hit the ground running," these individuals are expected to perform their jobs immediately upon hire.

The second approach to staffing is through organizational training. Organizations recognize that the nature of their work operations requires knowledge/skills not typically taught in vocational schools or universities. It is therefore unreasonable to expect new hires to possess organizationally-relevant knowledge/skills. Thus the responsibility falls to the organization itself to teach the new hires needed knowledge/skills. What the organization looks for in job candidates is the ability to learn and the desire to learn. Desirable candidates often manifest evidence of high intellectual ability needed for learning, and evidence of sustained learning over a fairly wide range of subject matter.

In brief, organizations typically face two fundamental choices in their staffing decisions: to select either knowledgeable/skilled individuals, or individuals with high potential to become knowledgeable/skilled. When the economy is struggling and good jobs are in great demand, organizations can afford to be extremely selective in extending offers of employment. Instead of choosing candidates with either high knowledge/skills or high potential, organizations can demand both. The chosen candidates will most likely be able to perform successfully after a very brief socialization to their new employer, as well as be readily able to acquire new knowledge and skills. The current economic conditions are most frustrating for many job applicants. If the candidates have a lengthy employment history, they may be rejected because they are perceived to lack the potential to develop through training (and because of reduced time the organization has to recoup its investment in the candidate). If the candidates are recent graduates, they may have vast potential, but they have limited knowledge/skills because of limited work experience. Many organizations prefer to "grow their own talent" through training, and favor younger workers in the labor market. But the state of the economy can raise the standard for selection into organizations to almost unattainable levels for job candidates. The best outcome for both knowledgeable/skilled individuals and individuals with high potential is an economic environment supporting full employment, allowing individuals to find organizations that value their respective assets.

Chapter Summary

- Organizational learning is the process by which employees as well as the entire organization acquire new skills to better adapt to the rapidly changing work world.
- Skill acquisition is the process by which individuals acquire declarative and procedural knowledge.
- Training employees to acquire new skills is best done in organizations that encourage employees to learn and give them the opportunity to use their new skills on the job.

- It is important to understand what deficiencies exist in individual and team performance and what resources and support are present in the organization prior to developing a training program.
- Many contemporary training methods use computer technology. Among the more frequently used are programmed instruction, intelligent tutoring systems, interactive multimedia, and virtual reality.
- Active learning approaches emphasize the trainee's role in his or her own development by encouraging them to ask questions, seek feedback, and reflect on their performance.
- Management development is the process of cultivating skills in upper-level employees, who affect the lives of many workers.
- Diversity training is designed to make employees understand how individuals with different backgrounds and experiences can contribute to the welfare of the organization.
- Expatriate training is designed to facilitate the adjustment of an employee who is serving in an international assignment.
- Sexual harassment training is designed to make employees understand the unacceptability of behavior in the workplace that is regarded to be sexual or offensive in nature.
- Mentoring is a process by which more established employees (mentors) facilitate the career development of less-experienced employees (protégés).
- Executive coaching is a one-on-one developmental relationship between an external coach and a manager designed to facilitate the manager's career progression.
- The key to successful learning is the transfer between what has been learned in training to behavior on the job. The four major criteria used to assess the effectiveness of training are reaction, learning, behavioral, and results.

Performance Management

Learning Objectives

- Understand the concept of performance management.
- Describe the performance management process.
- Describe the six purposes of performance management systems.
- Know the attributes of a legally defensible performance appraisal system.
- Understand the major rating errors and biases.
- Know the various types of absolute and relative rating systems.
- Explain the purpose of rater training.
- Understand the bases of rater motivation.
- Understand peer assessment, self-assessment, and 360-degree feedback.
- Describe the role of feedback giving, seeking, and reactions within performance management.
- Explain the rationale behind various reactions to performance management systems.

I n a widely read article entitled, "Putting People First for Organizational Success," Pfeffer and Veiga (1999) made a compelling argument that the organization with the better performing workforce will have a greater likelihood of being successful. Indeed, very few organizations can succeed without at least minimal employee performance. High-performing employees can greatly contribute to organizational performance. As such, individual performance is considered to be a *driver* of organizational performance. Accordingly, organizations are concerned about how well their employees are performing.

> **Performance management**
> The process of how an organization manages and aligns all of its resources to achieve high performance.

How can organizational decision makers know how well their employees are performing? And if employees aren't performing well, what can (or should) they do about it? The answers to these questions lie in the concept of performance management. According to Aguinis (2013), **performance management** is "a continuous process of identifying, measuring, and developing the performance of individuals and teams and aligning performance with the strategic goals of the organization" (p. 2). Within this definition, there are two main parts. First, there is the notion that performance management is a continuous process. The idea is that managing the performance of individuals and teams is not a one-time event. Rather, it is an ongoing process that involves establishing goals, observing and evaluating performance, and providing feedback and coaching to continuously develop individuals. Of particular relevance is the distinction between performance management and performance appraisal. While the terms are often used interchangeably in practice, there is a clear distinction between the two, with performance appraisal subsumed within the bigger concept of performance management. Generally speaking, performance appraisals are the evaluations of an individual's performance that occur periodically within organizations. They identify the person's strengths and weaknesses and in doing so suggest areas that are in need of development. Performance management, on the other hand, is an ongoing activity (den Hartog et al., 2004) that seeks to integrate goal setting along with ways in which the employee can be developed going forward. As Aguinis (2013) notes, "Performance appraisal is an important component of performance management, but it is just a part of a bigger whole because performance management is much more than just performance measurement" (p. 3).

The second main part of the definition of performance management concerns alignment. Fletcher (2008) described performance management as a shared vision within the organization, with all employees understanding how their individual performance contributes to organizational performance. Implicit in this view is the idea of multiple goals; in particular, the overall goals of the organization and the specific goal of each of its employees. When the goals of the organization and the goals of employees are *aligned*, individual performance contributes to organizational performance (Andrews et al., 2012). When the two sets of goals are not aligned, there is no connection between them. Under conditions of low alignment, it would be possible for all employees to be performing their jobs well, but the organization as a whole can fail. How is this possible? One explanation would be that the organization has set an unattainable goal for itself, or has an ineffective plan to reach its goal. As such, individual employees can do little to help the organization prosper.

The reverse is also possible. An organization can succeed despite poor individual performance by its employees. In this case, the organization has an attainable goal and a sound operating plan, and the organization succeeds in spite of its employees. If the employees were performing their jobs well, the organization would be even more successful. The concept of alignment is difficult to measure, but organizations seem to be aware when there is little connection between individual performance (of its employees) and overall organizational performance. Aguinis (2009) reported in a survey of organizational leaders that only about 12% of organizations believed there was a successful alignment between the two. Schiemann (2009) described some of the symptoms of misalignment. They include employees being caught up in many urgent but not important activities, a sense of burnout from working hard but accomplishing little, and high conflict among units within the organization.

The Performance Management Process

According to Kinicki et al. (2013), the process of performance management entails "defining, measuring, motivating, and developing the desired performance of employees" (p. 4). They provided a model of the performance management process that integrates numerous existing process models. As shown in Figure 7-1, the performance management process begins with the setting of goals and communication of performance expectations. Here, managers identify what it is they want employees to achieve and they communicate these expectations to employees. These criteria for successful job performance are ideally established through a careful work analysis. Recall that work analysis and job performance criteria were discussed in Chapter 3.

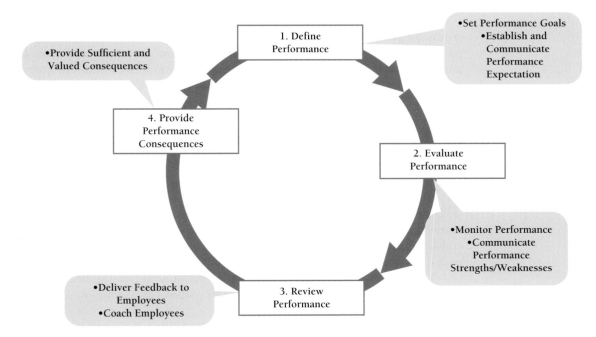

Figure 7-1 *Integrated performance management process*

Adapted from "Development and Validation of the Performance Management Behavior Questionnaire," by A. J. Kinicki, K. J. Jacobson, S. J. Peterson, and G. E. Prussia, in *Personnel Psychology* (2013). Reprinted by permission from Wiley Periodicals.

The second step in the performance management process is the evaluation of performance. This evaluation occurs through careful monitoring of an employee's performance combined with an assessment of the employee's strengths and weaknesses, whether in terms of the established performance standards or in comparison to other employees. These issues are a large focus of the current chapter and will be discussed in greater detail shortly.

Once performance is evaluated, the third step in the performance management process is to provide feedback to the employee about his or her performance. Both superior and subordinate are usually very uneasy about this step. Employees often get defensive about negative performance aspects. Superiors are often nervous about having to confront employees face-to-face with negative evaluations. If feedback is not given, however, or not given well, employee performance may actually decline rather than improve. We discuss feedback of appraisal information in greater detail later in this chapter. In addition, it is during this third stage that employees are provided coaching and other developmental opportunities to ensure future success. These developmental activities were described in Chapter 6.

The last step in the performance management process involves providing rewards to reinforce employee behaviors. Providing rewards helps emphasize what is valued by an organization while also encouraging employees to continue to exert effort on the appropriate tasks. Rewarding individuals for good performance, as well as not rewarding them for poor performance, is a key part of what is known as transactional leadership. According to Barling (2014), providing consequences that are contingent on the employee's performance are "crucial transactions" between managers and employees. You'll read more about transactional leadership in Chapter 13.

Once consequences are given, new goals are set and the revised expectations are communicated to employees. Performance is then evaluated based on those revised goals and expectations, feedback and coaching is provided, and new consequences are provided. In this manner, the performance management process continues in a recurring cycle that integrates numerous topics discussed throughout this book.

Purposes of Performance Management Systems

According to Cleveland et al. (1989), the results of performance appraisals are used for four broad purposes: 1) to make decisions between individuals (such as determining who should get promoted or who should be fired); 2) to make decisions within individuals (such as determining strengths and weaknesses of a single person); 3) to make systems maintenance decisions (such as determining organizational training needs or evaluating personnel systems); and 4) for documentation purposes (such as keeping track of actions and decisions to meet legal requirements).

Aguinis (2009) described six purposes of performance management systems, based in part on Cleveland et al.'s work. These six purposes are as follows:

Strategic.   The purpose of the human resources function in an organization is to maximize the contributions of employees to the goals of the organization, and assessments of employee job performance can play a major role in accomplishing that function. The issue of alignment that was discussed previously is critical. When individual and organizational goals are aligned, the performance management system communicates and reinforces what is most important for individuals to address. When individuals make improvements in these areas, the organization as a whole benefits.

Administrative.   Performance management systems are a key source of information for such things as making salary adjustments, deciding who should be promoted or recognized for exceptional performance, and identifying individuals who should be terminated. Appraisals identify the better-performing employees, and an employee who cannot perform well on his or her current job will not be considered for positive organizational outcomes, such as advancements in pay or promotion. For example, an employee who is judged to be performing in the top 10% of the workforce might get a 12% raise or a promotion. An employee who performs in the bottom 10% might get only a 2% raise, or may be one of the first to be laid off if there are reductions in force.

Communication.   Performance management systems are clear sources of information for employees. They tell employees what is expected of them, how well they are performing, and where they should focus their attention. Through formal and informal discussions, supervisors are able to communicate which activities are of critical importance and which activities require less attention.

Developmental.   According to DeNisi and Pritchard (2006), the ultimate goal of performance management is performance improvement. As part of this, a key element of successful performance management systems is that employees are provided with feedback that highlights their job-related strengths and weaknesses. Deficiencies or weaknesses then become the targets for coaching or training. Training should involve only those areas where poor performance can be attributed to the individual and not to aspects of the work environment. Also included here is the role of performance management systems in promoting employee engagement (to be discussed in Chapter 10). Scholars (Gruman & Saks, 2011; Mone & London, 2010) have suggested that designing performance management systems to focus on employee engagement will lead to higher levels of performance. As Gruman and Saks noted, "A focus on employee engagement in the performance management process may foster performance improvement beyond that achievable through a conventional focus on performance itself" (p. 124).

Organizational Maintenance.   Performance management systems are often used for workforce planning efforts, including succession planning. Succession planning is a concept in which fairly long-term projections (typically three to five years) about future staffing needs in an entire company are based on the anticipated promotion of current employees. It is possible to use information from performance management systems to determine how well employees within an organization are doing overall, and identify possible training needs for individuals and workgroups that will enable them to be ready for promotion at a later date. In addition, performance management systems help in the evaluation of various interventions. For example, if an organization invests in a training program for its salespeople, it is possible to see whether their performance improved following the program. If sales increased, the training program may be deemed a success. If performance remained the same or decreased, it provides some evidence that the training program may not be working as intended.

Documentation.   In many criterion-related validity studies, assessments of the criterion are derived from performance appraisals. Recall that the criterion is a measure of job performance, and that is what performance appraisals are supposed to measure. When I/O psychologists want to validate a new predictor test, they correlate test scores with criterion measures, which are often exhumed from a company's performance appraisal files. Thus, performance management systems help document the validity of predictor measures used for selection of applicants. In addition, formal performance appraisals provide a legally defensible basis for personnel decisions. As discussed in Chapter 5, personnel decisions must be based on reason, not caprice. There must be a defensible explanation for why some employees are promoted or discharged or receive differential pay raises compared with others. As will be discussed shortly, personnel decisions based on performance appraisals are subject to the same legal standards as tests. Both tests and performance evaluations are used as techniques for improving human resources. Although performance appraisals may trigger discordant reactions from some employees, the alternative of making personnel decisions with no rational basis is simply unacceptable.

It is important to note that performance management systems often serve multiple purposes concurrently. For example, information from appraisals may be used to provide developmental feedback and be used as a basis for salary decisions rather than simply for developmental purposes. Unfortunately, the "personnel development" and "salary administration" aspects of appraisal are often uncomfortable partners. Many employees attach far more meaning to pay raises because they are more immediate and instrumental than revelations about weaknesses on the job. If the two functions are combined in the same appraisal, employees can become defensive. When admitting weaknesses means getting a smaller raise, personnel development may take a backseat. In a classic article, Meyer et al. (1965) talked about the need for "split roles" for supervisors in conducting appraisals. One role is a counselor or coach in discussing employee development or performance improvement. The other is a judge in making salary decisions. Evidence shows that most supervisors cannot play both roles simultaneously. The problem may be addressed by having two appraisals—for example, one in January for employee development and the other in June for salary. Or the supervisor may handle development while the human resources department handles salary. Although both functions are important, it is customary practice that they not be conducted at the same time by the same person.

Performance Appraisal and the Law

Federal law on fair employment practices also pertains to performance appraisal. Unfair discrimination can occur not only on the predictor (test) side of the equation but also in the job behavior the test is trying to predict.

Malos (1998) reviewed many court cases involving alleged discrimination and found that charges of discrimination frequently related to the assessment of the employee's job performance. Charges of discrimination may be brought under the laws discussed in Chapter 5, including Title VII of the Civil Rights Acts of 1964 and 1991, the Age Discrimination in Employment Act, and the Americans with Disabilities Act. Litigation can also result from charges of employer *negligence* (breach of duty to conduct appraisals with due care), *defamation* (disclosure of untrue unfavorable performance information that damages the reputation of the employee), and *misrepresentation* (disclosure of untrue favorable performance information that presents a risk of harm to prospective employees or third parties).

Malos synthesized the findings from many court cases and arrived at recommendations for employers regarding both the content and the process of performance appraisals. The *contents* of performance appraisals are the criteria of job performance that are evaluated. Table 7-1 gives Malos' recommendations for legally sound performance appraisals. Conducting the appraisals on job-related factors, usually derived from a work analysis, is particularly important. Werner and Bolino (1997) likewise found that whether or not the company based its performance appraisals on criteria derived from work analyses was often a deciding factor in court rulings. Malos also made *procedural* recommendations for legally sound performance appraisals. These recommendations are presented in Table 7-2. Malos concluded by stating that as our economy continues

Table 7-1　*Content recommendations for legally sound performance appraisals*

Appraisal Criteria
■ Should be objective rather than subjective ■ Should be job-related or based on job analysis ■ Should be based on behaviors rather than traits ■ Should be within the control of the ratee ■ Should relate to specific functions, not global assessments

Source: From "Current Legal Issues in Performance Appraisal," by S. B. Malos, in J. W. Smither (Ed.), *Performance appraisal* (p. 80). Copyright © 1998 Jossey-Bass. Reprinted with permission.

Table 7-2　*Procedural recommendations for legally sound performance appraisals*

Appraisal Procedures
■ Should be standardized and uniform for all employees within a job group ■ Should be formally communicated to employees ■ Should provide notice of performance deficiencies and of opportunities to correct them ■ Should provide access for employees to review appraisal results ■ Should provide formal appeal mechanisms that allow for employee input ■ Should use multiple, diverse, and unbiased raters ■ Should provide written instructions for training raters ■ Should require thorough and consistent documentation across raters that includes specific examples of performance based on personal knowledge ■ Should establish a system to detect potentially discriminatory effect or abuses of the system overall

Source: From "Current Legal Issues in Performance Appraisal," by S. B. Malos, in J. W. Smither (Ed.), *Performance appraisal* (p. 83). Copyright © 1998 Jossey-Bass. Reprinted with permission.

to move toward a service and information emphasis, there will be the tendency to use subjective performance criteria, particularly at the professional and managerial levels. Also, more organizations are increasingly relying on multiple sources of evaluation (customers, subordinates, and peers). Using both subjective criteria and untrained raters can lead to discrimination claims that are difficult to defend. It is recommended that when such criteria and raters are used, they should be used in conjunction with objective criteria and trained raters whose input is given greater weight.

Judgmental Evaluations

Rating Errors and Biases

Serial position error
A type of rating error in which the rater has better recall of information that is presented at the beginning or end of a sequence, and has the worst recall of information in the middle of the sequence.

The most common means of appraising performance is through judgmental ratings. Because errors occur in making ratings, it is important to understand the major types of rating errors and biases that impact evaluations. In making appraisals, the rater may unknowingly commit errors in judgment. Serial position errors occur as a function of the sequence in which information is received. Contrast errors are a result of a faulty comparison of two (or more) individuals. Others, such as halo errors, leniency errors, and central-tendency errors, occur in part as a function of the rating scales used. Each of these errors stem from rater bias and misperception.

Serial position errors reflect the tendency for individuals to remember information when it is presented at a certain place within a sequence (or its serial position: e.g., first, second, last). Research has demonstrated that people are better able to recall information presented first (the *primacy effect*) or last (the *recency effect*) in a sequence. This means that raters will be more likely to recall information about individuals they observe first or last. Similarly, they will be better able to recall information early in one's relationship (e.g., first impressions) or information from events that just recently occurred. Thus, if evaluations are only occurring once every six months, the most recent behavior may be given more weight than behavior exhibited at other times.

Contrast error
A type of rating error in which the rater assesses the ratee as performing better (or worse) than he or she actually performed due to a comparison with another ratee who performed particularly poorly (or well).

Contrast error occurs when raters compare (or contrast) one individual with another when making evaluations. This would only be an error if individuals are supposed to be compared against a set standard rather than against one another. Managers are likely to have contrast effects when they rate numerous people within a short time period. If a manager evaluates a particularly strong employee, the employee that is rated afterwards may seem worse by comparison. If the manager rates the second employee lower than what he or she might have if the strong employee had not been rated previously, then a contrast error has occurred. The same issue arises when employees are rated higher than they should be simply because they are being compared to a weak employee.

Halo error
A type of rating error in which the rater assesses the ratee as performing well on a variety of performance dimensions, despite having credible knowledge of only a limited number of performance dimensions.

Halo errors are evaluations based on the rater's general opinions about an employee. Halo errors occur when the rater generally has a *favorable* attitude toward the employee that permeates all evaluations of this person. When a rater has a generally *unfavorable* attitude about an employee that permeates evaluations, it is referred to as a *horn* error. Typically the rater has strong feelings about at least one important aspect of the employee's performance. The feelings are then generalized to other performance factors, and the employee is judged (across many factors) as uniformly good or bad.

Whereas an employee truly may be good or bad across many areas, it is when these evaluations are based on insufficient information that it is considered an error. For example, a rater who is impressed by an employee's particularly good idea might allow those feelings to carry over to the evaluation of leadership, cooperation, motivation, and so on. This occurs even though the "good idea" is not related to these other factors. In general, halo errors are considered to be the most serious and pervasive of all rating errors (Cooper, 1981).

Research on halo error has revealed it is a more complex phenomenon than initially believed. Murphy and Anhalt (1992) concluded that halo error is not a stable characteristic of the rater or ratee, but rather is the result of an interaction of the rater, ratee, and evaluative situation. Balzer and Sulsky (1992) contended that halo error may not be a rating "error" so much as an indicator of how we cognitively process information in arriving at judgments of other people. That is, the presence of a halo does not necessarily indicate the ratings are inaccurate.

Leniency errors are yet another type of rating error that impacts evaluations. Just as some teachers are "hard graders" and others "easy graders," raters can be characterized by the leniency of their appraisals. Harsh raters give evaluations that are lower than the "true" level of ability (if it can be ascertained); this is called *severity* or *negative leniency*. Easy raters give evaluations that are higher than the "true" level; this is called *positive leniency*. These errors usually occur because raters apply personal standards derived from their own values or previous experience. Kane et al. (1995) found that the tendency to make leniency errors was stable with individuals; that is, people tend to be consistently lenient or harsh in their ratings. Bernardin et al. (2000) found that the most lenient raters were those who were low in conscientiousness and high in agreeableness.

Central-tendency error refers to the rater's unwillingness to assign extreme—high or low—ratings. In contrast to leniency and severity errors where individuals are rated as being unjustifiably high or low, everyone is "average," and only the middle (central) part of the scale is used with central-tendency errors. This may happen when raters are asked to evaluate unfamiliar aspects of performance. Rather than not respond, they play it safe and say the person is average in this "unknown" ability.

Worthy of note is the point that the absence of rating errors does not necessarily indicate *accuracy* in the ratings. Accuracy in performance appraisal refers to the extent to which ratings are valid measures of the "true" variable being measured. The "true" variable can refer to a global construct, such as overall job performance, or a dimension of job performance, such as interpersonal relations ability. The presence of the rating errors leads to inaccurate ratings, but accuracy involves other issues besides the removal of these three error types. I/O psychologists are seeking to develop statistical indicators of rating accuracy, some based on classical issues in measurement.

Rating Scales

Judgmental evaluations are commonly used for performance appraisal because finding relevant objective measures is difficult. Subjective assessments can apply to almost all jobs. Those who do the assessments are usually supervisors, but some use has also been made of self-assessment and peer assessment. A wide variety of measures have been developed, all intended to provide accurate assessments of how people are perform-

Leniency error
A type of rating error in which the rater assesses a disproportionately large number of ratees as performing well (positive leniency) or poorly (negative leniency) in contrast to their true level of performance.

Central-tendency error
A type of rating error in which the rater assesses a disproportionately large number of ratees as performing in the middle or central part of a distribution of rated performance in contrast to their true level of performance.

ing (Pulakos, 1997). There are three major types of rating scales used in performance appraisal:

1. Graphic rating scales
2. Employee-comparison methods
   a. Rank order
   b. Paired comparison
   c. Forced distribution
3. Behavioral checklists and scales
   a. Critical incidents
   b. Behaviorally anchored rating scale (BARS).

Graphic rating scales are the most commonly used method in performance appraisal. Individuals are rated on a number of traits or factors. The rater judges "how much" of each factor the individual has. Usually performance is judged on a 5- or 7-point scale, and the number of factors ranges between 5 and 20. The more common dimensions rated are quantity of work, quality of work, practical judgment, job knowledge, cooperation, and motivation. Examples of typical graphic rating scales are shown in Figure 7-2. Graphic rating scales are particularly susceptible to rating errors. As such, other methods of performance appraisal have been developed.

Employee-comparison methods involve individuals being compared with one another, not against some defined standard. Variance is thereby forced into the appraisals. Thus the concentration of ratings at one part of the scale caused by rating error is avoided. The major advantage of employee-comparison methods is the elimination of central-tendency and leniency errors because raters are compelled to differentiate among the people being rated. However, halo error is still possible because it manifests itself across multiple evaluations of the same person. All methods of employee comparison involve the question of whether variation represents true differences in performance or creates a false impression of large differences when they are in fact small. The three major employee-comparison methods are rank order, paired comparison, and forced distribution.

With the *rank-order method*, the rater ranks employees from high to low on a given performance dimension. The person ranked first is regarded as the "best" and the person ranked last as the "worst." However, we do not know how good the "best" is or how bad the "worst" is. We do not know the level of performance. For example, the Nobel Prize winners in a given year could be ranked in terms of their overall contributions to science. But we would be hard pressed to conclude that the Nobel laureate ranked last made the worst contribution to science. Rank-order data are all relative to some standard—in this case excellence in scientific research. Another problem is that it becomes quite tedious and perhaps somewhat meaningless to rank order large numbers of people. What usually happens is that the rater can sort out the people at the top and bottom of the pile. For those with undifferentiated performance, however, the rankings may be somewhat arbitrary.

With the *paired-comparison method*, each employee is compared with every other employee in the group being evaluated. The rater's task is to select which of the two is better on the dimension being rated. The method is typically used to evaluate

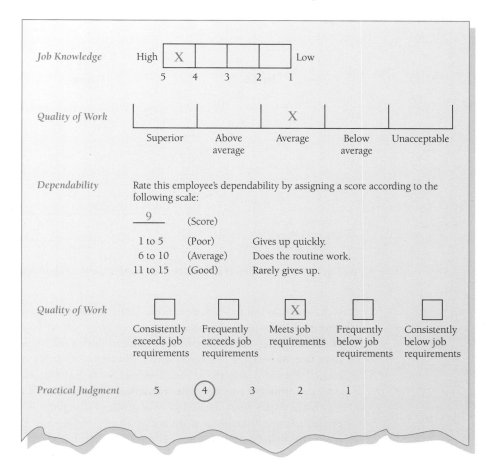

Figure 7-2 *Examples of graphic rating scales for various performance dimensions*

employees on a single dimension: overall ability to perform the job. The number of evaluation pairs is computed by the formula $n(n-1)/2$, where n is the number of people to be evaluated. For example, if there are 10 people in a group, the number of paired comparisons is $10(9)/2 = 45$. At the conclusion of the evaluation, the number of times each person was selected as the better of the two is tallied. The people are then ranked by the number of tallies they receive.

A major limitation is that the number of comparisons made mushrooms dramatically with large numbers of employees. If 50 people are to be appraised, the number of comparisons is 1,225; this obviously takes too much time. The paired-comparison method is best for relatively small samples.

The *forced-distribution method* is most useful when the other employee-comparison methods are most limited—that is, when the sample is large. Forced distribution is typically used when the rater must evaluate employees on a single dimension, but it can also be used with multiple dimensions. The procedure is based on the normal distribution and assumes that employee performance is normally distributed. The distribution

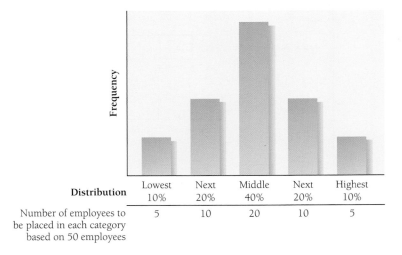

Distribution	Lowest 10%	Next 20%	Middle 40%	Next 20%	Highest 10%
Number of employees to be placed in each category based on 50 employees	5	10	20	10	5

Figure 7-3   *The forced-distribution method of performance appraisal*

is divided into five to seven categories. Using predetermined percentages (based on the normal distribution), the rater evaluates an employee by placing him or her into one of the categories. All employees are evaluated in this manner. The method "forces" the rater to distribute the employees across all categories (which is how the method gets its name). Thus it is impossible for all employees to be rated excellent, average, or poor. An example of the procedure for a sample of 50 employees is illustrated in Figure 7-3.

Some raters react negatively to the forced-distribution method, saying that the procedure creates artificial distinctions among employees. This is partly because the raters think that performance is not normally distributed but rather negatively skewed; that is, most of their employees are performing very well. The dissatisfaction can be partially allayed by noting that the lowest 10% are not necessarily performing poorly, just not as well as the others. The problem (as with all comparison methods) is that performance is not compared with a defined standard. The meaning of the differences among employees must be supplied from some other source.

One method of performance appraisal predicated on the forced distribution method is **top-grading** (Smart, 2005). The method involves identifying the bottom 10% of a company's workforce (as shown in Figure 7-3), and eliminating their positions. The loss of the bottom 10% of the workforce not only removes the lowest performing employees, but also serves to induce even higher performance in the remaining 90% of the workforce. This forced distribution method of evaluation is repeated year after year, with the result that the workforce gets progressively better, as well as progressively smaller. The slang term for top-grading is "rank and yank." Scullen et al. (2005) examined the effectiveness of the top-grading method of performance appraisal. The results of their study supported such a strategy for improving workforce quality, but its effectiveness diminished substantially beyond its initial years of implementation. Dominick (2009) reported the method lends itself to internal political maneuvering by managers that has little to do with performance. For example, managers may retain poor performing employees throughout the year just to have

Top-grading
A method of performance management whereby employees are graded on their overall contribution to the organization, and each year the bottom 10% of the employees are dismissed.

someone to rank at the bottom, sparing other employees from being "yanked." It is a statistical fact that no matter how well employees are performing, every year 10% of the workforce must be ranked in the bottom 10%. After repeated "yankings" the bottom 10% may well be performing their jobs successfully, and it is a matter of debate how much more work the surviving employees can absorb due to the annual departure of 10% of the workforce (see I/O Psychology and the Economy: *The Paradox of Top-Grading*).

Behavioral checklists and scales represent the most recent advances in performance appraisal. The key term is *behavior*. Behaviors are less vague than traits (such as "ambition" and "cooperativeness"). The greater the agreement on the meaning of the performance appraised, the greater the chance that the appraisal will be accurate. All of the methods in this category have their origin directly or indirectly in the critical-incidents method.

I/O Psychology and the Economy: *The Paradox of Top-Grading*

Few methods of performance appraisal have such a direct economic effect as does top-grading (or "rank and yank"). The paradox of the method is that it produces both positive and negative economic consequences simultaneously, benefiting the economic position of the organization and harming the economic position of the nation.

Assume an organization ranks its employees from high to low, and the bottom 10% are dismissed. What the organization gains economically is its total payroll (labor) costs are reduced. The magnitude of the reduction depends upon *which* employees are dismissed. If the dismissed employees have "above average" (within the organization) salaries, the cost savings are greater than 10%. If they have "below average" salaries, the cost savings are less than 10%. Let us assume the dismissals result in a 10% cost savings. In theory, the remaining 90% of the workforce will absorb most of the work performed by the dismissed 10%. The organization achieves what is called an "economic efficiency:" perhaps a 3% loss in work productivity, but a 10% reduction in cost. The surviving employees are fearful "they will be next" in the next annual round of "rank and yank," so they continue to work harder and smarter. The following year there is another round of dismissals, another 10% reduction in payroll expenses, but a greater loss in productivity, perhaps 8%. Eventually the cost of lower organizational productivity exceeds the cost savings achieved from having fewer employees to pay, and at this point the economic benefits from repeated reductions in personnel cease.

At the same time an organization is experiencing gains in economic efficiency from lowered payroll expenses, at the national level the economy suffers as increasingly more individuals become unemployed. If the dismissed employees remain unemployed, they receive unemployment benefits paid by the federal government. As increasingly more organizations engage in "rank and yank," increasingly more individuals become unemployed. Only if these dismissed workers find new employment elsewhere does the national economy not suffer. The question of economic efficiency is "efficiency for whom?" Actions that benefit the economic interests of a company can have the opposite effect at the national level. This stands in contrast with a booming economy, where organizational productivity is very robust and the national unemployment level is very low.

Critical incidents
Specific behaviors
indicative of good or bad
job performance.

Critical incidents are behaviors that result in good or poor job performance. Supervisors record behaviors of employees that greatly influence their job performance. They either keep a running tally of these critical incidents as they occur on the job or recall them at a later time. Critical incidents are usually grouped by aspects of performance: job knowledge, decision-making ability, leadership, and so on. The end product is a list of behaviors (good and bad) that constitute effective and ineffective job performance.

Each employee's performance can be described in terms of the occurrence of these critical behaviors. The supervisor can then counsel the employee to avoid the bad and continue the good behaviors. For example, a negative critical incident for a machine operator might be "leaves machine running while unattended." A positive one might be "always wears safety goggles on the job." Discussing performance in such clear terms is more understandable than using such vague statements as "poor attitude" or "careless work habits."

Behaviorally
anchored rating
scales (BARS)
A type of performance
appraisal rating scale in
which the scale points
are descriptions of
behavior.

Behaviorally anchored rating scales (BARS) are a combination of the critical-incidents and rating-scale methods. Performance is rated on a scale, but the scale points are anchored with behavioral incidents. The development of BARS is time-consuming, especially in reaching agreement on the job behaviors.

One of the major advantages of BARS is unrelated to performance appraisal. It is the high degree of involvement of the persons developing the scale. The participants must carefully examine specific behaviors that lead to effective performance. In so doing, they may reject false stereotypes about ineffective performances. The method has face validity for both the rater and ratee and also appears useful for training raters. However, one disadvantage is that BARS are job specific; that is, a different behaviorally anchored rating scale must be developed for every job. Furthermore, it is possible for employees to exhibit different behaviors (on a single performance dimension) depending on situational factors such as the degree of urgency.

The accuracy of judgmental evaluations in performance appraisal refers to the extent to which the ratings are valid measures of the "true" variable being measured. The "true" variable can refer to a global construct, such as overall job performance, or a dimension of job performance, such as interpersonal relations ability. One method of assessing the accuracy of judgmental data is to correlate them with performance appraisals from another method, such as objective production data. In studies that have conducted this type of analysis, the resulting correlations have been only moderate. Although these results may be interpreted to mean that judgmental data exhibit only moderate validity, the key question is whether the objective production data can be assumed to represent "true" performance. Objective production data might be incomplete or marginally relevant. Because we never obtain measures of the conceptual criterion (that is, "true" performance), we are forced to deal with imperfect measures that, not surprisingly, yield imperfect results. Research (e.g., Weekley & Gier, 1989) showed the existence of rater disagreement and halo error even among such expert raters as Olympic judges who were intensely trained to make accurate evaluations. DeNisi and Peters (1996) reported that instructing raters to keep a structured diary for continuous record keeping of performance (rather than using memory recall) produced more accurate assessments of the employees.

After many years of research (see Field Note 1: *Good Research Isn't Cheap*) on various types of performance appraisal rating scales, I/O psychologists have concluded that the variance in rated performance due to the rating scale format is slight, typically

Field Note 1: *Good Research Isn't Cheap*

Many times unexpected costs are associated with performance appraisal. Here is the story of one of the more unusual expenses I have ever encountered in a research study.

One of the uses of performance appraisal information is as a criterion of job performance. In turn, criteria of job performance may be used to validate selection tests. I had a colleague who needed to collect both performance appraisal (criterion) data and test score (predictor) data to validate a selection test battery for a company. He traveled to the company and had all the supervisors convene in the company cafeteria. He explained the nature of the performance ratings he wanted them to make. Then he explained that all their subordinates would be taking a 30-minute test, and the scores would be correlated with the supervisors' performance appraisal ratings, as is done in a concurrent criterion-related validity study. My colleague then asked the supervisors whether they wanted to take the same test their subordinates would be taking just to get a feel for what it

was like. They agreed. He passed out the test and informed them they would have 30 minutes to complete it. He wanted the testing procedure to be exact, giving everyone precisely 30 minutes. His watch did not have a second hand, so he was about to ask if he could borrow someone else's watch, when he spied the company's microwave oven on the wall in the cafeteria. He went over to the microwave, set the timer for 30 minutes, told the supervisors to begin the test, and started the microwave.

About 20 minutes into the test, a terrible odor began to fill the cafeteria. Somebody noticed it was coming from the microwave. My colleague had failed to place anything in the microwave when he started it, so for 20 minutes the microwave cooked itself, ultimately suffering terminal meltdown. The microwave cost $800 to replace and is one of the more unusual test-validation expense items I have ever heard of. Incidentally, the test turned out to be highly predictive of the performance appraisal ratings, so the exercise was not a complete waste.

less than 5%. Other sources of variance in rated performance are more substantial. These topics will be discussed next.

Rater Training

Rater error training The process of educating raters to make more accurate assessments of performance, typically achieved by reducing the frequency of halo, leniency, and central-tendency errors.

Raters can be trained to make better performance appraisals. Two of the most common types of rater training include rater error training and frame-of-reference training. **Rater error training** is a formal process in which appraisers are taught to make fewer halo, leniency, and central-tendency errors. Zedeck and Cascio (1982) considered the purpose for which performance appraisal ratings are made—merit raise, retention, and development—and found that training works better for some purposes than others. Training typically enhances the accuracy of performance appraisals as well as their acceptability to those who are being appraised.

"Barkley, I perceive my role in this institution not as a judge but merely as an observer and recorder. I have observed you to be a prize boob and have so recorded it."

One concern raised with rater error training is that the reduction of errors does not necessarily increase accuracy in ratings, which presumably is the ultimate goal of training raters. For example, Hedge and Kavanagh (1988) concluded that certain types of rater training reduce classic rating errors such as halo and leniency but do not increase rating accuracy. By increasing rater awareness of these effects, raters may actually over-correct their behaviors (such as becoming more severe to combat leniency). In addition, sometimes raters give uniformly high ratings to an employee that are in fact justified. That is, the employee truly performs well across many dimensions. Raters who are taught about halo effect, however, may "correct" themselves and provide more variation in their ratings, thereby resulting in decreased rather than increased accuracy. The relationship between rating errors and accuracy is uncertain because of our inability to know what "truth" is (Sulsky & Balzer, 1988).

Frame-of-reference training
The process of providing a common perspective and set of standards to all raters to increase the accuracy of their evaluations.

According to Smither (2012), the problems described above have led to a greater focus in rater training on increasing accuracy rather than on the reduction of errors. A particularly promising approach to this is **frame-of-reference training** (Sulsky & Day, 1992), which involves providing raters with common reference standards (i.e., frames) by which to evaluate performance. Raters are shown vignettes of good, poor, and average performances and are given feedback on the accuracy of their ratings of the vignettes. The intent of the training is to "calibrate" raters so that they agree on what constitutes varying levels of performance effectiveness for each performance dimension. According to Gorman and Rentsch (2009), the objective of frame-of-reference training is to provide raters a uniform standard (or a frame of reference) for making performance evaluations. The logic is that individuals can be trained to utilize the same standards of judgments as possessed by highly knowledgeable experts in rendering evaluations. Frame-of-reference training teaches raters "what to look for" in judging performance. Uggerslev and Sulsky (2008) noted that errors in judgment were typically the result of either under-weighting or over-weighting certain dimensions of job behavior (e.g., oral communication) compared to an ideal standard. The authors found frame-of-reference training helpful in improving under-weighting (teaching raters to pay more attention) than over-weighting (teaching raters to pay less attention). In a meta-analytic review of frame-of-reference training, Roch et al. (2012) found that frame-of-reference training is an effective rater training method that does appear to improve rating accuracy.

Rater Motivation

It is not unusual for the majority of employees in a company to receive very high performance evaluations. These inflated ratings are often interpreted as evidence of massive rater errors (i.e., leniency or halo) or a breakdown in the performance appraisal system. The typical organizational response to rating inflation is to make some technical adjustment in the rating scale format or to institute a new training program for raters. However, another explanation for rating inflation is unrelated to rater errors.

Murphy and Cleveland (1995) posited that the tendency to give uniformly high ratings is an instance of adaptive behavior that is, from the rater's point of view, an eminently logical course of action. These ratings are more likely to be a result of the rater's *unwillingness* to provide accurate ratings than of their *capacity* to rate accurately. If the situation is examined from the rater's perspective, there are many sound reasons to provide inaccurate ratings. **Rater motivation**, also referred to as *conscious rating distortion* (Spence & Keeping, 2011), refers to the deliberate distortion of ratings. These distortions occur when raters purposefully give ratees scores that are higher or lower than they actually deserve. These distortions typically occur to achieve some particular result.

Rater motivation
A concept that refers to organizationally-induced pressures that compel raters to distort their evaluations.

There are several reasons that raters may want to give unjustifiably lenient ratings. First, there are typically no rewards from the organization for accurate appraisals and few if any sanctions for inaccurate appraisals. Official company policies often emphasize the value of accurate performance appraisals, but organizations typically take no specific steps to reward this supposedly valued activity. Second, the most common reason cited for rating inflation is that high ratings are needed to guarantee promotions, salary increases, and other valued rewards. Low ratings, on the other hand, result in these rewards being withheld from subordinates. Raters are thus motivated to obtain valued rewards for their subordinates. Third, raters are motivated to give inflated ratings because the ratings received by subordinates are a reflection of the rater's job performance (Latham, 1986). One of the duties of managers is to develop their subordinates. If managers consistently rate their subordinates as less than good performers, it can appear that the managers are not doing their jobs. Thus high ratings make the rater look good and low ratings make the rater look bad. Fourth, raters tend to inflate their ratings because they wish to avoid the negative reactions that accompany low ratings (Klimoski & Inks, 1990). Negative evaluations typically result in defensive reactions from subordinates, which can create a stressful situation for the rater. The simplest way to avoid unpleasant or defensive reactions in appraisal interviews is to give uniformly positive feedback (i.e., inflated ratings). Giving everyone high ratings is perhaps seen by raters as a way to keep morale high and interpersonal relationships good (Barnes-Farrell, 2001). For example, as Wong and Kwong (2007) found, raters sometimes have the goal of increasing group harmony. When this is their goal, they tend to provide more uniformly inflated ratings across employees.

There are also several reasons that raters may provide employees with deflated ratings, or ratings lower than their performance might suggest they deserve. Aguinis (2013) suggested that raters may artificially lower their ratings of employees to shock employees and alert them that there is a problem that needs to be addressed. In addition, raters may deflate their ratings to teach an employee a lesson or send a signal that the employee may want to consider looking elsewhere for employment. Finally, Aguinis noted that raters might provide harsher ratings to provide compelling documentation in the event that the employee is terminated in the near future. The raters may be attempting to create a "paper trail" to justify their future actions by providing ratings that indicate performance is below standards. In this way, they may be attempting to avoid potential legal recourse resulting from a termination without cause (or terminations that are unrelated to misconduct).

Kozlowski et al. (1998) described "appraisal politics" in organizations. If there is a sense that most other raters are inflating their ratings of their subordinates, then a good rater has to play politics to protect and enhance the careers of his or her own subordinates. To the extent that a rating inflation strategy actually enhances the prospects of the better subordinates, it may be interpreted as being in the best interests of the organization to do so. Kozlowski et al. stated: "Indeed, if rating distortions are the norm, a failure to engage in appraisal politics may be maladaptive" (p. 176). Supporting this conclusion, Jawahar and Williams (1997) meta-analyzed performance appraisals given for administrative purposes (e.g., promotions) versus developmental or research purposes. Their results showed that performance appraisals conducted for administrative purposes were one-third of a standard deviation higher than those obtained for development or research purposes. As these authors stated, performance appraisals are much more lenient when those appraisals are "for keeps" (see Field Note 2: *Are High Ratings a "Problem"?*). X. Wang et al. (2010) concluded that raters can distort ratings to achieve desired goals. Raters lowered the performance ratings of high performers to achieve greater fairness (i.e., fewer differences among those being rated), and elevated the ratings of low performers to motivate them.

There is no simple way to counteract a rater's motivation to inflate ratings. The problem will not be solved by just increasing the capability of raters. In addition, the environment must be modified in such a way that raters are motivated to provide accurate ratings. Murphy and Cleveland believe accurate ratings are most likely to occur in environments where the following conditions exist:

Field Note 2: *Are High Ratings a "Problem"?*

Research on performance appraisal ratings has typically regarded high ratings as reflecting some kind of error. This error then becomes the focus of corrective action, as methods (i.e., different rating techniques, rater training) are applied to produce lower evaluations. However, an examination of just the statistical properties of ratings, apart from the organizational context in which they are rendered, fails to capture *why* they occur. As research has revealed, managers who give high evaluations of their employees are behaving in an eminently reasonable fashion, not making errors per se. Managers (or other supervisors) have a vested interest in the job performance of their subordinates. The subordinates are socialized and coached to exhibit desired behaviors on the job. Those who don't exhibit these behaviors are often dismissed. Those who do are rewarded with social approval, if nothing more than being allowed to retain their jobs. The performance of subordinates is also regarded as a measure of the manager's own job performance. It is then logical for a manager to cultivate an efficient work group. Finally, managers often feel a sense of sponsorship for their employees. They want their employees to do well and have in fact often invested a sizable portion of their own time and energy to produce that outcome. Thus, when it comes time for a formal performance review of their subordinates, managers often respond by rating them highly. Rather than errors of judgment, the high evaluations could represent little more than the outcome of a successful socialization process designed to achieve that very outcome.

- Good and poor performance are clearly defined.
- Distinguishing among workers in terms of their levels of performance is widely accepted.
- There is a high degree of trust in the system.
- Low ratings do not automatically result in the loss of valued rewards.
- Valued rewards are clearly linked to accuracy in performance appraisal.

The authors know of organizations in which *none* of these conditions is met, but they don't know of any in which *all* of them are met. It is clear that we need more research on the organizational context in which performance appraisals are conducted. Mero et al. (2007) also reported findings that underscored the importance of the context in which ratings are made. The authors found that more accurate ratings occur when raters are accountable to people of a higher status than themselves. If the raters are held accountable to people of a lower status than themselves, however, ratings were more likely to be inflated. These findings were stronger when ratings were presented face-to-face with employees, as opposed to in writing. The problem of rating inflation will ultimately be solved by changing the context in which ratings are made, not by changing the rater or the rating scale.

360-Degree Feedback

360-degree feedback
A process of evaluating employees from multiple rating sources, usually including supervisor, peer, subordinate, and self. Also called multisource feedback.

The technique of **360-degree feedback**, also called multisource feedback (MSF), is the practice of using multiple raters from different perspectives in the assessment of individuals. The term *360-degree feedback* derives from the geometric rationale for multiple-rater assessment, as shown in Figure 7-4. The target employee is evaluated by other individuals who interact in a social network. For example, feedback about a target employee may be solicited from the individual's coworkers, subordinates, customers, and superiors. The employee also provides self-assessments. The multiple raters make their assessments of the employee, and then the assessments are compared. The original purpose for 360-degree feedback was to enhance individuals' awareness of their strengths and weaknesses to guide developmental planning. However, it is increasingly being used as a method of performance appraisal (Bracken et al., 1997). According to Tornow (1993), 360-degree assessment activities are usually based on two key assumptions: (1) awareness of any discrepancies between how we see ourselves and how others see us enhances self-awareness, and (2) enhanced self-awareness is a key to maximum performance as a manager and thus becomes a foundation for management and leadership development programs.

It is particularly instructive to understand how *disagreement* among raters in 360-degree feedback is interpreted. The classic measurement perspective treats disagreement among raters as error variance—that is, something undesirable that reduces inter-rater reliability. With 360-degree feedback, however, differences in rater perspectives are regarded as potentially valuable and useful and are not treated as variations to be reduced. Such differences provide an opportunity for professional development and personal learning, to understand why individuals are perceived as they are by others (see Cross-Cultural I/O Psychology: *Cultural Differences in the Acceptability of Multisource Feedback*).

A disturbing finding regarding the accuracy of multisource feedback was reported by Scullen et al. (2000). Based on a large number of 360-degree assessments, the

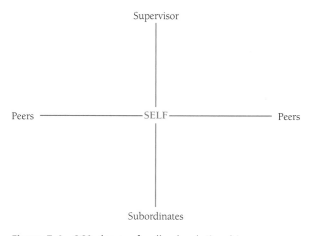

Figure 7-4   *360-degree feedback relationships*

Cross-Cultural I/O Psychology: *Cultural Differences in the Acceptability of Multisource Feedback*

As discussed in Chapter 6, the acceptability and usefulness of mentoring as a developmental method are influenced by cultural factors. Likewise, the acceptability and usefulness of some performance appraisal methods are also subject to cultural consideration. Multisource feedback (MSF) has been described as an "American product" based on the cultural values of the United States, including a strong sense of individualism and participative democracy. Individual achievement is regarded as a virtue, and opinions from a wide range of people are solicited in addressing social problems. As discussed previously, nations differ in power distance, and they also differ in individualism. Power distance influences who provides performance feedback and appraisals in an organization. In countries with a large power distance, employee appraisal is most often conducted by a person who has more power than the person being evaluated. Because there is the perception that managers and subordinates are unequal, it may be particularly inappropriate to have employees of less power evaluate their managers (the basis of subordinate evaluations). Conversely, employees in cultures with a small power distance are less dependent on their supervisors, and thus MSF systems including upward appraisals are likely to be more acceptable.

It is the inherent nature of performance appraisal to compare and contrast employees. This is the perceived intent of forced-choice rating methods. Employees who get higher evaluations often receive greater rewards (e.g., pay raise) than employees with lower evaluations. In an individualistic culture, this type of appraisal is acceptable because it affirms interpersonal competition for rewards. Cultures low on individualism, in contrast, place greater emphasis on group unity and maintaining harmonious group relations. A performance appraisal system that seeks to differentiate employees within a group is far less likely to be regarded as useful to the overall goals of the organization. Uncritically transplanting performance management processes developed in the United States to nations that have different cultural values is doomed to fail. Managerial techniques, as performance appraisal, are most effective when they are congruent with a country's cultural values.

authors partitioned the total amount of variance in the assessments into three components: the target's actual job performance, the raters' biases in the perception and recall of that performance, and random (uncontrollable) measurement error. The results revealed that only 25% of the variance in multisource feedback is attributable to the target's actual job performance, the intended object of the ratings. More than twice that amount of variance (54%) was due to rater bias in evaluating that performance. Thus the amount of performance-related variance is only moderate and differs by the perspective of the rater. The authors concluded that what multisource feedback measures is largely the idiosyncratic rating tendencies of the raters. In a related study, Hoffman et al. (2010) reported that performance ratings were more strongly influenced by idiosyncratic rating tendencies of individuals and the source of the ratings (peers, subordinates, supervisor) than the specific dimensions of behavior (e.g., leadership, interpersonal skills, etc.) being rated. Along these lines, Ng et al. (2011) found that subordinates tend to be more lenient and fall prey to halo errors more so than peers and superiors. Hoffman and Woehr (2009) concluded that multisource feedback given to managers on the basis of traditional behavioral dimensions (e.g., leadership, sociability, etc.) was not helpful in enhancing job performance. That is, managers could use the feedback to improve *themselves* along these dimensions (e.g., they could become more sociable), but such improvements would not necessarily translate into improved *job performance*. The rationale for the development purpose of multisource feedback is behavioral change will result in improved job performance. Perhaps feedback of a different type might be more facilitative of increasing job performance.

I/O psychologists are divided in their opinions about the use of 360-degree feedback for both developmental and administrative purposes. The term *feedback* suggests that the method is best suited for its original intent, providing developmental feedback to employees. However, in recent years some organizations have shifted to use 360-degree feedback for both developmental *and* administrative purposes. Balzer et al. (2004) presented various issues associated with using 360-degree feedback for dual purposes, as shown in Table 7-3. The major practical differences between the two purposes include source anonymity (i.e., the actual identity of the peers and subordinates), the implications of negative feedback, and adherence to legal guidelines. In short, both the employer's responsibilities and the employee's adaptive behavior differ as a function of how multisource feedback is used by the organization. Balzer et al. offered the following about multisource feedback (MSF) systems: "Decisions about the design and implementation of an MSF system may be quite different for the most frequently discussed purposes of the system: feedback versus administrative. It is therefore critical to determine carefully the purpose(s) of an MSF system, communicate the purpose(s) to all who will participate in the system, and carefully monitor adherence to the purpose(s)" (p. 405). Simply put, an organization should not state that multisource feedback is used for only developmental purposes and then discharge an employee because he or she got low evaluations (as from peers). Some experts think that over time it may be possible to gradually shift from development-only multisource feedback to a system that also is used for administrative decision making. Others are far less confident.

Table 7-3 *The effects of purpose on MSF systems*

Decision Points	Feedback Purposes	Administrative Purposes
1. Content of instrument	Tied to employee short- and long-term developmental needs	Tied to job description or established performance goals
2. Frequency of use	As needed	Consistent with performance review timetable
3. Source anonymity	Of less importance	Of critical importance
4. Threat/implications of negative feedback	Low (limited consequences)	High (potentially serious consequences)
5. Data ownership	Individual receiving feedback	Organization
6. Adherence to legal guidelines	Of less importance	Of great importance

Source: From Balzer, W. K., Greguras, G. J., and Raymark, P. H., "Multisource Feedback," in J. C. Thomas (Ed.), *Comprehensive handbook of psychological assessments*, Vol. 4. Copyright © 2004 John Wiley & Sons. This material is used by permission of John Wiley & Sons.

Feedback in Performance Management Contexts

As noted earlier, providing feedback is the third step in the performance management process. Without feedback, employee performance may actually decline rather than improve. Feedback on job performance has two properties: information and motivation. Feedback can tell the employee how to perform better as well as increase his or her desire to perform well. In this section, we discuss research related to giving and seeking feedback as well as typical reactions to feedback.

Giving Feedback

The process of giving feedback is an essential part of the performance management process. It is also one of the most difficult and most dreaded activities, by both supervisors and employees, mainly because not all feedback is likely to be positive in nature. Despite negative feedback's role in increasing substandard performance and guiding subsequent employee development, supervisors tend to dislike giving it. The reluctance or failure of individuals to communicate bad news is known as the "mum effect" and is a pervasive and problematic phenomenon (Rosen & Tesser, 1970). Marler et al. (2012) noted that individuals often avoid giving negative feedback in an effort to protect themselves and abide by organizational norms. According to Baron (1990), this tendency to delay giving negative feedback is likely to backfire, noting that "Managers often refrain from criticizing their subordinates until the frequency of severity of performance problems—and the managers' annoyance with them—rise to extremely high levels" (p. 235). When they do finally provide feedback, Baron notes that their emotions are high and the feedback that is provided is "often biting, sarcastic, and harsh" (p. 235). The destructive nature of the feedback detracts from the purpose of the message and all but ensures its rejection.

In a large-scale meta-analysis on the effects of feedback on performance, Kluger and DeNisi (1996) found that although feedback generally improves performance, roughly one-third of feedback interventions actually result in decreased, rather than increased, performance. They found that when feedback is directed at the self rather than at the task, the effectiveness of the feedback decreases. Thus, to be successful and result in performance improvement, feedback should be focused on behaviors and task, and not on the feedback recipient's traits or personal characteristics. In addition, Raver et al. (2012) found that individuals have to be careful when giving negative feedback, as it may be perceived as a personal attack, particularly for highly competitive individuals. They recommend training everyone within organizations on how to deliver feedback in considerate and nonthreatening ways.

Seeking Feedback

In addition to passively receiving feedback, employees can also actively seek feedback. With an increasing number of individuals working virtually and having less direct contact with their supervisors and peers, the only way that many people have of knowing how well they are doing is to proactively seek input from others. According to

Ashford et al. (2003), there are three motives people have for seeking feedback from others. These motives influence whether individuals will seek, and how they will seek, information from other people.

1. **Instrumental Motive**: Individuals may seek feedback from others to improve their performance. By finding out how others view their performance, employees have a better understanding of where they should focus their attention. Along these lines, organizational newcomers seek feedback relatively frequently at first, and then less so as they "learn the ropes" (Ashford & Cummings, 1985). In addition, people are more likely to seek feedback from sources they see as being credible, in part because they see the value of the feedback as being higher (Vancouver & Morrison, 1995).

2. **Ego-based Motive**: Individuals may also seek feedback to defend or enhance their views of themselves. Feedback can be very intimidating for people. To the extent it is negative, it has the potential to hurt one's self-image. As a result, it isn't surprising that many people avoid feedback altogether. Alternatively, employees may distort feedback or discount it if it fails to conform to their positive, ego-protective views of themselves. In general, individuals who are more confident in themselves and who think more highly of themselves are more likely to seek feedback (Bernichon et al., 2003).

3. **Image-based Motive**: Lastly, individuals may be motivated to seek feedback to make themselves look better to other people. For example, people might seek feedback from people when they are in a good mood or from people with whom they are friends to obtain positive feedback that makes them look good. Along these lines, individuals may be less likely to seek feedback if they believe the feedback will make them look bad.

In addition to the motives for feedback seeking, the organizational environment is important in determining the extent to which individuals will seek feedback. For example, Steelman et al. (2004) found that individuals are more likely to seek feedback in a supportive feedback environment. A supportive feedback environment is one in which the quality of feedback is high, sources are credible and available, people are considerate when delivering feedback, and feedback seeking is encouraged. Along these lines, van der Rijt et al. (2012) found that employees are more likely to seek feedback from their colleagues and their supervisor when they believe that mistakes and problems that may be brought up won't be held against them. The organizational culture can impact how feedback seeking is viewed. As London and Smither (2002) noted, some cultures may create the sense that feedback seeking is a sign of insecurity. Nevertheless, Ashford and Northcraft (1992) revealed that, unless they are poor performers already, individuals tend to be viewed more positively rather than negatively for seeking feedback from others.

Reactions to Feedback

According to Anderson and Jones (2000), "Responses to feedback regarding organizational behaviors and decisions more generally are among the most essential workplace issues" (p. 130). Ilgen and Davis (2000) discussed the importance of reactions to feedback, specifically addressing the attributions made in response to negative feedback. For example, they proposed that attributing negative feedback "to effort or situational conditions under the performer's control/influence are most likely to lead to improvements in future performance" (p. 555). That is, if somebody attributes negative feedback to something that is within their control, they are likely to exert more effort to remedy the issue. If, however, they believe that the feedback is about something that they can't influence, there is little reason to believe they will try to change their behaviors, and as such, performance is not likely to improve. Nease et al. (1999) also considered reactions to feedback to be an important predictor of performance. They noted that initial negative feedback leads to increased effort, but repeated negative feedback may result in decreased effort, lowered goals, rejection of the feedback, or withdrawal from the task.

Kinicki et al. (2004) asserted that "employees are unlikely to accept, desire to respond, or intend to respond to feedback based on information derived from an invalid or inaccurate appraisal system" (p. 1067). The acceptance of feedback and desire to seek self-improvement is also impacted by one's competence. Sheldon et al. (2014) conducted a series of studies and found that the least-skilled individuals were the most oblivious to their performance deficits, believing their performance to be better than it really was. When provided with explicit feedback about their deficiencies, these low-skilled individuals were likely to disparage and discount, or ignore, the feedback, and make fewer plans for self-improvements.

Reactions to Performance Management Systems

Performance appraisals have been described as "the organizational practice that managers and employees love to hate" (Culbertson et al., 2013, p. 35). Indeed, the dislike for them is so intense that people have called for their elimination within organizations (e.g., Culbert & Rout, 2010) or drastic transformation (see Social Media and I/O Psychology: *The Crowdsourced Performance Review*). Pulakos (2009) pointed out that employees often fail to see the value of performance management systems, reporting that less than a third of workers believe their organization's system actually helps them improve their performance.

In addition to employee and manager reactions to performance management systems as a whole, researchers have examined reactions to performance appraisals. These reactions include:

- the perceived accuracy or agreement with the evaluation,
- employee motivation following the appraisal,
- fairness perceptions regarding the appraisal,
- satisfaction with the appraisal, and
- perceived utility (or usefulness) of the appraisal.

Keeping and Levy (2000) noted that reaction criteria are almost always relevant, and an unfavorable reaction may doom the most carefully constructed performance management system. Fortunately, there are several things that managers can do to positively influence these reactions. For example, Cederblom (1982) found that three factors consistently contribute to effective performance appraisal interviews: the supervisor's knowledge of the subordinate's job and performance in it, the supervisor's support of the subordinate, and a welcoming of the subordinate's participation. In

Social Media and I/O Psychology: *The Crowdsourced Performance Review*

Crowdsourcing is a term that combines the word "crowd" with "outsourcing" and refers to the act of gathering input and help from a large group of people to accomplish a goal. With an entire online community at our fingertips, we see people solicit opinions to influence what products they should purchase, where they should eat dinner, and what hotel they should stay in while on vacation. As Eric Mosley, CEO of Globoforce, noted, "It's everywhere, from 'star rankings' on Amazon.com's product pages to services like Angie's List, Zagat.com, and TripAdvisor. Now, people make decisions based on feedback from dozens, hundreds, or tens of thousands of other people" (Mosley, 2013, p. 4).

Mosley has argued that using the "wisdom of crowds" can generate more influential performance reviews for employees. He notes that given the widespread use of crowdsourcing for all kinds of information, combined with the seemingly universal adoption of social media, is a natural fit to incorporate both into the workplace. He suggests that rather than rely on one-time evaluations of performance by a manager, performance reviews should be "informed by a yearlong narrative of [one's] accomplishments, skills, and behavior" (p. 3). These accolades can come from peers, customers, managers in other departments, direct reports, and so forth, and are simply meant to be an ongoing record of things an employee has done well. He refers to these various accolades as "social recognition" and suggests that by incorporating such recognition into a performance management system a culture of collaboration can be created. He further notes that using this crowdsourced means of gathering performance data should be more accurate and meaningful than traditional approaches that rely on a manager only valuing performance data. He notes that "Social recognition aggregates the opinions and thoughts of many individuals to arrive at a richer, more accurate conclusion than one person alone could attain" (p. 51).

Mosley notes that when applying a crowdsourced approach to performance management, the input should remain positive instead of negative. He notes that while negative feedback must be given at times, it is not something that should be made public and would create a negative, rather than positive, culture if implemented. He notes that managers should "praise in public, criticize in private" or else risk introducing "a toxic element to a culture you're trying to nurture" (pp. 165-166).

The closest relative to the crowdsourced review is 360-degree feedback, with the biggest difference being that rather than just having many people rate one person, the crowdsourced approach has many people rating many other people, including one another. In addition, 360-degree feedback is not typically focused only on positive recognition and is rarely made public (unless a person chooses to share his or her feedback). Thus, the notion of a crowdsourced performance review can be seen as a drastic departure from traditional performance reviews. Time will tell whether this approach gains momentum within the workplace.

particular, Cawley et al. (1998) found that employee participation for the sake of having one's "voice" heard was more important to the employee than participation for the purpose of influencing the end result. However, just conducting a performance appraisal interview will not resolve all problems in evaluating subordinate performance. Ilgen et al. (1981) found that even after the performance appraisal interview, subordinates and supervisors sometimes disagreed on the quality of subordinate performance, with subordinates feeling their performance was at a higher level.

In a review of performance evaluations, Greenberg (1986) identified seven characteristics that contribute to employees' accepting their evaluations and feeling they were fair:

1. Solicitation of employee input prior to the evaluation and use of it;
2. Two-way communication during the appraisal interview;
3. The opportunity to challenge/rebut the evaluation;
4. The rater's degree of familiarity with the ratee's work;
5. The consistent application of performance standards;
6. Basing of ratings on actual performance achieved; and
7. Basing of recommendations for salary/promotions on the ratings.

Furthermore, research by Kavanagh et al. (2007) similarly showed that performance management systems are more likely to be seen as fair to the extent that supervisors are seen as being neutral, employees are involved in the setting of objectives, and the system is clear and easily understood. Clearly there is much more to performance management than making a check mark on an appraisal instrument. Russell and Goode (1988) concluded that managers' reactions to performance management systems are affected by their overall satisfaction with them (that is, their attitude toward the systems' ability to document the performance of their subordinates) and the appraisal's improvement value. Likewise, Dickinson (1993) found that the most important determinant of employee attitudes about performance appraisal is the supervisor. When the supervisor is perceived as trustworthy and supportive, then attitudes about performance appraisal are favorable.

As Pulakos and O'Leary (2011) proclaimed, "Done effectively, performance management communicates what is important to the organization, drives employees to achieve results, and implements the organization's strategy. Done poorly, performance management not only fails to achieve these benefits but can also undermine employee confidence and damage relationships" (p. 147). Overall, there is nothing to be gained by conducting performance appraisals merely for the sake of doing so. At times, however, there can be the perception that more effort is placed into conducting performance appraisals than in making use of the information they provide. As stated by DeNisi and Sonesh (2011), "At all levels in the organization, there is often the feeling that appraisals are done because they have to be done but that nothing productive ever comes out of the process" (p. 255). There will be greater acceptability of the performance management system throughout the organization if tighter linkages can be attained between individual and organizational performance. Doing so will achieve the alignment that is fundamental to the concept of performance management (Hauenstein, 1998).

Chapter Summary

- Performance management is the process of aligning all of the organization's components to achieve high organizational performance.

- Performance appraisal is the evaluation of the organization's personnel component.
- Performance management systems are used to make important personnel decisions (such as retention and advancement) and as such are governed by fair employment laws.
- Supervisor ratings are the most common form of performance appraisal.
- I/O psychologists have developed various types of rating systems to evaluate job performance and have identified rating errors that occur with their use.
- Individuals can be trained to make higher-quality ratings; thus the judgment of employees is a skill that can be learned.
- An organization may have inhibiting factors that influence a rater's decision to give accurate and honest evaluations of employees.
- Appraisals of performance can be made by peers and subordinates (as well as oneself) in addition to supervisors.
- 360-degree feedback is an approach to performance evaluation based on a confluence of ratings from people at multiple organizational levels. The technique has been used for both developmental and administrative purposes.
- The process of giving and receiving feedback can be stressful and is related to how people react to their appraisals.
- When done well, performance management systems can have a beneficial impact on organizations, managers, and employees. When done poorly, they can backfire on all counts.

Organizations and Organizational Change

Chapter Outline

Learning Objectives

- Explain the classical and structural theories of organizations.
- Describe the components of social systems: roles, norms, and organizational culture.
- Understand the concept of person-organization fit.
- Explain downsizing, outsourcing, offshoring, and mergers and acquisitions.
- Explain the creation of global organizations.
- Discuss the rationale for organizational change.
- Understand why employees resist change.
- Understand the concept of corporate social responsibility.

Many academic disciplines have contributed to the study of organizations, including I/O psychology, sociology, economics, and political science. Their contributions tend to differ in the specific constructs that are investigated. The most common I/O psychological perspective is to examine individual behaviors and attitudes within an organizational context. First, it should be noted that it is not easy to grasp the meaning of an "organization." Organizations are abstract entities, yet they are real and in fact can be considered "alive." When an organization ceases to exist (such as a company that declares bankruptcy and goes out of business), it is not unusual to refer to the "death" of this formerly living entity. Authors have tried to use metaphors to understand the meaning of an organization (Morgan, 1997). Metaphors enhance the understanding of one concept by invoking reference to a more readily understood second concept. This technique has met with limited success in explaining organizations. One metaphor is to equate an organization with a person. People have a skeletal system and a circulatory system, concepts from physiology that are useful in understanding living organisms. Organizations possess characteristics (such as size and patterns of communication) that are general analogs of these physiological concepts; however, the metaphor is not totally accurate. What defines the boundary of where a person "ends" and his or her environment begins is our skin. Organizations, unlike humans, have no such boundary-defining characteristic as skin. Organizations have loose or porous boundaries where they "end" and their environments (legal, social, political, economic, etc.) begin. If you find that organizations are rather difficult to understand as entities, you are not alone. It is a challenge to those academic disciplines that study organizations to find useful ways to explain what they are.

Recall from Chapter 1 that for its first 70 years, the field was known simply as "industrial" psychology. There was substantial agreement as to what topics defined the field, which in turn led to the field's coalescence and emergence. However, "industrial" has a decidedly blue-collar, manufacturing, factory-based image to it, which many felt retarded the field's growth. In 1973, the name was officially changed to "industrial-organizational" psychology. While linguistically awkward, the "organizational" part of the name implied that the field's scientific and practical scope extended to non-manufacturing sectors of the economy as well. The body of knowledge reflecting "organizational" psychology is multidisciplinary in origin, and does not possess as clear a boundary as does its "industrial" counterpart. Indeed, Highhouse (2007) stated, "Documenting the history of the 'O' side of I-O psychology is made difficult by the fact that no one is really sure what constitutes organizational psychology" (p. 331). Despite its blurred origins and identity, "organizational" psychology is firmly affixed by hyphenation to its older "industrial" sibling. Schneider et al. (2011) offered this description of the origin of organizational psychology: "The focus was on the design of organizations that were effective through collective human attributes and actions and not on individual employees as the unit of theory or analysis" (pp. 375–376). This chapter will explain how an organization influences and shapes the behavior of its members. The concepts that will be examined (that is, the unit of analysis) shift from the individual to larger social collectivities.

One of the dominant themes of I/O psychology today is the need to be responsive and adaptable to changing conditions. This "need" has been described at both the individual level (in terms of personal flexibility) and the job level (continually evolving jobs require new tasks to be performed). This need to respond to change is particularly acute at the organizational level. Organizations are designed or created to perform work. As will be discussed in this chapter, organizations have both structural (how work processes are arranged) and social (the pattern of interactions among employees) components. As the work the organization performs is altered in response to external economic pressures, the organization must also change its structural and social components. Organizations are under constant pressure to change in response to their shifting environments. Helping organizations change is one of the major activities of I/O psychologists who work for consulting firms and businesses. As will be seen in this chapter, it is not easy to change the way an organization functions. Before the topic of organizational change is addressed, it is necessary to discuss how organizations operate.

Two Theories of Organizations

Organization
A coordinated group of people who perform tasks to produce goods or services, colloquially referred to as a company.

It is probably easier to state why organizations exist than to define what they are. In their simplest form, they exist as vehicles for accomplishing goals and objectives; that is, **organizations** are collectivities of parts that cannot accomplish their goals as effectively if they operated separately. How one chooses to examine the organizing process produces the various schools of thought or theories about organizations. We will limit our discussion to two prominent theories.

Classical Theory

Classical theory
A theory developed in the early 20th century that described the form and structure of organizations.

Classical theory, which emerged in the first few decades of the 20th century, focuses mainly on structural relationships in organizations. Classical theory begins with a statement of the basic ingredients of any organization and then addresses how the organization should best be structured to accomplish its objectives. There are four basic components to any organization:

1. **A system of differentiated activities**. All organizations are composed of the activities and functions performed in them and the relationships among these activities and functions. A formal organization emerges when these activities are linked together.

2. **People**. Although organizations are composed of activities and functions, people perform tasks and exercise authority.

3. **Cooperation toward a goal**. Cooperation must exist among the people performing their various activities to achieve a unity of purpose in pursuit of their common goals.

4. **Authority**. Authority is established through superior–subordinate relationships, and such authority is needed to ensure cooperation among people pursuing their goals.

Given that four ingredients are the basis of any organization, classical theory addresses the various structural properties by which the organization should best reach its goals. Four major structural principles are the hallmarks in the history of organizational theory.

Functional principle
The concept that organizations should be divided into units that perform similar functions.

Functional Principle.   The **functional principle** is the concept behind division of labor; that is, organizations should be divided into units that perform similar functions. Work is broken down to provide clear areas of specialization, which in turn improves the organization's overall performance. Similar work activities are often organized into departments, which enhances coordination of activities and permits more effective supervision and a more rational flow of work. It is the functional principle that accounts for the grouping of work functions into such units as production, sales, engineering, finance, and so on; these labels describe the primary nature of the work performed within each unit. The functional principle relates to the horizontal growth of the organization—that is, the formation of new functional units along the *horizontal* dimension.

Scalar principle
The concept that organizations are structured by a chain of command that grows with increasing levels of authority.

Scalar Principle.   The **scalar principle** deals with the organization's *vertical* growth and refers to the chain of command that grows with levels added to the organization. Each level has its own degree of authority and responsibility for meeting organizational goals, with higher levels having more responsibility. Each subordinate should be accountable to only one superior, a tenet referred to as the **unity of command**. Classical theorists thought the best way to overcome organizational fragmentation caused by division of labor was through a well-designed chain of command. Coordination among factions is achieved by people occupying positions of command in a hierarchy. Figure 8-1 shows a graphic representation of both the functional and scalar principles.

Unity of command
The concept that each subordinate should be accountable to only one supervisor.

Line/staff principle
The concept of differentiating organizational work into primary and support functions.

Line/Staff Principle.   One way to differentiate organizational work functions is by whether they are line or staff. **Line functions** have the primary responsibility for meeting the major goals of the organization, like the production department in a manufacturing organization. **Staff functions** support the line's activities but are regarded as subsidiary in overall importance to line functions. Typical staff functions are human resources and quality control. That is, although it is important to have good employees and to inspect products for their quality, the organization was not created to provide people with jobs or products to inspect. It was created to manufacture products (a line

Line functions
Organizational work that directly meets the major goals of an organization.

Staff functions
Organizational work that supports line activities.

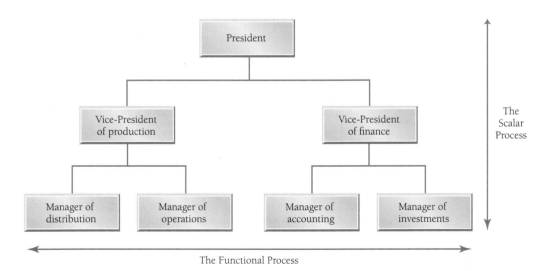

Figure 8-1   *The functional and scalar processes of an organization*

function), and human resources and quality control are two staff functions designed to support this larger goal.

Span-of-Control Principle.   The **span-of-control principle** refers to the number of subordinates a manager is responsible for supervising. A "small" span of control is 2 subordinates; a "large" span of control might be 15. Large spans of control produce flat organizations (that is, few levels between the top and bottom of the organization); small spans of control produce tall organizations (that is, many levels). Figure 8-2 is a diagram showing how the span of control affects the shape of the organization.

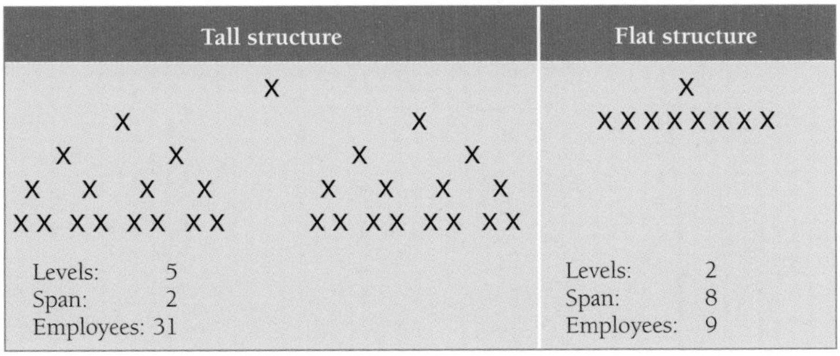

Span-of-control principle
The concept that refers to the number of subordinates a manager is responsible for supervising.

Tall structure	Flat structure
X	X
X X	X X X X X X X X
X X X X	
X X X X X X X X	
XX XX XX XX XX XX XX XX	
Levels: 5	Levels: 2
Span: 2	Span: 8
Employees: 31	Employees: 9

Figure 8-2   *Effect of span of control on organizational structure*

Classical theory is credited with providing the structural anatomy of organizations. It was the first major attempt to articulate the form and substance of organizations in a comprehensive fashion. There is little that is "psychological" about this view of organizations; indeed, none of the classical organizational theorists were psychologists. Although current organizational researchers regard classical theory as antiquated, its four principles are deeply ingrained in the real-life structure of organizations. Problems of line/staff relationships, number of organizational levels, division of labor, coordination, and spans of control are still of major concern today. Further thinking about organizations occurred because organizations were more complex than the four classical principles suggested. This desire to add richness and realism to understanding organizations gave rise to structural theory.

Structural Theory

Mintzberg (2008) greatly added to classical theory by proposing a comprehensive and lucid explanation of how organizations evolve to reach a certain form and shape. We refer to these characteristics as the **structure** or formal component of an organization. Various types of structure are possible, and an organization continuously seeks to find a structure that is an optimal match to its environment. That is, the structure of an organization is an adaptive mechanism that permits the organization to function in its surroundings. Organizations that have maladaptive structures will ultimately cease to exist. Because individuals assume roles within organizations, employees feel the brunt of change caused by the continuing evolution of an organization's structure. It is in this regard that I/O psychology is involved in matters of organizational structure.

Structure
The arrangement of work functions within an organization designed to achieve efficiency and control.

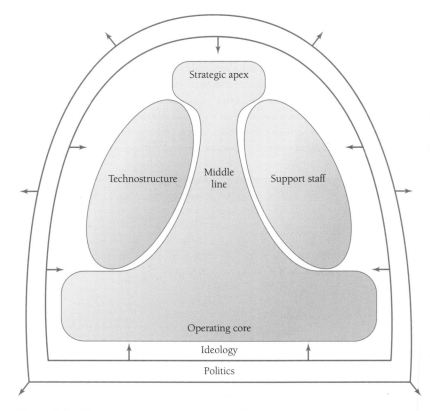

Figure 8-3 *The seven parts of an organization*

Source: From *Structuring of Organizations*, 1st ed., by H. Mintzberg. © 1979. Reprinted by
permission of Pearson Education, Inc., Upper Saddle River, NJ.

The Seven Basic Parts of an Organization.   Organizations are structured to define the interrelationships among their parts. Mintzberg (2008) proposed that all organizations consist of seven basic parts, as shown in Figure 8-3.

   1. **Operating core**. The operating core of an organization consists of those
employees who are responsible for conducting the basic work duties that give the
organization its defining purpose. In a manufacturing organization, it is the employees who transform raw goods (e.g., cloth) into a sellable product (e.g., apparel).
In a service organization (such as a dry cleaning store), it is the employees who
perform vital work functions (e.g., transform dirty clothes into clean clothes).

   2. **Strategic apex**. The strategic apex is responsible for the overall success of
the entire organization. The strategic apex is associated with the executive leadership of the organization. These employees have the responsibility and authority to
ensure that the larger goals of the organization are being met. Mintzberg referred
to the strategic apex as the "brain" of the organization.

   3. **Middle line**. The middle line represents those employees who have the
day-to-day authority for ensuring that the overall goals set by the strategic apex

are being carried out by the operating core. They are mid-level bosses, ranging from senior managers down to first-level supervisors. The chain of command that starts at the strategic apex and ends at the operating core runs directly through the middle line. An organizational hierarchy is created by the various levels that separate the operating core from the strategic apex.

4. **Technostructure**. The technostructure consists of those employees who possess specific technical expertise that facilitates the overall operation of the organization. These employees are specialists in areas of business that influence the organization, but these people do not perform the mainstream work of the organization (the operating core) nor are they members of top management (the strategic apex). Examples include such technical areas of expertise as accounting, human resources, information technology, and law.

5. **Support staff**. The support staff provides services that aid the basic mission of the organization and typically includes the mailroom, security, and janitorial services. Sometimes the members of the support staff and the technostructure are collectively regarded as meeting the "staff" function of an organization (vis-à-vis the line/staff distinction). However, there is a major distinction between the technostructure and the support staff. The members of the technostructure give advice to the organization, while the support staff performs services.

6. **Ideology**. All organizations are structured in response to a sixth factor that Mintzberg calls *ideology*. Ideology is a belief system that compels commitment to a particular value. Mintzberg refers to organizations that have a very strong ideology as having a "missionary" structure, but not necessarily in the religious sense. Rather, it is an organization that is singularly devoted to a particular mission, and all its actions are in pursuit of that mission. Examples include an organization that is directed to providing disaster relief for victims and an organization that is devoted to creative and innovative enterprises, such as an advertising agency or computer software designer. The ideology is the "glue" that holds the organization together. A strong ideology can produce high internal cohesion. Such organizations tend to have *few* formal rules and regulations, as they are not needed. The employees behave in accordance with their sincere conviction in the ideology of the organization, and can perform their work relatively independent of each other. All organizations have ideologies. However, in some organizations the ideology is strong enough to influence how the organization functions. In organizations with weak ideologies, its effects on individual behavior will not be pervasive. The effect of ideology within an organization is reflected in Figure 8-3 by the arrows pulling the organization together.

7. **Politics**. Mintzberg's seventh factor, *politics*, can be thought of as having the opposite effect of ideology. Ideology produces internal cohesion and provides a singular purpose to the organization; politics cause divisiveness and conflict. Politics are often the seeds of destruction within an organization. The basis for politics is the use of power that is neither formally authorized (as by a company president) or widely accepted within the organization. The use of political power pits individuals and groups against each other for the purpose of destabilizing the legitimate power base within the organization. Destabilizing legitimate power creates opportunities for selected individuals and groups to gain illegitimate power.

Mintzberg identified the tactics of power politics to include insurgency (active resistance or passive non-compliance with organizational initiatives), professing loyalty to someone in exchange for greater power, flaunting or feigning expertise to control organizational actions, and building temporary alliances with others to advance within the organization. As such, the total organization becomes an arena or theater in which power plays at all levels are considered fair game for enhancing one's position. Given the amount of energy spent on orchestrating internal political maneuvering, the likelihood of the organization fulfilling its primary purpose is greatly reduced. All organizations contain elements of politics. In a highly politicized organization the continuous tussles for illegitimate power become the organization's consuming activity. The effect of politics within an organization is reflected in Figure 8-3 by the arrows pulling the organization apart. The topic of organizational politics will be discussed in greater detail in Chapter 10.

Components of Social Systems

Social system
The human components of a work organization that influence the behavior of individuals and groups.

A **social system** is a structuring of events or happenings; it has no formal structure apart from its functioning. Physical or biological systems (cars or human beings) have structures that can be identified even when they are not functioning (electrical or skeleton structures); that is, they have both an anatomy and a physiology. A social system has no anatomy in this sense. When a social system stops functioning, no identifiable structure remains. It is hard for us to think of social systems as having no tangible anatomy because it is easier to understand concepts that have concrete and simple components. Social systems do indeed have components, but they are not concrete. They are sometimes referred to as the *informal* component of an organization. We will examine three of them—roles, norms, and organizational culture—while recognizing that they are abstract.

Roles

Role
A set of expectations about appropriate behavior in a position.

When an employee enters an organization, there is much for that person to learn: expected performance levels, recognition of superiors, dress codes, and time demands. Roles ease the learning process. **Roles** are usually defined as the expectations of others about appropriate behavior in a specific position. Each of us plays several roles simultaneously (parent, employee, club member, and so on), but the focus here will be on job-related roles.

There are five important aspects of roles. First, they are impersonal; the position itself determines the expectations, not the individual. Second, roles are related to task behavior. An organizational role is the expected behaviors for a particular job. Third, roles can be difficult to pin down. The problem is defining who determines what is expected. Because other people define our roles, opinions differ over what our role should be. How we see our role, how others see our role, and what we actually do may differ. Fourth, roles are learned quickly and can produce major behavior changes. Fifth, roles and jobs are not the same; a person in one job might play several roles.

Role conflict
The product of perceptual differences regarding the content of a person's role or the relative importance of its elements.

Role conflict occurs when an individual is faced with incompatible or competing demands. Individuals experiencing role conflict feel like they are being pulled in different directions and unable to easily meet all of the demands placed on them. For example, an employee who is asked by a supervisor to arrive at work early may experience role conflict if he or she also must drop children off at school at the same time. In this example, the individual's roles of employee and parent are conflicting. **Role ambiguity** refers to uncertainty about the behaviors to be exhibited in a role, or the boundaries that define a role. First-time parents often feel apprehensive about their performance in a role they have never previously fulfilled. Likewise with an employee who is asked to represent many other employees who hold a wide range of opinions or attitudes. **Role overload** occurs when an individual feels overwhelmed from having too many responsibilities. This sense of overload can occur from having too many demands within one particular role or from having too many roles in one's life. First-time parents, in addition to frequently experiencing role ambiguity, often feel overwhelmed in part because they now have a whole new role with demands and responsibilities that must be merged with their existing roles. This additional role may make them feel overly burdened by the total number of responsibilities placed on them. Another aspect is role differentiation. This is the extent to which different roles are performed by employees in the same subgroup. One person's job might be to maintain good group relations, such as a work-unit coordinator. His or her role might thus require providing emotional or interpersonal support to others. Another's role might be to set schedules, agendas, and meet deadlines; such a person is usually an administrator. When all the roles in a work group fit together like the pieces of a puzzle, the result is a smoothly running, effective group. However, all the pieces may not fit together.

Role ambiguity
Uncertainty about the behaviors to be exhibited in a role, or the boundaries that define a role.

Role overload
The feeling of being overwhelmed from having too many roles or too many responsibilities within a single role.

Norms

Norm
A set of shared group expectations about appropriate behavior.

Norms are shared group expectations about appropriate behavior. Whereas roles define what is appropriate for a particular job, norms define acceptable group behavior. Roles differentiate positions; norms establish the behavior expected of everyone in the group, such as when employees take coffee breaks, how much they produce, when they stop for the day, and what they wear. Norms are unwritten rules that govern behavior. A company may have a formal written rule against the use of personal cell phones during work time. If employees use their cell phones at work, there is a norm that sanctions such behavior in spite of the formal rule.

Norms have several important properties. First, there is "oughtness" or "should-ness;" that is, prescriptions for behavior. Second, norms are usually more obvious for behavior judged to be important for the group. A norm might exist for the time employees stop work before lunch, but there probably is no norm about what employees eat. Third, norms are enforced by the group. Much expected behavior is monitored and enforced through formal rules and procedures. With norms, group members regulate behavior. Sometimes formal rules and group norms clash. The rule prohibiting personal cell phone use and the group norm sanctioning personal cell phone use is one such example. Unless the organization imposes sanctions on personal cell phone users (that is, rule breakers), the group norm probably prevails.

There is a three-step process for developing and communicating norms. The norm must first be defined and communicated. This can be done either explicitly ("Here is the way we do things around here") or implicitly (the desired behavior is observed). Second, the group must be able to monitor behavior and judge whether the norm is being followed. Third, the group must be able to reward conformity and punish non-conformity. Conformity enhances the predictability of behavior within the group, which in turn promotes feelings of group cohesion.

Compliance with norms is enforced by positive reinforcement or punishment. Positive reinforcement can be praise or inclusion in group activities. Punishment can be a dirty look, a snide remark, or actual physical abuse. Workers who exceeded the group norm for productivity in the Hawthorne studies were hit on the arm, which was called "binging." Another form of punishment is exclusion from group activities. The group often tries to convince the nonconforming employee (referred to as a *deviant*) to change his or her behavior. The group tries to alter the deviant's opinion through increased communication, verbal or nonverbal. The clearer and more important the norm and the more cohesive the group, the greater the pressure. Eventually, the deviant either changes or is rejected. If rejected, the deviant becomes an *isolate*, and the pressure to conform stops. Because the group may need the isolate to perform work tasks, they usually reach a truce; the isolate is tolerated at work but excluded from

THE FAR SIDE®   By GARY LARSON

"Counterclockwise, Red Eagle! Always counter-clockwise!"

group activities and relationships. Obviously the isolate can quit the job and try to find a better match between his or her values and a group.

Finally, norms are not always contrary to formal organizational rules or independent of them. Sometimes norms can greatly promote organizational goals. For example, there may be a norm against leaving for home before a certain amount of work has been done. Although quitting time is 5:00 p.m., the group may expect employees to stay until 5:15 or 5:30 to finish a certain task. In this case, the deviant is one who conforms to the formal rule (that is, leaving at 5:00 p.m.) instead of the group norm. When group norms and organizational goals are complementary, high degrees of effectiveness can result.

Organizational Culture

The concept of culture was originally proposed by anthropologists to describe societies, but we have also found it useful to describe organizations. Within the field of I/O psychology, Schein (1965) is credited as being the first scholar to recognize the importance of organizational culture in explaining human behavior in the workplace. **Culture** is the languages, values, attitudes, beliefs, and customs of an organization. As can be inferred, it represents a complex pattern of variables that, when taken collectively, gives each organization its unique "flavor." Several definitions of organizational culture have been proposed, but the most straightforward was offered by Deal and Kennedy (1982): "The way we do things around here." As described by Schneider et al. (2011), organizational culture is reflected by what leaders pay attention to, measure, and control. It is embodied in the behaviors that leaders model for others, and on what basis leaders allocate rewards.

Ostroff et al. (2003) described the culture of an organization as having three layers. These three layers can be examined in any social collectivity, including a business organization, a social organization (e.g., a club), a church, or even a family.

Culture
The language, values, attitudes, beliefs, and customs of an organization.

1. **Observable artifacts**. Artifacts are the surface-level actions that can be observed from which some deeper meaning or interpretation can be drawn about the organization. Trice and Beyer (1993) identified four major categories of cultural artifacts: *symbols* (e.g., physical objects or locations); *language* (e.g., jargon, slang, gestures, humor, gossip, and rumors); *narratives* (e.g., stories, legends, and myths about the organization); and *practices* (e.g., rituals, taboos, and ceremonies). Although these artifacts are easy to observe, they are not necessarily easy to interpret or understand.

2. **Espoused values**. Espoused values are those beliefs or concepts that are specifically endorsed by management or the organization at large. Organizations per se do not possess values, but rather key individual leaders within the organization espouse these values. Two examples are "Safety is our top priority" and "We respect the opinions of all our employees." *Enacted* values are those that are converted into employee behavior. A perceived difference between espoused and enacted values can be a source of cynicism among employees. For example, despite the espoused values, actual safety efforts may be haphazard or employees may be criticized for speaking out.

3. **Basic assumptions**. Basic assumptions are unobservable and are at the core of the organization. They frequently start out as values but over time become so deeply ingrained that they are taken for granted. Basic assumptions are rarely confronted or debated and are extremely difficult to change. According to Ostroff et al., "Challenging basic assumptions produces anxiety and defensiveness because they provide security through their ability to define what employees should pay attention to, how they should react emotionally, and what actions they should take in various kinds of situations" (p. 569). Questioning a university about the value of education in society would represent a challenge to a basic assumption of academic institutions.

Culture may also be communicated through other channels, such as a company's intranet, official policies, mission statement, and any other means of value expression (see Social Media and I/O Psychology: *The New Water Cooler*).

Schein (1996) asserted that understanding the culture of an organization is critical to making sense of the behavior observed in the organization. A narrow description of behavior, divorced from the cultural context in which it occurs, is of limited value for understanding the organization. For example, Pratt and Rafaeli (1997) examined the types of clothes worn by members of a hospital staff to understand how the hospital

Social Media and I/O Psychology: *The New Water Cooler*

Once upon a time, people would gather around the office water cooler to discuss the previous evening's television shows and exchange details regarding the latest office gossip. The topics discussed and the fervor with which they captured individuals' attention was one way to gauge a company's culture. Were the conversations light-hearted and supportive or competitive and sprinkled with animosity? Did the discussions only occur when the boss was gone, or was he or she actively involved in the discourse?

Of course, the water cooler was and continues to simply be a metaphor for a gathering place in which people can chat about hot topics. Whereas individuals rarely stand around an actual water cooler anymore, the notion of a metaphoric water cooler exists, whether it be the office coffee maker, the photocopier, or a particularly outgoing receptionist's desk. Increasingly, the office water cooler is online, on various social media platforms. In addition, these virtual water coolers allow for the culture of an organization to be identified as employees communicate about their unique experiences and perceptions of the workplace.

Many organizations have begun to realize the role that social media can play in monitoring employees' views about the organization's culture. For example, through the use of internal platforms such as SharePoint, an application used by over three-quarters of Fortune 500 companies, companies can solicit input from employees and gauge the level of engagement and satisfaction within the workforce. In addition, organizations can utilize data mining of sites like Glassdoor.com in order to ascertain what topics are most discussed and how a company is viewed by its current and former employees. Thus, by keeping an eye on the new (virtual) water cooler, organizations can determine whether the culture they are striving for is the culture that is being realized in practice.

views itself. They found that the manner of dress among the staff was symbolic of their sense of organizational identity. Furthermore, differing views among staff members about dress were deeply felt. The authors offered the following two quotes from nurses working in the hospital:

> *Head nurse of a rehabilitation unit*: "Patients who wear pajamas and see hospital garb around them think of themselves as sick. If *they and their caretakers wear street clothes*, patients will think of themselves as moving out of the sick role and into rehabilitation. They will be ready for life outside the hospital. This is the rehab philosophy, and this is what makes this unit unique." [emphasis added]

> *Nurse on the evening shift of the same unit*: "We are medical and health professionals. We do professional work. We take care of sick patients, we deal with their bodily fluids and get their slime all over us. So we should all look like medical professionals; *we should be dressed in scrubs*." [emphasis added] (Pratt & Rafaeli, 1997, p. 862)

An organization's culture can be revealed in very subtle ways. Brown et al. (2005) discussed territoriality in organizations through the use of nameplates on doors and family photos on desks. They serve to establish a sense of an individual belonging to that organization by the implicit marking of "turf." Baruch (2006) described a ritual among business people from different organizations who meet for the first time: the exchange of business cards. Along with the individual's name on the card is often found the organization's logo, a visual symbol of its identity. The selection of a company's logo is to send a message, coded as a symbol. The message may seek to express such values as excellence, elitism, and innovation.

Anand (2006) proposed that the cartoons employees tape on their office doors not only reflect the organization's culture, but are also a production of it. The simple act of posting cartoons on doors is a message to the observer that such behavior (i.e., individual expression) is acceptable to the organization. The cartoons posted by individuals were statements of their own values, as the cartoons often portrayed cynicism and sarcasm presented as satire. Anand regarded the cartoons as artifacts of the organization's culture, and they offered insight into how individuals view the organization's values. Such artifacts are not easy to decipher and they can convey different meaning to the sender and receiver of the message. Despite their subtlety, they are expressions of value and have purpose.

Cameron and Quinn (2006) described how the culture of an organization is critically related to its effectiveness. That is, the culture of an organization serves to shape how the organization does what it does, and in so doing becomes a determinant of its success. Cameron and Quinn proposed the Competing Values Framework to describe four types of organizations. The organizations are guided by different (or competing) values. These values determine the indicators of effectiveness that the organization uses to judge itself, and in large part determine what is considered to be good and appropriate for the organization. The four types of organizations are shown in Figure 8-4.

Cameron and Quinn developed a framework on the basis of effectiveness standards. The four types of organizations define effectiveness in different ways, prefer different types of leaders, are guided by different values, and yield different cultures. *Competing cultures* assume their business environment is hostile, their leaders are tough and demanding, and use aggressive strategies to achieve productivity. A competing

Flexibility

<table>
<tr>
<td>

Type of culture: Collaborative

Type of organization: family business

Critical value: teamwork

Preferred leader: relationship builder

Effectiveness achieved through: loyalty and tradition

</td>
<td>

Type of culture: Creative

Type of organization: electronic products

Critical value: risk taking

Preferred leader: innovator

Effectiveness achieved through: new products

</td>
</tr>
<tr>
<td>

Type of culture: Controlling

Type of organization: fast food

Critical value: consistency of operations

Preferred leader: rule enforcer

Effectiveness achieved through: control and standardization

</td>
<td>

Type of culture: Competition

Type of organization: automotive

Critical value: aggressiveness

Preferred leader: tough and demanding

Effectiveness achieved through: defeating rivals

</td>
</tr>
</table>

Internal Focus (left side) — External Focus (right side)

Stability

Figure 8-4   *Competing Values Framework of organizational culture*

Adapted from *Diagnosing and changing organizational cultures* (rev. ed.), by K. L. Cameron and R. E. Quinn, 2006, Jossey-Bass.

culture is exemplified by the automobile industry. *Controlling cultures* assume the business environment is stable, their leaders emphasize the following of company policies and procedures, and effectiveness is achieved by standardization and control. The fast food industry is an example of a controlling culture. *Collaborative cultures* assume their business environment can best be managed through teamwork and by regarding customers as partners, their leaders emphasize developing relations, and effectiveness is achieved through loyalty and internal cohesiveness. The collaborative culture is represented by organizations that generally operate in smaller, niche markets (as a family-owned business). *Creative cultures* assume that their business environment is turbulent and dynamic, that their leaders emphasize innovation and creativity, and effectiveness is achieved by designing new products and services. The creative culture is exemplified by the high-tech electronics industry. Cameron and Quinn referred to their framework of organizational cultures as "competing values" because, as shown in Figure 8-4, the core values that guide the cultures are at opposite ends of a continuum. The vertical continuum is flexibility vs. stability, and the horizontal continuum is an internal vs. external focus. More importantly, there is nothing inherently superior about one value versus another. The values simply undergird how the organization tries to be effective. Furthermore, one can readily imagine how certain leader types, as the hard-charging competing type (for example), would not be a good match with a collaborative culture. The Competing Values Framework illustrates how the culture of an organization, based upon its values, is integrally related to not only the effectiveness of the organization, but how effectiveness is defined.

Hartnell et al. (2011) reached the following conclusion based on a meta-analysis of the relationship between organizational culture and organizational effectiveness:

It is important for executive leaders to consider the fit, or match, between strategic initiatives and organizational culture when determining how to embed a culture that produces competitive advantage. They should then espouse, enact, and reward the values and behaviors that are consistent with the desired culture. To this end, an organization's culture and strategy should be complementary such that they support the same mission . . . (p. 688)

Person-Organization Fit

Person-organization fit
The perception by both job candidates and the organization of the match between their respective values and goals.

As the research on organizational culture attests, organizations develop values that strongly influence employee behavior. When recruiting and selecting new employees, organizations consider (implicitly or explicitly) the likelihood an individual will be a good fit or match with the organization. The name for this match is **person-organization fit** (also called person-organization congruence). The process of gauging the degree of fit between the two parties is mutual. From the organization's perspective, it seeks to understand the candidate's values, skills, goals, and personality in attempting to predict the likely behavior of the candidate if hired. The degree of fit is ascertained by comparing the assessment of the candidate against the organization's values, expectations, and culture. If a strong match is perceived, the organization would extend a job offer to the candidate. Conversely, the candidate also gauges the degree of fit, but from the perspective of whether this particular organization is likely to deliver on the employment opportunities that the candidate seeks. If the candidate perceives a strong match, the job offer will be accepted. If not, the candidate will seek employment elsewhere, or enter into employment knowing it will be but for a short time (Kristof-Brown & Billsberry, 2013).

There is a strong link between organizational culture and person-organization fit. Schneider (1996) believes it is the people populating the organization who most define its culture. That is, people (e.g., employees) are not actors who fill predetermined roles in an established culture, but rather it is the personalities, values, and interests of these people over time that make the organization what it is. Schneider (1987) proposed what he calls the attraction–selection–attrition (ASA) cycle. The ASA cycle proposes that people with similar personalities and values are drawn to (attraction) certain organizations and hired into these organizations (selection), and people who don't fit into the pattern of shared values eventually leave the organization (attrition). This process occurs over time, however, not immediately.

Ehrhart et al. (2014) proposed that there are dimensions of culture that run deep throughout the organization, other dimensions may be specific to certain departments or levels of the organization, and other dimensions of culture that are weakly held. There would be low perceived person-organization fit if the candidate expressed values that are contrary to those deeply held throughout the organization. It is possible that a candidate might be regarded as a better fit with one department or branch of the organization compared to others. Jansen and Shipp (2013) recognized that time is a critical issue to understanding person-organization fit. There is no consensus as to how long it takes for a new employee to fit into a larger group, and how long a new employee will tolerate feeling like a misfit before action is taken (e.g., appealing to the organization for guidance or quitting). It will be recalled from Chapter 5 that *onboarding* is the process organizations use to shorten the time new employees need to feel that they fit. Achieving fit accelerates the adjustment process, facilitating increased job performance and reduced turnover.

Ostroff and Zahn (2012) concluded that the concept of person-organization fit is used by recruiters in gauging the match between candidates for specific jobs within the company and the organization as a whole. In an empirical study of person-organization fit, Arthur et al. (2006) found it to be more predictive of turnover ($r = .24$) than job performance ($r = .15$).

Downsizing, Outsourcing, and Offshoring

Downsizing
The process by which an organization reduces its number of employees to achieve greater overall efficiency.

One of the most radical and tumultuous ways an organization can change in response to pressures is called **downsizing**. An organization may believe it has too many employees to be responsive to its environment. The most common reason for the decision to cut jobs is the organization's conclusion that it can "do more with less" (i.e., have greater efficiency with fewer employees). For most organizations the single largest expense is the wages and salaries paid to their employees. By eliminating jobs, they reduce costs. Therefore some organizations have been compelled to cut jobs just to help assure their economic survival. The work that was done by the departed employees will have to be performed by the remaining employees or through technical changes in work processes (e.g., automation). Another term given to this process of cutting jobs is *reduction-in-force*. It is not uncommon for large organizations to reduce their size by several thousand employees at one time. Based on data from the U.S. Department of Labor, DeMeuse et al. (2011) reported, on average, 4,650 employees were laid off each business day from 2000–2007 in the United States. In the 30 months from January 2008 through June 2010, over 6 million U.S. workers were laid off, an average of almost 10,000 employees each business day (U.S. Department of Labor, 2010).

Where do the eliminated jobs come from within an organization? The five core parts of the organization are targeted, with the greatest losses typically coming from the middle line, technostructure, and support staff. Jobs can also be lost in the operating core, as jobs are automated or reassigned to other countries that pay lower wages. The strategic apex may be reduced, but generally the fewest jobs are lost at this level. Within the structure of an organization, job cuts can occur *horizontally* or *vertically*. A horizontal cut involves the loss of jobs within a department, but the department remains within the organization. For example, if there are 50 employees who work in the accounting department, the department might be slashed in half: 25 employees lose their jobs and 25 remain. A vertical cut involves the elimination of all jobs in the department. In this example, 50 employees have their jobs eliminated. The organization still needs the accounting function performed, but instead of having it performed by its own employees, the accounting function is outsourced to a professional accounting firm. **Outsourcing** the services performed by these individuals is less costly to the organization than hiring its own employees to perform these services.

Outsourcing
The process of eliminating jobs within the organization by having those work functions contracted to other organizations.

Offshoring
The process of eliminating jobs within the organization by having those work functions performed in cheaper labor markets overseas (offshore).

Yet another source of job loss is **offshoring**. The work performed domestically (often jobs in the operating core) is exported to cheaper labor markets in overseas countries. For example, DeMeuse et al. reported the average wage rate for U.S. production workers is $24 per hour, compared to 67¢ per hour for Chinese production workers. Even cheaper labor markets are found in Vietnam, Laos, and Cambodia.

It is common for decision making to become more decentralized following a downsizing. Figure 8-5 shows the top part of an organizational chart for a manufacturing

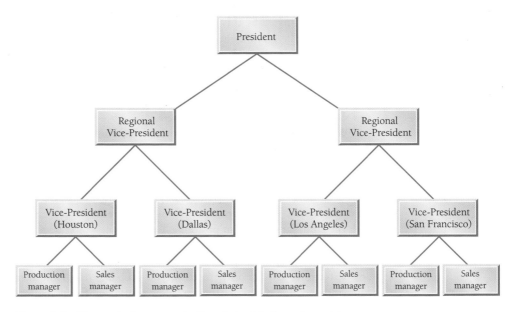

Figure 8-5   *Top part of an organizational chart before downsizing*

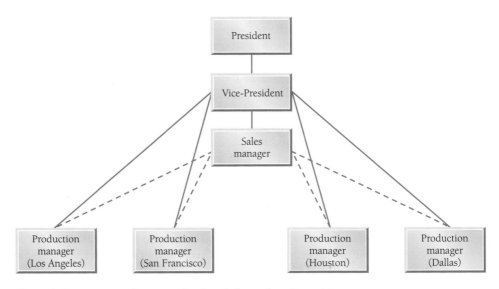

Figure 8-6   *Top part of an organizational chart after downsizing*

company before downsizing. The company is structured by both function (production and sales) and location (California and Texas). There are small spans of control. Each person below the president has two subordinates. A total of 15 people are needed to staff this part of the organization with such a configuration. Figure 8-6 shows the same company following reorganization—in this case, downsizing. A total of eight positions have been eliminated by this reorganization. The sales function has been consolidated into one job. The plant manager at each of the four locations now reports directly to the vice president. Each plant manager now also provides information directly to the sales manager (as indicated by the broken lines), but administratively the plant managers report to the vice president. The vice president now has a span of control of five. The positions lost in this reorganization are one vice president, three sales managers, and the entire layer of (middle) managers.

What consequences might we expect from this reorganization? There would be less administrative control from the loss of managerial jobs. There would be greater pressure on the organization's parts to coordinate with each other because of the loss of direct supervision. There would probably be more stress placed on the surviving employees to work harder and find new ways to do the work of the employees whose jobs were eliminated. The organization would have fewer salary expenditures associated with the elimination of eight positions. Eight people would be out of work.

How would you feel if you lost your job because you were fired? Probably not pleased, but in all likelihood you received some signals along the way that you were not performing satisfactorily. In turn, you probably had some control over whether you would change your job behavior. How would you feel if you lost your job because it was eliminated? You could have been an exemplary employee, but you lost your job through no fault of your own. *You* were not released; rather the *job* you were filling was eliminated to make the organization more efficient.

When organizations are contracting in size, the overall social order of employment is altered. If, as a rule, organizations reduce the number of middle managers needed to run the business, then these displaced middle managers will not simply find new jobs as middle managers in some other companies. Rather the *job* of middle manager is being reduced in frequency, necessitating holders of middle-management jobs to enter new jobs, not new positions in the same job family. This may necessitate professional retraining, learning new skills to fill jobs that continue to exist. Thus issues of organizational structure affect not only I/O psychology but also the sociology of employment and the economics of across-occupational mobility.

Feldman and Ng (2012), among others, have reported that severe job cuts do achieve short-term reductions in costs, but they do not achieve long-term profitability. Organizations typically grow in size because there is a demand for the products they make or services they perform. When the demand shrinks, it becomes necessary to eliminate jobs. However, there are less traumatic ways to achieve it than mass layoffs. One example is for the organization to offer an incentive for early retirement, as one month of severance pay for every year of employment with the company. Another possibility is when natural attrition occurs (e.g., an employee leaves to take a job elsewhere), the company does not hire a replacement. Massive job cuts serve to reduce a company's costs, but they also produce massive disruptions to the larger social order (see I/O Psychology and the Economy: *Job Loss*).

Mergers and Acquisitions

One strategy organizations can use in response to environmental pressures is to become smaller—that is, to downsize. Another strategy is to become larger. But rather

I/O Psychology and the Economy: *Job Loss*

As reported, job loss through layoffs, outsourcing, offshoring, and mergers and acquisitions has reached unprecedented levels. What are the reasons behind these enormous reductions in the workforce? There are many, but this discussion will be limited to two.

First, in the 1980s, eliminating jobs was an organizationally expedient (and perhaps fashionable) method for organizations to become more profitable or efficient. That is, they may have been performing acceptably, but they could have been doing better. Under intense pressure to reach ever-higher financial goals, jobs were targeted for elimination. Since the largest single expense item in most organizational budgets is payroll, by eliminating jobs, expenses can be substantially reduced. But to what degree is job loss a good way to improve organizational financial performance? DeMeuse et al. (2004) compared the financial performance (using multiple indicators) of companies that had downsized versus those who did not over a 12-year period. They found that the downsized companies incurred *lower* financial performance during the initial few years following downsizing (compared to the non-downsized companies). After about three years the financial performance of the downsized companies improved to a similar level of the non-downsized companies. At no time during the 12 years of the study did the group of downsized companies ever out-perform the non-downsized companies. Similar findings have been reported by other researchers.

What sense can be made of these findings? One interpretation might be that some companies may benefit financially by downsizing, perhaps depending on where the job loss occurred and whether surviving employees can increase their productive output. One critical question would be for how long these financial performance gains could be sustained. Given increased job stress and increased voluntary turnover, the gains might be short-lived. However, taken in their totality, it is clear that as a broad-based approach to improving organizational performance, downsizing is not a way to achieve that goal. As has been said about *corporate anorexia* (a metaphor for downsizing), being thinner does not mean being healthier.

Second, downsizing temporarily increases the likelihood of organizational survival in a bad economy. A useful way to think about the relationships among organizations is a (supply) chain. For example, suppose a company produces plastic tables and chairs. The company sells its products to major retail stores. The company buys the material used to make plastics from industrial chemical suppliers. When the economy entered a recessionary period, consumers cut back on discretionary spending. Few people regard plastic tables and chairs as a necessity. With fewer plastic tables and chairs being sold, there is less need to produce them. So the company lays off a portion of its workforce because of reduced orders. In turn, the company orders fewer chemicals from its suppliers. In turn, the chemical company lays off some of its employees because of reduced orders. Likewise, organizations that sell their products to industrial chemical suppliers reduce their workforces because of weakened sales. Following this sequential pattern, job loss flows up and down the myriad of organizational links in the chain. The process of eliminating jobs is caused by an economic contagion that ripples through virtually all sectors of the economy. The larger the company, the more jobs are potentially imperiled. Larger companies have the luxury of reducing payroll to survive, hoping for better days ahead. Small companies don't have many jobs to eliminate, and thus have fewer ways to reduce costs. As such, they face a greater risk.

than just becoming a larger version of what the organization already is, organizations can choose to "marry" another organization as a way of increasing their size. The logic behind an organizational marriage is similar to that of the marriage of individuals; that is, the overall quality of life for both parties will be enhanced.

Organizational marriages encompass both mergers and acquisitions. The technical distinction between a merger and an acquisition is slim. An **organizational merger** is the marriage or joining of two organizations of equal status and power. Their union is mutually decided. Both organizations think they will be more prosperous by their formal association with the other. An **acquisition** is the procurement of property (in this case, an organization) by another organization. The purchasing organization is in the dominant or more powerful role. Unlike a marriage of individuals, an acquisition can be a union between two organizations where only one party agrees to the new relationship. The dominant organization thus acquires an unwilling partner to enhance its financial status in what is called a *hostile takeover*. Other acquisitions are characterized by more friendly relations between the two organizations, but nevertheless the more powerful organization acquires the less powerful organization. The acquiring organization is referred to as the *parent*, and the organization being acquired is the *target*. For the purpose of this discussion, mergers and acquisitions will be portrayed as the combining of two companies, regardless of the difference in power between the two. There is relatively little research on this topic. What we do know applies mainly to the characteristics of the two organizations as they affect the quality of their marriage and the individual responses of employees to their organization being united with another.

Marks (2002) described three phases in the merger process: precombination, combination, and postcombination. Most of the emphasis in the precombination phase is on financial issues, such as what a target company is worth, tax implications, and expected returns on the investment. Little thought or concern is directed to psychological or cultural issues. In the combination phase individuals jockey for power and cultures clash as people focus on differences between the partners and which side won which battles. Conflict can erupt over even minor issues. Marks described this account:

In one health care merger, the two sides could not even agree on starting times for meetings. One organization's managers began 9:00 A.M. meetings promptly whereas

Organizational merger
The joining or combining of two organizations of approximately equal status and power.

Acquisition
The process by which one organization acquires or subsumes the resources of a second organization.

the other's managers only left their offices at the top of the hour, collected their papers, chatted with their assistants, and grabbed a cup of coffee before arriving at the conference room around 9:15. In the pre-merger culture this was no problem, because everyone knew that 9:00 A.M. meetings actually began at 9:15. But it infuriated counterparts from the partner organization, who described the tardiness as "disrespectful" and "undisciplined." Of course, the latecomers regarded their new partners as "uptight" and having "misplaced priorities." (p. 46)

It is in the postcombination phase that the importance of integrating the two cultures becomes acute. Declines in employee morale and customer satisfaction indicate there are other criteria of a successful merger besides initial financial appeal. Marks described the postcombination phase as steeped in concerns about implementation, and there is no predetermined date when the merger is declared to be "finalized." All parties involved in the merger must continue to understand and adapt to the new culture (and new company) that was birthed.

The International Labour Organization (2003) estimated that in the decade of the 1990s over 10 million workers lost their jobs due to mergers and acquisitions. This figure does not include job loss associated with small companies that were driven out of business because they could not compete with the new "super organizations" (such as large retail stores). DeMeuse et al. aptly summarized the relationship among organizations and employees facing the economic realities of today.

Old companies are closing or downsizing. Companies are buying each other. Others are forming strategic partnerships to gain market advantage or fend off competition. Businesses, communities, and—by default—employees are changing. A new reality is facing workers—a reality that can be exhilarating with unheard of opportunities for the agile and entrepreneurial. But it is also a reality that can be brutal for those seeking security or merely satisfaction with the status quo. (p. 729)

Hewlin (2009) described how chronic fear of job loss alters the expressed values of employees. Some employees feign support for organizational policies or otherwise act in an inauthentic manner to increase the perceived likelihood that they will not be targeted for job loss. The employees feign conformance to perceived organizational values so as not to stand out as being different, yet many organizations claim they value diversity of opinion.

In the past 35 years, we have had to address new aspects of organizational behavior about which we had little knowledge. The depth and magnitude of these issues on the psychology of work have had a profound impact on the profession of I/O psychology (see Field Note 1: *How Many Ways Can You Lose Your Job?*).

Global Organizations

The explosion in business being conducted on a global basis has given rise to a new type of organization—the global organization. Global organizations have all the properties of any organization (in terms of structural and social components) with the added feature that their physical locations and employees are distributed throughout the world. Global organizations are relatively new, emerging in the 1990s as a response to advances in computer technology, new trade agreements among nations,

Field Note 1: *How Many Ways Can You Lose Your Job?*

Employee turnover has been a point of great interest to I/O psychologists since the field's inception. Employees could either quit their jobs (classified as *voluntary* turnover), or be fired (classified as *involuntary* turnover). For the first 70–80 years of I/O psychology, involuntary turnover occurred primarily in one of three ways.

1. *Dismissal.* A person is fired and some other person fills the position.

2. *Automation.* Work that was performed manually is now performed by an automated process. In the late 1960s and early 1970s, computers were invented for widespread commercial (and ultimately, personal) use. The lament of many workers of that era was, "I was replaced by a computer."

3. *Loss of company.* An entire company is dissolved, either due to financial insolvency (bankruptcy) or because the owner simply "wants to get out of the business."

Following the radical changes in the business world in the 1980s, the number of reasons for job loss grew.

4. *Downsizing or reduction-in-force (RIF).* A decision to reduce the size of the workforce to reduce labor costs. For example, a company that has eight workers performing a job decides to eliminate two of the positions. The remaining six employees then have to do the work that was once performed by eight. The two workers who lost their jobs were "RIFed."

5. *Outsourcing.* Eliminating jobs by contracting with an outside company to provide a particular service at a reduced cost. Examples include security, food service, and maintenance.

6. *Mergers and acquisitions.* The elimination of jobs caused by the combination of two companies. The new, larger company does not need two sets of employees performing the same duties (often referenced as "redundant personnel"). Mergers and acquisitions occurred throughout the 20th century, but the decades of the 1980s and 1990s (in particular) were known as the era of "merger mania."

7. *Offshoring.* The reduction of costs by eliminating domestic jobs and having the work performed in another country at a lower wage. Examples include computer programming, manufacturing, and telephonic customer service.

When an employee is fired, another individual is hired to fill the position. There is no job loss to society as a whole. However, the remaining six reasons for job loss represent not only the basis for why people are unemployed, but also the disappearance of jobs from a national economy. From an individual perspective, people must find jobs to earn a living. From a societal perspective, for every position that is lost, a new position must be created to maintain the same overall level of employment. The term *job creation* is often associated with the development of new industries that provide jobs people can fill. Before a person can be a good fit with a job, there has to be a job that can be filled.

and the end of the Cold War. Chao and Moon (2005) described the magnitude of global business organizations in the contemporary work world. There are approximately 63,000 multinational corporations that employ 90 million individuals. These companies employ a diverse array of people who differ by race, ethnicity, religion, and gender. Groups constituting a "majority" or "minority" can vary across different geographic sites of the same company. Chao and Moon believe that trying to understand culture in terms of demographics (as by race, ethnicity, etc.) is an overly simplistic way to explain the values held by people. A purely demographic description tends to promote thinking that the members of the same group hold similar values, which is often not the case. The authors believe the "cultural mosaic" reflected in multinational companies must be understood at a deeper level than by demographic membership.

For many years organizations that conducted business overseas (i.e., importing and exporting supplies to and from other countries) had a single corporate headquarters (such as in the United States) and simply engaged in international commerce. As customer sales grew in offshore locations, the parent company found it critical to establish separate divisions in other countries. Thus a single company, such as IBM, had separate multinational business units in England, France, Australia, and so on. This type of organizational structure resulted in numerous disadvantages, including duplication of internal services and poor interdivisional communication. As new computer-based technology (such as the Internet) was created, people in one organization could operate on a worldwide basis as if they were (virtually) present and together. This technology created the possibility of a global organization, one that has a global organizational culture, structure, and communication process. In short, a global organization operates as if the entire world were a single entity. Thus the evolution of organizations doing business overseas has evolved from *international* to *multinational* to *global* (see Field Note 2: *"What's a Good Time to Get Together?"*).

The concept that nations have identifiable cultures that influence the conduct of business became more salient through the research of Geert Hofstede. Hofstede worked for IBM, a multinational organization that had offices in many countries around the world. The employees in each location were administered attitude and opinion surveys as part of their employment. Hofstede analyzed the data by nation and arrived at the conclusion there were reliable and meaningful differences among the responses to the surveys. Hofstede (1980) wrote a seminal book based on his research entitled *Culture's Consequences*, and he updated his findings in a later book (Hofstede, 2001). Hofstede identified four major dimensions that are useful in understanding cross-cultural differences. Some of the dimensions have already been described in this book.

1. **Power distance**. Power distance refers to the extent to which less powerful members of an organization expect and accept that power is distributed unequally. (Malaysia scores highest on power distance.)

2. **Individualism–collectivism**. Individualism refers to the belief that people in a society primarily look after themselves and their family members. Collectivism is the belief that people in a society are integrated into strong, cohesive in-groups, which throughout their lifetime protect them in exchange for unquestioning loyalty. (The United States scores highest on individualism.)

3. **Masculinity–femininity**. Masculinity stands for a society in which social gender roles generally tend to be distinct. Men are supposed to be assertive, tough, and focused on material resources; women are supposed to be more modest, tender, and concerned with the quality of life. Femininity stands for a society in which social gender roles overlap; both men and women are supposed to be modest, tender, and concerned with the quality of life. (Japan scores highest on masculinity.)

Field Note 2:   *"What's a Good Time to Get Together?"*

One of the consequences of conducting business globally is a greater awareness of the time differences in cities around the world. The world is divided into 24 time zones. In the continental United States there is a three-hour time difference between the East Coast and the West Coast. This time difference can be an annoyance for conducting business across time zones during the traditional business hours of 8:00 a.m. to 5:00 p.m. However, the "annoyance" gets magnified when business is conducted around the world. The use of electronic communication permits asynchronous virtual team meetings. But sometimes virtual team members have to conduct business synchronously; that is, they all have to communicate with each other at the "same time." What time might that be?

I know of a multinational company that has offices in New York, Rio de Janeiro, Rome, and Sydney. Selecting a convenient time when team members could all talk with each other was not easy. They finally agreed upon the following schedule for a weekly conference call: 6:00 a.m. in New York; 8:00 a.m. in Rio de Janeiro; 12:00 p.m. in Rome; and 9:00 p.m. in Sydney. The New York team member didn't like the early hour, and the Sydney team member didn't like the late hour. But any other time only made matters worse for someone. The time problem was compounded by the fact that some cities change time (as from standard time to daylight saving time) while other cities are always on the same time. Also, some cities around the world have times that differ by the half-hour, not the hour. For example, when it's 9:00 a.m. in New York, it's 7:30 p.m. in Calcutta. Most people around the world work during the day and sleep at night. However, "daytime" and "nighttime" lose some of their conventional meaning in global business.

4. **Uncertainty avoidance**. Uncertainty avoidance is the extent to which members of a culture feel threatened by uncertain or unknown situations. (Greece scores highest on uncertainty avoidance.)

Taras et al. (2010) conducted a major meta-analysis of Hofstede's theory based on over 600 individual studies. The authors found the concept of cultural tightness/looseness—the strength of social norms and the degree of sanctioning behavior within societies—influenced the impact of the four factors. Hofstede's four cultural factors exerted stronger influence over behavior in those nations that had tight cultures. In culturally tight societies, cultural norms and sanctions dictate behavior more than individual preferences and styles. In loose cultures, there is more variability in how people behave, indicative of less imposing cultural prescriptions.

Hofstede's theory has been challenged on several levels. One is culture can vary along more than four dimensions; in particular, the concept of time orientation—cultural values reflecting a greater preference for short-term versus long-term time perspectives. A stronger criticism is the theory itself is biased in favor of a Western value system for comparing and contrasting cultures (Ailon, 2008). That is, Hofstede's four cultural dimensions are supposedly purely descriptive, not implicitly evaluative. However, if avoiding uncertainty is not only different from accepting the ambiguous or unpredictable, it is worse, then cultures that do not avoid the uncertain are better than those that do. Critics contend that Western nations seem to fare better than Eastern nations on Hofstede's cultural dimensions. It is argued that Eastern nations would emerge more favorably if a different set of cultural values were used to differentiate nations (see Cross-Cultural I/O Psychology: *The Ecological Fallacy*).

Marquardt (2002) described how the diversity and differentiation created by multicultural employees can cause organizational tension that, if left unattended, can quickly lead to conflict in the global company. The key challenge is to build an organization in which there are core values that transcend specific cultures, uniform policies that are regarded as fair and reasonable, and consistent business practices that can be implemented globally but are respectful of local cultural customs. Marquardt stated,

> One of the greatest powers of a global company and an important source of its competitive advantage is its diversity. Diversity provides the requisite variety. Without this inherent complexity, global organizations would not survive. They would lack the creativity, energy, and talent to develop the level of problem-solving capability necessary to be successful and thrive in the chaos of the global environment. (pp. 270–271)

Cross-Cultural I/O Psychology: *The Ecological Fallacy*

The research by Hofstede (and others) on cross-cultural values has added greatly to our understanding of how people differ from each other. In Hofstede's research, value surveys were administered to thousands of individuals throughout the world. The results were aggregated (i.e., averaged) by nation, thereby producing a score for each nation on each dimension of culture. These analyses thus became the basis for understanding cross-cultural differences in values.

However, as is always the case with aggregated data, it is possible to misinterpret the results. One such error of interpretation is called the ecological fallacy. The *ecological fallacy* is to assume the results for a group (e.g., a nation) are accurate for an individual within the group. For example, Hofstede's research reveals that Greece scored highest on uncertainty avoidance. Imagine you meet a Greek manager, and accordingly you assume this person exhibits high uncertainty avoidance. You would be committing an ecological fallacy by ascribing the results for a group to a particular individual within the group. In reality, you would know nothing about the level of uncertainty avoidance exhibited by this individual. It is (statistically) possible that this person has, in fact, very *low* uncertainty avoidance.

The explanation for the ecological fallacy pertains to measures of central tendency and variation. The mean is the most representative score, but there is variation about the mean. Any one individual could be below, at, or above the mean. The only way the mean would be an accurate description of every individual would be if there were no variation in the data (i.e., the mean is a constant).

It would thus be possible to have two people from the same nation who are more dissimilar than two people from two different nations. Research findings based on group data should not be interpreted as describing every individual within the group. The ecological fallacy is not a statistical error but an error of interpretation.

Table 8-1   *Examples of Western and Non-Western values*

Western Values	Non-Western Values
Individualism	Collectivism, group
Achievement	Modesty
Equality, egalitarian	Hierarchy
Winning	Collaboration, harmony
Pride	Saving face
Respect for results	Respect for status, ascription
Respect for competence	Respect for elders
Time is money	Time is life
Action, doing	Being, acceptance
Systematic, mechanistic	Humanistic
Tasks	Relationships, loyalty
Informal	Formal
Directness, assertiveness	Indirectness
Future, change	Past, tradition
Control	Fate
Specific, linear	Holistic
Verbal	Nonverbal

Source: From Marquardt, M., "Around the World: Organization Development in the International Context," in J. Waclawski and A. H. Church (Eds.), *Organization development: A data-driven approach to organizational change* (San Francisco: Jossey-Bass, 2002). This material is used by permission of John Wiley & Sons, Inc.

The culture people grow up in causes them to see the world differently. We tend to believe that our view of the world is correct, which in turn leads us to think and act in certain ways. We can come to believe that other ways of thinking and acting are strange, bizarre, or unintelligible. For example, Europeans typically receive 30–40 paid vacation days per year. U.S. workers typically have fewer paid vacation days and many managerial-level employees do not use their full allotment of vacation time. It is not uncommon for managerial-level U.S. employees to work while on vacation through the use of modern electronic technology. Battista et al. (2010) referred to this practice as a "BlackBerry vacation," and observed it appears to be primarily an American custom. To most members of other cultures, the practice of "working while on vacation" is a contradiction in terms. Western (the United States, Canada, northern Europe, Australia, and New Zealand) and non-Western (the rest of the world) cultures reflect different sets of values that guide thinking and behavior. Table 8-1 lists some of these value differences.

Marquardt believes these differences in values can be reduced to four key dimensions that most affect the global organization:

1. **Leadership roles and expectations**. The democratic style of leadership is the hallmark of Western managers. Employees are encouraged and expected to voice their opinions to better serve the operation of the organization. Disagreements with managers are not uncommon, and employees are encouraged to challenge and question. In non-Western cultures managers are expected to make decisions rather than solicit opinions from employees. There are status differentials

based on title, and lower-level employees who speak out may be considered disrespectful. Managers act in a certain formal style or else they may lose credibility.

2. **Individualism and groups**. As extensive research has indicated, the United States is the most individualistic culture in the world. As a culture we greatly value independence, and successful task completion (or "getting the job done") is more important than relationships. The social interaction of different ages, genders, and races is consistent with Western values of equality and informality. Indeed, our employment laws (Civil Rights Act, Age Discrimination in Employment Act, Americans with Disabilities Act, etc.) are designed to achieve this very outcome. Non-Western cultures tend to be more group-oriented or collectivistic. Group members support each other in exchange for loyalty and acceptance in the group. Individuals identify on a personal level with the social network to which they belong. The social interaction of people of differing status may be seen as a means of subverting authority and power in the workplace and may cause embarrassment and loss of status.

3. **Communications**. Latin American, Middle Eastern, and southern European cultures value expressive communication styles. The passion with which they communicate is designed to establish and maintain social relations. Voices are raised to reflect emotions such as joy, anger, and excitement, and hugging and touching often accompany conversation. The Western style of communication places more emphasis on the factual accuracy of what is said. The primary goal is to reach an objective, unemotional conclusion that leads to actions being taken by the listener. Displays of emotion are thought to indicate a lack of professionalism and rationality. There can be extreme variability in communication styles across cultures in trying to make a point, ranging from intentional exaggeration of desire or intent in the Middle East to prolonged silence and pauses in Asian cultures. In short, there is ample opportunity for people of different cultures to misunderstand each other on the basis of their communication styles.

4. **Decision making and handling conflict**. Western cultures are highly action-oriented. We like to get work done, not waste time, and we derive pleasure from achievement. Western cultures prefer frankness and candor in dealing with conflict. We accept and expect conflict and use power to resolve our differences. Non-Western cultures are much more indirect in conveying disagreement or criticism. Greater emphasis is placed on avoiding conflict than on finding ways to resolve it. Circuitous, indirect communication is used in the desire to protect honor and avoid shame. The desire to avoid conflict is rooted in courtesy and respect. Age is often the deciding factor in determining the most important member in a group.

A broad-based view of culture in global organizations would be as follows. At one extreme, if everyone behaved the same, the world would operate under a single powerful culture. At the other extreme, if everyone behaved differently, our behavior would not be influenced by cultural values. Reality lies somewhere in the middle. As we enter the era of global organizations, what were once highly disparate cultures are producing some common ground as required to successfully run a business populated with employees from many nations. As stated by Erez (2011): "Under the surface of globalization, there is high variance in cultural values, histories, political regimes, religions, and external and climatic conditions that differentiate among cultures and require different patterns of cultural adaptations" (p. 841). Individuals who are members of global organizations must adopt the values of the particular company to be accepted as contributing organizational members. However, as individuals (in non-business roles) we do not surrender our own cultural identities that were shaped long before becoming socialized to a corporate culture.

Organizational Change

The first part of this chapter has dealt with the concept of an organization and its constituent components. The remainder will deal with an ever-widening area of I/O psychology—the process of effecting change in organizations. It is best to begin this section by considering why organizations exist in the first place. Organizations are created to fulfill some purpose or objective. They exist in a larger environment that encompasses economic, legal, and social factors. Thus there must be a sense of fit between the organization and the environment in which it exists.

Many business organizations were founded in the first half of the 20th century. They enjoyed a period of relative stability in the environments in which they operated. Although organizations had to respond to some environmental influences, for the most part the economic and social order was relatively stable until the 1980s. For the past 35 years, changes in the business world have accelerated to rates unparalleled in history. As the external world rapidly changes, so too must organizations. The process of altering organizations to be more adaptive and congruent with their business environments is called **organizational change**. The need for organizations to change in response to changing conditions was well captured by a business leader: "The rate of change internally has to be greater than the rate of change externally or else you're pedaling backward" (Martins, 2011, p. 691).

For reasons discussed in Chapter 1, the business world began to change in the 1980s. Among the forces responsible for the change were the adoption and diffusion of computers into work life, the evolving cultural diversity of the workforce, the emergence of advanced communication technologies, the globalization of business, and redistributions of economic power. Using the "peg and hole" analogy, we can think of organizations as "pegs" that must fit into ever-mutating business environments (the "holes"). There has always been a need for most organizations to change in response to environmental pressures, but the past 35 years has witnessed an ever-growing and expanding need for all organizations to respond to the pressures placed on them by transforming environmental conditions. What is different now than 35 years ago is: (1) the greater strength of environmental pressures prompting change, (2) the speed at which change must occur, (3) the acceptance that responsiveness to change is a continuous organizational process, and (4) the pervasiveness of organizations caught up and affected by changing environmental conditions. While there is resounding recognition of the need for change, it is not at all easy or clear how to do it.

There is a family-owned ice cream store in North Carolina that still sells ice cream the way it has for nine decades. On the surface it might appear that this little store has escaped the need to adjust in response to changes in the last 90 years. To a large extent this is true, although the store has been compelled to stock low-fat and no-fat

Organizational change
The methods by which organizations evolve to become more adaptive to pressing economic and social conditions.

dairy products to meet changing customer preferences. However, for the most part, this store is an "organizational dinosaur," one of the last of a rare breed that has not had to change with the times.

Church et al. (2002) noted that current organizational change strategies have become more grounded in business strategy, financial indicators, global trends, and customer research than interventions of a purely psychological nature. Burke (2008) candidly described what it is like to try to implement organizational change. "The implementation process is messy. Things don't proceed exactly as planned; people do things their own way, not always according to the plan; some people resist or even sabotage the process, and some people who would be predicted to support or resist the plan actually behave in just the opposite way" (p. 12).

Plowman et al. (2007) provided a vivid example of how organizational change actually occurs, including unanticipated outcomes that derived from unintended processes. The organization in question was a church. The desire for change began with some parishioners who were bored with the Sunday morning service. So instead of attending a traditional religious service, they decided to offer a free Sunday breakfast to homeless people. After five weeks of serving food, a physician in the group decided to also offer the homeless people free medical advice. This grew into the offering of eye-care, dental, and medical services. Within a few years, the church had created a separate social service organization. This organization obtained city funds to run a day care center for the homeless, serve approximately 200,000 meals per year, offer job training, and provide legal assistance. The homeless people sang in the church choir and served as ushers at the Sunday morning church service. This entire series of events started with a simple act of generosity.

This case described by Plowman et al. is not atypical in organizational change. The magnitude of the proposed intended change was small: to offer a free breakfast to some homeless people on Sunday mornings. Because there were no objections or resistance to the breakfast, the concept of accepting change got a toe-hold. Had the free breakfast idea been denied, none of the subsequent changes would have resulted. The success of the small intended change amplified the possibility for more radical changes. The entire process snow-balled, sustaining itself into continuous radical change. The sheer magnitude of the radical changes produced resistance and displeasure by other organizations. Some local businesses situated near the church objected to the amount of disruption the church's activities created in the neighborhood. However, the resistance came primarily after the new activities were fully operational.

The case provides insights into when resistance to change can best be overcome. Had the resistance emerged initially, the attempt at change may well have failed before it could even begin. After the change process produced momentum, further changes emerged, and the resistance was "too little too late" to stop it. In sum, both the process and the outcomes of organizational change could not have been envisioned at the outset, and the *timing* of events in the change process can be just as important as the nature of the events themselves.

Rousseau and Batt (2007) discussed not only the need for organizations to change, but also the need for society as a whole to change. The problems we face in the 21st century cannot necessarily be addressed with solutions that worked in the 20th century. The 21st century has produced greater life expectancy, lower job security, and major changes in how families function. There is an old saying; "We prefer the devil we know to the devil we don't know." We may know that old approaches and solutions are no longer effective, but we derive some comfort from them because they are familiar and known to us. New ideas pose a double threat: not only are we unfamiliar with them, they may be just as ineffectual as the old ideas. In short, while the need for change may be acute, there is often the temptation to stick with what is less threatening rather than venture into the more threatening (but also potentially more beneficial). Such is the paradox of organizational change and resistance to it.

An Example of the Need for Organizational Change

For more than 100 years the textile industry in the United States enjoyed economic prosperity. There was unending demand for textile products—people throughout the world need to clothe themselves. There was also a vast supply of a natural product, cotton, that was grown domestically. The raw cotton was transformed into cotton yarn, which in turn was woven into cotton fabrics (cloth). The cloth was then cut and sewn into shirts, pants, and other apparel. The United States literally "clothed the world" (or much of it) for a long time. Workers in the textile industry did not have to be highly skilled because neither the machinery for making yarn nor the looms for weaving cloth were complex. The work involved in cutting and stitching the cloth into apparel required even less technical skill. The typical wage of a textile worker in the United States in the 1980s was about $10 per hour.

Pressures on the textile industry to change began in the form of consumer demands for new types of yarn. This yarn did not grow from a natural plant but was created from a blend of cotton and synthetic fibers. The new yarn was less prone to shrink upon washing, more stain resistant, and more likely to retain its color with wear. The textile industry was forced to design a new line of manufacturing technology to produce these blended synthetic fibers. More technically competent workers were required to operate the new machinery. Some of the existing textile workers accepted the need to be trained, but others left the industry. New selection procedures had to be implemented to upgrade the skill requirements for new textile workers. This new yarn continued to be woven into cloth and then cut and sewn to create apparel.

Next came pressures from global competition. China developed a strong interest in entering the textile business. Because the yarn making process involved machinery and the Chinese could purchase this machinery as readily as any other country, large yarn producing textile companies were established in China. Because the quality of the finished yarn was comparable to yarn made in the United States, customers began to buy yarn from the Chinese because of lower costs. The lower cost was not evident in the fibers or machinery but in labor. A typical wage for a textile worker in China is approximately 80¢ per hour.

The Chinese began to flood the global market with yarn because U.S. companies could not compete with these low labor costs. Likewise, other countries built weaving operations that had lower labor costs. The third phase of the textile business, cutting and sewing cloth, was also shifted to Asia. In addition to lower wages, Asians (particularly women in Southeast Asia—Cambodia, Vietnam, and Laos) have smaller hands and fingers compared with Westerners. Their smaller features are ideally suited to the more delicate operations associated with turning cloth into apparel.

The U.S. textile industry was in dire shape. It could no longer compete with the Chinese in the manufacturing of yarn. The industry turned to political solutions to some of its problems. The textile industry lobbied the U.S. government to impose quotas and tariffs on goods made in China to give the Chinese less of a competitive edge. The U.S. government did impose quotas and tariffs on Chinese textile products but only for a limited time. The government gave the textile industry a temporary respite from its global economic problems. The textile industry then asked the government to extend the period of quotas and tariffs. However, the government has other concerns besides the welfare of the domestic textile industry. A larger, more grave issue of a geopolitical nature is facing our nation. The United States does not want to alienate China by extending the economic sanctions on textiles because China plays a vital political role for the United States. North Korea has nuclear weapons and is antagonistic in its relations to the United States. The United States believes that China, because of its geographic and political affinity with North Korea, can be instrumental in influencing North Korea's actions. As such, the fate of the domestic textile industry must be weighed against the strategic benefit of having a favorable relationship with China.

The U.S. textile industry has not ceased to exist, but the changes facing the industry are seismic. The U.S. textile industry now makes the textiles that are not made overseas. Among its leading products are fibers used in upholstery. By federal law the U.S. military must purchase U.S.-made textile products (uniforms, tents, etc.). The cut-and-sew functions of the textile industry are now performed almost exclusively overseas. The production of yarn in the United States is limited to specialty markets that are not (currently) met overseas. There has been a massive loss of jobs in the U.S. textile industry, estimated to be in excess of 500,000. The remaining U.S. textile companies have been compelled to invent new products (e.g., sweat-resistant fibers), use the latest and most efficient computer-based manufacturing techniques, and select and train a workforce that is vastly superior to its predecessors a mere generation ago. One of the consequences of living in a global economy is that oceans no longer offer protection or insulation. Geographically a country may be half a world away, but economically it is a computer click away. The essence of organizational change is to help organizations survive in a world that is evolving at an unrelenting pace.

Every U.S. company in the textile industry has had to change its culture from one of privileged position (everyone needs to wear our clothes) to the recognition that other nations can make high-quality goods cheaper. Virtually all U.S. textile companies have had to downsize to lower their costs. The remaining employees have had to find new ways to conduct their work. They have become empowered to make decisions about work problems and issues that previously were left to supervisors. There was massive resistance to all the changes that befell the industry. The resistance was met with an unassailable truth: either we change what we do and how we do it, or our jobs will be shipped overseas.

Corporate Social Responsibility

Across the evolutionary stages of I/O psychology there is a pattern of an ever-widening focus of attention and interest. In the early decades of I/O psychology the primary concern was on the individual. That is, how the person should be recruited, selected, trained, and evaluated. Changes in the business world prompted new ways to structure work, and teams were created to accomplish tasks once performed by individuals. The topic of teams and teamwork is the subject of Chapter 9. However, a work team is embedded within a larger social collectivity, the organization. As discussed earlier in this chapter, the birth of organizational psychology transformed our attention to the organization as an object of investigation. As such, organizations became the "endpoint" of the continuum of an ever-widening focus. However most recently, I/O scholars are now considering an even broader focus of our attention—how organizations contribute to the society or environment in which they are situated.

Corporate social responsibility
The obligation of organizations to take an active part in improving society.

The term for this area of inquiry is **corporate social responsibility**, a topic that has been previously examined in other disciplines, but is a relatively new area for I/O psychology. Corporate social responsibility can manifest itself in many ways. One example is corporate volunteering. Caligiuri et al. (2013) reported that most corporate volunteer programs involve companies sponsoring paid release time from work for interested employees to assist nonprofit organizations, such as the Red Cross and the United Way. Grant (2012) stated that over 90% of Fortune 500 companies run employee volunteering programs, encouraging employees to perform community service while being compensated on company time. Many programs require sustained participation, not a one-time contribution. Over the past 25 years employees of Disney have given more than five million hours to help nonprofit organizations.

However, no other societal issue has served as a catalyst for the growing importance of corporate social responsibility than has sustainability. Swim et al. (2011) summarized the problem as follows:

> Global climate change poses one of the greatest challenges facing humanity in this century. Earth's climate has changed in many ways over geological time, but for the first time, over the past century, human activity has become a significant cause of climate change. By burning fossil fuels, cutting and burning forests, and engaging in other environment-impacting activities, humans have changed the heat balance of Earth sufficiently that the global average temperature has moved outside the range that has characterized the 10,000 years of recorded human history. (p. 241)

Why should I/O psychology get involved in trying to address the global problems of sustainability? Over the years our discipline has learned why change is resisted, and what can be done to overcome it. We begin with a common definition of what we are addressing. Lowman (2013) reported the United Nations World Commission on Environment and Development defined sustainability as "being able to meet present needs without compromising the ability of future generations to meet their needs" (p. 35). As laudable and highly plausible as the goal of sustainability may be, there are psychological barriers to changing our behavior to make its attainment more likely. Gifford (2011) identified several barriers. Here are four:

1. *Immediacy* — we are more responsive to issues that produce current personal hardships. We postpone taking action on issues that affect us in the future.

2. *Technosalvation* — someone will think of something that will make it all work out.

3. *Perceived inequity* — it is not fair that I should change my lifestyle when people in other nations who cause more problems do not.

4. *Denial* — the behavior of people has nothing to do with climate change, and maybe the climate isn't really changing.

I/O psychology has learned that overcoming resistance to change is facilitated by having individuals serve as champions of the change process. Sonenshein (2012) referred to such people as "issue sellers — individuals who act as change agents inside mainstream business organizations by trying to convince others to direct attention and resources to issues" (p. 49). The leaders of the organization must make sustainability a top priority, repeating the message in both words and actions. Without both financial and human resources devoted to enacting sustainable behaviors, organizations will "look green" (to impress others) but not "be green" (DuBois et al., 2013). Sustainability must involve all employees so there is collective ownership of it. Haddock-Millar et al. (2012) described the creation of a program called "Planet Champion" at McDonald's UK. Employees came up with many useful ideas to support sustainability. Among them were placing all grills on stand-by when not in use, which reduced carbon dioxide emissions by 20,000 tons per year. By placing toasters on stand-by, McDonald's UK saved 30% of its energy costs per year. Stern (2011) addressed the importance for organizations including ecological impact criteria in making business decisions. Not only must organizations invent products that conserve energy, individuals must be willing to use the products. It is a matter of debate whether the government should provide financial incentives for organizations going green, or impose formal penalties for not going green.

Ones and Dilchert (2012) reduced the significance of sustainability to one sobering sentence: "If humanity does not survive in the face of resource shortages (for example, clean water and food supplies for nine billion individuals by 2050) and environmental calamities (such as climate change and destruction of the ecosystems), no organizations will remain" (p. 89).

Savitz and Weber (2006) proposed that sustainability is the intersection of economic ("profit"), social ("people"), and environmental ("planet") goals, as shown in Figure 8-7. We must find a way to strike a critical and delicate balance among the

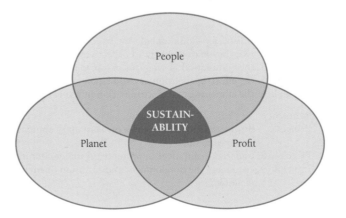

Figure 8-7 *The triple bottom line (profit, planet, and people) needed for environmental sustainability*

Adapted from *The triple bottom line*, by A. W. Savitz and K. Weber (2006). Reprinted with permission from Jossey-Bass.

three (Lombardo et al., 2013). The involvement of I/O psychology in corporate social responsibility is consistent with the Code of Ethics of psychologists — to promote human welfare. It is also consistent with the principles of humanitarian work psychology discussed in Chapter 1. Klein and Huffman (2013) concluded I/O psychology and environmental sustainability in organizations are "a natural partnership" (p. 3).

The recognition by I/O psychology to adopt a comprehensive perspective of organizational actions is consistent with the United Nations Global Compact (2008). The U.N. Global Compact is a set of policies and recommended actions for organizations to follow in the conduct of their business. The U.N. Global Compact is presented in Table 8-2. The intent of the Global Compact is to promote good by following principles pertaining to human rights, labor, environment, and anti-corruption. The U.N. has no authority to enforce organizational policies and actions. But the Global Compact does provide a specific set of initiatives for responsible organizations to follow, and as of 2014 it was endorsed by 8,000 organizations (including SIOP) representing 145 nations. In summation, there is a growing recognition of the need for organizations to conduct themselves in responsible ways for the betterment of mankind. When we speak of global organizations and a global economy, there are concomitant global consequences that follow from actions taken. I/O psychology has joined other scientific disciplines in recognizing our inherent global interdependence, and the need to pursue goals that historically were not part of our legacy.

Table 8-2   *United Nations Global Compact: The Ten Principles*

The Global Compact asks companies to embrace, support and enact, within their sphere of influence, a set of core values in the areas of human rights, labor standards, the environment, and anti-corruption:

Human Rights
   Principle 1: Businesses should support and respect the protection of internationally proclaimed human rights; and
   Principle 2: make sure that they are not complicit in human rights abuses.

Labor Standards
   Principle 3: Businesses should uphold the freedom of association and the effective recognition of the right to collective bargaining; and
   Principle 4: the elimination of all forms of forced and compulsory labor; and
   Principle 5: the effective abolition of child labor; and
   Principle 6: the elimination of discrimination in respect of employment and occupation.

Environment
   Principle 7: Businesses should support a precautionary approach to environmental challenges; and
   Principle 8: undertake initiatives to promote greater environmental responsibility; and
   Principle 9: encourage the development and diffusion of environmentally friendly technologies.

Anti-Corruption
   Principle 10: Businesses should work against corruption in all its forms, including extortion and bribery.

(copyright by the United Nations Global Compact. Reprinted with permission.)

Chapter Summary

- Organizations are complex social entities designed to achieve work-related objectives.
- Classical organizational theory defined the structure of an organization in terms of four principles: functional, scalar, line/staff, and span of control.
- Mintzberg proposed a theory of organizational structure consisting of seven parts: strategic apex, middle line, support staff, technostructure, operating core, ideology, and politics.
- Organizations are defined by a social system of roles, norms, and culture.
- Downsizing, outsourcing, offshoring, and mergers and acquisitions are contemporary sources of job loss.
- Person-organization fit is a useful framework for understanding why job candidates and companies are attracted to each other.
- The modern economy has given rise to global organizations that through electronic communication operate across time and space.
- Hofstede provided four classic dimensions useful in differentiating cultures around the world: power distance, individualism–collectivism, masculinity–femininity, and uncertainty avoidance.
- Organizations change continuously to adapt to their environments. Organizations can change suddenly and painfully, with downsizing being a major form of change.
- I/O psychology has recently recognized the need for organizations to contribute to the larger environment of which they are a part, the concept of corporate social responsibility.

Teams and Teamwork

Learning Objectives

- Explain why the use of teams is increasing.
- Explain what is meant by level of analysis.
- Explain the concept of teamwork.
- Describe the various types of teams.
- Describe how teams and team members develop over time.
- Describe the structure and processes of teams.
- Explain how teams make decisions and share mental models.
- Explain how personnel selection, training, and performance appraisal apply to teams.

The concept of teamwork dates to antiquity. As Kozlowski and Ilgen (2006) noted, "Teams of people working together for a common purpose have been a centerpiece of human social organization ever since our ancient ancestors first banded together to hunt game, raise families, and defend their communities. Human history is largely a story of people working together to explore, achieve, and conquer" (p. 77). Nevertheless, I/O psychologists have tended to make individuals, rather than teams, the object of their attention. That is, we have been concerned with finding the right person for the job, training the individual, and subsequently monitoring his or her performance on the job. Although the existence of informal work groups was acknowledged in the Hawthorne studies, for the most part interest in groups was limited to social psychology. However, since the 1980s, there has been a tremendous upsurge of interest in using work groups, not just individuals, as the organizing principle through which work is accomplished.

As described in the preceding chapter, organizations are designed for a purpose. Accordingly, the traditional structure of an organization (line/staff relationships, span of control, etc.) was created to conduct and monitor the flow of work. Such traditional organizational structures were effective for most of the 20th century. In the last two decades of the 20th century, however, several forces of a technological, economic, and demographic nature reached a confluence, prompting organizations to respond. These forces were discussed in Chapter 1 and reflect the changing nature of work. Greater global economic competition and rapid advances in communication technology forced organizations to change the way they performed their work operations. Some automobile companies developed a team approach to the production of cars compared with the traditional assembly-line approach. Products had to be developed and brought to market more quickly than in the past. Rapid changes in the business world compelled organizations to be more flexible and responsive to them. To increase flexibility, companies had to move away from tightly controlled organizational structures that often resulted in a relatively slow work pace. There was increased emphasis on organizations' need to respond quickly in what they did and how they did it. Organizations began to change their structure in response to these environmental forces and to use work teams to accomplish the organization's work (LePine, Hanson et al., 2000). Concurrently, the decision-making authority concerning the specific means of task accomplishment has been pushed down to these teams. The team members often must decide among themselves who will do the what, where, when, and how of work.

The evolution of teams and teamwork has compelled I/O psychology to address a host of new issues. As Tannenbaum et al. (2012) lamented, teams have become so commonplace that employees and managers "take them for granted and assume they will be effective" (p. 3). However, teams are *not* universally superior to individuals for conducting work across all relevant performance indices. For example, teams do not necessarily produce better quality decisions than do individuals. Indeed, Naquin and Tynan (2003) asserted it is a myth that companies that use teams are more effective than those that do not. Teams are not a panacea for all work-related ills. Naquin and Tynan believe that a "team halo effect" can exist in the work world. When people seek to understand team performance, they tend to give teams credit for their success. However, individuals (as opposed to the collective group) tend to receive the blame for poor team performance.

Some of what we have learned about individuals in the workplace generalizes to teams, but other issues are more specific to teams. There is nothing magical about transforming individuals into work teams. Teams are merely one means of performing work. In this chapter we will examine teams as a means of accomplishing work, including the factors that lead to successful team performance.

Level of Analysis

Level of analysis
The unit or level (individuals, teams, organizations, nations, etc.) that is the object of the researchers' interest and about which conclusions are drawn from the research.

A shift in the focus from individuals to teams as a means of conducting work also requires a shift in the conduct of I/O psychological research. Researchers can and do examine different entities as the object of their investigations. Historically I/O psychology focused on the individual with regard to such factors as desired KSAOs for employment, needed training, and standards of job performance. In such cases the level of analysis is the individual; that is, the conclusions drawn from the research are about individuals. However, research questions can also be posed at the team level of analysis and at the organizational level of analysis. Consider an organization that has 100 employees. A researcher may be interested in assessing the relationship between the degree to which employees feel a sense of organizational identification with the company and job performance. At the *individual* level of analysis, the researcher would have a sample size of 100 individuals, obtain measures of organizational identification and job performance, correlate the two variables, and arrive at a conclusion regarding the relationship between them. However, the 100 employees could also be organized into 25 four-person work teams. In this case the researcher would have a sample size of 25 (i.e., the 25 teams). Each team would be represented by a score reflecting its sense of organizational identification (as a team) and their work performance (as a team). The researcher would correlate these two variables and, based on a sample size of 25, arrive at a conclusion about the relationship between the two variables at the *team* level of analysis. It is also possible to study the relationship between organizational identification and performance at the *organizational* level of analysis. In this case the 100-employee company would be a sample size of 1. There would be one measure of organizational identification (for the entire company) and one measure of performance (for the entire company). The researcher would then have to collect data from additional organizations. The researcher would correlate these two variables, based on a sample size of however many organizations were in the study, and arrive at a conclusion about the relationship between the two variables at the *organizational* level of analysis. Figure 9-1 is a diagram showing these levels of analysis.

What *is* the relationship between organizational identification and performance? The answer depends on the level of analysis under consideration. It is possible to arrive at three different conclusions, depending on whether the level of analysis is the individual, team, or organization. Furthermore, some constructs do not exist at particular levels of analysis. Size is one example. Teams and organizations can differ in their size (i.e., number of members), but individuals cannot. For the most part, I/O psychologists have not focused their research interests on the organizational level of analysis. Studying complete organizations and their relationships with other organizations is more traditionally the province of sociology. There is often a link between a particular scientific discipline and the level of analysis of its research. The field of economics

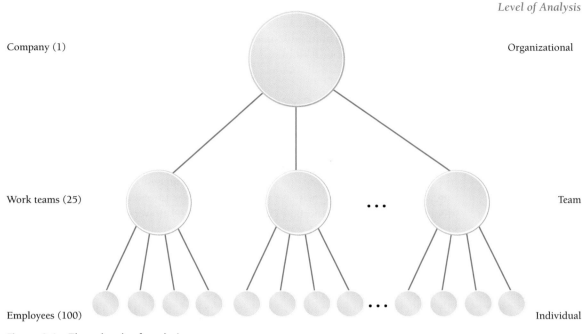

Company (1)   Organizational

Work teams (25)   Team

Employees (100)   Individual

Figure 9-1   *Three levels of analysis*

examines variables at the industry (petroleum, agriculture, manufacturing, etc.) level of analysis, and the field of political science frequently examines variables at the national level of analysis.

The term *micro* is often used to describe research at the individual level of analysis, while *macro* is used to describe research at the organizational level of analysis. Research at the team level of analysis is positioned somewhere between the micro and the macro. As Kozlowski and Bell (2003) stated, "Because teams occupy the intersection of the multilevel perspective, they bridge the gap between the individual and the organizational system as a whole" (p. 367). Rousseau and House (1994) proposed the term *meso* (meaning "in between," as in the word *mezzanine*) research. Meso research occurs in an organizational context where processes at two levels are examined simultaneously. Thus I/O researchers who study relationships between variables at both the individual and team levels of analysis are engaging in meso research. The entire area of multilevel research and theory is an emerging topic in our profession (e.g., Klein & Kozlowski, 2000). It addresses a fundamental dilemma in understanding human behavior in organizations; namely, we as individuals obtain employment in a larger social collectivity (an organization) and are often members of some smaller level of aggregation (such as a team, department, unit, or shift). The dilemma is to disentangle the sources of influence on our behavior from an individual, team, and organization perspective. It will also be recalled from Chapter 2 that meta-analysis is a frequently used method of research in which investigators combine the results from previously conducted research to distill a conclusion about a topic. Ostroff and Harrison (1999) cautioned that researchers must be clear about the level of analysis of their investigation.

Combining findings from original studies with different levels of analysis distorts the interpretation of the findings.

We can now move onto a discussion of teams and teamwork within organizations. The first question that we'll address is, "What is a team?"

Defining Characteristics of Work Teams

When discussing teams, one of the first things to consider is how they are different from groups, if at all. Whereas people often use the terms groups and teams interchangeably, there are clear characteristics of teams that make them unique and distinct from groups. West and Lyubovnikova (2012) suggest that inappropriately calling a group a team may hurt the ability to empower teams and set members up for disappointment. Nevertheless, as Cannon-Bowers and Bowers (2011) noted, "it is the defining characteristics and features of the construct that are important, not strictly the label" (p. 599). In this section we discuss those defining characteristics that make teams unique and distinct from groups.

Team

A social aggregation in which a limited number of individuals interact on a regular basis to accomplish a set of shared objectives for which they have mutual responsibility.

Teams are bounded social units that work within a larger social system—the organization. A work team has identifiable memberships (that is, members and nonmembers alike clearly know who is a member and who is not) and an identifiable task or set of tasks to perform. Tasks may include monitoring, producing, serving, generating ideas, and doing other activities. The team's work requires that members interact by exchanging information, sharing resources, and coordinating with and reacting to one another in accomplishing the group task. Furthermore, there is always some degree of interdependence within the members of a team, which is not always the case with mere groups of people. Moreover, as Kozlowski and Chao (2012) noted, "Like the different pieces in a jigsaw puzzle, diverse group identities can be compiled to create a picture or group that is not apparent from one piece or individual" (p. 347). By combining different perspectives and capitalizing on the strengths of the individual members, they are able to achieve results that exceed the pooled or combined results of all their members. As such, the whole is greater than the sum of the parts.

Another point worthy of mention is how many people it takes to form a team. While many scholars will consider a team to be two or more individuals working together, others believe a team must consist of at least three members and treat dyads (two-person units) separate from teams. Regardless, the issues discussed throughout this chapter apply to both dyads and teams of three or more individuals.

Principles of Teamwork

McIntyre and Salas (1995) conducted extensive research on U.S. Navy tactical teams and identified several principles of teamwork that are also relevant for other organizations that use teams. Five of the major principles are listed here.

Principle 1: *Teamwork implies that members provide feedback to and accept it from one another.* For teamwork to be effective, team members must feel free to provide feedback; that is, the climate within the group must be such that neither status nor power stands as an obstacle to team members providing feedback to one another.

Effective teams engage in tasks with an awareness of their strengths and weaknesses. When team leaders show the ability to accept constructive criticism, they establish a norm that this type of criticism is appropriate.

Principle 2: *Teamwork implies the willingness, preparedness, and proclivity to back fellow members up during operations.* Better teams are distinguishable from poorer teams in that their members show a willingness to jump in and help when they are needed, and they accept help without fear of being perceived as weak. Team members must show competence not only in their own particular area but also in the areas of other team members with whom they directly interact.

Principle 3: *Teamwork involves group members collectively viewing themselves as a group whose success depends on their interaction.* Team members must have high awareness of themselves as a team. Each member sees the team's success as taking precedence over individual performance. Members of effective teams view themselves as connected team members, not as isolated individuals working with other isolated individuals. Successful teams consist of individuals who recognize that their effectiveness is the team's effectiveness, which depends on the sum total of all team members' performance.

Principle 4: *Teamwork means fostering within-team interdependence.* Fostering team interdependence means the team adopts the value that it is not only appropriate but also essential for each team member (regardless of status within the team) to depend on every other team member to carry out the team's mission. Contrary to what may take place in the rest of the organization, interdependence is seen as a virtue, as an essential characteristic of team performance, not as a weakness.

Principle 5: *Team leadership makes a difference with respect to the performance of the team.* Team leaders serve as models for their fellow team members. If the leaders openly engage in teamwork (i.e., provide and accept feedback and supportive behavior) other team members are likely to do the same. Team leaders are vital and have tremendous influence on teams, and when team leaders are poor, so are the teams.

McIntyre and Salas believe these principles provide a theory of teamwork that must be incorporated into the organization's operating philosophy when implementing or improving team-based performance. Teamwork will take place within the organization to the extent that the organization fosters it and builds upon it.

Types of Teams

The term *team* has been used in many contexts to describe types of work operations, such as project teams, sales teams, new product teams, process improvement teams, cost-reduction teams, and so on (see Social Media and I/O Psychology: *Social Media Teams*). One way to differentiate teams is by their objectives. It is also possible to differentiate teams by other variables, such as the nature of their interactions (e.g., face-to-face vs. virtual). Larson and La Fasto (1989) proposed three basic types of teams (problem-resolution, creative, and tactical). In addition to these three, we present two additional types of teams that have emerged (*ad hoc* and virtual), as well as the concept of multiteam systems (or "team of teams").

Problem-resolution team
A type of team created for the purpose of focusing on solving ongoing problems or issues.

Problem-resolution teams are created for the purpose of focusing on solving ongoing problems or issues. Such teams require each member of the team to expect that

Social Media and I/O Psychology: *Social Media Teams*

Social media have become crucial for organizations, particularly with regard to their marketing and public relations. Organizations must have a clear and strong online presence to compete effectively in the digital world. While some organizations rely on individuals to maintain their online presence (often on top of other job responsibilities), many are turning to specialized teams of individuals who share the responsibility of managing the organization's Facebook and Twitter accounts, posting videos, photos, and promotional materials to YouTube, Instagram, and Pinterest, and writing blog posts, among other things. In short, these social media teams act as the digital face and voice of their organization.

A survey conducted by Ragan/NASDAQ OMX Corporate Solutions revealed that although many organizations use social media regularly, most feel they have more to learn and accomplish. Other organizations have become leaders in the social media realm. Taco Bell, for example, is ranked #1 on DigitalCoCo's Restaurant Social Media Index. Their social media team, which they refer to as "The Center for Social Excellence," is extremely active online. Their presence has created a passionate following, in part based on the team's ability to think creatively and engage customers in humorous yet constructive dialogue. They have even made waves (and attracted even more followers) by interacting with other notable brands. For example, in 2012 Old Spice's social media team tweeted "Why is it that 'fire sauce' isn't made with any real fire? Seems like false advertising." Taco Bell's social media team didn't miss a beat, tweeting, "@OldSpice is your deodorant made with really old spices?" To this, Old Spice's team quipped back, "@TacoBell Depends. Do you consider volcanos, tanks and freedom to be spices?" And with this simple exchange through social media, both organizations gained notoriety and an increased digital presence. Go teams!

interactions among members will be truthful and embody a high degree of integrity. Each member must believe that the team will be consistent and mature in its approach to dealing with problems. The members must have a high degree of trust in a process of problem resolution that focuses on issues, rather than on predetermined positions or conclusions. The authors cited diagnostic teams at the Centers for Disease Control as an exemplar of this type.

Creative team
A type of team created for the purpose of developing innovative possibilities or solutions.

Creative teams are responsible for exploring possibilities and alternatives, with the broad objective of developing a new product or service. A necessary feature of the team's structure is autonomy. For a creative team to function, it needs to have autonomy from systems and procedures as well as an atmosphere in which ideas are not prematurely quashed. Creative teams need to be insulated within the organizational structure to remain focused on the result to be achieved rather than on organizational processes. The IBM PC was developed by a creative team that endured many failures before arriving at a successful product. The design team needed protection from typical organizational pressures that reflect impatience with failure. The "incubation period" for the PC was many years and could not have been shortened by performance expectations imposed by others.

Tactical team
A type of team created for the purpose of executing a well-defined plan or objective.

Tactical teams are responsible for executing a well-defined plan. To do so there must be high task clarity and unambiguous role definition. The success of tactical teams depends on a high degree of responsiveness from team members, a clear understanding of who does what, and a clear set of performance standards. An example of a tactical team is a police SWAT team or a cardiac surgical team. Each operational procedure must be well defined, and each task must be highly focused and specific. Furthermore, the standards of excellence must be clear to everyone, and ways of measuring success or failure must be understood by the entire team.

We may add a fourth type of team, which is defined primarily by its limited life span. It is sometimes called an *ad hoc* (Latin for "to this") team and is basically a hybrid cross between a problem-resolution and a tactical team. An ***ad hoc* team** is created for a specific purpose, addressing itself "to this" particular problem. The team members are selected from existing employees in an organization, and after the team has completed its work, the team disbands. Thus membership in the team (and indeed the life span of the team itself) is finite and then the team no longer exists. *Ad hoc* teams are used in organizations that encounter unusual or atypical problems that require an atypical response (the creation of the *ad hoc* team). If the problem tends to recur, there may be pressure to establish the team on a longer-term basis, as a more formalized and permanent unit.

Lastly, a fifth type of team that has emerged is the **virtual team,** or those teams whose members "work together over time and distance via electronic media to combine effort and achieve common goals" (Hoch & Kozlowski, 2014, p. 390). According to Avolio et al. (2001), virtual teams have several defining characteristics. First, communication among team members primarily takes place electronically. The electronic communication processes use multiple communication channels, which may include text, graphic, audio, and video communication. Second, the team members are usually dispersed geographically. They may be in different cities, nations, or even continents. It is not unusual for the members of a virtual team to never meet face-to-face, which for some people may be a difficult obstacle to overcome (see Cross-Cultural I/O Psychology: *Human Interaction in Virtual Teams*). Third, virtual team members may interact synchronously or asynchronously. Synchronous interaction occurs when team members communicate at the same time, as in chat sessions or video conferencing. Asynchronous interaction occurs when team members communicate at different times, as through email or electronic bulletin boards. Purvanova (2014) reports that most virtual teams in a sample of published field studies relied on email to communicate, while the least frequently used means of communication was videoconferencing "mostly due to how expensive and cumbersome this technology still is" (p. 22). These findings may change, however, with ever-increasing technological advancements. Avolio et al. succinctly summarized the major differences between traditional and virtual teams as follows. "If we consider teams along a continuum, at one end of that continuum are teams that came from the same organization, same location, and interact face-to-face on a regular basis. At the other extreme end are teams of people who came from different organizations, geographical regions, cultures, and time zones, and are interacting via computer-mediated technology" (p. 340).

Mathieu et al. (2001) described how our lives are influenced by the interplay among various sets of teams operating in sequences. They are called **multiteam systems,** and they have become so ingrained in our society that we might not think of them as functioning in such a manner. Imagine there is a severe automobile accident where a life is in peril. Here is a likely sequence of actions by multiple teams: an emergency phone call reporting the accident is made to the police. The police department contacts the

---

Ad hoc team
A type of team created for a limited duration that is designed to address one particular problem.

Virtual team
A type of team in which the members, often geographically dispersed, interact through electronic communication and may never meet face-to-face.

Multiteam systems
Teams of teams that function interdependently to achieve overarching system-level goals.

Cross-Cultural I/O Psychology: *Human Interaction in Virtual Teams*

It will be recalled from Chapter 4 that the interview is universally the most popular means of assessing an applicant's suitability for employment. No other method comes close in acceptability and frequency of use. Even though the interview is not the most accurate means of making selection decisions, there is still great appeal in seeing someone face-to-face in the conduct of human interactions. The basis for this appeal is not fully understood, but it is deeply entrenched and has become an issue in virtual teams. Virtual team members interact through a variety of electronic-based communication media — email, audio-conferencing, videoconferencing, and so on. However, such methods are questionable substitutes for face-to-face meetings among team members. Earley and Gibson (2002) presented the following commentary by a virtual team member from Venezuela expressing his reaction to electronic communication with his team: "Now for that particular piece I really think we're going to need to come together as a group, you know face to face and have some kind of a workshop and work on that. Because there are just some pieces that need that continuity, if you know even if it is in a room eight hours or two or three days, you need to have that interaction, you need to get those juices flowing and not stop after a conference call. Just when you are like sort of warming up, you know the clock is ticking. Some point in time you just need that face to face" (p. 248).

Earley and Gibson stated that the most important and difficult issue in implementing a virtual team is managing the distances without losing the "humanity" and "personality" of the team itself. "There remains something quite primal and fundamental about humans when they encounter one another directly rather than through the mediated realm of email, video-conferences, and other electronic means" (p. 248). Earley and Gibson believe that electronic communication can substitute for face-to-face encounters *after* the team members have first met, but they doubt that electronic communication is an adequate substitution for direct encounters. As with the employment interview, we are left with the paradoxical finding that people place great faith in meeting each other in person, yet doing so does not necessarily result in higher-quality outcomes.

dispatch center of the fire department to send a crew to the scene. The police arrive at the scene to control the flow of traffic around the accident. The firefighters have the responsibility to extinguish any car fire that may have started or to apply retardant chemicals to leaking gasoline. Emergency medical technicians (EMTs), another team, work to extricate the victim from the crash. The victim is placed in an ambulance and rushed to the nearest hospital. At the hospital another team is standing by—the surgical team needed to perform a lifesaving operation. The surgical team might consist of nurses, anesthesiologists, medical technicians, and physicians. Following the surgery, the patient is admitted into the intensive care unit of the hospital and attended to by a recovery team of doctors and nurses.

According to Zaccaro et al. (2011), multiteam systems are characterized by the interdependency among teams that not only have their own team-level goals, but also have overarching system-level goals. Note the interconnectedness of the five teams that respond to this automobile accident, for example, and its consequences—police, fire, EMT, surgical, and recovery. Each team has a specific goal and follows a process that has beginning and ending points. Each team is specially trained to perform its tasks with great efficiency and under severe time pressure. Furthermore, one team cannot do its work until the preceding team in the sequence has finished its work. Furthermore, as Connaughton et al. (2011) point out, these teams must coordinate and communicate effectively to achieve the systems-level goal (i.e., to save lives, in the case of the automobile accident), despite having different cultures, norms, goals, and processes within each individual team. Mathieu et al. (2001) believe this "team of teams" concept involving coordination and communication among multiple teams is fertile for advancing our understanding from both scientific and practical perspectives.

Team Life Cycle

The ways in which individuals come together to form a team, and the stages they go through as the team develops is known as the team life cycle. The process of becoming a team is more complicated than simply putting individuals together into a group. It takes time for individuals to begin seeing themselves as a cohesive, functioning unit.

One of the best known models of team development was proposed by Tuckman (1965) and later revised by Tuckman and Jensen (1977). This model suggests that groups proceed through a predictable sequence of five stages. The first stage is the *forming* stage. In this stage, individuals come together, but still act more as individuals than as a cohesive unit. At this point, individuals are getting to know one another and do things to avoid conflict. There is a lot of uncertainty at this time, with individuals not knowing each other or what is expected of them. The forming stage is followed by the *storming* stage. In this stage, there is a great deal of interpersonal conflict and jockeying for position and status within the group. Next is the *norming* stage. This stage occurs once the team members understand their roles and have an agreed-upon goal and plan for accomplishing the goal. Members now understand their roles in the group and accept their positions. The fourth stage is the *performing* stage. This is when the team members coordinate their actions and behave as a cohesive, fully-functioning unit. Their actions are smooth and coordinated, and performance is optimal. The final stage is the *adjourning* stage. This stage occurs when the team is disbanding. At this point, the team has completed its task and members engage in reflection.

The five-stage model of group development is intuitively appealing. It is easy for individuals to think of teams they have been members of and identify these various stages as having occurred. However, the model doesn't hold true for all teams, and teams may progress through the model at different rates. For example, some teams may have a very short forming stage, moving quickly into the storming stage of conflict. In addition, the final two stages in the five-stage model of group development may not occur for all teams. Some teams may never become fully functioning and cohesive. Others may be permanent teams that never disband.

Socialization
The process of mutual adjustment between the team and its members, especially new members.

Life cycles within teams can also be examined for individuals within a team and how their adjustment impacts, and is impacted by, the team itself. **Socialization** is the process of mutual adjustment that produces changes over time in the relationship between a person and a team. It is the process a person goes through in joining a team, being on a team, and eventually leaving a team. Likewise, the team itself is affected by the arrival, presence, and departure of a team member. The socialization process can range from a formal orientation session to the team to informal one-on-one feedback between a senior team member and the newcomer. The relationship between a senior team member and a newcomer can take on many of the properties of the mentor–protégé relationship discussed in Chapter 6. New team members can be appraised by subtle observation of an older team member or by seeking feedback from the team. For example, "What does it take to be successful on this team?" and "Am I fitting in?"

Moreland and Levine (2001) proposed an explanatory framework for how socialization occurs. It is based on three psychological concepts: evaluation, commitment, and role transition. *Evaluation* involves attempts by the team and the individual to assess and maximize each other's value. This includes the team identifying the goals to which an individual can contribute, and the individual evaluating how participation on the team can satisfy his or her personal needs. Thus the evaluation process is mutual. *Commitment* is the sense of loyalty, union, and connection between the individual and the team. When the individual is committed to the team, he or she is likely to accept the team's goals, work hard to achieve them, and feel warmly toward the team. When a team is strongly committed to an individual, it is likely to accept that person's needs, work hard to satisfy them, and feel warmly toward the person. Changes in commitment transform the relationship between a team and an individual. These transformations are governed by specific levels of commitment that mark the boundaries between different membership roles the person could play in the team. Both the team and the individual try to initiate a *role transition* when commitment reaches a certain level. Figure 9-2 shows an individual's commitment to the team over time as he or she passes through five phases of team membership: investigation, socialization, maintenance, resocialization, and remembrance.

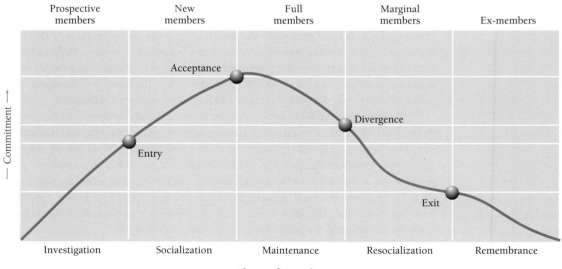

Figure 9-2   *The socialization process for team members*

Source: Adapted from "Socialization in Organizations and Work Groups," by R. L. Moreland and J. M. Levine, in M. E. Turner (Ed.), *Groups at work*, pp. 69–112. Mahwah, NJ: Lawrence Erlbaum Associates, 2001.

During the *investigation* phase, the team searches for individuals who can contribute to the achievement of team goals. Likewise, the individual, as a prospective member of the team, searches for a team that will be satisfying. If both parties achieve an initial sense of commitment, the investigation phase ends and the *socialization* phase begins. In this phase the individual assimilates into the team and the team accommodates itself to the individual. If both parties accept each other, the individual becomes a full member of the team. This acceptance marks the end of the socialization phase and the beginning of *maintenance*. Now both parties try to maximize their respective needs—the achievement of the team and the satisfaction of the individual. This phase lasts as long as both parties meet their needs. However, as commitment weakens between the team and individual, another role transition based on the divergence of commitment occurs, resulting in *resocialization*. During resocialization the team and the individual try again to influence each other so that the team's needs are more likely to be satisfied. If the resocialization process is not successful, team membership ends with a period of *remembrance*. The team recalls the individual's contributions to the achievement of its goals, and the individual recalls his or her experiences with the team. Over time, feelings of commitment between the team and the individual often stabilize, usually at a low level.

The socialization process presented by Moreland and Levine reveals the subtleties and phases of group dynamics. Both the individual and the team are mutually trying to influence each other to achieve the same purpose. The socialization process occurs over time, although the length of the time period varies across individuals and teams. Teams have "lives" based on the state of socialization of their members, and this socialization process is constantly evolving.

Team Structure

The structure of a team includes variables such as the number of members on the team, demographic composition, and experience of team members. A prominent theme in team structures is the diversity of its members. The term *diversity* is often associated with the gender, race, culture, and age of people. However, such is not strictly the case in describing diversity in a team. Research shows that successful teams manifest diversity in their members, where *diversity* literally means "differences." In what ways can diversity manifest itself among members on a team? Two manifestations are information diversity and value diversity. **Information diversity** refers to differences among the members in terms of what they know and what cognitive resources (e.g., factual knowledge, experiences) they can bring to the team. Successful teams often have a pooling of expertise or knowledge among their members. **Value diversity** reflects more fundamental differences among people with regard to tastes, preferences, goals, and interests. Differences in values among team members can be expressed in a wide range of issues, including the purpose of the team, the willingness to be an active team contributor, and the degree to which membership in the team is valued as a means of accomplishing work. Jehn et al. (1999) reported that informational diversity positively influenced team performance, but value diversity decreased member satisfaction with the team, intent to remain on the team, and commitment to the team. The authors also found the impact of diversity on team performance was dependent on the type of

Information diversity
The differences among team members in terms of what they know and what cognitive resources they can bring to the team.

Value diversity
Fundamental differences among team members with regard to tastes, preferences, goals, and interests.

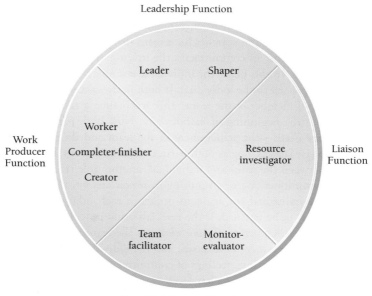

Figure 9-3   *Eight team roles distributed over four team functions*

task. If a task requires great speed and coordination, then information diversity may not positively influence team performance.

Some of the earliest research on team structure was conducted by Belbin (1981). Belbin proposed that diversity within a team was reflected in the members' filling different roles. Belbin proposed that effective teams were composed of members who served different roles on the team, and their roles were defined by the possession of selected mental ability and personality characteristics. Belbin studied eight-person teams and arrived at the following needed roles, which can be further reduced to four functions within a team: (1) leadership, (2) work producers, (3) internal team maintenance, and (4) liaison to people and resources outside of the team, as shown in Figure 9-3.

1. **A leader**. The leader of the team is responsible for the overall performance of the team, recognizes the team's strengths and weaknesses, and ensures that the best use is made of each team member's potential.

2. **A shaper**. A shaper influences the way in which team effort is applied, directs attention to the setting of objectives and priorities, and seeks to impose some shape or pattern on the outcome of team activities. Both the leader and shaper roles collectively define the team's direction and output.

3. **A worker**. A worker gets things done by turning concepts and plans into practical working procedures and carrying out agreed-upon plans systematically and efficiently.

4. **A creator**. A creator advances new ideas and strategies with special attention to major issues and looks for possible new ways to address problems confronting the team.

5. **A resource investigator**. This role reports on ideas, developments, and resources outside of the team and creates external contacts that may be useful to the team in its actions.

6. **A monitor-evaluator**. This role requires analyzing problems and evaluating ideas and suggestions so that the team stays focused on its task. This person often functions as a critic. The more numerous and complex suggestions become, the more important is the role of the monitor-evaluator.

7. **A team facilitator**. A team facilitator supports members in their strengths, helps compensate for their weaknesses, and improves communication between members by fostering team spirit.

8. **A completer-finisher**. This role actively searches for aspects of work that need more than the usual degree of attention and maintains a sense of urgency within the team.

It should be remembered, as described in Chapter 8, that these are different roles filled by individuals, and not necessarily different people. That is, although each of these roles may be critical to team success, a given individual can fulfill multiple roles. In teams of fewer than eight people, some team members must play more than one role. Belbin noted that a team can have more than one worker role and, as will be discussed in Chapter 13, more than one member can share the role of leader (Zaccaro et al., 2009). In addition, some roles are more likely pairs than others. That is, one person could well serve in both the worker and completer-finisher roles. Some pairs of roles filled by the same individual are less likely, such as facilitator and monitor-evaluator. Fisher et al. (1998) affirmed the validity of Belbin's team roles in teams with fewer than eight members and showed that the likelihood of individuals assuming a secondary role was based on their personalities.

Team Processes

As important as the structure of a team is to its functioning, the majority of research on teams has been directed to the processes that guide how teams function. The very nature of teamwork implies that individuals must coordinate their activities and manage interpersonal interactions to be successful. These operations within a team that permit it to function smoothly and efficiently are generally termed *team processes*. Marks et al. (2001) proposed a three-factor model of team processes that includes transition processes (behaviors and actions that focus on planning and evaluation), action processes (behaviors and actions that facilitate goal accomplishment), and interpersonal processes (behaviors and actions that concern managing team member affect/emotions). Although other models of team processes exist, researchers have found this particular model to be a better depiction of team processes compared to competing models (LePine et al., 2008).

Transition Processes

Transition processes include behaviors and actions that focus on planning and evaluation. According to Marks et al., these occur during time that is specifically set aside for such activities, such as during staff meetings or retreats. It is for this reason that Marks et al. call these transition process behaviors; they occur when a team is transitioning from one project or way of doing things to another. These behaviors include mission analysis, goal specification, and strategy formulation and planning.

Mission analysis.   When a team is given a task, team members must take the time to understand their charge and identify the resources and constraints that exist for the task. When considering these factors, the team is engaging in a mission analysis. As part of this analysis, the team members must look at their past performance to determine what worked and didn't work before. In addition, they must look forward to see if there might be anything that could impede their progress if they don't account for it. Marks et al. consider this to be a critical process for all teams. As they say, "teams that abbreviate or omit mission analysis activities run the risk of misguiding their attention and efforts until it is too late to recover" (p. 365).

Goal specification.   Along with the mission analysis, teams must set timelines and prioritize goals. Teams must be flexible, however, with timelines and priorities as situations change and obstacles may appear. As such, teams may need to redefine their goals periodically to continue making progress. In general, goals will be more effective for teams to the extent they are specific, attainable, and valued by team members. The issue of goal setting is discussed more in Chapter 12.

Strategy formulation and planning.   Teams must also be strategic in terms of their planning. They must create contingency plans in the event that their original plans don't work out as intended. To the extent that team members take the time to anticipate potential problems and actions they will take if those problems occur, they will be better equipped to deal more swiftly with the issues. In addition to creating a "Plan B" ahead of time, Marks et al. note that effective teams must be able to "decide 'on the fly' to reconsider, abandon, or adjust the original plan" (p. 366).

Action Processes

Action processes include behaviors and actions that facilitate goal accomplishment. These include activities that keep things running smoothly and efficiently. Coordination, monitoring, and backup behaviors are in this category.

Coordination behaviors.   Coordination behaviors involve the sharing of information to accomplish tasks. Key to coordination is communication. According to Yeatts and Hyten (1998), interpersonal communication in successful work teams is characterized by a consistent pattern. It is often described as open, frequent, and candid. Formal, regularly scheduled weekly meetings are held to discuss team progress. More informal communication occurs on a daily basis as team members discuss specific work issues. In high-performing groups, team members communicate problems they are having and freely solicit advice. They are not reluctant to discuss problems and concerns that might otherwise be artfully avoided. Continuous communication is regarded as not only acceptable but also desirable because it helps the team achieve results it might not attain otherwise. Nevertheless, there can be too much of a good thing. As Cannon-

Bowers and Bowers (2011) note: "Too few communication episodes may not allow sufficient information to be passed. Conversely, overabundant communication may add
so much workload to the team that it detracts from performance" (p. 620).

Monitoring behaviors.   For a team to reach its goals, the members need to know
how they are progressing toward the goals. Monitoring behaviors help accomplish this.
These behaviors include tracking and interpreting information to see how well a team
is doing in terms of reaching its objectives, and then sharing that information with all
team members. To the extent that team members know what is expected of them and
have an idea of how well they are doing, they can more easily and effectively achieve
their directives.

Backup behaviors.   According to Marks et al., backup behaviors are those actions
that are supportive in nature. For example, helping a teammate complete a task, coaching him or her to do the task, or actually doing the task for the teammate are all backup
behaviors. McIntyre and Salas (1995) describe such behaviors as being critically important for teams, noting that this type of behavior is "at the heart of teamwork, for it
makes the team truly operate as more than the sum of its parts" (p. 26). Nevertheless,
there are downsides to such behaviors within teams. For example, Barnes et al. (2008)
reported teams can incur costs associated with backing up teammates, which they
call "harmful help." Team members may neglect their own work to assist a chronically under-performing teammate. In addition, team members who know they will
be assisted by others may decrease their level of effort in subsequent tasks. Thus team
members can acquire a sense of "learned helplessness" in the conduct of their work
roles, secure in knowing other members will cover for them. In addition, Mueller and
Kamdar (2011) found that giving help to teammates was related to lower creativity for
those giving assistance. Thus, it is important to consider the costs of backup behaviors,
and only engage in them when the potential negative effects can be mitigated.

Interpersonal Processes

According to Marks et al., interpersonal processes include behaviors and actions that
concern managing team member affect/emotions. They suggested that these include
conflict management, motivation and confidence building, and affect management.

Conflict management.   Conflict among members is unavoidable in any team. According to Marks et al., conflict management behaviors include those behaviors that
prevent conflict from occurring as well as those that help members deal with conflict
once it does occur. It is important to note that not all conflict is bad. Yeatts and Hyten
pointed out there are two distinct types of conflict: beneficial and competitive. At the
root of *beneficial conflict* is the desire of two or more members with differing ideas and
interests to understand the views of the other. The team members try to understand
each other's perspective and seek to fashion a mutually satisfactory decision (see Field
Note 1: *Orchestrated Conflict*). Such experiences tend to strengthen relationships, as
members become more confident that future conflicts can also be resolved. In contrast, the basis of *competitive conflict* is the desire to win, to be judged "right" in a contest of opinions and values. The individuals in conflict regard the competition as a test

Field Note 1: *Orchestrated Conflict*

Conflict is often regarded as a negative influence among team members, but this is not always the case. Research reveals the positive value of beneficial conflict. Consider the following case in point. A university had a prime piece of land with an ideal location for many possible uses. An old building that stood on the property was razed, creating an opportunity for new use of the land. Many constituents of the university (students, faculty, alumni, financial supporters, etc.) held differing ideas about what use should be made of the land. The president of the university established an advisory committee to make a formal recommendation to the university on the best use of the land. However, the president did not want the ensuing land use debate to fall strictly along "party lines," such as students versus faculty. The president did not want to be perceived as favoring one party or subgroup over the rest in making the ultimate decision. The president was to select three faculty members to serve on the advisory committee. The list of possible names was reduced to four finalists, based on their expressed willingness to serve. Two strong-willed and highly opinionated professors who held similar beliefs about the land use were among the four finalists. The president chose one but not the other. When asked (privately) why both professors were not selected, the president replied, "They think too much alike. At times I believe they have two bodies but share the same brain." Here is one example where a decision was made to increase the likelihood of conflict within the group, in the belief that it would ultimately have a beneficial effect.

of their status, power, and credibility within the organization. Yeatts and Hyten found that high-performing work teams sought to diminish the manifestations of competitive conflict.

Conflict can also be categorized as *task conflict* (focused on work activities), *process conflict* (focused on how work activities are accomplished), and *relationship conflict* (focused on interpersonal dynamics). In a meta-analysis of the relationship between team member conflict and group performance, de Wit et al. (2012) found that task conflict was actually related to *higher* performance, especially when the team wasn't also experiencing relationship conflict. That is, task conflict can actually help a team perform better, particularly with regard to financial performance and the quality of its decisions. It is conflict that is focused on interpersonal relationships among team members that appears to be dysfunctional. Even so, not all task conflict is good either. Bradley et al. (2013) found that task conflict resulted in higher performance when teams were comprised of members who had high levels of openness to experience and emotional stability. When team members were low on these two personality characteristics, however, task conflict had a negative impact on group performance. Along these lines, Jackson and Joshi (2011) proposed the concept of "faultlines" within a team as a measure of understanding why member behavior may detract from the functioning of the team. Faultlines refer to subgroups emerging within the team. Subgroups may

form on the basis of shared attributes (as gender) or past work experiences. The critical question is the extent to which faultlines disrupt information sharing and interfere with team functioning. Some teams may rise above the presence of subgroups, while others may allow the subgroups to produce conflict within the team. For example, Bezrukova et al. (2012) found that informational faultlines, or subgroups that emerge based on knowledge, skill, and expertise, were related to performance problems.

Motivation and confidence building.   The second category of interpersonal processes described by Marks et al. are those aimed at creating a sense of collective confidence and motivation among the team members. These efforts would include such things as encouraging each other and creating a feeling of safety among members. Burke et al. (2010) discussed the importance of members cultivating a sense of psychological safety within the team. The team becomes a "safe harbor" for the expression of ideas and opinions that will not be treated with rebuke. Such a norm allows members to engage in interpersonal risk-taking that may advance the welfare of the team, as opposed to being reluctant to speak up about issues. These efforts, if successful, result in heightened *collective efficacy*, or a shared belief that the team can be successful. According to Bandura (2000), teams with a strong sense of collective efficacy tend to set more challenging goals and, when confronted with difficulties, keep on trying rather than giving up. In short, they are more likely to succeed. However, there does appear to be a caveat to this statement. Namely, Goncalo et al. (2010) found that it may be detrimental to teams if they experience collective efficacy too early in their life cycle. As they noted, "High levels of collective efficacy may be particularly problematic in the early phases of a group project because excessive confidence may lead to tunnel vision regarding long-term strategies or procedures that groups can use to approach complex tasks" (p. 15). As such, whereas collective efficacy is valuable for teams, it appears to be something that is better developed after team members have a chance to engage in a little conflict regarding processes and strategies.

Affect management.   The final category of interpersonal processes are those that deal with regulating team member emotions, including anger and frustration. According to Marks et al., these would include behaviors directed at calming members who may be stressed and helping increase morale and cohesion. Yeatts and Hyten defined *cohesion* as "the degree to which members of a team feel attached to their team and are compelled to stay in it" (p. 97). The attachment is posited to manifest itself in how the team performs its tasks, particularly as it relates to the accepted interdependence among team members. Team-oriented cohesion provides a safe environment in which members may express their opinions. Although at times some opinions may be regarded as dissenting, they are not viewed as threatening the cohesiveness of the team itself. There is research that suggests greater team cohesion may follow from successful team performance, as opposed to causing the performance to occur. Rewards that focus on team achievements are likely to enhance cohesion, whereas individual rewards encourage competition among team members, which weakens cohesion. Other teams and individuals within an organization often take notice of cohesive teams and sometimes express the desire to be members of a cohesive unit themselves. Cohesive teams have also been found to exert more influence than less cohesive teams in the running of the organization. Still, cohesion is not critical for success in all team tasks; it appears to be most crucial in tasks that require highly efficient and synchronized member interactions (Beal et al., 2003).

Related to the issue of managing emotions and building cohesion is the concept of trust. Trust is defined as the belief that even though you have no control over another person's behavior toward you, that person will behave in a way that benefits you. Schoorman et al. (2007) identified several components to trust. Trust develops over time, it is not necessarily mutual or reciprocal between parties, and it entails a willingness to be vulnerable to actions taken by the trusted party that may be harmful. Colquitt et al. (2007) differentiated trust, trust propensity, and trustworthiness. *Trust* is the intention to accept vulnerability based on positive expectations of the party being trusted. Trust is earned, and people differ in their threshold to be trusting. *Trust propensity* is a personality characteristic, a willingness to rely on others, and thus be vulnerable. *Trustworthiness* is the quality (often based on perceived integrity) of a party to be trusted. In general, trust develops slowly within a team, even among teams with stable memberships. It is also the most fragile of the interpersonal processes. Once betrayed, it is very difficult to restore. Despite that, Priem and Nystrom (2014) assert that distrust can occasionally be a good thing. For example, if a key member is seen as being untrustworthy, distrust by other members of that one member may actually help the rest of the team band together and overcome obstacles that may result from the untrustworthy member. Remaining blindly devoted to the member and giving him or her the "benefit of the doubt" may result in more harm. Alternatives to trust are close supervision and the continual monitoring of behavior.

Team Cognition

As we've just described, teams must plan, make decisions, solve problems, and generally think as a collective unit. How individuals think is reflected in their behavior, and the term given to the thinking process is *cognition*. A team is a social aggregation in which a limited number of individuals interact on a regular basis to accomplish a set of shared objectives for which they have mutual responsibility. The fusion of cognition (as a psychological process) and a team (as an interacting collectivity) produces the concept of *team cognition*, which reflects how the team acquires, stores, and uses information (Gibson, 2001). In the following sections we discuss two avenues of research related to team cognition that have received considerable attention: shared mental models and team decision making.

Shared Mental Models

Shared mental model
The cognitive processes held in common by members of a team regarding how they acquire information, analyze it, and respond to it.

The concept of **shared mental models** refers to team members having some degree of similarity in how they approach problems and evaluate potential solutions. They reflect the idea of being "on the same page" in terms of knowing what tasks to do and how to do them (Mohammed et al., 2010). Shared mental models are posited to influence the behavior of the group. For example, Fisher et al. (2012) found that when teams have these shared mental models, the team members are more likely to anticipate each other's actions and proactively share the workload and help one another. In turn, this implicit coordination is related to heightened team performance.

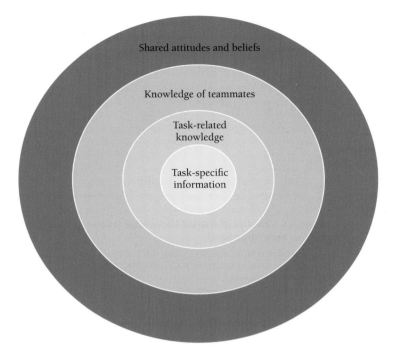

Figure 9-4   *Generalizability of four types of shared knowledge in mental models*

Cannon-Bowers and Salas (2001) addressed the fundamental question of what is actually shared among team members in establishing mental models. Four broad categories were identified: task-specific information, task-related knowledge, knowledge of teammates, and shared attitudes and beliefs, as shown in Figure 9-4. Each type of knowledge has increasingly broader generalizability across differing tasks. *Task-specific information* is shared information among team members that allows them to act without the need to discuss it. Task-specific information involves the particular procedures, sequences, actions, and strategies necessary to perform a task. It can be generalized only to other instances of similar tasks. *Task-related knowledge* refers to common knowledge about task-related processes, but it is not limited to a single task. It is more generalizable because it is knowledge of processes that applies to many specific tasks. *Knowledge of teammates* refers to how well the members understand each other, including their performance, strengths, weaknesses, and tendencies. Thus team members must learn how the collective expertise of the team is distributed across the members. This type of shared knowledge helps teammates compensate for one another, predict each other's actions, and allocate resources according to member expertise. The final category of *shared attitudes and beliefs* permits team members to arrive at comparable interpretations of the problems they face. It enhances team cohesion, motivation, and consensus. In summary, shared mental models do not refer to a unitary concept. It appears that all the types of knowledge in these four categories need to be shared in effective teams.

Figure 9-5 shows a graphic depiction of types of shared knowledge within a team. Knowledge can be common among members (i.e., everyone knows the same thing), as

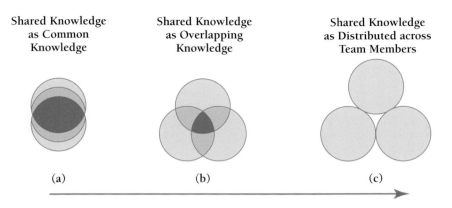

Figure 9-5   *Varieties of shared knowledge (circles represent knowledge held by individual team members)*

Source: Adapted from N. J. Cooke, J. C. Gorman, & L. J. Rowe (2009). An ecological perspective on team cognition (pp. 157–182). In E. Salas, G. F. Goodwin, & C. S. Burke (Eds.), *Team effectiveness in complex organizations*. New York: Psychology Press.

depicted in (a). Alternatively, knowledge can be distributed across team members according to expertise or role, as depicted in (c). In reality, knowledge is most likely not completely common nor distributed, but rather shared across members with some portions that are common and some distributed, as depicted in (b). Cannon-Bowers and Salas added there is also not a singular way that knowledge can be "shared" among team members. Some common knowledge must be held by all members of a team, particularly as it relates to the specific task. Other types of knowledge are shared by being distributed or apportioned across the team members. Certain knowledge is complex or specialized, and it is unrealistic to expect all members of a team to possess this level of knowledge equally. Thus what is important is that the knowledge resides within the team as a team, not held by each team member. Shared knowledge is common in military combat teams and surgical teams. Cross-training (where team members learn to perform the tasks of others) has been found to enhance shared mental models (Marks et al., 2002).

As compelling as the evidence is for shared mental models for effective team performance, there is a potential dark side to team members "thinking alike." The phenomenon is called **groupthink**. Noted problems in history that arose from groupthink are the Bay of Pigs invasion of Cuba in the 1960s and the explosion of the Challenger space shuttle in the 1980s. Groupthink refers to a deterioration in cognitive processing caused by team members feeling threatened by external forces. The defects in decision making include incomplete consideration of options and alternatives, poor information search, and selective information processing. Groupthink is a model of thinking in which team members consider consensus to be more important than rational, independent thinking. Choi and Kim (1999) noted that the conventional interpretation of groupthink is a negative influence on performance. However, although they found that some dimensions of the groupthink phenomenon (such as suppressing dissenting opinions) were related to negative team performance, some other dimensions (such as a strong sense of group identity) in fact were related to positive team performance.

Groupthink
A phenomenon associated with team decision making in which members feel threatened by forces external to the team, resulting in deterioration in the cognitive processing of information.

Turner and Horvitz (2001) concluded that groupthink is more likely found in teams that have a strong sense of social identity. In such cases team members often feel compelled to maintain and enhance their evaluation of the team and to protect the image of the team. When the image is questioned by a collective threat, the response among members is to seek concurrence about the threat and, by virtue of that, attain greater acceptance as *bona fide* team members. A threat to an individual member of a team is not as likely to engender groupthink as is a threat to the entire team. In short, effective team performance requires members to operate on similar or complementary knowledge bases, but under conditions of perceived threat to the team, groupthink often produces the opposite effect and can drive the team to undesirable behavior.

The amount of research on shared mental models is growing, but we still have much to learn about the process of forming a "team mentality" and how the performance of a team is affected by it. Marks et al. (2000) found that shared mental models provided teams with a common framework from which to perceive, interpret, and respond to novel environments. DeChurch and Mesmer-Magnus (2010) estimated that team cognition contributed more to team effectiveness than did motivation and cohesion. Successful teams develop a system for sharing information among the members, and the absence of team cognition cannot be compensated for by other important variables associated with teamwork.

Decision Making in Teams

Guzzo (1995) asserted that decision making in teams is different from individual decision making. In teams, information is often distributed unequally among members and must be integrated. Choosing among alternatives is made more complicated by having to integrate the often differing perspectives and opinions of team members. The integration process usually includes dealing with uncertainty, with the effects of status differences among members, and with the failure of one member to appreciate the significance of the information he or she holds. Ambiguity, time pressures, heavy workloads, and other factors may become sources of stress that affect the group's ability to perform its task.

Hollenbeck et al. (1996) described the development of a multilevel theory of team decision making. The theory is called *multilevel* because effective team decision making is related to characteristics of the individuals who make up the team, pairs of people within the team, and how the team functions as a team. The theory is based on three concepts. The first is the degree to which team members are adequately informed about the issue they are evaluating. Teams can be well informed on some decisions but poorly informed on others. The general level of how well informed the team is on the issues they must address is *team informity*. Second, teams are composed of individuals who differ in their ability to make accurate decisions. That is, some individuals can make poor decisions, while others typically make very accurate decisions. The concept of *staff validity* is the average of the individual team members' abilities to make accurate decisions. The final concept is *dyadic sensitivity*. A team leader must often listen to the differing opinions or recommendations of team members. The relationship between the leader and each team member is a dyad. The leader must be sensitive to weighing each team member's recommendation in reaching an overall decision. Thus an effective decision-making team leader knows which member's opinion should be given more weight than others. The theory has been tested with computer-simulated military command-and-control scenarios in which the team is asked to decide on the level of threat posed by a series of unidentified aircraft. The results revealed that the three concepts of team informity, staff validity, and dyadic sensitivity explained more variance in team-level decision-making accuracy than other concepts. The authors concluded that getting accurate information, making accurate recommendations, and ensuring that these recommendations are incorporated into the team's overall decision are the core requirements for effective decision making in teams.

Personnel Selection for Teams

Some of what I/O psychologists have learned about the selection of individuals into organizations is not wholly transferable to the selection of teams. Traditional work analytic methods identify the KSAOs needed for individual job performance, yet these methods tend to be insensitive to the social context in which work occurs. Teams, by definition, are social entities that interact in a larger social context. Klimoski and Jones (1995) believe that choosing team members on the basis of individual-task KSAOs alone is not enough to ensure optimal team effectiveness. Salas et al. (2002) asserted that successful team members need two general types of skills. *Taskwork skills* are those needed by team members to perform the actual task. Because team members must co-ordinate their actions and work independently, they must also possess *teamwork skills*. These are behavioral, cognitive, and attitudinal skills. As Salas et al. noted, "Although taskwork skills are the foundation for the operational side of performance, teamwork skills are the foundation for the necessary synchronization, integration, and social interaction that must occur between members for the team to complete the assigned goal" (p. 240).

Successful selection of team members requires identifying the best mix of personnel for effective team performance. Thus the selection requirements for particular individuals may involve complementing the abilities that other individuals will bring to the task. Creating the right mix can also mean considering those factors that account for interpersonal compatibility. Establishing team requirements involves identifying and assessing the congruence among members with regard to personality and values. Prieto (1993) asserted that five social skills are particularly critical for an individual to enhance the performance of the group:

1. Gain the group acceptance,

2. Increase group solidarity,

3. Be aware of the group consciousness,

4. Share the group identification, and

5. Manage others' impressions of him or her.

We are also learning about the relationship between personality variables and team effectiveness. Barry and Stewart (1997) reported that extraverts were perceived by other team members as having greater effect than introverts on group outcomes. Thus individuals with more reserved personalities may be less successful in getting the team to accept their ideas and suggestions. A related finding was reported by Janz et al.

(1997) pertaining to ability. They concluded that especially talented team members are likely to feel frustrated when they must work with lower-ability individuals on interdependent tasks. This may be particularly important given Aguinis and O'Boyle's (2014) belief that performance in organizations (and therefore teams) is not likely evenly distributed. Instead, they assert that there are likely a few star performers who do a disproportionate amount of the work. These individuals may become particularly frustrated with their teammates. Mumford et al. (2008) developed a selection test based on team roles similar to those described by Belbin. It is a 90-item situational judgment test (as described in Chapter 4) that assesses knowledge of team roles. Scores on the test explain between 7% - 20% of the variance in various aspects of team performance.

In general, research results suggest that individuals with outgoing and somewhat dominant personalities strongly influence the functioning of teams, yet a team composed of only those personality types may be thwarted by its own internal dynamics.

THE FAR SIDE® BY GARY LARSON

"I've got it, too, Omar ... a strange feeling like
we've just been going in circles."

Although this stream of research suggests that the "will do" factors of personality are critical for team success, the "can do" factors of ability cannot be dismissed or minimized. Cognitive and technical skills are also needed. Locke et al. (2001) quoted a leading business executive, who said, "A collaboration of incompetents, no matter how diligent or well-meaning, cannot be successful" (p. 503).

Research on teams has revealed other aspects of team performance that highlight the need for selected interpersonal skills. LePine, Colquitt, and Erez (2000) noted that teams often face situations that are not what they had anticipated. Then their success depends on their ability to adapt to these changing contexts. LePine (2003) reported that the most adaptable team members have the same profile of attributes identified in Chapter 5 as high individual performers. These team members were characterized by high cognitive ability, strong need for achievement, and an openness to new experiences. Similarly, as noted earlier, backup behaviors are unique supportive behaviors that are essential within teams. Team members should be willing to provide help to others when their own tasks demand less than their full attention and resources. According to Porter et al. (2003), the legitimacy of the need to back up team members often derives from an uneven workload distribution—some tasks in a team context are more demanding than others. Three personality factors predicted willingness to back up teammates: conscientiousness, emotional stability, and extraversion. Thus, within the context of team selection, these personality characteristics may become particularly relevant.

Training for Teams

Much of what we know about team training has come, directly or indirectly, from military applications. The military has been responsible primarily for advanced training technologies (such as intelligent tutoring systems) as well as strategies in team training, such as *cross-training*. Training team members on other team members' roles assumes that exposure to and practice on other teammates' tasks should result in better team member knowledge about task responsibilities and coordination requirements.

The logic of team training is the same as the logic of individual training, although the mechanisms are somewhat different. The process begins with a work analysis, but one aimed at the functioning of teams. Salas and Cannon-Bowers (1997) described a team task analysis as an extension of traditional task analysis to tasks that require coordination. SMEs are asked to provide information (e.g., ratings of difficulty, importance) on each task in which there is interdependency. The information obtained is then used to specify team training objectives and to develop realistic scenarios for practice.

The results of a team task analysis provide information about the knowledge, skills, and attitudes the team members must possess to be successful. Salas and Cannon-Bowers referred to these three as the *thinking, doing,* and *feeling* needed for the structure of team training, as shown in Figure 9-6. Identifying the criteria for team effectiveness serves to guide instructional activities in team training. The instructional activities focus on providing team members with shared mental models and knowledge structures. These activities are designed to foster common ways for team

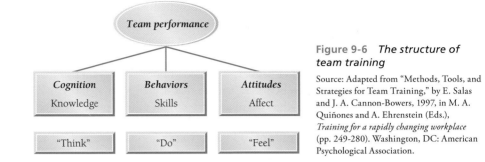

Figure 9-6 *The structure of team training*

Source: Adapted from "Methods, Tools, and Strategies for Team Training," by E. Salas and J. A. Cannon-Bowers, 1997, in M. A. Quiñones and A. Ehrenstein (Eds.), *Training for a rapidly changing workplace* (pp. 249-280). Washington, DC: American Psychological Association.

members to analyze information and make decisions. Moreover, training for teams can help with the processes discussed earlier, including how and when to engage in mission analyses, monitoring and coordination, and backup behaviors.

Performance Appraisal in Teams

Chapter 7 addressed the topic of performance management, primarily as it applies to individual employees. The same issues identified for individual performance appraisals have their counterpart for team appraisals. Moreover, there are some additional factors for teams not evidenced for individuals.

Jackson and LePine (2003) identified different responses of team members to the "weakest link" in their team. Team members tend to feel high levels of sympathy for a member who exhibits low performance for reasons that are beyond his or her control. Likewise, members feel low levels of sympathy for a team member who performs poorly because of factors under his or her control. If the group feels sympathy, they are more willing to train the poor performer or assist the individual by doing a portion of his or her tasks. But if the group feels little sympathy, they may attempt to motivate the low performer (perhaps with veiled threats) or to simply reject the individual.

A major issue in team performance appraisal is the extent to which individuals slacken their performance within the team. A team member may assume that individual slacking will not be noticed within the larger social context of a team, or that other members will elevate their performance within the team to achieve a satisfactory team level of performance. The term given to this phenomenon of slacking is social loafing, and it refers to the demotivating effect on individuals of working in a group or team context. When team outcomes are emphasized, individuals see less connection between their own contributions (time, effort, and skills) and the recognition and rewards they receive (Karau & Williams, 2001). Individual team members feel they have less incentive to work hard. Locke et al. (2001) identified three ways in which a lack of individual incentives can contribute to social loafing.

Social loafing
A phenomenon identified in teams in which certain individuals withhold effort or contributions to the collective outcome.

- **Free riding**. In some situations, social loafing derives from a desire to benefit (or free ride) from the efforts of others. When a team task makes individual contributions anonymous and rewards are shared equally, team members can reduce their own individual effort but still enjoy an equal share of the results. Thus social loafing is more likely to occur when team members believe their own contributions cannot be identified.

- **The "sucker" effect**. When conditions allow team members to take a free ride, some team members may assume that other group members will do so. Rather than be a "sucker" who contributes more than others, people reduce their effort to match the low level they expect from others. Mulvey and Klein (1998) observed the sucker effect in a study of college students working on team-level academic tasks.

- **Felt dispensability**. In some cases social loafing results from the feeling of being dispensable. Team members may feel dispensable when more able team members are available to accomplish the task or when they believe their efforts are redundant because they duplicate the contributions of others. When team members feel dispensable, they often reduce their effort.

Locke et al. observed that these three forms of social loafing share the following characteristics: (1) individual team members are concerned with the impact of their personal contributions on team performance; (2) team members expect some return on their effort; and (3) teamwork can weaken the links among individual effort, contributions to team success, and individual outcomes (see Field Note 2: *Teams in Education*). Therefore, although effective team processes (e.g., interaction, trust, cohesion) are important to achieve team success, it is individuals who make up teams and many organizational rewards (such as salary and career progression) are administered at the individual level.

Not all the research on team performance appraisal is limited to social loafing. Peer appraisals have been found to be effective at the individual level, and they also appear to have a positive influence at the team level. Druskat and Wolff (1999) found that developmental peer appraisals in work teams had a positive impact on team communication, task focus, and member relationships. As the volume of research on team performance appraisal grows, we will have a firmer basis on which to examine the generalizability of findings previously established in appraising individuals.

The issue of performance management for teams is certainly a tricky one. It will be recalled from Chapter 7 that one purpose of performance management is to identify performance differences across individuals and to reward them differentially. If we strive for teamwork and a sense of unity across team members, we should then *not* differentially reward the "best" individual team members. We will have to develop appraisal and reward processes that treat all members of a group as a single entity, not as individuals. Organizations get what they reward. If they choose to appraise and reward individual job performance, then they should not decry a lack of teamwork and cooperation among their employees (Kerr, 1995). With this in mind, Aguinis (2013) suggests that organizations that rely on teams should plan to manage the performance of both the teams *and* the individuals within those teams. He noted that by measuring both, individuals can be held accountable for their individual contributions while also being motivated to support the collective mission of the team. In addition, O'Leary et al. (2011) highlight the fact that individuals often belong to multiple teams simultaneously. As a result, it is important to consider how individuals should be evaluated and rewarded on the basis of their multiple team memberships and expectations.

Field Note 2: *Teams in Education*

Have you ever been in a class where one of the course requirements was some sort of team project or team presentation? How did you feel about the experience? Did you find it difficult to arrange a time when all the team members could meet? How did you decide who would be responsible for what within the group? Did you think everyone on the team "pulled their own weight" in the collective effort? Did you detect any social loafing among your team members? Did each member in the team have to evaluate every other team member's contribution to the final product? Did everyone on the team receive the same grade for the product of the team's work?

The use of teams in society is escalating (a phenomenon referred to as "groupism"), and their use in education as a learning mechanism for students is increasing as well. If you have ever participated in a team project for a class, your particular team members were probably specific to that class. However, there is a new approach to graduate education in business where students go through the entire degree program (not just in a class) as a team. The name given to this group of students is a "cohort." Each year the admitted students are regarded as a cohort; they all take the same classes in the same sequence and they all graduate at the same time as a group. It is expected that the students will stay in touch with each other after they graduate, as they share how they applied their graduate education in their respective careers. The concept of a cohort in education is designed to promote students learning from each other as students and continuing their education of each other after they graduate.

Concluding Comments

Salas et al. (2004) are of the opinion that the migration of work performed by individuals to teams will not abate. "Travelers seeking refuge from the accelerating storm of team research and practice and its associated roller coaster of complexities will not find sanctuary. In fact, as expressed by the second law of thermodynamics, chaos is always increasing" (p. 76). As the world becomes increasingly complex, organizations must find new ways to adapt to this complexity. Teams are viewed as one means of doing so. The conversion from an individual to a team perspective of work requires that we reexamine our knowledge about many facets of I/O psychology. Furthermore, although some of our concepts might generalize directly from individuals to teams, some procedures might be incompatible (e.g., Campion et al., 1996). We believe I/O psychology should gird itself for the journey of understanding how work performed by teams requires insight into new psychological concepts and existing concepts with unknown validity when generalized to teams (see I/O Psychology and the Economy: *Downsizing and Teamwork*). Salas, Priest et al. (2007) regard the growing use of teams to conduct work as an organizational response to a changing world. The past 30 years provided the strongest catalyst for I/O psychologists to understand teams and how teamwork functions. However, the actual use of teams as a means of accomplishing

I/O Psychology and the Economy: *Downsizing and Teamwork*

Downsizing is a common organizational response to the perceived need to reduce expenses and increase efficiency. The decision as to which employees are to be dismissed when the organization operates under the concept of work teams is not so easily determined. How would a team of, for example, seven members respond if two teammates were dismissed? The departure of the two team members could have a major impact on the concepts we know influence team performance, such as shared cognition. A team could ill-afford to lose members who possessed knowledge not shared with others. Likewise, perhaps the employees designated for dismissal were particularly skilled in maintaining intra-group relations. Could teams that incur loss of members adjust or adapt quickly, especially given the hallmark of teams is interdependence—everyone needs everyone else?

Perhaps the organization would seek to achieve its cost cutting not by dismissing selected individuals within teams, but by dismissing entire teams. If the organization recognizes that the functioning of teams depends upon the deliberately created attitudes, behaviors, and cognitions among team members, the performance of the entire team will suffer by the deletion of certain individuals. It is plausible some teams would be decimated by the loss of certain team members. The team might disband and the surviving team members would be reassigned to existing teams. As such, the teams that inherited new members would have to re-adjust and re-calibrate how they do what they do.

It might be argued that teams should be left intact. Given the amount of time and effort it takes to create the internal dynamics for successful team functioning, it would be more prudent from an economic sense to dismiss entire teams than selected individuals within the organization.

The tactic of organizations seeking to reduce costs through layoffs to achieve economic benefits has been practiced for over 35 years. The conversion to team-based work is not so well-established among contemporary organizations. Organizations achieve some measure of economic efficiency by reducing payroll costs. But the loss of operating efficiency to the organization would appear to be highly related to exactly which employees are dismissed when work is conducted using a team structure. The reduction of the organization's payroll would have fewer complicating problems if the employees were not aggregated into work teams.

work has been with us since long before the birth of I/O psychology. What is new about teams is our growing reliance on them to accomplish work that was once performed by individuals. Salas et al. stated, "It seems clear that after we compile all the lessons we have learned over the last century, one message is clear: industries, governments, and organizations count on teams . . . Teams have proven to be beneficial and will continue to proliferate as the complexity of our world increases. Teams always have and always will exist" (p. 432).

Chapter Summary

- Work teams are an adaptive response of organizations to the changing business world.
- Teams exist at a level of analysis that is in between the individual and the organization.
- There are five core principles pertaining to the processes that operate within the team.
- Teams can be differentiated based on their purpose and nature of interactions.
- Individuals proceed through a predictable series of stages as they become a part of the team and socialize within it.
- Teams have a definable structure as indexed by the roles members assume within a team.
- Teams function through important processes pertaining to planning and evaluation, goal facilitation, and interpersonal management.
- Teams must learn to make decisions that involve every member and result in the emergence of a team mentality.
- Issues such as personnel selection, training, and performance appraisal apply to teams, just as they do to individuals.
- The social processes that hold teams together and allow them to function are influenced by the cultural backgrounds of their members.

10 Affect, Attitudes, and Behavior at Work

Learning Objectives

- Explain the role of affect, moods, and emotions in the workplace.

- Explain the organizational attitudes of job satisfaction, work commitment, employee engagement, and organizational justice.

- Understand the concepts of organizational citizenship behavior and counterproductive work behavior and their relationships to other concepts.

- Understand the concept of organizational politics.

- Understand the concept of the psychological contract in employment and its changing nature.

The preceding chapters examined several conceptual approaches to organizations and teams, including their structure and the social mechanisms that enable them to function. This chapter will examine various psychological concepts that have emerged within organizations. In particular, the focus will be on concepts that not only have theoretical value but also have been found to influence a wide array of practical matters relating to work behavior. The title of this chapter, *Affect, Attitudes, and Behavior at Work*, is reflective of this large and multi-faceted topic.

Affect, Moods, and Emotions

For the most part I/O psychology has not addressed the emotional dimensions of work life, historically being more interested in cognitive issues (as witnessed by the amount of research on *g*). However, moods and emotions play an undeniable role in how we feel about life, including work. For example, Fisher and Ashkanasy (2000) noted that, "the study of emotions in the workplace has the potential to add an understanding of behavior in organizations" (p. 123). As Weiss (2002) highlighted, "Work . . . is a place where all our basic processes, including emotional processes, play out daily. People feel guilty at work, they feel angry, they feel happy, they feel anxious, often all in the same day. Events at work have real emotional impact on participants" (p. 1).

Affect

A broad range of feelings that encompass moods and emotions, typically described along a positive-negative continuum.

Moods and emotions fall under the broader term **affect**. The concept of *affect* refers to a broad range of feelings that are typically described along a positive–negative continuum. Affect can be conceptualized as either being a trait or a transient state. As a trait, it refers to a fundamental difference in how people view life, their general disposition, and attitude. People who are high on trait positive affect tend to be active, alert, enthusiastic, inspired, and interested. People who are high on trait negative affect, on the other hand, are pessimistic about life and "see the glass as half-empty rather than half-full." They have a tendency to feel anxious and fearful, as opposed to calm and serene.

Moods

General and long-lasting feelings not directed at a particular target.

Affect can also be described as being a momentary experience or transient state. In these cases, the terms that are typically used are moods and emotions. **Moods** refer to feelings that are general in nature and relatively long lasting. They are not necessarily directed at a particular object, but rather may exist without a person knowing its specific cause. As Frijda (2009) noted, moods "are about nothing specific or about everything—about the world in general" (p. 258). Fisher (2000) proposed that even though moods may not be directly controllable given their somewhat vague and diffuse causes, organizations may be successful in elevating employees' moods. For example, organizations could concentrate on providing a work environment free of minor irritations and hassles that produce frequent, if mild, feelings of frustration and annoyance.

Emotions

Discrete, target-specific feelings that are of relatively short duration.

Emotions are feelings that are more discrete and of shorter duration than moods, and are typically directed at a particular target. As Ekkekakis (2012) noted, "emotional events are elicited *by* something, are reactions *to* something, and are generally *about* something" (p. 322). Muchinsky (2000), drawing upon the research of Lazarus and Lazarus (1994), identified five categories of emotions, all of which are (or can be) manifested in the workplace. These five categories are presented in Table 10-1.

The emotions that individuals experience at work can impact their job performance. Shockley et al. (2012) found that happiness is related to higher job performance

Table 10-1   *Five categories of human emotions*

Category	Emotion
1. Positive	Happiness Love Pride
2. Negative	Sadness Hopelessness Despair
3. Existential	Anxiety Guilt Shame
4. "Nasty"	Anger Envy Jealousy
5. Empathetic	Gratitude Compassion Sympathy

Source: Adapted from *Passion and reason: Making sense of our emotions*, by R. S. Lazarus and B. N. Lazarus, 1994. New York: Oxford.

while sadness is related to lower performance. Rodell and Judge (2009) reported that anger was associated with greater counterproductive behaviors at work. Ilies et al. (2013) found that individuals who were made to feel guilty about engaging in counterproductive behaviors subsequently engaged in behaviors that benefitted the organization, in an apparent attempt to make up for the undesirable behaviors and alleviate their guilt.

Emotions also play a large role in decision making. As Lerner et al. (2013) noted, "People typically make some of the most consequential choices of their lives while in emotional states. Love drives a decision to propose or accept marriage; anger drives a decision to strike someone; fear drives a decision to abandon one's home in disaster" (p. 77). Lerner and Keltner (2000) noted that emotions impact how we appraise situations (who we blame vs. assign credit when bad and good events occur), influence how confident we are with our decisions, and color how we view risks. Reb et al. (2014) highlighted the role that emotions play in the performance appraisal process, noting that emotions affect which memories we recall and how much we are willing to process information. Murphy (2014) suggested that it may be possible to change how decision makers view tasks and situations to add or remove emotion from decision processes as needed.

In Chapter 3 we noted that organizations frequently require employees to engage in **emotional labor** by displaying certain emotions while at work. In our previous discussion, we noted that individuals may engage in surface acting in which they alter their outward emotional expression without actually changing how they truly feel. Alternatively, they may engage in deep acting in which they try to change their internal emotions to correspond to what is required of them. When individuals attempt to modify the emotions they are feeling, they are engaging in **emotion regulation**. Meta-analytic research by Hülsheger and Schewe (2011) revealed that surface acting is

Emotional labor
The requirement in some jobs that employees express emotions to customers or clients that are associated with enhanced performance in the job.

Emotion regulation
The attempts to control one's emotions or mood.

particularly harmful to one's well-being, attitudes toward work, and job performance, whereas deep acting does not appear to have the same negative consequences.

A related concept to emotional regulation that we first discussed in Chapter 4 is **emotional intelligence**. It has garnered a great deal of attention, and has been controversial within I/O psychology. Emotional intelligence reflects the ability to recognize emotions in oneself and in others and to control one's emotions in socially acceptable ways. A meta-analysis conducted by O'Boyle et al. (2011) revealed that emotional intelligence is positively related to job performance. In addition, emotional intelligence predicts job performance above and beyond cognitive ability and the Big 5 personality dimensions. In a separate meta-analysis, Joseph and Newman (2010) found that emotional intelligence was most predictive of performance in jobs that required emotional labor. Despite its apparent predictive capabilities, emotional intelligence remains a contentious subject for many psychologists. For example, Locke (2005) wrote an article titled "Why Emotional Intelligence is an Invalid Concept," in which he argued that emotional intelligence is better thought of as habits or skills rather than a form of intelligence. Nevertheless, the concept has endured, continuing to receive attention from both scholars and practitioners.

Emotions that are experienced by one person can spread to others, an effect known as **emotional contagion**. Individuals have an automatic tendency to mimic others with whom they interact, including their facial expressions and mannerisms. As such, when somebody is angry or sad, people nearby may also become angry or sad without necessarily realizing it. This emotional convergence between individuals happens for both positive and negative emotions and has very real consequences for the workplace. For example, Westman et al. (2013) conducted a study with Israeli soldiers in which trainers interviewed confederates pretending to be either a happy soldier or a distressed soldier. They found that trainers reported emotions in line with the soldiers they interviewed. Those interviewers who saw the happy soldier reported more positive emotions in themselves whereas those who saw the distressed soldier reported more negative emotions. They found that the effects for the positive crossover from soldier to interviewer were stronger than the effects for the negative crossover, suggesting that positive emotions may be more contagious than negative emotions.

Broaden-and-Build Theory of Positive Emotions

There has been an increased focus on the positive side of psychology, with a realization that historically much of the focus was on the dysfunctional, pathological side of psychology. The increased focus on positive constructs can be seen within the area of emotions by looking at Fredrickson's (2001) **broaden-and-build theory of positive emotions**. In her creation of the theory, Fredrickson sought to challenge the traditional assumptions that only negative emotions hold value for people. Certainly there is an advantage to experiencing fear or anger, as they would initiate the fight or flight mechanism necessary for survival. But what about positive emotions such as joy and gratitude? Fredrickson argued that they, too, were evolutionarily advantageous and increased the likelihood of survival.

According to the broaden-and-build theory, positive emotions broaden individuals' awareness and prompt them to think and act in more diverse ways than they might otherwise. Whereas negative emotions narrow one's thinking and actions in order to lead to a specific outcome (the fight or flight response), positive emotions expand one's views. In doing so, individuals are exposed to a wider range of resources.

Emotional intelligence
A construct that reflects a person's capacity to manage emotional responses in social situations.

Emotional contagion
The tendency for individuals to synchronize their emotions with others in their environment, experiencing and expressing another's emotions whether consciously or unconsciously.

Broaden-and-build theory of positive emotions
A theory that positive emotions prompt individuals to expand their thinking and action repertoires in ways that result in increased resources and enhanced functioning.

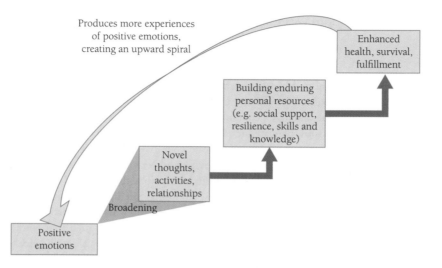

Figure 10-1   *Broaden-and-build theory of positive emotions*

Adapted from "Positive Emotions," by B. L. Fredrickson and M. A. Cohn, in M. Lewis, J. M. Haviland-Jones, and L. Feldman Barrett (Eds.), *Handbook of emotions* (3rd ed., pp. 777-796) (2008). Reprinted by permission from Guilford Press.

These resources can be cognitive (increased intellectual complexity), social (more high-quality friendships), psychological (greater resilience), or physical (heightened functioning of the immune system). These resources enable individuals to subsequently function more effectively. As Vacharkulksemsuk and Fredrickson (2013) summarized, "positive emotions function in the short term to *broaden* one's attention and awareness in ways that, over the long term, *build* one's basin of survival-promoting personal resources" (p. 45, italics in original).

Fredrickson suggests that as individuals experience positive emotions, and good things result, they will experience even more positive emotions that will lead to even better results in an ongoing upward spiral (as depicted in Figure 10-1). For example, Fredrickson (2000) found that experiencing positive emotions leads people to perceive more positive meaning in their life's events. This positive meaning in return leads to positive emotions. As such, a positive cycle is created that leads continuously upward. This theory has received considerable empirical support, demonstrating the importance of positive emotions within our work lives, and lives in general (Fredrickson, 2013).

Job Attitudes

Work-related attitudes are relatively enduring evaluations that individuals have of various aspects of employment, including their employer, their boss, and the job they hold (Schleicher et al., 2011). According to Judge et al. (2012), job attitudes have cognitive and affective components. They reflect internal evaluations or beliefs about something in the work domain (the cognitive component). In addition, they are emotionally charged, reflecting one's feelings about the object (the affective component). Attitudes can vary in both intensity and favorability, and they influence individual behavior.

This section presents an examination of four important attitudes employees hold about their work: how satisfied, committed, and engaged they are with their work, and how fair they view their work. Job satisfaction is the most frequently researched job attitude. Work commitment has also received a great deal of attention, but has been plagued to some extent by definitional confusion. As Klein (2014) notes, commitment has been viewed as everything from an attitude to an indicator of motivation to a feeling of congruence or identification. Similarly, employee engagement can be viewed as an attitude or a form of motivation. Lastly, although some authors (e.g., Ng & Feldman, 2010) view fairness perceptions as attitudes, others (e.g., Judge & Kammeyer-Mueller, 2012) view them as antecedents to attitudes rather than attitudes in their own right. We treat these concepts as attitudes, but encourage consideration of how they may be viewed differently depending on the questions being asked and the measures being used.

Job Satisfaction

Job satisfaction
The degree of pleasure an employee derives from his or her job.

Job satisfaction is an internal evaluation of the favorability of one's job (Judge et al., 2012). In short, it reflects the degree of pleasure an employee derives from his or her job. Because work is one of our major life activities, I/O psychologists have had a long-standing interest in job satisfaction. One hundred years ago employment conditions were, by today's standards, unacceptable. Work was often performed under unsafe conditions, work hours were very long, offices were not air-conditioned, and benefits we often take for granted today, such as paid vacations, medical insurance, and retirement contributions, did not exist. You might think that the employees of today, who enjoy more favorable working conditions, would be highly satisfied with their jobs; however, that is not the case. Although some employees derive great pleasure and meaning from their work, many others regard work as drudgery.

Why is this so? The answer lies in individual differences in expectations and, in particular, the degree to which a job meets one's expectations. Hulin and Judge (2003) asserted that an employee's affective reaction to a job is based on a comparison of the actual outcomes derived from the job with those outcomes that are expected. Dawis (2004) added that feelings of job satisfaction can change with time and circumstances. People differ in what is important to them, and this may also change for the same person. There are broad differences in what people expect from their jobs and thus broad reactions to them. As Hulin (1991) stated, "Jobs with responsibility may be dissatisfying to some because of the stress and problems that are associated with responsibility; others may find responsibility a source of positive affect. Challenging jobs may be satisfying to some because of how they feel about themselves after completing difficult job assignments; others may find such self-administered rewards irrelevant" (p. 460). Why people differ in their preferences for job outcomes is posited to be related to their developmental experiences and levels of aspiration. Alternatively stated, "What you seek from a job influences your satisfaction with it" (Warr & Clapperton, 2010, p. 19).

Research has revealed that people develop overall feelings about their jobs as well as about selected dimensions or facets of their jobs, such as their supervisor, coworkers, promotional opportunities, pay, and so on. I/O psychologists differentiate these two levels of feelings as *global job satisfaction* and *job facet satisfaction*, respectively. Considerable research has been devoted over the years to the measurement of job satisfaction.

The Job Descriptive Index (Smith et al., 1969) has been used to measure job satisfaction for more than 45 years, and it is regarded with professional esteem within I/O psychology (Kinicki et al., 2002). Likewise, the Minnesota Satisfaction Questionnaire (Weiss et al., 1967) is highly regarded within the profession. A version of the Minnesota Satisfaction Questionnaire is shown in Figure 10-2.

Ask yourself: How satisfied am I with this aspect of my job?

Very Sat. means I am very satisfied with this aspect of my job.

Sat. means I am satisfied with this aspect of my job.

N means I can't decide whether I am satisfied or not with this aspect of my job.

Dissat. means I am dissatisfied with this aspect of my job.

Very Dissat. means I am very dissatisfied with this aspect of my job.

On my present job, this is how I feel about . . .	Very Dissat.	Dissat.	N	Sat.	Very Sat.
1. Being able to keep busy all the time	☐	☐	☐	☐	☐
2. The chance to work alone on the job	☐	☐	☐	☐	☐
3. The chance to do different things from time to time	☐	☐	☐	☐	☐
4. The chance to be "somebody" in the community	☐	☐	☐	☐	☐
5. The way my boss handles subordinates	☐	☐	☐	☐	☐
6. The competence of my supervisor in making decisions	☐	☐	☐	☐	☐
7. Being able to do things that don't go against my conscience	☐	☐	☐	☐	☐
8. The way my job provides for steady employment	☐	☐	☐	☐	☐
9. The chance to do things for other people	☐	☐	☐	☐	☐
10. The chance to tell people what to do	☐	☐	☐	☐	☐
11. The chance to do something that makes use of my abilities	☐	☐	☐	☐	☐
12. The way company policies are put into practice	☐	☐	☐	☐	☐
13. My pay and the amount of work I do	☐	☐	☐	☐	☐
14. The chances for advancement on this job	☐	☐	☐	☐	☐
15. The freedom to use my own judgment	☐	☐	☐	☐	☐
16. The chance to try my own methods of doing the job	☐	☐	☐	☐	☐
17. The working conditions	☐	☐	☐	☐	☐
18. The way my coworkers get along with each other	☐	☐	☐	☐	☐
19. The praise I get for doing a good job	☐	☐	☐	☐	☐
20. The feeling of accomplishment I get from the job	☐	☐	☐	☐	☐

Figure 10-2   *Minnesota Satisfaction Questionnaire (short form)*

Source: From *Manual for the Minnesota Satisfaction Questionnaire*, by D. J. Weiss, R. V. Dawis, G. W. England, and L. H. Lofquist, © 1967. Minneapolis: Industrial Relations Center, University of Minnesota. Used by permission of Vocational Psychology Research, University of Minnesota. http://www.psych.umn.edu/psylabs/vpr

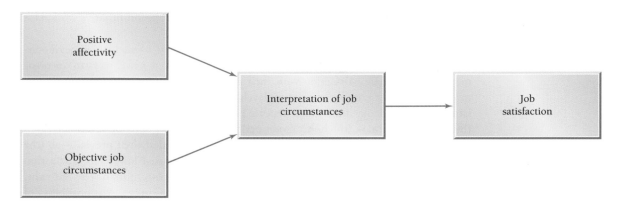

Figure 10-3   *Model of job satisfaction*

Source: Adapted from *Attitudes in and around organizations*, by A. P. Brief, p. 97. Copyright © 1998, Sage Publications, Inc. Adapted with permission of Sage Publications, Inc.

Over the past two decades we have grown to understand that how satisfied a person feels about his or her job is related to affect as much as to objective job conditions (e.g., level of pay, hours of work, and physical working conditions). Brief (1998) proposed a model of job satisfaction (as depicted in Figure 10-3) based on these two components (affect and objective job conditions), which led to an assessment or interpretation of the job circumstances. The interpretation is based on many considerations, including the perceived adequacy of the pay for the work performed, the level of stress on the job, and the match of the job to the person's skills and abilities. Recent research has confirmed the validity of affect in influencing one's job satisfaction.

Judge et al. (2002) established a linkage between personality factors and job satisfaction. Job satisfaction was found to correlate −.29 with emotional stability, .25 with extraversion, .02 with openness to experience, .17 with agreeableness, and .26 with conscientiousness. As a set these Big 5 personality dimensions had a multiple correlation coefficient of .41 with job satisfaction. Similarly Ilies and Judge (2003) proposed that feelings of job satisfaction are inheritable, based on a study of identical twins reared apart. In short, feelings of job satisfaction are related both to the objective conditions of work (that are under the control of the organization) and to the personality of the worker.

Bowling et al. (2005) offered an explanation of job satisfaction based on original research in sensation and perception. In a classic study from over 60 years ago, individuals were asked to judge the heaviness of several weights. Prior to judging the weights, the individuals lifted either a heavier or lighter weight relative to the weight of the target item. The judgment of the target item was found to be influenced by the weight of the previous item. Individuals adjusted their judgment of the target item by what they experienced before. That is, assume the target item weighs four ounces. If the previous item weighed two ounces, the target item was estimated to weigh more than four ounces. If the previous item weighed six ounces, the target item was estimated to weigh less than the four ounces. As such, our judgments are embedded in a relative context, and cannot be made independently of that context. The authors believe that how people feel about their jobs is also a contextual judgment. Individuals differ in their underlying personalities, and their sensitivity to positive and negative workplace events (i.e., the analog of lighter and heavier weights).

Boswell et al. (2009) found evidence for what they termed a "honeymoon-hangover effect" with regard to job satisfaction. They asked newcomers to an organization about their satisfaction with their prior job. They then asked the employees to report their current job satisfaction levels three months, six months, and one year later. They found that individuals reported their highest levels of job satisfaction at the three-month mark (the honeymoon period). Their job satisfaction levels decreased thereafter, however, to a level similar to what they reported at their previous job (the hangover). They further found that individuals who reported lower job satisfaction with their previous job were more likely to experience this pattern than were individuals who reported greater prior job satisfaction. Their findings suggest the possibility of a "set point" for job satisfaction. The findings from these studies suggest that organizational efforts to improve long-term job satisfaction in employees may be futile. Improvements in job satisfaction are possible, but their effects are likely to be short-lived, as the employees re-calibrate or re-adapt themselves to the new environment in which they find themselves.

The relationship between job satisfaction and important job-related criteria has been examined extensively. Three criteria will be presented: performance, turnover, and absence. The relationship between job satisfaction and job performance has been researched for more than 50 years. The reason is obvious—ideally we would like to be both productive and happy in our work. However, the relationship between satisfaction and performance is not as strong as we might imagine. Judge et al. (2001) conducted a meta-analysis that examined this relationship and reported the best estimate of their correlation to be .30. Based on this study the percentage of variance shared between these two concepts (r^2) is 9%, meaning 91% of the variance in one concept is *not* explained by the other. Its implication is that organizational attempts to enhance both worker satisfaction and performance *simultaneously* will likely be unsuccessful. The reason is that the two concepts are only mildly related. In fact, some organizational attempts to increase productivity (for example, cracking down on employees through tough supervisory practices) may decrease job satisfaction. Riketta (2008) provided meta-analytic evidence that job satisfaction is more likely to lead to job performance than job performance leading to job satisfaction.

Turnover and absence are often referred to as *withdrawal behavior* because they reflect the employee withdrawing from a noxious employment condition, either temporarily (absence) or permanently (turnover). The relationship between how much you like your job and whether you withdraw from it has attracted considerable interest among I/O psychologists. In general, the research shows that the more people dislike their job, the more likely they are to quit. The magnitude of the satisfaction–turnover correlation, on average, is about −.40. However, this relationship is influenced by several factors, including the availability of other work. People would rather endure a dissatisfying job than be unemployed (Hom & Kinicki, 2001). Conversely, when alternative employment is readily available, workers are more likely to leave dissatisfying jobs (Carsten & Spector, 1987).

The correlation between job satisfaction and absence is considerably smaller, approximately −.25 (Johns, 1997). Absence from work can be caused by many factors that have nothing to do with how much you like your job, including transportation

FRANK & ERNEST: © Thaves/Dist. by United Feature Syndicate, Inc.

problems and family responsibilities. However, when researchers control for methodological issues in the design of research addressing this relationship (including whether the absence from work is paid or unpaid, and whether organizational sanctions are imposed on absent workers), a mild but consistent negative relationship emerges between the two. A practical implication of the finding is that if you like your job, you are more likely to make the extra effort needed to get to work (as when you have a cold) than if you are dissatisfied with your job.

Judge et al. noted that job satisfaction is an important attitude to measure even without having to make a clear "business case" for it. That is, they argue that because jobs are important aspects of our lives, having a better understanding of our evaluations of them is reason enough to study job satisfaction. In addition, job satisfaction plays a role in obtaining overall life satisfaction. Thus, they conclude, "Regardless of whether a person considers his or her job a source of unremitting drudgery, acute frustration, or deep (even spiritual) fulfillment, it seems that job satisfaction is among the most important attitudes a person holds" (p. 519). Nevertheless, given the relatively meager relationship between job satisfaction and job outcomes, researchers have begun to redirect their efforts away from job satisfaction to other attitudes.

Work Commitment

Work commitment
The extent to which an employee feels a sense of allegiance to his or her work.

Work commitment is the extent to which an employee feels a sense of allegiance and loyalty to one or more targets within the sphere of employment. According to Klein et al. (2012), it is "a volitional psychological bond reflecting dedication to and responsibility for a particular target" (p. 137). The targets can include one's occupation or profession, the employing organization, a work team, or a particular component of one's job (e.g., being a good leader). According to Klein et al., commitment is just one of several types of bonds that may exist between a person and a target. They note that there are four types of bonds, which are summarized in Table 10-2.

First, there are *acquiescence bonds*, which are characterized by a perceived lack of alternatives. Employees who don't believe there are other jobs available for their skill sets may feel "stuck" with their organizations. Their bonds are more about compliance and resignation than volitional commitments to their organizations. Next, there are *instrumental bonds*. These bonds are primarily transactional in nature, with a focus on what might be lost if the target weren't in the picture. An employee who opts to remain in an occupation due to time, energy, money, etc. associated with education would be characterized as having an instrumental bond. He or she is accepting that a

Table 10-2 *A continuum of bond types*

	Acquiescence	Instrumental	Commitment	Identification
Defining feature	Perceived absence of alternatives	High cost or loss at stake	Volition, dedication, and responsibility	Merging of oneself with the target
How the bond is experienced	Resignation to the reality of the bond	Calculated acceptance of the bond	Embracement of the bond	Self-defined in terms of the bond

Adapted from "Reconceptualizing Workplace Commitment to Redress a Stretched Construct: Revisiting Assumptions and Removing Confounds," by H. J. Klein, J. C. Molloy, and C. T. Brinsfield, in *Academy of Management Review* (2012). Reprinted by permission from the Academy of Management.

bond exists based on a calculated examination of the costs and benefits of remaining versus leaving his or her particular occupation. *Commitment bonds* are next on the continuum, and reflect a choice to be dedicated to and responsible for a particular target. An employee who makes the conscious decision to be loyal to his or her supervisor is indicating a commitment to that individual. Choice is key here, and as such the employee will readily embrace the bond. Finally, *identification bonds* reflect a merging of an individual with a target. The bond is defined by the individual. An employee who considers the organization's values to be the same as his or hers may identify with the organization, creating a bond that reflects a psychological merging of the employee and organization.

One of the most popular ways to conceptualize commitment over the years was proposed by Allen and Meyer (1990). Their conceptualization includes three components. The *affective* component refers to the employee's emotional attachment to, and identification with, the target. The *continuance* component refers to commitment based on the costs that the employee associates with leaving the target. The *normative* component refers to the employee's feelings of obligation to remain with the target. In essence, affective commitment reflects allegiance based on liking the target, continuance commitment reflects allegiance because of a lack of viable alternatives, and normative commitment reflects allegiance to the target out of a sense of loyalty. Klein et al. noted that Allen and Meyer's conceptualization goes beyond commitment to include other types of bonds. Nevertheless, much of the existing research on work commitment has been based on this tripartite view.

For many years most research on work commitment was directed to the organization as a target of one's allegiance. However, more recent research (e.g., Meyer, 2009) has been directed toward other targets of commitment. The loss of job security in the contemporary workplace threatens why employees would commit to their organization. Through downsizing, outsourcing, offshoring, etc., employees can lose their jobs through no fault of their own (i.e., they are not fired), thereby weakening the basis of being in a committed relationship. Meyer examined the paradox of commitment—that organizational changes resulting in job loss can undermine employee commitment, yet commitment is essential for any re-configured organization (e.g., after downsizing) to succeed. The dilemma of how to inspire employee commitment in a work world of instability is captured in the following statement issued by Apple Computers regarding why individuals should select that organization as their employer:

Here's the deal Apple will give you: Here's what we want from you. We're going to give you a really neat trip while you're here. We're going to teach you stuff you couldn't learn anywhere else. In return we expect you to work like hell, buy the vision as long as you're here. We're not interested in employing you for a lifetime, because that's not the way we are thinking about this. It's a good opportunity for both of us that's probably finite. (Meyer, 2009, pp. 37–38)

To the extent this philosophy is embodied implicitly (if not explicitly) in the contemporary values of organizations, individuals will not exhibit commitment to organizations in exchange for long-term employment. The basis of commitment must be targeted to something else of value to the individual. In the case of Apple Computers, employee commitment should be offered ("buy the vision") in exchange for skill and knowledge acquisition that can generalize to other employment opportunities ("We're going to teach you stuff you couldn't learn anywhere else"). Becker et al. (2009) noted that the concept of commitment has not been rendered obsolete by the contemporary work world, but rather organizational commitment has been supplanted by commitment to other aspects or targets associated with employment.

Meyer (1997) asserted that organizational commitment reflects the employee's relationship with the organization and that it has implications for his or her decision to continue membership in the organization. Committed employees are more likely to remain in the organization than are uncommitted employees. However, as Solinger et al. (2008) noted, the construct of commitment does not necessarily explain *why* employees remain with their employer. Some behavior is habituated (i.e., we are in the habit of getting up, getting dressed, and going to work), which has nothing to do with commitment. Sample items from a questionnaire (Dunham et al., 1994) measuring organizational commitment are listed in Figure 10-4.

Based on a meta-analysis by Brown (1996), the average correlations between organizational commitment and other work-related constructs were as follows: .53 with overall job satisfaction, −.28 with turnover, and .67 with a personality construct similar to conscientiousness. Riketta (2002) estimated a correlation of .20 between

I really feel as if this organization's problems are my own.

This organization has a great deal of personal meaning for me.

Too much in my life would be disrupted if I decided I wanted to leave my organization now.

One of the major reasons I continue to work for this company is that leaving would require considerable sacrifice; another organization may not match the overall benefits I have here.

I think that people these days move from company to company too often.

I was taught to believe in the value of remaining loyal to one organization.

Figure 10-4 *Sample items from an organizational commitment questionnaire*

Source: From "Organizational Commitment: The Utility of an Integrated Definition," by R. B. Dunham, J. A. Grube, and M. B. Castaneda, 1994, *Journal of Applied Psychology, 79*, pp. 370–380.

organizational commitment and job performance based on a meta-analytic study. The general pattern of results reveals that job satisfaction and organizational commitment are substantially correlated with each other but only modestly correlated with performance and turnover. Thus organizational attitudes tend to be substantially intercorrelated. Performance is determined by ability, motivation, and situational constraints, whereas turnover is determined in part by external economic variables. The linkage between organizational attitudes and behavior is thus moderated by factors beyond the control of the individual.

Employee Engagement

Employee engagement
The degree to which a person feels invigorated, dedicated, and absorbed in his or her work.

Employee engagement is a complex, multi-faceted concept that draws upon many areas of I/O psychology. At a rudimentary level, engaged employees have very high levels of energy for their work and a strong sense of identity and attachment to their work. According to Macey and Schneider (2008), engagement is "a desirable condition, has an organizational purpose, and connotes involvement, commitment, passion, enthusiasm, focused effort, and energy" (p. 4).

Employee engagement has three dimensions (Schaufeli et al., 2002). The first is *vigor*, which is a sense of personal energy for work. Energy exists along a continuum, with vigor on one end and emotional exhaustion on the other. *Dedication* is the second dimension, which involves experiencing a sense of pride in one's work and challenge from it. The final dimension is *absorption*, reflecting the capacity to be engrossed in work and experiencing a sense of flow. Research by Demerouti and Cropanzano (2010) revealed that vigor was more predictive of job performance than either dedication or absorption.

As a way of conceptualizing employee engagement, some have regarded it as being on one end of the continuum of emotional responses to work, with burnout at the opposite end. *Burnout* is characterized by emotional exhaustion, cynicism, and feelings of reduced personal accomplishment. Maslach et al. (2001) suggested that engagement, which includes energy, involvement, and a sense of efficacy, are the positive counterparts to these burnout dimensions. Mills et al. (2012) suggest, however, that engagement is not the opposite of burnout, and that engagement may actually be more cognitive than emotional in nature.

Employee engagement is premised on the belief that individuals have the capacity to contribute far more to being productive than organizations typically allow them to be. Examples include allowing employees to take some risks in the conduct of their work, and not rebuke or censure them if their risk-taking leads to unsuccessful outcomes. The need to have a work environment that is supportive of work engagement was stated by Spreitzer et al. (2010): "Workers will be more engaged to the extent that they have the physical, political, financial, and social resources necessary to feel engaged and dedicated to their work" (p. 140). In short, employee engagement can be thought of as an interaction of individuals and work. Engagement can occur when both facilitate each other, and engagement will not occur when either (or both) thwarts each other. Employee engagement will not manifest itself if the employee just wants a paycheck and/or a job allows no discretion in individual decision making and behavior.

As was stated previously, employee engagement is a comprehensive concept that integrates many research findings from I/O psychology. The topic of alignment between individual job performance and organizational performance was discussed in Chapter 7. Mone and London (2010) believe organizations can use work engagement as a galvanizing principle around which greater alignment can be achieved. Organizations can develop performance management systems that more directly recognize and reward employees for contributing to organizational success. The greater linkage between individual and organizational performance would be achieved (in theory) by focusing more attention on how work is directed toward enhancing organizational performance, with less emphasis on the employee's performance within a narrowly defined job. In Chapter 8 the concept of organizational culture was discussed, and how the culture of an organization is directly related to its effectiveness. Organizations that want employees to thrive and become psychically immersed in their work must create a culture for engagement to occur. Chapter 11 will describe the many factors that contribute to psychological health through employment. At the core of employee engagement are concepts vital to leading a psychologically healthy life (e.g., thriving and personal fulfillment through work). Finally, several of the theories of work motivation that will be discussed in Chapter 12 are represented in employee engagement, including goal setting (to inspire performance) and work design (to create work environments that facilitate work engagement). In summation, employee engagement is highly inclusive of principles and concepts that psychological research has identified as contributing to achieving a high degree of congruence between individuals and work. It is most certainly a hybrid explanation of work behavior.

Critics of employee engagement as a concept contend that there is really nothing new to it, as it merely represents the confluence of previously established concepts under a new name (i.e., "old wine in a new bottle"). While there may be some justification for the criticism, the opposite scenario would be far more troubling. If employee engagement consisted of new concepts that had no demonstrated validity, it would be dismissed as fanciful. Macey et al. (2009) offered a reasoned caution about employee engagement. "Engagement implies something special—something at least a bit out of the ordinary and maybe even exceptional. Moreover, it sounds like something may be too good to be true, both for employee and employer" (p. 1). In a contemporary work world characterized by high employment instability, individuals may be grateful for any work, let alone engaged work. However, employee engagement is not proposed as a solution for job loss or unemployment. It represents a prescription for both employees and employers to derive the most value from each other during the tenure of their relationship.

Organizational Justice

Organizational justice
The theoretical concept pertaining to the fair treatment of people in organizations. The three types of organizational justice are distributive, procedural, and interactional.

Organizational justice is concerned with the fair treatment of people in organizations. Colquitt et al. (2001) believe that organizational justice has been among the most frequently researched topics in I/O psychology in the last two decades. This conclusion is justified because organizational justice has been found to be associated with many of the topics studied in I/O psychology, including performance, turnover, absenteeism, trust, job satisfaction, and organizational commitment.

Various configurations or typologies of organizational justice have been proposed over the years (e.g., Greenberg, 1993). However, the most current research and thinking on the topic have yielded the typology shown in Figure 10-5 (Colquitt, 2012), consisting of distributive, procedural, and interactional justice (which is further divided

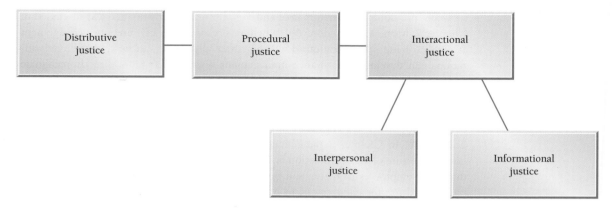

Figure 10-5   *Categories of organizational justice*

Distributive justice
The fairness with which the outcomes or results are distributed among members of an organization.

Procedural justice
The fairness by which means are used to achieve results in an organization.

into interpersonal and informational justices). **Distributive justice** refers to the fairness of the outcomes, results, or ends achieved. It is often difficult to reach a consensus on fairness, and there can be far-reaching implications for organizations from differing views on what constitutes fairness in their practices (see Field Note 1: *What is "Fair"?*).

The second major type of justice is **procedural justice**, which is the fairness of the means used to achieve the results. As the name suggests, it deals with the perceived fairness of the policies and procedures used to make decisions. In essence, the distinction between distributive and procedural justice is the difference between content and process that is basic to many philosophical approaches to the study of justice. According to Folger and Greenberg (1985), there are two dimensions to conceptualizing procedural justice. One emphasizes the role of the individual's "voice" in the process. Procedures are perceived to be fairer when affected individuals have an opportunity to either influence the decision process or offer input. Indeed, Schminke et al. (2000) found that higher levels of participation in decision making by employees within an organization were associated with higher levels of perceived procedural fairness. Gilliland and Chan (2001) reported that giving workers the opportunity to respond to their own performance evaluations, including the possibility of modifying them, is one of the most influential factors in their acceptability. The second dimension emphasizes the structural components of the process, whereby procedural justice is a function of the extent to which procedural rules are satisfied or violated. These procedural rules suggest that decisions should be made consistently, without personal biases, with as much accurate information as possible, and with an outcome that could be modified.

In applying the concept of procedural justice to a personnel selection system, for example, one could posit several components of what constitutes a "fair" selection process (Gilliland, 1993). Ideally the selection test should be job-related (or more precisely from the applicant's view, face valid), allow the candidate to demonstrate his or her proficiency, and be scored consistently across applicants. Furthermore, candidates should receive timely feedback on their application for employment, be told the truth, and be treated respectfully in the assessment process. Note that these procedural justice issues pertain to the selection process, not the outcome of whether the applicant

Field Note 1: *What Is "Fair"?*

What does it mean to be "fair"? Most certainly there are many ways to consider fairness, and I was party to one situation that evoked these multiple perspectives. A wealthy individual died and bequeathed $3,000,000 to a university to support students who attended the school. The university invested the $3,000,000 such that it earned 6% interest, or $180,000, per year. Thus every year the university could grant $180,000 to students to support their education, without having to use the original $3,000,000 gift. The university formed a committee to determine the most fair way of dispersing the $180,000 per year. I was a member of that committee. Three distinct schools of thought emerged as to what constituted the "most fair" disbursement of money.

The first school of thought was to grant a financial award to the most academically talented applicants. As indexed by high school grades and standardized test scores, the "best" applicants were to receive the financial support. This university had highly reputable programs in engineering and agriculture, majors that typically attract more men than women. Because these programs attracted many of the most highly qualified applicants to the university, and because the vast majority of these applicants were men, the financial award recipients would be very heavily represented by men.

Proponents of the second perspective pointed out that the university sought to embrace all groups in society—across genders, racial groups, age groups, the physically disabled, and so on. Therefore the financial support should be intentionally allocated to individual students who represent the various groups. In this way the university would show its support for recruiting a diverse student body.

The third perspective was to allocate the money based on financial need. It was proposed that the best use of the money would be to pay for students to obtain a college education who could not otherwise afford it. Therefore the recipients of the financial support would be the financially neediest students.

These were the three basic schools of thought on what was a "fair" strategy to disburse the money. I was struck not only by how different the recipients would be depending upon which strategy was followed, but also by the inherent plausibility of each strategy. That is, I felt each position had some intuitive appeal; each one made some sense to me. The three groups argued over such matters as the difference between a scholarship and financial aid, and what the intentions of the deceased benefactor were in disbursing his money. The final decision by the committee reflected a compromise—a (fair) resolution of conflicting standards of fairness. A portion of the funds was set aside to be allocated on the basis of need. The rest would be allocated on the basis of academic ability, with members of all the various groups represented. It was not a decision the committee enthusiastically endorsed, but one it could live with.

If you had been on that committee, what position would you have taken in allocating the funds? Why do you think your position is the "most fair" one?

Interactional justice
The fairness with which people are treated within an organization and the timeliness, completeness, and accuracy of the information received in an organization.

is accepted or rejected (which is a matter of distributive justice). Leventhal (1980) proposed six criteria by which procedures can be judged as fair: (1) consistent, (2) bias free, (3) accurate, (4) correctable in case of an error, (5) representative of all concerned, and (6) based on prevailing ethical standards.

A third major type of organizational justice has been identified, referred to as **interactional justice**. In turn, interactional justice has two components: interpersonal and informational. *Interpersonal justice* is manifested by showing concern for individuals and respecting them as people who have dignity. Ostensible displays of politeness and respect for citizens' rights enhance their perceptions of fair treatment by authorities, such as the police and the courts. As Folger and Skarlicki (2001) stated, it rarely costs anything to be polite. The lack of politeness, sensitivity, and caring for the emotional pain inflicted by organizations on employees only adds insult to injury. Folger and Skarlicki concisely summarized this point: "Politeness costs less than you think, and it stands to reap greater benefits than you might have realized. Paraphrased and shortened, politeness pays" (p. 116). Greenberg (2007) believes that many positive organizational outcomes can be derived from strongly promoting interactional justice: "The key is that being far more dignified and respectful to people than they expect cannot help but result in positive reactions . . . Importantly, these reactions are likely to be 'contagious' insofar as they contribute to a culture in which such positive acts are openly encouraged and in which violations are critically discouraged" (p. 172).

Informational justice is manifested by providing knowledge about procedures that demonstrate regard for people's concerns. People are given adequate accounts and explanations of the procedures used to determine desired outcomes. For explanations to be perceived as fair, they must also be recognized as genuine in intent (without any ulterior motives) and based on sound reasoning. Because it is typically the open sharing of information that promotes this form of organizational justice, the term *information* is used to identify it.

A study by Greenberg (1994) illustrates interpersonal and informational justice. Two announcements of a worksite smoking ban were made to employees of a large company. The announcements differed in the amount of information they gave about the need for the ban and the degree of interpersonal sensitivity shown for the personal impact of the ban. Some employees received a great deal of information about the reason for the smoking ban, while others received only the most cursory information. Furthermore, some employees received a personally sensitive message ("We realize that this new policy will be very hard on those of you who smoke. Smoking is an addiction, and it's very tough to stop. We are quite aware of this, and we do not want you to suffer"), while other employees received a message showing less personal concern ("I realize that it's tough to stop smoking, but it's in the best interest of our business to implement the smoking ban. And, of course, business must come first"). Immediately after the announcement, employees completed surveys on their acceptance of the ban. Although heavy smokers were least accepting of the ban, they showed the greatest incremental gain in acceptance after they received thorough information presented in a highly sensitive manner. Regardless of how much they smoked, all smokers recognized the procedural fairness associated with giving thorough information in a socially sensitive manner. By contrast, all nonsmokers' acceptance of the ban was uniformly unaffected by the way it was presented to them.

A major meta-analytic review of 25 years of organizational justice research by Colquitt et al. concluded that distributive justice, procedural justice, and the two types of interactional justice (interpersonal and informational) each contribute incremental variance to perceptions of fairness in the workplace. Although the different justice dimensions are not totally distinct, each reflects a facet of "what is fair." Greenberg (2007) observed that much of what is known about organizational justice has been discovered from its violation; that is, organizational injustice. Greenberg offered that because justice is expected as the norm, it is more informative to examine deviations from the norm (i.e., injustice) than behavior consistent with the norm (i.e., justice). Simons and Roberson (2003) concluded that the fair treatment of employees by organizations has important effects on individual employee attitudes, such as satisfaction and commitment, and on individual behaviors, such as absenteeism and citizenship behavior. Cohen-Charash and Spector (2001) reported that of the three major types of justice, procedural justice was most closely related to organizational attitudes and behaviors.

Behaviors

Individuals can engage in a variety of behaviors while at work. Whereas the vast majority of attention has been devoted to behaviors related to task performance, I/O psychologists have also examined "extra" behaviors that individuals engage in within organizations. Some of these behaviors can be beneficial to organizations, while others can cause harm to the organization and its constituents. Below, we examine organizational citizenship behavior, counterproductive work behavior, and political behavior, and the implications of each for individuals and organizations.

Organizational Citizenship Behavior

The classic approach to thinking about a job is in terms of the tasks that comprise it. In fact, one purpose of work analysis (as described in Chapter 3) is to identify these tasks. In turn, performance appraisal (as discussed in Chapter 7) is concerned with assessing how well employees perform the tasks that comprise their jobs. However, organizational researchers have discovered that some employees contribute to the welfare or effectiveness of their organization by going beyond the duties prescribed in their jobs. That is, they give extra discretionary contributions that are neither required nor expected. The most frequently used term for this phenomenon is **organizational citizenship behavior**. It is also referred to as *pro-social behavior, extra-role behavior,* and *contextual behavior.* We first mentioned citizenship behavior in Chapter 3 on criteria and again in Chapter 5 on personnel decisions. As noted in Chapter 3, organizational citizenship behavior can be directed at individuals or organizations. Organ (1994) referred to a person who engages in organizational citizenship behavior as a "good soldier."

Five dimensions to citizenship behavior have been supported by empirical research (LePine et al., 2002):

1. **Altruism** (also called *helping behavior*) reflects willfully helping specific people with an organizationally-relevant task or problem.

2. **Conscientiousness** refers to being punctual, having attendance better than the group norm, and judiciously following company rules, regulations, and procedures.

Organizational citizenship behavior Employee behavior that transcends job performance and is directed to the overall welfare of the organization.

3. **Courtesy** is being mindful and respectful of other people's rights.

4. **Sportsmanship** refers to avoiding complaints, petty grievances, gossiping, and falsely magnifying problems.

5. **Civic virtue** is responsible participation in the political life of the organization. Civic virtue reflects keeping abreast of not only current organizational issues but also more mundane issues, such as attending meetings, attending to in-house communications, and speaking up on issues. It has been suggested that civic virtue is the most admirable manifestation of organizational citizenship behavior because it often entails some sacrifice of individual productive efficiency.

Employees who exhibit pro-social behavior are highly valued by their managers. Indeed, they should be, because they contribute above and beyond the normal requirements and expectations of the job. Podsakoff et al. (2009) conducted a meta-analysis of the individual and organizational consequences of employees who engage in organizational citizenship behavior. Employees who were perceived as exhibiting citizenship behaviors received higher performance evaluations and pay raises, and had lower rates of absence, compared to employees who exhibited less citizenship behavior. The authors reported that across different organizational units, organizational citizenship behavior correlated .41 with unit productivity (objectively measured, not rated) and .42 with cost reduction.

Grant and Mayer (2009) proposed two motives for employees to engage in citizenship behaviors. One is to "do good" (citizenship) and the other is to "look good" (impression management). To do good is founded on the pro-social motive of contributing to the welfare of the organization beyond one's job duties, to be a "good soldier." To look good is to influence how others perceive you for self-serving reasons, to be a "good actor." Employees can be both good soldiers and good actors at the same time, but an individual is typically more driven by one motive over the other. Heilman and Chen (2005) examined the extent to which the altruism dimension of organizational citizenship behavior influenced the evaluations of male and female employees. Men who engaged in altruistic behavior on the job received higher evaluations than men who did not engage in altruistic behavior. Conversely, women who did not engage in altruistic behavior had lower evaluations than men who did not engage in altruistic behavior. The authors concluded that assisting others with tasks and going the "extra mile" (i.e., being a helper) is central to a female gender stereotype perception. Men who engage in helping others exceed the male gender stereotype perception, while women who help others are simply eliciting typical female behavior. In turn, these gender-based stereotypes influence the evaluations received by men and women on the job.

Are manifestations of such pro-social behavior a product of our individual dispositions (which are fairly immutable), or can organizations conduct themselves in ways that bring out such behavior in their employees? Research supports both the dispositional and situational antecedents of organizational citizenship behavior.

Support for dispositional antecedents comes from the Big 5 model of personality (as discussed in Chapter 4). Two of the Big 5 dimensions appear relevant to organizational citizenship behavior. One, agreeableness, pertains to the ease or difficulty one has in getting along with people, or how good-natured one is in interpersonal relationships. The second, conscientiousness, pertains to reliability, dependability, punctuality, and discipline. Evidence indicates that some people, given selected aspects of their personality, are more likely to engage in organizational citizenship behaviors than others. As McNeely and Meglino (1994) noted, organizations can promote pro-social behavior by selecting applicants who have high scores on agreeableness and conscientiousness. Managers include organizational citizenship behaviors in their evaluations of employee job performance. As expressed by Organ et al. (2011), "Therefore it would make sense for organizations to try to identify and select those job candidates who have a propensity to exhibit these behaviors" (p. 314).

The second explanation for organizational citizenship behavior—situational antecedents—has at its basis the concept of fairness. It is proposed that if employees believe they are treated fairly, then they are more likely to hold positive attitudes about their work. Organ (1988) hypothesized that fairness perceptions may influence pro-social behavior by prompting employees to define their relationship with the organization as a social exchange. In exchange for being treated fairly, it is proposed that employees would engage in discretionary gestures of organizational citizenship behavior. However, to the extent that unfairness is perceived in the relationship, the tendency would be to recast the relationship as a more rigidly-defined exchange. Thus, in a trusting relationship with the organization, the employee contributes more to the exchange than is formally required. However, to the degree the organization is perceived as lacking fairness, the employee retreats to contributing to the exchange only what he or she is obligated.

Another situational antecedent to organizational citizenship behaviors involves the concept of role stressors. Role stressors include role conflict, role ambiguity, and role overload as discussed in Chapter 8. Role conflict and ambiguity appear to be particularly relevant for citizenship behaviors. Specifically, Eatough et al. (2011) found that individuals were less likely to engage in organizational citizenship behaviors when they were experiencing role conflict or role ambiguity. Role overload appears to be a potential outcome of engaging in organizational citizenship behaviors. Bolino et al. (2010) found that individuals who felt pressured to engage in citizenship behaviors did, in fact, perform more pro-social behaviors, but also felt overloaded in their roles.

It should be clear that supervisors can directly influence employees' citizenship behavior. Moorman (1991) suggested that supervisors could increase citizenship behavior among their employees by increasing the fairness of their interactions with employees. Similarly, a supervisor could take steps to ensure role conflict and ambiguity are minimized. Organizations that are perceived as being equitable and that recognize desirable behavior in their employees reap the benefits of having employees engage in more citizenship behavior. Zellers and Tepper (2003) concluded: "Organizations that successfully attract and hire individuals with strong self-concepts comprised in part by values reflecting the importance of being a 'good citizen' may be able to reduce costly amounts of supervision since the individual is intrinsically motivated to be a 'good citizen' " (p. 415).

Despite the positive benefits for organizational citizenship behavior, some cautionary statements are needed. For example, Culbertson and Mills (2011) suggested that including ratings of citizenship behaviors in formal performance appraisals could have negative implications, including lower subsequent task performance, inaccurate ratings, and negative reactions regarding the fairness of the evaluation. In addition, it may be possible to have "too much of a good thing" when it comes to organizational citizenship behavior. Pierce and Aguinis (2013) suggested that such behavior may become dysfunctional if it interferes with the person's individual task performance.

There is a finite amount of time within a given workday. If an individual engages in pro-social behaviors to the point where not enough time is left to effectively complete assigned tasks, the benefits of the citizenship behaviors becomes questionable. Along these lines, Bergeron et al. (2013) found that spending time on actual task performance is more related to career outcomes (promotions, salary increases, and speed of advancement) than is citizenship behaviors. In addition, individuals who spent time engaging in citizenship behaviors had smaller salary increases and progressed more slowly within their organizations than did individuals who engaged in fewer such behaviors. It is important to note that time management skills may play a role here. Rapp et al. (2013) found that individuals who were skilled at time management were able to reap the benefits of engaging in helping behaviors, but those who weren't skilled at managing their time felt the negative impact on their task performance.

Counterproductive Work Behavior

Counterproductive work behavior
A broad range of employee behaviors that are harmful to other employees or the organization.

Counterproductive work behavior refers to a broad range of employee behaviors that negatively impact the organization and its constituents. According to Spector and Fox (2005), they are volitional in nature, meaning they are intended to cause harm. The phenomenon has also been called *workplace incivility, organizational deviance,* and *insidious workplace behavior* (Edwards & Greenberg, 2010). Campbell (2012) noted that deviant behaviors can be directed at harming either the organization or individuals, including oneself.

Counterproductive work behaviors can be grouped into several categories. *Verbal* behaviors are rudeness, ostracism, spreading rumors, and sarcasm. *Physical* behaviors include bullying and overt violence such as being kicked, beaten, or spat upon. *Sabotage* includes damage to a company's property, products, or reputation. *Work-directed* behaviors include lateness, excessive absence, theft, and working slowly (see I/O Psychology and the Economy: *The Cost of Counterproductive Work Behavior*). Finally, the most extreme form of organizational deviance is *workplace* (or *occupational*) *homicide*.

Counterproductive work behaviors can result from a number of factors. Tepper et al. (2008) reported that abusive supervisors who engage in the undermining and belittling of employees prompt organizational deviance. Organizational deviance can also result as a way to retaliate against somebody. For example, Scott et al. (2013) found that employees were likely to ignore and exclude other employees who they felt had been rude or demeaning in some way. Retaliatory acts are often rooted in feeling powerless to alter one's work environment. Seabright et al. (2010) developed a three-dimensional classification of one form of retaliation—sabotage. The authors classified acts of sabotage according to *severity* (minor/major), *recurrence* (one time/ongoing), and *visibility* (overt/covert). Insidious sabotage was described as minor, ongoing, and covert (as intentionally directing customer service calls to the wrong party). As the economy becomes increasingly service oriented, more acts of employee sabotage are directed toward customers. Skarlicki et al. (2008) described this exchange at an airport ticket counter, as originally reported in *Sweet Revenge: The Wicked Delights of Getting Even* (Barreca, 1997):

> His last words were, "If everybody working for this organization is as incompetent as you, no wonder your airline loses money." He then stormed off. I wished him a good flight as if nothing happened.

I/O Psychology and the Economy: *The Cost of Counterproductive Work Behavior*

Many factors contribute to how organizations set prices for the products they make and the services they provide. Three of the leading factors are the costs of labor, material, and marketing. Organizations carefully calculate all their costs, add in a profit margin, and the resulting total is the price that is charged to the customer. Any additional cost is passed on to the customer, resulting in a price increase.

Consider three forms of counterproductive work behavior discussed in this chapter: chronic lateness, unnecessary absence, and working slowly. These three serve to increase labor costs, because they add more time to produce a unit of work (e.g., manufacturing a product or serving a customer). Time is money. Sabotage directed toward the production process would also result in yet more time needed to make a car, as well as the cost of repairing the damage. Theft of tools or parts further drives up the cost of a car.

What is the net effect of these acts of organizational deviance on the final cost of a new car that we would purchase from a dealership? No one knows for certain what the added cost is, but here is an estimate. The average price of a new car in the United States is $30,000. A conservative estimate of the costs of deviant behavior is $500 per car, about 1.6% of the total price. Annual new car sales in the United States are about 14,000,000 units. $500 per car times 14,000,000 cars equals $7 billion in unnecessary costs that get passed on to the buying public; and that is for one year in one country and for one industry. Organizational deviance is not limited to autoworkers and the transportation industry. It occurs in all industries across the full range of occupations.

Companies pass on the costs of doing business to their customers. Customers, in turn, are employees of other companies. To the extent that counterproductive work behavior is represented throughout the entire economy, some employees contribute to unnecessary costs, and as customers we all pay unnecessary costs. Such is the paradox of organizational deviance. The actions of the "bad apple" employees produce consequences that adversely affect all of us. Counterproductive work behavior may be studied from an I/O psychological perspective, but its consequences are unequivocally economic in nature.

The little old lady behind him in line had heard everything, of course, as she sweetly asked how I managed to stay so polite and cheerful in the face of his behavior. I told her the truth. "He's going to Kansas City," I explained, "and his bags are going to Tokyo." She laughed and told me that I'd done the right thing. (p. 133)

In this case, the employee retaliated against the customer who was verbally abusive. In other cases, employees may retaliate against blameless customers who happen to be convenient targets. Skarlicki et al. proposed the possibility of organizations "firing customers" for their treatment of employees that can trigger a retaliatory response.

Bies et al. (1997) described what they call the "thermodynamics of revenge" in organizations. There is typically a sparking event of one of two types. One is a violation of rules, norms, or promises by the organization. An organizational agent changes the rules or criteria of decision making after the fact to justify a self-serving judgment. The second is status or power derogation, such as destructive criticism or public ridicule intended to embarrass the employee. The employee then "heats up" and experiences anger and bitterness, often feeling a need to satisfy a burning desire for revenge. This is followed by a "cooling down" phase, which can take several forms. One is *venting*, in which the employee talks heatedly and animatedly to friends, "blows off steam," and has little or no intention of acting out his or her feelings. A second is *dissipation*, where the employee gives the harm-doer the benefit of the doubt and searches for plausible explanations for the harm-doer's behavior. A third form is *fatigue*, in which employees maintain their negative feelings for long periods of time. These people do not forgive, forget, and let go. They often obsessively ruminate and express regret about not getting even with the harm-doer. The final form is *explosion*, which can manifest itself in the employee working harder to prove the critic wrong, mobilizing opposition to the harm-doer, or engaging in physical violence.

Workplace bullying has gained considerable attention within I/O psychology. Tehrani (2012) noted that bullying within organizations is complex given "there are a number of players, a range of motivations, hidden agendas and old scores to be settled" (p. 9). Bullying can involve a single bully targeting others or involve multiple bullies ganging up on one or more individuals. Jensen et al. (2014) noted that both high and low performers can be the targets of workplace aggression, but the type of aggression differed for each. They noted that "low performers are more likely to experience direct, 'in your face' aggression such as swearing, yelling, hostile body language, and threats, whereas excellent performers are more likely to experience subtle 'behind your back' aggression such as withholding information or resources, sabotage, or being avoided" (pp. 304–305).

Tehrani also noted that an organization's practices and policies may facilitate bullying, serving to "oppress, demean or humiliate the workforce" (p. 13). For example, a practice of requiring employees to indefinitely work beyond their assigned shifts when workflow is heavy, without concern for employees' needs, can be considered organizational bullying. In addition, the culture of the organization may create situations that allow greater incivility. Shore and Coyle-Shapiro (2012) suggested that employees who believe their organization has treated them deliberately and unnecessarily in a harmful manner will perceive the organization as being cruel. This perceived organizational cruelty is likely to lead to health and well-being problems for the employee as well as potential retaliatory behaviors.

It is the traditional perspective of I/O psychology to focus on individuals. Within the topic of organizational deviance, the conventional focus would be to assume individuals who engage in retaliatory acts are the "bad apples" in the barrel, who should be disciplined for the incivility. However, Kish-Gephart et al. (2010) offered an alternative perspective: organizations that embody a culture of "everyone for himself" which, in turn, produces a very broad range of behaviors. Among them are counterproductive work behaviors. The authors believe that organizational incivility can be the product of "bad barrels" that permit such behavior to occur in addition to "bad apples" within "good barrels." Along these lines, Ramsay et al. (2011) suggested that bullying may be either stifled or encouraged through the rules that teams set and how strongly members identify with their team. When team members identify strongly with a team that values respect and pro-social interactions, bullying won't be tolerated. If the team values aggression and disrespect, however, a team member who feels strongly connected to that team will be more likely to engage in interpersonally deviant behaviors.

Andersson and Pearson (1999) proposed a spiraling effect of incivility in the workplace. Workplace incivility is low-intensity deviant behavior with ambiguous intent to harm the target individual, in violation of workplace norms for mutual respect. Uncivil behaviors are characteristically rude and discourteous, displaying a lack of regard for others. The spiraling effect refers to the prospects that incivility can escalate into intense aggressive behavior. Glomb et al. (2002) stated, "Mildly aggressive acts can have great impact when they are experienced in quantity. . . . These overlapping effects build on each other, augmenting their impact. Eventually, repeated mild aggression can create considerable distress and oppression itself, such as that seen after periods of prolonged provocation or threat" (p. 229). Andersson and Pearson stated that the spiral of incivility often begins with a thoughtless act or a rude comment. This can be followed by a maligning insult, which prompts a counterinsult. If the spiral of escalation continues, threats of physical attack can follow, ultimately leading to violence. The authors believe there is a "tipping point" in the spiral where the accumulation of minor affronts escalates into coercive action. In a meta-analysis of workplace aggression, Hershcovis et al. (2007) found that coworkers were more likely than supervisors to be targets of workplace aggression. This finding may be attributable to coworkers having less retaliatory power than supervisors, as well as their greater representation within an organization.

Barclay and Aquino (2011) noted the increased use of computers in the workplace has produced a new form of aggression—**cyberaggression**. Cyberaggression, also referred to as *cyberbullying*, involves inflicting intentional harm to others through electronic media. A common form of cyberaggression is flaming, or the intentional use of insulting language through electronic means (email, blogs) designed to inflict harm. With the advancement of social media, cyberbullying has become a real threat for organizations (see Social Media and I/O Psychology: *The Cyberbully's Blog*). According to Weatherbee (2010), cyberaggression is a form of cyberdeviancy, which involves the misuse of technology to cause harm to the organization or its stakeholders. Cyberdeviance also includes cyberloafing, or the wasting of time by sending personal email and shopping online during company time.

Cyberaggression
Hostile or aggressive behavior at the workplace that occurs through electronic media.

Organizational Politics

Organizational politics
Behavior exhibited within organizations by employees that is driven by self-interest.

The concept of **organizational politics** is relatively new to the field of I/O psychology. It seeks to explain behavior within organizations that accounts for (among other things) how and why decisions get made. An idealistic view of organizations is that they are guided by rational and reasoned individuals who make decisions that solely enhance the welfare of the organization. That is, employees sublimate or negate their personal interests in favor of doing what is in the best interest of the organization. In reality, organizations are not populated with selfless individuals. Organizations are arenas for individual behavior to manifest itself, and people are motivated by many factors, including self-interest. Concerns about career progression and potential job loss are such examples. The concept of organizational politics examines how individuals use their organizational membership to enhance their self-interest.

Vigoda-Gadot and Drory (2006) described organizational politics as the capacity

Social Media and I/O Psychology: *The Cyberbully's Blog*

Bullies have been around since the dawn of time, inflicting pain and suffering on their victims. Even the sweet Peanuts character, Charlie Brown, suffers the wrath of Lucy, the bully who has tormented him on the comic book pages for over 50 years, most notably by constantly moving a football just as he goes to kick it. Bullies are not limited to playgrounds and comic strips, however. They now exist in the workplace, from the front lines to the boardrooms. Moreover, they exist online, in a world where they are shielded by a sense of anonymity combined with the possibility of widespread and instantaneous impact. As such, the cyberbully's harassment, although not face-to-face, has the potential to be just as damaging, if not more so, to his or her victims.

Social media blur the lines between work and non-work in many ways. Blogs are one way in which boundaries are obscured. Blogs (or web logs) emerged in the late 1990s, allowing individuals to provide commentary on a particular subject. Frequently interactive, they typically allow individuals to comment on the content, thereby establishing a social connection with others. Bloggers post seemingly anything they want, whenever they want, and as such the blog is fertile ground for cyberbullies—and for blurring the lines between work and non-work. The cyberbully should beware, however, as what is written outside of work could get him or her in trouble on the job. Furthermore, it could get the organization in trouble.

Take for example the unfortunate experience of a California probations employee who reported his coworker's misconduct on the job. A separate coworker created a blog away from work, using his personal computer. In this blog, employees started to post derogatory comments about the employee, who just happened to have a disability whereby he was born with a disfigured right hand that he usually attempted to keep hidden in his pocket. His coworkers referred to him as "the Rat" and his hand, as "the claw" in their blog posts. The posts become increasingly vulgar and highly inappropriate, and the employee filed a complaint. It was found that although the blog was created outside of work, it was clear that people were accessing the blog while on the job and that the employer was aware of this. In the end, the employer was found liable for having knowledge of the harassment and not taking sufficient steps to stop it. A jury awarded the employee over $800,000. So employers should beware of cyberbullying, as what happens outside of work may not stay outside of work.

and willingness of individuals within organizations to use power for the purpose of furthering their own interests. Self-serving behavior that may coincidentally enhance the welfare of other employees is the cornerstone of organizational politics. Fundamentally, organizational politics addresses the question of "who gets what, when, and how" (Lasswell, 1936). It has traditionally been portrayed by scholars as representing the dark side of behavior in organizations, involving such tactics as manipulation, coercion, deceit, and subversion. Indeed, as Hochwarter (2012) noted, the word politics is viewed by many "with disdain, conjuring up visions of shady behavior that is manipulative, divisive, and exclusively self-serving" (p. 27). However, Ferris and Treadway (2012) noted that the contemporary stance is to view organizational politics as neutral or even positive, more from the perspective of how decisions get made in organizations (see Field Note 2: *Beneficial Politics?*). The use of political tactics in organizations is widespread, and is often regarded as a fact of organizational life. A study by Buchanan (2008) found that 90% of managers they sampled agreed that "most managers, if they want to succeed, have to play politics at least part of the time" (p. 57). Ferris and Hochwarter (2011), in describing the ubiquity of organizational politics, cited a quote by former British Prime Minister Sir Winston Churchill: "When you mix people and power, you get politics" (p. 450). Nevertheless, organizations differ with regard to the frequency, intensity, and nature of its use.

Three aspects of organizational politics are noteworthy. One is the various forms of its occurrence. Beugne and Liverpool (2006) reported such tactics as by-passing the chain of command to gain approval for a particular decision, and creating norms of obligations and reciprocity (i.e., "you owe me"). Mintzberg (1989) described many political games played in organizations. The *budgeting game* is the awarding of a valued resource (money) to a department or unit in exchange for support or compliance. Implicit is the understanding that the following year's budget can be reduced for perceived lack of support. People who play the budgeting game often espouse the business version of the "Golden Rule"—"Those who control the gold, rule." The *expertise game* is the flaunting or feigning of technical knowledge, emphasizing it is critical and irreplaceable, for the purpose of influencing decision outcomes favorable to the same player. The basis of the expertise game is "knowledge is power," and the particular knowledge is hoarded by those who possess it. The *rival camps game* is typically played between two groups within an organization, such as production and sales. Individuals external to these two camps will form temporary alliances with one group in exchange for something of value to them. However, in the next political battle between the two camps, external individuals may "switch sides" in their support. The two rival camps are played off against each other by non-members, with the recipient of their support being the one who offers more in return than the other. As noted by Mintzberg, many of the games played do not seek to subvert the larger goals of the organization, but all games are designed to enhance the self-interests of those who play them.

A second area is devoted to understanding "political skill"—what attributes do people have that enable them to successfully engage in organizational politics? Liu et al. (2006) outlined four components of political skill. The first is *social astuteness*. Politically-skilled people have a well-crafted ability to observe social cues and to intuit the motives and values of other individuals. *Interpersonal influence*, the second component, is the capacity to take control of social encounters and do so with considerable ease. The third component, *building networks and forming coalitions*, is fundamental to organizational politics. A politically-skilled individual is not a renegade or rogue member of the organization, but someone who knows how to cultivate interpersonal resources to achieve desired outcomes. The final component is *projected virtue*. Politically-skilled individuals can disguise their true intentions, and project themselves to others as being virtuous in their motives. They may make emotional appeals to others for what is ostensibly the good of the organization, but such displays are disingenuous. Research by Blickle et al. (2011) revealed that political skill was predictive of job performance above and beyond personality and cognitive ability. In addition, Ferris et al. (2012) suggested that politically-skilled individuals are better able to adapt

Field Note 2: *Beneficial Politics?*

Organizational politics is typically associated with self-serving behavior that ignores the welfare of other people and the organization as a whole. However, sometimes the distinction between self-interest and organizational interest is not clear.

A company decided to invest very heavily in the professional development and education of three young high-potential employees. They would be sent to very expensive executive training programs both domestically and overseas, and would be individually mentored by the senior leaders of the company. The company was structured into five divisions. Each division was lead by a vice-president and each division advanced several candidates for possible selection. While each division wanted one of its people selected, with three openings and five divisions, it was understood that two divisions would not have a candidate selected. The selection committee consisted of the president and two senior vice-presidents. A sense of competition emerged among the divisions regarding selection of the three candidates.

The vice-president of one division privately lobbied the selection committee to choose *two* of his candidates. The selection committee did so. This meant that *three* divisions went unrepresented in the final selection. The vice-president had the reputation of being a "wheeler-dealer," a silky-smooth politician who frustrated (and sometimes angered) his fellow vice-presidents with his established track record of often getting his way. The selection of two of his people merely added to his political reputation. After about 18 months of professional development, the three individuals were deployed into

international assignments. Each one performed exceptionally well and the organization was affirmed it had made three correct personnel decisions.

In the context of organizational politics, one can question just how "self-serving" the vice-president was who lobbied to have two of his people chosen. It is certainly true that he enhanced his own reputation by the selection decisions. He furthered his image as someone who was a "player" within the company, and a force to be reckoned with. But ultimately, the company's interests were also well-served. The company got what it wanted—three top-flight people who became instrumental to the company's success. However, it could be argued that other candidates besides the chosen three would also have been successful if given the chance.

Andrews et al. (2009) noted that some circumstances call for people with high political skill, and the absence of such skill would be detrimental. Some individuals are elected to serve in governmental roles. Such elected people are called politicians. As described by Silvester (2008), "Politics and politicians are also at the heart of democracy; their performance affects the economic and social well-being of nations. Although professional politicians and their actions are often unpopular, acting politically is generally accepted as a legitimate and important part of their role. For politicians, politics *is* work, not an unacceptable or deviant activity" (pp. 107–108). In short, there are some situations where self-interest is clearly different from the interests of others. But there are other situations where the two may overlap, or the distinction is a matter of degree and not kind.

to their environments. Given the relationships between political skill and job performance and adaptability, Ferris et al. suggested that measures of political skill may be viable selection instruments.

The third area is how others respond to the tactics of organizational politics. Cropanzano and Li (2006) identified parallels between organizational politics and stress. They both are characterized by ambiguity, unpredictability, and an overall sense of uneasiness. The authors stated, "Both involve a certain perplexity as to *what* is going on and *when* it will occur" (p. 139). Organizational politics can undermine the principles of organizational justice and a sense of fair play. When used routinely throughout the organization, it can produce feelings of cynicism and apathy among employees. An organizational culture heavily steeped in organizational politics can invoke perceptions that few things are as they appear, backroom deals are how decisions get made, and people are foolish to believe what is publically espoused. Individuals who are recognized as political game-players are treated with suspicion, even on those occasions when their actions may not be self-serving. Such individuals may be recognized for their acumen in getting what they want, but their tactics create ill will among other employees. Chang et al. (2009) examined the relationships between perceptions of organizational politics and employee attitudes and behavior. Perceived politics correlated .43 with the desire to leave the organization, −.57 with job satisfaction, and −.54 with affective organizational commitment. This pattern of results is highly similar in direction and magnitude to how perceived violations of organizational justice influence employee attitudes and behavior.

The Psychological Contract

Psychological contract

The implied exchange relationship that exists between an employee and the organization.

Rousseau (1995) described the **psychological contract** as the exchange relationship between the individual employee and the organization. It is not a formal written contract between the two parties but an implied relationship based on mutual contributions. The psychological contract is the employee's perception of the reciprocal obligations that exist within the organization. The employees have beliefs about the organization's obligations to them as well as their obligations to the organization. Furthermore, as Rousseau (2011) observed, these perceptions of employer obligations may be in direct contrast to what employment laws stipulate about treatment of workers by organizations. That is, organizations are not legally obligated to provide what is at the heart of employee expectations. Thus employees may believe the organization has agreed to provide job security and promotional opportunities in exchange for hard work and loyalty by the employee. The contract is composed of a belief that some form of a promise has been made and that the terms and conditions of the contract have been accepted by both parties. Conway and Briner (2009) summarized the psychological contract as a useful construct in understanding organizational attitudes and behavior. "The psychological contract is used to explain employee behavior in two ways: by exploring how reciprocal promises oblige employee behavior to do things for their employer, and considering how employees react when they believe promises made to them are broken" (p. 71).

Dabos and Rousseau (2004) asserted that the psychological contract is founded on two principles: *mutuality* (the extent to which workers and employees share beliefs about specific terms of the exchange) and *reciprocity* (their commitments to each).

Dabos and Rousseau believe mutuality may be more easily achieved than reciprocity because there is no stated time frame in which the reciprocal commitments are to be made. For instance, an employer may indicate a willingness to develop an employee and support his or her career advancement. However, it may not be clear how and over what time period the employee is to make a reciprocal contribution to the employer. The psychological contract is made not once but is revised throughout the employee's tenure in the organization. The longer the relationship endures and the two parties interact, the broader the array of contributions that might be included in the contract. Rousseau and Parks (1993) found that employment itself is perceived as a promise (i.e., the implied contract of continued future employment) and that an employee's performance is perceived as a contribution (a way of paying for the promise). The use of downsizing, outsourcing, and other bases for job loss represent a severe violation of the psychological contract, because the organization has withdrawn employment despite the employee's willingness and capacity to perform work.

Rousseau (2011) suggested that psychological contracts lie along a continuum from the transactional to the relational. *Transactional contracts* are characterized by short time frames and specific obligations. Financial resources are the primary vehicle of exchange. *Relational contracts* are characterized by long-term relationships with diffuse obligations. Transactional contracts are predicated on total self-interest, whereas relational contracts implicitly acknowledge the value of the relationship itself, in which one party may put the immediate interests of the other party ahead of his or her own. At the relational end of the continuum, obligations are ambiguous and constantly evolving. These contracts are long term and exchange not only financial resources but also socioemotional resources such as loyalty and affiliation. Rousseau notes that, in general, relational obligations are associated with more positive outcomes whereas transactional obligations are associated with negative ones. For example, as shown in Figure 10-6, relational contracts are linked to pro-social behaviors and commitment to

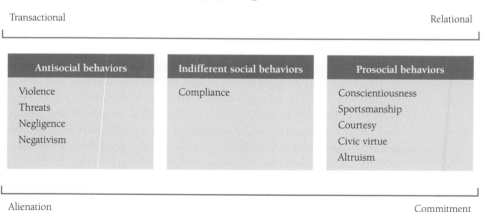

Figure 10-6 *Relationship between the psychological contract and the range of social behaviors*

Source: Adapted from "'Till Death Do Us Part . . .': Changing Work Relationships in the 1990s," by J. M. Parks and D. L. Kidder, 1994, in C. L. Cooper and D. M. Rousseau (Eds.), *Trends in organizational behavior*, Vol. 1 (p. 120), New York: Wiley.

the organization while transactional contracts are more related to antisocial behaviors and alienation from the organization.

There is an element of power in all contracts. Power can be distributed either equally (i.e., symmetrically) between the two parties or unequally (i.e., asymmetrically). Asymmetrical power is most common in employment relationships. Power asymmetries affect the perceived voluntariness of the exchange relationship, dividing the two parties into contract makers (relatively powerful) and contract takers (relatively powerless). As contract takers, employees cannot easily influence the employment relationship. This may result in a perceived loss of control in the relationship, which is likely to intensify feelings of mistreatment and injustice when violations are perceived. As the more powerful party, the employer can dictate terms of the contract to the less powerful employee, who must either accept them or exit the relationship.

Violations of the Psychological Contract

The psychological contract is violated (that is, breached) when one party in a relationship perceives that another has failed to fulfill the promised obligations. Table 10-3 lists typical organizational violations of the psychological contract and related example quotes from employees. The failure of one party to meet its obligations to another can be expected to erode both the relationship and the affected party's belief in the reciprocal obligations of the two parties. Violations by an employer may affect not only what an employee feels he or she is owed by the employer but also what an employee feels obligated to offer in return. Violation of a psychological contract undermines the very factors (e.g., trust) that led to the emergence of a relationship. If the employer reneges on an implied promise, the employer's integrity is questioned. Montes and Zweig (2009) concluded that employee perception of a contract breach is not a function of a broken promise by the organization, but rather whether the organization fulfills the employee's expectations. Expectations are derived from past work experiences, norms, and comparisons made to other employers. A violation signals that the employer's original motives to build and maintain a mutually beneficial relationship have changed or were false from the beginning. Cavanaugh and Noe (1999) and Turnley and Feldman (2000) found that violations of the psychological contract negatively influenced employees' intent to remain with the employer and job satisfaction. The psychological contract binds the employee and employer—a form of guarantee that if each does his or her part, then the relationship will be mutually beneficial. Thus violations weaken the bond.

What is the typical employee response to violations of the psychological contract? Robinson et al. (1994) found that psychological contracts become less relational and more transactional following violations. Employees turn away from the socioemotional aspects of work and focus on the monetary benefits of the relationship. This has the effect of increasing the psychological distance between the employee and the employer, making the contract more transactional. A sequential pattern of five employee responses to violations has been identified. The first is *voice*: employees voice their concerns over the violations and seek to reinstate the contract. Dulebohn (1997) found that employees are somewhat reluctant to use formal mechanisms of voice because they fear subsequent reprisal by management. People who use formal voice mechanisms (grievance or appeal systems) are often labeled as organizational dissenters and

Table 10-3   *Types of violation of the psychological contract*

Violation Type	Definition	Examples
Training/development	Absence of training or training experience not as promised	"Sales training was promised as an integral part of marketing training. It never materialized."
Compensation	Discrepancies in promised and realized pay, benefits, and bonuses	"Specific compensation benefits were promised. Either they were not given to me, or I had to fight for them."
Promotion	Promotion or advancement schedule not as promised	"I perceived a promise that I had a good chance of promotion to manager in one year. While I received excellent performance ratings, I was not promoted in my first year."
Job security	Promises not met regarding the degree of job security one could expect	"The company promised that no one would be fired out of the training program, that all of us were safe until placement. In return for this security we accepted lower pay. The company subsequently fired four people from the training program."
Feedback	Feedback and reviews inadequate compared with what was promised	"I did not receive performance reviews as promised."
People	Employer perceived as having misrepresented the type of people at the firm, in terms of things such as their expertise, work style, or reputation	"It was promised as dynamic and as having a challenging environment . . . rubbing elbows with some of the brightest people in the business . . . a lie. The true picture started to come out after the initial hype of working at one of the best 100 companies in the country had worn off."

Source: Adapted from "Violating the Psychological Contract: Not the Exception but the Norm." by S. L. Robinson and D. M. Rousseau, 1994. *Journal of Organizational Behavior*, 15, pp. 245–259.

experience retaliation. Instead, employees are more likely to use subtle influence tactics to affect procedural justice. If unsuccessful, voice is followed by *silence*. Silence connotes compliance with the organization, but a loss of commitment. Silence is followed by *retreat*, as indicated by passivity, negligence, and shirking of responsibility. *Destruction* may then occur, whereby employees retaliate against the employer through theft, threats, sabotage, and in extreme cases, homicide. Finally, in the *exit* stage, employees quit the organization or provoke the organization to dismiss them. Research has shown that justice perceptions play a role in responses to violations of the psychological contract. In particular, procedural justice is of primary importance to employees whose relational contract was violated. The use of fair and equitable procedures by organizations can lessen the impact of the contract violation on employees.

Zhao et al. (2007) conducted a meta-analysis of breaches to the psychological contract; that is, employee perceptions regarding the extent to which an organization has failed to fulfill its promises or obligations. Breaches of the psychological contract were associated with higher mistrust, lower job satisfaction, lower organizational commitment, lower pro-social behavior, and lower job performance compared with the perceptions by employees that their psychological contract was not breached. In addition, Ng et al. (2010) found a cascading effect such that the negative effects of psychological contract breaches strengthen over time. Downsizing, outsourcing, and offshoring produce lower job security for employees. Individuals can lose something vital to their welfare—gainful employment—even if the employees are performing their jobs satisfactorily. Control over our own lives is vital for our sense of well-being (a topic

Cross-Cultural I/O Psychology: *Cross-Cultural Influences on Organizational Attitudes and Behavior*

Organizational attitudes and behaviors are strongly affected by cross-cultural influences. Research on many of the topics addressed in this chapter revealed culture-specific interpretations and applications. Lam et al. (1999) found that employees in Hong Kong and Japan were more likely to regard some facets of *organizational citizenship behavior* as an expected or defined part of the job than were employees in the United States and Australia. Thus what employees in some cultures consider extra-role (discretionary) behavior, employees in other cultures consider in-role (expected) behavior. There are also cross-cultural differences in *job satisfaction* that are consistent with the individualism–collectivism dimension. Workers in collectivist cultures derive more satisfaction from the social, collegial aspects of work, whereas workers in individualistic cultures derive more satisfaction from opportunities for advancement and achievement. There are cultural differences in *organizational justice* as pertaining to preferences for the distribution of resources. In collectivistic cultures greater justice is achieved by distributing resources equally because it helps to preserve harmony. In individualistic cultures greater justice is achieved by distributing resources on the basis of merit, such as differential pay raises on the basis of job performance. Finally, the scope of *psychological contracts* also differs by culture. Schalk and Rousseau (2001) described how societal and cultural beliefs influence the kind of exchanges that are negotiable between an employee and employer. A manager in the United States might avoid hiring close friends or family members because of possible allegations of conflict of interest. In other cultures hiring family members or friends might be viewed as desirable because the person is not unknown to the hiring manager. In some countries employment relationships are formally specified or "spelled out" so there is little room for discretionary give-and-take. In other countries there may be much more room for individual negotiation between the two parties, with the associated problem of fewer institutional and guaranteed protections afforded by the lack of formal employment policies. There is substantial variability in manifestations of organizational attitudes and behavior in cultures throughout the world.

addressed in the next chapter). The perceived loss of control over our own job security compels employees to move down the continuum toward a more transactional relationship with their employer, with the resulting effect of less employee commitment and loyalty toward the employer.

Based on a multinational analysis, Rousseau and Schalk (2000) concluded that the psychological contract as a promise-based exchange is widely generalizable to a variety of societies. Given the rise of global business, cultural differences in the psychological contract will most likely continue to evolve. For example, traditionally Asians prefer to first establish a relationship between parties and then carry out business transactions, whereas Westerners prefer to create a relationship through repeated business transactions. In the future it is likely that both styles will manifest themselves in new and varied forms (see Cross-Cultural I/O Psychology: *Cross-Cultural Influences on Organizational Attitudes and Behavior*).

Chapter Summary

- Moods and emotions are contagious, frequently manifested in organizations, and impact individuals' job performance and decisions.
- Individuals in an organizational context develop attitudes and exhibit behaviors associated with their participation in the organization.
- Job satisfaction is one of the most frequently studied organizational attitudes. How much people like their jobs is associated with both their individual personalities and the objective characteristics of the work they perform.
- Work commitment is a bond that can be directed toward one's occupation, organization, team, or a particular component of one's job.
- Employee engagement is a hybrid construct that has gained an increasing amount of attention and draws upon many theories in I/O psychology.
- Individuals evaluate the fairness of outcomes, procedures, and interactions within the workplace. These evaluations are related to other attitudes and behaviors.
- The actions of employees in going beyond their formal job duties and responsibilities to contribute to the welfare of the organization are called organizational citizenship behaviors.
- Counterproductive work behavior includes insults, threats, bullying, lies, theft, sabotage, physical violence, and occupational homicide.
- The various behavioral tactics that individuals within an organizational context use to enhance their self-interests represent organizational politics.
- The psychological contract is the exchange relationship between the individual and the organization. Although unwritten, it is based on the expectations each party has of itself and of the other party.
- Violations of the psychological contract (i.e., when one party has not lived up to the expectations of the other) result in a wide range of behaviors that often distance the two parties in the relationship.

Workplace Psychological Health

Learning Objectives

- Understand the concept of psychological health and its five major components.
- Explain the different types of work stressors and their impact on employees.
- Explain the basis of work-family conflict and work-family enrichment.
- Discuss how work schedules affect workplace psychological health.
- Describe the stigmatizing effect of dirty work on employees.
- Understand how drug and alcohol abuse affect the workforce.
- Understand the psychological effects of unemployment.
- Understand the issues surrounding the exploitation of children in the global workforce.

The Origins of Workplace Psychological Health

It will be recalled from Chapter 1 that early in the 20th century the principles of scientific management determined how work was performed. Work was broken down into specific discrete tasks. Performing one task (like attaching a nut to a bolt) might be an entire job for a worker. By using many workers in sequence, each one performing a task, an organization made a complete product. Such production methods were efficient, training time was minimal, little skill was required, and a departed worker could easily be replaced. Scientific management principles intentionally tried to separate "thinking" from "doing" on the part of the worker. No consideration was given to employee emotions at work because it was assumed that emotions interfered with productive work. Designing work that involved repetitive actions, perhaps performing the same task once every ten seconds, led to mind-numbing boredom and fatigue. However, in the early years of the 20th century, that was the price a worker paid for having a production job. This model of work persisted for much of the century.

Over time the workforce became more educated. Having a high school diploma, which was relatively rare in the early 1900s, became a traditional standard of educational achievement by mid-century. Proportionately fewer workers were willing to accept jobs that were so divorced from the human component. By the 1930s a topic began to emerge (commonly referred to as "mental hygiene") that addressed the affective and emotional issues associated with work. The profession of counseling psychology recognized that many life-related adjustment problems had some connection to people's work lives. Nevertheless, there was still a wide gap between industrial psychology (which was concerned primarily with work productivity issues) and counseling psychology (which was concerned with adjustment and health-related issues). By the mid-20th century the discipline of **workplace psychological health** (also referred to as *occupational health*) began to crystallize.

Workplace psychological health
A broad-based concept that refers to the mental, emotional, and physical well-being of employees in relation to the conduct of their work.

The acceptability and legitimacy of workplace psychological health to I/O psychologists were facilitated by the publication of a book in 1965 by Arthur Kornhauser entitled *Mental Health of the Industrial Worker*. Kornhauser (an I/O psychologist) interviewed 400 Detroit auto workers about their work (which was still performed under the principles of scientific management). Zickar (2003) credited the emergence of the field of workplace health psychology to Kornhauser's landmark book. Since that time the field has begun investigating questions related to occupational health and to work-family conflict. According to Zickar, Kornhauser's research helped pave the way for other I/O psychologists interested in worker well-being. As Barling and Griffiths (2003) noted, by the end of the 20th century workplace health psychology was embracing the very opposite beliefs to those proposed by scientific management at the start of the 20th century. In short, it took approximately one hundred years to reach the conclusion that a productive workforce depends on (and thus is not independent of) the health of the workforce.

The need to be concerned about workplace health is evidenced by sobering statistics about work-related deaths, accidents, and diseases. Kaplan and Tetrick (2011) reported that 2.2 million workers worldwide die annually from workplace injuries and illnesses. Brough et al. (2009) estimated there are annually 270 million non-fatal industrial accidents and 160 million work-related diseases worldwide. The decade of the 1970s, as noted by Brotherton (2003), witnessed the passage of laws designed to reduce the frequency and severity of workplace accidents and illnesses by creating enforceable health and safety standards. They include, for example, the *Occupational Safety and Health Act* (U.S.), the *Health and Safety at Work Act* (U.K.), and the *Occupational Health and Safety Act* (Australia). These laws (and related legislative acts) primarily focused on reducing the negative health consequences of work. In this era, I/O psychology directed itself to the examination of safe (and unsafe) behavior in the workplace, and conditions that led to their occurrence.

By the end of the 20th century I/O psychology recognized the need to expand its focus from reducing accidents and illnesses to promoting workplace psychological health. Workplace psychological health builds upon the legacy of mental hygiene and occupational safety, but also embraces the concept that organizations should actively create work environments that facilitate personal well-being. Hofmann and Tetrick (2003) referred to a state of well-being as "flourishing" in life, indexed by being inspired to learn, to be reasonably independent, and by possessing self-confidence. Cleveland and Colella (2010) stated that organizations should include measures of workplace psychological health as criteria for judging their own success. "We argue that employees, their families, and their communities all have a vested interest in workplaces that promote physical and mental health and all have a vested interest in minimizing a range of negative outcomes" (p. 538). Tetrick et al. (2010) recommended that in addition to organizations having policies designed to enhance psychological health, they include assessments of health in evaluating job candidates. Healthcare is typically among the largest costs of all industrialized nations. It is simply cheaper to promote health than to pay the cost of poor health. It is thus advantageous to have both employers and employees contribute to fostering workplace psychological health.

The relationship between work and health is sufficiently powerful as to occasion new words entering a language. The word *workaholic* in English refers to a person who is pathologically addicted to performing work. In Japanese *karoshi* refers to death by overwork, and it is estimated 10,000 individuals each year in Japan die from overwork (Brough et al., 2009). We spend more of our lives engaged in work than any other single activity (including sleep, for many people). The topic of workplace psychological health recognizes the inextricable link between our work life and our well-being. In Chapter 1 the major fields of interest to I/O psychology were presented. Workplace psychological health is directed toward one of those fields, the quality of work life (Hammer & Zimmerman, 2011).

The Concept of Psychological Health

To fully delve into the concept of workplace psychological health, it is important to have a better understanding of what is meant by psychological health in general. The idea of psychological health, as opposed to psychological illness, comes from the push within the field of psychology to focus on the positive parts of human nature and behavior. According to Seligman and Csikszentmihalyi (2000), for the past 60 years psychology has become a science largely about healing and fixing what is broken. For example, clinical psychologists have been primarily interested in mental illness and social psychologists have focused their attention toward such topics as what makes good people do bad things and why people often fail to help others. Seligman and

Positive psychology
The study of the factors
and conditions in life
that lead to pleasurable
and satisfying outcomes
for individuals.

Csikszentmihalyi proposed that psychologists should come to understand what makes life worth living, not just how to cope with and heal from negative life events. They argued that psychologists should direct their attention toward what is called **positive psychology**. As Luthans (2002) noted, "The aim of positive psychology is to shift the emphasis away from what is wrong with people to what is right with people—to focus on strengths (as opposed to weaknesses), to be interested in resilience (as opposed to vulnerability), and to be concerned with enhancing and developing wellness, prosperity and the good life (as opposed to the remediation of pathology)" (p. 697).

With the push toward positive psychology has come the push for a focus on psychological health. No single definition of psychological health exists; it is easier to understand the meaning of psychological health by referencing its determinants. Societal standards contribute to the meaning of psychological health (with many derived from contemporary Western society) as well as standards proposed by the medical profession regarding psychological illness. We will not explore the varied contributions of these sources in conceptualizing psychological health. Rather, we will take an overall view of psychological health as proposed by Warr (2007) and focus on its five major components.

1. **Affective well-being**. Warr and Clapperton (2010) stipulated that psychological well-being has two dimensions: pleasure and activation (as shown in Figure 11-1). The combination of the pleasure and activation dimensions results in the following quadrants: Enthusiasm, Comfort, Anxiety, and Depression. For example, the lower left section of Figure 11-1 reveals terms such as *gloomy* and *fatigued*, reflecting both low pleasure and low activation. The highest levels of affective well-being are presented in the upper right section of the figure. Terms such as *alert* and *elated* indicate both high pleasure and high activation. In general, a person's affective well-being can be described in terms of the proportion of time spent in each of the four sections of Figure 11-1. Warr noted the word *happiness* is typically avoided by psychologists in their professional lives. Instead, terms like *well-being* or *positive affect* are typically used. Warr believes that happiness would be a more useful explanatory construct. "People are fascinated by the presence or absence of happiness, recognizing a strong personal relevance and wishing better to understand the experience" (p. 17). Warr cited a study that surveyed college students in 47 countries. Of all personal values, including wealth, health, and love, happiness was overwhelmingly rated the most important. Accordingly, Warr asserted that research on people in work organizations would have greater impact on a wider population if it were presented in terms of happiness or unhappiness, rather than the more technical terms frequently used by scientists.

2. **Competence**. Good psychological health is evidenced by being successful in various sectors of life's activities, such as relationships with others, gainful employment, and adaptability. The competent person has adequate psychological resources to deal with life's problems. It has been suggested that dealing with adversity in life provides a strong test of one's psychological health. A successful response to adversity requires a mixture of adaptive skills as well as beliefs and opinions that are consistent with reality.

3. **Autonomy**. Autonomy is the freedom to choose the path of one's own behavior. Psychologically healthy people have the capacity to express their values and preferences when choosing their actions. This contrasts sharply with the feel-

ing of being helpless when one is confronted with life's difficulties. The contribution of autonomy to psychological health appears to be given greater importance in Western than in Eastern cultures.

4. **Aspiration**. A psychologically healthy person is always striving to achieve a more desirable outcome. It is this sense of striving, being focused, and having a strong goal orientation that invigorates people to channel their energies. In striving to achieve personal goals, one may face stressful situations, and indeed one may create them by pursuing difficult challenges. Low levels of aspiration are associated with a sense of resignation and acceptance of one's current conditions, no matter how unsatisfying they may be.

5. **Integrated functioning**. The capstone dimension of psychological health is the most difficult to define and is most unlike the other four. Warr stated, "Integrated functioning concerns the person as a whole. People who are mentally healthy exhibit several forms of balance, harmony, and inner relatedness" (p. 59).

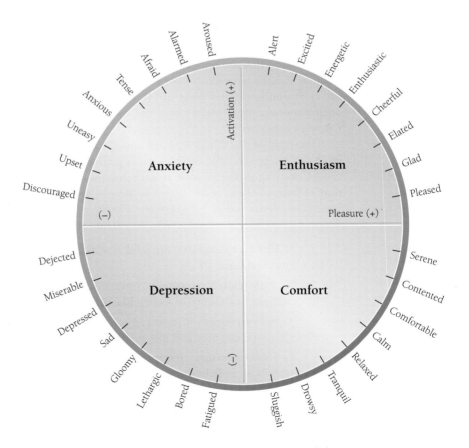

Figure 11-1 *Two-dimensional model of psychological well-being*

Adapted from *The joy of work? Jobs, happiness, and you,* by P. B. Warr and G. Clapperton, 2010. Reprinted with permission from Routledge.

Integrated functioning is the hallmark of psychologically healthy people in that they have found a way to balance the two. Integrated functioning is the most difficult goal to achieve as our lives are continuously pushed and pulled in competing directions.

Warr's portrayal of psychological health represents a comprehensive assessment of the major dimensions of psychological well-being. Competence, autonomy, and aspiration reflect aspects of a person's behavior in relation to the environment and often determine a person's affective well-being. For example, an inability to cope with current difficulties (a form of low competence) may give rise to distress (an aspect of low affective well-being). Affective well-being has its roots in medical criteria; the person reports feeling well and also not being impaired psychologically or physically. Integrated functioning, however, deals with the multiple relationships among the four components and covers broader issues.

Workplace Stress

Stressor

Anything that evokes a stress reaction.

Stress is a pervasive phenomenon, not only for one's work life but for life in general. It is also the biggest challenge to achieving psychological health. When individuals feel "stressed" they are not experiencing high levels of affective well-being. The stress reaction is characterized to a large extent by low pleasure and high activation (see Figure 11-1). Sonnentag and Frese (2013) note that, in general, job stress is related to low organizational commitment, higher turnover rates, and an increase in counterproductive work behaviors.

There are many things that can evoke stress reactions in the workplace. These **stressors** can be one-time events, such as getting fired or losing a large client, or they can be ongoing problems such as daily hassles or constantly having to deal with a rude colleague. They can be caused by people, technology, or any number of things (see Social Media and I/O Psychology: *The Stress Potential of Social Media at Work*). Sonnentag and Frese grouped work stressors into the following eight categories.

1. **Physical stressors** - Stressful aspects of the environment, such as aversive working conditions.

2. **Task-related stressors** - Aspects of one's task that create stress, such as interruptions, monotony, or feeling like there is too much to do in too little time.

3. **Role stressors** - Stressful aspects associated with one's role, including role conflict, role ambiguity, and role overload, as discussed in Chapter 8.

4. **Social stressors** - Interpersonal aspects that cause stress, such as conflicts with one's boss, bullying, and sexual harassment from a coworker.

5. **Work schedule-related stressors** - Aspects about one's work time arrangement that creates stress, such as shift work and overtime.

6. **Career-related stressors** - Stress-inducing aspects related to one's livelihood, including layoffs, unemployment, and a lack of career opportunities.

7. **Traumatic events** - Major incidents that cause stress, such as exposure to danger, natural disasters, and workplace homicide.

Social Media and I/O Psychology: *The Stress Potential of Social Media at Work*

Everywhere you turn there are references to social media. One need not be online to be reminded of the social world that awaits them there. News anchors invite you to follow them on Twitter, companies request that you like them on Facebook, and restaurants invite you to leave favorable reviews for them on Yelp. It seems that social media are inescapable, and when it comes to employees, can be potentially overwhelming.

Bucher et al. (2013) found that social media can be stressful for employees due to potential information overload, invasion, and uncertainty. First, they pointed out that individuals are constantly being inundated with information from a variety of social media outlets. As such, they may feel overwhelmed by the sheer amount of information they encounter. Second, individuals may feel like the constant exposure to social media, particularly as it pertains to work, may interfere with their non-work lives. As they note, "the advent of social media entails a blurring of boundaries between the private and the work domain, as the conversation on social media never rests and workers can be connected to it 24 hours a day on their (mobile) communication devices; this can lead to an invasion of work into the private domain and recreation time" (p. 1640). Lastly, because there are so many different social media outlets, all possibly conveying different – and perhaps competing – messages, it may be difficult for people to keep track of what is important and urgent. Thus, social media may create uncertainty, which can be stressful for employees as they try to navigate the workplace.

Currently, little research exists regarding how to manage social media to reduce its capacity to induce stress. Nevertheless, given the potential stress that social media can cause, individuals may want to consider how they can best manage their social media usage. Bucher et al. suggested we should learn how to limit the effects of social media that produce information overload (such as knowing how to turn off notification alerts). In short, despite its advantages and appeal, it may be healthy to disconnect from social media every now and then.

8. **Stressful change processes** - Stressors resulting from huge changes, such as mergers and acquisitions or the widespread implementation of new technology.

Challenge stressors
Job demands or characteristics that create positive feelings of achievement or fulfillment.

Hindrance stressors
Job demands or characteristics that are demotivating and hinder one's ability to achieve his or her goals.

Not all stressors impact people in the same way. Some stressors may actually result in increased performance, for example, whereas others might result in performance deficits. Cavanaugh et al. (2000) noted that job stressors can be separated into two broad categories: challenge stressors and hindrance stressors. **Challenge stressors** include job demands or characteristics that produce positive feelings, such as feelings of achievement or fulfillment. These would include such things as job overload, time pressures, or high levels of responsibility. **Hindrance stressors**, on the other hand, are demands or characteristics that are demotivating and problematic in that they hinder individuals' abilities to achieve their goals. These would include such things as concerns about job insecurity and organizational politics. A meta-analysis by LePine et al. (2005) revealed that challenge stressors positively impact performance while hindrance stressors negatively impact performance. Similarly, Podsakoff et al. (2007) found that hindrance stressors were negatively related to job satisfaction and organizational commitment and positively related to turnover whereas challenge stressors yielded opposite relationships with those same outcome variables.

Job demands-resources model
An explanatory model describing the ways in which resources can buffer the negative psychological and physical effects of job demands.

The impact of stressors on individuals can be lessened by the presence of resources the individuals have available to them. Demerouti et al. (2001) developed the **job demands-resources model** to explain how resources can provide a buffer against the stressors that individuals face. Individuals are faced with numerous demands throughout their day. With these demands come certain physiological and psychological costs. For example, as individuals are given more duties to perform, they may become physically tired and emotionally drained. Over time these demands and the physical and emotional toll that accompanies them may lead individuals to experience burnout. *Burnout* refers to the exhaustion and diminished interest in work that individuals feel after prolonged exposure to occupational stress. According to Demerouti et al., resources can help to buffer the impact of stressors and minimize the negative effects on one's health and motivation. Resources include anything that helps individuals achieve their goals, reduces the costs associated with job demands, and helps individuals grow and develop. This can include supervisor support, rewards, and feedback. Nahrgang et al. (2011) provided meta-analytic support that job demands such as risks and hazards are related to burnout whereas resources such as a supportive environment are related to engagement.

Personal characteristics can also serve as resources for managing stressful events. Not all individuals are impacted by stressors in the same ways or to the same extent. Some people are more resilient to their effects while others succumb to their negative effects more easily. What is happily busy for one person may be overwhelming for another. Tetrick and Peiró (2012) noted that stress reactions differ for individuals depending on their levels of resilience, tolerance for ambiguity, and perceptions of control. In general, those individuals who are higher on each of those characteristics tend to have fewer negative reactions to stressors.

Psychological capital
A personal resource consisting of hope, optimism, self-efficacy, and resilience that impacts one's psychological health and helps combat occupational stress.

Another personal resource available to individuals is their **psychological capital**. According to Luthans et al. (2007), psychological capital is "characterized by: (1) having confidence (self-efficacy) to take on and put in the necessary effort to succeed at challenging tasks; (2) making a positive attribution (optimism) about succeeding now and in the future; (3) persevering toward goals and, when necessary, redirecting paths to goals (hope) to succeed; and (4) when beset by problems and adversity, sustaining and bouncing back and even beyond (resilience) to attain success" (p. 3). Avey et al. (2009) found that psychological capital was related to fewer job stress symptoms in a sample of 416 working adults. Furthermore, in a meta-analysis of the literature, Avey et al. (2011) demonstrated that psychological capital is related to heightened psychological well-being, job satisfaction, organizational commitment, organizational citizenship behaviors, and job performance as well as lower anxiety and job stress. Thus, individuals with greater psychological capital are likely to demonstrate lower stress and heightened psychological health while individuals who lack hope, are unsure of themselves, are pessimistic about the future, and are unable to bounce back from problems are likely to have more stress and lower psychological health.

Balancing Work and Non-Work

Sigmund Freud was once asked what he thought a "normal" person should be able to do well. He is reported to have said "Lieben und Arbeiten" ("to love and to work;"

Field Note 1: *The Meaning of Work*

Why do people work? This seemingly simple question has been debated for centuries from many perspectives, including religion, economics, psychology, and philosophy. Some religious doctrine teaches that work is a form of punishment for our original sin. Work is an obligation or duty toward building God's kingdom. Work is thus good, and hard work even better. Work is noble because of its taxing nature and because it is a hardship that strengthens our character. Religious teachings also emphasized work as a means of controlling and restraining our passions. Lack of work, or idleness, fosters unhealthy impulses, which deflect us from more admirable pursuits. Thus work is thought of as an arduous process, deliberately filled with hardships, a means of facilitating our personal development. The view from an economic perspective is that work provides us with the financial resources to sustain life and the aspiration to improve the quality of our material life. The most commonly accepted interpretation of *work*—the exchange of labor services for pay—clearly reflects an economic viewpoint. Work has psychological meaning as well, giving us a source of identity and union with other individuals, in addition to being a source of personal accomplishment. Work also has the effect of providing a temporal rhythm to our lives. Our work gives us our time structure—when we have to leave for work and when we are off work to pursue other activities. Finally, work even provides a philosophical explanation of our mission in life: to derive meaning from creating and giving service to others. As can be inferred, there is no one answer to the question of why we work, but its multiple meanings provide a basis to understand why work is so important.

Erickson, 1963, p. 265). Freud believed that it is through one's family that love-related needs are gratified and that work has a more powerful effect than any other aspect of human life in binding a person to reality. Therefore Freud's call for a normal person to love and to work can be interpreted as an emphasis on both work and family for healthy psychological functioning (Quick et al., 1992). Work and the role it plays in our lives has been a subject of interest and controversy down through recorded history (see Field Note 1: *The Meaning of Work*). Opinions about work are highly varied, as reflected in the following three quotations:

- "Work consists of whatever a body is obligated to do. Play consists of whatever a body is not obligated to do."—Mark Twain

- "The world is full of willing people; some willing to work, the rest willing to let them."—Robert Frost

- "The first sign of a nervous breakdown is when you start thinking your work is terribly important."—Milo Bloom

A person's work and occupational stature play a critical role in an individual's sense of identity, self-esteem, and psychological well-being. Work is the central and defining characteristic of life for most individuals. Work may have intrinsic value, instrumental value, or both. The intrinsic value of work is the value an individual finds in performing the work, in and of itself. The instrumental value of work is in providing the necessities of life and serving as a channel for the individual's talents, abilities, and knowledge. It has been suggested that the split in a person's work and home identities dates back to the Industrial Revolution of the mid-19th century. It was then that it became necessary for a person to leave the home and "go to work."

Interest in family-related issues by I/O psychologists has manifested itself primarily in the past 30 years. For many years we tended to limit our focus to work-related issues (e.g., tasks, jobs, occupations, organizations) and left the subject of domestic matters (e.g., family) to other areas of professional study. However, I/O psychologists began to see legitimate linkages or connections between the two spheres of work and family and thus have expanded our areas of inquiry.

Zedeck (1992) described the following three topics as targets of work-family research.

- *The effect of work on family.* This area examines what impact work factors have on family matters. To express this relationship in terms of research design, *work* is regarded as the independent variable and *family* is the dependent variable. This perspective is most typical of I/O psychological research.

- *The effect of family on work.* This perspective is the opposite of the former and generally focuses on how structural or developmental aspects of the family have an impact on work behavior. For example, some researchers have viewed family life as a "shock absorber:" if home life is positive, it blocks disappointment at work. Others view family responsibility as a major determinant of work absenteeism and tardiness.

- *The work–family interaction.* This third perspective views work and family as interacting and concludes that there is no simple or direct link between work and family matters. One view of the family–work interaction concerns the compatibility or incompatibility of family–work relationships and their impact on other processes, such as the transition between roles.

Whether the responsibilities and obligations of work and family interfere with one another or benefit one another has been a topic of great interest to work-family researchers. On the one hand, one's work and family roles can interfere with one another and cause problems. The feeling of having too little time or energy to complete all tasks in both life domains can feel overwhelming and wreak havoc on an individual. On the other hand, the money earned from work can certainly help make home life easier. Furthermore, having a job can make you a more interesting person at home, giving you things to talk about with your loved ones. Thus, the interactions between work and family can result in either *negative spillover*, in which one domain hinders the other, or *positive spillover*, in which one domain benefits the other. These two forms of spillover result in work-family conflict and work-family enrichment, respectively. These two constructs are discussed in more detail below.

Work-family conflict
The result of conflicting demands between work and family making it difficult to effectively participate in both domains.

Work-family Conflict

Work-family conflict is the result of having conflicting demands of work and family responsibilities. According to Allen (2013), work-family conflict has its theoretical basis in the scarcity hypothesis, which states that individuals have a finite amount of resources (time, energy, attention). When too much of one resource is allocated to a particular domain, the other suffers. For every hour that an employee spends working, there is one less hour the person can devote to his or her family life. Similarly, when a person is experiencing a great deal of stress at home, he or she may not have the energy to perform as effectively at work. The result of these situations is work-family conflict. This conflict can be viewed as bi-directional with both work and family interfering with one another, or can be described directionally, with work interfering with family or family interfering with work.

Researchers have also demonstrated that work-family conflict can have a considerable negative impact on one's psychological and physical health. Work-family conflict is related to poor eating habits, weight gain, lower sleep quality and quantity, and increased alcohol abuse (Allen & Armstrong, 2006; M. Wang et al., 2010). Based on a broad national survey of employees, Frone (2000) reported that employees who reported experiencing work-family conflict were up to 30 times more likely to experience a clinically significant psychological health problem than were employees who reported no work-family conflict. In addition, work-family conflict results in negative outcomes for both work and family domains. Amstad et al. (2011) demonstrated that where conflict is seen as originating (from work-to-family or family-to-work) is important when predicting outcomes. They found that work-to-family conflict is more strongly associated with work-related outcomes such as lower job satisfaction, organizational commitment, and performance while family-to-work conflict is more strongly associated with family-related outcomes, including lower satisfaction with one's marriage and family. Allen noted that the reason the origin of the conflict seems to matter is because that is where the blame for the conflict is attributed. So, when individuals see work as causing the conflict, their satisfaction and commitment with their work suffers. This explains to some extent why I/O psychologists have focused a greater deal of attention toward work interfering with family rather than family interfering with work.

Given the negative consequences of work-family conflict, researchers have devoted considerable attention to understanding who is most likely to experience conflict, and under what circumstances it is likely to occur. Byron (2005) conducted a meta-analysis of work-family conflict antecedents and, in line with the notion that people "blame" the domain seen as causing the conflict, found that work demands are related to work-to-family conflict whereas family demands are related to family-to-work conflict. Byron further found that the number of children at home was a strong predictor of both directions of work-family conflict. Ford et al. (2007) found that families with children experienced a stronger negative relationship between hours of work per week and family satisfaction. Employees without children were better able to sustain a satisfactory family life despite long work hours. In addition, Byron found that single parents report more conflict than do married parents. Lastly, while it is often believed that women experience more work-family conflict than men, her results demonstrated that men and women actually report very similar levels of conflict.

MacDermid et al. (2002) noted that psychologists tend to study enduring characteristics of people (such as cognitive ability and personality) when it may be short-term phenomena that best explain feelings of work-family conflict. They noted: "Although we cognitively recognize the presence of conflict most of the time, we feel it only some of the time" (pp. 402–403). MacDermid et al. believe that a better understanding of our emotions may help explain the causes of work-family conflict because the transfer of emotions (e.g., anger) across situations tends to occur over very short intervals, such

Reality Check: © United Features Syndicate, Inc.

as a few hours or days. Livingston and Judge (2008) concluded that one consequence of work-family conflict may be guilt. Explained in terms of emotions, one basis for the appeal of flexible work hours and increased vacation time is they may reduce feelings of guilt among people incurring work-family conflict.

Casper et al. (2007) noted that most of our knowledge about work-family conflict is based upon the traditional concept of a family, and employees working in managerial and professional jobs. We know far less about single-parent families and members of other types of occupations. Dierdorff and Ellington (2008) examined occupational differences in work-family conflict. They found greater conflict in occupations that require substantial interactions between people to accomplish work. Jobs such as police detectives, firefighters, and medical practitioners produced higher work-family conflict than taxi drivers, insurance examiners, and bank tellers. Jobs that induce low work-family conflict offer an opportunity for individuals to leave their work at the office. The authors proposed that individuals can seek membership in certain occupations because of their reduced possibility of producing work-family conflict.

Work-family Enrichment

In line with the push toward positive psychology, work-family researchers have focused their attention on the benefits of individuals participating in multiple roles. As

Morganson et al. (2013) highlight, many concepts have emerged to describe the positive relationship between one's work and personal life, with the fundamental idea being that the positive spillover between work and family can enrich, enhance, and facilitate one another. Crain and Hammer (2013) defined **work-family enrichment** as "the degree to which experiences in one role improve the quality of life in the other role, through the transfer of resources or positive affect from one role to the other" (p. 305). According to Greenhaus and Powell (2006), individuals acquire a variety of resources from different role experiences. For example, in addition to material resources like money, work also helps individuals gain skills and broaden their perspectives, develop their social network, and generate greater psychological resources such as self-efficacy. With these additional resources, individuals are better able to manage the interactions between their multiple roles. In addition, work and family are likely enriched by the other through an affective pathway. Positive affect that is generated in one domain, such as work, can spill over to the other domain. For instance, an employee who receives accolades from his boss may develop a good mood at work that transfers over to his home life, thereby enriching his interactions with his family.

In their review of the literature, Crain and Hammer reported that work-family enrichment has been shown to be impacted by work-related variables (such as family-supportive supervisors and job resources) and nonwork-related variables (such as spousal support and community involvement). Michel et al. (2011) conducted a meta-analysis on the relationship between Big 5 personality dimensions and work-family enrichment and found that extraversion, agreeableness, conscientiousness, and openness to experience are related to higher levels of enrichment.

Similar to the notion that individuals appear to "blame" a particular domain for causing conflict, Voydanoff (2005) suggested that people will credit their enhanced performance in one role to the resources generated in the other. Thus, whereas negative outcomes were associated with the originating domain with work-family conflict, positive benefits would be associated for work-family enrichment. In line with this, Crain and Hammer found that more studies showed that enrichment originating in the family (vs. work) was related to family satisfaction, while enrichment originating at work (vs. family) was related to lower turnover intentions. However, McNall et al. (2010) found that both directions of enrichment were related to job satisfaction and organizational commitment. In addition, they found that both directions are related to increased physical and mental health.

Ilies et al. (2011) proposed the concept of work-family interpersonal capitalization, which they defined as "an active response to positive work events that involves sharing or discussing such events with one's spouse or partner at home" (p. 118). They suggested that by simply sharing the positive events that occur at work with loved ones at home, individuals are able to highlight their resources and affirm their self-worth. In addition, by sharing their experiences, they are able to relive and savor the positive experience, thereby enhancing their mood. This good mood could be contagious to their partner, ultimately facilitating positive work-family interactions. Culbertson et al. (2012) found that the more people talked with their partner about the good things that happened at work, the more their work engagement facilitated their work-family interactions. When people capitalized on their work experiences by sharing them with their loved ones, they felt like their work was helping them function more effectively at home.

Work-family enrichment
The extent to which work and family roles enhance and facilitate one another's functioning.

Work-family Interventions

Nations differ in the extent to which they have policies that help employees manage their work-family interactions. Hammer and Zimmerman (2011) stated, "The United States is the only industrialized nation without a formal paid leave program in response to the birth or adoption of a child. For example, in Europe and Japan maternity leave is state supported until children reach school age" (p. 403). The *Family and Medical Leave Act* offers *unpaid* job-protected leaves of absence for up to 12 weeks in the United States during any 12-month period for childbirth, adoption, foster care placement, or care for oneself or immediate family member (child, spouse, parent) for a serious health condition. Other nations provide new parents with *paid* leaves for up to 14 weeks (and in some cases, longer). In addition, the United States lags behind other countries in terms of publicly-funded childcare assistance programs and mandated paid sick leave policies (Allen, 2013). According to Williams (2010), "Failures of public policy are a key reason that Americans face such acute work-family conflict" (p. 8).

Individual and organizational interventions have been shown to be effective at reducing work-family conflict and helping enhance work-family enrichment. Hornung et al. (2008) noted that some individuals create what are known as "idiosyncratic deals" with their employers; special arrangements meant to help them meet their personal needs and preferences. For example, an employee may ask to start and end the workday earlier to allow him or her to pick up a child from school. Alternatively, employees may negotiate with their managers for training opportunities that may not be available to others (such as a special workshop). According to Morganson et al. (2013), "Idiosyncratic deals become an important individual coping strategy in situations where organizational policy and support are lacking" (p. 218). Organizations can also be impactful in helping employees effectively integrate their work and family roles. Baltes and Heydens-Gahir (2003) noted that changes in the social pattern of worker participation have forced companies to make accommodations to their workers. These accommodations are directed toward reducing the conflict between work and family, which if ignored, ultimately lead to lower efficiency in the workplace. Such inefficiency is reflected in more tardiness, absenteeism, turnover, and stress-related reductions in job performance. Frone (2003) cited flexible work hours, compressed workweeks, working at home, and leaves of absence as examples of organizational initiatives to reduce work-family conflict (see Field Note 2: *Artificial Energy*). Hammer et al. (2013) noted that simply having formal work-family benefits in place helps retain employees and increases their commitment and satisfaction, even when employees don't use the benefits themselves.

Onsite or near-site childcare centers have been developed to reduce work-family conflict. Companies may develop such centers exclusively for their own employees or in a consortium with other employees for use by several participating companies. Approximately 1,400 onsite or near-site childcare centers are sponsored by employers in the United States. Although their number is growing, many companies are too small to have the resources to provide such a center. Spector et al. (2007) reported findings of particular relevance to global organizations. The creation of flexible working hours and organization-based childcare were created in response to lowering work-family conflict. However, these interventions were based upon the needs of employees in predominately Western cultures. The authors found that in Asian, Eastern European, and

Field Note 2: *Artificial Energy*

An adage from clinical psychology is, "Some disorders are best detected by their disguise." A parallel statement from I/O psychology might be, "Some work-related problems are best detected by our attempts to address them." In the on-going battle to fulfill the demands on our time, including trying to balance work-family conflict, one of the resources we sacrifice is sleep time. While individuals differ in the amount of sleep needed to feel rested and rejuvenated, the average is about 8 hours. The time needed to complete all our self-imposed duties often requires a sacrifice of something else, and often what is sacrificed is the seemingly unproductive time we devote to sleep. So we "cheat," trading an hour or two of sleep for another hour or two for performing work or personal tasks. What is the consequence? We are often sleepy, fatigued, and inattentive. Recognizing this widespread condition, many artificial stimulant products have been created to combat chronic tiredness. These products include highly caffeinated beverages that are touted to "provide energy" or "boost stamina." Products designed to achieve the same effect also are marketed in the form of food or over-the-counter medications. It is questionable what the consumer demand would be for these products if we felt less sleep-deprived. In short, tampering with the normal rhythm of our lives produces unwanted side effects. Many of the currently available products used to address these side effects were not commercially available one generation ago.

Latin American countries, parents of employees often live in close proximity to their children and grandchildren. This older generation is a resource not as readily available to employees in Western cultures. Accordingly, there would be less of a need for organizations to provide means of reducing work-family conflict in these parts of the world (see Cross-Cultural I/O Psychology: *Organizational Paternalism*).

Major and Germano (2006) commented on the relationship between an ever-changing work world and the unchanging responsibility to achieve balance between our work and family lives. "It is rather ironic that in this discussion of the changing nature of work the one thing that has not changed is the notion that work-family behavior is the employee's problem to solve. Until social and political movements aimed at reducing work hours and protecting personal time gain momentum, it is up to individual employees to be their own best advocates in pursuing accommodations that create a desirable work-family interface" (p. 32).

Flexible Work Arrangements

The concept of flexible work arrangements allows individuals more discretionary control regarding when and where work is performed. As succinctly stated by Allen et al. (2010), "Work is viewed as something that gets done, not a place" (p. 379). Flexible work arrangements offer temporal flexibility (when work is done) and spatial flexibility

Cross-Cultural I/O Psychology: *Organizational Paternalism*

Western culture draws a clear distinction between the work and non-work spheres of our lives. Although in theory we can partition our lives into two separate realms, in reality they may not easily mesh. We speak of the need to balance our work and non-work roles, having time and energy for both. When the two roles clash, we speak of role conflict. Technology permits employees to embed one role inside another – the concept of working from home or telework.

Non-Western cultures adopt more of a holistic approach to life. That is, there is less of a clear segmentation between work and non-work. The concept of organizations assuming a *paternalistic* (derived from the Latin word, *pater*, meaning father) demeanor is traditional in non-Western cultures. Aycan (2000) described organizational paternalism: "The role of the supervisor is to provide care, protection, and guidance to the subordinate both in work and non-work domains" (p. 466). Namazie and Tayeb (2006) noted that "employees view their managers and sympathetic brothers and sisters as compassionate fathers and mothers who are frequently involved in their employees' private lives and family matters" (p. 29). In a literal sense of the word, a collectivistic cultural value incorporates work and non-work domains into a whole.

Aycan and Gelfand (2012) identified a subtle artifact of paternalistic organizations. In Western cultures religion is a private and individual matter. In the context of employment in the United States, religion is typically referenced only in regard to religious holidays and religion being a legally protected group. Aycan and Gelfand observed that in the Latin American culture the presence of religious images and sculptures are common in the workplace. The U.S. was founded on the separation of church and state (government). There is an associated desire to separate church from the workplace.

(where work is done). More specifically, flexible work allows employees to determine where they work, when they start and stop work, which days or shifts they work, and how many hours they work (Kossek & Michel, 2011). Shockley and Allen (2012) found that employees are more motivated to use flexible work arrangements to avoid distractions and be more efficient in their work than use such arrangements to manage competing work and family obligations. Nevertheless, flexible work does provide employees more discretion in how they manage work-family conflict.

Kossek and Michel cited one of the earliest adoptions of flexible work occurring in 1930 during the Great Depression. The Kellogg Company, the largest maker of cereal, wanted to reduce growing unemployment by converting from three 8-hour shifts to four 6-hour shifts. It was reported that employee morale increased, there were fewer industrial accidents, and work productivity increased. Many years later there are other ways to facilitate flexible work arrangements. Most of them are technology based. The use of laptop computers, tablets, and cell phones allows work to be conducted independent of any physical location. New words have entered our language reflective of the contemporary work world, such as *teleworker* (a person who works outside of a traditional physical location using electronic technology) and *flexplace* (any location, as one's home, a café, or even a vacation resort where work can be performed). Kossek and Michel suggested the meaning of "flexible work" may shift over time as it becomes increasingly more common. While flexible work can offer greater personal control over people's lives, it is not without limitations. For example, Golden et al. (2008) reported teleworking produced social isolation from other employees and supervisors. One of the benefits of traditional employment is it provides face-to-face contact with cowork-ers, and allows people to become members of a social network. Such opportunities are not as readily available to employees who work out of their homes.

Non-traditional work arrangements include flextime, compressed workweeks, and shift work. Each has produced positive and negative consequences for both employers and employees.

Flexible Work Hours

Flextime
A schedule of work hours that permits employees flexibility in when they arrive at and leave work.

One variation in flexible work schedules is flexible working hours, popularly known as **flextime**. According to Kossek and Michel, 56% of U.S. employers offer flextime to their workers. The main objective of flextime is to create an alternative to the tradi-tional fixed working schedule by giving workers some choice in arrival and departure times. The system is usually arranged so that everyone must be present during certain designated hours ("coretime"), but there is latitude in other hours ("flexband"). For example, coretime may be 9:00 a.m. to 3:00 p.m. and flexband may be 6:00 a.m. to 6:00 p.m. Some employees may start working at 9:00 a.m. and work until 6:00 p.m.; some may end at 3:00 p.m. by starting at 6:00 a.m.; others work any combination in between (see Figure 11-2). Flexible working hours may alleviate problems with family commitments, recreation, second jobs, commuting, and stress.

Narayanan and Nath (1982) examined the impact of flextime at two organiza-tional levels: lower-level and professional employees. They concluded that flextime pri-marily benefited lower-level employees by giving them more flexibility in their sched-ules. For professional employees, the flextime system merely formalized the already existing informal system they had with the company. In a six-year study of flextime, Dalton and Mesch (1990) reported large reductions in employee absenteeism com-pared with a control group that had regular work hours. However, the rates of turn-over in the two groups were the same.

Allen et al. (2013) found meta-analytic evidence that the availability of flextime policies is related to reduced work-family conflict whereas the actual use of such poli-cies is unrelated to work-family conflict. They surmised that the reason for this finding is that having flextime policies in place may provide employees with a sense of control regarding whether they use the policies or not. This would presumably impact the ex-tent to which they see their work as interfering with their family lives. Actually using the policies, however, may increase *or* decrease control because some employees may be using flextime by choice whereas others may be forced to use it (e.g., being told they have to telecommute).

Although there is ample evidence that flextime benefits individuals (Gottlieb et al., 1998), it is likely to be detrimental to the functioning of teams. If employees

Flexible Start Time		Core Time		Flexible Stop Time
6 a.m.	9 a.m.	12 p.m.	3 p.m.	6 p.m.

Figure 11-2 *Schedule of flexible work hours*

must work as a team, the individualized schedules that flextime permits may limit the continuity of the team. However, additional research is needed to address this issue.

Compressed Workweek

Employees traditionally have worked 8 hours a day, 5 days a week, for a 40-hour workweek. Some employees work 10 hours a day for 4 days, popularly known as the "4/40." Kossek and Michel reported that 15% of U.S. employers have compressed workweeks, and they are most frequently evidenced in law enforcement and health-care occupations.

There are several obvious advantages to a compressed workweek for both the individual and the organization. Individuals have a three-day weekend, which gives them more recreation time, the chance to work a second job, more time for family life, and so on. However, the possible drawbacks include worker fatigue, fewer productive hours, and more accidents. Baltes et al. (1999) concluded on the basis of a meta-analysis that there are mixed effects of the compressed workweek related to the specific outcome criterion in question. For example, compressed workweeks seem to increase job satisfaction, but they do not lead to reductions in absences. Furthermore, working extended hours can create disturbances in workers' eating patterns. In line with this, Caruso et al. (2004) found that shift work was associated with digestive problems, cardiovascular disease, and weight gain.

In a major review of the 4/40, Ronen and Primps (1981) concluded that the work schedule had a positive effect on home and family life as well as on leisure and recreation. There appeared to be no change in employee job performance, however. There were mixed results with regard to absenteeism, and worker fatigue definitely increased.

A few studies have been reported on reactions to a 12-hour shift, typically noon to midnight and then midnight to noon. The results are mixed. Breaugh (1983) reported that nurses on 12-hour shifts experienced substantial fatigue associated with the longer hours. However, the midnight-to-noon shift felt more out of phase with physiological and social rhythms than did the noon-to-midnight shift. Pierce and Dunham (1992) reported significant improvements in attitudes toward the work schedule, general affect, and fatigue in a sample of police officers who switched from a rotating 8-hour-shift work schedule to a fixed 12-hour schedule. Duchon et al. (1994) examined underground miners who switched from an 8-hour to a 12-hour schedule. The miners reported improved sleep quality with the new schedule, but fatigue had either no change or only slight improvement. The findings from such studies may be influenced by the variety of jobs examined in the research.

Shift Work

Not all employees work from 8:00 a.m. to 5:00 p.m., Monday through Friday. The nature of the services performed may necessitate other schedules. Police officers, firefighters, and healthcare providers must supply 24-hour-a-day service. In industrial manufacturing, some technology requires constant monitoring and operation. It isn't practical to shut off furnaces, boilers, and chemical process operations at 5:00 p.m. just because workers go home. In those cases it is advantageous to have different shifts

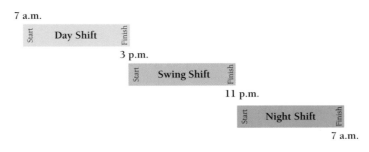

Figure 11-3   *Sample shift work schedule*

work around the clock. Jex et al. (2013) note that approximately 40% of employees in the United States are engaged in shift work, with men and racial minorities more likely to have these nonstandard schedules. Psychologists have become interested in how different hours (or **shift work**) affect occupational health.

There are no uniform shift-work hours; companies use different shifts (see Figure 11-3). Usually a 24-hour day is divided into three 8-hour work shifts, like 7:00 a.m.–3:00 p.m. (day shift), 3:00 p.m.–11:00 p.m. (swing shift), and 11:00 p.m.– 7:00 a.m. (night shift). Some companies have employees work just one shift, but workers generally don't like the swing and night shifts, so many firms rotate the shifts. Employees may work two weeks on the day shift, two weeks on the swing shift, and then two weeks on the night shift. A shift workweek need not be Monday through Friday. Also, there may be an uneven number of days off between shifts, like two days off after the swing shift and three after the night shift.

Shift workers experience many problems in physiological and social adjustment. Most physiological problems are associated with interruptions of the circadian rhythm. Smith et al. (2003) explained that the circadian rhythm has an evolutionary basis:

> Life on earth has evolved in an environment subject to regular and pronounced changes produced by planetary movements. The rotation of the earth on its own axis results in the 24-hour light/dark cycle, whereas its rotation around the sun gives rise to seasonal changes in light and temperature. During the process of evolution, these periodic changes have become internalized, and it is now widely accepted that living organisms possess a "body clock," such that organisms do not merely respond to environmental changes but actively anticipate them. (p. 164)

Because most people work during the day and sleep at night, shift workers also have social problems. They often experience difficulties with children, marital relationships, and recreation. For example, Smith et al. found that divorces and separations were 50% more frequent in night-shift workers than in any other group of workers. Health issues are also a concern. The World Health Organization (2007) concluded that working the night shift is related to a higher incidence of cancer. Our bodies respond to light and dark cycles through production of melatonin, a hormone that regulates sleep cycles and bolsters the immune system. Artificial light cannot make up for the qualities of natural light, nor can sleeping during the day make up for the darkness of nighttime sleep. Frost and Jamal (1979) reported that shift workers experienced

Shift work
A non-traditional work pattern in which an operation functions 24 hours per day. Typical work shifts are 7:00 a.m. to 3:00 p.m., 3:00 p.m. to 11:00 p.m., and 11:00 p.m. to 7:00 a.m.

less need fulfillment, were more likely to quit their jobs, and participated in fewer voluntary organizations.

Research indicates that shift work has a strong influence on the lives of people who perform it. As long as certain industries require 24-hour-a-day operations, psychologists will continue searching for ways to improve this particularly difficult person-environment fit. Social problems may be lessened by changing some existing patterns in the community; however, physiological problems will be more difficult to overcome. Monk et al. (1996) noted that shift workers must face three enduring conditions of *biochronology:* (1) human beings and society are diurnal (awake in the day, asleep in the night), (2) daylight has a cueing effect to initiate wakefulness, and (3) the circadian system is slow to adjust to night work. Any organizational or social policy designed to assist shift workers must address these conditions. At least one major source of physiological difficulty is the rotation of workers across shifts. If workers were assigned to a fixed shift (day, swing, or night), their behavior would be consistent, which would help them adjust to the circadian rhythms. Some people prefer to work afternoons or nights, so part of the solution may be personnel selection. Workers could choose a shift; if enough workers of the appropriate skill level were placed in the shift of their choice, that would meet both individual and organizational needs. Rotating shift work produces many adjustment problems. There is also evidence (Knauth, 1996) that backward rotation (from day to night to swing shifts) is more difficult to adjust to than forward rotation (from day to swing to night). Barnes and Wagner (2009) examined a naturally occurring "shift" in work hours, the conversion to daylight saving time, that affects most workers (some geographic areas don't alter time). In daylight saving time, the clock is advanced forward, typically resulting in one less hour of sleep. In a 24-year study of coal miners, the first Monday following the time switch, there were more workplace injuries and injuries of greater magnitude compared to other work days. Conversely, on the Monday following the switch back to standard time (when an hour of sleep can be gained), there were no changes in injury quantity or severity compared to other work days.

The findings attest to the costs of fatigue and adjustment associated with nocturnal work routines. In fact, Freese and Okonek (1984) reported that some people who have reached the emotional, psychological, and physical breaking point because of rotating shift work are told by their physicians to find jobs with traditional work hours. G. Costa (1996) estimated that 20% of workers have to leave shift work in a short time because of serious disturbances; those who remain show different and varying levels of adaptation and tolerance. Tepas (1993) concluded that organizations should design educational programs for shift workers and their families to better prepare them for the demands imposed by this work schedule.

The Stigma of Dirty Work

Dirty work describes work that most people would rather not perform due to some aspect of the job that society finds repulsive, distasteful, or degrading (Ashforth & Kreiner, 1999). When individuals engage in dirty work, they are seen as being tainted. According to Ashforth et al. (2007), taint can occur from having direct contact with dirty or deadly environments (e.g., garbage collector), having contact with stigmatized individuals (e.g., homeless shelter manager), or engaging in activities seen as deviant or immoral (e.g., exotic dancer). These taint types are classified as physical, social, and moral taint, respectively.

According to Bergman and Chalkley (2007), stigmas are "characteristics or marks that are devalued in some social contexts, leading to prejudice against the person who possesses the mark" (p. 251). They note that each type of taint that is associated with dirty work is theorized to leave stigmatizing marks on individuals, which can stick to them even after they no longer perform the dirty work. This "stickiness" is the result of other individuals attributing the marks' cause to inherent characteristics of the marked individual. Whereas other sources of stigma (e.g., age, disability) may be perceived to be beyond one's control, occupations are perceived as choices rather than results of circumstances (Kreiner et al., 2006). As such, the decision to engage oneself in a tainted job is often seen as a direct reflection of the person and therefore difficult to remove even after the person has long left the job.

Bergman and Chalkley proposed that morally-tainted dirty work will have more stickiness than other kinds of dirty work because immoral acts are seen as illustrative of the individual's true character. Physical and social taint will have less stickiness because of the tainted individual's willingness to do what others are not willing to do but should (or must) be done, thus making the person appear somewhat altruistic. In addition, social taint should have even less stigmatization because the morality of helping others further offsets the stickiness.

Baran et al. (2012) noted that even jobs that are not normally seen as dirty can take on dirty characteristics depending on the tasks involved. They gave the example of a management consultant: "This would generally not be considered dirty work in that no apparent stigma exists. If, however, the management consultant's primary job task is to assist organizations in terminating workers' employment (a task with considerable social and moral taint), the job perhaps takes on characteristics of dirty work and may, therefore, be subject to stigmatization" (p. 599). Baran et al. examined 499 employees working at animal shelters, jobs that are not necessarily dirty, but do involve one particularly dirty task for some—animal euthanasia. They found that employees who were responsible for conducting animal euthanasia had greater stress reactions than employees who were not responsible for such tasks. They were also more reluctant to discuss their work than were their counterparts. However, these same employees reported more psychological investment in their work, suggesting that engaging in the stigmatized task was a form of identification—a way to unite themselves to others within the profession and separate themselves from those not in the profession. Lopina et al. (2012) also examined animal shelter employees who were responsible for euthanizing animals and found that those who were given more access to information about the nature of the job prior to being hired were less likely to leave the job prematurely. In addition, those who believed in the value of the job were less likely to exit the job.

Adams (2012) noted that views toward stigmatized jobs and industries can change over time. He described how the cosmetic surgery and tattoo industries have gone from being seen as deviant to having relative mainstream acceptance in society. Whereas cosmetic surgeons were often described as "beauty doctors" and seen as disreputable, he notes that plastic surgeons have "found a new legitimacy as respectable medical professionals" (p. 156). Similarly, he notes that whereas tattoos were once associated with marginal groups and sideshow spectacles, they have gained a more widespread acceptance, being donned by members of all classes. Nevertheless, tattoos have not gained total acceptance, as evidenced by the belief that not all are suitable for employment (Burgess & Clark, 2010). Thus a stigma may remain within the workplace for those with tattoos, if not for the artists themselves.

Alcohol and Drug Abuse in the Workplace

Alcoholism and drug abuse are global problems affecting all arenas of life. Furthermore, it has been estimated that there are more than 10 million alcoholic American workers. Tyson and Vaughn (1987) reported that approximately two-thirds of the people who enter the workforce have used illegal drugs. Marlatt and Witkiewitz (2010) noted that, "More than 70% of current illicit drug users and heavy drinkers are employed full time. Thus, the large majority of substance abusers in the United States are in the workplace" (p. 600). Moore (1994) offered this concise statement: "Alcohol and work. This has always been an uneasy relationship. Genius may be fired by wine. More commonplace talent is often fired because of it" (p. 75). Whereas the Americans with Disabilities Act regards former drug use as a disability and thus provides legal protection to former drug users, current drug users are not covered by the law.

Due to the sensitivity and confidentiality of substance abuse, we do not have a very strong research foundation on which to base our knowledge. That is, it is difficult to collect reliable and valid data on substance abuse, given the delicacy of the issue. What follows is a brief overview of some of the major dimensions of this complex social problem.

Substance abuse
The ingestion of a broad array of substances (such as alcohol, tobacco, or drugs) that are deemed to have a harmful effect on the individual.

The term **substance abuse** covers a broad array of substances but usually includes alcohol, prescription drugs, and illegal drugs. Some people include tobacco (both smoking and chewing), but most of our knowledge is limited to alcohol and illegal drugs. Frone (2013) noted that it is important to distinguish between *workforce* substance use and impairment and *workplace* substance use and impairment. Workforce substance use and impairment concerns alcohol and drug use away from work by members of the working population. In general, I/O psychologists are interested in what happens during work and/or what impacts workplace behavior. As such, we are more interested in workplace substance use and impairment, or the consumption of alcohol or drugs immediately prior to coming to work or during work such that their work is negatively impacted.

In an extensive review of several large data collection efforts on substance use and abuse, Frone concluded that although workforce alcohol use is prevalent, workplace alcohol use is relatively rare within the United States, noting that 92% of the American workforce does not report any alcohol use before or during the workday on average. Furthermore, for those who admit to drinking at work, it is infrequent (such as an occasional drink during lunch). Similarly, he reported that illicit drug use was not prevalent, with close to 97% of the workforce not reporting any use of illegal substances during or within two hours of starting work. Nevertheless, even small percentages of the workforce can be reflective of large numbers. For example, although only 8% of the workforce reported alcohol use before or during work, that constitutes a little over 10.3 million workers! Similarly, the 3% of the workforce using illicit drugs before or during work constitutes close to 4 million workers. Thus, by any reasonable standard, substance abuse is a major problem in industry today.

Frone reported that certain segments of the U.S. workforce had much higher usage rates than the national average. For example, substance use and abuse is more common among men than women, and both workforce and workplace alcohol and drug use tends to decrease with age. In addition, he reports that employees within arts, entertainment, sports, and media tend to engage in more alcohol and drug use than individuals in other broad occupational categories.

Although I/O psychologists may approach the topic of substance abuse from several perspectives, a primary area of concern is performance impairment—that is, the extent to which substance abuse contributes to lower job performance. We do know that cognitive skills such as vigilance, monitoring, reaction time, and decision making are adversely affected by many kinds of drugs. We do not know, however, whether these drugs simply lengthen the amount of time needed to perform these cognitive functions, or whether they cause attention to be focused on irrelevant or competing stimuli. In addition, Frone (2013) notes that very little is known regarding the influence of hangovers on cognitive and psychomotor functioning. Jobs that involve the use of these skills in areas like the transportation industry (for example, pilots and railroad engineers) have regrettably contributed to our knowledge through tragic accidents. Some drugs (such as anabolic steroids) have been found to enhance aspects of physical performance (most notably, strength and speed), but their long-term effects can be very harmful to the user.

Substance abuse has long-term negative relationships to work adjustment, both as a cause and as an effect. Galaif et al. (2001) conducted a longitudinal study of polydrug use (alcohol, marijuana, and cocaine). They found that polydrug use predicted lower job satisfaction four years later and that job instability (i.e., being fired or laid off) predicted subsequent substance abuse. Frone noted that although low to moderate doses of alcohol and drugs typically cause positive emotional experiences (which is the reason they are often repeated later), high levels of consumption often lead to negative emotional experiences, particularly for naive users.

Workplace substance abuse is influenced by several factors. Bacharach et al. (2002) found that problem drinking was based on a permissive norm that was part of the workplace culture. Individuals who wanted to be accepted by coworkers matched or exceeded the drinking level of the referent group. Frone (2008) examined the relationship between job insecurity (i.e., feelings of possible impending loss of employment) and substance abuse. Job insecurity was substantially related to both the frequency and quantity of alcohol use during the work day, but only to the frequency of illicit drug use. Substance abuse occurring *before* the start of work is postulated to have a numbing or dampening effect on work stress; its use *after* work is postulated to be a release from stress. Frone found illicit drug use both before and after work, while alcohol abuse was primarily limited to after work. It was proposed that the differential timing was due to the likelihood of detection at the worksite (i.e., the smell of alcohol on one's breath).

Economic issues are also salient to drug use. Bennett et al. (1994) noted that organizations typically address the problem of drug use at work in two ways. The first is drug testing, designed to exclude drug users from the workplace. Frone (2013) noted that a large proportion of U.S. organizations test employees for alcohol and illicit drugs, but that the number is on the decline in part because tests as typically administered cannot determine use or impairment during the workday. Instead, they simply reveal that a substance has been used at some point in the recent past, which could have been while not at work. The second means of addressing the problem of drug use at work is through employee assistance programs (EAPs). EAPs started mostly after World War II to rehabilitate veterans who came home with alcohol abuse problems. Drug abuse treatment was added to the EAPs mainly after the Vietnam War for veterans returning with drug problems. Currently EAPs address all kinds of adjustment, stress, and family problems faced by workers. Such programs are mandated by the federal government for all employers who receive more than a specified amount of federal funding. Bennett et al. found that organizations in geographic areas with high unemployment rates are more likely to use pre-employment drug testing, whereas worksites with low turnover more often provide an EAP. Cooper et al. (2003) believe the role of EAPs in organizations will expand in the future to include issues of work-family conflict. Such programs will be expected to support the investment organizations make in their employees and the value they place on a healthy workforce.

It is difficult for I/O psychologists to conduct high-quality research on substance abuse. Given ethical concerns, alcohol or drugs can be administered in an experimental setting only under the most restrictive conditions. Reliance on self-report measures is problematic, given the factors of social desirability and accuracy. Civil and legal issues are also associated with drug testing, both in this country and internationally, particularly pertaining to the constitutional rights of individuals to refuse to submit to drug testing. As with most complex social problems, researchers and scholars from many professions (such as pharmacology, toxicology, law, and genetics) must take an interdisciplinary approach to addressing these issues. Although I/O psychologists will contribute only a small piece of the total picture, we envision our efforts as concentrated in two traditional areas: individual assessment and performance measurement. Perhaps in 20 years an evaluation of working conditions may also include the propensity of certain jobs to induce substance abuse and the likelihood your coworker is under the influence of drugs or alcohol. Whether we are ready for it or not, we believe society will expect I/O psychologists to provide information on problems our predecessors could scarcely have imagined.

The Psychological Effects of Unemployment

As was discussed in Chapter 8, the possibility of job loss is a major concern for the contemporary worker. Millions of employees have lost their jobs through downsizing, outsourcing, offshoring, and mergers and acquisitions. Perilous economic conditions have resulted in large-scale job loss both domestically and globally. What have we learned about the meaning of work to individuals as a result of involuntary unemployment? This section will address the primarily negative psychological effects of unemployment.

Jahoda (1981) asserted that being employed has both intended and unintended consequences for the individual. Earning a living is the most obvious intended consequence of employment, but the primary psychological meaning of work derives from the unintended or latent consequences. The five important latent consequences of employment are: (1) imposition of a time structure on the waking day, (2) regular shared experiences and contacts with people outside the nuclear family, (3) the linking of individuals to goals and purposes, (4) the definition of aspects of personal status and identity, and (5) the enforcement of activity. Jahoda believed that these unintended consequences of employment reflected enduring human needs. Accordingly, when one is unemployed and is deprived of these functions, one's needs are unsatisfied. It is thus argued that employment is the major institution in society that reliably and effectively provides these supports to psychological well-being. Research by Van Hoye and Lootens (2013) provides support for the notion that individuals who are able to maintain some time structure while unemployed are more likely to experience greater well-being.

Fryer and Payne (1986) offered a different explanation for why unemployment is psychologically devastating based upon a loss of discretionary control. Their explanation is heavily tied to the loss of income associated with unemployment. Financial problems are an outstanding worry for most unemployed people, and lack of money is one of the underlying causes of problems in maintaining relationships. While the loss of adequate income is certain for most unemployed people, there is also uncertainty about how long the low income will persist. The poor resources of the unemployed cause them to have much less discretion or freedom to pursue various decision options, such as food or clothes to purchase. The act of choosing is severely restricted by unemployment. Attempting to solve problems with limited resources frequently means that the quality of the solution is poorer, which can engender a sense of failure and lowered self-esteem. Thus the loss of financial resources limits choices, thereby enhancing feelings of limited control over one's life. In turn, lowered psychological health follows from this condition (see I/O Psychology and the Economy: *Psychological Well-Being and the Economy*).

Wanberg et al. (2011) noted that unemployment requires considerable self-regulation of effort and emotion. Individuals must sustain effort for long periods of time, despite rejections and the tedium of the job search process. Furthermore, they must regulate their emotions. Job search involves putting oneself on the line and dealing with feelings about being judged harshly, evaluated critically, and ultimately rejected. In their study that examined unemployed people over a 20-week period, Wanberg et al. found some individuals who were able to limit the extent to which they engaged in negative self-talk (beating themselves up over their situation). Those who had strategies for staying on course with their job search (such as setting goals) had better mental health and a higher job search intensity than those who were self-defeating or lacked motivational control. Gowan et al. (1999) concluded that individuals who can manage the negative emotions associated with job loss may appear to be stable and confident in interviews and thus improve their chances of receiving job offers. A quasi-experiment by van Hooft and Noordzij (2009) compared two goal orientations among unemployed job seekers. One focused on learning goals, trying to increase competence by acquiring a new skill. The other focused on demonstrating current competence to gain a positive response from a prospective employer. The learning goal approach resulted in greater re-employment. The authors proposed that the process of finding a new job is a learning experience in itself, thus the learning goal orientation was more congruent with becoming re-employed.

Wanberg (1997) suggested the best intervention programs for unemployed individuals incorporate exercises that promote feelings of self-esteem, optimism, and

I/O Psychology and the Economy: *Psychological Well-Being and the Economy*

As discussed in the text, prolonged unemployment produces a wide array of psychological ills incurred by those who have lost employment. But the survivors of job loss also incur stress often induced by having to work harder to offset the lost productivity of the departed workers. Working harder may also be perceived as a way to reduce the likelihood of being laid off in the next round of job cuts. But there can be a heavy price to be paid for all in a poor economy.

Healthcare providers have identified patterns between human behavior and the economy. Following job loss, there is an increase in anxiety and depression, followed by increased levels of alcohol and drug consumption. There is an increase in calls to crisis hotlines. Complaints of psychosomatic ills such as stomach ulcers and headaches increase. There is increased usage of company-sponsored Employee Assistance Programs. There is an increase in people treated for addictions. Some people forgo traditional treatment and seek less-expensive alternatives as support groups, yoga, and meditation. Financial contributions to charities and non-profit organizations decline in stressful economic periods.

Suicide rates also increase in such economic times. The spike in suicides during the Great Recession in Europe resulted in a new term entering the language—"economic suicides." The prevalence of economic suicides in Ireland prompted one mobile telephone company to give up its advertising space at soccer stadiums to promote a suicide prevention campaign.

Most of us need to work for a living. A psychologically healthy life is achieved, in part, by balancing our work and non-work lives. Full employment is vital to healthy and well-functioning societies.

control as well as job-seeking skills. Wanberg et al. (2010) developed a measure for unemployed job seekers to aid them in their job search. The measure, called "Getting Ready for Your Next Job," helps job seekers gain insight into their job search intensity and clarity, their level of confidence and stress regarding the job search, barriers and support that exist for them as they search for a job, and how the search is going. Interested individuals can view the measure at *www.ynj.csom.umn.edu*.

Given the difficulties associated with being unemployed and the lost resources, it is not surprising that unemployment has been consistently linked to lower psychological health. Murphy and Athanasou (1999) conducted a meta-analysis of longitudinal studies examining how employment affects one's psychological health. The results revealed an average correlation coefficient of .54 between gaining employment and improved psychological well-being, and an average correlation of .36 between losing employment and decreased psychological health. In addition, McKee-Ryan et al. (2005) conducted a meta-analytic study of psychological and physical well-being during unemployment. The authors concluded, "In cross-sectional studies unemployed individuals had lower well-being than employed individuals. In longitudinal studies well-being declines as individuals move from employment to unemployment, but improves as individuals move from unemployment to re-employment" (p. 67). In a meta-analysis comparing unemployed individuals with employed individuals, Paul and Moser (2009) similarly found that unemployed individuals had significantly lower levels of psychological health than their employed counterparts. Furthermore, a greater proportion of the people in the unemployed sample could be deemed clinically distressed. Luhmann et al. (2014) examined job loss for individuals in relationships and found that the loss of a job caused decreases in life satisfaction for both the individual and his or her partner, particularly when the couple had children. In sum, it appears that job loss and unemployment produce a cascade of worry, uncertainty, and financial restrictions, as well as family difficulties.

Child Labor and Exploitation

We conclude this chapter with a facet of workplace psychological health that is rarely addressed by I/O psychologists. It pertains to the health of children who are compelled to work. Our awareness of child labor, a disturbing and deplorable aspect of work life, comes from increased interest in global business practices (Piotrkowski & Carrubba, 1999). Although child labor is relatively rare (and illegal in most circumstances) in the United States, it is not in many other countries, and some U.S. companies utilize child labor in developing countries to make their products.

Child labor

The pattern of compelling children under the age of 15 to perform labor that is harmful to their overall health and psychological well-being.

Child labor refers to economic activities carried out by persons under 15 years of age. The International Labour Organization (ILO) estimated that in 2012 there were 168 million children worldwide, or 11% of all children, engaged in child labor. Furthermore, 85 million children work in hazardous jobs that endanger their physical and mental health and safety. Child labor is most common in developing countries, particularly in Asia, Africa, and Latin America. But it occurs in wealthy countries as well. Child workers typically are found in agriculture, working long hours, sometimes under inhumane and hazardous conditions for little or no pay. In Zimbabwe some children work 60 hours per week picking cotton or coffee. In Nepal children work on tea estates, some for up to 14 hours per day. In its most extreme form, the exploitation of working children takes the form of slavery or forced labor, still practiced in parts of Asia and Africa. Children's work may be pledged by parents for payment of a debt, the children may be kidnapped and imprisoned in brothels or sweatshops, or they may be given away or sold by families. Child labor is evidenced in the United States by children trafficking drugs in inner-city neighborhoods.

The ILO (2004) estimated that 10 million children worldwide are forced to work in slavelike conditions as domestic servants in private homes. In parts of Africa, Central America, and Asia, girls as young as 8 work 15 hours a day, every day, for little or no pay. The ILO report found that South Africa had the highest number of children working as servants, more than 2 million. Other countries with high numbers were Indonesia, Brazil, and Pakistan. The child workers, who are employed in homes where having servants is a sign of social status, are sometimes sexually abused. The study found that some children forget their own names after simply being called "girl" or "boy" for years. When they are considered too old, many children are evicted by their employers and live on the streets because they have no idea where or how to find their families.

The U.S. Department of Labor (2006) issued a report examining the use of child labor in 137 nations. The study revealed that child labor is common throughout much of the world. The study limited itself only to the *worst forms* of child labor, as these are universally regarded as the most offensive and objectionable forms of work, even for adults. The worst forms of child labor were specifically described as follows:

A. All forms of slavery or practices similar to slavery, such as the sale or trafficking of children, debt bondage, serfdom, or forced or compulsory recruitment of children for use in armed conflict;

B. The use, procuring, or offering of a child for prostitution, for the production of pornography or for pornographic purposes;

C. The use, procuring, or offering of a child for illicit activity in the production or trafficking of drugs; and

D. Work by its nature or the circumstances in which it is carried out, is likely to harm the health, safety, or morals of children. (p. 1)

Girls are primarily trafficked for commercial sexual exploitation, domestic services, or forced marriage. Boys are trafficked mostly for the purpose of exploitative labor in agriculture, mining, manufacturing, organized begging, and armed conflict. The massive earthquake and tsunami in December 2004 resulted in the deaths of thousands of parents whose surviving children became at great risk to exploitative labor. The tsunami destroyed many schools that provided an alternative venue for children other than work. The report concluded: "The creation of good new jobs for adults can increase the chances that children will be able to stay in school rather than engage in hazardous work to help support their families . . . When governments pressure the elimination of the worst forms of child labor and the promotion of basic education as national priorities, they make an important investment in their country's children and in the potential of their national economies" (p. 9).

According to Piotrkowski and Carrubba. child labor is harmful when it interferes with healthy development by imposing inappropriate physical and social demands on children, directly exposes children to noxious conditions that harm them physically or psychologically, and is detrimental to children's full social and psychological development. Children are especially vulnerable to dangerous or stressful working conditions because they are emotionally, physically, and cognitively immature. Child laborers are too young to understand the physical and psychological hazards they face and are too powerless to escape them. The plight of children around the world confronted with extreme family poverty and crime as precursors to forced labor has been the subject of major initiatives by the United Nations.

Piotrkowski and Carrubba summarized their review of child labor with the following sober conclusion:

> The economic exploitation and maltreatment of defenseless young children are violations of their basic human rights. Even when permitted by law, child labor may be harmful. Insofar as child labor abuses are tied to family poverty, they cannot be tackled alone, without regard for the economic needs of these families. The idea that children are primarily of sentimental value, rather than of economic value, is a fairly recent historical development. Parents may not understand the harms associated with child labor, believing instead that they have a right to make use of all their human resources. Although child labor may help individual families in their day-to-day ef-

forts to survive, ultimately it perpetuates the cycle of poverty. As such, it has enormous social costs. In depriving children of their rights and subjecting them to harm, exploitative child labor has enormous human costs. (p. 151)

We doubt the subject of child labor will become a dominant issue among I/O psychologists, in part because of its inherent social repulsiveness. However, it underscores one of the major reasons we work: our services have economic and instrumental value. As adults we have the free will to decide how and where we will offer our services to enhance our economic standing in life. Children, on the other hand, do not possess this free will. They are compelled to work to enhance the economic standing of others.

Chapter Summary

- The topic of workplace psychological health emerged in I/O psychology as we came to understand that both work and family issues contribute to our overall welfare.
- There are five major components to psychological health.
- The workplace can be very stressful for some individuals, and have negative consequences for both individuals and organizations.
- Understanding the conflict and enrichment between the work and family spheres of our lives is a major activity of I/O psychologists.
- Organizations try to alleviate work-family conflict by providing flexible work hours and onsite day care centers.
- Some work operations must be performed continuously. Employees who work non-traditional work shifts are generally less healthy than traditional day workers.
- Some jobs and tasks are seen as repulsive, distasteful, or degrading and can be stigmatizing for people, leading to negative outcomes.
- Alcohol and drug abuse affects millions of employees in the workplace.
- The psychological effects of unemployment can be severe, especially over a prolonged time period. Unemployment is a problem of global proportions.
- The illicit exploitation of child labor around the world is estimated to involve 168 million children between the ages of 5 and 14.

12 Work Motivation

Chapter Outline

Learning Objectives

- Explain five critical concepts central to work motivation.
- Understand the conceptual basis and degree of empirical support for these work motivation theories: biological-based, flow, self-determination, expectancy, equity, goal-setting, self-regulation, and work design.
- Provide an overview and synthesis of the work motivation theories.
- Understand the points of convergence among the work motivation theories.
- Give practical examples of applying motivational strategies.

Have you ever known a person who appears "driven" to perform well or succeed? Perhaps you would describe yourself in that way. Such people may or may not have more ability than others, but it appears they are willing to work harder or expend more effort. The capacity and willingness to expend effort is the motivational or "will do" component of behavior. Diefendorff and Chandler (2011) offered this observation: "Motivation has an abstruse, intangible, shape-shifting quality that makes it perhaps one of the most difficult constructs to study in all of psychology" (p. 65). Furthermore, it is one of the most vexing constructs to measure, particularly in an employment setting (Ployhart, 2008). Tests that have been designed to measure the motivation of job applicants often contain questions that are prone to response distortion. That is, the desired answer is rather obvious, and applicants fake their responses to increase the likelihood they will be hired. Psychologists refer to this attribute or trait as ambition, or being motivated. Motivation is not directly observable; it must be inferred from an analysis of a continuous stream of behaviors. As Mitchell and Daniels (2003) stated, "Motivation is a core construct. To understand why people behave the way they do in organizations, one must know something about motivation" (p. 225).

Work motivation refers to the domain of motivational processes directed to the realm of work. Pinder (2008) offered this definition:

> Work motivation is a set of energetic forces that originate both within as well as beyond an individual's being, to initiate work-related behavior, and to determine its form, direction, intensity, and duration. (p. 11)

There are three noteworthy components to this definition. First, *direction* addresses the choice of activities we make in expending effort. We might choose to work diligently at some tasks and not at others. For example, if you're motivated to do well on an exam, you would likely focus your attention on studying the relevant material, whereas if you're not motivated you might become easily distracted by other activities. Second, *intensity* refers to how hard we choose to work, or how much effort we choose to expend. If you are truly motivated to do well on an exam, you would be willing to try hard to understand the material. Third, duration (more commonly referred to as *persistence)* reflects motivation over time, as opposed to a one-time choice between courses of action (direction) or high levels of effort aimed at a single task (intensity). The idea is that it might not be enough to read the book and try hard to do well on an exam, but you might also have to keep on trying. So, if you're really motivated to do well on an exam, you would be more willing to spend your evenings studying for the test to ensure you performed well. Each of the three dimensions of motivation has direct implications for both organizations and individuals. As expressed by Kanfer et al. (2008), "To change behavior one must change motivation" (p. 6).

As a general rule, motivation is often thought of as being intrinsically or extrinsically driven. Intrinsic motivation is the drive to do things simply for the sake of doing them. Here, the reasons for engaging in an activity are internally derived. Extrinsic motivation, on the other hand, is dictated by the prospect of some instrumental outcome and is externally derived. For example, the motivation that people have to read books or run may be intrinsic or extrinsic. Some people are intrinsically motivated, wanting to read or go for a jog simply because they enjoy such activities. Others, however, may only read or run when there is something of value to gain or lose. For example, some people only read when they are assigned to do so for a class and their grade depends on it. Similarly, some people may only run when someone (or something) is chasing them or to pass a required fitness test.

Klehe and Anderson (2007) identified a distinction between the upper limit of what people can do (maximum performance) versus what they will do (typical performance). One conception of motivation is that it accounts for the difference between typical and maximum performance. Individuals with high ability may be able to sustain an acceptable level of typical performance, but they would be capable of much greater (i.e., maximum) performance if they were sufficiently motivated to perform at this higher level. They stand in sharp contrast with other individuals who have to work very hard to be successful because they lack high ability. The degree to which greater effort can compensate for lesser ability in attaining satisfactory performance varies across jobs. Individuals with high ability can also seek out jobs that don't require high effort if averse to working hard. Dalal and Hulin (2008) described the complex interplay between ability and motivation. Some people who work hard may have to do so because they lack the innate ability to perform well. Alternatively, we tend to persevere in tasks when we derive gratification from their completion. Relatively few people would repeatedly engage in behavior for which they lacked requisite abilities, unless situational factors compelled them to do so. We know relatively little about the trade-off between ability and motivation for behavior exhibited over a prolonged time period.

Five Critical Concepts in Motivation

It is relatively easy to misunderstand or confuse several concepts critical to work motivation. The distinctions among these concepts are not always discernible, or at the least they can become blurred. To help you differentiate them throughout the chapter, five critical concepts will be articulated next.

- **Behavior**. Behavior is the action from which we infer motivation. The behavior in question may be typing speed, firing a rifle at a target, or engaging in any of a broad constellation of human activities.
- **Performance**. Performance entails some evaluation of behavior. The basic unit of observation is behavior, but coupled with the behavior is an assessment of the behavior as judged against some standard. If the behavior is typing 60 words per minute, a judgment can be made as to whether this *level of performance* is adequate or inadequate to hold a job. Thus the behavior is appraised within some organizational context, and 60 words per minute might represent adequate performance in some jobs and inadequate performance in others. Many organizational theories tend to be concerned with performance, not just behavior. Performance, however, is determined by factors that transcend behavior.
- **Ability**. Ability is one of three determinants of behavior. It is generally regarded as fairly stable within individuals and may be represented by a broad construct like intelligence or a more specific construct like physical coordination.
- **Situational factors**. Situational factors are the second determinant of behavior. They are environmental influences and opportunities that facilitate or constrain behavior

Frank and Ernest   by Bob Thaves

I THINK OF MYSELF AS BEING IN MOTIVATION RESEARCH -- EVERY MORNING I WONDER WHY I GO TO WORK.

THAVES 2-11

Frank & Ernest: © Thaves/Dist. by Newspaper Enterprise Association, Inc. Reprinted with permission.

(and ultimately performance). Examples include tools, equipment, procedures, and the like, which if present, facilitate behavior, and if absent, diminish it. If no situational constraints are present, it is possible to maximize behavior. Individual behavior manifests itself in some environmental or situational context that influences the conduct of behavior but is beyond the control of the individual.

- **Motivation**. Motivation is the third determinant of behavior. You can think of ability as reflecting what you *can* do, motivation as what you *will* do (given your ability), and the situational factors as what you are *allowed* to do.

Each of the three determinants is critical to the manifestation of behavior. Behavior is at a maximum when a person has high ability, exhibits high motivation, and is in an environment that is supportive of such behavior. The judgment of "poor performance" could be attributed to four factors. First, the organization in which the behavior occurs may have high standards; the same behavior in another organization may receive a more positive evaluation. Second, the individual may lack the needed ability to exhibit the desired behavior. Third, the individual may lack the motivation to exhibit the desired behavior. Fourth, the individual may lack the needed resources or opportunity to exhibit the behavior.

Work Motivation Theories

Over the past 50 years there has been a profusion of work motivation theories. In the past 10 to 20 years, however, attempts have been made to identify consistency in the psychological constructs that underlie the theories. As will be witnessed, certain psychological constructs coalesce more readily across theories than others.

Whereas there are dozens of theories of motivation, only eight theories of work motivation will be presented here. They differ markedly in the psychological constructs that are hypothesized to account for motivation. Each theory will be presented along with a summary of some of the supporting empirical research. At the conclusion of this presentation, there will be a discussion of points of convergence among the theories and the fundamental perspectives that have been taken in addressing work motivation.

Biological-Based Theory

In Chapter 2, we noted that I/O psychologists have begun to delve into the area of the brain with a focus on organizational neuroscience. Researchers have now explored the physiological bases of many organizational phenomena, including motivation. The **biological-based theory of motivation** examines the role of physiological responses (such as activity in the brain's neurons) and inherited traits (such as the Big 5 personality dimensions discussed in Chapter 4) in the determination of motivation. There is certainly reason to believe that motivation may have a physiological element, determined by factors outside of our control. Researchers have found, for example, that when individuals make mistakes, there is a unique response within the brain's neurons that occurs approximately 50 milliseconds after the mistake is made, even when people are unaware of making the error (Hajcak, 2012). This neural response occurs in a portion of the prefrontal cortex that is connected to the limbic and frontal regions of the brain. In addition to changes in basic neural responses, errors lead to an engagement of the sympathetic nervous system such that one's heart rate briefly slows immediately following a mistake (Hajcak et al., 2004). As Hajcak noted, "errors can jeopardize an organization's safety and thus are motivationally salient events" (p. 102). Thus, individuals appear to be motivated at a physiological level to avoid errors.

As further evidence of the biological basis of motivation, Ridley (1999) described the mapping of the human genome, particularly with reference to the gene *D4DR*, which is a component of chromosome 11. This gene determines how receptive neurons are to dopamine, which in turn controls neural electrical discharge and regulates the flow of blood to the brain. Ridley stated, "To simplify grossly, dopamine is perhaps the brain's motivational chemical. Too little and the person lacks initiative and motivation. Too much and the person is easily bored and frequently seeks new adventures. Here perhaps lies the root of a difference in 'personality'" (p. 163). Erez and Eden (2001) succinctly summarized this orientation toward the origins of human behavior: "Although for us as psychologists the jump from chemicals to motivation to personality is a bit abrupt, the trend is clear: We are drawing nearer to the dream—or nightmare—of chemistry-based motivation" (p. 7).

Recall that a contemporary interpretation of personality is represented in the Big 5 theory. With regard to motivation, one personality factor of considerable interest to I/O psychologists is conscientiousness, which can also be thought of as the "will to achieve" (Digman & Takemoto-Chock, 1981). This name implies that individuals who are attentive to detail, rule abiding, and honest also exhibit high ambition. Likewise, Erez and Isen (2002) found that people with positive affect performed better and exhibited more persistence than people with negative affect. This area of research indicates that our willingness to expend effort is a defining component of our personality. Kanfer and Heggestad (1997) refer to this personality factor as "trait achievement."

Becker and Menges (2013) noted that "a growing body of neuroscience research indicates that much of the brain processing that shapes workplace attitudes, emotions, and behavior takes place outside of conscious awareness" (p. 220). Along these lines, Ilies et al. (2006) provided comprehensive empirical evidence to support the proposition that genetic factors influence work motivation. In short, what drives us to pursue certain tasks, exert effort, and persist over time may in part be a function of our physiological make-up.

Biological-based theory of motivation A theory that presumes motivation is genetically predisposed, determined by one's physiology and traits.

Flow Theory

Have you ever felt so deeply engaged in an activity that you seemingly forgot about everything but the activity itself? Perhaps you've found yourself still engrossed in a book at 3:00 a.m., unaware that the night had turned to morning. This is the premise behind **flow theory**. The expression "time flies when you're having fun" is certainly relevant to this theory, as is the feeling of being "in the zone."

Flow is a mental and emotional state of optimal sensation, characterized by focused attention, a clear mind, distortion of time, a loss of self-consciousness, and intense intrinsic enjoyment (Csikszentmihalyi, 1990). In many ways, flow can be thought of metaphorically as "intrinsic motivation on steroids." As Csikszentmihalyi notes, flow "is so enjoyable that people will do it even at great cost, for the sheer sake of doing it" (p. 4). When in a state of flow, a person becomes psychically "lost" through immersion. They feel in complete control, with their actions seeming almost spontaneous and automatic.

According to Nakamura and Csikszentmihalyi (2009), to experience flow, there are three necessary preconditions that must be in place. First, there must be a balance between the challenge of the task and the skills of the person performing the task. If the task requirements exceed skill levels, frustration and anxiety are likely to ensue. If skills exceed the task requirements, then boredom or apathy is likely. It is only when both the needs of the task and the abilities of the individual are high that flow will occur. Figure 12-1 depicts the ways in which challenge and skill level combinations are related, with sample activities that fall into each category.

A second precondition for flow to occur is the need for there to be clear goals. Individuals must understand what is required of them for the activity at hand. If it isn't clear what must be done, feelings of uncertainty and self-consciousness will result, making it unlikely that flow is experienced. Lastly, there must be clear and immediate

Flow theory
A theory of motivation that suggests that individuals will experience an intense level of enjoyment, concentration, and lack of self-awareness when actively engaged in activities that have clear goals, unambiguous feedback, and a match between one's skills and the challenge of the task.

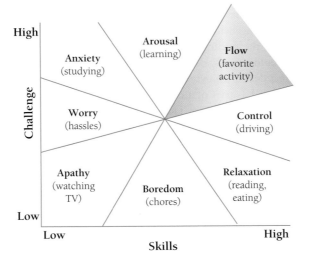

Figure 12-1 *Challenge and skill combinations per flow theory*

Adapted from *Finding flow: The psychology of engagement with everyday life*, by M. Csikszentmihalyi, (1997). New York: Basic Books.

feedback that is inherent in the task itself for flow to be possible. Individuals are driven to reduce uncertainty in their environments and make sense of their surroundings (see Field Note 1: *Sensemaking*). The presence of unambiguous feedback reaffirms one's actions and reduces uncertainty, allowing an individual to let go and become fully immersed in an activity.

It appears that some people are more apt to experience flow than are other individuals. Mosing et al. (2012) examined flow proneness (or the tendency to experience flow) in 444 pairs of adult twins and found evidence for a genetic basis for flow experiences. Ullén et al. (2012) found that flow proneness is related to emotional stability and conscientiousness such that individuals who are emotionally unstable are less likely to experience flow, whereas individuals who are high on conscientiousness are more prone to experience flow.

There has been a good deal of support for the beneficial aspects of being in flow at work. Salanova et al. (2006) found that work-related flow is related to heightened self-efficacy. Kuo and Ho (2010) found employees who perceived themselves to be in flow at work reported having higher quality customer service performance. However, Demerouti (2006) found that the relationship between flow and performance was dependent on whether an individual is conscientious or not. Specifically, she found that flow was related to heightened task and citizenship performance for employees who were high in conscientiousness, but unrelated when employees were low in conscientiousness. There is also evidence that flow is beneficial for work-family interactions. For example, Demerouti et al. (2012) examined 83 people over a period of four consecutive days and found that when individuals experienced flow at work and then went home and were psychologically detached from work, they were more invigorated and less exhausted at home compared to people who experienced lower levels of flow during the workday.

Self-Determination Theory

Self-determination theory
A theory of motivation based on the fulfillment of basic needs to experience intrinsic motivation.

As noted earlier, motivation is often categorized as being either intrinsic or extrinsic in nature. A long-held belief and heavily researched concept is the *undermining effect*, which is the finding that adding external incentives to a task that was initially enjoyable could actually decrease intrinsic motivation. Take for example a student who gains a great deal of enjoyment from reading. Yet, when an instructor assigns a certain book to be read as part of a course requirement, the student feels less than enthused. Said differently, the extrinsic factors have diminished the student's intrinsic motivation for reading. Why might this be? **Self-determination theory** is a theory of motivation that helps to resolve some of the issues of when extrinsic motivators (rewards and incentives) may result in positive versus negative outcomes. More specifically, the theory proposes that individuals have three basic needs that result in intrinsic motivation if they are fulfilled. These needs are:

1. **Autonomy**: People want to feel like they have a say in what it is they do. When they feel like they have the discretion to make their own choices, they are more likely to derive enjoyment from a task.

2. **Competence**: As a general rule, people prefer to feel capable of doing things. When they feel like they are able to perform successfully and experience mastery over a task, they are more likely to gain a sense of enjoyment in doing it.

Field Note 1: *Sensemaking*

Weick (2001) proposed a concept he called *sensemaking*. It is not directly a theory of motivation, but it explains many facets of human behavior. The term "sensemaking" should be interpreted literally: it is the process by which we make sense of our lives and the world around us. We are driven (i.e., motivated) to understand phenomena in our lives, and the lack of making sense of something is often troubling to us. For example, how often have you thought or said these words about something you experienced in your life?

"It just doesn't make sense to me."

"If only I could figure it out."

"Why would someone do something like that?"

"It just doesn't add up."

"I don't understand that at all."

Each statement addresses Weick's fundamental concept of sensemaking. We feel compelled to derive meaning and understanding from experiences in our lives—understanding, not necessarily approval or disapproval. Sensemaking implies there is no single objective truth we are searching for (as a combination to a lock or safe), but rather something personal that allows us the comfort of understanding a problem or issue that may initially seem unfathomable. Fay (1990) has portrayed life as a puzzling terrain and "there is nobody here but us scratching around trying to make our experience and our world as comprehensible to ourselves in the best way we can" (p. 38). The terrain we seek to understand is continuously changing, a condition no more evident than that witnessed by the seismic changes in the business world over the past 35 years. As explained in Chapter 10, the rupturing of the traditional psychological contract of employment "just doesn't make any sense" to the generation that entered the work world prior to the current turbulent period in society. Why would an organization *not* value loyalty and hard work in exchange for job security? All that employees can ever give to their employer is "100% of the brains and hearts," but even that no longer guarantees continued employment. Society was compelled to understand that the traditional psychological contract made sense under one set of economic conditions (i.e., relative stability, immunity from economic problems in other parts of the world, primarily local competition for goods, etc.). Under a different set of economic conditions (i.e., high instability, global economic interdependence, and the availability of cheaper goods a computer click away), the traditional psychological contract no longer made sense. Now employees have become expendable, regardless of their job proficiency and organizational loyalty. The cost of employees (i.e., labor costs) are often the single largest expense item in a corporate budget. Organizations found they had to cut back on their expenses to compete in the global economy, and in so doing the prevailing model of employment was cut with it.

Weick's conception of sensemaking is grounded in philosophy as well as psychology. Informational justice (as discussed in Chapter 10) is fundamentally about providing information to employees in a fair and equitable manner. Its overall goal is to help people make sense of events in their organization. The quest to make sense of our world is an unending process. We are probably more sensitized to when things don't make sense to us than when they do. It is the absence of understanding that motivates us to try to comprehend our world. We often feel relieved when we finally make sense out of something and can remain disquieted when we don't.

3. **Relatedness**: Feeling connected to others is the final basic need proposed by self-determination theory. People have a desire for interaction and belongingness, and when they feel connected to others they are more likely to experience intrinsic motivation.

When these needs are met, intrinsic motivation flourishes and the direction, intensity, and persistence of effort is heightened. However, according to Ryan and Deci (2000), it is when extrinsic rewards undermine these basic needs that intrinsic motivation will be lessened. Consider the earlier example of the student whose intrinsic motivation for reading diminished after being assigned a book to read for class. According to self-determination theory, one possible explanation is that the student doesn't have as much autonomy as he or she usually does. In addition to not getting to choose the book, the teacher likely imposed a deadline for having the book read. In addition, perhaps the deadline or content of the book is such that the student doesn't feel like it is within his or her abilities. That is, feelings of competence may be lower for this particular book than they are for the books that the student would typically choose to read. In short, these factors have undermined the student's intrinsic motivation by negatively impacting the student's basic self-determination needs.

Ryan and Deci also noted that extrinsic motivators can vary considerably in terms of how controlled versus autonomous they are. On the one end, rewards may be very externally regulated, based on outside rewards and punishments. For example, a soldier who typically enjoys running may be forced to run as part of a physical training requirement for the military. Failure to do the run will result in a negative evaluation. Motivators such as these would be the most likely to hinder intrinsic motivation, as feelings of autonomy are drastically reduced. On the other end of the continuum, extrinsic motivators can be integrated into the person's own value system, and less likely to detract from feelings of autonomy. For example, an individual may run in part because of the health benefits associated with the activity. If the person values good health, the extrinsic benefit of getting in shape won't be as detrimental to the enjoyment of the activity due to the ties to the personally prescribed values. The importance of tying extrinsic motivations to values can be seen with work conducted by Grant (2008), who found that firefighters and fundraisers performed better and were more productive and persistent with their efforts when they were driven by a synergistic combination of intrinsic motivation and pro-social values.

Cerasoli et al. (2014) conducted a meta-analysis of 183 studies over 40 years that offers some clear insight. They found that intrinsic motivation mattered more for the quality of one's performance, or how well somebody does something, whereas extrinsic motivation was a better predictor of quantity of performance, or how much somebody gets accomplished. Furthermore, they found that intrinsic motivation was related to overall performance even when there were incentives in place. This is counter to the undermining effect discussed earlier. However, when incentives were directly linked to performance (such as sales commissions and performance bonuses), intrinsic motivation was less related to performance than when the incentives were indirectly linked (such as with base salaries, which aren't directly related to actual performance levels). The authors concluded that managers should feel comfortable using external incentives that are directly tied to performance when tasks are simple, productivity is of utmost concern, and/or compliance of certain behaviors is key for performance and safety. This is because having these direct links between performance and the incentives will likely make the person focus exclusively on reaching the specific goal (to receive the incentive). However, this over-emphasis on reaching the goal may diminish creativity, autonomy, teamwork, and efforts to enhance learning, while also leading to the possibility of an increase in unethical and counterproductive behavior. As such, a close examination of the trade-offs for presenting and using incentives within the workplace is necessary.

It has been argued that focusing solely on either intrinsic or extrinsic motivation within the workplace is shortsighted given the two typically coexist. It is not uncommon for individuals to enjoy their work, and given the positive associations with high levels of job satisfaction discussed in Chapter 10, it would seem optimal for this to be the case. Nevertheless, people expect to be paid for their work, as well as organizations being legally required to do so. Incentivizing individuals to increase their performance is standard practice in many organizations. As such, figuring out how and when rewards and incentives can lead to positive rather than negative effects is a worthwhile endeavor, and makes self-determination theory important for organizational scholars.

Expectancy Theory

Expectancy theory
A theory of motivation based on the perceived degree of relationship between how much effort a person expends and the performance that results from that effort.

Expectancy
Within expectancy theory, the belief that effort leads to performance.

Instrumentality
Within expectancy theory, the belief that performance will lead to an outcome.

Expectancy theory is a cognitive theory of motivation put forth by Vroom (1964) that suggests that employees are rational decision makers who will expend effort on activities that lead to desired rewards. At its most simplest level, expectancy theory suggests that effort is a function of the employee's beliefs that (1) effort will lead to performance, (2) performance will lead to an outcome, and (3) the outcome is valued. To the extent that employees hold these beliefs, they should be motivated to exert effort.

The first belief, that effort leads to performance, is termed **expectancy**, and answers the question, "How likely is it that my effort will lead to performance?" In some jobs there may seem to be no relationship between how hard you try and how well you do. In others there may be a very clear relationship: the harder you try, the better you do. In general, expectancy theory proposes that people must see a relationship (an expectancy) between how hard they try and how well they perform. If expectancy is low, it will make very little difference to them whether they work hard because effort and performance seem unrelated. In short, effort will seem futile. The idea of expectancy also explains why work motivation can be very high in jobs where employees perceive very high expectancies. On assembly lines, the group performance level is determined by the speed of the line. No matter how hard a person works, he or she cannot produce any more until the next object moves down the line. The employee soon learns that he or she need only keep pace with the line. Thus there is no relationship between individual effort and performance. Alternatively, sales jobs are characterized by high expectancy. Salespeople who are paid on commission realize that the harder they try (the more sales calls they make), the better is their performance (sales volume). Thus, expectancy theory predicts that motivation is highest in jobs that have high expectancies.

The second belief, that performance will lead to an outcome, is termed **instrumentality**. *Instrumentality* is defined as the perceived degree of relationship between performance and outcome attainment. It answers the question, "How likely is it that performance will lead to certain job outcomes?" Instrumentality exists in the employee's mind. Thus, whether or not performance will *actually* lead to certain outcomes is not the point. What matters is whether the employee *believes* that the connection or relationship is real. For example, if a person thinks that pay increases are highly conditional on performance, then the instrumentality associated with that outcome (a pay raise) is very high. If an employee thinks that being transferred is unrelated to job performance, then the instrumentality associated with that outcome (a transfer) is zero. According to expectancy theory, for motivation to occur a person must believe that there is some relationship between job performance and attainment of outcomes (instrumentalities must be high). If a person does not see performance as a means of obtaining an outcome, increased effort simply won't seem worth it. Reward practices and the supervisor are crucial in establishing high instrumentalities. If a supervisor says, "Your performance has been very good lately; therefore, I will reward you with a raise (or promotion)," the individual will see that the attainment of a pay raise or a promotion is conditional on (instrumental to) good performance. Conversely, if a supervisor says, "We don't give pay raises or promotions on the basis of performance; we grant them only on the basis of seniority," the individual will not be motivated to perform well to attain these outcomes. Perhaps the only motivation is to work hard enough not to be fired, so these outcomes would eventually be attained through longer service with the organization. When outcomes are made contingent on performance and the individual understands this relationship, expectancy theory predicts that job performance will be enhanced.

Valence
Within expectancy theory, the extent to which outcomes are valued.

Finally, the third belief that is essential for effort to be exerted, that the outcomes are valued, is known as **valence**. *Valences* are the employee's feelings about the outcomes and are usually defined in terms of attractiveness or anticipated satisfaction. They answer the question, "How valuable or attractive are the job outcomes to me?" If the outcomes are seen as attractive, the employee assigns a positive valence to them. If they are seen as negative, they are given negative valences. Lastly, if the employee feels indifferent about an outcome, that outcome would have a valence of zero. Whether an outcome is seen as positive or negative (or neutral) depends on the person and situation. For example, a manager may try to incentivize employees by offering a certain parking spot to whomever is deemed "employee of the month." For some people, this might be seen as a valuable outcome, particularly if there is limited nearby parking available. Others may not find such an outcome very valuable. For example if they use public transportation to get to work or could have an even better spot on their own, such an enticement may have little value, or even be seen as a worse option. Thus, valences will vary by person, situation, and outcome (see Cross-Cultural I/O Psychology: *Cross-Cultural Differences in Incentives*). Figure 12-2 shows the types of questions someone might ask to determine if he or she is motivated to try harder per expectancy theory.

Expectancy theory is a highly rational and conscious explanation of human motivation. The theory has also been used to make predictions in other contexts that involve decisions besides choosing levels of effort. Also included are how people choose an occupation and how they choose to engage in one particular task over others. People are assumed to behave in a way that will maximize their expected gains (attainment of outcomes) from exhibiting certain job behaviors and expending certain levels of effort. To the extent that behavior is not directed toward maximizing gains in a rational, systematic way, the theory will not be upheld. Whenever unconscious motives deflect behavior from what a knowledge of conscious processes would predict,

Cross-Cultural I/O Psychology: *Cross-Cultural Differences in Incentives*

Given the documented differences across cultures with regard to values and attitudes, it is not surprising that workers around the world have different preferences for incentives and rewards. Sanchez-Runde and Steers (2003) described some of these differences identified through cross-cultural research. Individual-based incentive pay (e.g., financial bonuses for meritorious performance) is commonly used in the United States. It is designed to accentuate and reward differences among workers. A study found that Asian companies that adopted this Western strategy for motivation met with substantial problems. A merit-based reward system that would reduce the pay of less productive workers would also cause them to lose face and disrupt group harmony. Giving all employees the same bonus irrespective of merit defeated the intent of the incentive system and substantially escalated labor costs. Another form of incentive pay is compensation-at-risk. Instead of a fixed salary, managers can opt to place a portion of their salary "at risk." The practical implication is if the managers perform well, their total pay will be greater than what they would have earned with a fixed salary. The converse is also true, however, with poorer performance resulting in less pay. One study found that American managers were more risk-oriented; some were willing to convert 100% of their pay to at-risk compensation. European managers were much more risk-averse; they would seldom commit more than 10% of their pay to at-risk compensation.

Another study reported that Swedes typically preferred additional time off for superior performance instead of additional income, whereas if given a choice, Japanese workers prefer financial incentives (with a strong preference for group-based incentives). Japanese workers tend to take only about half of their paid holidays because taking all the time available may show a lack of commitment to the group. Sanchez-Runde and Steers stated that Japanese workers who take their full vacations or refuse to work overtime are labeled *wagamama* ("selfish"). "As a result, *karoshi* (death by overwork) is a serious concern in Japan, while Swedes see taking time off as part of an inherent right to a healthy and happy life" (p. 366).

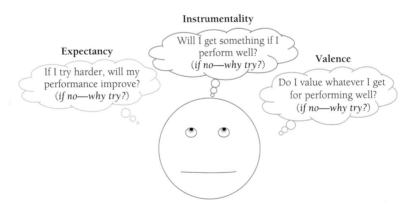

Figure 12-2   *The types of questions one might ask in expending effort according to expectancy theory*

expectancy theory will not be predictive. Research suggests that people differ in the extent to which their behavior is motivated by rational processes. This was apparent in an early study by Muchinsky (1977). This study examined the extent to which expectancy theory predicted the amount of effort college students put into each of their courses. While the average validity of the theory for all students was .52 it ranged from −.08 to .92 for individual students. Thus the theory accurately predicted the expenditure of effort by some students but was unable to predict it for others. This supports the idea that some people have a very rational basis for their behavior, and thus the theory works well for them; others appear to be motivated more by unconscious factors, and for them the theory does not work well (Stahl & Harrell, 1981).

In addition, and related to this, van Eerde and Thierry (1996) meta-analyzed 77 studies and found that expectancy theory seems better at predicting the levels of effort an individual will expend on different tasks than at predicting gradations of motivation across different people. Furthermore, they concluded that reduced conceptualization of the theory (not involving the measurement of all the components) resulted in superior predictions of effort compared with the complete model. Lastly, they found that expectancy, instrumentality, and valence beliefs were better at predicting intentions and preferences (psychological indicators of motivation) than they were at predicting actual performance, effort, or choices (behavioral indicators of motivation).

On a practical level, people do not go through life carefully determining specific valence, instrumentality, and expectancy values. For this very reason, expectancy theory is often criticized as being overly calculative. As Grant and Shin (2012) note, "Although the theory is reasonably effective in predicting motivation and behavior, it creates a caricature of how employees actually make decisions and experience motivation" (p. 507). Nevertheless, given its theoretical parsimony and the intuitive appeal of its underlying concepts, expectancy theory remains one of the dominant explanations of work motivation in I/O psychology.

Equity Theory

Equity theory
A theory of motivation based on the comparison of one's inputs to outcomes with those of another person to determine if a situation is fair. These determinations of equity dictate subsequent actions taken.

Equity theory suggests that motivation exists in a social context, and is based on how fair individuals see situations and interactions. This theory proposed by Adams (1963, 1965) states that employees intuitively make comparisons between themselves and others to determine how hard to work. The comparisons involve *inputs*, or contributions they make to a situation (like their level of effort, knowledge, or specific skill set), and the *outcomes* they receive (like pay, recognition, or other benefits). In general, there should be a match between their inputs and outcomes such that increases in one should lead to increases in the other. In short, an individual would compare his or her ratio of inputs to outcomes with the ratio of inputs and outcomes of another person, such as a coworker. If they perceive the ratios are equal, they see the situation as equitable, or fair. If, however, they feel there is a mismatch between the ratios of inputs and outcomes, they will feel distress and will be motivated to reduce the inequity. For example, assume you have a job in which you earn $15 an hour. You are talking with your coworker and discover that you both make the same amount of money for doing the same job. Your inputs and outcomes are the same as your coworker's inputs and outcomes; therefore you would likely see that as being fair. In equity theory's terms, you perceive that there is *equity*. Imagine you compare your inputs and outcomes with another more experienced coworker who makes $20 an hour. Although this coworker makes more than you do (greater outcomes), you note that this person also has more experience than you do (greater inputs). Thus, you would still perceive that there is equity.

What if, however, you discovered that your first coworker makes $2 more per hour than you for doing the same amount of work? In this case, the ratios of inputs to outcomes don't match because your coworker is getting more than you (more outcomes) despite having the same level of inputs (as far as you can tell). In this situation, you perceive that there is *inequity*, or unfairness. It is important to note that ratios are compared, not just inputs or outcomes. That is, you might perceive equity if your coworker makes more money than you, but also has more experience. Figure 12-3 shows how comparing ratios of inputs to outcomes is much like placing the ratios on a scale. When the scale tips to one side (because one person's ratio is higher than the other), there is inequity. When the ratios are the same, the scale is even and equity is perceived.

According to equity theory, feelings of *inequity* motivate individuals to take action to make things equitable, or fair. If you feel like you are under-rewarded (or your ratios are less than those of your coworker), you may try to restore equity by (1) reducing your inputs (slacking off) or (2) increasing your outcomes (whether by asking for a raise or doing so unethically like stealing from the organization). You could also reduce the feelings of inequity by (3) distorting your perceptions of the situation. For example, you could modify your thinking so that you believe your coworker is actually doing more than you originally believed. For example, you may decide that your coworker is required to perform tasks that nobody likes to do. Alternatively, he or she might make more money than you, but you get other benefits that your coworker doesn't get (such as preferred hours, a parking space, and greater recognition for your work). By changing how you think about the comparison, you fashion the ratio of your coworker's inputs to outcomes so as to match the ratio of your inputs to outcomes. Of course, you could also make yourself feel better by (4) changing the person with whom you compare yourself, or (5) leaving the situation (by quitting).

Much of the support for equity theory comes from it being the basis for organizational justice perceptions (described in Chapter 10). Recall that justice perceptions

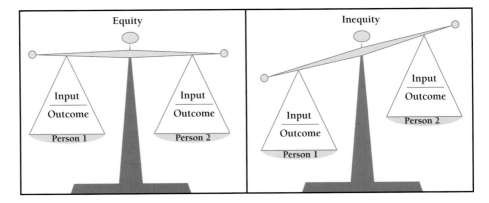

Figure 12-3 *Comparison of input/outcome ratios to determine equity and inequity according to equity theory*

refer to how fair people perceive outcomes (distributive justice), the ways in which decisions regarding outcomes are reached (procedural justice), and the ways in which people are treated (interactional justice).

What should be clear at this point is that a large part of whether an individual views a situation as being equitable or not depends on the person with whom they are making their comparisons. When making comparisons, employees could choose to look at others (such as coworkers) or themselves (such as comparing what they now earn vs. what they earned in a previous job). They could also choose to look internally (such as coworkers in their current organization) or look externally (to colleagues at different organizations). In addition, comparisons don't even have to be made with actual people for feelings of inequity to result. According to Folger (1986), thoughts of "what might have been" can serve as the basis for comparison. If employees *imagine* that an outcome could have been much better than it actually was given their level of input, they will likely feel inequity in the form of resentment. The most important consideration is that individuals used for comparison purposes be realistic. It would be unrealistic, for example, for an entry-level employee to use the CEO of the organization or fanciful imagined outcomes for the basis of comparisons.

In the examples thus far, inequity has been framed as under-reward without much thought given to over-reward. The reason for this is simple. Although equity theory suggests that *any* inequity — whether due to under-reward or over-reward — should result in motivation to restore equity, there is simply less empirical support for the notion that inequity in one's favor leads to such action. It would seem that people are more likely to act to restore equity when they are the ones at a *disadvantage*. According to Huseman et al. (1987), individuals differ in their preference for equity (or tolerance for inequity; King et al., 1993). This **equity sensitivity** predicts the extent to which individuals will be likely to take action when faced with inequity. On one end of the continuum are *benevolents*, or those individuals with a greater tolerance for under-reward. On the other end are *entitleds*, or those that have a greater preference for being over-rewarded (or higher outcome/input ratio compared to others). In the middle are *equity sensitives*, or those individuals who prefer to have equal ratios. According to this view, benevolent and equity sensitive employees would be likely to take action to reduce inequity that was due to perceived over-reward, whereas entitled employees would be content with such inequity.

Equity sensitivity
The individual differences that people have regarding their preference for equity (or tolerance for inequity).

Goal-Setting Theory

Goal-setting theory
A theory of motivation based on directing one's effort toward the attainment of specific goals that have been set or established.

Goal-setting theory is based on directing one's effort toward the attainment of specific goals that have been set or established. Its basic premise is that setting clear, specific, and challenging goals leads to enhanced task performance by way of increased performance motivation. Goals are what the individual is consciously trying to attain, particularly as they relate to future objectives. According to Locke and Latham (2002), goals influence all indicators of motivation, including direction, intensity, and persistence of effort. They indicate where a person should direct efforts, how much effort is needed, and for how long. In addition, they encourage the development of novel task strategies to accomplish goals.

Goal-setting theory is one of the most widely studied theories of motivation. As such, much is known regarding what makes goals effective versus ineffective. For example, it has become fairly well-established that specific (vs. vague) goals lead to higher performance (Locke & Latham, 2002; Mitchell, 1997). In general, goals direct attention and action, and identify the target of intended behavior. Thus, when they are stated specifically, the focus of the person's effort becomes well defined.

It has been well-documented that difficult (vs. easy) and attainable (vs. unattainable) goals lead to greater performance levels (Locke & Latham, 2002; Mitchell, 1997). For example, Locke and Latham (1990) found a significant, positive relationship between goal difficulty and motivation, which remained positive up to the point at which either a participant's skill level was no longer sufficient to attain the goal (i.e., it became unattainable), or the individual became uncommitted to its achievement. Furthermore, they reported that specifying challenging goals led to greater levels of motivation than did a simple "do your best" instruction. The reason difficulty seems to matter is because if a goal is difficult, it normally requires more effort, over a longer period of time, to be attained. Thus, the difficulty of a goal can be expected to impact an individual's intensity and persistence of effort. In addition, goal setting requires the development of a task-related strategy. When people contemplate a goal, they must also consider the means for its attainment, especially when the goal is seen as difficult. It may be that harder tasks are more likely to stimulate more strategy development than are easy tasks.

In addition to goals varying in terms of specificity and difficulty, goals can also differ in terms of their content. For example, goals can be categorized as learning goals (those aimed at increasing development) or performance goals (those aimed at demonstrating competence). Schmidt et al. (2013) point out that "both learning and performance goals are important, as well as the ability to pursue the right goals at the right time; employees and organizations that strike an adequate balance are likely to be the most effective" (p. 316). Nevertheless, individuals appear to have a tendency to approach tasks with certain goals in mind. This tendency is a trait known as **goal orientation**. There are two general goal orientations that people have. The first is learning goal orientation, which is a tendency to approach tasks with the objective of learning for its own sake. The second is performance goal orientation, which involves approaching or avoiding tasks with the goal of gaining favorable judgments or avoiding negative judgments from others. Payne et al. (2007) meta-analyzed many studies and found that individuals with high levels of learning goal orientation (vs. those with low levels) tend to perform better on tasks. On the other hand, they found that individuals who tend to approach tasks with the goal of avoiding negative judgments from others are more likely to perform poorly than those who don't approach tasks with this mindset.

Goal orientation
The way in which individuals approach or avoid goals in achievement situations.

The relationship between goals and performance is also impacted by how committed individuals are to the goals. In general, when individuals are more committed to goals, they are more likely to exert more effort and persevere over time. As Locke and Latham (2002) noted, goal commitment is enhanced when individuals believe they can attain the goal and when such goal attainment is seen as important. In addition, individuals are typically more committed to self-set or participatively-set (vs. assigned) and publicly declared (vs. those kept private) goals. It seems that having a voice in setting the goal and/or announcing a goal to others creates a sense of importance for individuals that isn't there otherwise.

Finally, the impact of goals on performance is also impacted by the nature of the task as well as feedback regarding progress toward one's goals. Regarding the nature of the task, research has revealed that goals are more effective for simple (vs. complex) tasks and tasks that are independent (vs. interdependent). As for feedback, research has consistently demonstrated that people who receive feedback on how well they are doing are more likely to accomplish their goals. Locke and Latham (2002) note that feedback is important because it helps individuals know if they need to adjust the level or direction of effort or utilize different strategies to reach their goals. In short, feedback tells us whether our efforts are "on target."

Overall, you should be struck by the elegance and simplicity of goal-setting theory. As Latham and Locke (1991) observed, goal-setting theory lies within the domain of purposefully directed action. The theory focuses on why some people perform better on work tasks than others. If the people are equal in ability and situational conditions, then the explanation for the difference must be motivational. The theory states that the simplest and most direct motivational explanation of why some people perform better than others is that they have different performance goals. The difficulty and specificity of the goal influence performance, as do the amount and nature of feedback. There are some differences in performance between goals that are assigned and those that are self-selected. Different types of people also prefer different types of goals, but it is clear that goal setting in general elicits better performance.

There is also evidence that goal setting is effective for groups (e.g., Pritchard et al., 1988). Group goals can be more difficult to attain, however, because in many cases the success of the overall group depends on more than just the success of individual members. A basketball team may set a goal of winning a certain number of games in a season, but its success is determined by more than just the number of points each player scores. Player coordination and integration must also be considered. One player might help the team by passing, another by rebounding, and the others by shooting.

Locke and Latham (2002) asserted that the principles of goal-setting theory generalize widely. Overall, results from an impressive number of studies has demonstrated that setting specific, difficult goals leads to increased performance on a wide range of variables, including quantity, quality, and time spent. The effects of goal setting are long-lasting, and the theory is applicable to individuals, groups, and entire organizations. Not surprisingly then, Locke and Latham concluded: "goal-setting theory is among the most valid and practiced theories of employee motivation in organizational psychology" (p. 714). Nevertheless, it is important to note that goal setting is not without criticism. Ordóñez et al. (2009) suggest that goal setting can have harmful effects. They argue that if a goal is too challenging, it may hurt one's self-efficacy and decrease the individual's motivation. In addition, they caution that goal setting may harm cooperation, lead to tunnel vision, and increase risk taking and competition. Along these lines, Van Mierlo and Kleingeld (2010) found that increased time pressure from goals made people take more risks, which is potentially disastrous depending on the situation. Furthermore, and in part related to the argument that goals may unduly increase competition, goal setting may lead to unethical behavior. Schweitzer et al. (2004) found that participants in a laboratory study who were given goals were more likely to distort how productive they were than were participants who were simply asked to do their best, particularly if they just barely missed reaching those goals. Thus, despite its advantages for motivation, goal setting has some potentially deleterious effects.

Self-Regulation Theories

There is not a single theory of self-regulation. Rather, a family of theories share some basic commonalities. As stated by Vancouver et al. (2010), "Self-regulation theories have become the dominant perspective for understanding motivation, particularly in applied areas of psychology" (p. 986). A complete description of all the theories and an examination of the specific formulations by which they differ are beyond the scope of this book. What follows is an explanation of the basic concepts of self-regulation theories.

The name of this family of theories, *self-regulation*, implies that individuals play an active role in monitoring their own behavior, seeking feedback, responding to the feedback, and forming opinions regarding their likelihood of success in future endeavors. At the core of the theory is the idea of goals. Diefendorff and Lord (2008) summarized the theory: "Self-regulation has been most commonly used to try to understand how goals are set, the process by which goals influence behavior, the reasons for goal attainment or nonattainment, and how goals are revised or new goals are set" (p. 153). It is presumed that people consciously set goals for themselves that guide and direct their behavior toward the attainment of these goals. Furthermore, individuals engage in a process of self-monitoring or self-evaluation; that is, they are aware of their progress in pursuit of the goals they have set. Their awareness of their progress is facilitated by receiving feedback. Feedback is information about how successful or "on target" the individual is in progressing toward the goal attainment. The feedback can and often does produce a discrepancy between the individual's current status in pursuing a goal and the desired or needed status to attain the goal. In essence, the feedback can provide an "error message" that the individual is off-track in pursuit of the goal. It is at this point that the individual responds to the information provided by the feedback. The individual's response can be in the form of altering behavior so as to reduce the magnitude of the discrepancy between the current progress toward attaining the goal and the needed progress toward goal attainment. Alternatively, the feedback received by the individual can show little or no discrepancy between the actual and desired status in the path toward goal attainment. If the discrepancy is small, the individual has enhanced self-efficacy, or the belief in one's capabilities and capacity to perform successfully, which results in greater self-confidence that the goal can and will be attained. However, large discrepancies result in a loss of self-efficacy, which decreases the individual's sense of confidence that the goal will be attained. When the discrepancies are large, the individual may engage in goal revision, a process of readjusting or modifying the initial goal to an easier or ambitious level. Finally, life is a process of repeatedly pursuing goals in one form or another. With each success we experience in attaining the goals we set, we gain a greater collective sense of self-efficacy. Goal attainment acquires a degree of perceived generalizability, meaning the individual thinks that future goals are more likely to be attained because of his or her success in attaining past goals.

Ilies and Judge (2005) found evidence of self-regulation in goal setting. Goals are initially set, but following negative feedback goal levels were adjusted downward and raised following positive feedback. Thus the nature of the feedback received becomes a mechanism for the self-regulation of behavior. For example, assume an individual

Self-regulation theories
Theories of motivation based on the setting of goals and the receipt of accurate feedback that is monitored to enhance the likelihood of goal attainment.

Self-efficacy
The belief in one's capabilities and capacity to perform successfully.

sets a goal of losing 30 pounds by dieting and exercising. The 30-pound weight loss is scheduled to occur over a 10-week period, with a loss of 3 pounds per week for 10 weeks. The feedback comes from weighing on a scale. If after 2 weeks, for example, the individual had not lost 6 pounds, a different pattern of eating and exercising may follow. If the individual continued not to meet the weight-loss goal over the ensuing weeks, the individual may revise the stated goal to perhaps 20 pounds over the 10-week period, or extend the 30-pound weight loss over a longer period of time, to perhaps 20 weeks. To the extent the individual is successful in meeting the weight-loss goal, the individual's self-efficacy about personal weight loss is enhanced (he or she would feel more capable of achieving weight loss success in the future). Furthermore, the sense of self-efficacy regarding the weight loss could generalize to other goals in other aspects of life.

Self-regulation theories provide a rich conceptual basis to understand how individuals become motivated to pursue various goals and why they persevere in their pursuit of the goals. Although some components of self-regulation theories have not been expressed in earlier theories of motivation, self-regulation theories have several concepts associated with previous theories. The importance of setting goals and consciously focusing on their attainment is supported by early research on goal-setting theory. The association between expending effort in pursuit of a goal and ultimately attaining the goal is reflected in the concept of expectancy from expectancy theory. Furthermore, repeated success in goal attainment results in higher self-efficacy, which is the analog in expectancy theory of perceiving a strong relationship between effort and performance. The research on self-regulation theories reveal that we are more likely to be committed to goals that we regard as particularly significant and important to us than trivial goals. In short, much of self-regulation theories are a distillation of previous motivational theories buttressed with new concepts (most notably the feedback/expectation discrepancy; Kluger, 2001) not found in other theories. Furthermore, they emphasize how cognitive processes become translated or activated in behavior (Lord & Levy, 1994).

Self-regulation theories have been tested in a wide variety of contexts. Examples include how children learn in school (Zimmerman, 1995), career choice and development (Hackett, 1995), and treatment of addictive behaviors (Marlatt et al., 1995). The general pattern of results is very positive. Among the more supportive findings is the perceived importance of personal causation and control over goal pursuit. Self-regulation theories clearly position the individual as the agent responsible for striving to attain the goal.

As noted earlier, there are multiple manifestations of self-regulation theories. Not all of the manifestations make identical predictions of behavior in specific circumstances (e.g., Phillips et al., 1996). Nevertheless, the theories reach the following conclusions about people (Bandura & Locke, 2003):

- They form intentions that include plans and strategies for attaining them.
- They set goals for themselves and anticipate the likely outcomes of possible actions to guide and motivate their efforts.
- They adapt personal standards and monitor and regulate their actions by self-reactive influences.

- They reflect on their efficiency, the soundness of their thoughts and actions, and the meaning of their pursuits and make corrective adjustments if necessary.

The concept of self-efficacy does indeed appear to be a useful and insightful way for us to understand our participation, performance, and persistence in a wide range of human endeavors.

Work Design Theory

Work design theory
A theory of motivation based on the presence of dimensions or characteristics of jobs that foster the expenditure of effort.

Job enrichment
The process of designing work so as to enhance individual motivation to perform the work.

The **work design theory** of motivation is based on the presence of dimensions or characteristics of jobs that foster the expenditure of effort. This theory proposes that, given the proper design of jobs, work can facilitate motivation in individuals. According to this view, there are characteristics or attributes of jobs that are more (or less) motivating than others. The number of these attributes and their identification have been the subject of extensive research. The process of designing jobs to possess those attributes that are motivating is called **job enrichment**.

Hackman and Oldham (1976) proposed the job characteristics model that best exemplifies this approach to motivation. It is among the most heavily researched theories in the history of I/O psychology. The model specified the particular *job characteristics* (also called *core job dimensions*) that induce motivation:

1. **Skill variety**—the extent to which a job requires a number of different activities, skills, and talents;

2. **Task identity**—the degree to which a job requires completion of a whole, identifiable piece of work—that is, doing a job from beginning to end, with visible results;

3. **Task significance**—the job's impact on the lives or work of other people, whether within or outside the organization;

4. **Autonomy**—the degree of freedom, independence, and discretion in scheduling work and determining procedures that the job provides; and

5. **Task feedback**—the degree to which carrying out the activities required results in direct and clear information about the effectiveness of performance.

The job characteristics model proposes that the five core job attributes induce critical psychological states that establish the basis of enriched and meaningful work. The model also proposed that certain types of people respond more favorably to enriched work than others, most notably those people who had a strong need for personal growth through work. The job characteristics model is credited with advancing the concept that work itself can be designed to have motivating properties, and that the motivation of individuals is not independent of a work context. As expressed by Grant et al. (2011), "Job design is an actionable feature of organizational context. Managers typically have more influence and control over job design than they do over culture, structure, relationships, technology, and people themselves" (p. 419). Although the job characteristics model was found to be limited by problems of measurement, the historical value of the model for advancing research on job design was substantial. There can be a mismatch between the knowledge and skills of employees and work that is boring, monotonous, and emotionally deadening. The contribution of the work context to motivation can be conspicuous by both its presence and absence. Grant et al. quoted the manager of a call center who recognized what effect the tedium of work had on the employees: "This may not be a good place to study motivation because there isn't any" (p. 417).

The value of the core job attributes is embodied in the concept of *job crafting*. Many jobs permit some degree of latitude on the part of employees as to how the job is performed. The employer is concerned with the outcome of the job (i.e., whether the work gets accomplished), and is less concerned about *how* the employee structures the process of work. Job crafting is the process of allowing employees to make subtle modifications in the boundaries of their tasks and interpersonal relationships to provide more autonomy and feedback. That is, how work is performed reflects an interactionistic perspective between the psychological needs or preferences of individuals and the required output of the job. In essence, job crafting permits some psychological flexibility in how work is performed, and in so doing, can lead to greater psychological health (Bond et al., 2008). As expressed by Grant et al. (2011), "Employees are active architects, not merely passive recipients of a job" (p. 433).

Work design theory asserts that it is properties of the job or the workplace that foster motivation in people. In short, motivation is not a durable personal attribute or a trait that some people possess more of than others, but rather a variable attribute that can be enhanced if properly and intentionally designed within a work environment.

Rather than just trying to identify and select highly motivated job applicants, organizations can also design work in a way that fosters or facilitates motivation. Indeed, support for the value of the core job dimensions to enhance motivation has been evidenced in many empirical studies. For example, Humphrey et al. (2007) conducted a meta-analysis of research that examined the five core job dimensions. The authors found the five motivational characteristics of work explained 25% of the variance in job performance, 34% in job satisfaction, and 24% in organizational commitment. They concluded that the motivating properties of work (and thus how work can be designed to increase motivation) have meaningful implications for important constructs in I/O psychology. The implication is that organizations need not be passive in their desire to identify motivated employees. By the way they design work, organizations can help achieve the very outcomes they strive to attain.

Worthy of note is that while some jobs can be redesigned to enhance worker motivation to perform them, other jobs cannot be altered in any meaningful way (see Field Note 2: *Packing Light Bulbs*). As Morgeson and Humphrey (2006) concluded, the motivational characteristics of work reflect the underlying mental demands of work. For example, the job of parking lot attendant is monotonous because it involves little information processing. As such, this job would best be staffed with employees who are content with the lack of stimulation inherent in the highly repetitive nature of the tasks performed. Other jobs, as an air traffic controller, already have a very high level of information processing, and adding to it would only increase stress. There is also the issue of matching abilities and pay to the job characteristics. Campion and Berger (1990) reported that jobs characterized by higher scores on the core job dimensions were associated with higher aptitudes and higher pay. Thus, when organizations want

Field Note 2: *Packing Light Bulbs*

As the research on work design has revealed, some jobs cannot be designed to be stimulating, motivating, and challenging. Some jobs are very routine, involving highly repetitive actions, and not much can be done to enhance their appeal. Yet, unglamorous as they may be, these jobs may be vital to an organization.

A company manufactured a special type of light bulb used primarily by commercial photographers. The bulbs were very delicate and fragile, and had a relatively brief life-span. It was imperative that the bulbs be packed in pre-formed casing, one bulb per pack. Four individually packed light bulbs would be placed in a larger case for shipping to retail stores. The company tried an automated packing system, but the breakage rate of the fragile bulbs was unacceptably high. It then tried packing the light bulbs by hand, but the employee turnover rate was excessive and attributed to the tedious nature of the work. The company decided it needed people to pack the light bulbs, but needed to find workers who would not want more intellectual stimulation from the job than it could possibly provide. A facility for mentally handicapped people was contacted by the company. One of the goals of the facility was to find work their members could perform. The company hired six individuals with limited mental capability. The new workers found the job of packing light bulbs to be within their range of capability. In the first eight years of staffing the job with mentally handicapped workers, the company incurred turnover of only one packer; a much lower rate of turnover than for any other area of the company. The light bulb packers are very proud of their contributions to the company and the company is equally proud of the packers. The packers acquired the status of heroes within the company, and represent a success story of the employability of handicapped workers. This was a case of *not* redesigning a job to make it more stimulating, but rather finding employees who were sufficiently challenged by the job to perform it successfully and to continue performing it.

to make jobs more motivating, it should be realized that they will need people with more ability, and should be prepared to pay them accordingly.

In summary, the work design theory of motivation represents a classic contribution of I/O psychology toward understanding human behavior in the workplace. Achieving a good fit between the "peg and hole" can also be facilitated by altering (or redesigning) the shape of the hole.

Synthesis of Work Motivation Theories

It may be overwhelming at this point to consider the number of theories of work motivation that have been presented. Furthermore, after studying these various theories, one can reasonably ask whether any unifying themes run through them and whether one is "better" than another. Let's tackle the issue of unifying themes first. It should be clear at this point that the biggest unifying theme that cuts across each of the theories is the capacity of the different perspectives to account for the key components of motivation. Each theory provides an understanding of how the direction, intensity, and persistence of behavior is impacted by various factors, whether internal or external to the individual.

In addition, the theories of work motivation that have been presented here can be synthesized in terms of their conceptual proximity to action. Kanfer (1992) proposed that theories of motivation can be examined along a continuum ranging from distal (i.e., distant) to proximal (i.e., near) in terms of the constructs examined. *Distal* constructs such as personality exert indirect effects on behavior. *Proximal* constructs begin with the individual's goals and characteristics of the workplace that directly influence behavior. Figure 12-4 portrays the motivation constructs and associated theories arrayed along the distal/proximal continuum proposed by Kanfer.

As illustrated by the arrangement of the motivational theories in Kanfer's framework, the array of explanations for motivation range from genetic predisposition to the characteristics of jobs. At the extreme distal end is the construct of genetics/heredity. As noted earlier, this view takes the approach that motivation is determined by factors inherent in each of us, and largely outside of our control. Also on the more distal end are flow theory and self-determination theory. Given that individuals differ in their

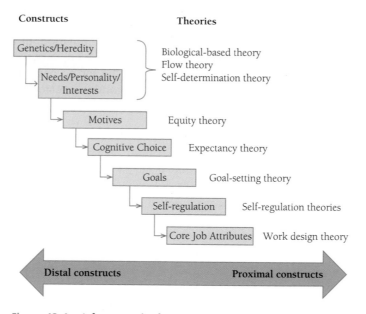

Figure 12-4　*A framework of motivation constructs and theories*

Adapted from "Work Motivation: New Directions in Theory and Research," by R. Kanfer, 1992, in C. L. Cooper and I. T. Robertson (Eds.), *International review of industrial and organizational psychology*, p. 4, London: Wiley.

propensity to experience flow, we put it on the more distal side of the continuum. In addition, self-determination theory is placed here given its view that motivation can be influenced by our own intrinsic interest (which is based on whether basic needs are met) in an activity as well as through extrinsic means.

As we continue down the continuum toward proximal constructs, there is increasing reliance on the assumption that people have clear motives for their behaviors and make conscious, deliberate, controllable choices about how much effort they choose to expend. This is the antithesis of a genetic/dispositional orientation toward motivation. Proximal theories are heavily predicated upon a cognitive explanation for motivation. Expectancy theory postulates that individuals are consciously aware of the results or outcomes they wish to attain, perceive relationships between their behavior and attaining those outcomes, and also perceive a relationship between their effort and their behavior. The theory elevates motivation to a conscious choice made by the individual.

Equity theory and goal-setting theory are other examples of this orientation. Like expectancy theory, equity theory proposes that individuals are rational decision makers who calculate fairness beliefs on the basis of how they see themselves and others treated. Their motivation is a direct result of these cognitive assessments. Furthermore, goal-setting theory offers motivation as an opportunity to engage in self-control or self-regulation. Goal-setting theory postulates that one way we can take some control over our life is to decide how hard we are willing to work. Locke (1991) offered this description of how important individual choice or volition is in our lives:

> For example, people can choose . . . what their needs are and how to satisfy them; what values they should pursue and the validity of the values other people have told them to pursue; whether and how to apply their values to a specific situation; what goals to set, how to develop plans to reach them, and whether to commit to the goals and plans; what their performance capacity is for a specific task and how to raise it; what their performance means and who is responsible for it; the adequacy of their rewards and the relation of these rewards to their values; the causes of their affective reactions to their performance and rewards; and how to modify these reactions (e.g., by changing their performance or changing their value standards). (pp. 297–298)

Self-regulation theories of motivation are extensions and modifications of goal-setting theory. Self-regulation theories also involve consciously setting goals, then obtaining feedback on the degree to which the individual is on target in pursuit of the goal, and then using that feedback to modify or maintain the chosen paths of action to goal attainment. The process of self-monitoring or self-evaluation clearly is predicated upon a conscious, rational, deliberate strategy of using information to guide behavior.

Finally, work design theory specifies there are dimensions or components of the job itself that induce motivation. Although there are individual differences with regard to how people will respond to these job characteristics, it is the properties of the work environment itself that facilitate energized behavior. Work design theory contains the most proximal constructs, constructs that in fact can be designed or structured by the organization to induce motivation. A general summary of the major theories of work motivation discussed in this chapter is presented in Table 12-1.

Table 12-1   *Summary and organizational applicability of work motivation theories*

Theory	Source of Motivation	Organizational Applicability
Biological-based theory	Physiological factors and inherited traits	Limited: Traits that are related to higher motivation can be assessed for personnel selection.
Flow theory	Enjoyment of a task that has clear goals, unambiguous feedback, and a match between the challenge of the task and a person's skill level	Moderate: Whereas goals can be clarified and feedback provided, not all tasks can be matched to one's skill level, therefore limiting the extent to which flow can be facilitated.
Self-determination theory	Desire to fulfill the basic needs of autonomy, competence, and relatedness	Strong: Theory provides input into how and when incentives can lead to positive rather than negative effects at work.
Expectancy theory	Relationship among effort-performance links, performance-reward links, and desired outcomes	Strong: Theory provides a rational basis for why people expend effort, although not all behavior is consciously determined as postulated.
Equity theory	Drive to reduce feelings of tension caused by perceived inequity	Moderate-strong: Fairly strong links to organizational justice, but feelings of inequity can be reduced through means other than increased motivation.
Goal-setting theory	Intention to direct behavior in pursuit of acceptable goals	Strong: Ability to set goals is not restricted to certain types of people or jobs.
Self-regulation theories	Self-monitoring of feedback designed to enhance goal attainment	Strong: Organizations can provide directive feedback to individuals to facilitate goal attainment.
Work design theory	Attributes of jobs that can facilitate motivation among people with a strong need to achieve	Moderate: Not all jobs can be designed to be stimulating or motivating.

The Impact of Time on Work Motivation

As can be seen from the various theories, motivation is not a static concept. Instead of existing in a single, unchanging state, it is impacted by the individual, the situation, and an interaction of the two. It is reasonable, then, that it would also be impacted by issues of time. For example, motivation is impacted when the time to complete a task is restricted through deadlines. Goals often include deadlines. Schmidt et al. (2013) noted that short deadlines are typically more difficult than longer deadlines and create a sense of urgency, which can increase the commitment that people have toward their goals. Deadlines can also be problematic, however, in that there is evidence that they can impair creativity (Amabile et al., 2002). In addition, as noted earlier, time pressures may increase risk taking (Van Mierlo & Kleingeld, 2010).

Social Media and I/O Psychology: *Cyberloafing*

A startling infographic was released in 2012 by LearnStuff that suggests 6 out of 10 people visit social media sites while at work, and are interrupted on average every 10.5 minutes by instant messages, tweets, and Facebook messages. Moreover, they report it then takes those interrupted employees 23 minutes to get back on task. Furthermore, they estimate that on average each social media user costs their employer $4,452 a year in lost productivity! While having information at our fingertips and access to a massive social network has its advantages, it can clearly also wreak havoc on employee motivation. This act of wasting time at work on the Internet is known as *cyberloafing*.

Cyberloafing can be thought of as an indicator of low work motivation. If individuals are directing their efforts on activities that are unrelated to their work, they are clearly not motivated. Moreover, according to Wagner et al. (2012), this appears to be even more the case when people haven't slept well or have had less sleep than usual. Indeed, they found an increased level of cyberloafing on the Monday following daylight saving time. Apparently, having one less hour of sleep than normal was related to more cyberloafing at a national level!

So, besides hoping their employees are well-rested, what can organizations do to decrease cyberloafing and redirect employee motivation back to work activities? A study by Ugrin and Pearson (2013) found that simply having policies in place to deter social media use will likely be ineffective. Instead, they note that individuals will only be persuaded to cease their social media usage when policies are coupled with a belief that they are likely to be caught and they are aware that severe punishments have actually been enforced in the past. Nevertheless, they caution that threatening employees with a severe punishment (e.g., they could be fired) can run the risk of being seen as overly harsh and decreasing morale.

Related to the topic of deadlines is the concept of procrastination. According to Steel (2007), procrastination is when individuals "voluntarily delay an intended course of action despite expecting to be worse off for the delay" (p. 66). Rather than focus on a particular task, they opt to focus on other activities (see Social Media and I/O Psychology: *Cyberloafing*). Steel referred to procrastination as the "quintessential self-regulatory failure" (p. 65) and noted that it is extremely prevalent, with references to procrastination dating back thousands of years. As an explanation for why procrastination occurs, Steel and König (2006) noted that outcomes that occur in the distal future are likely to be discounted relative to outcomes occurring more immediately. As such, activities for which an outcome won't occur for a while will likely be put off until later. van Eerde (2003) meta-analytically found that individuals who had high levels of conscientiousness and self-efficacy were less likely to procrastinate compared to individuals low on conscientiousness and self-efficacy. DeArmond et al. (2014) found that individuals were more likely to procrastinate when their workloads were heavy, in part because the excessive amounts of work made them fatigued and psychologically detached from their work. Nguyen et al. (2013) collected data from over 22,000 people and found that procrastination was related to lower salaries, shorter durations of employment, and a greater likelihood of being unemployed.

Planning fallacy
The tendency to
underestimate how long
it will take to complete
a task.

Unfortunately, people often underestimate how long it will take for them to complete a task, a phenomenon known as the **planning fallacy**. According to Buehler et al. (2010), the estimate the people have for how long an activity will take is more related to when they start the activity than when they finish. So, if they don't think a task will take very long to finish, individuals will delay starting it. One reason for tasks taking longer than planned is because of interruptions. As Schmidt et al. noted, "When interruptions can occur, delays in task completion can occur despite the best of intentions" (p. 327). One strategy that has been found to reduce the planning fallacy is to "unpack" tasks into subtasks (Kruger & Evans, 2004). By identifying the various components that comprise the larger task, individuals are much better at accurately predicting how long a task will take. In addition, Buehler et al. (2012) found that the planning fallacy was reduced when people took a third-person perspective when imagining a task rather than a first-person view. They suggested that taking this third-person perspective made individuals less likely to be overly optimistic in their plans and made them consider potential obstacles that they might not have otherwise.

The Application of Motivational Strategies

After eight approaches to work motivation have been presented, it is almost inevitable to ask which theory has the greatest practical value or, perhaps more to the point, which theory will "work" for you. There is no simple answer to this question, but some practical guidelines are available to assist in the decision. Mitchell (1997) referred to this process as "matching" motivational strategies with varying organizational contexts.

Mitchell stated that we must begin with a general assessment of the situation we face and then systematically narrow our focus. There are three major determinants to human behavior: ability, motivation, and situational factors (including constraints). The most obvious beginning point for our assessment is constraints. Constraints are obstacles or impediments that limit the range of our behavior. It would be our initial goal to remove the constraints, or at the least reduce their limiting effect on our behavior. The lack of a needed piece of equipment (e.g., a computer) is an example of a situational constraint. Gaining access to a computer might readily improve your behavior in a way that "trying harder" might not.

If your behavior is not constrained or limited, the next step is to examine whether you have sufficient skills and abilities to engage in the desired behavior. Perhaps you have a computer, but you don't have the knowledge, ability, or sufficient training to use it. If lack of ability does not appear to be a major issue, the problem may have a large motivational component. In short, there is nothing preventing you from engaging in the behavior and you have the ability to engage in the behavior, but you are unwilling or uninterested in doing so. However, there are several types of motivational issues to consider. If you feel bored or indifferent, the motivational issue is one of arousal. If you are interested and try to succeed but your efforts result in failure, perhaps your energies are being channeled in the wrong direction. If you are going in the wrong direction to achieve your goal, trying harder will not result in success. Alternatively, some successful behaviors require a high intensity of motivation. In this context "trying harder" would be an appropriate strategy because moderate levels of effort may not be adequate to attain the desired outcome.

Finally, there is also a persistence dimension to motivation. Some outcomes can be achieved by engaging in short but intense bursts of energy (e.g., getting a good grade by "cramming" the night before the exam). Other outcomes can be achieved only by persistence and dedicated effort over the long haul, not by a sudden burst of motivation. Becoming physically fit through proper exercise and diet is an example of an outcome that can be achieved only through persistence.

Self-regulation theories provide additional insights into how we can change our behavior in a positive direction (Diefendorff & Lord, 2008). First, rather than dwelling on our mistakes and the negative emotions they produce in us, we should regard our mistakes as an opportunity to learn. This same concept is the basis for *error management training* discussed in Chapter 6. Second, the ability to sustain motivation is strongly influenced by emotions. When we attain a personal goal, we should reward ourselves with something that induces a positive mood. Alternatively, when we don't reach a personal goal, we should deny ourselves the reward. Third, we should recognize that interruptions distract our attention, and we should actively structure our workplace and time to minimize them. Doing so will increase the likelihood we will remain "on target" and stay focused. Mitchell et al. (2008) described the importance of *pacing* and *spacing* in the allocation of time and effort to accomplish goals that have deadlines. *Pacing* pertains to how we regulate ourselves in pursuit of a single goal, and *spacing* is how we allocate our time and effort in pursuing multiple goals. The authors advocate creating a plan that identifies tasks that are particularly difficult and important, while deadlines create a sense of accountability and urgency. The plan fosters sensitivity to the discrepancy between tasks completed and their projected dates of completion, thereby informing us as to whether we are ahead or behind schedule. Vancouver et al. (2010) noted that most research on goal choice and goal striving has focused on a single goal, but in real life we are often confronted with pursuing multiple goals simultaneously. These authors proposed a formal model that explained the strategy people use in allocating their motivational resources in pursuing multiple goals.

While the field of I/O psychology has advanced the state of our knowledge about work motivation, we have much to learn (see I/O Psychology and the Economy: *Inflation and Work Motivation*). In particular, the question of how to sustain motivation (the perseverance dimension) is under-researched. Kanfer (2009) noted the contrast between short-term and long-term contexts. An athletic coach may give an inspiring talk before the start of a contest that lasts a few hours. Such a context is very different from most work environments where effort must be sustained to achieve goals over weeks and months. In the contemporary work world organizations face turbulent environments. Changing business conditions can require organizations to reduce employment, yet the surviving employees of a layoff must sustain their motivation. Kanfer stated that we know more about enhancing short-term bursts of motivation for maximal performance, but we are less knowledgeable of how to maintain consistent effort over a long-term period. Diefendorff and Chandler (2011) concluded, "The changing nature of the world economy, organizations, jobs, and the way companies do business suggests that the factors that shape motivation and the challenges organizations face in improving motivation are likely to change" (p. 114). This view of motivation is highly consistent with many areas of I/O psychology—the 21st century has brought unparalleled change to our understanding of the modern work world.

I/O Psychology and the Economy: *Economic Inflation and Work Motivation*

The topic of work motivation provides an opportunity to examine a different type of linkage between I/O psychology and the economy. While our attention has been drawn to a recessionary economy, another economic condition is *inflation*. Inflation is *not* the opposite of recession, but economists generally believe that as the effects of an economic recession recede, the likelihood of inflation increases.

Inflation is an increase in the cost of goods and services over a specified time period (for example, three months). When price levels increase, each unit of currency purchases proportionally less. Thus inflation weakens the power of money to purchase goods and services. In the United States one index of inflation is the Consumer Price Index; essentially a measure of what it costs to purchase a defined set of items. As the cost of these items increases, the increase is reflected in a rising Consumer Price Index. Inflation is indexed across a broad spectrum of purchasable items.

There are numerous reasons why people work; different scientific disciplines have offered various explanations (see Field Note 1 in Chapter 11). As described by Kaufman (2008), economists believe that financial incentives are critical to understanding why people work, and to a large extent, how hard they work. It is with money derived through employment that we can purchase the goods and services needed to live our lives.

Psychologists recognize the importance of money in work motivation, but we believe other factors are more critical. I/O psychological research has revealed the importance of stimulating work, opportunities for personal growth, and feeling a sense of purpose and accomplishment as the primary reasons why people work. However, these more psychological reasons for work motivation are premised on individuals having relatively fixed or static costs for goods and services in their lives. When the economy enters an inflationary period, the costs of goods and services is not static, but escalating. In response, the importance of money becomes greater to employees as more money is needed to pay for the same goods and services.

How do employees go about getting paid more money for the work they perform? Most organizations award pay raises on an *annual* basis. Asking your employer for a mid-year pay raise to offset inflation will most likely be summarily rejected. An alternative solution would be for you to cut back on your total purchases; in essence, to accept a lower standard of living. Another approach would be to find another job that paid more money, but there may be new costs associated with switching employers. Yet another strategy might be to exchange more of your time for more money, as by working overtime or taking on a second job.

During times of high inflation, unionized employees (to be discussed in Chapter 14) have successfully bargained for a provision in the labor contract that specifies the company will make mid-year increases in wages and salaries to offset the effects of inflation. Such increases are called *cost-of-living-adjustments* (COLAs). The COLAs are paid independent of merit performance, the usual reason for a pay raise. There is also a link between the cost of goods and services and money paid to employees. As individuals we tend to separate what we are paid (income) from what we spend (expenses). From an organizational perspective, income for employees is another cost paid by employers to operate the business—labor costs. The effect of paying more money to employees to offset inflation actually adds to the level of inflation, as the company must now charge more for the goods or services it provides to

$ £
¥ €

I/O Psychology and the Economy: *Economic Inflation and Work Motivation*
(continued)

offset its increased labor costs. The compounding and interacting effects of increased labor costs offsetting increased consumer prices results in what is called the *wage-price spiral.* That is, the increased cost of goods and services prompts an increase in labor costs, which in turn produces yet another increase in the cost of goods and services, and so on.

As research has shown, there are no simple or singular reasons for why people work. Certainly money is one reason. But employees and organizations do not exist in a vacuum, unaffected by larger-scale issues of an economic nature. An inflationary economy increases the importance of money as it takes more of it to maintain the same standard of living.

Chapter Summary

- Work motivation is one of the most fundamental and critical issues in understanding the way people behave in organizations.
- Motivation is a very complex topic, and various theories have been proposed to explain why people behave as they do.
- One set of theories posits that people differ in their motivation because of innate personality differences, perhaps of a genetic origin.
- Individuals are likely to experience the intense form of intrinsic motivation known as flow when they have clear goals, unambiguous feedback, and both the challenge of the task and the individual's skill levels are high.
- Self-determination theory suggests that when individuals have the basic needs of autonomy, competence, and relatedness met, they will be more likely to experience intrinsic motivation.
- According to equity theory, when individuals perceive a situation as unfair, they will be motivated to restore the equity.
- The expectancy theory of motivation posits that individuals establish a linkage between what they want to attain, how well they must perform to get what they want, and how hard they must work to perform at that level.
- The goal-setting theory of motivation states that people intentionally set goals for themselves and then direct their behavior to attain the desired goal.
- A set of theories pertaining to the self-regulation theory of motivation assert that people set goals for themselves and then engage in a process of self-monitoring. The feedback they receive tells them whether they are "on target" in achieving their goals, and then they will adjust their effort and behavior accordingly.
- The work design theory of motivation posits that the capacity for motivation lies not within people but within the work environment. Jobs can be designed in a way that motivates the people who perform them.
- The various theories of work motivation offer practical techniques that can be applied to enhance motivation.
- Work motivation is impacted by time elements, including deadlines and procrastination.
- Recent research on motivation is directed toward understanding the process by which people adapt to their ever-changing jobs.

CHAPTER

13 Leadership

Chapter Outline

Learning Objectives

- Describe the major theoretical approaches to the study of leadership: trait, behavioral, power and influence, contingency, full-range leadership model, authentic leadership, servant leadership, implicit leadership, and substitutes for leadership.
- Understand the points of convergence among the leadership approaches.
- Describe the dark side of leadership.
- Explain how leadership is evidenced in teams.
- Understand cross-cultural leadership issues.
- Understand diversity issues in leadership.
- Understand the concept of entrepreneurship.

When you think of leadership, many ideas might come to mind. Your thoughts might relate to power, authority, and influence. Maybe you think of actual people, such as Washington, Lincoln, or Churchill. Or perhaps you think of behaviors engaged in by effective leaders. The concept of leadership evokes a multitude of thoughts, all of which in some way address the causes, symptoms, or effects of leadership. Bennis (2007) framed the concept of leadership in terms of three factors. "Leadership is grounded in a relationship. In its simplest form, it is a tripod—a leader or leaders, followers, and the common goal they want to achieve. None of these three elements can survive without the others" (pp. 3–4).

Barling et al. (2011) stated, "Leadership is a fascinating and controversial topic, about which much is known and much remains to be learned" (p. 183). This general description of leadership is highly similar to work motivation (as discussed in Chapter 12)—both topics have intrigued I/O psychology since the founding of the discipline. The intense desire to know what makes a leader effective, and the pervasive interest in the topic of leadership in general, is perhaps summarized best by Birnbaum (2013), who notes, "Even if we can't precisely define or articulate its substance, we know that 'leadership' is a real, if rare phenomenon. We sense it when it is present, and when it is missing its absence is palpable" (p. 261). He further romanticizes the notion of leadership and its importance by stating, "Human groups succumb to entropy and fall apart without the energy provided by leadership" (p. 263). This chapter will examine how I/O psychologists have tried to grapple with the multifaceted concept of leadership, particularly as it relates to behavior in the world of work.

Researchers have approached the concept of leadership from many different perspectives. Some researchers have examined what strong leaders are like as people by looking at demographic variables, personality traits, skills, and so on. Without followers, there can be no leaders; accordingly, some researchers have examined leader–follower relationships. Presumably "strong" leaders accomplish things that "weak" leaders do not; thus other researchers have focused on the effects of leadership. An interesting question addresses contextual effects in leadership—for example, is leadership of a prison more demanding than leadership of a business organization? Thus the situation in which leadership occurs has attracted much attention. Although the diversity of interests in the domain of leadership research expands our basis of understanding, it also creates ambiguity as to exactly what leadership is all about.

It is also a matter of scientific debate whether "leadership" is different from "management" or "administration." Historically and practically, these terms have been used interchangeably. For example, one might readily encounter this sentence: "The leaders of the company manage its resources and are responsible for its administration." A slight variation would be: "The management of the company administers its operations by providing leadership." Are these terms really synonymous? Some researchers think not, believing that management requires administrative oversight but not necessarily the manifestation of leadership. Leadership implies providing a vision of the future and inspiring others to make that vision a reality. As such, a large component of leadership is implicitly future-oriented. In contrast, management and administration refer more to present-oriented activities. According to some scholars, leadership has a heroic, larger-than-life quality that differentiates it from related concepts. Some people believe that individuals can be trained to be managers, but leaders possess unique qualities that may not be developed in everyone. This debate of whether leaders are born or made is evidenced in some of the theories presented here.

Leadership researchers have also given considerable attention to the question of how important leaders are to leadership. Often the focus is on the traits and behaviors of leaders and how that impacts leader emergence and effectiveness. Recent theorists, however, have also questioned the extent to which followers matter, as well as the degree to which the situation in which the leaders are in matters. Within this area, scholars are seeking to answer the questions of why some leaders seem to be able to effectively lead some people but not others and why some leaders are effective in some situations but not others. Hollander (2009), for example, described leadership as a process that is inextricably linked to the needs and goals of followers. Casual observation suggests that some people are easier for leaders to work with than others.

In general, leadership is of interest to the I/O practitioner as well as to the scientist. In fact, leadership is one of the richer areas of interplay between the two; it has had a healthy influx of ideas from both camps. Identifying and developing leaders are major concerns of organizations today. Companies often train their higher-level personnel in skill areas (interpersonal relations, decision making, planning, etc.) that directly affect their performance as leaders. In Greensboro, North Carolina, there is an organization called the Center for Creative Leadership whose purpose is to enhance, through training, the leadership skills of key business personnel. Not surprisingly, the military is also greatly concerned with leadership. It sponsors a wide variety of research projects that have the potential for enhancing our understanding of this subject. In summary, the balance between the theory and practice of leadership is fairly even as a result of this dual infusion of interest.

Theoretical Approaches to Leadership

Numerous theoretical approaches have been developed to explain leadership. In fact, more theories of leadership exist than there is room in this book to present. We focus on the approaches that have been the most dominant historically and currently.

The Trait Approach

Trait approach
A conception that leadership is best understood in terms of traits or dispositions held by an individual that are accountable for the observed leadership.

The **trait approach** is the oldest conception of leadership. Zaccaro et al. (2004) defined leader traits as "relatively stable and coherent integration of personality characteristics that foster a consistent pattern of leadership performance across a variety of group and organizational situations. These characteristics reflect a range of stable individual differences, including personality, temperament, motives, cognitive abilities, skills, and expertise" (p. 104). Day and Zaccaro (2007) added that personality traits do not "cause" behavior, but are labels or terms used to make sense of behaviors. In this view of leadership, effective leaders are described as possessing characteristics (traits) that are associated with leadership talents. The list of such traits is extensive and often includes personality characteristics such as being decisive, dynamic, outgoing, assertive, strong, bold, and persuasive. Various other traits have also been proposed as related to the acceptance of a leader, including being tall, good-looking, poised, articulate, confident, and authoritative. The constellation of traits in a person can prompt others to regard the person as "born to lead" or a "natural leader." Research by Kirkpatrick and Locke (1991) revealed that although the presence of such traits is associated with people in leadership positions, their presence does not guarantee success.

An extension of the trait approach to leadership is that certain traits are more (or less) important for success because of their influence on behaviors of importance to leaders. The classic research of McClelland and his colleagues (e.g., McClelland & Boyatzis, 1982) identified three motives or needs that drive the behavior of leaders. They are the *need for power*, the *need for achievement*, and the *need for affiliation*. In this sense requisite leadership traits are represented not as attributes that people possess, but as the underlying basis for why they behave as they do. The need for power is reflected in the desire to influence other people, to control events, and to function in a position of formal authority. The need for achievement is evidenced in the desire to solve problems, attain results, and accomplish objectives. The need for affiliation is manifested in the desire to associate or affiliate with other people in a social context, to provide guidance and support for them, and to derive gratification from helping others to succeed. These three needs are classics in the field of personality, where one's personality is defined from the perspective of the dominant needs that drive leader behavior.

Other research on personality as a basis for explaining leadership has also been conducted. Hoffman et al. (2011) examined the role of various traits, such as self-confidence, dominance, and achievement orientation on leadership effectiveness. They found evidence that these traits were "able to distinguish effective from ineffective leaders lending credence to the hypothesis that to some extent, leaders are born, not made" (p. 365). They also examined individual differences, such as interpersonal skills, oral and written communication, and decision making. They found that these more malleable characteristics similarly predicted leader effectiveness, supporting the notion that leaders can be developed.

In general, the trait approach was dominant in the early days of leadership research, then fell out of favor for a long time, and only lately has regained some credibility through the recent advances in personality assessment. Traits offer the potential to explain why people seek leadership positions and why they act the way they do when they occupy these positions. It is now evident that some traits and skills increase the likelihood of leadership success, even though they do not ensure it. Despite this progress, the utility of the trait approach for understanding leadership is limited by the elusive nature of traits. Traits interact with situational demands and constraints to influence a leader's behavior, and this behavior interacts with other situational variables to influence group process variables, which in turn affect group performance. It is therefore difficult to understand how leader traits can affect subordinate motivation or group performance unless we examine how traits are expressed in the actual behavior of leaders. Emphasis on leadership behavior ushers in the next era of research on leadership.

Behavioral approach
A conception that leadership is best understood in terms of the actions taken by an individual in the conduct of leading a group.

The Behavioral Approach

The **behavioral approach** to leadership shifts the focus from traits that leaders possess to specific behaviors or actions in which leaders engage. Whereas the trait approach addresses the extent to which leaders are born, the behavioral approach addresses the extent to which leaders are made.

A major contribution to the behavioral approach to leadership was made in the 1950s by researchers at Ohio State University. Their research is regarded as classic among efforts to understand the phenomenon of leadership. The researchers asked workers to describe the actions of their supervisors in leadership situations. Based on the results, two critical leadership factors were identified. One relates to how the leader gets work accomplished. This factor was named *initiation of structure* and addresses the means by which leaders provide direction or structure to get workers to accomplish tasks. The second factor addresses how the leader interacts on a personal level with workers. This factor was named *consideration* and concerns the people-oriented aspects of leadership (i.e., being considerate of others). Sixty years after its original development, researchers are still reporting evidence of its value. Judge et al. (2004) conducted a meta-analysis of studies that examined the validity of initiation of structure and consideration. Initiation of structure was highly correlated with leader effectiveness, while consideration was predictive of workers being satisfied with their leader.

Over the years the behavioral approach was expanded to include other dimensions of leadership besides those originally identified in the Ohio State studies. Research from the behavioral approach has identified specific leader behaviors that are associated with effective leadership. Two such behaviors are monitoring the employees' work and providing clarification on ambiguous issues. Researchers discovered that although monitoring is an important leadership behavior, it alone does not account for effective leadership. Monitoring an employee's work may identify a problem, but it is also necessary to find a solution to the problem. Likewise, clarifying a work problem by delegating assignments to different employees will be effective only if the employees accept their assignments and have the skills needed to perform them. It became evident that the behavioral approach (i.e., the identification of specific leader behaviors) interacted in complex ways with other factors, such as the skill level of the employees. In short, although the behavioral approach identified critical leader behaviors, the process of being an effective leader was more complicated than simply eliciting those behaviors. In particular, it was concluded that how a leader exercises power and influence with subordinates is particularly important to understand. This realization led to the next phase of leadership research [see Social Media and I/O Psychology: *Follow the Leader (on Twitter)*].

The Power and Influence Approach

Power and influence approach
A conception that leadership is best understood by the use of the power and influence exercised by a person with a group.

The **power and influence approach** is yet another way of conceptualizing leadership. The trait approach focused on what attributes a leader possesses; the behavioral approach focused on what a leader does. The power and influence approach asserts that leadership is an exercise of power by one person (the leader) over other people (the subordinates). Furthermore, how the leader exercises power is by influencing the subordinates to behave in certain ways. As such, this approach to leadership attempts to understand the meaning of power and the tactics of influence.

Power and Leader Effectiveness.   Power manifests in many ways. French and Raven (1960) developed a classic taxonomy that proposed five bases of power: reward, coercive, legitimate, expert, and referent (see Figure 13-1).

Social Media and I/O Psychology: *Follow the Leader (on Twitter)*

There is a famous proverb that states, "He who thinks he leads, but has no followers, is only taking a walk." It would seem that social media, and Twitter in particular, may be taking this proverb to a whole new level. Leaders from all over the world have found a powerful platform in Twitter as a way of speaking to, and engaging with, their followers. World leaders such as U.S. President Barack Obama (@BarackObama) and India's Prime Minister Narendra Modi (@NarendraModi) have millions of followers each. The presidency of Mexico (@PresidenciaMX) sends an average of 70 tweets a day. Pope Francis (@Pontifex) has thousands of retweets for every tweet he sends. In short, world leaders are active and influential on Twitter.

Organizational leaders have also begun to find a voice on Twitter. With over 1.5 million followers, Arianna Huffington (@ariannahuff), President and Editor-in-Chief of the Huffington Post Media Group, uses her influence on Twitter to provide tips on balancing one's work and family. With close to 160,000 followers, Jeff Weiner (@JeffWeiner), CEO of LinkedIn, tweets about technology, recruitment, and social media. Then there's Elon Musk (@ElonMusk), co-founder of SpaceX, PayPal, SolarCity, and Tesla Motors, who reaches out to his close to one million followers with tweets about the future of space and high-speed travel.

While followers on Twitter are certainly not necessary for a leader to be successful, it is another way in which leaders can broaden their impact and strengthen their influence. Furthermore, and perhaps more the case of how Twitter and leadership are related, the number of Twitter followers may be reflective of one's influence outside of social media. For example, Warren Buffett, Chairman and CEO of Berkshire Hathaway and one of the world's wealthiest people, has only tweeted five times (with his first tweet being "Warren is in the house") yet has amassed over 870,000 followers!

Figure 13-1 *Graphic illustration of five bases of power*

1. **Reward power**. This is the capacity to offer positive incentives for desirable behavior. To the extent that you can provide something of value to somebody, you have power over them. This could include promotions, raises, vacations, good work assignments, and so on. In general, power to reward an employee is defined by the formal authority inherent in a superior's role.

2. **Coercive power**. This is the capacity to punish undesirable behavior. Dismissal, docking of pay, reprimands, and unpleasant work assignments are examples. To the extent that you can sanction others in this way, you have power over them. Like reward power, this capacity to punish is also defined by formal authority and policies inherent in the organization.

3. **Legitimate power**. Sometimes referred to as *authority*, this means that the employee believes the organization's power over him or her is legitimate. Norms and expectations help define the degree of legitimate power. If a boss asks an individual to work overtime, this would likely be seen as legitimate, given the boss's authority. However, if a coworker makes the same request, it might be turned down. The coworker has no legitimate authority to make the request, although the individual might agree out of friendship.

4. **Expert power**. This base of power relies on expertise that an individual has in a given area. If others rely on you for your knowledge and judgments, you have power. Consultants, for example, are called on to help handle problems because they are seen as experts in certain areas. The source of expert power is the perceived experience, knowledge, or ability of a person. It is not formally sanctioned in the organization.

5. **Referent power**. This is the most abstract type of power. One employee might admire another, want to be like that person, and want to be approved of by him or her. That person is a *referent*, someone the employee refers to. The source of referent power is the referent's personal qualities. Cultural factors may contribute to these qualities. Younger people will often defer to an older person partly because age, to some, is a personal quality that engenders deference. Norms can also generate referent power. An employee may wish to identify with a particular group and will bow to the group's expectations.

Yukl (1994) noted that the success of an influence attempt is a matter of degree. It produces three qualitatively distinct outcomes. *Commitment* describes an outcome in which an individual (the target) enthusiastically accepts a request from another individual (the agent) and makes a great effort to carry out the request effectively. *Compliance* describes an outcome in which the target is willing to do what the agent asks but is apathetic rather than enthusiastic about it and makes only a minimal effort. *Resistance* describes an outcome in which the target person is opposed to the request, rather than merely indifferent about it, and actively tries to avoid carrying it out.

Some researchers have proposed that the manner in which power is exercised largely determines whether it results in enthusiastic commitment, passive compliance, or stubborn resistance. Effective leaders use combinations of power in a subtle fashion that minimizes status differentials and avoids threats to the self-esteem of subordinates. In contrast, leaders who exercise power in an arrogant and manipulative manner are likely to engender resistance.

Individuals differ in the extent to which they use the various bases of power. Authoritarian managers rely on reward and coercive power. Managers with a participative style rely on expert and referent power. Members of the military frequently rely heavily on the legitimate power inherent in military rank. Stahelski et al. (1989) reported that university administrators use referent and expert power more than legitimate, reward, or coercive power to influence professors.

Ragins and Sundstrom (1989) examined gender differences in the path to power within organizations. They concluded that power seems to grow incrementally through the accumulation of multiple resources over the span of a career. For women, the path to power contains many impediments and barriers that create an obstacle course. The path to power for men contains fewer obstacles that derive from their gender and may actually have sources of support unavailable to their female counterparts.

The Contingency Approach

Contingency approach
A conception that leadership is best understood in terms of the actions taken by an individual in the conduct of leading a group.

The **contingency approach** to leadership moves away from a focus on the leaders and their behaviors and influence to one that also includes a consideration of the situation in which leadership is occurring. Theories that fall under this approach assume that the leader's traits and behaviors that will be most effective will be contingent upon, or depend on, what is happening in the environment. According to contingency theories, it is not enough to simply think about the leader in isolation. Instead, you must consider the leader, the followers, and the situation together. Barling (2014) described this in terms of a fire metaphor: "Leaders constitute the spark, followers the flammable material, and the situation the oxygen—and without an appropriate mix of all three components, nothing of much significance will ever happen!" (p. 292).

Fiedler's contingency model
A contingency approach to leadership that suggests a leader's effectiveness will depend on the interaction between his or her leadership style and the favorability of the situation.

The most comprehensive leadership theory that takes a contingency approach is Fiedler's (1967) **contingency model**. Fiedler proposed that leaders have a relatively fixed leadership style based on their personality. Fiedler developed a personality scale that reveals the leader's orientation. The leader is classified as being either task-oriented or relationship-oriented (or a mix of the two).

Once the leader's style is identified, it is important to determine the favorability of the situation, as this is what will determine whether the leader's style will be effective or ineffective. The favorability of the situation is determined by three factors: leader-member relations, the degree of task structure, and the leader's position power. When all three of these are high — the followers respect and trust the leader, the task is clear and structured, and the leader's position grants him or her clear authority and power — the situation is said to be most favorable. When all three of these are low, the situation is most unfavorable. According to Fiedler, task-oriented leaders are more effective under these extreme conditions of favorability and unfavorability. Relationship-oriented leaders are more effective under the intermediate conditions (such as when task structure and position power are low but leader-member relations are high).

There are several other theories that take a contingency approach to leadership, including one that suggests the effectiveness of a leader depends on the level of confidence and ability of the followers (i.e., situational leadership theory). Another theory that suggests a leader should provide different leadership styles depending on the situation, with a goal of helping followers achieve their goals. The common theme that cuts across all contingency theories is the consideration of the situation when examining leader effectiveness.

The various theories within the contingency approach to leadership have received support over the years. The emphasis, however, has shifted and fewer researchers are focusing on this particular approach. In fact, Rumsey (2013) noted that trait, behavioral, and contingency theories have all received far less attention, making way for a "new genre of leadership" (p. 462). Nevertheless, while these approaches to leadership have waned, the realization that the interaction between leaders, followers, and the situation is important has remained. A more recent approach to understanding situations is to consider the adaptive nature of the leader. As Shamir (2013) highlights, theorists now acknowledge that leaders operate in contexts that are "more varied, complex, dynamic, and unpredictable" (p. 348). As such, he notes that the current emphasis is on a leader's ability to adapt to a wide variety of situations and circumstances. The idea is that a leader who is more adaptable will be more effective regardless of the context. Thus, it is not that the situation doesn't matter. On the contrary, the point is that the situation *does* matter, but because the situation is continuously changing, the leader needs to be ready and able to adapt as the need arises.

Leader-Member Exchange Theory

Leader–member exchange theory
A theory of leadership based on the nature of the relationship between a leader and members of the group he or she leads.

Another approach to leadership is one that takes into account the relationships between leaders and their followers. According to **leader–member exchange theory** (LMX), leaders differentiate their followers in terms of (1) their competence and skill, (2) the extent to which they can be trusted (especially when not being watched by the leader), and (3) their motivation to assume greater responsibility within the unit (Dansereau et al., 1975). Followers (termed "members" in this theory) with these attributes develop high-quality relationships with the leader and become part of the *in-group*. In-group members go beyond their formal job duties and take responsibility for completing tasks that are most critical to the success of the work group. In return, they receive more attention, support, and sensitivity from their leaders. Members who do not have these attributes are in the *out-group*; they do the more routine, mundane tasks and have a more formal relationship with the leader. Leaders influence out-group members by using formal authority, but this is not necessary with in-group members. Thus leaders and followers use different types and degrees of influence depending on whether the follower is in the in-group or out-group. As expressed by Liden et al. (1997): "Quite simply, members who receive more information and support from the leader and who engage in tasks that require challenge and responsibility are expected to have more positive job attitudes and engage in more positive behaviors than members whose support is limited to what is required by the employment contract" (p. 60).

Research has revealed how LMX theory is useful in explaining dimensions of organizational behavior. Furst and Cable (2008) found that when there is a strong LMX relationship, employees trust their manager and offer less resistance to organizational change. Henderson et al. (2008) reported that the greater the LMX relationship, the greater the employee's commitment to the psychological contract that bonds the individual to the organization.

It is important to consider how other people in the organization play a role in the exchange relationships between leaders and members. Martin et al. (2010) proposed that each exchange relationship is a bi-directional lens through which both parties see each other in the work context. Because employees are situated within an organizational hierarchy (with others above and below them), each relationship is its own lens. Thus an individual within an organization views others through multiple lenses, like a kaleidoscope. Along these lines, Hu and Liden (2013) found that individuals compare their LMX relationship with the relationships that the leader has with other individuals. They found that when people feel they have a better relationship with their leader than their teammates have with the leader, they are more confident in their ability to perform their job, which leads to better job performance, more citizenship behaviors, and higher job satisfaction. In addition to teammates' LMX relationships having an impact, the presence of multiple leaders is also an important consideration. Vidyarthi et al. (2014) noted that when an employee has two leaders, each exchange relationship exists with the other in mind. When they are aligned with one another, the member is more satisfied and less likely to leave the organization. When they are misaligned, however, the member is less satisfied and more likely to quit.

More than any other theory of leadership, LMX emphasizes the importance of the relationship between each leader and each follower. Recent conceptualizations have expanded this to include the need for leaders to forge relationships and alliances beyond the follower. That is, the traditional LMX conceptualization noted that each leader and follower have their own exchange relationships that vary in quality. Leader-member pairs that have higher quality relationships have what are essentially informal contracts in which it is understood that the leader will help and support the member and the member, in turn, will help and support the leader. Graen (2013) provided an updated version of LMX, termed *Leader Motivated Xcellence*, which proposes that strategic alliances are formed by leaders with individuals within and outside of the organization that are mutually beneficial to fulfillment of the leader's and the organization's goals. Thus, exchange relationships exist beyond just the leader and his or her followers, but also between the leader and his or her peers, supervisors, and other internal and external constituents. To date, research on this updated view of LMX theory is lacking. Time will tell whether it gains acceptance among leadership researchers.

Full-Range Leadership Theory

Transformational leadership
A conception that leadership is the process of inspiring a group to pursue goals and attain results.

The next leadership theory addresses the distinction between a manager and a leader perhaps better than any other leadership theory. Avolio (2011) describes the full-range leadership theory as consisting of three separate groups of behaviors that form the full spectrum of leadership. At the highest end of the spectrum is **transformational leadership**, which is a view of leadership that involves influence by a leader over subordinates, but the effect of the influence is to empower subordinates who also become leaders in the process of transforming the organization. According to this perspective, a successful leader transforms the members into believing in themselves, generating confidence in their respective abilities, and elevating their self-expectations. In short, a transformational leader's success is indexed by the group's capacity to function at a much higher level of performance than previously evidenced. A transformational leader unleashes the power and harnesses the talent within a group to help it be successful. Understanding this conversion process is the object of research on transformational leadership.

Bass (1998) suggested that transformational leaders make followers feel more aware of their own importance and value to the success of the group. Followers are expected to sublimate their self-interests for the overall benefit of the group. The desire to be trusted and respected by the leader prompts the group to respond with greater effort and commitment to achieve a common goal.

Transformational leaders behave in ways to achieve superior results by using one or more of the five components of transformational leadership (Avolio, 2011).

- **Attributed charisma.** The term charisma comes from the Greek word *kharisma*, meaning "gift of grace" and implies that a charismatic leader possesses a divinely inspired gift. Followers see leaders as powerful and charming, able to inspire devotion. There is a clear emotional element inherent in charisma. For example, as Gardner and Avolio (1998) suggested, effective charismatic leaders are able to manipulate and use their environments in ways that generate an emotional reaction in their followers. For example, a leader may stage a presentation by giving a speech in front of a building that has symbolic significance for the followers (see Field Note 1: *Use of Props by Leaders*). Thus, whether a leader is charismatic or not is more determined through gut feelings and emotional ties than through logical decisions and systematic thought processes.

- **Idealized influence.** Transformational leaders behave in ways that make them role models for their followers. Unlike charisma, their influence is driven by how followers attribute their beliefs and values rather than by their charm and personal appeal. While attributed charisma refers to follower's perceptions of the leader as being larger than life, idealized influence refers to the behaviors leaders engage in that reflect this confidence and allow them to be admired, respected, and trusted. In essence, this involves "walking the talk," or backing up one's values and beliefs with actions that accurately reflect them.

- **Inspirational motivation.** Transformational leaders behave in ways that motivate and inspire those around them by providing meaning and challenge to their followers' work. Leaders get followers involved in envisioning attractive future states; they create clearly communicated expectations that followers want to meet.

- **Intellectual stimulation.** Transformational leaders stimulate their followers' efforts to be innovative and creative by questioning assumptions, reframing problems, and approaching old situations in new ways. These leaders encourage their followers to question the status quo and challenge their own assumptions. New ideas and creative problem solutions are solicited from followers, who are included in the process of addressing problems and finding solutions.

- **Individualized consideration.** Transformational leaders pay special attention to each individual follower's needs for advancement and growth by acting as a coach or mentor. Followers and colleagues are developed to successively higher levels of potential. Individual differences in needs and desires are recognized, and the leader's own behavior demonstrates acceptance of these differences.

Transactional leadership
A conception that leadership involves providing rewards and punishments in exchange for certain behaviors of followers.

The next set of leadership behaviors in the full-range leadership theory include transactional behaviors. **Transactional leadership** consists of managerial and supervisory behaviors that focus on providing rewards and punishments to enact change in

Field Note 1: *Use of Props by Leaders*

Current research has studied the use of props by leaders and the "staging" of activities designed to enhance communication effectiveness. Several examples of props have been used by U.S. political leaders. When Richard Nixon was Vice-President of the United States, he was accused of inappropriately accepting gifts from people who wanted Nixon to use his influence on their behalf. In his defense Nixon appeared on television holding a cocker spaniel puppy named "Checkers." Nixon explained that he returned all the gifts he had received, except the dog, which he noted had become the family pet. The talk by Nixon while holding the dog became long remembered as "Nixon's Checkers speech."

When Dwight Eisenhower was President, he gave a speech on television to outline his philosophy of leadership. A camera was mounted above Eisenhower's head pointing downward at the top of his desk. Eisenhower took a piece of string out of his pocket and then demonstrated that if he pulled the string, it would fol-

low his fingers. But if he pushed the string, it would go nowhere. Equating the nation with the string, Eisenhower conveyed that he wanted to lead the nation to prosperity, not push it from behind.

Earl Butz was Secretary of Agriculture under President Nixon. Butz appeared before a congressional committee to explain the financial budget of the Department of Agriculture. While seated before the committee, Butz pulled a loaf of sliced bread out of a paper bag. He proceeded to stack the slices in various sized piles, demonstrating symbolically how the Department of Agriculture budget was allocated to various directives.

In these examples leaders used a dog, a piece of string, and a loaf of bread as props to explain issues of considerable complexity. The props were remembered long after people had forgotten the content of the speeches. It has been suggested that business leaders should learn to utilize some of the techniques of theater directors in show business to enhance their impact through the use of staging.

followers. There are clearly defined expectations for both leaders and followers, with associated consequences (see Figure 13-2). There are three components that comprise transactional leadership.

- **Contingent reward**. Transactional leaders engage in exchange relationships with their followers. When employing contingent reward behaviors, they provide rewards if followers perform in ways that are desired. The rewards can be economic (e.g., bonuses), emotional (e.g., praise), or tangible (e.g., a certificate). Although this form of leadership is fairly effective, it is considered less effective than transformational leadership.

- **Active management-by-exception**. The exchange relationships that transactional leaders use can also be based on punishments, as in the case of active management-by-exception. When engaging in these behaviors, leaders actively search for mistakes and deviations from the rules, and take corrective action in the form of punishments as they find the problems.

Figure 13-2 *Badge clearly expressing the leader-follower relationship*

- **Passive management-by-exception**. This is the lowest form of transactional leadership. Similar to active management-by-exception, leaders provide punishment for undesirable behaviors. These leaders are passive, however, rather than active in their pursuit of problems. They wait for issues to arise before intervening.

According to Barling (2014), transactional leadership "might best be viewed as an oxymoron: While many of these behaviors are necessary (e.g., contingent reward), they derive from one's formal position and reflect good management, not leadership" (p. 9). This brings us to the lowest end of the full-range leadership spectrum, **laissez-faire leadership**, which is essentially the absence of leadership. The term "laissez faire" literally means "allow to do." Laissez-faire leaders are hands-off with their followers, allowing others to make decisions and abdicating their own authority. This is the most inactive form of leadership, often considered to be non-leadership. Indeed, a failure to provide direction to followers and the avoidance of responsibility is arguably not even good management. Hinkin and Schriesheim (2008) examined the consequences of leaders failing to make decisions when others perceived that actions should have been taken. The authors found that employees were less satisfied with their supervisors when they failed to reward good performance or failed to punish poor performance. Thus, employees expect leaders to make critical decisions when circumstances call for them.

In a summary of the literature on the full-range leadership theory (see Figure 13-3), Walumbwa and Wernsing (2013) cited a considerable number of studies demonstrating that transformational leadership is consistently related to employee satisfaction and performance across a variety of situations and cultures. Moreover, a study by MacKenzie et al. (2001) showed that transformational leadership behaviors had a much stronger effect on performance and citizenship behaviors of agents in an insurance company than did transactional leadership behaviors. Not surprisingly, active and passive management-by-exception and laissez-faire leadership behaviors are largely ineffective.

Laissez-faire leadership
A form of non-leadership in which managers deflect all responsibility and leave followers on their own.

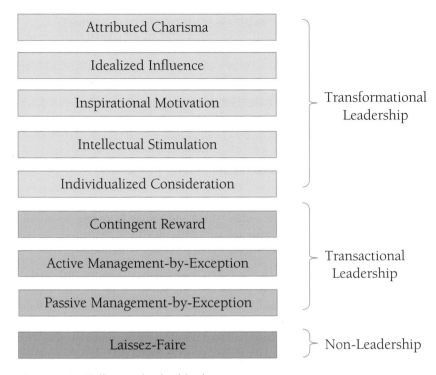

Figure 13-3   *Full-range leadership theory*

Considering the amount of research in support of transformational leadership, two points should be made. First, Bass (1985) noted that transformational leadership builds on transactional leadership. As such, leaders who engage in both types of behaviors are typically more effective than those who only engage in only one set of behaviors. Second, Barling clarifies that leaders don't have to engage in all forms of transformational behaviors at all times. As he noted, "outstanding leaders do not engage in the right behaviors *all* the time, but they rarely miss the opportunity to do so at the *right* time" (p. 20).

Authentic leadership
A conception that leaders who are self-aware, transparent in their relationships with others, unbiased in their decision making, and internally moral will be more trusted, and therefore more effective.

Authentic Leadership

A newer leadership perspective that has its roots in transformational leadership, positive psychology, and ethics is that of **authentic leadership**. This particular theory focuses on leaders being genuine in their thoughts and actions. According to Avolio et al. (2007), authentic leadership has four main components:

   1. Self-awareness: Leaders must be aware of their own strengths and weakness and how their views of themselves compare to views others have of them. Without being self-aware, a leader can't be "true to oneself," which is a key part of being authentic (May et al., 2003).

2. **Relational transparency**: Authentic leaders present themselves to others as they truly are, rather than as fake portrayals of themselves. This means that they don't try to appear better than they really are, but instead share their doubts, insecurities, and vulnerabilities alongside their strengths and accomplishments. In short, they are open and honest with their followers.

3. **Balanced processing**: Authentic leaders analyze information and come to decisions in very unbiased ways. To obtain a balanced view of issues, they solicit information from others, even if it is unlikely to go in their favor. In doing so, they are able to maintain high levels of integrity in their decision making.

4. **Internalized moral perspective**: A strong internal moral compass is a key aspect of authentic leaders. They think and behave in accordance with a value system that is guided by internal standards. As Walumbwa and Wernsing noted, authentic leaders "think and behave in a more pro-social and ethical manner even when confronted with difficult ethical challenges, because they tend to act in line with their highly developed value structures" (p. 396).

Barling clarified that "leaders are not simply 'authentic' or 'inauthentic'; they vary in the extent to which they are authentic or not" (p. 13). In addition, Avolio (2010) noted that leaders can be developed to become more authentic. By engaging in such activities as self-reflection and discussion about case studies involving moral dilemmas, leaders can become more sensitive to the consequences of their decisions and more confident in their ability to make moral decisions. Wagner (2013) suggested that such training would help prepare leaders to proactively handle ethical crises within their organizations.

Servant Leadership

Servant leadership
A conception that leadership involves putting the needs of followers ahead of one's own needs.

Another approach to leadership that has overlap with transformational, authentic, and LMX leadership theories is **servant leadership** theory. Originally introduced by Robert Greenleaf (Greenleaf, 1970), it has gained renewed attention in recent years. Servant leaders place a strong emphasis on ethics and relationships between themselves and their followers. They put the interests of followers ahead of their own and strive to develop employees, not simply to help the organization but to truly help the employees. According to Liden et al. (2008), servant leaders focus on empowering followers and helping them grow and succeed. In addition, they care about the communities in which they reside, not just their own organization and its employees.

Servant leaders' selfless focus on their followers appears to result in positive outcomes. For example, Walumbwa et al. (2010) examined 815 employees and 123 supervisors and found that servant leadership was related to employees: a) having more commitment to the supervisor, b) feeling more confident in their abilities to perform well, c) having higher justice perceptions, and d) believing there was a greater focus on customer service within the organization. In turn, these perceptions and beliefs were related to more organizational citizenship behaviors. Thus, it appears that servant leaders entice their followers to go above and beyond normal task requirements by influencing employees' attitudes and beliefs.

Servant leadership also appears to influence teams and organizations as a whole in addition to individuals. For example, Hu and Liden (2011) found that servant leadership is related to groups believing they are highly capable, which in turn is related to higher levels of group performance. In addition, Peterson et al. (2012) examined servant leadership behaviors of chief executive officers (CEOs) and found that CEO servant leadership predicted firm performance. That is, CEOs that focused their attention on the long-term prosperity of their firms and the development of their employees achieved superior financial results. Peterson et al. speculated that servant leaders, by showing that they care more about the organization's success than their own personal success and demonstrate that they value honesty more than profits, promote a benevolent climate that generates employee commitment and makes them want to perform better.

Implicit Leadership Theory

A radically different view of leadership than what has been presented thus far is that leadership exists only in the mind of the beholder, usually the follower. It may be that "leadership" is nothing more than a label we attach to a set of outcomes; that is, we observe a set of conditions and events and make the attribution that leadership has occurred or exists. Unlike the previous theories presented, **implicit leadership theory** regards leadership as a subjectively perceived construct rather than an objective entity. Implicit leadership theory is also referred to as the *attribution theory of leadership* or *social information processing theory*.

> **Implicit leadership theory**
> A conception that leadership is a perceived phenomenon as attributed to an individual by others.

Lord and his associates have made the greatest contribution to this view of leadership. For example, Lord et al. (1982) concluded that individuals hold conceptions of prototypical leaders (that is, what they think leaders are like) and then evaluate actual leaders according to their conceptions. People judged as "good" leaders are likely to be those whose actions and demeanors conform to the conception we hold. Thus "effectiveness" in leadership is determined not objectively but through the confirmation of expectations. Phillips and Lord (1981) discovered that individuals develop global impressions of leader effectiveness and then use those global impressions to describe specific dimensions of leader behavior. Thus individuals make confident judgments of behavior they have had no opportunity to observe, in much the same way halo error operates in performance appraisal. Meindl and Ehrlich (1987) discussed what they called "the romance of leadership" as it relates to assessments of organizational performance. In their study, participants gave better evaluations to performance outcomes attributed to leadership factors than they gave to the same outcomes when they were attributed to non-leadership factors. The authors concluded that leadership has assumed a heroic, larger-than-life quality in people's minds. Meindl and Ehrlich believe leadership may serve a symbolic role, causing people to feel assured and confident that the fate and fortune of an organization are in good hands. Thus the authors contended that leadership may not account for as much of an organization's success as we believe, but "leadership" has a symbolic value in producing subordinate support, which may then paradoxically produce organizational effectiveness (see I/O Psychology and the Economy: *How the Economy Influences Political Leaders*).

Lord and Brown (2004) asserted leadership is best understood from the perspective of followers. Leadership is viewed as a process through which one person, the leader, changes the way followers envision themselves. A follower-centered perspective of leadership is deemed most insightful because it is through followers' reactions and

I/O Psychology and the Economy: *How the Economy Influences Political Leaders*

The relationship between leadership and the economy is most evident when viewed through the lens of history, particularly political history.

As evidenced from the research on implicit leadership, people believe in the power of leaders to influence the general quality of life. It can be a matter of debate whether any individual leader truly has the power to effectuate large-scale change, particularly resulting in enduring positive outcomes. There is an adage that people "vote their wallets" in elections. In the United States, most presidents are re-elected to a second four-year term of office. If voters are generally satisfied with their overall economic standing, incumbent presidents typically receive a mandate to remain in office. In the 20th century, only four U.S. presidents were not re-elected to a second term of office. In three cases, economic issues were at the heart of the leadership change (the fourth case involved a third party candidate that split the votes). In 1932 the U.S. (and the world) was in the grips of the Great Depression. President Herbert Hoover failed to win re-election, losing to a relative political unknown, Franklin Delano Roosevelt. Roosevelt was credited with leading the nation out of its worst economic crisis in history. Roosevelt was subsequently re-elected three times (1936, 1940, and 1944) and his continuous re-elections prompted an amendment to the U.S. Constitution limiting the presidency to two terms. In the election of 1980 incumbent president Jimmy Carter was opposed by Ronald Reagan. At the time the nation was facing record levels of economic inflation. In a televised debate between the two candidates, Reagan concluded his presentation with a knock-out statement that focused the voter's attention. Reagan said to the television audience: "Are you better off than you were four years ago?" Most people weren't, and Carter was voted out of office. In the election of 1992 President George H. W. Bush was opposed by William Jefferson Clinton. Bush was favored to win re-election because of foreign policy developments that led to the end of the Cold War between the United States and the USSR. However, the nation was facing a recession, and Clinton's campaign strategist, James Carville, uttered a riveting catchphrase that focused voter attention on domestic issues: "It's the economy, stupid." Clinton decisively defeated Bush in the election.

Beleaguered economic conditions have often been the basis for why individuals have risen to political leadership. In some cases these individuals rose to become heroic leaders, while others became tyrants who led their nations to despair. In the hyper-competitive world of corporate business, leaders are replaced because they failed to live up to the financial expectations held by stakeholders of the organization. In some circumstances it appears people will more readily tolerate some degree of perceived organizational corruption (dismissing it as "politics as usual") than be economically harmed. The overall quality of our lives is linked to the state of economic or financial well-being, particularly when we feel a decline or loss compared to a previous state in our lives. Rightly or wrongly we hold leaders accountable for our well-being and imbue them with the power to change our lives.

behaviors that leadership attempts succeed or fail. It is proposed that followers regulate their own behavior as a result of the meaning derived from leadership acts. Thus a useful way to gauge the effectiveness of leaders is through the self-identity of followers. Epitropaki and Martin (2004) believe leaders should be made aware of how followers conceptualize effective leadership. Followers tend to regard effective leaders as sensitive, intelligent, dedicated, and dynamic (and not manipulative, domineering, or pushy). Epitropaki and Martin stated that leaders should be trained to present themselves as followers want to see them.

Substitutes for Leadership

Kerr and Jermier (1978) asked what it is that employees need to maximize in seeking organizational and personal outcomes. They concluded that employees seek both guidance and good feelings from their work settings. Guidance usually comes from role or task structuring; good feelings may stem from any type of recognition. The authors feel that although these factors must be present, they do not necessarily have to come from a superior. Other sources may provide guidance and recognition as well. In these cases the need for formal leadership is lessened. The authors reference **substitutes for leadership** and highlight the point that a leader is merely one vehicle for providing these services. Indeed, some organizations have abandoned formal supervisory positions as increasingly more work is performed by employees organized into teams (as discussed in Chapter 9). Podsakoff et al. (1996) reported that leaders and substitutes for leadership can simultaneously affect work groups. For example, leaders can create less need for formal supervision by carefully selecting employees who can function relatively independently. The authors concluded that such substitutes have very important effects on the work group, but they do not diminish the role of the leader. Dionne et al. (2002) and Muchiri and Cooksey (2011) reached similar conclusions—that substitutes for leadership cannot fully replace the role of the leader.

There is evidence that the concept of leadership does not have to be vested in a formal position. Howell and Dorfman (1981) tested whether leader substitution can replace or "act in the place of" a specific leader. They examined whether having a closely knit cohesive work group and tasks that provide feedback concerning performance can take the place of a formal leader. The authors found partial support for the substitution of leadership, giving some credence to the idea that leadership need not always reside in a person. Pierce et al. (1984) provided further support for leader substitutes. They examined four environmental sources from which employees get structure and direction in how to perform their work: the job itself, technology, the work unit, and the leader. The authors found that only when the first three sources of structure were weak did the influence of the leader strongly affect employees. It seems that employees can derive typical leader qualities (that is, structure and direction) from inanimate sources in their environments and that leadership functions need not be associated with someone in authority. It is therefore possible to envision a successfully operating leaderless group in which the job itself provides direction in what to do (initiating structure) and the work group members support and tend to one another (consideration).

There is also evidence that some individuals are capable of directing themselves, a concept called *self-leadership*. Manz (1986) found that some employees could lead

Substitutes for leadership
The conception that there are sources of influence in an environment that can serve to act in place of, or be substitutes for, formal leadership.

themselves if their values and beliefs were congruent with those of the organization. In summary, the research on substitutes for leadership suggests that leadership can be thought of as a series of processes or functions that facilitate organizational and personal effectiveness. These processes or functions need not necessarily emanate from a person in a formal leadership role, but may be derived from characteristics of the work being performed by the group members.

Points of Convergence Among Approaches

Despite the profusion of leadership approaches and related empirical findings, Yukl (1994) noted there is some convergence in the findings from different lines of leadership research. Yukl identified three consistent themes.

Importance of Influencing and Motivating.   Influence is the essence of leadership. Yukl stated that leaders are heavily involved in influencing the attitudes and behaviors of people, including subordinates, peers, and outsiders. The array of influence tactics available to a leader are all designed to induce followers to pursue selected goals and objectives. How leaders use power and their own personal needs affect the type of influence attempts they make. Skillful leaders provide an appealing vision for the future and inspire people to pursue it.

Importance of Maintaining Effective Relationships.   Yukl asserted that leaders recognize the importance of cooperative relationships among people and are skillful in achieving that outcome. Organizations operate more effectively when employees work within an environment of trust, loyalty, and mutual respect. Employees are more satisfied with leaders who demonstrate concern for their needs and values. Alternatively, leaders who regard organizations as simply arenas for their own self-enhancement are likely to alienate the very people who can make the organization be successful.

Importance of Making Decisions.   Decisions are made in the present but their consequences occur in the future. A leader who makes good decisions is skillful in shaping the future. Such talent is the hallmark of a good leader. Several of the traits and skills that predict leadership effectiveness are relevant for decision making. Leaders with extensive technical knowledge and cognitive skills are more likely to make high-quality decisions. These skills are important for analyzing problems, identifying causal patterns and trends, and forecasting likely outcomes of different strategies for attaining objectives. It is typically impossible for one leader to possess all the information needed to make an informed decision. Consequently, the ability to obtain relevant information, the skill to know the differential importance of the information as it relates to a given decision, and the capacity to weigh various decision options are all critical leadership skills. Self-confidence and tolerance for ambiguity and stress help leaders cope with the responsibility for making major decisions on the basis of incomplete information.

Dark Side of Leadership

According to Craig and Kaiser (2013), leadership theories have traditionally examined factors that enhance leadership through their presence, such as certain traits, behaviors, or relationships with followers. These views have been considered the "bright side" approach to leadership. A starkly different view that has been steadily gaining momentum by leadership scholars is the "dark side" approach, which examines factors that can make leaders more effective through their *absence*. It is not simply the lack of "bright side" features (e.g., charisma, monitoring behaviors) that can make a leader destructive. Instead, as Craig and Kaiser note, the dark side of leadership is "the presence or operation of factors that actively undermine desirable leadership processes and outcomes" (p. 440).

In Chapter 4 (in the discussion of the Dark Triad), we noted that some leaders may be "snakes in suits" (Babiak & Hare, 2006), or exhibit high levels of psychopathy. Similar to this, there is evidence that narcissists tend to rise within organizations given their confidence levels and willingness to step on others to get ahead. Given the negative effects of these dark personality traits, it should be easy to see why not all leaders may act in the best interests of their followers. Indeed, Hogan et al. (1990) cautioned that there can be a "dark side" to charismatic leaders. Because they have excellent social skills, sometimes to the point of being charming, they are readily liked by their followers. But sometimes lurking behind the mask of likability is a person with pronounced adjustment problems, such as the psychopaths and narcissists. Only after these people fail in their leadership roles do we ever learn of their maladjustment, which was cleverly concealed by their ability to manipulate people to like them.

Whether it is because of some personality trait or maladjustment, one thing is clear: some leaders are toxic, creating stress and wreaking havoc on those who refuse to follow their directives. In Chapter 11 we discussed workplace bullying and noted that the bully can be one's leader. The issue of abusive supervision, or the "sustained display of hostile verbal and nonverbal behaviors, excluding physical contact" (Tepper, 2000, p. 178), has attracted much interest among researchers in recent years. One reason for this increased focus is because of the level of devastation that such leaders can cause. For example, Tepper found that employees exposed to abusive supervision were less satisfied with their jobs and their lives, had greater work-family conflict, and experienced heightened psychological distress. In addition, and not surprisingly, they were more likely to quit their jobs. Similarly, Aryee et al. (2007) found that employees with abusive supervisors had low emotional attachment with their organization and tended to engage in few organizational citizenship behaviors. Tepper et al. (2006) estimated that the costs to employers in the United States due to the effects of abusive supervision is $23.8 billion annually.

Unruly, abusive, and unethical leaders can also lead to potential legal harm as well as damage to the organization's reputation. Consider, for example, a case from 2011 in which a full-time cashier who worked for the convenience store QC Mart in Iowa quit her job due to a "hostile work environment and intolerable working conditions" (Pinto, 2011). She quit after her employer issued a memo (see Figure 13-4) regarding a "new contest" in which employees were to "guess the next cashier who will be fired!" The memo described the rules of the contest and a promise of $10 cash for the right choice. This supervisor was clearly being abusive in his use of power. The case led to

NEW CONTEST – GUESS THE NEXT CASHIER WHO WILL BE FIRED!!!   To win our game, write on a piece of paper the name of the next cashier you believe will be fired. Write their name (the person who will be fired), today's date, today's time, and your name. Seal it in an envelope and give it to the manager to put in my envelope. Here's how the game will work. We are doubling our secret shopper efforts, and your store will be visited during the day **AND** at night several times a week. Secret shoppers will be looking for cashiers wearing a hat, talking on a cell phone, not wearing a QC Mart shirt, having someone hanging around/behind the counter, and/or no car personal car parked by the pumps after 7:00 pm, among other things. If the name in your envelope has the right answer, you will win **$10.00 CASH**. Only one winner per firing unless there are multiple right answers with the exact same name, date, and time. Once we fire the person, we will open all the envelopes, award the prize, and start the contest again. **AND NO FAIR PICKING MIKE MILLER FROM ROCKINGHAM. HE WAS FIRED AROUND 11:30 AM TODAY FOR WEARING A HAD AND TALKING ON HIS CELL PHONE. GOOD LUCK!!!!!!**

Figure 13-4   *Memo issued by convenience store manager exhibiting abusive supervision* (linguistic errors in original)

litigation and bad press for the convenience store — two things no organization ever wants.

Finally, when discussing the dark side of leadership, it is important to consider the role of followers and the environment. In much the same way that the bright side theorists have argued for the importance of followers and the situation, so too have the dark side scholars. Padilla et al. (2007) suggested that there is a "toxic triangle of destructive leadership," noting that a devious, toxic leader needs to have susceptible followers and conducive environments in order to accomplish their (destructive) goals. According to Thoroughgood et al. (2012), susceptible followers can be conformers or colluders. Conformers are those followers who are "prone to obedience, and thus do not engage in destructive behavior alone" while "colluders actively contribute to the leader's mission" (p. 902). They noted that one way to reduce the impact of destructive leadership is to "promote strong, independent followers who will challenge destructive leaders and develop healthy organizational processes and practices" (p. 911). Along these lines, Nandkeolyar et al. (2014) found that conscientious individuals and individuals who were apt to engage in avoidant coping (such as skipping work or daydreaming) were less likely to be negatively impacted by abusive supervisors.

Leadership in Teams

The focus on leadership has long considered the ways that individuals are led, and what leaders can do to best meet their needs. With the ever-increasing use of teams within organizations, however, there has been a similarly growing interest in leading teams.

In Chapter 9, we noted that some of what we know about individuals in the workplace generalizes to teams while others do not. The topic of leadership is one of those areas in which we see some stark differences between individuals and teams.

Within a team setting, the leader cannot simply focus only on the individuals that comprise the team. Instead, the leader must focus on the functioning of the team as a whole. According to Kozlowski et al. (2009), leading teams requires adaptability. Leadership must evolve as the team evolves and develop along with the team. Whether a team is in its planning phases or is actively performing, the leader must be able to make accommodations and address the team's needs accordingly (Morgeson et al., 2010).

One concept that has received considerable attention is that of **shared leadership**. Here, the focus is less on specific leaders, and more on leadership in general (Shuffler et al., 2013). The "shared" element of shared leadership reflects the point that, with a team, there may be more than one person who takes on a leadership role. Who the leader is may depend on what the team is experiencing at the moment. Leadership could be evenly dispersed among all of the members of the team. Alternatively, the team members could take turns being the leader as needed. According to a meta-analysis conducted by Wang et al. (2014), teams that engage in shared leadership appear to be more satisfied and committed to their teams and engage in more cooperation and helping behaviors. Moreover, although the effects weren't as strong, shared leadership is related to both subjective and objective performance measures. These effects seem to be particularly true when the work is complex.

The importance of team leadership appears to also be a function of the environment. Graen (2013) noted that team leadership will be less important when the team is in a calm environment. When the team is in danger of clear physical or psychological harm, however, team leadership becomes essential. For example, a team of firefighters may be more likely to rely on outside administration as the point of authority when they are not actively involved in fighting fires. When they are in harm's way, however, and are risking their lives for the lives of others, the leadership from within the team is more likely to be of utmost importance. According to Graen, this reliance on one another's teammates in times of crisis may be a "survival mechanism from our hunter-gather history," noting that without this trust and reliance, "our ancestors may not have survived the hunt of wooly mammoths" (p. 176).

In Chapter 9, we also discussed multiteam systems, or multiple teams that interact with one another to accomplish higher-level goals. According to Zaccaro et al. (2011), leaders of these "team of teams" must not only be concerned with the functioning of each team, including how individual members coordinate and cooperate with one another, but they must also manage the interactions between each of the separate teams. Furthermore, and along these lines, it is important for leaders to consider how they treat each team for which they are responsible. For example, Luciano et al. (2014) found that when leaders of multiple teams paid more attention to certain teams, those teams felt more empowered and subsequently performed better. Thus, as Mathieu et al. (2001) noted, leaders of multiteam systems must care about and respond to the needs of each individual team as well as all of the teams (i.e., the system). If a leader has too small of a focus, or doesn't consider the needs of all individuals and teams, he or she will likely be ineffective in coordinating activities and will be limited in terms of effectiveness.

Shared leadership
Leadership within a team whereby team members distribute leadership roles among the different members of the team rather than relying on a single individual to serve as the sole leader.

Cross-Cultural Leadership Issues

For many years most of what we knew about cross-cultural leadership issues derived from international business. For example, one company might conduct business in two countries (such as the United States and Japan). Research findings indicated which leadership practices would and would not generalize across the two nations. However, we are now in the era of global business, where commerce is conducted on a worldwide basis (see Field Note 2: *One CEO's Office*). A major study was completed on leadership and culture. It is called *GLOBE*, an acronym for Global Leadership and Organizational Behavior Effectiveness. The goal of the massive research project was to address how culture is related to societal, organizational, and leadership effectiveness. The researchers measured the practices and values of managers in different industries (financial services, food processing, telecommunications, etc.) and organizations (951 of them) within 62 societies representing 59 nations (alphabetically from Albania to

Field Note 2: *One CEO's Office*

A description of one chief executive officer's (CEO) office gives a glimpse into how the business world has changed. This CEO is head of one of the largest textile companies in the United States. Twenty years ago the office of his predecessor had a map of the United States hanging on the wall. Inserted into the map were colored push-pins. The blue pin was the site of the corporate headquarters of the company where his office was located. Red pins indicated eight manufacturing facilities located in a three-state area, all in the southeastern United States. Green pins represented regional warehouses, and yellow pins showed the locations of major customers. That was twenty years ago.

Today there is a new CEO and two new maps hang on the wall. The first is a map of the world, showing the various local times compared to 12:00 p.m. at the corporate headquarters. The company now has business operations in Brazil, Honduras, Ireland, Israel, South Africa, Hong Kong, and Thailand. The second map is of China. China will be the location for many future business dealings, currently in various stages of negotiation and development. The company is now as familiar with such major cities in China as Beijing, Guangzhou, and Shanghai as it is with New York, Chicago, and Los Angeles. The map of China highlights railroad lines, major highways, and rivers that can be used to transport goods to airports and deep-water ports for ultimate distribution around the world. Twenty years ago the focus and field of vision of the company was the United States, as embodied in the map of the United States. Today the company has a global perspective; it thinks globally and views the world as one big marketplace. China will soon be the epicenter of its global business operations. Gone are the different colored push-pins, and conspicuously absent from the wall is the map of the United States. Whereas the previous CEO was not concerned with global business, the current CEO cannot be concerned with only domestic business.

Zimbabwe). The initial product of their work was a book (House et al., 2004) that represents our best understanding of cross-cultural issues in leadership.

House et al. drew upon the research of Hofstede (2001) in establishing major cultural dimensions (such as power distance, individualism–collectivism, and uncertainty avoidance) as well as proposing some additional dimensions. Understandably, the results of the research are complex and multifaceted; however, here are some of the major findings:

- In some cultures the concept of leadership is denigrated. Members of the culture are highly suspicious of individuals who are in positions of authority for fear they will acquire and abuse power. In these cultures substantial constraints are placed on what individuals in positions of authority can and cannot do. Alternatively, in some cultures the concept of leadership is romanticized and leaders are given exceptional privileges and status and are held in great esteem.
- Twenty-two leadership traits were identified as being universally desirable. Two examples are decisiveness and foresight.
- Eight leadership traits were identified as being universally undesirable. Two examples are irritability and ruthlessness.
- Many leadership traits were culturally contingent, being desirable in some cultures and undesirable in others. Two examples are ambition and elitism.
- Members of different cultures share common observations and values about what constitutes effective and ineffective leadership. Six styles of leadership were identified: charismatic, team-oriented, participative, autonomous, humane-oriented, and self-protective. Although all cultures recognized these six leadership styles, they were seen as differentially contributing to outstanding leadership. Anglo and Nordic European cultures, for example, tend to see charismatic and participative leadership styles as being particularly effective. Asian and Sub-Saharan African cultures are more favorably disposed to humane-oriented and self-protective leadership styles. Middle Eastern cultures do not place great value on team-oriented and participative styles for achieving success.

The researchers found clear cultural underpinnings to the way societies generate and distribute wealth and take care of their people. The findings indicate that decisions designed to change the way governments operate or the way societies allocate their resources must take into consideration cultural issues. House et al. found that certain leadership traits (such as integrity) were universally endorsed, but they question whether the leader behaviors associated with this trait would be common across cultures. For example, in one culture a leader with high integrity might be regarded as someone who gives great thought and consideration to an issue before making a decision. In another culture high integrity by a leader might be manifested by soliciting a wide range of opinions from others before making a decision. Weir (2010) described a major difference in leadership values between Western and Middle Eastern cultures. In the Middle East, interpersonal relationships (especially among those in positions of power) are based upon establishing and maintaining a strong sense of honor between the parties. Both parties engage in practices of giving and preserving a sense of shared honor that is the basis for their extended relationship. In the Western culture,

Cross-Cultural I/O Psychology: *Participative Leadership and Power Distance*

Among the concepts that I/O psychologists have studied, leadership probably best exemplifies the power of culture in influencing attitudes and behavior. The GLOBE project revealed there is no one style of leadership that is universally regarded to be effective. The greatest variation across cultures involves participative leadership – the inclusion of others in making decisions that affect their lives.

Western culture is highly accepting of participative leadership. The right to vote is a form of power, giving people voice in matters that concern them. More than any other value, the effectiveness of participative leadership rests with the cultural value of power distance. In nations with lower power distance (as the U.S.), elected political leaders emerge from the population at large. Similarly, business leaders typically exhibit a career path of advancement up through the ranks of an organization. The gap or distance between leaders and those being led is small.

In high power distance cultures, participative leadership is not regarded as effective. The authority to make decisions is granted to only a few individuals at the top. Leaders are of a special class in the social order, often members of royalty or nobility. They are granted the deference to lead as a birthright, or because of their greater experience, wealth, or power. As such, making decisions without consulting others is their privilege.

Lower power distance implies equality (or nearly so), the basis for the acceptance of participative leadership. High power distance implies vast inequality, rendering participative leadership as both unacceptable and ineffective.

relationships are founded more on the perceived instrumental value of the relationship (i.e., what is to be gained from the relationship). There is a strong recognition that the relationship will endure only to the extent both parties have something to gain from the exchange, which may be for a limited period of time.

The manifestation of specific behaviors from culturally endorsed traits awaits further research in the GLOBE project. The myriad of findings from the GLOBE study will provide us with a much better understanding of how cultural issues influence a wide range of human behavior. As Lowe and Gardner (2000) stated, most leadership research has had a technological, modern, and U.S. bias. The GLOBE project will help us understand leadership from other perspectives from around the world (see Cross-Cultural I/O Psychology: *Participative Leadership and Power Distance*).

Diversity Issues in Leadership

There have been substantial economic, political, and social changes within the United States since the passage of the Civil Rights Act in 1964. By prohibiting some forms of discrimination in the workplace, the U.S. labor market has shifted and the nature of leadership has changed. For example, the national economy experienced a shift from manufacturing to service jobs (Offerman & Gowing, 1990). In addition, there have been changes to the demographic makeup, such as the ratio of women to men in the workforce moving to nearly equal numbers. The labor market for skilled workers has tightened, and there will be increased competition for talented personnel. As noted in Chapter 8, as organizations shrink, fewer middle managers will be needed and the responsibilities of first-line managers will expand.

As the labor market has shifted, barriers for members of certain groups have become apparent. There is evidence, for example, that women are underrepresented in managerial positions and, in particular, the chief executive positions within organizations (O'Neil et al., 2008). The issue, however, isn't limited to managerial ranks. Eagly and Carli (2007) used the metaphor "glass labyrinth" to describe the hurdles that women face at all levels of an organization, as opposed to the misnomer "glass ceiling" that implies that women progress evenly and then suddenly and unexpectedly encounter resistance to advancement. Along these lines, Hoobler et al. (2014) found that both male and female managers viewed female subordinates as having lower career motivation, seemingly supporting the view that "men are viewed as more suited for management careers ('think leader, think male')" (p. 720).

Chemers and Murphy (1995) noted that one explanation for gender differences in leadership is cultural. This view holds that because of their roles as family caretakers, women are socialized to be sensitive, nurturing, and caring. When they carry that socialization over into organizational roles, women are likely to be warm, considerate, and democratic leaders. Rosette and Tost (2010) explained how gender roles influence perceptions of leadership styles. The *agentic* or male gender role is to be competent, aggressive, independent, decisive and forceful. The *communal* or female gender role is to be kind, concerned, and sympathetic to the needs of others. The concept of leadership has typically been defined in terms of masculine characteristics. Rosette and Tost noted that there can be a backlash against women leaders who exhibit more agentic characteristics. As such, there can be a double standard in leadership: men don't have to be communal but women have to be both. Ayman and Korabik (2010) observed that there is a growing recognition of the importance of communal skills among leaders. While Western leadership styles emphasize achievement, the Eastern leadership style more heavily values the importance of relationships. The era of global business has made us more aware of the criticality of organizational success being dependent on collaboration with others and building strong relationships. As such, it is proposed the female role may be more suited to leadership than in the past.

Lyness and Heilman (2006) noted that one explanation often put forth as to why there are relatively few women in top-level managerial jobs is "lack of fit." Men are stereotypically viewed as forceful, achievement-oriented, and tough. Women are stereotypically viewed as caring, relationship-oriented, and kind. Accordingly, men are often perceived as a better fit. The authors compared performance evaluations and promotions for men and women. Those women who were promoted had higher performance ratings than men, suggesting stricter standards for promotion were applied to women. There appears to be no empirical basis for the disproportionately small representation of women in top leadership jobs in the United States. Eagly et al. (2003) found only small male–female differences in leadership. Furthermore, women's typical leadership styles tend to be more transformational than those of men, which have been found to be predictive of effectiveness. Lyness (2002) documented reasons why women and racial minorities experience difficulties with participating in leadership development activities, including being slotted into jobs that don't facilitate advancement, having problems obtaining influential mentors or sponsors, and being excluded from informal networks where critical information and career opportunities are shared. Lyness commented, "I have been struck by how much more we seem to know about barriers for women and people of color than about how best to overcome the barriers" (p. 265).

Entrepreneurship

Entrepreneurship
The process by which individuals pursue opportunities and organize resources that can lead to new job creation and business growth.

All business organizations were created by individuals who at some point in time thought they had a "good idea." Such individuals who started these businesses are called *entrepreneurs*, and *entrepreneurship* is the underlying concept of business creation. Although **entrepreneurship** has been addressed for over 100 years, there has been renewed interest in the topic, particularly when society has been confronted with massive job loss (Baron & Henry, 2011). It is believed that a greater understanding of how businesses are created will lead to the development of new organizations (often called "start-up" companies) that will grow and prosper. Such organizations would not only add value to society by the products and services they offer, but also as a source of employment. However, not all entrepreneurial activities enhance social welfare. Gottschalk (2009) described how organized crime, across many different cultures, follows the same basic principles of entrepreneurship found in successful legal businesses. Gottschalk stated that the only differentiating characteristic is the readiness of criminal entrepreneurs to use physical violence to attain their goals. The similarities between legal and illegal enterprises also extend to how they are structured to be effective. Levitt and Dubner (2005) quoted a member of a London street gang called the *Black Disciples* that sold crack cocaine within a twelve-square-block area:

> So how *did* the gang work? An awful lot like most American businesses, actually, though perhaps none more so than McDonald's. In fact, if you were to hold a McDonald's organizational chart and a Black Disciples org chart side by side, you could hardly tell the difference. (p. 99)

I/O psychologists have recently become drawn into the study of entrepreneurship because of its growing emergence in society, and because I/O psychology has much to offer in understanding entrepreneurship. Successful entrepreneurs have much in common with successful leaders, although they are not identical. At the heart of entrepreneurship is innovation; thinking of new ways or methods to extract value out of an opportunity that presents itself. Shane (2003) describes a six-step process that is the basis for entrepreneurship:

1. **Existence of opportunity**. There must be an opportunity to provide a new product or service that is desired, or to improve upon an existing one.

2. **Discovery of opportunity**. A person must perceive this opportunity to exist. Not perceived, the opportunity is "missed." When a person perceives an opportunity when in fact there is none, the perception is an "illusion."

3. **Decision to pursue the opportunity**. A person must decide whether the opportunity is of sufficient magnitude to warrant the expenditure of time, money, and skill needed to pursue it.

4. **Resource acquisition**. Once the decision is made to pursue the opportunity, a person has to marshal the resources needed for its pursuit.

5. **Entrepreneurial strategy**. Strategy is the process by which a person can convert or transform the opportunity, upon application of the resources, into a product or service valued by others.

6. **Organizing process**. The organizing process is the means by which the entrepreneurial strategy is enacted. It may involve the founding of a new organization, or some other process of pursuing the opportunity that previously did not exist.

With the exception of the existence of an objective opportunity (which naturally occurs in the environment), the remaining five steps all involve a human component. That is, each requires a person who: sees the opportunity; decides to act upon it; obtains the needed resources; develops a strategy; and develops an organizing process to create the new product or services. It is this strong human component to entrepreneurship that interests I/O psychologists. Entrepreneurship is highly interdisciplinary. Reliance on one scientific discipline to understand a topic that cuts across disciplines is rarely effective. For example, the 4th step (resource acquisition) entails the procurement of money needed to pursue the opportunity. This step is typically the domain of investment management. There are individuals who will provide the needed money for some entrepreneurial activity. Such people are called "venture capitalists," and it is their goal to identify a potentially lucrative opportunity, invest their money (capital) in it, and share in the success of the venture. As noted by Shane, research that focuses only on the financial dimension of entrepreneurship fails to understand the importance of the individual entrepreneur whose idea is being supported. Likewise, an examination of the psychological profile (e.g., intelligence, personality, values, etc.) of successful entrepreneurs fails to understand the situations in which they operate. We might think of entrepreneurship as a special case of "the peg and the hole," where the criterion of fit is successful innovation.

There is disagreement within I/O psychology about whether entrepreneurship is truly different from leadership (Antonakis & Autio, 2007). Vecchio (2003) believes that entrepreneurship is nothing more than leadership embedded within an entrepreneurial organization. However, there is evidence that highly creative individuals who inspire innovation are not necessarily skilled in other leadership dimensions, such as interpersonal skills. In addition, Zhao and Seibert (2006) conducted a meta-analysis of personality factors that differentiated entrepreneurs compared to a sample of traditional business managers. Entrepreneurs were found to be more conscientious and open to new experiences than their managerial counterparts.

A compelling finding from the study of entrepreneurs is their high rate of failure. Shane reported that nearly half of all entrepreneurs fail to even complete their organizing efforts (Step 6). The goal of all businesses is to grow and prosper. However, the initial goal is just to survive, and research indicates organizational survival is more the exception than the rule. The reasons for failure rest in each of the steps proposed by Shane. While I/O psychology cannot contribute to understanding entrepreneurship from a financial perspective, it can contribute from a human perspective. A blending of knowledge from different fields is necessary to understand entrepreneurship. Baron et al. (2007) concluded: "In sum, it seems clear that the benefits of closer ties between

The Born Loser: © United Feature Syndicate, Inc.

I/O psychology and entrepreneurship are indeed reciprocal in nature. Both fields can gain measurably from such links" (p. 369).

Concluding Comments

As was discussed earlier, sometimes research investigations meld major topics of interest to I/O psychologists. A notable example by Chan and Drasgow (2001) combined motivation and leadership in a study that addressed the motivation to lead. Chan and Drasgow proposed the existence of a personality construct that explains why some people seek leadership positions. Using sophisticated analytic methods, the authors identified three types of people who desire to lead others. The first type sees themselves as having leadership qualities: they are outgoing and sociable (i.e., extraverts), they value competition and achievement, and they are confident in their own leadership abilities. The second type does not expect rewards or privileges to flow from leading but consents to do so because of their agreeable disposition. They value harmony in the group, irrespective of their own leadership experience or self-efficacy. The third type does not necessarily see themselves as having leadership qualities but is motivated to lead by a sense of social duty and obligation. The study revealed that the motivation to lead is not a unidimensional construct, but rather people can be drawn to leadership roles for different types of reasons.

Hackman and Wageman (2007) believe that leadership research has been adversely affected by seeking answers to simplistic questions that belie the inherent complexity of leadership. They believe the answers researchers get about leadership depend upon the questions asked, and the right questions need to be asked. For example, we should not ask what are the traits of leaders, but instead how do leaders' personal attributes interact with situational properties to shape outcomes. The most useful and insightful questions are based upon the simultaneous consideration of the multiple components of leadership, not just any one component in isolation of the others. Although several approaches have been taken to understand leadership, all reach the same conclusion that leadership is a vital process in directing work within organizations. There appear to be boundary conditions regarding when formal leadership is most effective as well as the processes leaders use to galvanize the members of their organizations. It is also insightful that current thinking about leadership considers leaders as not only heroes but also as hero makers. Thus leadership need not be a phenomenon vested exclusively in upper-level positions, but rather is a contagious process that can manifest itself throughout all levels of an organization. It is concluded that people not only need leaders but also want them in their lives. We feel comforted by the presence of strong, effective, yet approachable leaders, and we place our trust in them (Dirks & Ferrin, 2002). The breadth of topics addressed in this chapter attests to the complexity of leadership; it is a phenomenon that has intrigued us throughout the history of civilization.

Chapter Summary

- Leadership is a topic that has intrigued humankind since antiquity.
- The trait approach to leadership posits that effective leaders possess certain personality attributes that make them effective.
- The behavioral approach to leadership posits that leadership is a learned skill and that demonstrating key behaviors is the basis of effective leadership.
- Power and influence theories of leadership assert that leadership is a process that stems from the shared relationship between parties, and leadership is associated with effectively managing that relationship.
- The contingency approach suggests that the context must be taken into consideration because the extent to which a leader is effective will depend on what is happening in the environment.
- Leader-member exchange theory posits that leaders and followers establish relationships with each other, and that the level of trust, support, and types of responsibilities provided to followers by their leaders is in part based on the quality of these relationships.
- The full-range leadership theory asserts that there is a wide spectrum of leadership behaviors, ranging from laissez-faire behaviors (which essentially reflect non-leadership) to transactional behaviors (which are based on exchanges of rewards or punishments depending on performance) to transformational behaviors (which are higher-level behaviors meant to transform the follower into something greater than what he or she was before).
- Authentic leadership theory focuses on the leader being self-aware, genuine in their thoughts and actions, and making decisions that are unbiased and based on a strong set of internal values.
- Servant leadership theory suggests that effective leaders put the needs of their followers above their own, help their followers grow and succeed, and show a clear concern for the communities in which they reside.
- Implicit leadership theory asserts that the concept of leadership exists primarily in the minds of followers. As such, "leadership" is not so much real as implied by a set of actions that are taken or decisions that are made. It is proposed that people are comforted by the idea of having powerful leaders who will protect and help them, thus legitimating their existence.
- The concept of substitutes for leadership is that the functions provided by leadership need not be vested in a person. Characteristics of the work can substitute for the need to have a leader.
- There are factors that can make leaders less effective, and can result in a toxic, abusive form of leadership that has a negative impact on followers.

- Leading teams requires a focus on not only the functioning of individuals, but also on the team as a whole and the coordination of teams with other teams.
- There are vast cross-cultural differences in what people want from their leaders and what styles of leadership are acceptable.
- There appears to be some barriers to leadership that exist for individuals based on gender, race, and other group membership characteristics.
- Entrepreneurship represents a context in which leadership can be examined as a means of creating new jobs through innovation.

Union/Management Relations

Chapter Outline

Learning Objectives

- Describe the nature and formation of a labor union.
- Explain the functions of a labor contract.
- Understand the strategies of impasse resolution in the collective bargaining process.
- Describe responses to impasse.
- Describe the nature of grievances and grievance arbitration.
- Describe behavioral research on union/management relations.
- Understand why organized labor is declining in the United States.

Over the years I/O psychologists have studied a broad range of topics relating to work. Strangely enough, one not often addressed is union/management relations. This area cannot be dismissed as "tangential" to work; for many organizations, union-related issues are among the most crucial. Many authors have observed that there is a great imbalance in I/O psychologists' interest between union and management problems. The two are not mutually exclusive, but I/O psychology seems more aligned with management. A listing of some of the professional activities of I/O psychologists testifies to this: managerial consulting, management development, use of assessment centers to identify those with management ability, and cross-cultural managerial issues. However, it is not as if I/O psychologists have spurned advances from unions. Over 50 years ago Shostak (1964) described the relationship as "mutual indifference." Not much has changed over the past half-century. Unions appear reluctant to approach I/O psychologists for help in solving their problems. Rosen and Stagner (1980) think this is caused partly by the belief that I/O psychologists are not truly impartial and partly by reluctance to give outsiders access to union data.

The reasons for the unions' attitudes are numerous. One explanation is that the development of industrial psychology is closely tied to the work of Frederick Taylor. Criticisms of "Taylorism" have been raised by union workers; they see it as exploiting workers to increase company profits. There can be an adversarial relationship between unions and management, a "we/they" perspective. Unions may still see I/O psychologists as a partner of "them." Also, some factors may appear to place I/O psychologists more in the management camp. I/O psychologists are often placed in management-level positions. Management invariably sees the need for, explains the problems to, and pays the consultant. In short, I/O psychology has been more involved with management than with unions (to the point that some authors refer to I/O psychology as a "management tool"). This is most apparent in the conspicuous absence of psychological research on unions. However, another reason was presented by Zickar and Kostek (2013). One of the major contributions of I/O psychology to employment has been the development and use of psychological assessments of job candidates, the results of which are used to make personnel selection decisions. One notable type of psychological assessment is the personality test. Zickar (2001) described an unethical application of personality testing: **union-busting**. The author noted "that management, in collaboration with some I/O psychologists, initially used personality inventories, not to predict job performance, but to screen potential employees who might be likely to affiliate with unions" (p. 149). Zickar added,

Union-busting
A derogatory term used to describe actions taken to prevent a labor union from representing employees.

> Regardless of the genesis of this practice, it is clear that by the late 1930s psychologists . . . were marketing these [personality] scales for union busting. This alliance with management helped fuel labor's suspicion of social scientists . . . This partisanship made it difficult for psychologists who wished to implement policies that would ease the tensions between labor and management. Labor unions became suspicious of even the best intentioned psychologists. (p. 161)

A list of the major reasons unions distrust I/O psychologists was offered by Huszczo et al. (1984) and is presented in Table 14-1.

In the state of New York psychologists became unionized. Verdi (2000) posed this question: "Why are highly trained, certified, licensed, and well-compensated

Table 14-1   *Reasons unions distrust I/O psychologists*

They are associated with management.

They are associated with F. W. Taylor's scientific management (i.e., emphasis on efficiency, time and motion studies).

Unions are ignored in textbooks and journals of I/O psychology.

They are moralistic intellectuals who want social reform.

Methods (e.g., attitude surveys) have been used to avoid or beat union organizing attempts or to lower pay demands.

They are associated with job enrichment techniques that interfere with job classification and standards systems.

Methods of psychological testing emphasize differentiation among workers (hence, anti-solidarity and anti-seniority systems).

Many psychologists have not had work experiences similar to union members, which causes suspicion and communication barriers.

Source: From "The Relationship Between Psychology and Organized Labor: Past Present, and Future," by G. E. Huszczo, J. G. Wiggins, and J. S. Currie, 1984, *American Psychologist, 39*, pp. 432–440.

individuals who have earned the right to work in their chosen specialties as entrepreneurs seeking to unionize?" (p. 31). The answer was that the 3,200 members of the New York State Psychological Association were frustrated by their lack of power in dealing with managed healthcare. The psychologists became members of a powerful labor union, the American Federation of Teachers, which has more than 400,000 members. As members of a large union, they now have a stronger voice in negotiating issues regarding their employment, one of the classic reasons workers join unions. Yet Verdi reported that psychologists had some stereotypical concerns about unions: "There is the loss of status—people view union members as individuals who work with their hands and not their heads for a living" (p. 32). Yet even professions that historically have not been aligned with unions turn to them for help with employment-related matters (see Field Note 1: *Why Study Unions?*).

Bownas (2000) described the fundamental similarity in the motives of both the union and management:

> The kinds of motives that drive union spokespeople in organizations are no different from those that motivate corporate management. Sometimes the different vantage points from which the two groups operate cause them to reach different conclusions about specific outcomes, but the underlying motives are the same. We all try to maximize personal outcomes (such as power, prestige, and influence) and to maximize the outcomes of constituents and other loyal followers. (p. 197)

This chapter will examine the nature of unions, the factors that influence union/management relations, recent research on unions, how unionization affects many topics discussed earlier, and the future of labor unions.

Field Note 1: *Why Study Unions?*

I believe that unions have been given inadequate attention by educators. When the topic of labor unions comes up, students are more likely to have heard of Jimmy Hoffa (a union leader with reputed criminal connections) than Walter Reuther (a major contributor to organized labor). Why? There are probably many reasons, but one seems fundamental. Schools, colleges, and higher education in general are founded on scholarly intellectual values. They produce learned people, many of whom rise to become business leaders. Unions, on the other hand, got their start representing less educated workers, rank-and-file employees, rather than business leaders. Rightly or wrongly, unions have had the image of representing the "common man" in labor over the "privileged intellectuals." Some union leaders become suspicious and skeptical of the motives of formally educated people, feeling they are more likely to share values held by management.

Few psychology textbooks in this country offer more than a passing look at organized labor. It seems the "we/they" dichotomy between labor and management has filtered down into textbook writing; unions simply are infrequently discussed in books. This book, in fact, is one of the few I/O psychology textbooks that devotes a chapter to union/management issues. However, the anti-intellectual attitude that some unions hold is costing them in ways beyond exposure in education. Unions rarely hire outside professionals; they generally promote from within their own ranks. If you were an I/O psychologist who wanted to work full time for a union, I doubt you would have many employment possibilities. Furthermore, unions are currently experiencing a decline in membership, an unprecedented number of unions are being decertified, and unions are losing their effectiveness in negotiating for desired employment conditions. In short, I think unions need some fresh ideas. They could benefit from organizational change interventions. But unless they are willing to look beyond their own ranks for expertise, I doubt that they (like any organization) will have sufficient internal strength to pull themselves up by the bootstraps. The paradoxical split between I/O psychology (the study of people at work) and labor unions (which represent a significant portion of workers) has been detrimental to both parties.

What Is a Union?

Union
A labor organization with defined members whose purpose is to enhance the welfare of its members in their employment relationship with the company.

Unions are organizations designed to promote and enhance the social and economic welfare of their members. Basically, unions were created to protect workers from exploitation. Unions originally sprang from the abysmal working conditions in this country more than 100 years ago. Workers got little pay, had almost no job security, had no benefits, and, perhaps most important, worked in degrading and unsafe conditions. Unions gave unity and power to employees. This power forced employers to deal with workers as a group. Certain federal laws compelled employers to stop certain activities (such as employing children) and engage in others (such as making Social Security contributions). Collectively, labor unions and labor laws brought about many changes in the workplace. For example, Blyton (2008) reported that the length of the average workweek in the United Kingdom over the past century was heavily influenced by the power of labor unions. At the start of the 20th century, the standard workweek was 54 hours. This was followed later by the 48-hour and 44-hour workweeks, and by the 1960s the 40-hour workweek was standard. By 2004 the average workweek was 37.2 hours, with considerably greater hours being evidenced in managerial and professional occupations. Although the problems facing the North American worker today are not as severe as they were 75 to 100 years ago, unions continue to give a sense of security and increased welfare to their members (see Field Note 2: *Is History Repeating Itself?*). Guest (2008) reported that at the start of the 20th century, issues of employee welfare were primarily directed to such factors as hours of work, pay, and methods of dispute resolution. However, Guest noted, in the 21st century the concept of worker welfare has expanded to include smoking bans at the worksite, healthy eating at work, and provisions for gyms and health checks.

Why do workers join unions? What can unions accomplish? According to several authors, unions have consistently contributed to the attainment of certain outcomes. Based upon labor research, unions have made these contributions to worker welfare:

- They have increased wages; in turn, employers have raised the wages of some non-union workers.

- They have bargained for and gotten benefits such as pensions, insurance, vacations, and rest periods.

Field Note 2: *Is History Repeating Itself?*

In the early years of the 20th century, the use of child labor was prevalent in the United States, particularly in large cities. Children toiled for long hours (10–12 hours per day) in unsafe conditions (poor air to breathe, no heating or cooling) and for minuscule wages (pennies per hour) in what were called "sweat shops." Eventually state and federal labor laws were enacted to prohibit child labor. Then 80–90 years later some U.S. companies moved their production facilities to other countries that had no child labor laws. In some factories children again work long hours in unsafe conditions for minuscule wages (less than $1 per hour). How do you feel about this prac-tice? Should U.S. companies follow U.S. labor laws in other countries where the laws are much different, particularly with regard to child labor? Should social pressure (e.g., economic boycotts) be exerted against companies that use child labor? Some companies argue that the reduced costs they incur by using child labor are passed on to consumers in the form of lower costs of the products. How should companies in particular and our society as a whole balance economic gain and social conscience? We are finding that history is repeating itself; the conditions that spawned labor laws in this country many years ago are now being exploited by some companies in other countries.

Figure 14-1 *Badge worn by unionized workers advocating equality of treatment for all employees*

- They have provided formal rules and procedures for discipline, promotion, wage differentials, and other important job-related factors. This has led to less arbitrary treatment of employees.

There are other reasons as well: unions can provide better communication with management, better working conditions, increased employee unity, and higher morale. Other authors cite social reasons, like belonging to a group with whom workers can share common experiences and fellowship. Schiavone (2008) advocated that unions make social justice issues, such as bargaining for better childcare, primary negotiating concerns. Unions that pursued social justice issues were found to attract more members than unions that bargained over traditional economic issues. Matters of social justice have an appeal to a wide constituency, which is the base from which unions derive power. Thus there are both economic and personal reasons for joining unions.

Figure 14-1 shows a badge worn by unionized employees. It identifies three employment issues desired by union members: a full pension after 30 years of service to the company; that workers receive pay on days when they are sick and cannot attend work; and the use of personal time away from work that is not counted as vacation time. But note the one word on the badge that is in the largest font — "equal." The foundation of labor unions is equal treatment across all workers. That is, it would be unacceptable to the union if some workers got sick pay and others didn't, some got personal time and others didn't, and so forth. Equality of treatment is the basis of *solidarity* (i.e., a feeling of unity that binds members of the labor union together).

Unions as Organizations

The percentage of unionized employees in the national workforce has been steadily declining over the past 70 years. It is now 12%, about 14.5 million workers. The reasons for the decline will be discussed later in the chapter. The largest labor union is

Figure 14-2   *Badge identifying shop steward (United Seamstresses of America)*

the National Education Association (3.2 million members). Other large unions are the International Brotherhood of Teamsters and the United Steelworkers. Historically unions were strongest among blue-collar employees, but now white-collar workers (particularly government employees and teachers) are the dominant union base.

Each union has a headquarters, but its strength is its many locals. A local may represent members in a geographic area (for example, all tollbooth collectors in Philadelphia) or a particular plant (for example, Amalgamated Beef Packers at Armour's Dubuque, Iowa, slaughterhouse). The local elects officials. If it is large enough, it affords some officials full-time jobs. Other officials are full-time company employees who may get time off for union activities. The shop, or union, steward has a union position equivalent to that of a company supervisor (see Figure 14-2). The steward represents the union on the job site; he or she handles grievances and discipline. Usually the steward is elected by union members for a one-year term.

A union represents an organization (for example, a labor organization) within another organization (the company). The local depends on the company for its existence. Large companies often have a multiunion labor force and thus multiple organizations within themselves. In this case the employer must deal with several collectively organized groups—for example, production workers, clerical workers, and truck drivers. Each union negotiates separately, trying to improve the welfare of its members. A large, multiunion employer is a good example of how organizations are composed of interdependent parts. Each union has a certain degree of power, which can influence the behavior of the total organization.

Union members pay dues, which are the union's chief resource. The union can also collect money for a strike fund, a pool that members can draw from if they are on strike and do not get paid. (Strikes will be discussed in more detail shortly.) Unions use their funds to offer members such things as special group automobile insurance rates or union-owned vacation facilities. Unions are highly dependent on their members. Increased membership gives a union more bargaining clout, generates more revenue, and provides a greater range of services for members. Without members, a union

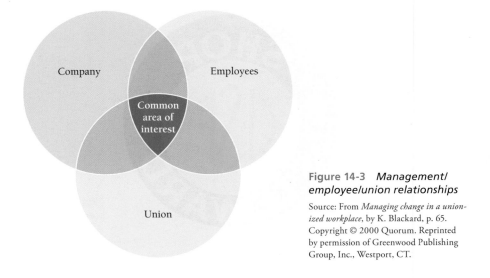

Figure 14-3 *Management/ employee/union relationships*

Source: From *Managing change in a union- ized workplace*, by K. Blackard, p. 65. Copyright © 2000 Quorum. Reprinted by permission of Greenwood Publishing Group, Inc., Westport, CT.

cannot exist; indeed, declining membership can threaten its very survival. Figure 14-3 is a graphic representation of the relationship between the company, the union, and the employees.

The Formation of a Union

National Labor Relations Act
The most influential federal law influencing union/management relations in collective bargaining.

National Labor Relations Board
An agency of the federal government that has oversight responsibility for enforcing laws pertaining to union/ management relations.

Authorization card
A card employees sign authorizing an election to determine whether a union will represent employees in the collective bargaining process.

The formation of labor unions is governed by laws across different nations; there is no universal procedure. In the United States the most influential federal law pertaining to labor unions is the **National Labor Relations Act** (NLRA) that was enacted by Congress in 1935. The NLRA established the rights of employers and employees engaged in collective bargaining. When employees in the United States want to consider being represented by a labor union, they follow a standard procedure. First, they invite representatives to solicit union membership. Federal law allows organizers to solicit membership as long as this does not endanger employees' safety or performance. Solicitations usually occur over lunch or at break time. It is illegal for employers to threaten physically, interfere with, or harass organizers. It is also illegal to fire employees for pro-union sentiments.

Both the union and the company typically mount campaigns on behalf of their positions. The union emphasizes how it can improve the workers' lot. The company's countercampaign stresses how well off the employees already are, the costs of union membership, and the loss of freedom. Then a federal agency, the **National Labor Relations Board** (NLRB), becomes involved. The NLRB sends a hearing officer to oversee the union campaign and monitor developments.

There is a two-step process that certifies a labor union to represent employees in their relationship with the company. First, employees are asked to sign cards authorizing a union election. If fewer than 30% sign the **authorization cards**, the process ends. If 30% or more sign, the second step begins. An election is held to determine whether a union will represent the employees. The NLRB officer must determine which employees are eligible to be in the union and thus eligible to vote. Management personnel (supervisors, superintendents, and managers) are excluded. The hearing officer schedules the election, provides secret ballots and ballot boxes, counts the votes, and certifies the election. This expression of voter preference is termed a **certification election**. If more than 50% of the voters approve, the union is voted in. If the union loses the election, it can repeat the entire process at a later date. A union that loses a close election will probably do so. Hepburn and Barling (2001) reported that employees who abstained from voting in a union representation election possessed less extreme work and union attitudes and believed less in the ability of their vote to affect the election outcome, compared with employees who did vote in the election. Carefully note who determines the outcome of a certification election: the employees who vote. If 100 employees are declared eligible to vote, 30 employees vote in favor of the union, 20 employees vote against the union, and 50 employees do not vote, the union becomes certified to represent all 100 employees.

Employees will support a union to the extent that it will obtain outcomes important to them without prohibitive costs. Over 70 years ago Bakke (1945) stated this most eloquently:

> The worker reacts favorably to union membership in proportion to the strength of his belief that this step will reduce his frustrations and anxieties and will further his opportunities relevant to the achievement of his standards of successful living. He reacts unfavorably in proportion to the strength of his belief that this step will increase his frustrations and anxieties and will reduce his opportunities relevant to the achievement of such standards. (p. 38)

Tetrick et al. (2007) proposed an explanation of why workers join unions (see Figure 14-4). The process begins by workers regarding a labor union as being instrumental in helping them to attain the results or outcomes they desire. If such union instrumentality is accepted, a labor union will be supported. To the extent that the labor union continues to remain instrumental in attaining the desired outcomes, workers will exhibit loyalty to the union. Tetrick et al. extended the concept of organizational citizenship behaviors (as discussed in Chapter 10) to become "union citizenship behaviors." The two constructs are composed of similar dimensions, including active participation, exerting a voice, and demonstrating civic virtue. The difference is that the behaviors are directed to the union as a means of contributing to its effectiveness. The workers view the union as being essential to their well-being, and thus they contribute

Certification election
An election in which employees vote to determine whether a union will represent them in the collective bargaining process.

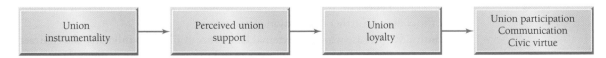

Figure 14-4   *A model of union participation*

Source: From L. E. Tetrick, L. M. Shore, L. N. McClurg, and R. J. Vandenberg, 2007. "A Model of Union Participation: The Impact of Perceived Union Support, Union Instrumentality, and Union Loyalty," *Journal of Applied Psychology*, 92, 820–828.

to the maintenance of the social exchange relationship with management. Buttigieg et al. (2007) reported similar findings regarding the instrumentality of unions to help achieve greater procedural justice within the organization.

Godard (2008) reported that union formation was primarily determined by three factors: (1) dissatisfaction with one's job; (2) general attitudes towards unions; and (3) union instrumentality. However, if workers do not support the concept of third-party representation (i.e., a labor union), they will more readily endure dissatisfying jobs than pursue an alternative deemed unacceptable.

The Labor Contract

Labor contract
A formal agreement between labor and management that specifies the terms and conditions of employment.

Once a union is recognized, its officials are authorized to negotiate a **labor contract**. This is a formal agreement between union and management that specifies the conditions of employment over a set period.

Both sides prepare a preliminary list of what they want included; the union presents its *demands* and the employer its *offers*. The union tends to ask for more than it knows it can get; management tends to offer less. While both sides seek a satisfactory agreement, they often resort to bombast, which is a hallmark of such negotiations.

Union officials may allege that management is making huge profits and taking advantage of workers. Management may allege that malicious union leaders have duped the good workers and that their policies may force the company into bankruptcy. Over time, both sides usually come to an agreement; the union often gets less than it wanted and management gives more. When agreement is not reached (an **impasse**), other steps are taken, as will be discussed.

Impasse
A point in the collective bargaining process at which both the union and management conclude they are unable to reach an agreement in the formation of a labor contract.

Contract negotiations take place between two teams of negotiators. The union side typically consists of local union officials, shop stewards, and perhaps a representative of the national union. Management usually fields a team of a few human resource and production managers, who follow preset guidelines. The contract contains many articles; there are also many issues to bargain over. The issues can generally be classified into five categories: compensation and working conditions, employee security, union security, management rights, and contract duration. Table 14-2 gives examples of these issues and the positions typically taken by each side.

In the process each bargaining team checks with its members to see whether they will compromise on the initial positions. Social media is one way through which union members can communicate with each other during contract negotiations (see Social Media and I/O Psychology: *Members Unite . . . Online*). Each side may be willing to yield on some points but not others. Eventually they reach a tentative agreement. Union members then vote on the contract. If they approve it, the contract is *ratified* and remains in effect for the agreed-on time (typically two to three years). If members reject the contract, further negotiation is necessary.

Both sides will use whatever external factors are available to influence the contract in their favor. If there is high unemployment and the company can easily replace workers who go on strike, management has an advantage. If the company does much of its business around Christmas, the union may choose that time to negotiate a contract, knowing the company can ill afford a strike then. Each side looks for factors that will bolster its position.

Table 14-2 *Typical bargaining issues and positions taken by union and management*

Issue	Union's Position	Management's Position
Compensation	Higher pay, more benefits, cost-of-living adjustments	Lower company expenditures, not yielding to all union demands
Employee security	Seniority is the basis for promotions, layoffs, and recall decisions	Merit or job performance is the basis for these decisions
Union security	A union shop in which employees must join the union when hired	An open shop in which employees can choose to join the union
Management rights	Union wants more voice in setting policies and making decisions that affect employees	Management feels certain decisions are its inherent right and does not want to share them with the union
Contract duration	Shorter contracts	Longer contracts

Social Media and I/O Psychology: *Members Unite... Online*

There is evidence that members of trade unions are more intense users of the Internet than their non-unionized counterparts. And for good reason. Social media allow unions to make information readily available to members and activists. Social media sites also help in recruiting and mobilizing union memberships. In addition, through social media, union members can move beyond traditional trade union discourses and practices to more novel and impactful means of negotiations that allow for new and unique forms of power and representation.

Take for example the power of social media for organizing protests and campaigns. Information can spread rapidly through various social media channels, and a flash mob (a group of people who assemble suddenly in a public place) can be summoned to support employees who are on strike. Moreover, demonstrations can be organized to a far larger scale than what was possible a mere decade ago. For example, in May of 2014, fast food workers in 150 U.S. cities and 33 countries staged various flash mobs, protests, and walkouts in an effort to rally for higher wages.

Demonstrations can even be made virtually, as has been the case for protestors on Second Life, an online 3D virtual world in which individuals can interact. Protestors have staged strikes within Second Life, having their avatars (their virtual representations of themselves) meet at a specified rallying point to carry out online what they may not have been able to do in the real world. Famous movements like Occupy Wall Street have taken to Second Life with official places to protest. At one point there was even a special "Union Island" created to allow trade unionists from around the globe a place to meet and access resources about labor unions in general. Indeed, it is clear that technological advances and the advent of social media have altered the landscape of union and management relations.

Collective Bargaining and Impasse Resolution

Collective bargaining
The process by which labor and management negotiate a labor contract.

Whether the **collective bargaining** process runs smoothly often depends on the parties' approaches. Pruitt (1993) distinguished between distributive and integrative bargaining postures. *Distributive bargaining* is predominant in the United States. This assumes a win/lose relationship; whatever the employer gives the union, the employer loses, and vice versa. Because both sides are trying to minimize losses, movement toward a compromise is often painful and slow. The alternative is *integrative bargaining*. Both sides work to improve the relationship while the present contract is in effect. Contract renewal is not seen as the time and place for confrontation. Instead, both parties seek to identify common problems and propose acceptable solutions that can be adopted when the contract expires. Labor and management collaboratively seek "win-win" situations to the issues they face. Although it is not always a strict either/or decision, distributive bargaining is far more characteristic of union/management relations than is integrative bargaining.

What happens if the two parties cannot reach an agreement? In some cases the labor contract may stipulate what will be done if an impasse is reached. In other cases union and management must jointly determine how to break the impasse. In either case there are three options, all involving third parties: mediation, fact-finding, and arbitration.

Mediation
A method of dispute settlement in which a neutral third party offers advice to the union and management to help them agree on a labor contract.

Mediation.   Mediation is the most frequently used and informal third-party option. A neutral third party (a mediator) assists union and management in reaching voluntary agreement. A mediator has no power to impose a settlement; rather, he or she facilitates bringing both parties together. A mediator functions like marriage counselor in trying to resolve conflict between the parties.

Where do mediators come from? The Federal Mediation and Conciliation Service (FMCS) has a staff of qualified mediators. An organization may contact FMCS for the services of such a person. The mediator need not be affiliated with FMCS; any third party acceptable to labor and management may serve. Generally, however, both parties prefer someone who has training and experience in labor disputes, so FMCS is often used.

How a mediator intervenes is not clear-cut. Mediation is voluntary; thus no mediator can function without the trust, cooperation, and acceptance of both parties. Acceptance is important because an effective mediator obtains confidential information that the parties have withheld from each other. If the information is used indiscriminately, the parties' bargaining strategy and leverage could be weakened. The mediator tries to reduce the number of disputed issues; ideally, he or she reaches a point where there are no disputes at all. Gelfand et al. (2011) reported mediators can be thwarted in bringing both parties to agreement if there is a *fixed-pie* perception. A fixed-pie perception is the belief that one party's gain will be achieved only at the expense of the other party's loss. A mediator can possibly offset this perception by offering ideas where both sides can gain, or by proposing the two parties trade off issues (i.e., give and get) in multi-issue cases. The mediator encourages information sharing to break the deadlock. Without a mediator, it is often difficult for parties to "open up" after assuming adversarial roles. The mediator facilitates the flow of information and progress toward compromise. If the mediator is unsuccessful, both parties may engage in the next phase: fact-finding.

Fact-finding
A method of dispute settlement in which a neutral third party makes public the respective positions of labor and management with the intention that the public will influence the two sides to resolve their disputes in establishing a labor contract.

Arbitration
A method of dispute settlement in which a neutral third party resolves the dispute between labor and management by using a decision that is typically final and binding on both parties.

Interest arbitration
A type of arbitration used to resolve disputes between labor and management in the formation of a labor contract.

Conventional arbitration
A form of arbitration in which the arbitrator is free to fashion whatever decision is deemed most fair in resolving a dispute.

Final-offer arbitration
A form of arbitration in which the arbitrator is obligated to accept the final offer of either the union or management in their dispute.

Total-package arbitration
A form of final-offer arbitration in which the arbitrator is obligated to accept either the union's position or management's position on every issue in dispute between the parties.

Issue-by-issue arbitration
A form of final-offer arbitration in which the arbitrator is obligated to accept either the union's position or management's position on an issue-by-issue basis in disputes between the parties.

Fact-finding.   Fact-finding is more formal than mediation. A qualified mediator may also serve as a fact-finder, but his or her role is different. In fact-finding the third party reviews the facts, makes a formal recommendation to resolve the dispute, and makes the recommendation public. It is presumed that if the recommendation is public, the parties will be pressured to accept it or use it for a negotiated settlement.

However, fact-finding has typically not produced the desired pressure. Public interest is aroused only when a strike threatens or actually imposes direct hardship on the public.

Fact-finding may be most useful when one party faces internal differences and needs recommendations from an expert to overcome opposition to a settlement. There appears to be a difference in the effectiveness of fact-finding between private- and public-sector employers. In the public sector fact-finding has met with limited success. Parties learn that rejecting a fact-finding recommendation is not politically or economically costly, so they are unlikely to value the opinion of the fact-finder. In the private sector, fact-finding can be helpful primarily because the final technique of settlement (arbitration) is strongly opposed by unions and management. However, fact-finding is not used very often in the private sector.

Arbitration.   Arbitration is the final and most formal settlement technique. Both parties must abide by the decision of the neutral third party. "Final and binding" is usually associated with arbitration. The use of arbitration may be stipulated in the labor contract; it may also be agreed on informally. This is called **interest arbitration** because it involves the interests of both parties in negotiating a new contract.

Arbitrators must have extensive experience in labor relations. The American Arbitration Association (AAA) maintains the standards and keeps a list of qualified arbitrators. Arbitrators listed by AAA can also serve as mediators listed by FMCS. Effective mediators, fact-finders, and arbitrators all need the same skills. What distinguishes the services is the clout of the third party.

There are many forms of interest arbitration. With voluntary arbitration, the parties agree to the process. It is most common in the private sector to settle disputes that arise while a contract is still in effect. Compulsory arbitration is legally required. It is most common in the public sector.

There are other types of arbitration. With **conventional arbitration**, the arbitrator creates the settlement he or she deems appropriate. In **final-offer arbitration**, the arbitrator must select the proposal of either union or management; no compromise is possible. For example, suppose the union demands $12 per hour and the company offers $10. In conventional arbitration the arbitrator could decide on any wage but would probably split the difference and decide on $11. In final-offer arbitration the arbitrator must choose the $10 or the $12. An additional variation also holds for final-offer arbitration. The arbitrator may make the decision with **total-package arbitration**: he or she chooses the complete proposal of either the company or the union on all issues. The decision may also be made with **issue-by-issue arbitration**: the arbitrator might choose the company wage offer but select the union demand on vacation days. Decisions on voluntary versus compulsory arbitration, conventional versus final-offer arbitration, and total-package versus issue-by-issue arbitration are determined by law for public-sector employers and by mutual agreement in the private sector.

Interest arbitration is more common in the public sector. Historically, the private sector has been opposed to outside interference in resolving labor problems that are "private" affairs. Thus private-sector employers will readily seek the advice of a media-tor but shun strategies that require certain courses of action. The public sector, how-ever, is quite different. Bus drivers, for example, may be permitted to strike because the public can find other means of transportation. Alternatively, firefighters, for example, perform a service vital to the welfare of society. The cessation of their services due to a labor strike could have a devastating effect on the general public. As such, firefighters would be prohibited by law from using a labor strike as a bargaining tactic. Therefore, other means of reaching a settlement (e.g., fact-finding and arbitration) are made avail-able to them.

Responses to Impasse

Consider the situation in which union and management cannot resolve their disputes. They may or may not have used a mediator. Assume the private sector is involved be-cause mediation, fact-finding, and arbitration might be required in the public sector. What happens if the two parties cannot agree?

In collective bargaining both sides can take actions if they are not pleased with the outcome. These actions are tactics with which to bring about favorable settlements.

The union can call for a **labor strike**. Union members must vote for a strike. If members support a strike and no settlement is reached, they will stop work at a par-ticular time. That point is typically the day after the current contract expires (literally, 12:01 a.m.). Taking a strike vote during negotiations brings pressure on management to agree to union demands.

The right to strike is a very powerful tactic. A company's losses from a long strike may be greater than the concessions made in a new contract. Also, unions are skilled in scheduling their strikes (or threatening to do so) when the company is particularly vulnerable (such as around Christmas for the airline industry). If employees do strike, the company is usually closed down completely. There may be limited production if management performs some jobs. It is also possible to hire workers to replace those on strike. These replacements are called "scabs" (see Figure 14-5). Given the time it takes to recruit, hire, and train new workers, replacements will not be hired unless a long strike is predicted.

Labor strike
A cessation of work activities by unionized employees as a means of influencing management to accept the union position in a dispute over the labor contract.

Figure 14-5 *Badge worn by unionized ironworkers expressing contempt for scab workers*

The Wizard Of ID

By permission of John L. Hart FLP and Creators Syndicate, Inc.

Although a strike hurts management, it is frustrating for the workers as well. Because they are not working, they do not get paid. The employees may have contributed to a strike fund, but such funds usually pay only a fraction of regular wages. A strike is the price employees pay to get their demands. It sometimes also limits their demands. By the time a union faces a strike, it is usually confronted with two unpalatable options. One is to accept a contract it does not like; the other is to strike. Employees may seek temporary employment while they are on strike, but such jobs are not always available. On the basis of labor economists' studies of the costs of strikes to both employees and employers, strikes rarely benefit either party. Sometimes the company suffers more; in other cases the union does. There are rarely any consistent "winners" in a strike.

One study examined some of the dynamics associated with strikes. Stagner and Effal (1982) examined the attitudes of unionized automobile workers at several times, including when contracts were being negotiated, during an ensuing strike, and seven months after the strike ended. The authors found that union members on strike (1) had a higher opinion of the union and its leadership than before the strike, (2) evaluated the benefit package more highly after the strike, (3) became more militant toward the employer during the strike, and (4) reported more willingness to engage in union activities. The results of this study support predictions based on theories of conflict and attitude formation.

Cloutier et al. (2013) examined the attitudes of unionized professors in a North American university. After being unable to reach an agreement with the university over such employment issues as pay equality and perceived university support of the faculty, the professors voted to go on strike. The researchers used the Internet to measure changes in attitudes of the professors during the labor dispute. The initial decision to go on strike was supported by 59% of the professors. The primary reason for going on strike was the rational desire to improve faculty employment conditions. Five weeks into the strike, another 20% (now 79% of the faculty) voted to continue the strike based on the emotional desire to punish the university for not agreeing to the union's original demands. After the union bargaining committee succeeded in fashioning a settlement favorable to the professors, 99% of the faculty voted to accept the negotiated settlement. The research results revealed that over time union members' resolve to prolong a labor strike became strengthened by emotional commitment to the process of collective bargaining.

Management is not totally defenseless in the case of a strike. If it anticipates a strike, it might boost production beforehand to stockpile goods. Most public-sector employees, on the other hand, perform services, and services cannot be stockpiled. Sometimes a strike uncovers information about the quality of the workforce. When one company replaced strikers with temporary help, new production records were set. In this case the strike revealed a weakness in the employees. Kelloway et al. (2008) examined third-party support for striking workers. Individuals in a community can show support for striking workers by blowing their car horns as they drive by the picket line, wearing a lapel button supporting the strikers, or writing a letter to the editor of a newspaper supporting the strikers. These individuals supported a labor strike in the belief that their actions would influence the outcome of a strike. Supportive individuals were found to be those who supported labor unions in general, or who felt management's offer to the workers was unfair. Kelloway et al. suggested union leaders should work on projecting their image to the public, creating a reservoir of goodwill that might result in public support for a strike.

A strike is not the only option available to the union. **Work slowdowns** have also been used in which workers operate at lower levels of efficiency. They may simply put out less effort and thus produce less, or they may be absent to reduce productivity. Because strikes are illegal in the police force, police officers who are dissatisfied with their contracts may call in sick *en masse* with what has become known as the "blue flu." Such tactics can exert pressure on management to yield to union demands.

Sabotage is another response to impasse in negotiations. A factory increased production from 2,000 to 3,000 units per day by modifying a drill press. Wages were not raised, however, and workers resented it. They found that bumping the sheet metal against the drill would eventually break the drill. Then the employee handling the drill would have to wait idly for a replacement. By some curious accident, average production continued at around 2,000 units per day. Management got the "message." Although sabotage is not a sanctioned union activity like a strike, it is a way of putting pressure on management to accept demands.

Management also has a major tactic to get the union to acquiesce. It is called a **lockout** and is considered the employer's equivalent of a strike. The company threatens to close if the union does not accept its offer. Employees cannot work and thus "pay" for rejecting the employer's offer. A threatened lockout may cause a majority of workers to pressure a minority holding out against a contract issue. Like strikes, lockouts are costly to both the company and the union, and they are not undertaken lightly. They are management's ultimate response to an impasse.

Before this section ends, note that strikes, slowdowns, sabotage, and lockouts represent failures in the collective bargaining process. These actions are taken because a settlement was *not* reached. Like most responses to frustration, they are rarely beneficial in the long run. Some unions may want to "teach the company a lesson;" some companies want to break a union. But the two parties have a symbiotic relationship. A company cannot exist without employees; without a company, employees have no jobs. Collective bargaining reflects the continual tussle for power, but neither side can afford to be totally victorious. If a union exacts so many concessions that the company goes bankrupt, it will have accomplished nothing. As Estey (1981) put it, "Labor does not seek to kill the goose that lays the golden eggs; it wants it to lay more golden eggs, and wants more eggs for itself" (p. 83). If management drives employees away by not

---

Work slowdown
A tactic used by some employees to influence the outcome of union/management negotiations in which the usual pace of work is intentionally reduced.

Sabotage
A tactic used by some employees to influence the outcome of union/management negotiations in which company equipment is intentionally damaged to reduce work productivity.

Lockout
Action taken by management against unionized employees to prevent them from entering their place of work as a means of influencing the union to accept the management position in a dispute over the labor contract.

I/O Psychology and the Economy: *The Effect of Work Stoppages on the Economy*

As discussed within the context of collective bargaining, both union and management have tactics that can be used to influence agreement on a new labor contract. However, the ultimate tactic used by both parties is the threat of a work stoppage. For the union, the work stoppage is a strike. For management, the work stoppage is a lockout. However, other individuals and organizations who are not directly involved in the labor dispute can and do get caught in the wake of a work stoppage.

Consider a work stoppage among mass transportation workers in a large urban area. Possibilities include subway operators, bus drivers, taxi drivers, and bridge toll booth operators. Employees in urban areas rely on mass transportation to get to work. When they are prevented from doing so, all organizations dependent on public commutation for their employees suffer. Many big city residents do not own a car; there are also a limited (and very expensive) number of parking places in a big city. In New York City it currently costs $15.00 per hour for use of a parking garage. Companies that use extensive air travel as part of their business operations are similarly influenced by work stoppages involving airline pilots, flight attendants, and baggage handlers.

The effect of work stoppages in suburban and rural areas takes a different form. Many small cities may have a few large businesses as the primary source of employment. Other smaller companies in town rely on the employees of these large businesses for their own livelihood. During a work stoppage, workers do not get paid, so they must conserve their money. Discretionary spending, as for dry-cleaning, dining out, clothing, attending movies, travel, house maintenance, etc., is greatly curtailed or eliminated. Spending on necessities as food, utilities, and medical needs are also reduced. In prolonged work stoppages, there is a risk of lending institutions foreclosing on mortgage holders for not making house payments. After the second or third month of non-payment, foreclosure proceedings typically begin.

The transfer of money is the lubricant by which society functions. Think of a work stoppage as a (temporary) clot that interferes with the flow of money in a community, just as a blood clot interferes with the circulatory system in our body. Most work stoppages eventually get resolved, and the system returns to normal. The longer the work stoppage lasts, the greater is the likelihood of damage to individuals and organizations that have little in reserve to weather such an interruption in the flow of money. In extreme cases, there is no "return to normal." One response to striking workers is to move the company to a different geographic area, or to offshore jobs. Similarly, one response to a lockout is for individuals to find employment elsewhere. You can think of these extreme cases as work stoppage developing into work cessation.

A seemingly isolated labor dispute between two parties can produce immediate consequences for others who are not directly involved in it. The high degree of organizational interdependence in society is most notably when one component of it ceases to function.

making enough concessions, it will not have a qualified workforce. Industrial peace is far more desirable for all parties than warfare. Conflict can provide opportunities for change and development; if conflict gets out of hand, it can be devastating.

Collective bargaining is a delicate process. Neither side should lose sight of the total economic and social environment, even though short-term, narrow issues are often at the heart of disputes (see I/O Psychology and the Economy: *The Effect of Work Stoppages on the Economy*).

Grievances

Collective bargaining is mainly directed toward resolving disputes over new labor contracts; however, disputes also occur over contracts that are in effect. No matter how clearly a labor contract is written, disagreements can arise over its meaning. Developing a clear and precise contract involves writing skills in their highest form. Despite the best intentions of those involved, events occur that are not covered clearly in a labor contract. For example, companies often include a contract clause stating that sleeping on the job is grounds for dismissal. A supervisor notices that an employee's head is resting on his arms and his eyes are closed. The supervisor infers the employee is asleep and fires him. The employee says he was not sleeping but felt dizzy and chose to rest for a moment rather than risk falling down. Who is right?

Grievance
A formal complaint made by an employee against management alleging a violation of the labor contract in effect.

If the supervisor dismissed the employee, the employee would probably file a **grievance**, or formal complaint. The firing decision can be appealed through a grievance procedure, which is usually a provision of a labor contract. First, the employee and supervisor try to reach an understanding. If they do not, the shop steward represents the employee in negotiating with the supervisor. This is often done whether or not the steward thinks the employee "has a case;" above all, the steward's job is to represent union members. If it is not resolved, the case may then be taken to the company's director of industrial relations, who hears testimony from both sides and issues a verdict. This may be a compromise—such as the employee keeps his job but is put on probation. The final step is to call in an arbitrator. He or she examines the labor contract, hears testimony, and renders an opinion. This process is called rights or **grievance arbitration**; it involves the rights of the employee. The labor contract usually specifies that union and management share the cost of arbitration, which may be $2,000 per hearing. This is done to prevent all grievances from being routinely pushed to arbitration. Each side must believe it has a strong case before calling in an arbitrator.

Grievance arbitration
A type of arbitration used in resolving disputes between labor and management in interpretation of an existing labor contract. Also called rights arbitration.

The arbitrator must be acceptable to both sides; this means he or she must be seen as neither pro-union nor pro-management. The arbitrator may decide in favor of one side or issue a compromise decision. The decision is final and binding. If an arbitrator hears many cases in the same company and repeatedly decides in favor of one side, he or she may become unacceptable to the side that always loses. Articles of the labor contract that are repeated subjects of grievance (due mainly to ambiguous language) become prime candidates for revision in the next contract.

Think of grievances as a somewhat contaminated criterion of the quality of union/management relations. In general, when the working relationship is good, there are fewer grievances. However, in some organizations work problems are resolved informally between the conflicting parties and never develop into formal grievances.

Although formal grievances are usually indicative of conflict, their absence does not always reflect a problem-free work environment. Also, the more ambiguous the labor contract, the more likely conflicts will ensue. A poorly written or inconsistently interpreted contract invites grievances. There can be much grievance activity in a recently unionized organization; employees use grievances to "test" management's knowledge of the labor contract. Particularly in the public sector, where collective bargaining is more recent, government employees are expected to act as "management" even though they may have little or no training in dealing with labor. This can contribute to errors in contract administration. Gordon and Bowlby (1989) found that employees were more likely to file a grievance when management actions against them were perceived as a threat and when the employees attributed the discipline to a manager's personal disposition (animus toward a worker). Employees were less likely to file a grievance when they perceived managers as simply following rules that required punishment for the specific worker behavior.

Employee concern over capricious management decisions is one of the major reasons employees opt for union representation. Fryxell and Gordon (1989) reported that the amount of procedural justice afforded by a grievance system was the strongest predictor of employee satisfaction with a union. Gordon and Bowlby (1988) also challenged the assertion that grievances are best resolved at the lowest step of the grievance process. Grievants who won their cases at higher levels of the grievance process showed greater faith in the fairness and perceived justice of the dispute resolution process. Klaas (1989) reported that at higher levels in the grievance process managers were influenced by the grievant's work history as documented in performance appraisals, even when that history was not relevant to evaluating the merits of the grievance. Olson-Buchanan (1996) found that, consistent with procedural justice, employees who had access to a grievance system were more willing to continue working for the organization.

There is also a growing use of arbitration to resolve disputes in nonunion companies. Richey et al. (2001) reported that in the past 20 years there has been a huge increase in employment litigation, with a corresponding increase in company costs and negative publicity. With the increased number of lawsuits in the courts, there has been growing support for *alternative dispute resolution* procedures among employees, legislators, and the courts. Arbitration is being proposed as a means of resolving disputes between employees and employers. The arbitration process may be voluntary (i.e., the employee has the option to submit the dispute to an impartial arbitrator) or mandatory (i.e., the employee is required to submit any dispute to an impartial arbitrator as a condition of employment at the company). Likewise, the outcome of the arbitration process can be nonbinding (meaning if the arbitrator's judgment does not satisfy the employee, the employee can choose to pursue the dispute in court) or binding (meaning the outcome of the arbitration process is final and binding and may not be pursued in court). Richey et al. found that job applicants were more inclined to view an employer negatively if they used either mandatory or binding arbitration as a means of resolving disputes. The finding was interpreted as limiting avenues of procedural justice for employees.

In conclusion, although there is much publicity about strike-related issues, union members think the union's highest priority should be enhancing their welfare. Unions serve many purposes; however, the most pressing need they fill is to ensure fair treatment in employment. Of course, this is a primary reason that unions appeal to workers.

Influence of Unions on Nonunionized Companies

Even if they do not have unionized employees, companies are still sensitive to union influence. Companies that are unresponsive to employees' needs invite unionization. A nonunion company that wants to remain so must be receptive to its workers' ideas and complaints. If a company can satisfy its employees' needs, a union is unnecessary; that is, if the company does voluntarily what a labor union would force it to do. A given community or industry often has a mix of union and nonunion companies. If unionized employees get concessions from management on wages, benefits, hours, and so on, these become reference points for nonunionized employees. Thus, for example, a nonunion company may feel compelled to raise wages to remain competitive. If a labor contract calls for formal grievance procedures, a nonunion company may well follow suit. Workers are aware of employment conditions in other companies, which gives them a frame of reference for judging their own. If a company does not offer comparable conditions, employees may see a union as a means of improving their welfare. This is not to say that nonunion companies must offer identical conditions. There are costs associated with a union (for example, dues); a nonunion company might set wages slightly lower than those paid in a unionized company so the net effect (higher wages minus dues) is comparable. What economists call the **union/nonunion wage differential** has been the subject of extensive research. Jarrell and Stanley (1990) reported that the union/nonunion wage differential varied with the national unemployment rate and ranged from 8.9% to 12.4%. The higher wages for unionized employees get passed on to customers of the companies through the higher costs for goods produced or services supplied. It is argued that the higher cost of union labor is offset by higher work quality. Figure 14-6 shows a badge worn by supporters of the United

Union/nonunion wage differential
The average difference in wages paid to union versus nonunion employees across an industry or geographic area for performing the same jobs.

Figure 14-6 *Badge worn by supporters of the United Association (UA)*

Association (UA), a labor union representing welders and plumbers. Notice the "tools of the trade" for their respective members: a welding torch and a wrench. The slogan of the union shown on the badge ("There is no substitute for U.A. skilled craftsmen") reflects its belief in the quality of its members' work.

Although a prudent nonunion employer keeps abreast of employment conditions in the community and the industry, a company cannot act to keep a union out "at all costs." For example, an employer cannot fire a worker without penalty just because he or she supports a union. The history of labor relations is full of cases of worker harassment by unions or management to influence attitudes toward unionization. But both sides can suffer for breaking the law.

Behavioral Research on Union/Management Relations

Thus far this chapter has examined the structure of unions, collective bargaining, and various issues in union/management relations. For the most part, psychological issues have not been discussed. With the exception of grievances, there is little behavioral research on union/management relations. However, over the past few decades, interest in this area has increased. We are beginning to see an interdisciplinary approach to topics that historically were treated with parochialism. This section will examine research on union/management relations with a strong behavioral thrust.

Employee Support for Unions

Numerous studies have examined why employees support a union, particularly with regard to personal needs and job satisfaction. Feuille and Blandin (1974) sampled the attitudes toward unionization of more than 400 college professors at a university experiencing many financial and resource cutbacks. The items measured satisfaction with areas like fairness of the university's personnel decisions, adequacy of financial support, representation of faculty interests in the state legislature, and salary. The professors were also asked to rate their inclination to accept a union. Professors who were dissatisfied with employment conditions were much more likely to support a union. Respondents also were consistent in their attitudes toward a union and their perceptions of its impact and effectiveness. Proponents of a union saw it as an effective way to protect employment interests and as having a positive impact. In general, results indicated that unionization is more attractive as employment conditions deteriorate.

Using a similar research design and sample, Bigoness (1978) correlated measures of job satisfaction with disposition to accept unionization. Bigoness found that feelings of dissatisfaction correlated with acceptance of unionization. In particular, dissatisfaction with work, pay, and promotions each correlated .35 with attitude toward unionization. Additionally, unionization was more appealing to people who were less involved in their jobs. Combining all predictor variables in a multiple regression equation, Bigoness accounted for more than 27% of the variance in attitudes toward unionization.

Hamner and Smith (1978) examined union activity in 250 units of a large organization. In half the units there had been some union activity; the other half had no activity. Using an immense sample of more than 80,000 employees, the authors found that employee attitudes predicted the level of unionization activity. The strongest predictor was dissatisfaction with supervision. Schriesheim (1978) found that pro-union voting in a certification election was positively correlated with dissatisfaction; also, dissatisfaction with economic issues was more predictive than dissatisfaction with noneconomic factors. Furthermore, research by Youngblood et al. (1984) and Zalesny (1985) showed the importance of two other factors in union support. The first factor is attitude toward collective bargaining in general. The more acceptable unions in general are to a person, the more likely he or she will vote for unionization. The second factor is attitude toward unions as being instrumental in enhancing worker welfare. Employees may not be satisfied with their employment conditions, but they may feel that unions can do little to aid them.

These studies show that dissatisfaction with employment conditions is predictive of support for unionization. The more satisfied workers are, the less likely they are to think a union is necessary or that it can improve their welfare. These results are not surprising. They reveal the types of dissatisfaction associated with a disposition toward unions. Some authors tout the social benefits of unions (for example, association with similar people), but it is mainly the perceived economic advantages that give unions their appeal. Not all support for unions, however, is based on dissatisfaction with economic conditions. Hammer and Berman (1981) found that the faculty at one college wanted a union mainly because they distrusted administrative decision making and were dissatisfied with work content. Pro-union voting was motivated by the faculty's desire to have more power in dealing with the administration. The decision to support a union is grounded in theories of organizational justice. Aryee and Chay (2001) found that perceived union support and union instrumentality were closely linked to workers' desire for procedural justice. Similarly, Fuller and Hester (2001) reported support for unionization on the basis of interactional justice—in this case, higher-quality interactions between employees and management.

Union Influence

What influence do unions have on enhancing employee welfare? Various studies have produced different conclusions. Cameron (1982) examined this in 41 colleges; faculty were unionized in 18 colleges and nonunionized in 23. Cameron proposed nine criteria of effectiveness for a college, including student academic development, faculty and administrator satisfaction, and ability to acquire resources. Nonunionized colleges were significantly more effective on three of the nine criteria; unionized colleges were not significantly more effective on any. Cameron also collected attitude data from faculty members on four factors relating to their work. These results are presented in Figure 14-7. Faculty power and "red tape" were seen as increasing since unionization; collegiality was seen as decreasing. The study revealed some major differences in the effectiveness of union and nonunion colleges; however, the cause was not determined. Unionization may cause colleges to be less effective, which would be a strong argument against unions. However, less effective colleges may turn to unions for improvement, which is obviously an argument supporting unionization.

Fullagar et al. (1995) tested the proposition that new organizational members are socialized to consider joining a union. There are two types of socialization. The first is *institutional*, which refers to the collective and formal practices organizations use to

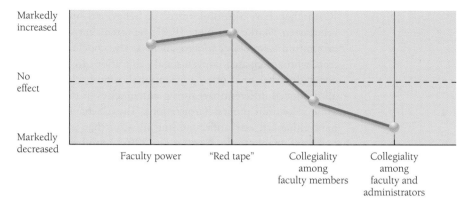

Figure 14-7   *Perceptions of the effects of faculty unionization*

From "The Relationship Between Faculty Unionism and Organizational Effectiveness," by K. Cameron, 1982, *Academy of Management Journal*, 25, p. 13.

provide newcomers with a common set of experiences and information to elicit standardized responses. In contrast, *individual* socialization practices are idiosyncratic and informal. Individual socialization is informal in that learning takes place on the job through interactions with other organizational members. Fullagar et al. found that individual socialization practices had a positive impact on both affective and behavioral involvement in the union. Institutional socialization practices were shown to be either ineffective or counterproductive. The practical implications are that important interactions occur between union officials and new members in developing new members' affective attachment to the union and later participation in union activities. Informal and individual socialization tactics may be undertaken by active or interested rank-and-file members and not necessarily by union stewards. Institutional socialization efforts (e.g., an orientation program to the union) seemingly are more effective in increasing awareness, whereas individual socialization efforts are more effective in producing involvement (Fullagar et al., 1994).

Dispute Settlement

I/O psychologists have examined the process by which disputes are settled in both laboratory and field settings. As in some other areas of I/O research, the generalizability of laboratory findings in this area is somewhat limited. Gordon et al. (1984) think the value of laboratory studies is to prepare people for undertaking actual collective bargaining in the future and to help develop questionnaires for later field use in dispute settlement. They noted that the limitations of laboratory and field research on dispute settlement are the classic ones discussed in Chapter 2. There is questionable generalizability from laboratory studies, and field studies fail to identify causal relationships.

Several studies have looked at mediation and arbitration as means of settling disputes. Neale (1984) determined that when the costs of arbitration are high, negotiators are more likely to reach a resolution on their own before they resort to arbitration. However, when cost is not much of an issue, they are more likely to accept arbitration.

Researchers have also discovered the behavioral implications of the different types of arbitration. Starke and Notz (1981) reported that subjects who anticipated final-offer arbitration were closer to agreement at the conclusion of their bargaining than subjects who anticipated conventional arbitration. In fact, Grigsby and Bigoness (1982) concluded that final-offer, conventional, total-package, and issue-by-issue arbitration all produced different bargaining outcomes even though they are all variations of the same resolution process (arbitration). These behavioral studies on dispute settlement have enhanced our understanding in ways that traditional labor economic research has been unable to do. Brett et al. (2007) found that the words people use in online dispute resolution affected the likelihood of settlement. The authors studied disputes between buyers and sellers on eBay, an online auction service. Settlement was more likely when parties engaged in face-saving gestures, as by providing a possible causal account for the misunderstanding between the two parties. Conversely, settlement was less likely when parties felt attacked by verbal expressions of negative emotions or by making demands.

Conlon et al. (2002) have experimented with hybrid means of dispute settlement. The criteria for dispute resolution include getting the two parties to resolve their own differences and having both parties feel some measure of satisfaction in the resulting outcome. Conlon et al. noted that mediation is generally more effective as a means of dispute settlement when it is followed by binding arbitration (compared with mediation alone). That is, when both parties know (and have agreed in advance) that a settlement will be made for them by a third party (an arbitrator), they are more likely to reach a voluntary agreement on their own. Conlon et al. proposed a hybrid means of dispute settlement where arbitration *precedes* (not follows) mediation. The three-phase process worked as follows. In phase one the two parties present their cases to an arbitrator, who then makes a ruling. The ruling is sealed in an envelope and is not revealed to the two parties. In the second phase the two parties engage in traditional mediation with no third party present. A precise time period is set for the two parties to reach an agreement. Conlon et al. (2007) noted that with a fixed time period set for the mediation phase, neither party can afford to engage in posturing or delays. Any wasted time in the mediation phase increases the likelihood a settlement will not be reached, thereby placing control of the settlement in the hands of the arbitrator. If the two sides reach an agreement, the dispute is settled and the arbitrator's (unknown) ruling is rendered moot. However, if the two parties do not resolve their dispute in mediation, the third phase of the process is to make the arbitrator's ruling known to both parties, and they are both obligated to accept it. It was reported that this hybrid method of "putting the cart before the horse" did result in successful voluntary agreements in the mediation phase, and was often used in highly contested disputes.

Commitment to the Union

The concept of employee commitment to a union addresses the notion of dual allegiance: can a person be loyal to both a labor union and the employing company? Researchers have examined the antecedents of both union and company commitment.

Union commitment
The sense of identity and support unionized employees feel for their labor union.

Our understanding of **union commitment** was enhanced through a major study by Gordon et al. (1980). These authors developed a questionnaire for measuring commitment that was completed by more than 1,800 union members. Responses were statistically analyzed, and union commitment was found to be composed of four dimensions: loyalty, responsibility to the union, willingness to work for the union, and belief in unionism. The research had at least two major benefits for unions. First, unions could use the questionnaires to assess the effect of their actions and estimate solidarity, especially before negotiations. Second, the research revealed the importance of socialization to new union members. The authors found that union commitment increases when both formal and informal efforts are made to involve a member in union activities soon after joining. Coworker attitudes and willingness to help are crucial to the socialization process. Improving the socialization of new members improves their commitment, which is one index of union strength. Klandermans (1989) found the scale useful for understanding unionism in the Netherlands.

Mellor (1990) studied membership decline in 20 unions. The unions with the greatest decline in membership showed the strongest commitment to the union by the surviving members. Members in locals with more severe losses expressed a greater willingness to participate in future strikes. Fullagar and Barling (1989) reported that union loyalty was best predicted by union instrumentality, extrinsic job dissatisfaction, and early socialization experiences with unions. The authors proposed that greater union loyalty resulted in more formal participation in union activities. In a study of dual allegiance, Margenau et al. (1988) found that satisfied workers felt allegiance to both the company and the union, whereas dissatisfied workers showed allegiance only to the union.

Tetrick (1995) proposed that union commitment occurs in a context of organizational rights that are provided by the union as well as organizational citizenship behaviors on the part of union members. Tetrick stated that the degree of commitment to the union can be understood in terms of the psychological contract between the employee and the organization, and the role the union plays in maintaining this relationship. Sverke and Kuruvilla (1995) identified two dimensions that explain why employees are committed to a union. The first is *instrumentality*, the perceived value or usefulness associated with union membership. The second is *ideology*, the individual's acceptance and support of the ideals or principles upon which labor unions are based.

Sverke and Sjoberg (1995) developed a typology of union members' commitment to the union based on these two dimensions, as shown in Figure 14-8. Each dimension (instrumentality and ideology) is divided into two levels, high and low, resulting in a four-cell classification model. The *alienated member* is the noncommitted member who is likely to be nonparticipative and who might intend to withdraw membership. The *instrumental member* can be expected to retain membership and to support union activities directed at improving wages and working conditions. Members committed primarily because of their pro-union ideology (*ideological members*) support and take part in union activities, such as attending meetings. The *devoted member* category, representing members with high degrees of commitment on both dimensions, is postulated to contain the most active union members. Other forms of union participation activities include holding office, serving on union committees, and voting in elections (Kelloway et al., 1995).

Finally, Gordon and Ladd (1990) provided a cautionary note about professional ethics to researchers studying dual allegiance. They said researchers should be fully aware of the reasons that either the union or the company would encourage research

Ideological commitment to the union

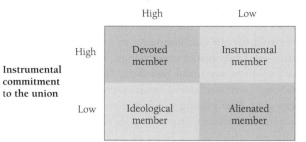

Figure 14-8   *Typology of union commitment*

Source: Adapted from "Union Membership Behavior: The Influence of Instrumental and Value-Based Commitment," by M. Sverke and A. Sjoberg, 1995, (pp. 229–254), in L. E. Tetrick and J. Barling (Eds.), *Changing employment relations.* Washington, DC: American Psychological Association.

on allegiance. I/O psychologists should not allow themselves to be "used" by either side to further their own aims by conducting such research. A similar point, as noted earlier, was raised by Zickar (2001) regarding how I/O psychologists were involved in union-busting by using personality tests to detect "pro-union" job candidates.

I/O Psychology and Labor Relations

Hartley (1992) proposed that there are many areas where I/O psychology might contribute to the field of labor relations. These include many of the issues already examined, including why workers join unions, dispute settlement, and dual commitment. Four traditional I/O psychology topics are examined from a labor union perspective: personnel selection, training, leadership development, and organizational change.

Union shop
A provision of employment stipulating that new employees must join the union that represents employees following a probationary period.

Open shop
A provision of employment stipulating that, although new employees need not join the union that represents employees, in lieu of union dues they must pay a fee for their representation.

Personnel Selection and Promotion.   In both union and nonunion companies, management determines the knowledge, skills, and abilities needed to fill jobs. The human resources office usually determines fitness for employment in lower-level jobs. For higher-level jobs, responsibility is spread through various units of the company. However, in a union company the labor contract may stipulate that those hired for jobs represented by the union must join the union after a probationary period. This is a **union shop**; the employee has no choice about joining (see Figure 14-9). Currently 24 states have "right to work" laws prohibiting compulsory union membership as a condition of continued employment. In other unionized companies the employee has the choice of joining a union; these are agency or **open shops**. However, considerable pressure can be put on an employee to join. In many cases it is to the employee's advantage to join the union for the benefits and protection it affords.

Union influence in personnel selection can affect both applicants and companies. Those who do not endorse unions (or who are uncertain about them) might not apply for jobs in unionized companies. Obviously, the applicant pool for unionized companies would be smaller if such feelings are widespread. The extent of this problem varies with anti-union sentiment and availability of other jobs.

Figure 14-9 *Badge worn by unionized employees expressing support for a union shop*

Union influence can also work in reverse. One company prided itself on remaining nonunionized. It believes unionization is encouraged by employees who have prior union experience, and therefore it carefully screens job applicants for union membership. Those who have been members are not considered (however, they are not told why). The company wants applicants who have the talent needed, but it places a higher priority on avoiding unions. Whether the company can continue this practice without adversely affecting the quality of its workforce will depend on the job openings and the number of applicants for employment with the company. Thus, from the perspectives of both the applicants and the company, unions can and do ultimately influence who gets hired.

One of the classic differences between unions and management is their preference for determining how employees will be promoted or advanced to higher jobs. The clear preference of management is merit, as determined by an assessment of current job performance. It will be recalled from Chapter 7 that performance appraisals are conducted for use in making promotion decisions. Unions, in contrast, prefer seniority as the basis for subsequent job moves. Bownas (2000) described the basis for the preference as follows:

> Once an employee becomes a dues-paying member of a union, the union generally prefers seniority as the sole criterion for subsequent job moves. Seniority has two attractive features for its proponents: it's completely objective and it comes to all members who have the patience to wait for it. Union representatives can argue for one member and against another on the basis of seniority without disparaging or offending either of them, and unions will go to extreme lengths to avoid being put in the position of articulating disparities between the value of two of their members. (p. 204)

A compromise position between merit and seniority is "qualified seniority." The employees must first meet some standard of proficiency (such as passing a job knowledge test), and among those who pass, the employee with the most seniority is promoted into the job. Union leaders have suggested using the ultimate measure of a person's suitability for employment, the job tryout, for *all* jobs. From the union perspective this method affords equal opportunity for all members, with final retention based on documented performance in the tryout period. As Bownas (2000) noted, job tryouts are usually too costly and impractical in terms of training, development, and performance management. However, the logic of such a selection method is unassailable in theory: there is no need to predict (by use of a test, interview, work sample, etc.) behavior on the job when you can actually insert people into jobs and see how they perform. In practice this idea ignores the problem of having multiple applicants for few openings as well as the consequences of making errors in the tryout period.

Personnel Training.   One area in which unions have significant influence is personnel training. One of the oldest forms is **apprentice training**, and unions have a long history of this kind of training, especially in trades and crafts. Apprenticeship is governed by law; at the national level it is administered by the Department of Labor. The Office of Apprenticeship Training, Employer, and Labor Services (OATELS) works closely with unions, vocational schools, state agencies, and others. According to the U.S. Department of Labor (2010), there are more than 30,000 apprentice programs employing over 488,000 apprentices. Apprentices go through a formal program of training and experience. They are supervised on the job and are given the facilities needed for instruction. There is a progressive wage schedule over the course of apprenticeship, and the individual is well versed in all aspects of the trade.

Most apprentice programs are in heavily unionized occupations (such as construction, manufacturing, and transportation); thus unions work closely with OATELS. For example, Figure 14-10, shows the cooperation among various organizations and agencies in the carpentry trade. Although not all unions are involved in apprentice programs, the linkage between unions and apprenticeship is one of the oldest in the history of American labor.

Leadership Development.   Often employees elected to leadership roles within their unions (e.g., shop stewards) or within the organization (e.g., supervisors) have had little developmental instruction in how to behave in a position of leadership. Several studies used the tenets of procedural justice as a basis to explain the concept of organizational fairness. Cole and Latham (1997) used a development exercise to teach supervisors to take effective disciplinary action with employees. The supervisors were placed into either a training group or a control group. Following simulated role-playing exercises derived from organizational incidents, both unionized employees and disciplinary subject matter experts (managers, union officials, and attorneys) rated the trained supervisors higher on disciplinary fairness than the supervisors in the control group. Skarlicki and Latham (1996) examined whether training union officers in the skills necessary for implementing principles of organizational justice would increase citizenship behaviors on the part of members of a labor union. The results showed that three months after training, the perceptions of union fairness among members whose leaders were in the training group were higher than among members whose leaders were in the control group. Skarlicki and Latham (1997) taught shop stewards methods of procedural justice using cases based on organizational incidents. The training improved knowledge of what constitutes fairness and may result in fewer grievances among employees regarding alleged unfairness in work. These examples illustrate how

---

Apprentice training
A method of training in which the trainee learns to perform a job by serving under the supervision of an experienced worker who provides guidance, direction, and support.

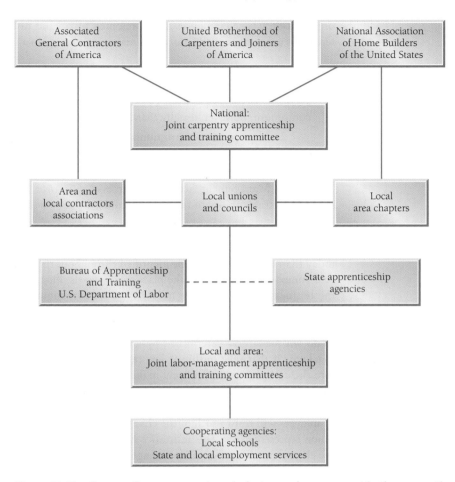

Figure 14-10   *Cooperation among unions, industry, and government in the apprentice-ship system of the carpentry trade*

Source: From *Apprenticeship: Past and present* (p. 25) by U.S. Department of Labor, 1994. Washington, DC: U.S. Government Printing Office.

concepts such as procedural justice and organizational citizenship behavior can be used to improve the quality of leadership in organizations with labor unions.

Hammer et al. (2009) examined the relationship between union leadership and member attitudes. The authors concluded that union leaders should make sure their members see the connection between the actions union leadership is taking to achieve desired employment outcomes and the attainment of those outcomes. Workers seek unions to represent them in employment relations because they perceive the union as being valuable in doing so. In turn, effective labor unions should send a "union utility" message back to their members. Namely, the union is delivering on what the members want, and without the union, the members would be receiving less.

Organizational Change.   As was discussed in Chapter 8, it is difficult to bring about change in any organization. It is even more difficult to bring about change in an organization whose employees are represented by a labor union. Blackard (2000) offered this assessment of the process of managing change in a unionized workplace:

1. Labor/management relationships have evolved over time and fall somewhere on a continuum between open warfare and efforts to create labor/management partnerships. Even those relationships near the partnership end of the continuum, however, usually manifest some discord.

2. Management in a unionized workplace is governed by laws that do not apply in a nonunion environment. These laws, particularly those relating to bargaining and labor contracts, are a major factor in the management of change.

3. Management faces more sources of resistance, more reasons for resistance, and a greater ability to resist in a unionized than a nonunion workplace. (p. 6)

Blackard noted that the need for organizations to change in response to changing environmental conditions (international competition, increasing costs, etc.) is greater today than ever before, a theme identified throughout this book. However, in a unionized company change must take place at two levels. First, management must make all the business changes that are necessary to remain competitive in the rapidly changing world. Second, it needs to change its relationship with its union. A union is in a position to delay, prevent, or make such changes more difficult, and what it elects to do will be largely determined by its relationship with management. According to Blackard, if that relationship is less than positive, management must improve it before the company can effectively make the many business changes that are required. Typically business changes lead to fewer jobs, different roles and responsibilities for existing jobs, new or revised work rules, and changes in pay, benefits, and work hours. Employees will resist much of the change, both individually and through their elected union representatives. This resistance will confirm their union as a legitimate force in the change process and require management to work not only with employees but also with the union that represents them.

A union may refuse to discuss a company proposal that affects an issue covered by a previously negotiated labor contract, such as wages, hours, or conditions of work. In such a case, the matter is closed to discussion and the union could exercise its right to have a "deal be a deal" until the scheduled termination of the labor contract in effect, which might be several years in the future. When the contract expires, the company may, after appropriate bargaining, implement planned changes at the risk of other union resistance tactics. The psychology of union resistance to change is predicated, in part, upon the union not wanting to appear irrelevant in the relationship between employees and the company (see Figure 14-3). Individuals are often reluctant to change because the change represents some loss (or perceived loss) of control over their lives.

The union, therefore, can become an instrument for increasing employee control, even to the possible long-term detriment of the employees. If the union shows little resistance to proposed management changes, the very viability of the union as an agent of the employees can be questioned. Blackard contends there is a gap in our knowledge about organizational change in unionized companies. Consider Figure 14-11. It is a badge made by a labor union (the United Steelworkers of America) expressing protest against a safety program initiated by management. The name given to the

Figure 14-11   *Badge worn by union members expressing contempt for a management program on behavioral safety*

program was "Behavioral Safety;" the program was designed to encourage workers to behave safely in steel factories. The union badge represents a defiant statement against the Behavioral Safety program ("No B.S."). While the labor union was in favor of reducing work-related injuries to their members, the union resented the assumption that the behavior of their members was responsible for the injuries ("Don't Blame Workers"). The union's explanation for the work-related injuries incurred by their members pertained to factors under the control of management ("Eliminate Hazards"). This badge is symbolic of what Blackard described as unions offering resistance to proposed management changes (i.e., a safety program designed to reduce work-related injuries), even if the change was for the workers' benefit. If the union supported the safety program, the instrumental value of the union as an agent of the employees could be questioned.

What is the Future of Labor Unions?

As mentioned previously, in the United States membership in labor unions has steadily declined over the past 70 years. The highwater mark for unionized employees was around 35% of the total workforce in 1945. Sweet and Meiksins (2013) reported that it is only because 37% of government employees are unionized (compared to 7% of the private sector) that the total percentage of unionized employees in the workforce today is still in double digits (12%).

Sweet and Meiksins proposed several reasons for the decline in labor unions. First, the percentage of the workforce employed in manufacturing, a traditional labor stronghold, is declining. Companies that manufactured products are finding more favorable economic conditions in other countries, the topic of offshoring, discussed in Chapter 8. Most prominent is the cost of labor. Many countries do not have minimum wage laws. Employees in Southeast Asia typically work for less than $1.00 per hour. Immense cost savings to employers are achieved by exporting jobs to cheaper labor markets. Also, corporate tax rates differ markedly across nations. For example, when a large manufacturing company shifted its corporate headquarters from the U.S. to Bermuda, its annual corporate tax was reduced from $40 million owed to the United States government to $27,653 owed to Bermuda (Johnston, 2004).

Second, the sectors of the economy that are growing (e.g., customer service, healthcare) have shown little interest in having its employees be represented by labor unions. Employers in those sectors have become increasingly resistant to organizing attempts by voluntarily offering the types of employment conditions that unions achieve for their members. Employers like to tout their attractiveness through such reports as the "Best Places to Work" (Glassdoor, 2014). The vast majority of these highly rated companies are union-free; it is highly unlikely a union presence could make major improvements in employment conditions.

Third, proponents of organized labor claim the union-management playing field is far from even, with labor being greatly disadvantaged by current federal laws. For example, employers can require all workers to attend anti-union informational meetings on company time, but unions are not allowed to do the same. While laws prohibit employers from firing workers who express pro-union sentiments, the consequences for doing so are not severe.

Finally, the nature of employment has changed in the 21st century. Today workers are less likely to devote their entire career to a single employer compared to decades ago. Also, the era of huge companies (employing thousands of workers each) have given way to relatively small employers. Approximately 52% of the U.S. workforce is employed by companies that have fewer than 500 employees; furthermore, 75% of new job growth in the nation is with small employers (Conte & Carr, 2012). Being smaller, there is more capacity for cooperation between workers and management, with a corresponding reduction in a "them vs. us" mentality. The very nature of work itself is characterized by a different structure than in the past. Work is now routinely conducted across nations. For example, a U.S. owned company has a production plant in the Philippines using German-made equipment to process raw material from Argentina that is assembled in Vietnam and transported to worldwide markets by ships from South Korea. Through the Internet information transmission is now continuous and immediate. Time, when we work and when we sleep, is irrelevant to global commerce. It is always "work time" in some part of the world, a cornerstone of the new global economy. Labor unions in the United States have not evolved at the same rate of change as the world of business.

Do these changing global conditions render labor unions obsolete? Not at all. Labor unions will have to develop different strategies for attracting new members and appealing to the growing sectors of the national economy to once again serve a prominent role in the U.S. economy. Labor unions are but a means to an end. Organized labor has long advocated principles that would be the foundation of a better society for all. Work plays a central role, perhaps the defining role, in any healthy society. As Yates (2009) described, most of us need jobs to thrive. Unemployment, particularly long-term unemployment, has corrosive consequences for humanity. Many people desire meaningful work, jobs that utilize the full range of talent that we have to offer. Underemployment often leads to alienation and aversion to work. Lastly, we need to balance work and non-work activities to sustain psychological health. Neither unemployment, underemployment, nor a subscription to overemployment (working 60–80 hours per week) leads to a fulfilling life. In short, there is no shortage of problems in the contemporary work world. The pressing issue for labor unions is whether they can offer viable solutions to employment problems in the new global economy. While organized labor would be facilitated by new legislation favorable to their goals, ultimately the value of labor unions will be what it has always been: offering workers a higher quality of life with their presence than their absence.

Labor union representation in other countries is typically much higher than in the United States. For example, it is almost 80% in Belgium, 60% in Denmark, and 30% in the U.K. (Hayter & Stoeveska, 2011). The average employee in Europe works 1,640 hours per year and gets five weeks of vacation; the average worker in the U.S. works 1,900 hours per year and gets two weeks of vacation (Lichtenstein, 2013). In reference to organized labor in the U.S., Sweet and Meiksins stated, "evidence suggests that unions have lost much of their teeth" (p. 43). It is a matter of debate whether labor

Cross-Cultural I/O Psychology: *The International Trade Union Confederation*

Many individual labor unions within a nation are members of a larger organization of similar unions, called a *federation*. The largest union federation in the United States is the American Federation of Labor – Congress of Industrial Organizations (AFL-CIO). In 2006 a world-wide federation of unions was created: The International Trade Union Confederation (ITUC), headquartered in Belgium. The representative from the United States to the ITUC is the AFL-CIO. Currently the ITUC has members from 161 nations representing 176 million workers. The ITUC advocates labor unions as a way to increase human rights, non-discrimination, prohibitions against child labor, and fair treatment of all workers.

The ITUC conducted a survey of 139 nations regarding their treatment of workers. The survey was based on 97 specific criteria that assessed two broad factors. The first was the degree to which nations have laws protecting the rights of workers to join labor unions, engage in collective bargaining, and the right to strike. The second factor was the degree to which there are violations of these basic worker rights, and whether there are government sanctions for violators. Scores on the 97 criteria were aggregated to produce a rating on a scale of 1-5, with 1 being the best rating. Nations with a rating of 1 had many laws to protect the rights of workers, reported few violations of these rights, and government sanctions were imposed on violators. A nation that received a rating of 5 had few or no laws in place to protect worker rights, reported massive violations, and no governmental sanctions. Denmark received a perfect evaluation, and was one of several Scandinavian nations (as well as France and Germany) to receive a rating of 1. Nations receiving a rating of 2 included Japan and Switzerland. Canada and the United Kingdom were among the nations that received a rating of 3. Nations receiving a rating of 4 included Mexico and the United States. China and India (the two most populous nations) were among those that received a rating of 5 (India is a member of ITUC; China is not).

One major finding was a nation's level of economic development was not related to its score. For example, the tiny island nation of Barbados received a score of 1; the Republic of Korea (South Korea) received a score of 5. While the United States has laws designed to protect the rights of workers, the primary basis of its low rating was the frequency of reported violations and the lack of government sanctions for violations. The ITUC cited one U.S. company that compels its workers to wear electronic ankle bracelets to monitor their activity at the worksite.

unions in the U.S. will be able to muster the resources and appeal that they once held, especially in comparison to other developed nations in the world (see Cross-Cultural I/O Psychology: *The International Trade Union Confederation*).

Pocock (2008) reflected on how labor unions were originally developed to decrease the disparity between two segments of society (management—the "haves," and the workers—the "have nots"). Labor unions bargained for outcomes (e.g., higher wages, better benefits) to reduce the inequality between the two. However, increased global commerce in the 21st century has produced a new form of the haves and the have nots.

Growing global trade has been accompanied by widening inequality between countries. Work—or its absence—significantly shapes these inequalities with many citizens unable to find work, or enough of it, when they want it. Unemployment is high in many countries and as former U.N. Secretary General Kofi Annan stated, "The best anti-poverty program is employment. And the best road to economic empowerment and social well-being is decent work" (Pocock, pp. 573–574).

It remains to be seen if in the 21st century emerging nations will turn to labor unions to improve their economic welfare, as happened with industrialized nations at the start of the 20th century. It should also be noted that labor unions are specifically referenced in the United Nations Global Compact (Table 8–3) in Chapter 8.

Chapter Summary

- Labor unions were created to improve the quality of work life.
- I/O psychology does not have a favorable image in the eyes of labor unions.
- Labor unions are found throughout the world. Countries differ greatly in the extent to which their respective workforces are represented by labor unions.
- Labor unions appeal to workers to the extent the unions are perceived as being instrumental in achieving desired outcomes.
- A labor contract specifies the terms and conditions of the employment relationship.
- Mediation, fact-finding, and arbitration are means of resolving disputes between the parties in a labor contract.
- Strikes and lockouts are the responses both sides can use to put pressure on the other to accept the terms of a labor contract.
- Grievances are complaints filed by workers alleging a violation of the labor contract by management.
- Employees differ in the strength of their commitment to a labor union.
- Labor unions typically have represented manufacturing employees. As our economy moves toward a service economy, union influence has declined in the United States. However, with the emergence of global businesses composed of unionized employees in their own respective countries, it is possible the future will witness new forms and types of labor unions that stretch across national boundaries.

Glossary

Acquisition The process by which one organization acquires or subsumes the resources of a second organization.

Actual criteria The operational or actual standards that researchers measure or assess. Often contrasted with conceptual criteria.

Ad hoc team A type of team created for a limited duration that is designed to address one particular problem.

Adaptive behavior A range of behaviors that enable employees to increase their capacity to cope with organizational change.

Adverse impact A type of unfair discrimination in which the result of using a particular personnel selection method has a negative effect on protected group members compared with majority group members. Often contrasted with disparate treatment.

Affect A broad range of feelings that encompass moods and emotions, typically described along a positive-negative continuum.

Affirmative action A social policy that advocates members of protected groups will be actively recruited and considered for selection in employment.

Apprentice training A method of training in which the trainee learns to perform a job by serving under the supervision of an experienced worker who provides guidance, direction, and support.

Arbitration A method of dispute settlement in which a neutral third party resolves the dispute between labor and management by using a decision that is typically final and binding on both parties.

Armed Services Vocational Aptitude Battery (ASVAB) A test developed in the 1980s by I/O psychologists for the selection and placement of military personnel.

Army Alpha An intelligence test developed during World War I by I/O psychologists for the selection and placement of military personnel.

Army Beta A nonverbal intelligence test developed during World War I by I/O psychologists to assess illiterate recruits.

Army General Classification Test (AGCT) A test developed during World War II by I/O psychologists for the selection and placement of military personnel.

Assessment center A technique for assessing job candidates using a series of structured, group-oriented exercises that are evaluated by raters.

Authentic leadership A conception that leaders who are self-aware, transparent in their relationships with others, unbiased in their decision making, and internally moral will be more trusted, and therefore more effective.

Authorization card A card employees sign authorizing an election to determine whether a union will represent employees in the collective bargaining process.

Banding A method of interpreting test scores such that scores of different magnitude in a numeric range or band (e.g., 90–95) are regarded as being equivalent.

Base rate The percentage of current employees in a job who are judged to be performing their jobs satisfactorily.

Behavior modeling A method of training that makes use of imitative learning and reinforcement to modify human behavior.

Behavioral approach A conception that leadership is best understood in terms of the actions taken by an individual in the conduct of leading a group.

Behavioral criteria A standard for judging the effectiveness of training that refers to changes in performance that are exhibited on the job as a result of training.

Behaviorally anchored rating scale (BARS) A type of performance appraisal rating scale in which the scale points are descriptions of behavior.

Benchmarking The process of comparing a company's products or procedures with those of the leading companies in an industry.

Big 5 personality theory A theory that defines personality in terms of five major factors: emotional stability, extraversion, openness to experience, agreeableness, and conscientiousness. Also referred to as the "Five-Factor" theory of personality.

Biographical information A method of assessing individuals in which information pertaining to past activities, interests, and behaviors in their lives is considered.

Biological-based theory of motivation A theory that presumes motivation is genetically predisposed, determined by one's physiology and traits.

Broaden-and-build theory of positive emotions A theory that positive emotions prompt individuals to expand their thinking and action repertoires in ways that result in increased resources and enhanced functioning.

Business games A method of training that simulates a business environment with specific objectives to achieve and rules for trainees to follow.

Categorical variables Objects of study that do not inherently have numerical values associated with them, as gender. Often contrasted with quantitative variables.

Central-tendency error A type of rating error in which the rater assesses a disproportionately large number of ratees as performing in the middle or central part of a distribution of rated performance in contrast to their true level of performance.

Certification election An election in which employees vote to determine whether a union will represent them in the collective bargaining process.

Challenge stressors Job demands or characteristics that create positive feelings of achievement or fulfillment.

Child labor The pattern of compelling children under the age of 15 to perform labor that is harmful to their overall health and psychological well-being.

Citizenship behavior Employee behavior that transcends job performance and is directed to the overall welfare of the organization.

Classical theory A theory developed in the early 20th century that described the form and structure of organizations.

Classification The process of assigning individuals to jobs based on two or more test scores.

Collective bargaining The process by which labor and management negotiate a labor contract.

Competency modeling A process for determining the human characteristics (i.e., competencies) needed to perform successfully within an organization.

Compressed workweek A schedule of work hours that typically involves more hours per day and fewer days per week. An example is 10 hours per day, 4 days per week.

Computer-based training A method of training that utilizes computer technology to enhance the acquisition of knowledge and skills.

Computerized adaptive testing (CAT) A form of assessment using a computer in which the questions have been precalibrated in terms of difficulty, and the examinee's response (i.e., right or wrong) to one question determines the selection of the next question.

Conceptual criterion The theoretical standard that researchers seek to understand.

Construct validity The degree to which a test is an accurate and faithful measure of the construct it purports to measure.

Content validity The degree to which subject matter experts agree that the items in a test are a representative sample of the domain of knowledge the test purports to measure.

Contingency approach A conception that leadership is best understood in terms of the actions taken by an individual in the conduct of leading a group.

Contrast error A type of rating error in which the rater assesses the ratee as performing better (or worse) than he or she actually performed due to a comparison with another ratee who performed particularly poorly (or well).

Conventional arbitration A form of arbitration in which the arbitrator is free to fashion whatever decision is deemed most fair in resolving a dispute. Often contrasted with final-offer arbitration.

Corporate social responsibility The obligation of organizations to take an active part in improving society.

Correlation coefficient A statistical index that reflects the degree of relationship between two variables.

Counterproductive work behavior A broad range of employee behaviors that are harmful to other employees or the organization.

Creative team A type of team created for the purpose of developing innovative possibilities or solutions.

Criteria Standards used to help make evaluative judgments.

Criterion contamination The part of the actual criterion that is unrelated to the conceptual criterion.

Criterion cutoff A standard that separates successful from unsuccessful job performance.

Criterion deficiency The part of the conceptual criterion that is not measured by the actual criterion.

Criterion relevance The degree of overlap or similarity between the actual criterion and the conceptual criterion.

Criterion variable A variable that is a primary object of a research study; it is forecasted by a predictor variable.

Criterion-related validity The degree to which a test forecasts or is statistically related to a criterion.

Critical incidents Specific behaviors indicative of good or bad job performance.

Cross-cultural psychology An area of research that examines the degree to which psychological concepts and findings generalize to people in other cultures and societies.

Culture The language, values, attitudes, beliefs, and customs of an organization.

Cyberaggression Hostile or aggressive behavior at the workplace that occurs through electronic media.

Dark triad A cluster of three personality disorders associated with counterproductive work behavior: Machiavellianism, narcissism, and psychopathy.

Data mining An emerging secondary research method in I/O psychology that looks for patterns of association among the measured items in very large data sets.

Declarative knowledge A body of knowledge about facts and things. Often compared with procedural knowledge.

Deductive method A research process in which conclusions are drawn about a specific member of a class of objects or people based on knowledge of the general class under investigation. Often contrasted with the inductive method.

Dependent variable A variable whose values are influenced by the independent variable.

Development The process through which the knowledge and skills of employees are enhanced but for which there is no immediate use.

Disparate treatment A type of unfair discrimination in which protected group members are afforded differential employment procedures compared to members of other groups. Often contrasted with adverse impact.

Distributive justice The fairness with which the outcomes or results are distributed among members of an organization.

Diversity A goal of staffing whereby demographic differences in society are reflected in the workforce.

Diversity training A method of training directed at improving interpersonal sensitivity and awareness of differences among employees.

Diversity-validity dilemma The paradox of organizations being unable to simultaneously hire the most qualified applicants and members of the full range of demographic groups that populate society.

Downsizing The process by which an organization reduces its number of employees to achieve greater overall efficiency.

Drug testing A method of assessment typically based on an analysis of urine that is used to detect illicit drug use by the candidate.

Dynamic performance criteria Aspects of job performance that change (increase or decrease) over time.

Emic An approach to researching phenomena that emphasizes knowledge derived from the participants' awareness and understanding of their own culture. Often contrasted with etic.

Emotion regulation The attempts to control one's emotions or mood.

Emotional contagion The tendency for individuals to synchronize their emotions with others in their environment, experiencing and expressing another's emotions whether consciously or unconsciously.

Emotional intelligence A construct that reflects a person's capacity to manage emotional responses in social situations.

Emotional labor The requirement in some jobs that employees express emotions to customers or clients that are associated with enhanced performance in the job.

Emotions Discrete, target-specific feelings that are of relatively short duration.

Employee engagement The degree to which a person feels invigorated, dedicated, and absorbed in his or her work.

Entrepreneurship The process by which individuals pursue opportunities and organize resources that can lead to new job creation and business growth.

Equity sensitivity The individual differences that people have regarding their preference for equity (or tolerance for inequity).

Equity theory A theory of motivation based on the comparison of one's inputs to outcomes with those of another person to determine if a situation is fair. These determinations of equity dictate subsequent actions taken.

Equivalent-form reliability A type of reliability that reveals the equivalence of test scores between two versions or forms of the test.

Error-management training A system of training in which employees are encouraged to make errors, and then learn from their mistakes.

Ethnography A research method that utilizes field observations to study a society's culture.

Etic An approach to researching phenomena that emphasizes knowledge derived from the perspective of a detached objective investigator in understanding a culture. Often contrasted with emic.

Executive coaching An individualized developmental process for business leaders provided by a trained professional (the coach).

Expatriate A person native to one country who serves a period of employment in another country.

Expectancy Within expectancy theory, the belief that effort leads to performance.

Expectancy theory A theory of motivation based on the perceived degree of relationship between how much effort a person expends and the performance that results from that effort.

External validity The degree to which the relationships evidenced among variables in a particular research study are generalizable or accurate in other contexts.

Face validity The appearance that items in a test are appropriate for the intended use of the test by the individuals who take the test.

Fact-finding A method of dispute settlement in which a neutral third party makes public the respective positions of labor and management with the intention that the public will influence the two sides to resolve their disputes in establishing a labor contract.

Faking The behavior of job applicants to falsify or fake their responses to items on personality inventories to create a favorable impression.

False negatives A term to describe individuals who were incorrectly rejected for employment as they would have been successful employees.

False positives A term to describe individuals who were incorrectly accepted for employment as they became unsuccessful employees.

Fiedler's contingency model A contingency approach to leadership that suggests a leader's effectiveness will depend on the interaction between his or her leadership style and the favorability of the situation.

Final-offer arbitration A form of arbitration in which the arbitrator is obligated to accept the final offer of either the union or management in their dispute. Often contrasted with conventional arbitration.

Flextime A schedule of work hours that permits employees flexibility in when they arrive at and leave work.

Flow theory A theory of motivation that suggests that individuals will experience an intense level of enjoyment, concentration, and lack of self-awareness when actively engaged in activities that have clear goals, unambiguous feedback, and a match between one's skills and the challenge of the task.

Frame-of-reference training The process of providing a common perspective and set of standards to all raters to increase the accuracy of their evaluations.

Functional Job Analysis (FJA) A method of work analysis that describes the content of jobs in terms of People, Data, and Things.

Functional principle The concept that organizations should be divided into units that perform similar functions.

g The symbol for "general mental ability," which has been found to be predictive of success in most jobs.

Generalizability The extent to which conclusions drawn from one research study spread or apply to a larger population.

Goal orientation The way in which individuals approach or avoid goals in achievement situations.

Goal-setting theory A theory of motivation based on directing one's effort toward the attainment of specific goals that have been set or established.

Grievance A formal complaint made by an employee against management alleging a violation of the labor contract in effect.

Grievance arbitration A type of arbitration used in resolving disputes between labor and management in interpretation of an existing labor contract. Also called rights arbitration.

Groupthink A phenomenon associated with team decision making in which members feel threatened by forces external to the team, resulting in deterioration in the cognitive processing of information.

Halo error A type of rating error in which the rater assesses the ratee as performing well on a variety of performance dimensions, despite having credible knowledge of only a limited number of performance dimensions.

Hawthorne studies A series of research studies that began in the late 1920s at the Western Electric Company and ultimately refocused the interests of I/O psychologists on how work behavior manifests itself in an organizational context.

Hindrance stressors Job demands or characteristics that are demotivating and hinder one's ability to achieve his or her goals.

Hostile environment harassment A legal classification of sexual harassment in which individuals regard conditions in the workplace (such as unwanted touching or off-color jokes) as offensive. Often compared with *quid pro quo* harassment.

Humanitarian work psychology The practice of I/O psychology directed to the societal goal of improving employment for all mankind.

I/O psychology An area of scientific study and professional practice that addresses psychological concepts and principles in the work world.

Impasse A point in the collective bargaining process at which both the union and management conclude they are unable to reach an agreement in the formation of a labor contract. Impasse (literally meaning "blockage") triggers the use of other means (besides negotiation) to resolve the dispute between the parties.

Implicit leadership theory A conception that leadership is a perceived phenomenon as attributed to an individual by others.

Independent variable A variable that can be manipulated to influence the values of the dependent variable. Usually used in the context of experimental research. Similar to a predictor variable. Often contrasted with a dependent variable.

Inductive method A research process in which conclusions are drawn about a general class of objects or people based on knowledge of a specific member of the class under investigation. Often contrasted with the deductive method.

Information diversity The differences among team members in terms of what they know and what cognitive resources they can bring to the team.

Instrumentality Within expectancy theory, the belief that performance will lead to an outcome.

Integrity test A type of test that purports to assess a candidate's honesty or character.

Intelligent tutoring systems A sophisticated type of computer-based training that uses artificial intelligence to customize learning to the individual.

Interactional justice The fairness with which people are treated within an organization and the timeliness, completeness, and accuracy of the information received in an organization.

Interactive multimedia training A type of computer-based training that combines visual and auditory information to create a realistic but non-threatening environment.

Interest arbitration A type of arbitration used to resolve disputes between labor and management in the formation of a labor contract.

Internal validity The degree to which the relationships evidenced among variables in a particular research study are accurate or true. Often contrasted with external validity.

Internal-consistency reliability A type of reliability that reveals the homogeneity of the items comprising a test.

Inter-rater reliability A type of reliability that reveals the degree of agreement among the assessments provided by two or more raters.

Issue-by-issue arbitration A form of final-offer arbitration in which the arbitrator is obligated to accept either the union's position or management's position on an issue-by-issue basis in disputes between the parties. Often contrasted with total-package final-offer arbitration.

Job A set of similar positions in an organization.

Job demands-resources model An explanatory model describing the ways in which resources can buffer the negative psychological and physical effects of job demands.

Job enrichment The process of designing work so as to enhance individual motivation to perform the work.

Job family A grouping of similar jobs in an organization.

Job satisfaction The degree of pleasure an employee derives from his or her job.

Knowledge compilation The body of knowledge acquired as a result of learning.

KSAOs An abbreviation for "knowledge, skills, abilities, and other" characteristics. Often used in the context of work analysis.

Labor contract A formal agreement between labor and management that specifies the terms and conditions of employment.

Labor strike A cessation of work activities by unionized employees as a means of influencing management to accept the union position in a dispute over the labor contract.

Laboratory experiment A type of research method in which the investigator manipulates independent variables and assigns subjects to experimental and control conditions.

Laissez-faire leadership A form of non-leadership in which managers deflect all responsibility and leave followers on their own.

Leader–member exchange theory A theory of leadership based on the nature of the relationship between a leader and members of the group he or she leads.

Learning The process by which change in knowledge or skills is acquired through education or experience.

Learning criteria A standard for judging the effectiveness of training that refers to the amount of new knowledge and skills acquired through training.

Leniency error A type of rating error in which the rater assesses a disproportionately large number of ratees as performing well (positive leniency) or poorly (negative leniency) in contrast to their true level of performance.

Level of analysis The unit or level (individuals, teams, organizations, nations, etc.) that is the object of the researchers' interest and about which conclusions are drawn from the research.

Licensure The process by which a professional practice is regulated by law to ensure quality standards are met to protect the public.

Line functions Organizational work that directly meets the major goals of an organization.

Line/staff principle The concept of differentiating organizational work into primary and support functions.

Linkage analysis A technique in work analysis that establishes the connection between the tasks performed and the human attributes needed to perform them.

Lockout Action taken by management against unionized employees to prevent them from entering their place of work as a means of influencing the union to accept the management position in a dispute over the labor contract.

Management development The process by which individuals serving in management or leadership positions enhance their talents to better perform the job.

Mediation A method of dispute settlement in which a neutral third party offers advice to the union and management to help them agree on a labor contract.

Mentor Typically a more senior or experienced person who helps to professionally develop a less experienced person (the protégé).

Meta-analysis A quantitative secondary research method for summarizing and integrating the findings from original empirical research studies.

Moods General and long-lasting feelings not directed at a particular target.

Multiple correlation A statistical index used to indicate the degree of predictability (ranging from 0 to 1.00) in forecasting the criterion on the basis of two or more other variables.

Multiteam systems Teams of teams that function interdependently to achieve overarching system-level goals.

National Labor Relations Act The most influential federal law influencing union/management relations in collective bargaining.

National Labor Relations Board An agency of the federal government that has oversight responsibility for enforcing laws pertaining to union/management relations.

Nepotism An approach to personnel staffing whereby family members receive preferential treatment because of birth or marriage.

Norm A set of shared group expectations about appropriate behavior.

Objective performance criteria A set of factors used to assess job performance that are (relatively) factual in character. Examples are days absent, units of production, and sales volume.

Observation A type of research method in which the investigator monitors employees for the purpose of understanding their behavior and culture.

Occupational Information Network (O*NET) An online computer-based source of information about jobs.

Offshoring The process of eliminating jobs within the organization by having those work functions performed in cheaper labor markets overseas (offshore).

Open shop A provision of employment stipulating that, although new employees need not join the union that represents employees, in lieu of union dues they must pay a fee for their representation. Often contrasted with a union shop.

Organization A coordinated group of people who perform tasks to produce goods or services, colloquially referred to as a company.

Organizational analysis Part of the training needs assessment in which the organization's strategic objectives and the availability of resources and support are identified.

Organizational change The methods by which organizations evolve to become more adaptive to pressing economic and social conditions.

Organizational citizenship behavior Employee behavior that transcends job performance and is directed to the overall welfare of the organization.

Organizational justice The theoretical concept pertaining to the fair treatment of people in organizations. The three types of organizational justice are distributive, procedural, and interactional.

Organizational merger The joining or combining of two organizations of approximately equal status and power.

Organizational neuroscience The scientific study of neural activity as evidenced in organizational attitudes and behavior.

Organizational politics Behavior exhibited within organizations by employees that is driven by self-interest.

Outsourcing The process of eliminating jobs within the organization by having those work functions contracted to other organizations.

Peer assessment A technique of performance appraisal in which individuals assess the behavior of their peers or coworkers. Peer assessments include nominations, ratings, and rankings.

Peer nomination A technique of appraising the performance of coworkers by nominating them for membership in a group.

Peer ranking A technique of appraising the performance of coworkers by ranking them on a dimension of their job behavior.

Peer rating A technique of appraising the performance of coworkers by rating them on a dimension of their job behavior.

Performance management The process of how an organization manages and aligns all of its resources to achieve high performance.

Person analysis Part of the training needs assessment in which the people who need training are identified.

Personnel selection The process of determining those applicants who are selected for hire versus those who are rejected.

Person-organization fit The perception by both job candidates and the organization of the match between their respective values and goals.

Placement The process of assigning individuals to jobs based on one test score.

Planning fallacy The tendency to underestimate how long it will take to complete a task.

Polygraph An instrument that assesses responses of an individual's central nervous system (heart rate, breathing, perspiration, etc.) that supposedly indicate giving false responses to questions.

Position A set of tasks performed by a single employee. For example, the position of a secretary is often represented by the tasks of typing, filing, and scheduling. There are usually as many positions in an organization as there are employees.

Position Analysis Questionnaire (PAQ) A method of work analysis that assesses the content of jobs on the basis of approximately 200 items in the questionnaire.

Positive psychology The study of the factors and conditions in life that lead to pleasurable and satisfying outcomes for individuals.

Power and influence approach A conception that leadership is best understood by the use of the power and influence exercised by a person with a group.

Predictor cutoff A score on a test that differentiates those who passed the test from those who failed; often equated with the passing score on a test.

Predictor variable A variable used to predict or forecast a criterion variable.

Primary research methods A class of research methods that generates new information on a particular research question.

Problem-resolution team A type of team created for the purpose of focusing on solving ongoing problems or issues.

Procedural justice The fairness by which means are used to achieve results in an organization.

Procedural knowledge A body of knowledge about how to use information to address issues and solve problems. Often compared with declarative knowledge.

Programmed instruction The most basic computer-based training that provides for self-paced learning.

Protected group A designation for members of society who are granted legal status by virtue of a demographic characteristic, such as race, sex, national origin, color, religion, age, and disability.

Protégé Typically a more junior and less experienced person who is helped and developed in his or her career by a more experienced person (the mentor).

Psychological capital A personal resource consisting of hope, optimism, self-efficacy, and resilience that impacts one's psychological health and helps combat occupational stress.

Psychological contract The implied exchange relationship that exists between an employee and the organization.

Psychometric Literally, the measurement ("metric") of properties of the mind (from the Greek word "psyche"). The standards used to measure the quality of psychological assessments.

Qualitative research A class of research methods in which the investigator takes an active role in interacting with the subjects he or she wishes to study. Often contrasted with quantitative research methods.

Quantitative variables Objects of study that inherently have numerical values associated with them, such as weight. Often contrasted with categorical variables.

Quasi-experiment A type of research method for conducting studies in field situations where the researcher may be able to manipulate some independent variables.

Questionnaire A type of research method in which subjects respond to written questions posed by the investigator.

Quid pro quo harassment A legal classification of harassment in which specified organizational rewards are offered in exchange for sexual favors. Often compared with hostile environment harassment.

Rater error training The process of educating raters to make more accurate assessments of performance, typically achieved by reducing the frequency of halo, leniency, and central-tendency errors.

Rater motivation A concept that refers to organizationally-induced pressures that compel raters to distort their evaluations.

Reaction criteria A standard for judging the effectiveness of training that refers to the reactions or feelings of individuals about the training they received.

Recruitment The process by which individuals are solicited to apply for jobs.

Reliability A standard for evaluating tests that refers to the consistency, stability, or equivalence of test scores. Often contrasted with validity.

Research A formal process by which knowledge is produced and understood.

Research design A plan for conducting scientific research for the purpose of learning about a phenomenon of interest.

Results criteria A standard for judging the effectiveness of training that refers to the economic value that accrues to the organization as a function of the new behaviors exhibited on the job.

Role A set of expectations about appropriate behavior in a position.

Role ambiguity Uncertainty about the behaviors to be exhibited in a role, or the boundaries that define a role.

Role conflict The product of perceptual differences regarding the content of a person's role or the relative importance of its elements.

Role overload The feeling of being overwhelmed from having too many roles or too many responsibilities within a single role.

Role playing A training method directed primarily at enhancing interpersonal skills in which training participants adopt various roles in a group exercise.

Sabotage A tactic used by some employees to influence the outcome of union/management negotiations in which company equipment is intentionally damaged to reduce work productivity.

Scalar principle The concept that organizations are structured by a chain of command that grows with increasing levels of authority.

Scientist-practitioner gap The difference between scientific research findings on organizations and their management versus organizations are actually managed.

Scientist–practitioner model A model or framework for education in an academic discipline based on understanding the scientific principles and findings evidenced in the discipline and how they provide the basis for professional practice.

Secondary research methods A class of research methods that examines existing information from research studies that used primary methods.

Selection ratio A numeric index ranging between 0 and 1.00 that reflects the selectivity of the hiring organization in filling jobs; the number of job openings divided by the number of job applicants.

Self-assessment A technique of performance appraisal in which individuals assess their own behavior.

Self-determination theory A theory of motivation based on the fulfillment of basic needs to experience intrinsic motivation.

Self-efficacy The belief in one's capabilities and capacity to perform successfully.

Self-regulation theories Theories of motivation based on the setting of goals and the receipt of accurate feedback that is monitored to enhance the likelihood of goal attainment.

Self-regulatory training A system of training in which employees are prompted to monitor and adjust their actions and reactions during training.

Serial position error A type of rating error in which the rater has better recall of information that is presented at the beginning or end of a sequence, and has the worst recall of information in the middle of the sequence.

Servant leadership A conception that leadership involves putting the needs of followers ahead of one's own needs.

Sexual harassment Unwelcome sexual advances, requests for sexual favors, and other verbal or physical conduct of a sexual nature that creates an intimidating, hostile, or offensive work environment.

Shared leadership Leadership within a team whereby team members distribute leadership roles among the different members of the team rather than relying on a single individual to serve as the sole leader.

Shared mental model The cognitive processes held in common by members of a team regarding how they acquire information, analyze it, and respond to it.

Shift work A non-traditional work pattern in which an operation functions 24 hours per day. Typical work shifts are 7:00 a.m. to 3:00 p.m., 3:00 p.m. to 11:00 p.m., and 11:00 p.m. to 7:00 a.m.

Situational exercise A method of assessment in which examinees are presented with a problem and asked how they would respond to it.

Situational interview A type of job interview in which candidates are presented with a hypothetical problem and asked how they would respond to it.

Situational judgment test A type of test that describes a problem to the test taker and requires the test taker to rate various possible solutions in terms of their feasibility or applicability.

Social loafing A phenomenon identified in teams in which certain individuals withhold effort or contributions to the collective outcome.

Social system The human components of a work organization that influence the behavior of individuals and groups.

Socialization The process of mutual adjustment between the team and its members, especially new members.

Society for Industrial and Organizational Psychology (SIOP) The professional organization that represents I/O psychologists in the United States.

Span-of-control principle The concept that refers to the number of subordinates a manager is responsible for supervising.

Staff functions Organizational work that supports line activities.

Stressor Anything that evokes a stress reaction.

Structure The arrangement of work functions within an organization designed to achieve efficiency and control.

Structured interview A format for the job interview in which the questions are consistent across all candidates. Often contrasted with the unstructured interview.

Subject matter expert (SME) A person knowledgeable about a topic who can serve as a qualified information source. Often associated with individuals who provide work analytic information.

Subjective performance criteria A set of factors used to assess job performance that are the product of someone's (e.g., supervisor, peer, customer) judgment of these factors.

Substance abuse The ingestion of a broad array of substances (such as alcohol, tobacco, or drugs) that are deemed to have a harmful effect on the individual.

Substitutes for leadership The conception that there are sources of influence in an environment that can serve to act in place of, or be substitutes for, formal leadership.

Tactical team A type of team created for the purpose of executing a well-defined plan or objective.

Task The lowest level of analysis in the study of work; a basic component of work (such as typing for a secretary).

Task analysis Part of the training needs assessment in which the tasks that require training are identified.

Task-oriented procedure A procedure or set of operations in work analysis designed to identify important or frequently performed tasks as a means of understanding the work performed. Often contrasted with worker-oriented procedure.

Taxonomy A classification of objects designed to enhance understanding of the objects being classified.

Team A social aggregation in which a limited number of individuals interact on a regular basis to accomplish a set of shared objectives for which they have mutual responsibility.

Test–retest reliability A type of reliability that reveals the stability of test scores upon repeated applications of the test.

Theory A statement that proposes to explain relationships among phenomena of interest.

360-degree feedback A process of evaluating employees from multiple rating sources, usually including supervisor, peer, subordinate, and self. Also called multisource feedback.

Top-grading A method of performance management whereby employees are graded on their overall contribution to the organization, and each year the bottom 10% of the employees are dismissed.

Total-package arbitration A form of final-offer arbitration in which the arbitrator is obligated to accept either the union's position or management's position on every issue in dispute between the parties. Often contrasted with issue-by-issue final-offer arbitration.

Training The process through which the knowledge and skills of employees are enhanced for an immediate job or role.

Training needs assessment A systematic process of identifying and specifying training requirements. Consists of organizational, task, and person analyses.

Trait approach A conception that leadership is best understood in terms of traits or dispositions held by an individual that are accountable for the observed leadership.

Transactional leadership A conception that leadership involves providing rewards and punishments in exchange for certain behaviors of followers.

Transfer of training The application of knowledge and skills learned in training back to the job.

Transformational leadership A conception that leadership is the process of inspiring a group to pursue goals and attain results.

True negatives A term to describe individuals who were correctly rejected for employment as they would have been unsuccessful employees.

True positives A term to describe individuals who were correctly selected for hire because they became successful employees.

Union A labor organization with defined members whose purpose is to enhance the welfare of its members in their employment relationship with the company.

Union commitment The sense of identity and support unionized employees feel for their labor union.

Union shop A provision of employment stipulating that new employees must join the union that represents employees following a probationary period. Often contrasted with an open shop.

Union/nonunion wage differential The average difference in wages paid to union versus nonunion employees across an industry or geographic area for performing the same jobs.

Union-busting A derogatory term used to describe actions taken to prevent a labor union from representing employees.

Unity of command The concept that each subordinate should be accountable to only one supervisor.

Unstructured interview A format for the job interview in which the questions are different across all candidates. Often contrasted with the structured interview.

Utility A concept reflecting the economic value (expressed in monetary terms) of making personnel decisions.

Valence Within expectancy theory, the extent to which outcomes are valued.

Validity A standard for evaluating tests that refers to the accuracy or appropriateness of drawing inferences from test scores. Often contrasted with reliability.

Validity coefficient A statistical index (often expressed as a correlation coefficient) that reveals the degree of association between two variables. Often used in the context of prediction.

Validity generalization A concept that reflects the degree to which a predictive relationship empirically established in one context spreads to other populations or contexts.

Value diversity Fundamental differences among team members with regard to tastes, preferences, goals, and interests.

Variable An object of study whose measurement can take on two or more values.

Virtual reality training A type of computer-based training that uses three-dimensional computer-generated imagery.

Virtual team A type of team in which the members, often geographically dispersed, interact through electronic communication and may never meet face-to-face.

Work analysis A formal procedure by which the content of work is defined in terms of activities performed and attributes needed to perform the work.

Work commitment The extent to which an employee feels a sense of allegiance to his or her work.

Work design theory A theory of motivation based on the presence of dimensions or characteristics of jobs that foster the expenditure of effort.

Work samples A type of personnel selection test in which the candidate demonstrates proficiency on a task representative of the work performed in the job.

Work slowdown A tactic used by some employees to influence the outcome of union/management negotiations in which the usual pace of work is intentionally reduced.

Worker-oriented procedure A procedure or set of operations in work analysis designed to identify important or frequently utilized human attributes as a means of understanding the work performed. Often contrasted with task-oriented procedure.

Work-family conflict The result of conflicting demands between work and family making it difficult to effectively participate in both domains.

Work-family enrichment The extent to which work and family roles enhance and facilitate one another's functioning.

Workplace psychological health A broad-based concept that refers to the mental, emotional, and physical well-being of employees in relation to the conduct of their work (also called occupational health).

References

Ackerman, P. L. (1987). Individual differences in skill learning: An integration of psychometric and information processing perspectives. *Psychological Bulletin, 102,* 3–27.

Ackerman, P. L. (1992). Predicting individual differences in complex skill acquisition: Dynamics of ability determinants. *Journal of Applied Psychology, 77,* 598–614.

Ackerman, P. L., & Kanfer, R. (1993). Integrating laboratory and field study for improving selection: Development of a battery for predicting air traffic controller success. *Journal of Applied Psychology, 78,* 413–432.

Adams, J. (2012). Cleaning up the dirty work: Professionalization and the management of stigma in the cosmetic surgery and tattoo industries. *Deviant Behavior, 33,* 149–167.

Adams, J. S. (1963). Toward an understanding of inequity. *Journal of Abnormal and Social Psychology, 67,* 422–436.

Adams, J. S. (1965). Inequity in social exchange. In L. Berkowitz (Ed.), *Advances in experimental social psychology* (Vol. 2, pp. 267–299). New York: Academic Press.

Adis, C. S., & Thompson, J. C. (2013). A brief primer on neuroimaging methods for industrial/organizational psychology. In J. M. Cortina & R. S. Landis (Eds.), *Modern research methods for the study of behavior in organizations* (pp. 405–442). New York: Routledge.

Aguinis, H. (2009). An expanded view of performance management. In J. W. Smither & M. London (Eds.), *Performance management* (pp. 1–44). San Francisco: Jossey-Bass.

Aguinis, H. (2013). *Performance management* (3rd ed.). Upper Saddle River, NJ: Pearson.

Aguinis, H., & Henle, C. A. (2002). Ethics in research. In S. G. Rogelberg (Ed.), *Handbook of research methods in industrial and organizational psychology* (pp. 34–56). Malden, MA: Blackwell.

Aguinis, H., & O'Boyle, E., Jr. (2014). Star performers in twenty-first century organizations. *Personnel Psychology, 67,* 313–350.

Ailon, G. (2008). Mirror, mirror on the wall: *Culture's Consequences* in a value test of its own design. *Academy of Management Review, 33,* 885–904.

Allen, N. J., & Meyer, J. P. (1990). The measurement and antecedents of affective, continuance, and normative commitment to the organization. *Journal of Occupational Psychology, 63,* 1–18.

Allen, T. D. (2013). The work-family role interface: A synthesis of the research from industrial and organizational psychology. In N. Schmitt, & S. Highhouse (Eds.), *Handbook of psychology* (Vol. 12): *Industrial and organizational psychology* (pp. 698–718). New York: John Wiley & Sons.

Allen, T. D., & Armstrong, J. (2006). Further examination of the link between work-family conflict and physical health: The role of health-related behaviors. *American Behavioral Scientist, 49,* 1204–1221.

Allen, T. D., Eby, L. T., Poteet, M. L., Lentz, E., & Lima, L. (2004). Career benefits associated with mentoring for protégés: A meta-analysis. *Journal of Applied Psychology, 89,* 127–136.

Allen, T. D., Johnson, R. C., Kiburz, K. M., & Shockley, K. M. (2013). Work-family conflict and flexible work arrangements: Deconstructing flexibility. *Personnel Psychology, 66,* 345–376.

Allen, T. D., Shockley, K. M., & Biga, A. (2010). Work and family in a global context. In K. Lundby (Ed.), *Going global* (pp. 377–401). San Francisco: Jossey-Bass.

Alliger, G. M., Lilienfeld, S. O., & Mitchell, K. E. (1995). The susceptibility of overt and covert integrity tests to coaching and faking. *Psychological Science, 7,* 32–39.

Amabile, T., Hadley, C. N., & Kramer, S. J. (2002). Creativity under the gun. *Harvard Business Review, 80,* 52–61.

American Psychological Association (2010). 2010 amendments to the 2002 "Ethical Principles of Psychologists and Code of Conduct." *American Psychologist, 65,* 493.

Amstad, F. T., Meier, L. L., Fasel, U., Elfering, A., & Semmer, N. K. (2011). A meta-analysis of work-family conflict and various outcomes with a special emphasis on cross-domain versus matching-domain relations. *Journal of Occupational Health Psychology, 16,* 151–169.

Anand, N. (2006). Cartoon displays as autoproduction of organizational culture. In A. Rafaeli & M. G. Pratt (Eds.), *Artifacts and organizations* (pp. 85–100). Mahwah, NJ: Erlbaum.

Anderson, C. D., Warner, J. L., & Spencer, C. C. (1984). Inflation bias in self-assessment examinations: Implications for valid employee selection. *Journal of Applied Psychology, 69,* 574–580.

Anderson, J. R. (1985). *Cognitive psychology and its implications* (2nd ed.). New York: Freeman.

Anderson, L. J., & Jones, R. G. (2000). Affective, behavioral, and cognitive acceptance of feedback: Individual difference moderators. In N. M. Ashkanasy & C. E. Haertel (Eds.), *Emotions in the workplace: Research, theory, and practice* (pp. 130–140). Westport, CT: Quorum.

Andersson, L. M., & Pearson, C. M. (1999). Tit for tat? The spiraling effect of incivility in the workplace. *Academy of Management Review, 24,* 452–471.

Andrews, M. C., Kacmar, K. M., & Harris, K. J. (2009). Got political skill? The impact of justice on the importance of political skill for job performance. *Journal of Applied Psychology, 94,* 1427–1437.

Andrews, R., Boyne, G. A., Meier, K. J., O'Toole, L. J., & Walker, R. M. (2012). Vertical strategic alignment and public service performance. *Public Administration, 90,* 77–98.

Antonakis, J., & Autio, E. (2007). Entrepreneurship and leadership. In J. R. Baum, M. Frese, & R. A. Baron (Eds.), *The psychology of entrepreneurship* (pp. 189–208). Mahwah, NJ: Erlbaum.

Arnold, D. W. (2001). Seventh circuit rules favorably regarding use of banding. *The Industrial-Organizational Psychologist, 39*(1), 153.

Arthur, W. A., Jr., & Bennett, W. (1995). The international assignee: The relative importance of factors perceived to contribute to success. *Personnel Psychology, 48,* 99–114.

Arthur, W. A., Jr., & Day, E. A. (2011). Assessment centers. In S. Zedeck (Ed.), *APA handbook of industrial and organizational psychology* (Vol. 2, pp. 205–235). Washington, DC: APA.

Arthur, W. A., Jr., & Villado, A. J. (2008). The importance of distinguishing between constructs and methods when comparing predictors in personnel selection research and practice. *Journal of Applied Psychology, 93,* 435–442.

Arthur, W. A., Jr., & Woehr, D. (2013). No steps forward, two steps back: The fallacy of trying to "eradicate" adverse impact? *Industrial and Organizational Psychology, 6,* 438–442.

Arthur, W. A., Jr., Bell, S. T., Villado, A. J., & Doverspike, D. (2006). The use of person-fit in employment decision making: An assessment of its criterion-related validity. *Journal of Applied Psychology, 91,* 786–801.

Arthur, W. A., Jr., Bennett, W., Edens, P. S., & Bell, S. T. (2003). Effectiveness of training in organizations: A meta-analysis of design and evaluation features. *Journal of Applied Psychology, 88,* 234–245.

Aryee, S., & Chay, Y. W. (2001). Workplace justice, citizenship behavior, and turnover intentions in a union context: Examining the mediating role of perceived union support and union instrumentality. *Journal of Applied Psychology, 86,* 154–160.

Aryee, S., Chen, Z. X., Sun, L., & Debrah, Y. A. (2007). Antecedents and outcomes of abusive supervision: Test of a trickle-down model. *Journal of Applied Psychology, 92,* 191–201.

Ashford, S. J., & Cummings, L. L. (1985). Proactive feedback seeking: The instrumental use of the information environment. *Journal of Occupational Psychology, 58,* 67–79.

Ashford, S. J., & Northcraft, G. B. (1992). Conveying more (or less) than we realize: The role of impression-management in feedback seeking. *Organizational Behavior and Human Decision Processes, 53,* 310–334.

Ashford, S. J., Blatt, R., & VandeWalle, D. (2003). Reflections on the looking glass: A review of research on feedback-seeking behavior in organizations. *Journal of Management, 29,* 773–799.

Ashforth, B. E., & Kreiner, G. E. (1999). How do you do it? Dirty work and the challenge of constructing a positive identity. *Academy of Management Review, 24,* 413–434.

Ashforth, B. E., Kreiner, G. E., Clark, M. A., & Fugate, M. (2007). Normalizing dirty work: Managerial tactics for countering occupational taint. *Academy of Management Journal, 50,* 149–174.

Austin, J. T., & Villanova, P. (1992). The criterion problem: 1917–1992. *Journal of Applied Psychology, 77,* 836–874.

Avery, D. P., McKay, P. F., & Hunter, E. M. (2012). Demography and disappearing merchandise: How older workers influence retail shrinkage. *Journal of Organizational Behavior, 33,* 105–120.

Avey, J. B., Luthans, F., & Jensen, S. M. (2009). Psychological capital: A positive resource for combating employee stress and turnover. *Human Resource Management, 48,* 677–693.

Avey, J. B., Reichard, R. J., Luthans, F., & Mhatre, K. H. (2011). Meta-analysis of the impact of positive psychological capital on employee attitudes, behaviors, and performance. *Human Resource Development Quarterly, 22,* 127–152.

Avolio, B. J. (2010). Pursuing authentic leadership development. In N. Nohria & R. Khurana (Eds.), *Handbook of leadership theory and practice* (pp. 739–768). Boston, MA: Harvard Business Press.

Avolio, B. J. (2011). *Full range leadership development.* Los Angeles: Sage.

Avolio, B. J., Gardner, W. L., & Walumbwa, F. O. (2007). *Authentic leadership scale* (ALQ version 1.0 self). Redwood City, CA: Mind Garden.

Avolio, B. J., Kahai, S., Dumdum, R., & Sivasubramaniam, N. (2001). Virtual teams: Implications for e-leadership and team development. In M. London (Ed.), *How people evaluate others in organizations* (pp. 337–358). Mahwah, NJ: Erlbaum.

Aycan, Z. (Ed.) (2000). *Management, leadership, and human resource practices in Turkey.* Ankara: Turkish Psychological Association Press.

Aycan, Z., & Gelfand, M. J. (2012). Cross-cultural organizational psychology. In S. W. J. Kozlowski (Ed.), *The Oxford handbook of organizational psychology* (Vol. 2, pp. 1103–1160). New York: Oxford University Press.

Aycan, Z., & Kanungo, R. N. (2001). Cross-cultural industrial and organizational psychology: A critical appraisal of the field and future directions. In N. Anderson, D. S. Ones, H. K. Sinangil, & C. Viswesvaran (Eds.), *Handbook of industrial, work, and organizational psychology* (Vol. 1, pp. 385–408). London: Sage.

Ayman, P., & Korabik, K. (2010). Leadership: Why gender and culture matter. *American Psychologist, 65,* 157–170.

Babiak, P., & Hare, R. D. (2006). *Snakes in suits: When psychopaths go to work.* New York: ReganBooks.

Bacharach, S. B., Bamberger, P. A., & Sonnenstuhl, W. J. (2002). Driven to drink: Managerial control, work-related risk factors, and employee problem drinking. *Academy of Management Journal, 45,* 637–658.

Baker, T. N., & Gebhardt, D. L. (2012). The assessment of physical capabilities in the workplace. In N. Schmitt (Ed.) *The Oxford handbook of personnel assessment and selection* (pp. 274–296). New York: Oxford University Press.

Bakke, E. W. (1945). Why workers join unions. *Personnel, 22,* 37–46.

Baldwin, T. T., & Ford, J. K. (1988). Transfer of training: A review and directions for future research. *Personnel Psychology, 41,* 63–105.

Baldwin, T. T., Ford, J. K., & Blume, D. B. (2009). Transfer of training 1998–2008: An updated review and agenda for future research. In G. P. Hodgkinson & J. L. Ford (Eds.), *International review of industrial and organizational psychology* (Vol. 24, pp. 41–70). Chichester, UK: Wiley-Blackwell.

Baltes, B. B., & Heydens-Gahir, H. A. (2003). Reduction of work-family conflict through the use of selection, optimization, and compensation behaviors. *Journal of Applied Psychology, 88,* 1005–1018.

Baltes, B. B., Briggs, T. E., Huff, J. W., Wright, J. A., & Neuman, G. A. (1999). Flexible and compressed workweek schedules: A meta-analysis of their effects on work-related criteria. *Journal of Applied Psychology, 84,* 496–513.

Balzer, W. K., & Sulsky, L. M. (1992). Halo and performance appraisal research. *Journal of Applied Psychology, 77,* 975–985.

Balzer, W. K., Greguras, G. J., & Raymark, P. H. (2004). Multisource feedback. In J. C. Thomas (Ed.), *Comprehensive handbook of psychological assessment* (Vol. 4, pp. 390–411). Hoboken, NJ: Wiley.

Bandura, A. (2000). Exercise of human agency through collective efficacy. *Current Directions in Psychological Science, 9,* 75–78.

Bandura, A., & Locke, E. A. (2003). Negative self-efficacy and goal effects revisited. *Journal of Applied Psychology, 87,* 87–99.

Bangerter, A., Roulin, N., & Konig, C. J. (2012). Personnel selection as a signaling game. *Journal of Applied Psychology, 97,* 719–738.

Banks, G. C., & McDaniel, M. A. (2012). Meta-analysis as a validity summary tool. In N. Schmitt (Ed.), *The Oxford handbook of personnel assessment and selection* (pp. 156–175). New York: Oxford University Press.

Baran, B. E., Rogelberg, S. G., Lopina, E. C., Allen, J. A., Spitzmüller, C., & Bergman, M. (2012). Shouldering a silent burden: The toll of dirty tasks. *Human Relations, 65,* 597–626.

Baranowski, L. E., & Anderson, L. E. (2006). Examining rating source variation in work behavior and KSA linkages. *Personnel Psychology, 58,* 1041–1054.

Barclay, L. J., & Aquino, K. (2011). Workplace aggression and violence. In S. Zedeck (Ed.), *APA handbook of industrial and organizational psychology* (Vol. 3, pp. 615–640). Washington, DC: APA.

Barling, J. (2014). *The science of leadership: Lessons from research for organizational leaders.* New York, NY: Oxford University Press.

Barling, J., & Griffiths, A. (2003). A history of occupational health psychology. In J. C. Quick & L. E. Tetrick (Eds.), *Handbook of organizational health psychology* (pp. 19–34). Washington, DC: American Psychological Association.

Barling, J., Christie, A., & Hoption, C. (2011). Leadership. In S. Zedeck (Ed.), *APA handbook of industrial and organizational psychology* (Vol. 1, pp. 183–240). Washington, DC: APA.

Barnes, C. M., & Wagner, D. T (2009). Changing to daylight saving time cuts into sleep and increases workplace injuries. *Journal of Applied Psychology, 94,* 1305–1317.

Barnes, C. M., Hollenbeck, J. R., Wagner, D. T., DeRue, D. S., Nahrgang, J. D., & Schwind, K. M. (2008). Harmful help: The costs of backing-up behavior in teams. *Journal of Applied Psychology, 93,* 529–539.

Barnes-Farrell, J. L. (2001). Performance appraisal: Person perception processes and challenges. In M. London (Ed.), *How people evaluate others in organizations* (pp. 135–154). Mahwah, NJ: Erlbaum.

Baron, R. A. (1990). Countering the effects of destructive criticism: The relative efficacy of four interventions. *Journal of Applied Psychology, 75*, 235–245.

Baron, R. A., & Henry, R. A. (2011). Entrepreneurship: The genesis of organizations. In S. Zedeck (Ed.), *APA handbook of industrial and organizational psychology* (Vol. 1, pp. 241–273). Washington, DC: APA.

Baron, R. A., Frese, M., & Baum, J. R. (2007). Research gains: Benefits of closer links between I/O psychology and entrepreneurship. In J. R. Baum, M. Frese, & R. A. Baron (Eds.), *The psychology of entrepreneurship* (pp. 347–373). Mahwah, NJ: Erlbaum.

Barreca, R. (1997). *Sweet revenge: The wicked delights of getting even.* New York: Berkley.

Barrick, M. R., & Mount, M. K. (1991). The Big Five personality dimensions and job performance: A meta-analysis. *Personnel Psychology, 44*, 1–26.

Barrick, M. R., & Mount, M. K. (2012). Nature and use of personality in selection. In N. Schmitt (Ed.), *The Oxford handbook of personnel assessment and selection* (pp. 225–251). New York: Oxford University Press.

Barrick, M. R., Shaffer, J. A., & DeGrassi, S. W. (2009). What you see may not be what you get: Relationships among self-presentation tactics and ratings of interview and job performance. *Journal of Applied Psychology, 94*, 1394–1411.

Barrick, M. R., Swider, B. W., & Stewart, G. L. (2010). Initial evaluations in the interview: Relationships with subsequent interviewer evaluations and employment offers. *Journal of Applied Psychology, 95*, 1163–1172.

Barry, B., & Stewart, G. L. (1997). Composition, process, and performance in self-managed groups: The role of personality. *Journal of Applied Psychology, 82*, 62–78.

Bartram, D. (2005). The great eight competencies: A criterion-centric approach to validation. *Journal of Applied Psychology, 90*, 1185–1203.

Bartram, D., & Burke, E. (2013). Industrial/organizational testing case studies. In J. A. Wollack & J. J. Fremer (Eds.), *Handbook of test security* (pp. 313–332). New York: Routledge.

Baruch, Y. (2006). On logos and business cards: The case of UK universities. In A. Rafaeli & M. G. Pratt (Eds.), *Artifacts and organizations* (pp. 181–198). Mahwah, NJ: Erlbaum.

Bass, B. M. (1985). *Leadership and performance beyond expectations.* New York: Free Press.

Bass, B. M. (1998). *Transformational leadership.* Mahwah, NJ: Erlbaum.

Battista, M., Pedigo, P., & Desrosiers, E. (2010). Navigating the complexities of a global organization. In K. Lundby (Ed.), *Going global* (pp. 1–21). San Francisco: Jossey-Bass.

Bazerman, M. H. (2005). Conducting influential research: The need for prescriptive implications. *Academy of Management Research, 30*, 25–31.

Beal, D. J., Cohen, R. R., Burke, M. J., & McLendon, C. L. (2003). Cohesion and performance in groups: A meta-analytic clarification of construct relations. *Journal of Applied Psychology, 88*, 989–1004.

Beal, D. J., Trougakos, J. P., Weiss, H. M., & Green, S. G. (2006). Episodic processes in emotional labor: Perceptions of affective delivery and regulation strategies. *Journal of Applied Psychology, 91*, 1053–1065.

Becker, T. E., & Colquitt, A. L. (1992). Potential versus actual faking of a biodata form: An analysis along several dimensions of item type. *Personnel Psychology, 45*, 389–406.

Becker, T. E., Klein, H. J., & Meyer, J. P. (2009). Commitment in organizations: Accumulated wisdom and new directions. In H. J. Klein, T. E. Becker, & J. P. Meyer (Eds.), *Commitment in organizations* (pp. 419–452). New York: Taylor & Francis.

Becker, W. J., & Cropanzano, R. (2010). Organizational neuroscience: The promise and prospects of an emerging discipline. *Journal of Organizational Behavior, 31*, 1055–1059.

Becker, W. J., & Menges, J. I. (2013). Biological implicit measures in HRM and OB: A question of how not if. *Human Resource Management Review, 23*, 219–228.

Beehr, T. A., Ivanitskaya, L., Hansen, C. P., Erofeev, D., & Gudanowski, D. M. (2001). Evaluation of 360 degree feedback ratings: Relationships with each other and with performance and selection predictors. *Journal of Organizational Behavior, 22*, 775–788.

Behnke, S. H., & Moorehead-Slaughter, O. (2012). Ethics, human rights, and interrogation. In J. H. Lawrence & M. D. Matthews (Eds.), *The Oxford handbook of military psychology* (pp. 50–62). New York: Oxford University Press.

Beier, M. E., & Kanfer, R. (2010). Motivation in training and development: A phase perspective. In S. W. J. Kozlowski & E. Salas (Eds.), *Learning, training, and development in organizations* (pp. 65–98). New York: Routledge.

Belbin, R. M. (1981). *Management teams.* New York: Wiley.

Bell, B. S., & Federman, J. E. (2010). Self-assessments of knowledge: Where do we go from here? *Academy of Management Learning & Education, 9*, 342–347.

Bell, B. S., & Kozlowski, S. W. J. (2010). Toward a theory of learner-centered training design: An integrative framework of active learning. In S. W. J. Kozlowski & E. Salas (Eds.), *Learning, training, and development in organizations* (pp. 263–300). New York: Routledge.

Benjamin, L. T., Jr. (1997). Organized industrial psychology before Division 14: The ACP and the AAAP (1930–1945). *Journal of Applied Psychology, 82*, 459–466.

Benjamin, L. T., Jr. (2006). Hugo Münsterberg's attack on the application of scientific psychology. *Journal of Applied Psychology, 91,* 414–425.

Bennett, G. K. (1980). *Test of mechanical comprehension.* New York: Psychological Corporation.

Bennett, N., Blum, T. C., & Roman, P. M. (1994). Pressure of drug screening and employee assistance programs: Exclusive and inclusive human resource management practices. *Journal of Organizational Behavior, 15,* 549–560.

Bennis, W. (2007). The challenges of leadership in the modern world. *American Psychologist, 62,* 2–5.

Berdahl, J. L., & Aquino, K. (2009). Sexual behavior at work: Fun or folly? *Journal of Applied Psychology, 94,* 34–47.

Berdahl, J. L., & Raver, J. L. (2011). Maintaining, expanding, and contracting the organization. In S. Zedeck (Ed.), *APA handbook of industrial and organizational psychology* (Vol. 3, pp. 641–669). Washington, DC: American Psychological Association.

Bergeron, D. M., Shipp, A. J., Rosen, B., & Furst, S. A. (2013). Organizational citizenship behavior and career outcomes: The cost of being a good citizen. *Journal of Management, 39,* 958–984.

Bergman, M. E., & Chalkley, K. M. (2007). "Ex" marks a spot: The stickiness of dirty work and other removed stigmas. *Journal of Occupational Health Psychology, 12,* 251–265.

Bernardin, H. J., Cooke, D. K., & Villanova, P. (2000). Conscientiousness and agreeableness as predictors of rating leniency. *Journal of Applied Psychology, 85,* 232–236.

Bernardin, H. J., Hagan, C. M., Kane, J. S., & Villanova, P. (1998). Effective performance management. In J. W. Smither (Ed.), *Performance appraisal* (pp. 3–48). San Francisco: Jossey-Bass.

Bernichon, T., Cook, K. E., & Brown, J. D. (2003). Seeking self-evaluative feedback: The interactive role of global self-esteem and specific self-views. *Journal of Personality and Social Psychology, 84,* 194–204.

Berry, C. M., & Sackett, P. R. (2009). Faking in personnel selection: Tradeoffs in performance versus fairness resulting from two cut-score strategies. *Personnel Psychology, 62,* 835–863.

Berry, C. M., Ones, D. S., & Sackett, P. R. (2007). Interpersonal deviance, organizational deviance, and their common correlates: A review and meta-analysis. *Journal of Applied Psychology, 92,* 410–424.

Berry, C. M., Sackett, P. R., & Wiemann, S. (2007). A review of recent developments in integrity test research. *Personnel Psychology, 60,* 271–301.

Beugne, C. D., & Liverpool, P. R. (2006). Politics as determinants of fairness perceptions in organizations. In E. Vigoda-Gadot & A. Drory (Eds.), *Handbook of organizational politics* (pp. 122–135). Cheltenham, UK: Edward Elgar.

Bezrukova, K., Thatcher, S. M. B., Jehn, K. A., & Spell, C. S. (2012). The effects of alignments: Examining group faultlines, organizational cultures, and performance. *Journal of Applied Psychology, 97,* 77–92.

Bhutta, C. B. (2012). Not by the book: Facebook as a sampling frame. *Sociological Methods & Research, 41,* 57–88.

Biddle, D. A. (2008). Are the Uniform Guidelines outdated? Federal guidelines, professional standards, and validity generalization (VG). *The Industrial-Organizational Psychologist, 45*(4), 17–23.

Bies, R. J., Tripp, T. M., & Kramer, R. M. (1997). At the breaking point. In R. A. Giacalone & J. Greenberg (Eds.), *Antisocial behavior in organizations* (pp. 18–36). Thousand Oaks, CA: Sage.

Bigoness, W. J. (1978). Correlates of faculty attitudes toward collective bargaining. *Journal of Applied Psychology, 63,* 228–233.

Bingham, W. V. (1917). Mentality testing of college students. *Journal of Applied Psychology, 1,* 38–45.

Binning, J. F., & Barrett, G. V. (1989). Validity of personnel decisions: A conceptual analysis of the inferential and evidential bases. *Journal of Applied Psychology, 74,* 478–494.

Birnbaum, R. (2013). Genes, memes, and the evolution of human leadership. In M. G. Rumsey (Ed.), *The Oxford handbook of leadership* (pp. 243–266). New York: Oxford University Press.

Blackard, K. (2000). *Managing change in a unionized workplace.* Westport, CT: Quorum.

Blanchard, P. M., & Thacker, J. W. (2004). *Effective training: Systems, strategies, and practices* (2nd ed.). Upper Saddle River, NJ: Prentice Hall.

Blickle, G., Kramer, J., Schneider, P. B., Meurs, J. A., Ferris, G. R., Mierke, J., Witzki, A. H., & Momm, T. D. (2011). Role of political skill in job performance prediction beyond general mental ability and personality in cross-sectional and predictive studies. *Journal of Applied Social Psychology, 41,* 488–514.

Blum, M. L., & Naylor, J. C. (1968). *Industrial psychology: Its theoretical and social foundations.* New York: Harper & Row.

Blyton, P. (2008). Working time and work-life balance. In P. Blyton, N. Bacon, J. Fiorito, & E. Heery (Eds.), *Industrial relations* (pp. 513–528). Thousand Oaks, CA: Sage.

Bobko, P., & Roth, P. L. (2010). An analysis of the methods for assessing and indexing adverse impact: A disconnect between academic literature and some practice. In

J. L. Outtz (Ed.), *Adverse impact: Implications for organizational staffing and high stakes selection* (pp. 29–49). New York: Routledge.

Bobko, P., & Roth, P. L. (2012). Reviewing, categorizing, and analyzing the literature on black-white mean differences for predictors of job performance: Verifying some perceptions and updating/correcting others. *Personnel Psychology, 66,* 91–126.

Bolino, M. C., Klotz, A. C., Turnley, W. H., & Harvey, J. (2013). Exploring the dark side of organizational citizenship behavior. *Journal of Organizational Behavior, 34,* 542–559.

Bolino, M. C., Turnley, W. H., Gilstrap, J. B., & Suazo, M. M. (2010). Citizenship under pressure: What's a "good soldier" to do? *Journal of Organizational Behavior, 31,* 835–855.

Bond, F. W., Flaxman, P. E., & Bunce, D. (2008). The influence of psychological flexibility on work redesign: Mediated moderation of a work reorganization intervention. *Journal of Applied Psychology, 93,* 645–654.

Bono, J. E., Purvanova, R. K., Towler, A. J., & Peterson, D. B. (2009). A survey of executive coaching practices. *Personnel Psychology, 62,* 361–404.

Boswell, W. R., Shipp, A. J., Payne, S. C., & Culbertson, S. S. (2009). Changes in newcomer job satisfaction over time: Examining the pattern of honeymoons and hangovers. *Journal of Applied Psychology, 94,* 844–858.

Boutelle, C. (2004). New *Principles* encourage greater accountability for test users and developers. *The Industrial-Organizational Psychologist, 41*(3), 20–21.

Bowling, N. A., Beehr, T. A., Wagner, S. H., & Libkuman, T. M. (2005). Adaptation-level theory, opponent process theory, and dispositions: An integrated approach to the stability of job satisfaction. *Journal of Applied Psychology, 90,* 1044–1053.

Bownas, D. A. (2000). Selection programs in a union environment: A commentary. In J. F. Kehoe (Ed.), *Managing selection in changing organizations* (pp. 197–209). San Francisco: Jossey-Bass.

Bracken, D. W., Dalton, M. A., Jako, R. A., McCauley, C. D., & Pollman, V. A. (1997). *Should 360-degree feedback be used only for developmental purposes?* Greensboro, NC: Center for Creative Leadership.

Bradley, B. H., Klotz, A. C., Postlethwaite, B. E., & Brown, K. G. (2013). Ready to rumble: How team personality composition and task conflict interact to improve performance. *Journal of Applied Psychology, 98,* 385–392.

Brand, C. (1987). The importance of general intelligence. In S. Modgil & C. Modgil (Eds.), *Arthur Jensen: Consensus and controversy* (pp. 251–265). New York: Falmer.

Brandon, S. E. (2011). Impacts of psychological science on national security agencies post-9/11. *American Psychologist, 66,* 495–506.

Brannick, M. T., & Levine, E. L. (2002). *Job analysis.* Thousand Oaks, CA: Sage.

Brannick, M. T., Levine, E. L., & Morgeson, F. P. (2007). *Job and work analysis* (2nd ed.). Thousand Oaks, CA: Sage.

Breaugh, J. A. (1983). The 12-hour work day: Differing employee reactions. *Personnel Psychology, 36,* 277–288.

Breaugh, J. A. (2012). Employee recruitment: Current knowledge and suggestions for future research. In N. Schmitt (Ed.), *The Oxford handbook of personnel assessment and selection* (pp. 68–87). New York: Oxford University Press.

Breaugh, J. A., Macan, T. J., & Grambow, D. M. (2008). Employee recruitment: Current knowledge and directions for future research. In G. P. Hodgkinson & J. L. Ford (Eds.), *International review of industrial and organizational psychology* (Vol. 23, pp. 45–82). Chichester, UK: Wiley-Blackwell.

Brett, J. M., & Stroh, L. K. (2003). Working 60 plus hours a week: Why do managers do it? *Journal of Applied Psychology, 88,* 67–78.

Brett, J. M., Olekalns, M., Friedman, R., Goates, N., Anderson, C., & Lisco, C. C. (2007). Sticks and stones: Language, face, and online dispute resolution. *Academy of Management Journal, 50,* 85–99.

Brief, A. P. (1998). *Attitudes in and around organizations.* Thousand Oaks, CA: Sage.

Brotherton, C. (2003). The role of external policies in shaping organizational health and safety. In D. A. Hofmann & L. E. Tetrick (Eds.), *Health and safety in organizations* (pp. 372–396). San Francisco: Jossey-Bass.

Brough, P., O'Driscoll, M., Kalliath, T., Cooper, C. L., & Poelmans, S. A. (2009). *Workplace psychological health: Current research and practice.* Cheltenham, UK: Elgar.

Brown, G., Lawrence, T. B., & Robinson, S. L. (2005). Territoriality in organizations. *Academy of Management Review, 30,* 577–594.

Brown, K. G., & Sitzmann, T. (2011). Training and employee development for improved performance. In S. Zedeck (Ed.), *APA handbook of industrial and organizational psychology* (Vol. 2, pp. 469–504). Washington, DC: APA.

Brown, S. P. (1996). A meta-analysis and review of organizational research in job involvement. *Psychological Bulletin, 120,* 235–255.

Brutus, S., Gill, H., & Duniewicz, K. (2010). State of science in industrial and organizational psychology: A review of self-reported limitations. *Personnel Psychology, 63,* 907–936.

Bryan, W. L. (1904). Theory and practice. *Psychological Review, 11,* 71–82.

Bryan, W. L., & Harter, N. (1897). Studies in the physiology and psychology of the telegraphic language. *Psychological Review, 4,* 27–53.

Bryan, W. L., & Harter, N. (1899). Studies of the telegraphic language. *Psychological Review, 6,* 345–375.

Buchanan, D. (2008). You stab my back, I'll stab yours: Management experience and perceptions of organizational political behaviour. *British Journal of Management, 19,* 49–64.

Bucher, E., Fieseler, C., & Suphan, A. (2013). The stress potential of social media in the workplace. *Information, Communication & Society, 16,* 1639–1667.

Buehler, R., Griffin, D., Lam, K. C. H., & Deslauriers, J. (2012). Perspective on prediction: Does third-person imagery improve task completion estimates? *Organizational Behavior and Human Decision Processes, 117,* 138–149.

Buehler, R., Peetz, J., & Griffin, D. (2010). Finishing on time: When do predictions influence completion times? *Organizational Behavior and Human Decision Processes, 111,* 23–32.

Buhrmester, M., Kwang, T., & Gosling, S. D. (2011). Amazon's Mechanical Turk: A new source of inexpensive, yet high quality, data? *Perspectives on Psychological Science, 6,* 3–5.

Burgess, M., & Clark, L. (2010). Do the "savage origins" of tattoos cast a prejudicial shadow on contemporary tattooed individuals? *Journal of Applied Social Psychology, 40,* 746–764.

Burghart, G., & Finn, C. A. (2011). *Handbook of MRI scanning.* St. Louis: Elsevier Mosby.

Burke, C. S., Shuffler, M. L., Salas, E., & Gelfand, M. (2010). Multicultural teams: Critical team processes and guidelines. In K. Lundby (Ed.), *Going global* (pp. 46–82). San Francisco: Jossey-Bass.

Burke, W. W. (2008). *Organizational change: Theory and practice* (2nd ed.). Thousand Oaks, CA: Sage.

Buster, M. A., Roth, P. L., & Bobko, P. (2005). A process for content validation of education and experienced-based minimum qualifications: An approach resulting in federal court approval. *Personnel Psychology, 58,* 771–799.

Buttigieg, D. M., Deery, S. J., & Iverson, R. D. (2007). An event history analysis of union joining and union leaving. *Journal of Applied Psychology, 92,* 829–839.

Byron, K. (2005). A meta-analytic review of work-family conflict and its antecedents. *Journal of Vocational Behavior, 62,* 169–198.

Caligiuri, P., & Hippler, T. (2010). Maximizing the success and retention of international assignees. In K. Lundby (Ed.), *Going global* (pp. 333–376). San Francisco: Jossey-Bass.

Caligiuri, P., Mencin, A., & Hang, K. (2013). Win-win-win: The influence of company-sponsored volunteerism programs on employees, NGOs, and business units. *Personnel Psychology, 66,* 825–860.

Callinan, M., & Robertson, I. T. (2000). Work sample testing. *International Journal of Selection and Assessment, 8,* 248–260.

Cameron, K. L. (1982). The relationship between faculty unionism and organizational effectiveness. *Academy of Management Journal, 25,* 6–24.

Cameron, K. L., & Quinn, R. E. (2006). *Diagnosing and changing organizational cultures* (rev. ed.). San Francisco: Jossey-Bass.

Campbell, J. P. (1990). The role of theory in industrial and organizational psychology. In M. D. Dunnette & L. M. Hough (Eds.), *Handbook of industrial and organizational psychology* (2nd ed., Vol. 1, pp. 39–74). Palo Alto, CA: Consulting Psychologists Press.

Campbell, J. P. (1996). Group differences and personnel decisions: Validity, fairness, and affirmative action. *Journal of Vocational Behavior, 49,* 122–158.

Campbell, J. P. (2007). Profiting from history. In L. L. Koppes (Ed.), *Historical perspectives in industrial and organizational psychology* (pp. 441–457). Mahwah, NJ: Erlbaum.

Campbell, J. P. (2012). Behavior, performance, and effectiveness in the twenty-first century. In S. W. J. Kozlowski (Ed.), *The Oxford handbook of organizational psychology,* (Vol. 1, pp. 159–194). New York: Oxford University Press.

Campbell, J. P., & Knapp, D. J. (2010). Project A: 12 years of R & D. In J. L. Farr & N. T. Tippins (Eds.), *Handbook of employee selection* (pp. 865–886). New York: Routledge.

Campion, J. E. (1972). Work sampling for personnel selection. *Journal of Applied Psychology, 56,* 40–44.

Campion, M. A. (1991). Meaning and measurement of turnover: Comparison of alternative measures and recommendations for research. *Journal of Applied Psychology, 76,* 199–212.

Campion, M. A., Fink, A. A., Ruggeberg, B. J., Carr, L., Phillips, G. M., & Odman, R. B. (2011). Doing competencies well: Best practices in competence modeling. *Personnel Psychology, 64,* 225–262.

Campion, M. A., & Berger, C. J. (1990). Conceptual integration and empirical test of job design and compensation relationships. *Personnel Psychology, 43,* 525–554.

Campion, M. A., Papper, E. M., & Medsker, G. J. (1996). Relations between work team characteristics and effectiveness: A replication and extension. *Personnel Psychology, 49,* 429–452.

Cannon-Bowers, J. A., & Bowers, C. (2010). Synthetic learning environments: On developing a science of simulation, games, and virtual worlds for training. In S. W. J. Kozlowski & E. Salas (Eds.), *Learning, training, and development in organizations* (pp. 229–262). New York: Routledge.

Cannon-Bowers, J. A., & Bowers, C. (2011). Team development and functioning. In S. Zedeck (Ed.), *APA handbook of industrial and organizational psychology* (Vol. 1, pp. 597–650). Washington, DC: APA.

Cannon-Bowers, J. A., & Salas, E. (2001). Reflections on shared cognition. *Journal of Organizational Behavior, 22,* 195–202.

Cappelli, P., & Keller, J. (2013). Classifying work in the new economy. *Academy of Management Review, 38,* 575–596.

CareerBuilder (2013). Thirty-eight percent of workers have dated a co-worker, finds CareerBuilder survey. Retrieved August 12, 2014, from http://www.careerbuilder.com/share/aboutus/pressreleasesdetail.aspx?id=pr803&sd=2/13/2014&ed=02/13/2014

Carr, S. C., MacLachlan, M., & Furnham, A. (Eds.) (2012). *Humanitarian work psychology.* New York: Palgrave Macmillan.

Carsten, J. M., & Spector, P. E. (1987). Unemployment, job satisfaction, and employee turnover: A meta-analytic test of the Muchinsky model. *Journal of Applied Psychology, 72,* 374–381.

Caruso, C. C., Hitchcock, E. M., Dick, R. B., Russo, J. M., & Schmit, J. M. (2004). *Overtime and extended work shifts: Recent findings on illnesses, injuries, and health behaviors.* Cincinnati, OH: U. S. Department of Health and Human Services, Centers for Disease Control and Prevention, National Institute for Occupational Safety and Health. DHHS (NIOSH) Publication No. 2004–143.

Cascio, W. F. (2007). Evidence-based management and the marketplace of ideas. *Academy of Management Journal, 50,* 1009–1012.

Cascio, W. F., & Aguinis, H. (2008). Research in industrial and organizational psychology from 1963 to 2007: Changes, choices, and trends. *Journal of Applied Psychology, 93,* 1062–1081.

Cascio, W. F., & Fogli, L. (2010). The business value of employee selection. In J. L. Farr & N. T. Tippins (Eds.), *Handbook of employee selection* (pp. 235–252). New York: Routledge.

Cascio, W. F., Alexander, R. A., & Barrett, G. V. (1988). Setting cutoff scores: Legal, psychometric, and professional issues and guidelines. *Personnel Psychology, 41,* 1–24.

Casper, W. J., Eby, L. T., Bordeaux, C., Lockwood, A., & Lambert, D. (2007). A review of research methods in IO/OB work-family research. *Journal of Applied Psychology, 92,* 28–41.

Cassell, C., & Symon, G. (2011). Assessing "good" qualitative research in the work psychology field: A narrative analysis. *Journal of Occupational and Organizational Psychology, 84,* 633–650.

Cavanaugh, M. A., & Noe, R. A. (1999). Antecedents and consequences of relational components of the new psychological contract. *Journal of Organizational Behavior, 20,* 323–340.

Cavanaugh, M. A., Boswell, W. R., Roehling, M. V., & Boudreau, J. W. (2000). An empirical examination of self-reported work stress among U.S. managers. *Journal of Applied Psychology, 85,* 65–74.

Cawley, B. D., Keeping, L. M., & Levy, P. E. (1998). Participation in the performance appraisal process and employee reactions: A meta-analytic review of field investigations. *Journal of Applied Psychology, 83,* 615–633.

Cederblom, D. (1982). The performance appraisal interview: A review, implications and suggestions. *Academy of Management Review, 7,* 219–227.

Cederblom, D., & Lounsbury, J. W. (1980). An investigation of user acceptance of peer evaluations. *Personnel Psychology, 33,* 567–580.

Cerasoli, C. P., Nicklin, J. M., & Ford, M. T. (2014). Intrinsic motivation and extrinsic incentives jointly predict performance: A 40-year meta-analysis. *Psychological Bulletin, 140,* 980–1008.

Chan, K. Y., & Drasgow, F. (2001). Toward a theory of individual differences and leadership: Understanding the motivation to lead. *Journal of Applied Psychology, 86,* 481–498.

Chang, C. H., Rosen, C. C., & Levy, P. E. (2009). The relationship between perceptions of organizational politics and employee attitudes, strain, and behavior: A meta-analytic examination. *Academy of Management Journal, 52,* 779–801.

Chao, G. T., & Moon, H. (2005). The cultural mosaic: A metatheory for understanding the complexity of culture. *Journal of Applied Psychology, 90,* 1128–1140.

Chemers, M. M., & Murphy, S. E. (1995). Leadership and diversity in groups and organizations. In M. M. Chemers, S. Oskamp, & M. A. Costanzo (Eds.), *Diversity in organizations: New perspectives for a changing workforce* (pp. 157–188). Thousand Oaks, CA: Sage.

Choi, J. N., & Kim, M. U. (1999). The organizational applications of groupthink and its limitations in organizations. *Journal of Applied Psychology, 84,* 297–306.

Christian, M. S., Edwards, B. D., & Bradley, J. C. (2010). Situational judgment tests: Constructs assessed and a meta-analysis of their criterion-related validities. *Personnel Psychology, 63,* 83–117.

Chrobot-Mason, D., & Quiñones, M. A. (2002). Training for a diverse workplace. In K. Kraiger (Ed.), *Creating, implementing, and managing effective training and development* (pp. 117–159). San Francisco: Jossey-Bass.

Church, A. H. (2001). Is there a method to our madness? The impact of data collection methodology on organizational survey results. *Personnel Psychology, 54,* 937–969.

Church, A. H., Waclawski, J., & Berr, S. A. (2002). Voices from the field: Future directions for organization development. In. J. Waclawski & A. H. Church (Eds.), *Organization development* (pp. 321–336). San Francisco: Jossey-Bass.

Clark, R. C., & Mayer, R. E. (2008). *e-Learning and the science of instruction* (2nd ed.). San Francisco: Pfeiffer.

Clause, C. S., Mullins, M. E., Nee, M. T., Pulakos, E., & Schmitt, N. (1998). Parallel test form development: A procedure for alternative predictors and an example. *Personnel Psychology, 51,* 193–208.

Cleveland, J. N., & Colella, A. (2010). Criterion validity and criterion deficiency: What we measure well and what we ignore. In J. L. Farr & N. T. Tippins (Eds.), *Handbook of employee selection* (pp. 551–567). New York: Routledge.

Cleveland, J. N., Murphy, K. R., & Williams, R. E. (1989). Multiple uses of performance appraisal: Prevalence and correlates. *Journal of Applied Psychology, 74,* 130–135.

Clifford, J. P. (1994). Job analysis: Why do it, and how should it be done? *Public Personnel Management, 23,* 321–338.

Cloutier, J., Denis, P. L., & Bilodeau, H. (2013). The dynamics of strike votes: Perceived justice during collective bargaining. *Journal of Organizational Behavior, 34,* 1016–1038.

Cohen-Charash, Y., & Spector, P. E. (2001). The role of justice in organizations: A meta-analysis. *Organizational Behavior and Human Decision Processes, 86,* 278–321.

Cohn, L. D., & Becker, B. J. (2003). How meta-analysis increases statistical power. *Psychological Methods, 8,* 243–253.

Cole, N. D., & Latham, G. P. (1997). Effects of training in procedural justice on perceptions of disciplinary fairness by unionized employees and disciplinary subject matter experts. *Journal of Applied Psychology, 82,* 699–705.

Colella, A. J., McKay, P. F., Daniels, S. R., & Signal, S. M. (2012). Employment discrimination. In S. W. J. Kozlowski (Ed.), *The Oxford handbook of organizational psychology* (Vol. 2, pp. 1034–1102). New York: Oxford University Press.

Collins, J. M., & Schmidt, F. L. (1993). Personality, integrity, and white collar crime: A construct validity study. *Personnel Psychology, 46,* 295–311.

Colquitt, J. A. (2012). Organizational justice. In S. W. J. Kozlowski (Ed.), *The Oxford handbook of organizational psychology,* (Vol. 1, pp. 526–547). New York: Oxford University Press.

Colquitt, J. A., Conlon, D. E., Wesson, M. J., Porter, C. O., & Ng, K. Y. (2001). Justice at the millennium: A meta-analytic review of 25 years of organizational justice research. *Journal of Applied Psychology, 86,* 425–445.

Colquitt, J. A., Scott, B. A., & LePine, J. A. (2007). Trust, trustworthiness, and trust propensity: A meta-analytic test of their unique relationships with risk taking and job performance. *Journal of Applied Psychology, 92,* 909–927.

Conlon, D. E., Meyer, C. J., Lytle, A. L., & Willaby, H. W. (2007). Third party interventions across cultures: No "one best choice." In J. J. Martocchio (Ed.), *Research in personnel and human resources management* (pp. 309–349). Oxford, UK: JAI.

Conlon, D. E., Moon, H., & Ng, K. Y. (2002). Putting the cart before the horse: The benefits of arbitrating before mediating. *Journal of Applied Psychology, 87,* 978–984.

Connaughton, S. L., Williams, E. A., & Shuffler, M. L. (2011). Social identity issues in multi-team systems: Considerations for future research. In S. J. Zaccaro, M. A. Marks, & L. A. DeChurch (Eds.), *Multiteam systems: An organizational form for dynamic and complex environments* (pp. 109–140). New York: Taylor & Francis.

Connelly, B. S., & Ones, D. S. (2010). An other perspective on personality: Meta-analytic interpretation of observers' accuracy and predictive validity. *Psychological Bulletin, 136,* 1092–1122.

Conte, C., & Carr, A. R. (2012). *Outline of the U.S. economy.* Washington, DC: U.S. Department of State.

Conway, N., & Briner, R. B. (2009). Fifty years of psychological contract research: What do we know and what are the main challenges? In G. P. Hodgkinson & J. L. Ford (Eds.), *International review of industrial and organizational psychology* (Vol. 24, pp. 71–130). Chichester, UK: Wiley-Blackwell.

Cooke, N. J., Gorman, J. C., & Rowe, L. J. (2009). An ecological perspective on team cognition. In E. Salas, G. F. Goodwin, & C. S. Burke (Eds.), *Team effectiveness in complex organizations* (pp. 157–182). New York: Taylor & Francis.

Cooper, C. L., Dewe, P., & O'Driscoll, M. (2003). Employee assistance programs. In J. C. Quick & L. E. Tetrick (Eds.), *Handbook of organizational health psychology* (pp. 289–304). Washington, DC: American Psychological Association.

Cooper, W. H. (1981). Ubiquitous halo. *Psychological Bulletin, 90*, 218–244.

Costa, G. (1996). The impact of shift and night work on health. *Applied Ergonomics, 27*, 9–16.

Costa, P. T. (1996). Work and personality: Use of the NEO-PI-R in industrial/organizational psychology. *Applied Psychology: An International Review, 45*, 225–241.

Côté, S., van Kleef, G. A., & Sy, T. (2013). The social effects of emotional regulation in organizations. In A. A. Grandey, J. M. Diefendorff, & D. E. Rupp (Eds.), *Emotional labor in the 21st century* (pp. 79–100). New York: Routledge.

Courtright, S. H., McCormick, B. W., Postlethwaite, B. E., Reeves, C. J., & Mount, M. K. (2013). A meta-analysis of sex differences in physical ability: Revised estimates and strategies for reducing differences in selection contexts. *Journal of Applied Psychology, 98*, 623–641.

Craig, S. B., & Kaiser, R. B. (2013). Destructive leadership. In M. G. Rumsey (Ed.), *The Oxford handbook of leadership* (pp. 439–454). New York: Oxford University Press.

Crain, T. L., & Hammer, L. B. (2013). Work-family enrichment: A systematic review of antecedents, outcomes, and mechanisms. In A. B. Bakker (Ed.), *Advances in positive organizational psychology*, (Vol. 1, pp. 303–328). Bingley, UK: Emerald.

Crook, T. R., Todd, S. Y., Combs, J. G., & Woehr, D. J. (2011). Does human capital matter? A meta-analysis of the relationship between human capital and firm performance. *Journal of Applied Psychology, 96*, 443–456.

Cropanzano, R., & Li, A. (2006). Organizational politics and workplace stress. In E. Vigoda-Gadot & A. Drory (Eds.), *Handbook of organizational politics* (pp. 139–160). Cheltenham, UK: Edward Elgar.

Crosby, F. J., & VanDeVeer, C. (Eds.). (2000). *Sex, race, & merit*. Ann Arbor: University of Michigan Press.

Csikszentmihalyi, M. (1990). *Flow: The psychology of optimal experience*. New York: Harper and Row.

Csikszentmihalyi, M. (1997). *Finding flow: The psychology of engagement with everyday life*. New York: Basic Books.

Culbert, S. A., & Rout, L. (2010). *Get rid of the performance review! How companies can stop intimidating, start managing – and focus on what really matters*. New York: Business Plus.

Culbertson, S. S. (2011). The academic's forum: I-O coverage in general psychology courses. *The Industrial and Organizational Psychologist, 49*(2), 62–65.

Culbertson, S. S., & Mills, M. J. (2011). Negative implications for the inclusion of citizenship performance in ratings. *Human Resource Development International, 14*, 23–38.

Culbertson, S. S., Krome, L. R., McHenry, B. J., Stetzer, M. W., & van Ittersum, K. (2013). Performance appraisals: Mend them, don't end them. In M. Paludi (Ed.), *The psychology for business success* (Vol. 4, pp. 35–51). Westport, CT: Praeger Press.

Culbertson, S. S., Mills, M. J., & Fullagar, C. J. (2012). Work engagement and work-family facilitation: Making homes happier through positive affective spillover. *Human Relations, 65*, 1155–1177.

Cullen, M. J., Muros, J. P., Rasch, R., & Sackett, P. R. (2013). Individual differences in the effectiveness of error management training for developing negotiation skills. *International Journal of Selection and Assessment, 21*, 1–21.

Cunningham, M. R., Wong, D. T., & Barbee, A. P. (1994). Self-presentation dynamics on overt integrity tests: Experimental studies of the Reid Report. *Journal of Applied Psychology, 79*, 643–658.

Dabos, G. E., & Rousseau, D. M. (2004). Mutuality and reciprocity in the psychological contracts of employees and employers. *Journal of Applied Psychology, 89*, 52–72.

Daft, R. L. (1983). Learning the craft of organizational research. *Academy of Management Review, 8*, 539–546.

Dalal, R. S., & Hulin, C. L. (2008). Motivation for what? A multivariate dynamic perspective of the criterion. In R. Kanfer, G. Chen, & R. D. Pritchard (Eds.), *Work motivation: Past, present, and future* (pp. 63–100). New York: Routledge.

Dalton, D. R., & Mesch, D. J. (1990). The impact of flexible scheduling on employee attendance and turnover. *Administrative Science Quarterly, 35*, 370–387.

Dalton, D. R., Aguinis, H., Dalton, C. M., Bosco, F. A., & Pierce, C. A. (2012). Revisiting the file drawer problem in meta-analysis: An assessment of published and nonpublished correlation matrices. *Personnel Psychology, 65*, 221–249.

Daniel, M. H. (1997). Intelligence testing. *American Psychologist, 52*, 1038–1045.

Danielson, C. C., & Wiggenhorn, W. (2003). The strategic challenge for transfer: Chief learning officers speak out. In E. F. Holton & T. T. Baldwin (Eds.), *Improving learning transfer in organizations* (pp. 16–38). San Francisco: Jossey-Bass.

Dansereau, F., Graen, G., & Haga, W. (1975). A vertical dyad linkage approach to leadership in formal organizations. *Organizational Behavior and Human Performance, 13*, 46–78.

Dawis, R. V. (2004). Job satisfaction. In J. C. Thomas

(Ed.), *Comprehensive handbook of psychological assessment* (Vol. 4, pp. 470–481). Hoboken, NJ: Wiley.

Day, D. V., & Zaccaro, S. J. (2007). Leadership: A critical historical analysis of the influence of leader traits. In L. L. Koppes (Ed.), *Historical perspectives in industrial and organizational psychology* (pp. 383–405). Mahwah, NJ: Erlbaum.

De Angelis, K., & Segal, D. R. (2012). Minorities in the military. In J. H. Laurence & M. D. Matthews (Eds.), *The Oxford handbook of military psychology* (pp. 325–343). New York: Oxford University Press.

De Corte, W., Sackett, P. R., & Lievens, F. (2011). Designing Pareto-optimal selection systems: Formalizing the decisions required for selection system development. *Journal of Applied Psychology, 96*, 907–926.

de Wit, F. R. C., Greer, L. L., & Jehn, K. A. (2012). The paradox of intragroup conflict: A meta-analysis. *Journal of Applied Psychology, 97*, 360–390.

Deal, T., & Kennedy, A. (1982). *Corporate cultures*. Reading, MA: Addison-Wesley.

DeArmond, S., Matthews, R. A., & Bunk, J. (2014). Workload and procrastination: The roles of psychological detachment and fatigue. *International Journal of Stress Management, 21*, 137–161.

DeChurch, L. A., & Mesmer-Magnus, J. R. (2010). The cognitive underpinnings of effective teamwork: A meta-analysis. *Journal of Applied Psychology, 95*, 32–53.

Demerouti, E. (2006). Job characteristics, flow, and performance: The moderating role of conscientiousness. *Journal of Occupational Health Psychology, 11*, 266–280.

Demerouti, E., & Cropanzano, R. (2010). From thought to action: Employee work engagement and job performance. In A. B. Bakker & M. P. Leiter (Eds.), *Work engagement: A handbook of essential theory and research* (pp. 147–163). New York: Psychology Press.

Demerouti, E., Bakker, A. B., Nachreiner, F., & Schaufeli, W. B. (2001). Job demands-resources model of burnout. *Journal of Applied Psychology, 86*, 499–512.

Demerouti, E., Bakker, A. B., Sonnentag, S., & Fullagar, C. J. (2012). Work-related flow and energy at work and at home: A study on the role of daily recovery. *Journal of Organizational Behavior, 33*, 276–295.

DeMeuse, K. P., Bergmann, T. J., Vanderheiden, P. A., & Roraff, C. E. (2004). New evidence regarding organizational downsizing and a firm's financial performance: A long-term analysis. *Journal of Managerial Issues, 16*, 155–177.

DeMeuse, K. P., Marks, M. L., & Dai, G. (2011). Organizational downsizing, mergers and acquisitions, and strategic alliances: Using theory and research to enhance practice. In S. Zedeck (Ed.), *APA handbook of industrial and organizational psychology* (Vol. 3, pp. 729–768). Washington, DC: APA.

den Hartog, D. N., Boselie, P., & Paauwe, J. (2004). Performance management: A model and research agenda. *Applied Psychology: An International Review, 53*, 556–569.

DeNisi, A. S., & Peters, L. H. (1996). Organization of information in memory and the performance appraisal process: Evidence from the field. *Journal of Applied Psychology, 81*, 717–737.

DeNisi, A. S., & Pritchard, R. D. (2006). Performance appraisal, performance management and improving individual performance: A motivational framework. *Management and Organization Review, 2*, 253–277.

DeNisi, A. S., & Sonesh, S. (2011). The appraisal and management of performance at work. In S. Zedeck (Ed.), *APA handbook of industrial and organizational psychology* (Vol. 2, pp. 255–279). Washington, DC: APA.

Dickinson, T. L. (1993). Attitudes about performance appraisal. In H. Schuler, J. L. Farr, & M. Smith (Eds.), *Personnel selection and assessment* (pp. 141–162). Hillsdale, NJ: Erlbaum.

Diefendorff, J. M., & Chandler, M. M. (2011). Motivating employees. In S. Zedeck (Ed.), *APA handbook of industrial and organizational psychology* (Vol. 3, pp. 65–136). Washington, DC: APA.

Diefendorff, J. M., & Lord, R. G. (2008). Goal-striving and self-regulation processes. In R. Kanfer, G. Chen, & R. D. Pritchard (Eds.), *Work motivation: Past, present, and future* (pp. 151–196). New York: Routledge.

Dierdorff, E. C., & Ellington, J. K. (2008). It's the nature of work: Examining behavior-based sources of work-family conflict across occupations. *Journal of Applied Psychology, 93*, 883–892.

Dierdorff, E. C., & Morgeson, F. P. (2009). Effects of descriptor specificity and observability on incumbent work analysis ratings. *Personnel Psychology, 62*, 601–628.

Dierdorff, E. C., & Surface, E. A. (2007). Placing peer ratings in context: Systematic influences beyond ratee performance. *Personnel Psychology, 60*, 93–126.

Digman, J. M., & Takemoto-Chock, N. K. (1981). Factors in the natural language of personality: Re-analysis and comparison of six major studies. *Multivariate Behavioral Research, 16*, 149–170.

Dineen, B. R., & Soltis, S. M. (2011). Recruitment: A review of research and emerging directions. In S. Zedeck (Ed.), *APA handbook of industrial and organizational psychology* (Vol. 2, pp. 43–66). Washington, DC: APA.

Dionne, S. D., Yammarino, F. J., Atwater, L. E., & James, L. R. (2002). Neutralizing substitutes for leadership theory: Leadership effects and common-source bias. *Journal of Applied Psychology, 87*, 454–464.

Dipboye, R. L., Macan, T., & Shahani-Denning, C. (2012). The selection interview from the interviewer and applicant perspectives: Can't have one without the other. In N. Schmitt (Ed.), *The Oxford handbook of personnel assessment and selection* (pp. 323–352). New York: Oxford University Press.

Dirks, K. T., & Ferrin, D. L. (2002). Trust in leadership: Meta-analytic findings and implications for research and practice. *Journal of Applied Psychology, 87*, 611–628.

Dobrow, S. R. (2013). Dynamics of calling: A longitudinal study of musicians. *Journal of Organizational Behavior, 34*, 431–452.

Dobrow, S. R., & Tosti-Kharas, J. (2011). Calling: The development of a scale measure. *Personnel Psychology, 64*, 1001–1049.

Dominick, P. G. (2009). Forced rankings: Pros, cons, and practices. In J. W. Smither & M. London (Eds.), *Performance management* (pp. 411–444). San Francisco: Jossey-Bass.

Dorsey, D. W., Cortina, J. M., & Luchman, J. (2010). Adaptive and citizenship-related behaviors at work. In J. L. Farr & N. T. Tippins (Eds.), *Handbook of employee selection* (pp. 463–488). New York: Routledge.

Doverspike, D., & Arthur, W. A., Jr. (2012). The role of job analysis in test selection and development. In M. A. Wilson, W. Bennett, S. G. Gibson, & G. M. Alliger (Eds.), *The handbook of work analysis* (pp. 381–399). New York: Routledge.

Dovidio, J. F., & Gaertner, S. L. (1996). Affirmative action, unintentional racial biases, and intergroup relations. *Journal of Social Issues, 52*, 51–75.

Druskat, V. A., & Wolff, S. B. (1999). Effects and timing of developmental peer appraisals in self-managing work groups. *Journal of Applied Psychology, 84*, 58–74.

DuBois, C. L., Astakhova, M. N., & DuBois, D. A. (2013). Motivating behavior change to support organizational environmental sustainability goals. In A. H. Huffman & S. R. Klein (Eds.), *Green organizations: Driving change with I-O psychology* (pp. 186–207). New York: Routledge.

DuBois, D. A. (2002). Leveraging hidden expertise: Why, when, and how to use cognitive task analysis. In K. Kraiger (Ed.), *Creating, implementing, and managing effective training and development* (pp. 80–114). San Francisco: Jossey-Bass.

Duchon, J. C., Keran, C. M., & Smith, T. J. (1994). Extended workdays in an underground mine: A work performance analysis. *Human Factors, 36*, 258–268.

Dudley-Meislahn, N., Vaughn, E. D., Sydell, E. J., & Seeds, M. A. (2013). Advances in knowledge measurement. In J. M. Cortina & R. S. Landis (Eds.), *Modern research methods for the study of behavior in organizations* (pp. 443–481). New York: Routledge.

Dulebohn, J. H. (1997). Social influences in justice evaluations of human resources systems. In G. R. Ferris (Ed.), *Research in personnel and human resources management* (Vol. 15, pp. 241–292). Greenwich, CT: JAI Press.

Dunham, R. B., Grube, J. A., & Castaneda, M. B. (1994). Organizational commitment: The utility of an integrated definition. *Journal of Applied Psychology, 79*, 370–380.

Eagly, A. H., & Carli, L. L. (2007). *Through the labyrinth: The truth about how women become leaders.* Boston, MA: Harvard Business School Press.

Eagly, A. H., Johannesen-Schmidt, M. C., & van Engen, M. L. (2003). Transformation, transactional, and laissez-faire leadership styles: A meta-analysis comparing women and men. *Psychological Bulletin, 129,* 569–591.

Earley, P. C., & Gibson, C. B. (2002). *Multinational work teams.* Mahwah, NJ: Erlbaum.

Eatough, E. M., Chang, C. H., Miloslavic, S. A., & Johnson, R. E. (2011). Relationship of role stressors with organizational citizenship behavior: A meta-analysis. *Journal of Applied Psychology, 96*, 619–632.

Ebel, R. L. (1972). *Essentials of educational measurement.* Englewood Cliffs, NJ: Prentice Hall.

Eby, L. T. (2011). Mentoring. In S. Zedeck (Ed.), *APA handbook of industrial and organizational psychology* (Vol. 2, pp. 503–526). Washington, DC: APA.

Eby, L. T. (2012). Workplace mentoring: Past, present, and future perspectives. In S. W. J. Kozlowski (Ed.), *The Oxford handbook of organizational psychology* (Vol. 1, pp. 615–642). New York: Oxford University Press.

Eby, L. T., Allen, T. D., Hoffman, B., Baranik, L. E., Sauer, J. B., Baldwin, S., Morrison, A., Kinkade, K. M., Maher, C. P., Curtis, S., & Evans, S. C. (2013). An interdisciplinary meta-analysis of the potential antecedents, correlates, and consequences of protégé perceptions of mentoring. *Psychological Bulletin, 139*, 441–476.

Edwards, J. R., & Bagozzi, R. P. (2000). On the nature and direction of relationships between constructs and measure. *Psychological Methods, 5*, 155–174.

Edwards, M. S., & Greenberg, J. (2010). What is insidious workplace behavior? In J. Greenberg (Ed.), *Insidious workplace behavior* (pp. 3–28). New York: Routledge.

Ehrhart, M. G., Schneider, B., & Macey, W. H. (2014). *Organizational climate and culture.* New York: Routledge.

Ekkekakis, P. (2012). Affect, mood, and emotion. In G. Tenenbaum, R. C. Eklund, & A. Kamata (Eds.), *Measurement in sport and exercise psychology* (pp. 321–332). Champaign, IL: Human Kinetics.

Ellis, S., Mendel, R., & Nir, M. (2006). Learning from successful and failed experience: The moderating role of kind of after-event review. *Journal of Applied Psychology, 91*, 669–680.

Epitropaki, O., & Martin, R. (2004). Implicit leadership theories in applied settings: Factor structure, generalizability, and stability over time. *Journal of Applied Psychology, 89*, 293–310.

Equal Employment Opportunity Commission. (1980). Discrimination because of sex under Title VII of the Civil Rights Act of 1964, as amended; adoption of interim interpretive guidelines. *Federal Register, 45,* 25024–25025.

Erez, A., & Isen, A. M. (2002). The influence of positive affect on the components of expectancy motivation. *Journal of Applied Psychology, 87*, 1055–1067.

Erez, M. (2011). Cross-cultural and global issues in organizational psychology. In S. Zedeck (Ed.), *APA handbook of industrial and organizational psychology* (Vol. 3, pp. 807–854). Washington, DC: APA.

Erez, M., & Eden, D. (2001). Introduction: Trends reflected in work motivation. In M. Erez, U. Kleinbeck, & H. Thierry (Eds.), *Work motivation in the context of a globalizing economy* (pp. 1–8). Mahwah, NJ: Erlbaum.

Erickson, E. H. (1963). *Childhood and society* (2nd ed.). New York: Norton.

Estey, M. (1981). *The unions: Structure, development, and management* (3rd ed.). New York: Harcourt Brace Jovanovich.

Estrada, A. X. (2012). Gay service personnel in the U.S. military. In J. H. Laurence & M. D. Matthews (Eds.), *The Oxford handbook of military psychology* (pp. 344–364). New York: Oxford University Press.

Evans, D. C. (2003). A comparison of other-directed stigmatization produced by legal and illegal forms of affirmative action. *Journal of Applied Psychology, 88*, 121–130.

Fan, J., & Wanous, J. P. (2008). Organizational and cultural entry: A new type of orientation program for multiple boundary crossings. *Journal of Applied Psychology, 93*, 1390–1400.

Fan, J., Gao, D., Carroll, S. A., Lopez, F. J., Tian, T. S., & Meng, H. (2012). Testing the efficacy of a new procedure for reducing faking on personality tests within selection contexts. *Journal of Applied Psychology, 97*, 866–880.

Farr, J. L., & Tesluk, P. E. (1997). Bruce V. Moore: First president of Division 14. *Journal of Applied Psychology, 82*, 478–485.

Farrell, J. N., & McDaniel, M. A. (2001). The stability of validity coefficients over time: Ackerman's (1988) model and the general aptitude test battery. *Journal of Applied Psychology, 86*, 60–79.

Fay, B. (1990). Critical realism? *Journal for the Theory of Social Behaviour, 20*, 33–41.

Feldman, D. C., & Ng, T. W. (2012). Selecting out: How firms choose workers to lay off. In N. Schmitt (Ed.), *The Oxford handbook of personnel assessment and selection* (pp. 849–864). New York: Oxford University Press.

Ferguson, C. J., & Brannick, M. T. (2012). Publication bias in psychological science: Prevalence, methods for identifying and controlling, and implications for the use of meta-analyses. *Psychological Methods, 17*, 120–128.

Ferris, G. R., & Hochwarter, W. A. (2011). Organizational politics. In S. Zedeck (Ed.), *APA handbook of industrial and organizational psychology* (Vol. 3, pp. 435–459). Washington, DC: APA.

Ferris, G. R., & Treadway, D. C (2012). Politics in organizations: History, construct specification, and research directions. In G. R. Ferris & D. C. Treadway (Eds.), *Politics in organizations: Theory and research considerations* (pp. 3–26). New York: Routledge.

Ferris, G. R., Treadway, D. C., Brouer, R. L., & Munyon, T. P. (2012). Political skill in the organizational sciences. In G. R. Ferris & D. C. Treadway (Eds.), *Politics in organizations: Theory and research considerations* (pp. 487–528). New York: Routledge.

Fetterman, D. M. (1998). Ethnography. In L. Bickman & D. J. Rog (Eds.), *Handbook of applied social research methods* (pp. 473–504). Thousand Oaks, CA: Sage.

Feuille, P., & Blandin, J. (1974). Faculty job satisfaction and bargaining sentiment: A case study. *Academy of Management Journal, 17*, 678–692.

Fiedler, F. E. (1967). *A theory of leadership effectiveness.* New York: McGraw-Hill.

Fine, S. A., & Cronshaw, S. F. (1999). *Functional job analysis.* Mahwah, NJ: Erlbaum.

Fisher, C. D. (2000). Mood and emotions while working: Missing pieces of job satisfaction? *Journal of Organizational Behavior, 21*, 185–202.

Fisher, C. D., & Ashkanasy, N. M. (2000). The emerging role of emotions in work life: An introduction. *Journal of Organizational Behavior, 21*, 123–129.

Fisher, D. M., Bell, S. T., Dierdorff, E. C., & Belohlav, J. A. (2012). Facet personality and surface-level diversity as team mental model antecedents: Implications for implicit coordination. *Journal of Applied Psychology, 97*, 825–841.

Fisher, S. G., Hunter, T. A., & Macrosson, W. D. (1998). The structure of Belbin's team roles. *Journal of Occupational & Organizational Psychology, 71*, 283–288.

Fleishman, E. A., & Quaintance, M. K. (1984). *Taxonomies of human performance.* Orlando, FL: Academic Press.

Fletcher, C. (2008). *Appraisal, feedback, and development* (4th ed.). New York: Routledge.

Folger, R. (1986). Rethinking equity theory: A referent cognitions model. In H. W. Bierhoff, R. L. Cohen, &

J. Greenberg (Eds.), *Justice in social relations* (pp. 145–162). New York: Plenum Press.

Folger, R., & Greenberg, J. (1985). Procedural justice: An interpretive analysis of personnel systems. In K. Rowland & G. Ferris (Eds.), *Research in personnel and human resources management* (Vol. 3, pp. 141–183). Greenwich, CT: JAI Press.

Folger, R., & Skarlicki, D. P. (2001). Fairness as a dependent variable: Why tough times can lead to bad management. In R. Cropanzano (Ed.), *Justice in the workplace* (Vol. 2, pp. 97–120). Mahwah, NJ: Erlbaum.

Ford, J. K., & Kraiger, K. (1995). The application of cognitive constructs and principles to the instructional systems model of training: Implications for needs assessment, design, and transfer. In C. L. Cooper & I. T. Robertson (Eds.), *International review of industrial and organizational psychology* (Vol. 10, pp. 1–48). New York: Wiley.

Ford, J. K., Quiñones, M., Sego, D., & Speer, J. (1991). *Factors affecting the opportunity to use trained skills on the job.* Paper presented at the 6th annual conference of the Society for Industrial and Organizational Psychology, St. Louis.

Ford, M. T., Heinen, B. A., & Langkamer, K. L. (2007). Work and family satisfaction and conflict: A meta-analysis of cross-domain relations. *Journal of Applied Psychology, 92,* 57–80.

Foster, D. (2013). Security issues in technology-based testing. In J. A. Wollack & J. J. Fremer (Eds.), *Handbook of test security* (pp. 39–83). New York: Routledge.

Foster, J., Gaddis, B., & Hogan, J. (2012). Personality-based job analysis. In M. A. Wilson, W. Bennett, S. G. Gibson, & G. M. Alliger (Eds.), *The handbook of work analysis* (pp. 247–264). New York: Routledge.

Fredrickson, B. L. (2000). Cultivating positive emotions to optimize health and well-being. *Prevention & Treatment, 3,* 1–25.

Fredrickson, B. L. (2001). The role of positive emotions in positive psychology: The broaden-and-build theory. *American Psychologist, 56,* 218–226.

Fredrickson, B. L. (2013). Updated thinking on positive ratios. *American Psychologist, 68,* 814–822.

Fredrickson, B. L., & Cohn, M. A. (2008). Positive emotions. In M. Lewis, J. M. Haviland-Jones, & L. F. Barrett (Eds.), *Handbook of emotions* (3rd ed., pp. 777–796). New York: Guilford Press.

Freese, M., & Okonek, K. (1984). Reasons to leave shiftwork and psychological and psychosomatic complaints of former shiftworkers. *Journal of Applied Psychology, 69,* 509–514.

French, J. R. P., & Raven, B. (1960). The basis of social power. In D. Cartwright & A. F. Zander (Eds.), *Group dynamics* (2nd ed., pp. 607–623). Evanston, IL: Row Peterson.

Frijda, N. H. (2009). Mood. In D. Sender & K. R. Scherer (Eds.), *The Oxford companion to emotion and the affective sciences* (pp. 258–259). New York: Oxford University Press.

Frone, M. R. (2000). Work-family conflict and employee psychiatric disorders: The national comorbidity survey. *Journal of Applied Psychology, 85,* 888–895.

Frone, M. R. (2003). Work-family balance. In J. C. Quick & L. E. Tetrick (Eds.), *Handbook of organizational health psychology* (pp. 143–162). Washington, DC: American Psychological Association.

Frone, M. R. (2008). Employee substance use? The importance of temporal context in assessments of alcohol and illicit drug use. *Journal of Applied Psychology, 93,* 199–206.

Frone, M. R. (2013). *Alcohol and illicit drug use in the workforce and workplace.* Washington, DC: American Psychological Association.

Frost, P. J., & Jamal, M. (1979). Shift work, attitudes and reported behaviors: Some association between individual characteristics and hours of work and leisure. *Journal of Applied Psychology, 64,* 77–81.

Fryer, D., & Payne, R. (1986). Being unemployed: A review of the literature on the psychological experience of unemployment. In C. L. Cooper & I. Robertson (Eds.), *International review of industrial and organizational psychology* (Vol. 1, pp. 235–278). London: Wiley.

Fryxell, G. E., & Gordon, M. E. (1989). Workplace justice and job satisfaction as predictors of satisfaction with union and management. *Academy of Management Journal, 32,* 851–866.

Fullagar, C., & Barling, J. (1989). A longitudinal test of a model of the antecedents and consequences of union loyalty. *Journal of Applied Psychology, 74,* 213–227.

Fullagar, C., Clark, P., Gallagher, D., & Gordon, M. E. (1994). A model of the antecedents of early union commitment: The role of socialization experiences and steward characteristics. *Journal of Organizational Behavior, 15,* 517–533.

Fullagar, C. J. A., Gallagher, D. G., Gordon, M. E., & Clark, P. F. (1995). Impact of early socialization on union commitment and participation: A longitudinal study. *Journal of Applied Psychology, 80,* 147–157.

Fuller, J. B., Jr., & Hester, K. (2001). A closer look at the relationship between justice perceptions and union participation. *Journal of Applied Psychology, 86,* 1096–1106.

Furst, S. A., & Cable, D. M. (2008). Employee resistance to organizational change: Managerial influence tactics and leader-member exchange. *Journal of Applied Psychology, 93*, 453–462.

Galaif, E. R., Newcomb, M. D., & Carmona, J. V. (2001). Prospective relationships between drug problems and work adjustment in a community sample of adults. *Journal of Applied Psychology, 86*, 337–350.

Gardner, W. L., & Avolio, B. J. (1998). The charismatic relationship: A dramaturgical perspective. *Academy of Management Review, 23*, 32–58.

Gebhardt, D. L., & Baker, T. A. (2010). Physical performance tests. In J. L. Farr & N. T. Tippins (Eds.), *Handbook of employee selection* (pp. 277–298). New York: Routledge.

Gelfand, M. J., Fulmer, C. A., & Severance, L. (2011). The psychology of negotiation and mediation. In S. Zedeck (Ed.), *APA handbook of industrial and organizational psychology* (Vol. 3, pp. 495–554). Washington, DC: APA.

Gelfand, M. J., Raver, J. L., & Ehrhart, K. H. (2002). Methodological issues in cross-cultural organizational research. In S. G. Rogelberg (Ed.), *Handbook of research methods in industrial and organizational psychology* (pp. 216–246). Malden, MA: Blackwell.

George, G., Haas, M., & Pentland, A. (2014). Big data and management. *Academy of Management Journal, 57*, 321–326.

Gephart, R. P., Jr. (2013). Doing research with words: Qualitative methodologies in industrial/organizational psychology. In J. M. Cortina & R. S. Landis (Eds.), *Modern research methods for the study of behavior in organizations* (pp. 265–317). New York: Routledge.

Gettman, H. J., & Gelfand, M. J. (2007). When the customer shouldn't be king: Antecedents and consequences of sexual harassment by clients and customers. *Journal of Applied Psychology, 62*, 757–770.

Ghiselli, E. E., & Brown, C. W. (1955). *Personnel and industrial psychology.* New York: McGraw-Hill.

Gibson, C. B. (2001). From knowledge accumulation to accommodation: Cycles of collective cognition in work groups. *Journal of Organizational Behavior, 22*, 121–134.

Gifford, R. (2011). The dragons of inaction: Psychological barriers that limit climate change mitigation and adaptation. *American Psychologist, 37*, 589–615.

Gilliland, S. W. (1993). The perceived fairness of selection systems: An organizational justice perspective. *Academy of Management Review, 18*, 694–734.

Gilliland, S. W., & Chan, D. (2001). Justice in organizations: Theory, methods, and applications. In N. An-derson, D. S. Ones, H. K. Sinangil, & C. Viswesvaran (Eds.), *Handbook of industrial, work, and organizational psychology* (Vol. 2, pp. 143–165). London: Sage.

Gilliland, S. W., & Steiner, D. D. (2012). Applicant reactions to testing and selection. In N. Schmitt (Ed.), *The Oxford handbook of personnel assessment and selection* (pp. 629–666). New York: Oxford University Press.

Glassdoor (2014). *Best Places to Work.* www.glassdoor.com. Accessed May 27, 2014.

Glomb, T. M., Steele, P. D., & Arvey, R. D. (2002). Office sneers, snipes, and stab wounds: Antecedents, consequences, and implications of workplace violence and aggression. In R. G. Lord, R. J. Klimoski, & R. Kanfer (Eds.), *Emotions in the workplace* (pp. 227–259). San Francisco: Jossey-Bass.

Gloss, A. E., & Thompson, L. F. (2013). I-O psychology without borders: The emergence of humanitarian work psychology. In J. Olson-Buchanan, L. K. Bryan, & L. F. Thompson (Eds.), *Using industrial-organizational psychology for the greater good: Helping those who help others* (pp. 353–393). New York: Routledge.

Godard, J. (2008). Union formation. In P. Blyton, N. Bacon, J. Fiorito, & E. Heery (Eds.), *Industrial relations* (pp. 377–405). Thousand Oaks, CA: Sage.

Golden, T. D., Veiga, J. F., & Dino, R. N. (2008). The impact of professional isolation on teleworker job performance and turnover intentions: Does time spent teleworking, interacting face-to-face, or having access to communication-enhancing technology matter? *Journal of Applied Psychology, 93*, 1412–1421.

Goncalo, J. A., Polman, E., & Maslach, C. (2010). Can confidence come too soon? Collective efficacy, conflict and group performance over time. *Organizational Behavior and Human Decision Processes, 113*, 13–24.

Gordon, M. E., & Bowlby, R. L. (1988). Propositions about grievance settlements: Finally, consultation with grievants. *Personnel Psychology, 41*, 107–124.

Gordon, M. E., & Bowlby, R. L. (1989). Reactance and intentionality attributions as determinants of the intent to file a grievance. *Personnel Psychology, 42*, 309–330.

Gordon, M. E., & Ladd, R. T. (1990). Dual allegiance: Renewal, reconsideration, and recantation. *Personnel Psychology, 43*, 37–69.

Gordon, M. E., Philpot, J. W., Burt, R. E., Thompson, C. A., & Spiller, W. E. (1980). Commitment to the union: Development of a measure and an examination of its correlates. *Journal of Applied Psychology, 65*, 479–499.

Gordon, M. E., Schmitt, N., & Schneider, W. G. (1984). Laboratory research on bargaining and negotiations: An evaluation. *Industrial Relations, 23*, 218–233.

Gorman, C. A., & Rentsch, J. R. (2009). Evaluating frame-of-reference rater training effectiveness using performance schema accuracy. *Journal of Applied Psychology, 94*, 1336–1344.

Gottfredson, L. S. (2009). Logical fallacies used to dismiss the evidence on intellectual testing. In R. P. Phelps (Ed.), *Correcting fallacies about educational and psychological testing* (pp. 11–65). Washington, DC: APA.

Gottlieb, B. H., Kelloway, E. K., & Barham, E. (1998). *Flexible work arrangements.* Chichester: Wiley.

Gottschalk, P. (2009). *Entrepreneurship and organised crime: Entrepreneurs in illegal business.* Cheltenham, UK: Edward Elgar.

Gowan, M. A., Riordan, C. M., & Gatewood, K. D. (1999). Test of a model of coping with involuntary job loss following a company closing. *Journal of Applied Psychology, 84*, 75–86.

Graen, G. B. (2013). Overview of future research directions for team leadership. In M. G. Rumsey (Ed.), *The Oxford handbook of leadership* (pp. 167–183). New York: Oxford University Press.

Grandey, A. A., Fisk, G. M., & Steiner, D. D. (2005). Must "service with a smile" be stressful? The moderating role of personal control for American and French employees. *Journal of Applied Psychology, 90*, 893–904.

Grant, A. M. (2008). Does intrinsic motivation fuel the prosocial fire? Motivational synergy in predicting persistence, performance, and productivity. *Journal of Applied Psychology, 93*, 48–58.

Grant, A. M. (2012). Giving time, time after time: Work design and sustained employee participation in corporate volunteering. *Academy of Management Review, 37*, 589–615.

Grant, A. M., & Shin, J. (2012) Work motivation: Directing, energizing, and maintaining effort (and research). In R. M. Ryan (Ed.), *The Oxford handbook of human motivation* (pp. 505–519). New York, NY: Oxford University Press.

Grant, A. M., Cavanagh, M. J., Parker, H. M., & Passmore, J. (2010). The state of play in coaching today: A comprehensive review of the field. In G. P. Hodgkinson & J. L. Ford (Eds.), *International review of industrial and organizational psychology* (Vol. 25, pp. 125–167). Chichester, UK: Wiley-Blackwell.

Grant, A. M., Fried, Y., & Juillerat, T. (2011). Work matters: Job design in classic and contemporary perspectives. In S. Zedeck (Ed.), *APA handbook of industrial and organizational psychology* (Vol. 1, pp. 417–454). Washington, DC: APA.

Grant, D. M., & Mayer, D. M. (2009). Good soldiers and good actors: Prosocial and impression management mo-

tives as interactive predictors of affiliative citizenship behavior. *Journal of Applied Psychology, 94*, 900–912.

Greenberg, J. (1986). Determinants of perceived fairness of performance evaluations. *Journal of Applied Psychology, 71*, 340–342.

Greenberg, J. (1993). The social side of fairness: Interpersonal and informational classes of organizational justice. In R. Cropanzano (Ed.), *Justice in the workplace: Approaching fairness in human resource management* (pp. 79–103). Hillsdale, NJ: Erlbaum.

Greenberg, J. (1994). Using socially fair treatment to promote acceptance of a work site smoking ban. *Journal of Applied Psychology, 79*, 288–297.

Greenberg, J. (2007). Positive organizational justice: From fair to fairer—and beyond. In J. E. Dutton & B. R. Ragins (Eds.), *Exploring positive relationships at work* (pp. 159–178). Mahwah, NJ: Erlbaum.

Greenberg, J., & Scott, K. S. (1996). Why do workers bite the hands that feed them? Employee theft as a social exchange process. In B. M. Staw & L. L. Cummings (Eds.), *Research in organizational behavior* (Vol. 18, pp. 111–156). Greenwich, CT: JAI.

Greenhaus, J. H., & Powell, G. N. (2006). When work and family are allies: A theory of work-family enrichment. *Academy of Management Review, 31*, 72–92.

Greenleaf, R. K. (1970). *The servant as leader.* Newton Centre, MA: The Robert K. Greenleaf Center.

Gregori, A., & Baltar, F. (2013). Ready to complete the survey on Facebook. Web 2.0 as a research tool in business studies. *International Journal of Marketing Research, 55*, 131–148.

Greguras, G. J., Robie, C., Schleicher, D. J., & Goff, M. (2003). A field study of the effects of rating purpose on the quality of multisource ratings. *Personnel Psychology, 56*, 1–22.

Griepentrog, B. K., Harold, C. M., Holtz, B. C., Klimoski, R. J., & Marsh, S. M. (2012). Interpreting social identity and the theory of planned behavior: Predicting withdrawal from an organizational recruitment process. *Personnel Psychology, 65*, 723–753.

Griffith, R. L., & Robie, C. (2013). Personality testing and the "F-word." In N. D. Christiansen & R. P. Tett (Eds.), *Handbook of personality at work* (pp. 253–280). New York: Routledge.

Griffith, R. L., & Wang, M. (2010). The internationalization of I-O psychology: We're not in Kansas anymore. *The Industrial-Organizational Psychologist, 48*(1), 41–45.

Grigsby, D. M., & Bigoness, W. J. (1982). Effects of mediation and alternative forms of arbitration on bargaining behavior: A laboratory study. *Journal of Applied Psychology, 67*, 549–554.

Groth, M., Hennig-Thurau, T., & Walsh, G. (2009). Customer reactions to emotional labor: The roles of employee acting strategies and customer detection accuracy. *Academy of Management Journal, 52*, 958–974.

Groth, M., Hennig-Thurau, T., & Wang, K. (2013). The customer experience of emotional labor. In A. A. Grandey, J. M. Diefendorff, & D. E. Rupp (Eds.), *Emotional labor in the 21st century* (pp. 127–152). New York: Routledge.

Gruman, J. A., & Saks, A. M. (2011). Performance management and employee engagement. *Human Resource Management Review, 21*, 123–136.

Guenole, N. (2014). Maladaptive personality at work: Exploring the darkness. *Industrial and Organizational Psychology, 7*, 85–97.

Guest, D. (2008). Worker well-being. In P. Blyton, N. Bacon, J. Fiorito, & E. Heery (Eds.), *Industrial relations* (pp. 529–547). Thousand Oaks, CA: Sage.

Guion, R. M. (1998a). *Assessment, measurement, and prediction for personnel decisions.* Mahwah, NJ: Erlbaum.

Guion, R. M. (1998b). Some virtues of dissatisfaction in the science and practice of personnel selection. *Human Resource Management Review, 8*, 351–366.

Gutman, A. (2003). The *Grutter, Gratz, & Costa* rulings. *The Industrial-Organizational Psychologist, 41*(2), 117–127.

Gutman, A. (2004). Ground rules for adverse impact. *The Industrial-Organizational Psychologist, 41*(3), 109–119.

Gutman, A. (2012). Legal constraints on personnel selection decisions. In N. Schmitt (Ed.), *The Oxford handbook of personnel assessment and selection* (pp. 686–720). New York: Oxford University Press.

Gutman, A., & Dunleavy, E. M. (2012). Documenting work analysis projects: A review of strategy and legal defensibility for personnel selection. In M. A. Wilson, W. Bennett, S. G. Gibson, & G. M. Alliger (Eds.), *The handbook of work analysis* (pp. 139–167). New York: Routledge.

Guzzo, R. A. (1995). Introduction: At the intersection of team effectiveness and decision making. In R. A. Guzzo & E. Salas (Eds.), *Team effectiveness and decision making in organizations* (pp. 1–8). San Francisco: Jossey-Bass.

Hackett, G. (1995). Self-efficacy in career choice and development. In A. Bandura (Ed.), *Self-efficacy in changing societies* (pp. 232–258). New York: Cambridge.

Hackman, J. R., & Oldham, G. R. (1976). Motivation through the design of work: Test of a theory. *Organizational Behavior and Human Performance, 16, 250–279*.

Hackman, J. R., & Wageman, R. (2007). Asking the right questions about leadership. *American Psychologist, 62*, 43–47.

Haddock-Millar, J., Muller-Camen, M., & Miles, D. (2012). Human resource development initiatives for managing environmental concerns at McDonald's UK.

In S. E. Jackson, D. S. Ones, & S. Dilchert (Eds.), *Managing human resources for environmental sustainability* (pp. 341–361). San Francisco: Jossey-Bass.

Hajcak, G. (2012). What we've learned from mistakes: Insights from error-related brain activity. *Current Directions in Psychological Science, 21*, 101–106.

Hajcak, G., McDonald, N., & Simons, R. (2004). Error-related psychophysiology and negative affect. *Brain and Cognition, 56*, 189–197.

Haladyna, T. M. (1999). *Developing and validating multiple-choice test items* (2nd ed.). Mahwah, NJ: Erlbaum.

Hall, G. S. (1917). Practical relations between psychology and the war. *Journal of Applied Psychology, 1*, 9–16.

Hall, G. S., Baird, J. W., & Geissler, L. R. (1917). Foreword. *Journal of Applied Psychology, 1*, 5–7.

Hambrick, D. C. (2007). The field of management's devotion to theory: Too much of a good thing? *Academy of Management Journal, 50*, 1346–1352.

Hammer, L. B., & Zimmerman, K. L. (2011). Quality of work life. In S. Zedeck (Ed.), *APA handbook of industrial and organizational psychology* (Vol. 3, pp. 399–431). Washington, DC: APA.

Hammer, L. B., Van Dyck, S. E., & Ellis, A. M. (2013). Organizational policies supportive of work-life integration. In D. Major & R. Burke (Eds.), *Handbook of work-life integration among professionals: Challenges and opportunities* (pp. 288–309). Cheltenham, UK: Edward Elgar.

Hammer, T. H., & Berman, M. (1981). The role of noneconomic factors in faculty union voting. *Journal of Applied Psychology, 66*, 415–421.

Hammer, T. H., Bayazit, M., & Wazeter, D. L. (2009). Union leadership and member attitudes: A multi-level analysis. *Journal of Applied Psychology, 94*, 392–410.

Hamner, W. C., & Smith, F. J. (1978). Work attitudes as predictors of unionization activity. *Journal of Applied Psychology, 63*, 415–421.

Hanges, P. J., & Wang, M. (2012). Seeking the Holy Grail in organizational science: Uncovering causality through research design. In S. W. J. Kozlowski (Ed.), *The Oxford handbook of organizational psychology* (Vol. 1, pp. 79–116). New York: Oxford University Press.

Harms, P. D., & Lester, P. B. (2012). Boots on the ground: A first-hand account of conducting psychological research in combat. *The Industrial-Organizational Psychologist, 49*(3), 15–21.

Harrell, T. W. (1992). Some history of the Army General Classification Test. *Journal of Applied Psychology, 77*, 875–878.

Harris, L. (2000). Procedural justice and perceptions of fairness in selection practice. *International Journal of Selection and Assessment, 8*, 148–157.

Harris, W. G., Jones, J. W., Klion, R., Arnold, D. W., Camara, W., & Cunningham, M. R. (2012). Test publishers' perspective on "An updated meta-analysis:" Comment on Van Iddekinge, Roth, Raymark, and Odle-Dusseau (2012). *Journal of Applied Psychology, 97*, 531–536.

Hartley, J. F. (1992). The psychology of industrial relations. In C. L. Cooper & I. T. Robertson (Eds.), *International review of industrial and organizational psychology* (Vol. 7, pp. 201–243). London: Wiley.

Hartnell, C. A., Ou, A. Y., & Kinicki, A. (2011). Organizational culture and organizational effectiveness: A meta-analytic investigation of the competing values framework's theoretical suppositions. *Journal of Applied Psychology, 96*, 677–694.

Harvey, R. J., & Lozada-Larsen, S. R. (1988). Influence of amount of job descriptive information on job analysis rating accuracy. *Journal of Applied Psychology, 73*, 457–461.

Hauenstein, N. M. A. (1998). Training raters to increase the accuracy of appraisals and the usefulness of feedback. In J. W. Smither (Ed.), *Performance appraisal* (pp. 404–444). San Francisco: Jossey-Bass.

Hausknecht, J. P., & Langevin, A. M. (2010). Selection for service and sales jobs. In. J. L. Farr & N. T. Tippins (Eds.), *Handbook of employee selection* (pp. 765–780). New York: Routledge.

Hausknecht, J. P., & Wright, P. M. (2012). Organizational strategy and staffing. In N. Schmitt (Ed.), *The Oxford handbook of personnel assessment and selection* (pp. 147–155). New York: Oxford University Press.

Hausknecht, J. P., Halpert, J. A., Di Paolo, N. T., & Gerrard, M. O. (2007). Retesting in selection: A meta-analysis of coaching and practice effects for tests of cognitive ability. *Journal of Applied Psychology, 92*, 373–385.

Hayles, V. R. (1996). Diversity training and development. In R. L. Craig (Ed.), *The ASTD training and development handbook: A guide to human resource development* (3rd ed., pp. 104–123). New York: McGraw-Hill.

Hayter, S., & Stoeveska, V. (2011). *Trade union density and collective bargaining coverage: International statistical inquiry 2008–09.* Geneva: International Labor Organization.

Hedge, J. W., & Kavanagh, M. J. (1988). Improving the accuracy of performance evaluations: Comparison of three methods of performance appraisal training. *Journal of Applied Psychology, 73*, 68–73.

Hedlund, J., & Sternberg, R. J. (2000). Practical intelligence: Implications for human resources research. In G. R. Ferris (Ed.), *Research in personnel and human resources management* (Vol. 19, pp. 1–52). New York: Elsevier.

Heilman, M. E. (1996). Affirmative actions' contradictory consequences. *Journal of Social Issues, 52*(4), 105–109.

Heilman, M. E., & Alcott, V. B. (2001). What I think you think of me: Women's reactions to being viewed as beneficiaries of preferential selection. *Journal of Applied Psychology, 86*, 574–582.

Heilman, M. E., & Chen, J. J. (2005). Same behavior, different consequences: Reactions to men's and women's altruistic citizenship behavior. *Journal of Applied Psychology, 90*, 431–441.

Heilman, M. E., Block, C. J., & Lucas, J. A. (1992). Presumed incompetent? Stigmatization and affirmative action efforts. *Journal of Applied Psychology, 77*, 536–544.

Hemphill, H., & Haines, R. (1997). *Discrimination, harassment, and the failure of diversity training.* Westport, CT: Quorum.

Henderson, D. J., Wayne, S. J., Shore, L. M., Bommer, W. H., & Tetrick, L. E. (2008). Leader-member exchange, differentiation, and psychological contract fulfillment: A multi-level examination. *Journal of Applied Psychology, 93*, 1208–1219.

Henrich, J., Heine, S. J., & Norenzayan, A. (2010). The weirdest people in the world? *Behavioral and Brain Sciences, 33*, 61–135.

Hepburn, C. G., & Barling, J. (2001). To vote or not to vote: Abstaining from voting in union representation elections. *Journal of Organizational Behavior, 22*, 569–591.

Hershcovis, M. S., Turner, N., Barling, J., Arnold, K. A., Dupre, K. E., Inness, M., LeBlanc, M. M., & Sivanathan, N. (2007). Predicting workplace aggression: A meta-analysis. *Journal of Applied Psychology, 92*, 228–238.

Hesketh, B. (2001). Adapting vocational psychology to cope with change. *Journal of Vocational Behavior, 59*, 203–212.

Hewlin, P. F. (2009). Wearing the cloak: Antecedents and consequences of creating facades of conformity. *Journal of Applied Psychology, 94*, 727–741.

Highhouse, S. (2007). Applications of organizational psychology: Learning through failure or failure to learn? In L. L. Koppes (Ed.), *Historical perspectives in industrial and organizational psychology* (pp. 331–352). Mahwah, NJ: Erlbaum.

Highhouse, S. (2008). Stubborn reliance on intuition and subjectivity in employee selection. *Industrial and Organizational Psychology, 1*, 333–342.

Highhouse, S. (2011). Was the addition of sex to Title VII a joke? *The Industrial-Organizational Psychologist, 48*(3), 102–107.

Highhouse, S., & Nolan, K. P. (2012). One history of the assessment center. In D. J. Jackson, C. E. Lance, &

B. J. Hoffman (Eds.), *The psychology of assessment centers* (pp. 25–44). New York: Routledge.

Highhouse, S., Stierwalt, S., Bachiochi, P., Elder, A. E., & Fisher, G. (1999). Effects of advertised human resource management practices on attraction of African American applicants. *Personnel Psychology, 52*, 425–442.

Hinkin, T. R., & Schriesheim, C. A. (2008). An examination of "nonleadership:" From laissez-faire leadership to leader reward omission and punishment omission. *Journal of Applied Psychology, 93*, 1234–1248.

Hoch, J. E., & Kozlowski, S. W. J. (2014). Leading virtual teams: Hierarchical leadership, structural supports, and shared team leadership. *Journal of Applied Psychology, 99*, 390–403.

Hochwarter, W. A. (2012). The positive side of organizational politics. In G. R. Ferris & D. C. Treadway (Eds.), *Politics in organizations: Theory and research considerations* (pp. 27–65). New York: Routledge.

Hoffman, B. J., & Woehr, D. J. (2009). Disentangling the meaning of multisource performance rating source and dimension factors. *Personnel Psychology, 62*, 735–765.

Hoffman, B. J., Lance, C. E., Bynum, B., & Gentry, W. A. (2010). Rater source effects are alive and well after all. *Personnel Psychology, 63*, 119–151.

Hoffman, B. J., Woehr, D. J., Maldagen-Youngjohn, R., & Lyons, B. D. (2011). Great man or great myth? A quantitative review of the relationship between individual differences and leader effectiveness. *Journal of Occupational and Organizational Psychology, 84*, 347–381.

Hoffman, C. C., & McPhail, S. M. (1998). Exploring options for supporting test use in situations precluding local validation. *Personnel Psychology, 51*, 987–1003.

Hofmann, D. A., & Tetrick, L. E. (2003). The etiology of the concept of health: Implications for "organizing" individuals and organizational health. In D. A. Hofmann & L. E. Tetrick (Eds.), *Health and safety in organizations* (pp. 1–26). San Francisco: Jossey-Bass.

Hofstede, G. (1980). *Culture's consequences: International differences in work-related values.* Beverly Hills, CA: Sage.

Hofstede, G. (2001). *Culture's consequences* (2nd ed.): *Comparing values, behaviors, institutions, and organizations across nations.* Thousand Oaks, CA: Sage.

Hofstee, W. K. (2001). Intelligence and personality: Do they mix? In J. M. Collis & S. Messick (Eds.), *Intelligence and personality: Bridging the gap in theory and measurement* (pp. 43–60). Mahwah, NJ: Erlbaum.

Hogan, R. T. (1991). Personality and personality measurement. In M. D. Dunnette & L. M. Hough (Eds.), *Handbook of industrial and organizational psychology* (2nd ed.,

Vol. 2, pp. 873–919). Palo Alto, CA: Consulting Psychologists Press.

Hogan, R. T., & Hogan, J. (1992). *Hogan Personality Inventory.* Tulsa, OK: Hogan Assessment Systems.

Hogan, R. T., Raskin, R., & Fazzini, D. (1990). The dark side of charisma. In K. E. Clark & M. B. Clark (Eds.), *Measures of leadership* (pp. 343–354). West Orange, NJ: Leadership Library of America.

Hollander, E. P. (2009). *Inclusive leadership: The essential leader-follower relationship.* New York: Routledge.

Hollenbeck, J. R., LePine, J. A., & Ilgen, D. R. (1996). Adapting to roles in decision-making teams. In K. R. Murphy (Ed.), *Individual differences and behaviors in organizations* (pp. 300–333). San Francisco: Jossey-Bass.

Holton, E. F., & Baldwin, T. T. (2003). Making transfer happen: An active perspective on learning transfer systems. In E. F. Holton & T. T. Baldwin (Eds.), *Improving learning transfer in organizations* (pp. 3–15). San Francisco: Jossey-Bass.

Hom, P. W., & Kinicki, A. J. (2001). Toward a greater understanding of how dissatisfaction drives employee turnover. *Academy of Management Journal, 44*, 975–987.

Hom, P. W., Mitchell, T. R., Lee, T. W., & Griffeth, R. W. (2012). Reviewing employee turnover: Focusing on proximal withdrawal states and an expanded criterion. *Psychological Bulletin, 138*, 831–858.

Honts, C. R. (1991). The emperor's new clothes: Application of polygraph tests in the American workplace. *Forensic Reports, 4*, 91–116.

Honts, C. R., & Amato, S. L. (2002). Countermeasures. In M. Kleiner (Ed.), *Handbook of polygraph testing* (pp. 251–264). San Diego: Academic Press.

Hoobler, J. M., Lemmon, G., & Wayne, S. J. (2014). Women's managerial aspirations: An organizational development perspective. *Journal of Management, 40*, 703–730.

Hornung, S., Rousseau, D. M., & Glaser, J. (2008). Creating flexible work arrangements through idiosyncratic deals. *Journal of Applied Psychology, 93*, 655–664.

Hough, L., & Dilchert, S. (2010). Personality: Its measurement and validity for employee selection. In J. L. Farr & N. T. Tippins (Eds.), *Handbook of employee selection* (pp. 299–320). New York: Routledge.

House, R. J., Hanges, P. J., Javidan, M., Dorman, P. W., & Gupta, V. (Eds.). (2004). *Culture, leadership, and organizations: The GLOBE study of 62 societies.* Thousand Oaks, CA: Sage.

Howard, A., & Lowman, R. L. (1985). Should industrial/organizational psychologists be licensed? *American Psychologist, 40*, 40–47.

Howell, J. P., & Dorfman, P. W. (1981). Substitutes for leadership: Test of a construct. *Academy of Management Journal, 24,* 714–728.

Howell, W. C., & Cooke, N. J. (1989). Training the human information processor: A review of cognitive models. In I. L. Goldstein (Ed.), *Training and development in organizations* (pp. 121–182). San Francisco: Jossey-Bass.

Hu, J., & Liden, R. C. (2011). Antecedents of team potency and team effectiveness: An examination of goal and process clarity and servant leadership. *Journal of Applied Psychology, 96,* 851–862.

Hu, J., & Liden, R. C. (2013). Relative leader-member exchange within team contexts: How and when social comparison impacts individual effectiveness. *Personnel Psychology, 66,* 127–172.

Huang, J. L., Ryan, A. M., Zabel, K. L., & Palmer, A. (2014). Personality and adaptive performance at work: A meta-analytic investigation. *Journal of Applied Psychology, 99,* 162–179.

Huffcutt, A. I., & Culbertson, S. S. (2011). Interviews. In S. Zedeck (Ed.), *APA handbook of industrial and organizational psychology* (Vol. 2, pp. 185–203). Washington, DC: APA.

Huffcutt, A. I., Conway, J. M., Ruth, P. L., & Stone, N. J. (2001). Identification and meta-analytic assessment of psychological constructs measured in employment interviews. *Journal of Applied Psychology, 86,* 897–913.

Huffman, A. H., Watrous-Rodriguez, K. M., Henning, J. B., & Berry, J. (2009). "Working" through environmental issues: The role of I/O psychologists. *The Industrial-Organizational Psychologist, 47*(2), 27–36.

Hulin, C. L. (1991). Adaptation, persistence, and commitment in organizations. In M. D. Dunnette & L. M. Hough (Eds.), *Handbook of industrial and organizational psychology* (2nd ed., Vol. 2, pp. 445–505). Palo Alto, CA: Consulting Psychologists Press.

Hulin, C. L. (2014). Work and being: The meanings of work in contemporary society. In J. K. Ford, J. R. Hollenbeck, & A. M. Ryan (Eds.), *The nature of work* (pp. 9–33). Washington, DC: APA.

Hulin, C. L., & Judge, T. A. (2003). Job attitudes. In W. C. Borman, D. R. Ilgen, & R. J. Klimoski (Eds.), *Handbook of psychology* (Vol. 12): *Industrial and organizational psychology* (pp. 255–276). Hoboken, NJ: Wiley.

Hülsheger, U. R., & Schewe, A. F. (2011). On the costs and benefits of emotional labor: A meta-analysis spanning three decades of research. *Journal of Occupational Health Psychology, 16,* 361–389.

Humphrey, S. E., Nahrgang, J. D., & Morgeson, F. P. (2007). Integrating motivational, social, and contextual work design features: A meta-analytic summary of theoretical extensions of the work design literature. *Journal of Applied Psychology, 92,* 1332–1356.

Hunter, J. E., & Schmidt, F. L. (1990). *Method of meta-analysis: Correcting error and bias in research findings.* Newbury Park, CA: Sage.

Huseman, R. C., Hatfield, J. D., & Miles, E. W. (1987). A new perspective on equity theory: The equity sensitivity construct. *Academy of Management Review, 12,* 222–234.

Huszczo, G. E., Wiggins, J. G., & Currie, J. S. (1984). The relationship between psychology and organized labor: Past, present and future. *American Psychologist, 39,* 432–440.

Ilgen, D. R., & Davis, C. A. (2000). Bearing bad news: Reactions to negative performance feedback. *Applied Psychology: An International Review, 49,* 550–565.

Ilgen, D. R., Peterson, R. B., Martin, B. A., & Boeschen, D. A. (1981). Supervisor and subordinate reactions to performance appraisal sessions. *Organizational Behavior and Human Performance, 28,* 311–330.

Ilies, R., & Judge, T. A. (2003). On the heritability of job satisfaction: The mediating role of personality. *Journal of Applied Psychology, 88,* 750–759.

Ilies, R., & Judge, T. A. (2005). Goal regulation across time: The effects of feedback and affect. *Journal of Applied Psychology, 90,* 453–467.

Ilies, R., Arvey, R. D., & Bouchard, T. J. (2006). Darwinism, behavioral genetics, and organizational behavior: A review and agenda for future research. *Journal of Organizational Behavior, 27,* 121–141.

Ilies, R., Keeney, J., & Scott, B. A. (2011). Work-family interpersonal capitalization: Sharing positive work events at home. *Organizational Behavior and Human Decision Processes, 114,* 115–126.

Ilies, R., Peng, A. C., Savani, K., & Dimotakis, N. (2013). Guilty and helpful: An emotion-based reparatory model of voluntary work behavior. *Journal of Applied Psychology, 98,* 1051–1059.

International Labour Organization (2003). *The employment effects of mergers and acquisitions in commerce.* Geneva: Author.

International Labour Organization. (2004). *Helping hands or shackled lives? Understanding child domestic labour and responses to it.* Geneva: Author.

Internetworldstats (2014). *www.internetworldstats.com/stats.htm.* Accessed January 20, 2014.

Jackson, C. L., & LePine, J. A. (2003). Peer responses to a team's weakest link: A test and extension of LePine and Van Dyne's model. *Journal of Applied Psychology, 88,* 459–475.

Jackson, S. E., & Joshi, A. (2011). Work team diversity. In S. Zedeck (Ed.), *APA handbook of industrial and organi-*

zational psychology (Vol. 1, pp. 651–686). Washington, DC: APA.

Jaffe, S. R., Strait, L. B., & Odgers, C. L. (2012). From correlates to causes: Can quasi-experimental studies and statistical innovations bring us closer to identifying the causes of anti-social behavior? *Psychological Bulletin, 138,* 272–295.

Jahoda, M. (1981). Work, employment, and unemployment: Values, theories and approaches in social research. *American Psychologist, 36,* 184–191.

James L. R., & McIntyre, H. H. (2010). Situational specificity and validity generalization. In J. L. Farr & N. T. Tippins (Eds.), *Handbook of employee selection* (pp. 909–920). New York: Routledge.

Jansen, K. J., & Shipp, A. J. (2013). A review and agenda for incorporating time in fit research. In A. L. Kristof-Brown & J. Billsberry (Eds.), *Organizational fit: Key issues and new directions* (pp. 195–221). Malden, MA: Wiley.

Janz, B. D., Colquitt, J. A., & Noe, R. A. (1997). Knowledge worker team effectiveness: The role of autonomy, interdependence, team development, and contextual support variables. *Personnel Psychology, 50,* 877–904.

Jarrell, S. B., & Stanley, T. D. (1990). A meta-analysis of the union–nonunion wage gap. *Industrial and Labor Relations Review, 44,* 54–67.

Jawahar, I. M., & Williams, C. R. (1997). Where all the children are above average: The performance appraisal purpose effect. *Personnel Psychology, 50,* 905–925.

Jayne, M. E., & Rauschenberger, J. M. (2000). Demonstrating the value of selection in organizations. In J. F. Kehoe (Ed.), *Managing selection in changing organizations* (pp. 123–157). San Francisco: Jossey-Bass.

Jeanneret, P. R., D'Egidio, E. L., & Hanson, M. A. (2004). Assessment and development opportunities using the Occupational Information Network (O*NET). In J. C. Thomas (Ed.), *Comprehensive handbook of psychological assessment* (Vol. 4, pp. 192–202). Hoboken, NJ: Wiley.

Jehn, K. A., Northcraft, G. B., & Neale, M. A. (1999). Why differences make a difference: A field study of diversity, conflict, and performance in workgroups. *Administrative Science Quarterly, 44,* 741–763.

Jenkins, J. G. (1946). Validity for what? *Journal of Consulting Psychology, 10,* 93–98.

Jensen, J. M., Patel, P. C., & Raver, J. L. (2014). Is it better to be average? High and low performance as predictors of employee victimization. *Journal of Applied Psychology, 99,* 296–309.

Jex, S. M., Swanson, N., & Grubb, P. (2013). Healthy workplaces. In N. Schmitt, & S. Highhouse (Eds.), *Handbook of psychology* (Vol. 12): *Industrial and organi-*

zational psychology (pp. 615–642). New York: John Wiley & Sons.

Jobvite (2012). *Jobvite social recruiting survey.* Retrieved September 1, 2014 from http://web.jobvite.com/Social_Recruiting_Survey-2012–13.html

Johns, G. (1994). How often were you absent? A review of the use of self-reported absence data. *Journal of Applied Psychology, 79,* 574–591.

Johns, G. (1997). Contemporary research on absence from work: Correlates, causes, and consequences. In C. L. Cooper & I. T. Robertson (Eds.), *International review of industrial and organizational psychology* (Vol. 12, pp. 115–173). Chichester: Wiley.

Johnston, D. C. (2004). *Perfectly legal: The covert campaign to rig our tax system to benefit the super rich — and cheat everybody else.* New York: Portfolio.

Jones, D. A., Willness, C. R., & Madey, S. (2014). Why are job seekers attracted by corporate social performance? Experimental and field tests of three signal-based mechanisms. *Academy of Management Journal, 57,* 383–404.

Jones, R. G. (Ed.) (2012). *Nepotism in organizations.* New York: Routledge.

Jonsen, K., & Ozbilgin, M. (2014). Models of global diversity management. In B. M. Ferdman & B. R. Deane (Eds.), *Diversity at work: The practice of inclusion* (pp. 364–390). San Francisco: Jossey-Bass.

Joseph, D. L., & Newman, D. A. (2010). Emotional intelligence: An integrative meta-analysis and cascading model. *Journal of Applied Psychology, 95,* 54–78.

Judge, T. A., & Kammeyer-Mueller, J. D. (2012). Job attitudes. *Annual Review of Psychology, 63,* 341–367.

Judge, T. A., Heller, D., & Mount, M. K. (2002). Five-factor model of personality and job satisfaction: A meta-analysis. *Journal of Applied Psychology, 87,* 530–541.

Judge, T. A., Higgins, C. A., Thoresen, C. J., & Barrick, M. R. (1999). The big five personality traits, general mental ability, and career success across the life span. *Personnel Psychology, 52,* 621–652.

Judge, T. A., Hulin, C. L., & Dalal, R. S. (2012). Job satisfaction and job affect. In S. W. J. Kozlowski (Ed.), *The Oxford handbook of organizational psychology* (Vol. 1, pp. 496–525). New York: Oxford University Press.

Judge, T. A., Piccolo, R. F., & Ilies, R. (2004). The forgotten ones? The validity of consideration and initiating structure in leadership research. *Journal of Applied Psychology, 89,* 36–51.

Judge, T. A., Thoresen, C. J., Bono, J. E., & Patton, G. K. (2001). The job satisfaction–job performance relationship: A qualitative and quantitative review. *Psychological Bulletin, 127,* 376–407.

Kagitcibasi, C., & Berry, J. W. (1989). Cross-cultural psychology: Current research and trends. *Annual Review of Psychology, 40,* 493–531.

Kane, J. S., Bernardin, H. J., Villanova, P., & Peyrefitte, J. (1995). Stability of rater leniency: Three studies. *Academy of Management Journal, 38,* 1036–1051.

Kanfer, R. (1992). Work motivation: New directions in theory and research. In C. L. Cooper & I. T. Robertson (Eds.), *International review of industrial and organizational psychology* (Vol. 7, pp. 1–53). London: Wiley.

Kanfer, R. (2009). Work motivation: Identifying new use-inspired research directions. *Industrial and Organizational Psychology: Perspectives on Science and Practice, 2,* 77–93.

Kanfer, R., & Ackerman, P. L. (1989). Motivation and cognitive abilities: An integrative/aptitude–treatment interaction approach to skill acquisition. *Journal of Applied Psychology, 74,* 657–690.

Kanfer, R., & Heggestad, E. D. (1997). Motivational traits and skills: A person-centered approach to work motivation. In B. M. Staw & L. L. Cummings (Eds.), *Research in organizational behavior* (Vol. 19, pp. 1–56). Greenwich, CT: JAI Press.

Kanfer, R., Chan, G., & Pritchard, R. D. (2008). The three C's of work motivation: Content, context, and change. In R. Kanfer, G. Chen, & R. D. Pritchard (Eds.), *Work motivation: Past, present, and future* (pp. 1–16). New York: Routledge.

Kaplan, S., & Tetrick, L. E. (2011). Workplace safety and accidents: An industrial and organizational psychology perspective. In S. Zedeck (Ed.), *APA handbook of industrial and organizational psychology* (Vol. 1, pp. 455–472). Washington, DC: APA.

Kapp, K. M., & O'Driscoll, T. (2010). *Learning in 3D.* San Francisco: Pfeiffer.

Karau, S. J., & Williams, K. D. (2001). Understanding individual motivation in groups: The collective effort model. In M. E. Turner (Ed.), *Groups at work* (pp. 113–142). Mahwah, NJ: Erlbaum.

Katzell, R. A., & Austin, J. T. (1992). From then to now: The development of industrial-organizational psychology in the United States. *Journal of Applied Psychology, 77,* 803–835.

Kaufman, B. E. (2008). Work motivation: Insights from economics. In R. Kanfer, G. Chen, & R. D. Pritchard (Eds.), *Work motivation: Past, present, and future* (pp. 588–600). New York: Routledge.

Kavanagh, P., Benson, J., & Brown, M. (2007). Understanding performance appraisal fairness. *Asia Pacific Journal of Human Resources, 45*(2), 132–150.

Keeping, L. M., & Levy, P. E. (2000). Performance appraisal reaction: Measurement, modeling, and method bias. *Journal of Applied Psychology, 85,* 708–723.

Kehoe, J. F. (2002). General mental ability and selection in private sector organizations. A commentary. *Human Performance, 15,* 96–106.

Keith, N., & Frese, M. (2008). Effectiveness of error management training: A meta-analysis. *Journal of Applied Psychology, 93,* 59–69.

Kelloway, E. K., Catano, V. M., & Carroll, A. E. (1995). The nature of member participation in local union activities. In L. E. Tetrick & J. Barling (Eds.), *Changing employment relations* (pp. 333–348). Washington, DC: American Psychological Association.

Kelloway, E. K., Francis, L., Catano, V. M., & Dupre, K. E. (2008). Third-party support for strike actions. *Journal of Applied Psychology, 93,* 806–817.

Kerr, S. (1995). On the folly of rewarding A, while hoping for B. *Academy of Management Executive, 9,* 7–14.

Kerr, S., & Jermier, J. M. (1978). Substitutes for leadership: Their meaning and measurement. *Organizational Behavior and Human Performance, 22,* 375–403.

Khanna, C., Medsker, G. J., & Ginter, R. (2013). 2012 income and employment survey results for the Society for Industrial and Organizational Psychology. *The Industrial-Organizational Psychologist, 51*(1), 18–31.

Kidd, S. A. (2002). The role of qualitative research in psychological journals. *Psychological Methods, 7,* 126–138.

King, W. C., Miles, E. W., & Day, D. D. (1993). A test and refinement of the equity sensitivity construct. *Journal of Organizational Behavior, 14,* 301–317.

Kinicki, A. J., Jacobson, K. J. L., Peterson, S. J., & Prussia, G. E. (2013). Development and validation of the Performance Management Behavior Questionnaire. *Personnel Psychology, 66,* 1–45.

Kinicki, A. J., McKee-Ryan, F. M., Schriesheim, C. A., & Carson, K. P. (2002). Assessing the construct validity of the Job Descriptive Index: A review and meta-analysis. *Journal of Applied Psychology, 87,* 14–32.

Kinicki, A. J., Prussia, G. E., Wu, B., & McKee-Ryan, F. M. (2004). A covariance structure analysis of employees' response to performance feedback. *Journal of Applied Psychology, 89,* 1057–1069.

Kirkpatrick, D. L. (1976). Evaluation of training. In R. L. Craig (Ed.), *Training and development handbook: A guide to human resource development* (2nd ed., pp. 1–26). New York: McGraw Hill.

Kirkpatrick, S. A., & Locke, E. A. (1991). Leadership: Do traits matter? *Academy of Management Executive, 5*(2), 48–60.

Kish-Gephart, J. J., Harrison, D. A., & Trevino, L. K. (2010). Bad apples, bad cases, and bad barrels: Meta-analytic evidence about sources of unethical decisions at work. *Journal of Applied Psychology, 95,* 1–31.

Klaas, B. S. (1989). Managerial decision making about employee grievances: The impact of the grievant's work history. *Personnel Psychology, 42,* 53–68.

Klahr, D., & Simon, H. A. (1999). Studies of scientific discovery: Complementary approaches and convergent findings. *Psychological Bulletin, 125,* 524–543.

Klandermans, B. (1989). Union commitment: Replications and tests in the Dutch context. *Journal of Applied Psychology, 74,* 869–875.

Klehe, U.-C., & Anderson, N. (2007). Working hard and working smart: Motivation and ability during typical and maximum performance. *Journal of Applied Psychology, 92,* 978–992.

Klein, H. J. (2014). Distinguishing commitment bonds from other attachments in a target-free manner. In J. K. Ford, J. R. Hollenbeck, & A. M. Ryan (Eds.), *The nature of work* (pp. 117–146). Washington, DC: American Psychological Association.

Klein, H. J., Molloy, J. C., & Brinsfield, C. T. (2012). Reconceptualizing workplace commitment to redress a stretched construct: Revisiting assumptions and removing confounds. *Academy of Management Review, 37,* 130–151.

Klein, K. J., & Kozlowski, S. W. J. (2000). *Multilevel theory, research, and methods in organizations.* San Francisco: Jossey-Bass.

Klein, S. R., & Huffman, A. H. (2013). I-O psychology and environmental sustainability in organizations: A natural partnership. In A. H. Huffman & S. R. Klein (Eds.), *Green organizations: Driving change with I-O psychology* (pp. 3–16). New York: Routledge.

Klimoski, R. J., & Inks, L. (1990). Accountability forces in performance appraisal. *Organizational Behavior and Human Decision Processes, 45,* 194–208.

Klimoski, R. J., & Jones, R. G. (1995). Staffing for effective group decision making: Key issues in marketing people and teams. In R. A. Guzzo & E. Salas (Eds.), *Team effectiveness and decision making in organizations* (pp. 291–332). San Francisco: Jossey-Bass.

Klimoski, R. J., & Strickland, W. J. (1977). Assessment centers—Valid or merely prescient? *Personnel Psychology, 30,* 353–361.

Kluger, A. N. (2001). Feedback-expectation discrepancy, arousal and locus of cognition. In M. Erez, U. Kleinbeck, & H. Thierry (Eds.), *Work motivation in the context of a globalizing economy* (pp. 111–120). Mahwah, NJ: Erlbaum.

Kluger, A. N., & DeNisi, A. (1996). The effects of feedback interventions on performance: A historical review, a meta-analysis, and a preliminary feedback intervention theory. *Psychological Bulletin, 119,* 254–284.

Kluger, A. N., Reilly, R. R., & Russell, C. J. (1991). Faking biodata tests: Are option-keyed instruments more resistant? *Journal of Applied Psychology, 76,* 889–896.

Knauth, P. (1996). Designing better shift systems. *Applied Ergonomics, 27,* 39–44.

Kolmstetter, E. (2003). I-O's making an impact: TSA transportation security screener skill standards, selection system, and hiring process. *The Industrial-Organizational Psychologist, 40*(4), 39–46.

Komaki, J. L. (1986). Toward effective supervision: An operant analysis and comparison of managers at work. *Journal of Applied Psychology, 71,* 270–279.

Komaki, J. L. (1998). When performance improvement is the goal: A new set of criteria for criteria. *Journal of Applied Behavior Analysis, 31,* 263–280.

Komar, S., Brown, D. J., Komar, J. A., & Robie, C. (2008). Faking and the validity of conscientiousness: A Monte Carlo investigation. *Journal of Applied Psychology, 93,* 140–154.

Koppes, L. L. (1997). American female pioneers of industrial and organizational psychology during the early years. *Journal of Applied Psychology, 82,* 500–515.

Koppes, L. L. (2002). The rise of industrial-organizational psychology: A confluence of dynamic forces. In D. K. Freedheim (Ed.), *History of psychology* (pp. 367–389). New York: Wiley.

Koppes, L. L. (Ed.) (2007). *Historical perspectives in industrial and organizational psychology.* Mahwah, NJ: Erlbaum.

Koppes, L. L., & Pickren, W. (2007). Industrial and organizational psychology: An evolving science and practice. In L. L. Koppes (Ed.), *Historical perspectives in industrial and organizational psychology* (pp. 3–35). Mahwah, NJ: Erlbaum.

Kornhauser, A. W. (1965). *Mental health of the industrial worker: A Detroit study.* New York: Wiley.

Kossek, F. R., & Michel, J. S. (2011). Flexible work schedules. In S. Zedeck (Ed.), *APA handbook of industrial and organizational psychology* (Vol. 1, pp. 535–572). Washington, DC: APA.

Kotter, J. P. (1988). *The leadership factor.* New York: Free Press.

Kozlowski, S. W. J., & Bell, B. S. (2003). Work groups and teams in organizations. In W. C. Borman, D. R. Ilgen, & R. J. Klimoski (Eds.), *Handbook of psychology* (Vol. 12): *Industrial and organizational psychology* (pp. 333–375). Hoboken, NJ: Wiley.

Kozlowski, S. W. J., & Chao, G. T. (2012). The dynamics of emergence: Cognition and cohesion in work teams. *Managerial and Decision Economics, 33,* 335–354.

Kozlowski, S. W. J., & Ilgen, D. (2006). Enhancing the effectiveness of work groups and teams. *Psychological Science in the Public Interest, 7,* 77–124.

Kozlowski, S. W. J., Chao, G. T., & Morrison, R. F. (1998). Games raters play: Politics, strategies, and impression management in performance appraisal. In J. W. Smither (Ed.), *Performance appraisal* (pp. 163–208). San Francisco: Jossey-Bass.

Kozlowski, S. W. J., Watola, D. J., Jensen, J. M., Kim, B. H., & Botero, I. C. (2009). Developing adaptive teams: A theory of dynamic team leadership. In E. Salas, G. F. Goodwin, & C. S. Burke (Eds.), *Team effectiveness in complex organizations: Foundations, extensions, and new directions* (pp. 113–155). San Francisco: Jossey-Bass.

Kraiger, K. (2008). Transforming our models of learning and development: Web-based instruction as enabler of third-generation instruction. *Industrial and Organizational Psychology, 1,* 454–467.

Kraiger, K., & Culbertson, S. S. (2013). Understanding and facilitating learning: Advancements in training and development. In N. Schmitt, & S. Highhouse (Eds.), *Handbook of psychology* (Vol. 12): *Industrial and organizational psychology* (pp. 244–261). New York: John Wiley & Sons.

Kraiger, K., & Jung, K. M. (1997). Linking training objectives to evaluation criteria. In M. A. Quiñones & A. Ehrenstein (Eds.), *Training for a rapidly changing workplace* (pp. 151–176). Washington, DC: American Psychological Association.

Kram, K. E. (1985). *Mentoring at work.* Glenview, IL: Scott Foresman.

Krapohl, D. J. (2002). The polygraph in personnel screening. In M. Kleiner (Ed.), *Handbook of polygraph testing* (pp. 217–236). San Diego: Academic Press.

Kraut, A. I. (2010). Foreword. In K. Lundby (Ed.), *Going global* (pp. xi-xiii). San Francisco: Jossey-Bass.

Kravitz, D. A., & Klineberg, S. L. (2000). Reactions to two versions of affirmative action among Whites, Blacks, and Hispanics. *Journal of Applied Psychology, 85,* 597–611.

Kreiner, G. E., Ashforth, B. E., & Sluss, D. M. (2006). Identity dynamics in occupational dirty work: Integrating social identity and system justification perspectives. *Organization Science, 17,* 619–636.

Kristof-Brown, A. L., & Billsberry J. (2013). Fit for the future. In A. L. Kristof-Brown & J. Billsberry (Eds.), *Organizational fit: Key issues and new directions* (pp. 1–18). Malden, MA: Wiley.

Kruger, J., & Evans, M. (2004). If you don't want to be late, enumerate: Unpacking reduces the planning fallacy. *Journal of Experimental Social Psychology, 40,* 586–598.

Kuncel, N. R., & Sackett, P. R. (2014). Resolving the assessment center validity problem (as we know it). *Journal of Applied Psychology, 99,* 38–47.

Kuo, T. H., & Ho, L. A. (2010). Individual difference and job performance: The relationships among personal factors, job characteristics, flow experience, and service quality. *Social Behavior and Personality, 38,* 531–552.

Lam, S. S., Hui, C., & Law, K. S. (1999). Organizational citizenship behavior: Comparing perspectives of supervisors and subordinates across four international samples. *Journal of Applied Psychology, 84,* 594–601.

Landers, R. N., Sackett, P. R., & Tuzinski, K. A. (2011). Retesting after initial failure, coaching rumors, and warnings against faking in online personality measures for selection. *Journal of Applied Psychology, 96,* 202–210.

Landy, F. J. (1992). Hugo Münsterberg: Victim or visionary? *Journal of Applied Psychology, 77,* 787–802.

Landy, F. J. (1997). Early influences on the development of industrial and organizational psychology. *Journal of Applied Psychology, 82,* 467–477.

Landy, F. J., & Vasey, J. (1991). Job analysis: The composition of SME samples. *Personnel Psychology, 44,* 27–50.

Larson, C. E., & La Fasto, F. M. (1989). *Teamwork.* Newbury Park, CA: Sage.

Lasswell, H. (1936). *Politics: Who gets what, when, how?* New York: Whittlesey.

Latham, G. P. (1986). Job performance and appraisal. In C. L. Cooper & I. T. Robertson (Eds.), *International review of industrial and organizational psychology* (Vol. 1, pp. 117–155). London: Wiley.

Latham, G. P., & Kinne, S. B. (1974). Improving job performance through training in goal setting. *Journal of Applied Psychology, 59,* 187–191.

Latham, G. P., & Locke, E. A. (1991). Self-regulation through goal-setting. *Organizational Behavior and Human Decision Processes, 50,* 212–247.

Lawler, E. E. (2007). Why HR practices are not evidence-based. *Academy of Management Journal, 50,* 1033–1036.

Lazarus, R. S., & Lazarus, B. N. (1994). *Passion and reason: Making sense of our emotions.* New York: Oxford.

LearnStuff (2012). Social media at work. Retrieved August 12, 2014, from http://www.learnstuff.com/social-media-at-work/

Lee, N., Senior, C., & Butler, M. J. (2012). The domain of organizational cognitive neuroscience: Theoretical and empirical challenges. *Journal of Management, 38,* 921–931.

Lee, T. W., Mitchell, J. R., & Harman, W. S. (2011). Qualitative research strategies in industrial and organizational psychology. In S. Zedeck (Ed.), *APA handbook of industrial and organizational psychology* (Vol. 1, pp. 73–83). Washington, DC: APA.

Lefkowitz, J. (2003). *Ethics and values in industrial-organizational psychology.* Mahwah, NJ: Erlbaum.

Lefkowitz, J. (2012). From humanitarian to humanistic work psychology. In S. C. Carr, M. MacLachlan, & A. Furnham (Eds.), *Humanitarian work psychology* (pp. 103–125). New York: Palgrave Macmillan.

LePine, J. A. (2003). Team adaptation and postchange performance: Effects of team composition in terms of members' cognitive ability and personality. *Journal of Applied Psychology, 88,* 27–39.

LePine, J. A., Colquitt, J. A., & Erez, A. (2000). Adaptability to changing task contexts: Effects of general cognitive ability, conscientiousness, and openness to experience. *Personnel Psychology, 53,* 563–593.

LePine, J. A., Erez, A., & Johnson, D. E. (2002). The nature and dimensionality of organizational citizenship behavior: A critical review and meta-analysis. *Journal of Applied Psychology, 87,* 52–65.

LePine, J. A., Hanson, M. A., Borman, W. C., & Motowidlo, S. J. (2000). Contextual performance and teamwork: Implications for staffing. In G. R. Ferris (Ed.), *Research in personnel and human resources management* (Vol. 19, pp. 53–90). New York: Elsevier.

LePine, J. A., Piccolo, R. F., Jackson, C. L., Mathieu, J. E., & Saul, J. R. (2008). A meta-analysis of teamwork processes: Tests of a multidimensional model and relationships with team effectiveness criteria. *Personnel Psychology, 61,* 273–307.

LePine, J. A., Podsakoff, N. P., & LePine, M. A. (2005). A meta-analytic test of the challenge stressor-hindrance stressor framework: An explanation for inconsistent relationships among stressors and performance. *Academy of Management Journal, 48,* 764–775.

Lerner, J. S., & Keltner, D. (2000). Beyond valence: Toward a model of emotion-specific influences on judgment and choice. *Cognition and Emotion, 14,* 473–493.

Lerner, J. S., Li, Y., & Weber, E. U. (2013). The financial costs of sadness. *Psychological Science, 24,* 72–79.

Levashina, J., Hartwell, C. J., Morgeson, F. P., & Campion, M. A. (2014). The structured employment interview: Narrative and quantitative review of the research literature. *Personnel Psychology, 67,* 241–293.

Levashina, J., Morgeson, F. P., & Campion, M. A. (2012). Tell me some more: Exploring how verbal ability and item verifiability influence responses to biodata questions in a high-stakes selection context. *Personnel Psychology, 65,* 359–383.

Leventhal, G. S. (1980). What should be done with equity theory? New approaches to the study of fairness in social relationships. In K. Gergen, M. Greenberg, & R. Willis (Eds.), *Social exchange: Advances in theory and research* (pp. 27–55). New York: Plenum Press.

Levine, E. L., & Sanchez, J. I. (2012). Evaluating work analysis in the 21st century. In M. A. Wilson, W. Bennett, S. G. Gibson, & G. M. Alliger (Eds.), *The handbook of work analysis* (pp. 127–138). New York: Routledge.

Levine, E. L., Ash, R. A., & Levine, J. D. (2004). Judgmental assessment of job-related experience, training, and education for use in human resource staffing. In J. C. Thomas (Ed.), *Comprehensive handbook of psychological assessment* (Vol. 4, pp. 269–296). Hoboken, NJ: Wiley.

Levine, J. D., & Oswald, F. L. (2012). O*NET: The Occupational Information Network. In M. A. Wilson, W. Bennett, S. G. Gibson, & G. M. Alliger (Eds.), *The handbook of work analysis* (pp. 281–301). New York: Routledge.

Levitt, S. D., & Dubner, S. J. (2005). *Freakonomics: A rogue economist explores the hidden side of everything.* London: Allen Lane.

Lichtenstein, N. (2013). *State of the union: A century of American labor* (revised ed.). Princeton, NJ: Princeton University Press.

Liden, R. C., Sparrowe, R. T., & Wayne, S. J. (1997). Leader–member exchange theory: The past and potential for the future. In G. R. Ferris (Ed.), *Research in personnel and human resources management* (Vol. 15, pp. 47–120). Greenwich, CT: JAI Press.

Liden, R. C., Wayne, S. J., Zhao, H., & Henderson, D. (2008). Servant leadership: Development of a multidimensional measure and multi-level assessment. *The Leadership Quarterly, 19,* 161–177.

Lievens, F., & Chan, D. (2010). Practical intelligence, emotional intelligence, and social intelligence. In J. L. Farr & N. T. Tippins (Eds.), *Handbook of employee selection* (pp. 339–355). New York: Routledge.

Lievens, F., & Klimoski, R. J. (2001). Understanding the assessment centre process: Where are we now? In C. L. Cooper & I. T. Robertson (Eds.), *International review of industrial and organizational psychology* (Vol. 16, pp. 245–286). West Sussex, England: Wiley.

Lievens, F., & Patterson, F. (2011). The validity and incremental validity of knowledge tests, low-fidelity simulations, and high-fidelity simulations for predicting job performance in advanced-level high-stakes selection. *Journal of Applied Psychology, 96,* 927–940.

Lievens, F., & Sackett, P. R. (2012). The validity of interpersonal skills assessment via situational judgment tests for predicting academic success and job performance. *Journal of Applied Psychology, 97*, 460–468.

Lievens, F., Sanchez, J. I., Bartram, D., & Brown, A. (2010). Lack of consensus among competence ratings of the same occupations: Noise or substance? *Journal of Applied Psychology, 95*, 562–571.

Lilienfeld, S. O. (2012). Public skepticism of psychology. *American Psychologist, 67*, 111–129.

Lindsey, A., King, E., McCausland, T., Jones, K., & Dunleavy, E. (2013). What we know and don't: Eradicating employment discrimination 50 years after the Civil Rights Act. *Industrial and Organizational Psychology, 6*, 391–413.

Liu, Y., Ferris, G. R., Treadway, D. C., Prati, M. L., Perrewé, P. L., & Hochwarter, W. A. (2006). The emotion of politics and the politics of emotions. In E. Vigoda-Gadot & A. Drory (Eds.), *Handbook of organizational politics* (pp. 161–186). Cheltenham, UK: Edward Elgar.

Livingston, B. A., & Judge, T. A. (2008). Emotional responses to work-family conflict: An examination of gender role orientation among working women. *Journal of Applied Psychology, 93*, 207–216.

Locke, E. A. (1991). The motivation sequence, the motivation hub, and the motivation core. *Organizational Behavior and Human Decision Processes, 50*, 288–299.

Locke, E. A. (2005). Why emotional intelligence is an invalid concept. *Journal of Organizational Behavior, 26*, 425–431.

Locke, E. A., & Latham, G. P. (1990). *A theory of goal setting and task performance.* Englewood Cliffs, NJ: Prentice Hall.

Locke, E. A., & Latham, G. P. (2002). Building a practically useful theory of goal setting and task motivation: A 35-year odyssey. *American Psychologist, 57,* 705–717.

Locke, E. A., Jirnauer, D., Roberson, Q., Goldman, B., Latham, M. E., & Weldon, E. (2001). The importance of the individual in an age of groupism. In M. E. Turner (Ed.), *Groups at work* (pp. 501–528). Mahwah, NJ: Erlbaum.

Locke, K., & Golden-Biddle, K. (2002). An introduction to qualitative research: Its potential for industrial and organizational psychology. In S. G. Rogelberg (Ed.), *Handbook of research methods in industrial and organizational psychology* (pp. 99–118). Malden, MA: Blackwell.

Lombardo, M. M., & McCauley, C. D. (1988). *The dynamics of management derailment* (Tech. Report No. 134). Greensboro, NC: Center for Creative Leadership.

Lombardo, T., Schneider, S., & Bryan, L. K. (2013). Corporate leaders of sustainable organizations: Balancing profit, planet, and people. In J. Olson-Buchanon, L. K. Bryan, & L. F. Thompson (Eds.), *Using industrial-organizational psychology for the greater good: Helping those who help others* (pp. 75–109). New York: Routledge.

London, M., & Smither, J. W. (2002). Feedback orientation, feedback culture, and the longitudinal performance management process. *Human Resource Management Review, 12*, 81–100.

Lopina, E. C., Rogelberg, S. G., & Howell, B. (2012). Turnover in dirty work occupations: A focus on pre-entry individual characteristics. *Journal of Occupational and Organizational Psychology, 85*, 396–406.

Lord, R. G., & Brown, D. L. (2004). *Leadership processes and follower self-identity.* Mahwah, NJ: Erlbaum.

Lord, R. G., & Levy, P. E. (1994). Moving from cognition to action: A control theory perspective. *Applied Psychology: An International Review, 43,* 335–367.

Lord, R. G., Foti, R. J., & Phillips, J. S. (1982). A theory of leadership categorization. In J. G. Hunt, U. Sekaran, & C. Schriesheim (Eds.), *Leadership: Beyond establishment views* (pp. 104–121). Carbondale, IL: Southern Illinois University Press.

Lowe, K. B., & Gardner, W. L. (2000). Ten years of *The Leadership Quarterly*: Contributions and challenges for the future. *The Leadership Quarterly, 11,* 459–514.

Lowman, R. L. (2013). Is sustainability an ethical responsibility of I/O and consulting psychologists? In A. H. Huffman & S. R. Klein (Eds.), *Green organizations: Driving change with I-O psychology* (pp. 34–54). New York: Routledge.

Lubinski, D., & Dawis, R. V. (1992). Aptitudes, skills, and proficiencies. In M. D. Dunnette & L. M. Hough (Eds.), *Handbook of industrial and organizational psychology* (2nd ed., Vol. 3, pp. 1–59). Palo Alto, CA: Consulting Psychologists Press.

Luciano, M. M., Mathieu, J. E., & Ruddy, T. M. (2014). Leading multiple teams: Average and relative external leadership influences on team empowerment and effectiveness. *Journal of Applied Psychology, 99*, 322–331.

Luhmann, M., Weiss, P., Hosoya, G., & Eid, M. (2014). Honey, I got fired! A longitudinal dyadic analysis of the effect of unemployment on life satisfaction in couples. *Journal of Personality and Social Psychology, 107*, 163–180.

Luria, G., & Kalish, Y. (2013). A social network approach to peer assessment: Improving predictive validity. *Human Resource Management, 52*, 537–560.

Luthans, F. (2002). The need for and meaning of positive organization behavior. *Journal of Organization Behavior, 23*, 695–706.

Luthans, F., Youssef, C. M., & Avolio, B. J. (2007). *Psychological capital: Developing the human competitive edge.* New York, NY: Oxford University Press.

Lyness, K. S. (2002). Finding the key to the executive suite: Challenges for women and people of color. In R. Silzer (Ed.), *The 21st century executive* (pp. 229–273). San Francisco: Jossey-Bass.

Lyness, K. S., & Heilman, M. E. (2006). When fit is fundamental: Performance evaluations and promotions of upper-level female and male managers. *Journal of Applied Psychology, 91*, 777–785.

MacDermid, S. M., Seery, B. L., & Weiss, H. M. (2002). An emotional examination of the work-family interface. In R. G. Lord, R. J. Klimoski, & R. Kanfer (Eds.), *Emotions in the workplace* (pp. 402–427). San Francisco: Jossey-Bass.

Macey, B. (2002). The licensing of I-O psychologists. *The Industrial-Organizational Psychologist, 39*(3), 11–13.

Macey, W. H., & Schneider, B. (2008). The meaning of employee engagement. *Industrial and Organizational Psychology: Perspectives on Science and Practice, 1*, 3–30.

Macey, W. H., Schneider, B., Bandera, K. M., & Young, S. A. (2009). *Employee engagement.* Malden, MA: Wiley-Blackwell.

Machin, M. A. (2002). Planning, managing, and optimizing transfer of training. In K. Kraiger (Ed.), *Creating, implementing, and managing effective training and development* (pp. 263–301). San Francisco: Jossey-Bass.

MacKenzie, S. B., Podsakoff, P. M., & Rich, G. A. (2001). Transformational and transactional leadership and salesperson performance. *Journal of the Academy of Marketing Science, 29*, 115–134.

Madera, J. M., Hebl, M. R., & Martin, R. C. (2009). Gender and letters of recommendation for academia: Agentic and communal differences. *Journal of Applied Psychology, 94*, 1591–1599.

Madill, A., & Gough, B. (2008). Qualitative research and its place in psychological science. *Psychological Methods, 13*, 254–271.

Mael, F. A. (1991). A conceptual rationale for the domain and attributes of biodata items. *Personnel Psychology, 44*, 763–792.

Mael, F. A., Connerly, M., & Morath, R. A. (1996). None of your business: Parameters of biodata invasiveness. *Personnel Psychology, 49*, 613–650.

Mainiero, L. A., & Jones, K. J. (2013). Sexual harassment versus workplace romance: Social media spillover and textual harassment in the workplace. *Academy of Management Perspectives, 27*, 187–203.

Major, D. A., & Germano, L. M. (2006). The changing nature of work and its impact on the work-home interface. In F. Jones, R.J. Burke, & M. Westman (Eds.), *Work-life balance: A psychological perspective* (pp. 13–38). Hove, UK: Taylor & Francis.

Malos, S. B. (1998). Current legal issues in performance appraisal. In J. W. Smither (Ed.), *Performance appraisal* (pp. 49–94). San Francisco: Jossey-Bass.

Manz, C. C. (1986). Self-leadership: Toward an expanded theory of self-influence. *Academy of Management Review, 11*, 585–600.

Marchant, G., & Robinson, J. (1999). Is knowing the tax code all it takes to be a tax expert? On the development of legal expertise. In R. J. Sternberg & J. A. Howath (Eds.), *Tacit knowledge in professional practice* (pp. 3–20). Mahwah, NJ: Erlbaum.

Margenau, J. M., Martin, J. E., & Peterson, M. M. (1988). Dual and unilateral commitment among stewards and rank-and-file union members. *Academy of Management Journal, 31*, 359–376.

Marks, M. A., Mathieu, J. E., & Zaccaro, S. J. (2001). A temporally based framework and taxonomy of team processes. *Academy of Management Review, 26*, 356–376.

Marks, M. A., Sabella, M. J., Burke, C. S., & Zaccaro, S. J. (2002). The impact of cross-training on team effectiveness. *Journal of Applied Psychology, 87*, 3–13.

Marks, M. A., Zaccaro, S. J., & Mathieu, J. E. (2000). Performance implications of leader briefings and team-interaction training for team adaptation to novel environments. *Journal of Applied Psychology, 85,* 971–986.

Marks, M. L. (2002). Mergers and acquisitions. In J. W. Hedge & E. D. Pulakos (Eds.), *Implementing organizational interventions: Steps, processes, and best practices* (pp. 43–77). San Francisco: Jossey-Bass.

Marlatt, G. A., & Witkiewitz, K. (2010). Update on harm-reduction policy and intervention research. *Annual Review of Clinical Psychology, 6*, 591–606.

Marlatt, G. A., Baer, J. S., & Quigley, L. A. (1995). Self-efficacy and addictive behavior. In A. Bandura (Ed.), *Self-efficacy in changing societies* (pp. 289–315). New York: Cambridge.

Marler, L. E., McKee, D., Cox, S., Simmering, M., & Allen, D. (2012). Don't make me the bad guy: Self-monitoring, organizational norms, and the Mum Effect. *Journal of Managerial Issues, 24*, 97–116.

Marquardt, M. (2002). Around the world: Organization development in the international context. In J. Waclawski & A. H. Church (Eds.), *Organization development: A data-driven approach to organizational change* (pp. 266–285). San Francisco: Jossey-Bass.

Martin, B. O., Kolomitro, K., & Lam, T. C. M. (2014). Training methods: A review and analysis. *Human Resource Development Review, 13*, 11–35.

Martin, R., Epitropaki, O., Thomas, G., & Topakas, A. (2010). A review of leader-member exchange research: Future prospects and directions. In G. P. Hodgkinson &

J. L. Ford (Eds.), *International review of industrial and organizational psychology* (Vol. 25, pp. 35–88). Chichester, UK: Wiley-Blackwell.

Martin, S. L., & Terris, W. (1991). Predicting infrequent behavior: Clarifying the impact on false-positive rates. *Journal of Applied Psychology, 76,* 484–487.

Martins, L. L. (2011). Organizational change and development. In S. Zedeck (Ed.), *APA handbook of industrial and organizational psychology* (Vol. 3, pp. 691–728). Washington, DC: APA.

Martocchio, J. J., & Harrison, D. A. (1993). To be there or not to be there: Questions, theories, and methods in absenteeism research. In G. R. Ferris (Ed.), *Research in personnel and human resources management* (Vol. 11, pp. 259–329). Greenwich, CT: JAI Press.

Maslach, C., Schaufeli, W. B., & Leiter, M. P. (2001). Job burnout. *Annual Review of Psychology, 52,* 397–422.

Mateer, F. (1917). The moron as a war problem. *Journal of Applied Psychology, 1,* 317–320.

Mathieu, J. E., Marks, M. A., & Zaccaro, S. J. (2001). Multi-team systems. In N. Anderson, D. S. Ones, H. K. Sinangil, & C. Viswesvaran (Eds.), *Handbook of industrial, work, & organizational psychology* (Vol. 2, pp. 289–313). London: Sage.

Maurer, T. J., & Solamon, J. M. (2006). The science and practice of a structured employment interview coaching program. *Personnel Psychology, 59,* 433–456.

Maxwell, J. A. (1998). Designing a qualitative study. In L. Bickman & D. J. Rog (Eds.), *Handbook of applied social research methods* (pp. 69–100). Thousand Oaks, CA: Sage.

May, D. R., Chan, A. Y. L., Hodges, T. D., & Avolio, B. J. (2003). Developing the moral component of authentic leadership. *Organizational Dynamics, 32,* 247–260.

Mayer, J. D., Salovey, P., & Caruso, D. R. (2002). *Mayer-Salovey-Caruso Emotional Intelligence Test (MSCEIT)* User's manual. Toronto: MHS Publishers.

Mayer, J. D., Salovey, P., & Caruso, D. R. (2008). Emotional intelligence: New ability or eclectic traits? *American Psychologist, 63,* 503–517.

McCall, M. W., & Bobko, P. (1990). Research methods in the service of discovery. In M. D. Dunnette & L. M. Hough (Eds.), *Handbook of industrial and organizational psychology* (2nd ed., Vol. 1, pp. 381–418). Palo Alto, CA: Consulting Psychologists Press.

McCarthy, J. M., Van Iddekinge, C. H., Lievens, F., Kung, M.-C., Sinar, E. F., & Campion, M. A. (2013). Do candidate reactions relate to job performance or affect criterion-related validity? A multi-study investigation of relations among reactions, selection, test scores, and job performance. *Journal of Applied Psychology, 98,* 701–719.

McClelland, D. C., & Boyatzis, R. E. (1982). Leadership motive pattern and long term success in management. *Journal of Applied Psychology, 67,* 737–743.

McCormick, E. J., & Jeanneret, P. R. (1988). Position Analysis Questionnaire (PAQ). In S. Gael (Ed.), *The job analysis handbook for business, industry, and government* (Vol. 2, pp. 825–842). New York: Wiley.

McCrae, R. R., & Costa, P. T. (1987). Validation of the five-factor model of personality across instruments and observers. *Journal of Personality & Social Psychology, 56,* 586–595.

McCrae, R. R., & Costa, P. T. (1997). Personality trait structure as a human universal. *American Psychologist, 52,* 509–516.

McDaniel, M. A., Hartman, N. S., Whetzel, D. L., & Grubb, W. L., III. (2007). Situational judgment tests, response instructions, and validity: A meta-analysis. *Personnel Psychology, 60,* 63–91.

McDaniel, M. A., Kepes, S., & Banks, G. C. (2011). The *Uniform Guidelines* are a detriment to the field of personnel selection. *Industrial and Organizational Psychology, 4,* 494–514.

McDaniel, M. A., Morgeson, F. P., Finnegan, E. B., Campion, M. A., & Brauerman, E. P. (2001). Use of situational judgment tests to predict job performance: A clarification of the literature. *Journal of Applied Psychology, 86,* 730–740.

McDaniel, M. A., Rothstein, H. R., & Whetzel, D. L. (2006). Publication bias: A case study of four test vendors. *Personnel Psychology, 59,* 927–953.

McDaniel, M. A., Whetzel, D. L., Schmidt, F. L., & Maurer, S. D. (1994). The validity of employment interviews: A comprehensive review and meta-analysis. *Journal of Applied Psychology, 79,* 599–616.

McFarland, L. A. (2013). Applicant reactions to personality tests: Why do applicants hate them? In N. D. Christiansen & R. P. Tett (Eds.), *Handbook of personality at work* (pp. 281–298). New York: Routledge.

McGrath, R. E., Mitchell, M., Kim, B. H., & Hough, L. (2010). Evidence for response bias as a source of error variance in applied settings. *Psychological Bulletin, 136,* 450–470.

McIntyre, R. M., & Salas, E. (1995). Measuring and managing for team performance: Lessons from complex environments. In R. A. Guzzo & E. Salas (Eds.), *Team effectiveness and decision making in organizations* (pp. 9–45). San Francisco: Jossey-Bass.

McKee-Ryan, F. M., Song, Z., Wanberg, C. R., & Kinicki, A. J. (2005). Psychological and physical well-being during unemployment: A meta-analytic study. *Journal of Applied Psychology, 90,* 53–76.

McManus, M. A., & Brown, S. H. (1995). Adjusting sales results measures for use as criteria. *Personnel Psychology, 48,* 391–400.

McNall, L. A., Nicklin, J. M., & Masuda, A. D. (2010). A meta-analytic review of the consequences associated with work-family enrichment. *Journal of Business Psychology, 25,* 381–396.

McNeely, B. L., & Meglino, B. M. (1994). The role of dispositional and situational antecedents in prosocial organizational behavior: An examination of the intended beneficiaries of prosocial behavior. *Journal of Applied Psychology, 79,* 836–844.

Meindl, J. R., & Ehrlich, S. B. (1987). The romance of leadership and the evaluation of organizational performance. *Academy of Management Journal, 30,* 91–109.

Mellor, S. (1990). The relationship between membership decline and union commitment: A field study of local unions in crisis. *Journal of Applied Psychology, 75,* 258–267.

Mero, N. P., Guidice, R. M., & Brownlee, A. L. (2007). Accountability in a performance appraisal context: The effect of audience and form of accounting on rater response and behavior. *Journal of Management, 33,* 223–252.

Meyer, H. H. (1980). Self-appraisal of job performance. *Personnel Psychology, 33,* 291–296.

Meyer, H. H., Kay, E., & French, J. R. P., Jr. (1965). Split roles in performance appraisal. *Harvard Business Review, 43,* 123–129.

Meyer, J. P. (1997). Organizational commitment. In C. L. Cooper & I. T. Robertson (Eds.), *International review of industrial and organizational psychology* (Vol. 12, pp. 175–228). Chichester, England: Wiley.

Meyer, J. P. (2009). Commitment in a changing world of work. In H. J. Klein, T. E. Becker, & J. P. Meyer (Eds.), *Commitment in organizations* (pp. 37–68). New York: Routledge.

Michel, J. S., Clark, M. A., & Jaramillo, D. (2011). The role of the Five Factor model of personality in the perceptions of negative and positive forms of work-nonwork spillover: A meta-analytic review. *Journal of Vocational Behavior, 79,* 191–203.

Mills, M. J. (2012). The beginnings of industrial psychology: The life and work of Morris Viteles. *The Industrial-Organizational Psychologist, 49*(3), 39–44.

Mills, M. J., Culbertson, S. S., & Fullagar, C. J. (2012). Conceptualizing and measuring engagement: An analysis of the Utrecht Work Engagement Scale. *Journal of Happiness Studies, 13,* 519–545.

Mintzberg, H. (1979). *Structuring of organizations.* Upper Saddle River, NJ: Pearson Education.

Mintzberg, H. (1989). *Mintzberg on management: Inside our strange world of organizations.* New York: Free Press.

Mintzberg, H. (2008). *Structure in sevens.* Upper Saddle River, NJ: Prentice-Hall.

Mitchell, J. L., & McCormick, E. J. (1990). *Professional and managerial position questionnaire.* Logan, UT: PAQ Services.

Mitchell, T. R. (1997). Matching motivational strategies with organizational contexts. In B. M. Staw & L. L. Cummings (Eds.), *Research in organizational behavior* (Vol. 19, pp. 57–149). Greenwich, CT: JAI Press.

Mitchell, T. R., & Daniels, D. (2003). Motivation. In W. C. Borman, D. R. Ilgen, & R. J. Klimoski (Eds.), *Handbook of psychology* (Vol. 12): *Industrial and organizational psychology* (pp. 225–254). Hoboken, NJ: Wiley.

Mitchell, T. R., Harman, W. S., Lee, T. W., & Lee, D.-Y. (2008). Self-regulation and multiple deadline goals. In R. Kanfer, G. Chen, & R. D. Pritchard (Eds.), *Work motivation: Past, present, and future* (pp. 197–231). New York: Routledge/Taylor Francis.

Mohammed, S., Ferzandi, L., & Hamilton, K. (2010). Metaphor no more: A 15-year review of the team mental model construct. *Journal of Management, 36,* 876–910.

Molloy, J. C., & Noe, R. A. (2010). "Learning" a living: Continuous learning for survival in today's talent market. In S. W. J. Kozlowski & E. Salas (Eds.), *Learning, training, and development in organizations* (pp. 333–362). New York: Routledge.

Mone, E. M., & London, M. (2010). *Employee engagement through effective performance management.* New York: Routledge.

Monk, T. H., Folkard, S., & Wedderburn, A. I. (1996). Maintaining safety and high performance on shiftwork. *Applied Ergonomics, 27,* 17–23.

Montes, S. D., & Zweig, D. (2009). Do promises matter? An exploration of the role of promises in psychological contract breach. *Journal of Applied Psychology, 94,* 1243–1260.

Moon, H., Choi, B., & Jung, J. (2012). Previous international experience, cross-cultural training, and expatriates' cross-cultural adjustment: Effects of cultural intelligence and goal orientation. *Human Resource Development Quarterly, 23,* 285–330.

Moore, D. A. (1994). Company alcohol policies: Practicalities and problems. In C. L. Cooper & S. Williams (Eds.), *Creating healthy work organizations* (pp. 75–96). Chichester, England: Wiley.

Moorman, R. H. (1991). Relationship between organizational justice and organizational citizenship behaviors: Do fairness perceptions influence employee citizenship? *Journal of Applied Psychology, 76,* 845–855.

Moreland, R. L., & Levine, J. M. (2001). Socialization in organizations and work groups. In M. E. Turner (Ed.), *Groups at work* (pp. 69–112). Mahwah, NJ: Erlbaum.

Morgan, G. (1997). *Images of organizations.* Thousand Oaks, CA: Sage.

Morganson, V. J., Culbertson, S. S., & Matthews, R. A. (2013). Individual strategies for navigating the work-life interface. In D. Major & R. Burke (Eds.), *Handbook of work-life integration among professionals: Challenges and opportunities* (pp. 205–224). Cheltenham, UK: Edward Elgar.

Morgeson, F. P., & Campion, M. A. (1997). Social and cognitive sources of potential inaccuracy in job analysis. *Journal of Applied Psychology, 82,* 627–655.

Morgeson, F. P., & Dierdorff, E. C. (2011). Work analysis: From technique to theory. In S. Zedeck (Ed.), *APA handbook of industrial and organizational psychology* (Vol. 2, pp. 3–41). Washington, DC: APA.

Morgeson, F. P., & Humphrey, S. E. (2006). The work design questionnaire (WDQ): Developing and validating a comprehensive measure for assessing job design and the nature of work. *Journal of Applied Psychology, 91,* 1321–1339.

Morgeson, F. P., Campion, M. A., Dipboye, R. L., Hollenbeck, J. R., Murphy, K., & Schmitt, N. (2007). Reconsidering the use of personality tests in personnel selection contexts. *Personnel Psychology, 60,* 683–729.

Morgeson, F. P., DeRue, D. S., & Karam, E. P. (2010). Leadership in teams: A functional approach to understanding leadership structures and processes. *Journal of Management, 36,* 5–39.

Mosing, M. A., Magnusson, P. K. E., Pedersen, N. L., Nakamura, J., Madison, G., & Ullén, F. (2012). Heritability of proneness for psychological flow experiences. *Personality and Individual Differences, 53,* 699–704.

Mosley, E. (2013). *The crowdsourced performance review: How to use the power of social recognition to transform employee performance.* New York: McGraw-Hill.

Motowidlo, S. J., Hanson, M. A., & Crafts, J. L. (1997). Low-fidelity simulations. In D. L. Whetzel & G. R. Wheaton (Eds.), *Applied measurement methods in industrial psychology* (pp. 241–260). Palo Alto, CA: Consulting Psychologists Press.

Mount, M. K. (1984). Psychometric properties of subordinate ratings of managerial performance. *Personnel Psychology, 37,* 687–702.

Muchinsky, P. M. (1977). A comparison of within- and across-subjects analyses of the expectancy-valence model for predicting effort. *Academy of Management Journal, 20,* 154–158.

Muchinsky, P. M. (2000). Emotions in the workplace: The neglect of organizational behavior. *Journal of Organizational Behavior, 21,* 801–805.

Muchinsky, P. M. (2004). Mechanical aptitude and spatial ability testing. In J. C. Thomas (Ed.), *Comprehensive handbook of psychological assessment* (Vol. 4, pp. 21–34). Hoboken, NJ: Wiley.

Muchinsky, P. M. (2013). Three bold ideas. *The Industrial-Organizational Psychologist, 51*(2), 152–157.

Muchinsky, P. M., & Raines, J. M. (2013). The overgeneralized validity of validity generalization. *Journal of Organizational Behavior, 34,* 1057–1060.

Muchiri, M. K., & Cooksey, R. W. (2011). Examining the effects of substitutes for leadership on performance outcomes. *Leadership & Organization Development Journal, 32,* 817–836.

Mueller, J. S., & Kamdar, D. (2011). Why seeking help from teammates is a blessing and a curse: A theory of help seeking and individual creativity in team contexts. *Journal of Applied Psychology, 96,* 263–276.

Mulvey, P. W., & Klein, H. J. (1998). The impact of perceived loafing and collective efficacy in group goal processes and group performance. *Organizational Behavior & Human Decision Processes, 74,* 62–87.

Mumford, M. D., & Stokes, G. S. (1992). Developmental determinants of individual action: Theory and practice in applying background measures. In M. D. Dunnette & L. M. Hough (Eds.), *Handbook of industrial and organizational psychology* (2nd ed., Vol. 3, pp. 61–138). Palo Alto, CA: Consulting Psychologists Press.

Mumford, T. V., Van Iddekinge, C. H., Morgeson, F. P., & Campion, M. A. (2008). The team role test: Development and validation of a team role knowledge situational judgment test. *Journal of Applied Psychology, 93,* 250–267.

Münsterberg, H. (1913). *Psychology and industrial efficiency.* Boston: Houghton Mifflin.

Murphy, G. C., & Athanasou, J. A. (1999). The effect of unemployment on mental health. *Journal of Occupational & Organizational Psychology, 72,* 83–99.

Murphy, K. R. (1996). Individual differences and behavior in organizations: Much more than *g.* In K. R. Murphy (Ed.), *Individual differences and behavior in organizations* (pp. 3–30). San Francisco: Jossey-Bass.

Murphy, K. R. (1997). Meta-analysis and validity generalization. In N. Anderson & P. Herriot (Eds.), *International handbook of selection and assessment* (pp. 323–342). Chichester, England: Wiley.

Murphy, K. R. (1999). The challenge of staffing a post-industrial workplace. In D. R. Ilgen & E. D. Pulakos (Eds.), *The changing nature of performance* (pp. 295–324). San Francisco: Jossey-Bass.

Murphy, K. R. (2003). The logic of validity generalization. In K. R. Murphy (Ed.), *Validity generalization: A critical review* (pp. 1–30). Mahwah, NJ: Erlbaum.

Murphy, K. R. (2009). Content validation is useful for many things, but validity isn't one of them. *Industrial and Organizational Psychology, 2,* 453–464.

Murphy, K. R. (2014). Apollo, Dionysus, or both?: The evolving models and concerns of JDM. In S. Highhouse, R. S. Dalal, & E. Salas (Eds.), *Judgment and decision making at work* (pp. 347–361). New York: Routledge.

Murphy, K. R., & Anhalt, R. L. (1992). Is halo error a property of the rater, ratees, or the specific behaviors observed? *Journal of Applied Psychology, 77,* 494–500.

Murphy, K. R., & Cleveland, J. N. (1995). *Understanding performance appraisal: Social, organizational, and goal-based perspectives.* Thousand Oaks, CA: Sage.

Murphy, K. R., Cronin, B. E., & Tam, A. P. (2003). Controversy and consensus regarding the use of cognitive ability testing in organizations. *Journal of Applied Psychology, 88,* 660–671.

Murphy, K. R., Deckert, P. J., & Hunter, S. T. (2013). What personality does and does not predict and why: Lessons learned and future directions. In N. D. Christiansen & R. P. Tett (Eds.), *Handbook of personality at work* (pp. 633–650). New York: Routledge.

Murphy, K. R., Dzieweczynski, J. L., & Zhang, Y. (2009). Positive manifold limits the relevance of content-matching strategies for validating selection test batteries. *Journal of Applied Psychology, 94,* 1018–1031.

Murphy, K. R., Osten, K., & Myors, B. (1995). Modeling the effects of banding in personnel selection. *Personnel Psychology, 48,* 61–84.

Murphy, K. R., Thornton, G. C., & Prue, K. (1991). Influence of job characteristics on the acceptability of employee drug testing. *Journal of Applied Psychology, 76,* 447–453.

Murray, H. A., & MacKinnon, D. W. (1946). Assessment of OSS personnel. *Journal of Consulting Psychology, 10,* 76–80.

Naglieri, J. A., Drasgow, F., Schmit, M., Handler, L., Prifitera, A., Margolis, A., & Velasquez, R. (2004). Psychological testing on the Internet: New problems, old issues. *American Psychologist, 59,* 150–162.

Nahrgang, J. D., Morgeson, F. P., & Hofmann, D. A. (2011). Safety at work: A meta-analytic investigation of the link between job demands, job resources, burnout, engagement, and safety outcomes. *Journal of Applied Psychology, 96,* 71–94.

Nakamura, J., & Csikszentmihalyi, M. (2009). Flow theory and research. In S. J. Lopez & C. R. Snyder (Eds.), *The Oxford handbook of positive psychology* (2nd ed., pp. 195–206). New York: Oxford University Press.

Nam, K. A., Cho, Y., & Lee, M. (2014). West meets East? Identifying the gap in current cross-cultural training research. *Human Resource Development Review, 13,* 36–57.

Namazie, P., & Tayeb, M. (2006). Human resource management in Iran. In P. S. Budhwar & K. Mellahi (Eds.), *Managing human resources in the Middle East* (pp. 20–39). New York: Routledge.

Nandkeolyar, A. K., Shaffer, J. A., Li, A., Ekkirala, S., & Bagger, J. (2014). Surviving an abusive supervisor: The joint roles of conscientiousness and coping strategies. *Journal of Applied Psychology, 99,* 138–150.

Naquin, C. E., & Tynan, R. O. (2003). The team halo effect: Why teams are not blamed for their failures. *Journal of Applied Psychology, 88,* 332–340.

Narayanan, V. K., & Nath, R. (1982). Hierarchical level and the impact of flextime. *Industrial Relations, 21,* 216–230.

Neale, M. A. (1984). The effects of negotiation and arbitration cost salience on bargainer behavior: The role of the arbiter and constituency in negotiator judgment. *Organizational Behavior and Human Performance, 34,* 97–111.

Nease, A. A., Mudgett, B. O., & Quiñones, M. A. (1999). Relationships among feedback sign, self-efficacy, and acceptance of performance feedback. *Journal of Applied Psychology, 84,* 806–814.

Newell, S., & Tansley, C. (2001). International uses of selection methods. In C. L. Cooper & I. T. Robertson (Eds.), *International review of industrial and organizational psychology* (Vol. 16, pp. 195–213). Chichester, England: Wiley.

Newman, D. A., Jacobs, R. R., & Bartram, D. (2007). Choosing the best method for local validity estimation: Relative accuracy of meta-analysis versus a local study versus Bayes-analysis. *Journal of Applied Psychology, 92,* 1394–1413.

Newton, P. E., & Shaw, S. D. (2013). Standards for talking and thinking about validity. *Psychological Methods, 18,* 301–319.

Ng, K. Y., Koh, C., Ang, S., Kennedy, J. C., & Chan, K. Y. (2011). Rating leniency and halo in multisource feedback ratings: Testing cultural assumptions of power distance and individualism-collectivism. *Journal of Applied Psychology, 96,* 1033–1044.

Ng, T. W. H., & Feldman, D. C. (2010). The relationships of age with job attitudes: A meta-analysis. *Personnel Psychology, 63,* 677–718.

Ng, T. W. H., Feldman, D. C., & Simon, S. K. (2010). Psychological contract breaches, organizational commitment, and innovation-related behaviors: A latent growth modeling approach. *Journal of Applied Psychology, 9,* 744–751.

Nguyen, B., Steel, P., & Ferrari, J. R. (2013). Procrastination's impact in the workplace and the workplace's impact on procrastination. *International Journal of Selection and Assessment, 21,* 388–399.

Nickels, B. J. (1994). The nature of biodata. In G. S. Stokes, M. D. Mumford, & W. A. Owens (Eds.), *Biodata hand-*

book: *Theory, research, and use of biographical information in selection and performance prediction* (pp. 1–16). Palo Alto, CA: Consulting Psychologists Press.

Noe, R. A. (2010). *Employee training and development* (5th ed.). Alexandria, VA: ASTD Press.

Noe, R. A., & Ford, J. K. (1992). Emerging issues and new directions for training research. In K. Rowland & G. Ferris (Eds.), *Research in personnel and human resource management* (Vol. 10, pp. 345–384). Greenwich, CT: JAI Press.

Normand, J., Salyards, S. D., & Mahoney, J. J. (1990). An evaluation of preemployment drug testing. *Journal of Applied Psychology, 75,* 629–639.

Nyfield, G., & Baron, H. (2000). Cultural context in adopting selection practices across borders. In J. F. Kehoe (Ed.), *Managing selection in changing organizations* (pp. 242–268). San Francisco: Jossey-Bass.

O'Boyle, E. H., Jr., Forsyth, D. R., Banks, G. C., & McDaniel, M. A. (2012). A meta-analysis of the dark triad and work behavior: A social exchange perspective. *Journal of Applied Psychology, 97,* 557–579.

O'Boyle, E. H., Jr., Humphrey, R. H., Pollack, J. M., Hawver, T. H., & Story, P. A. (2011). The relation between emotional intelligence and job performance: A meta-analysis. *Journal of Organizational Behavior, 32,* 788–818.

O'Brien, K. E., Biga, A., Kessler, S. R., & Allen, T. D. (2010). A meta-analytic investigation of gender differences in mentoring. *Journal of Management, 36,* 537–554.

O'Keeffe, J. (1994). Disability, discrimination, and the Americans with Disabilities Act. In S. M. Bruyere & J. O'Keeffe (Eds.), *Implications of the Americans with Disabilities Act for psychology* (pp. 1–14). New York: Springer.

O'Leary, M., Mortensen, M., & Woolley, A. (2011). Multiple team memberships: A theoretical model of its effects on productivity and learning for individuals and teams. *Academy of Management Review, 36,* 461–478.

O'Neil, D. A., Hopkins, M. M., & Bilimoria, D. (2008). Women's careers at the start of the 21st century: Patterns and paradoxes. *Journal of Business Ethics, 80,* 727–743.

Offerman, L. R., & Basford, T. E. (2014). Inclusive human resource management. In B. M. Ferdman & B. R. Deane (Eds.), *Diversity at work: The practice of inclusion* (pp. 229–259). San Francisco: Jossey-Bass.

Offerman, L. R., & Gowing, M. K. (1990). Organizations of the future. *American Psychologist, 45,* 95–108.

Oh, I.-S., Wang, G., & Mount, M. K. (2011). Validity of observer ratings of the five-factor model of personality traits: A meta-analysis. *Journal of Applied Psychology, 96,* 762–773.

Olson-Buchanan, J. B. (1996). Voicing discontent: What happens to the grievance filer after the grievance? *Journal of Applied Psychology, 81,* 52–63.

Ones, D. S., & Dilchert, S. (2012). Employee green behaviors. In S. E. Jackson, D. S. Ones, & S. Dilchert (Eds.), *Managing human resources for environmental sustainability* (pp. 85–116). San Francisco: Jossey-Bass.

Ordóñez, L. D., Schweitzer, M. E., Galinsky, A. D., & Bazerman, M. H. (2009). Goals gone wild: The systematic side effects of overprescribing goal setting. *Academy of Management Perspectives, 23,* 6–16.

Organ, D. W. (1988). *Organizational citizenship behavior: The good soldier syndrome.* Lexington, MA: Lexington Books.

Organ, D. W. (1994). Organizational citizenship behavior and the good soldier. In M. G. Rumsey, C. B. Walker, & J. H. Harris (Eds.), *Personnel selection and classification* (pp. 53–68). Hillsdale, NJ: Erlbaum.

Organ, D. W., Podsakoff, P. M., & Podsakoff, N. P. (2011). Expanding the criterion domain to include organizational citizenship behavior: Implications for employee selection. In S. Zedeck (Ed.), *APA handbook of industrial and organizational psychology* (Vol. 2, pp. 281–323). Washington, DC: APA.

Osicki, M., & Kulkarni, M. (2010). Recruitment in a global workplace. In K. Lundby (Ed.), *Going global* (pp. 113–142). San Francisco: Jossey-Bass.

Ostroff, C., & Fulmer, A. (2014). Variance as a construct: Understanding variability beyond the mean. In J. K. Ford, J. R. Hollenbeck, & A. M. Ryan (Eds.), *The nature of work* (pp. 185–210). Washington, DC: APA.

Ostroff, C., & Harrison, D. A. (1999). Meta-analysis, level of analysis, and best estimates of population correlations: Cautions for interpreting meta-analytic results in organizational behavior. *Journal of Applied Psychology, 84,* 260–270.

Ostroff, C., & Zhan, Y. (2012). Person-environment fit in the selection process. In N. Schmitt (Ed.), *The Oxford handbook of personnel assessment and selection* (pp. 252–273). New York: Oxford University Press.

Ostroff, C., Kinicki, A. J., & Tamkins, M. M. (2003). Organizational culture and climate. In W. C. Borman, D. R. Ilgen, & R. J. Klimoski (Eds.), *Handbook of psychology* (Vol. 12): *Industrial and organizational psychology* (pp. 565–593). Hoboken, NJ: Wiley.

Oswald, F. L., & Hough, L. M. (2011). Personality and its assessment in organizations. Theoretical and empirical assessments. In S. Zedeck (Ed.), *APA handbook of industrial and organizational psychology* (Vol. 2, pp. 153–184). Washington, DC: APA.

Outtz, J. L. (2011). The unique origins of advancements in selection and personnel psychology. In S. Zedeck (Ed.),

APA handbook of industrial and organizational psychology (Vol. 2, pp. 445–465). Washington, DC: APA.

Overton, R. C., Harms, H. J., Taylor, L. R., & Zickar, M. J. (1997). Adapting to adaptive testing. *Personnel Psychology, 50,* 171–185.

Padilla, A., Hogan, R., & Kaiser, R. B. (2007). The toxic triangle: Destructive leaders, susceptible followers, and conducive environments. *The Leadership Quarterly, 18,* 176–194

Parks, J. M., & Kidder, D. L. (1994). Till death do us part . . . : Changing work relationships in the 1990s. In C. L. Cooper & D. M. Rousseau (Eds.), *Trends in organizational behavior* (Vol. 1, p. 111–136). New York: Wiley.

Paul, K. I., & Moser, K. (2009). Unemployment impairs mental health: Meta-analyses. *Journal of Vocational Behavior, 74,* 264–282.

Payne, S. C., & Pariyothorn, M. M. (2007). I-O psychology in introductory psychology textbooks: A survey of authors. *The Industrial-Organizational Psychologist, 44*(4), 37–42.

Payne, S. C., Youngcourt, S. S., & Beaubien, J. M. (2007). A meta-analytic examination of the goal orientation nomological net. *Journal of Applied Psychology, 92,* 128–150.

Pearlman, K. (2009). Unproctored internet testing: Practical, legal, and ethical concerns. *Industrial and Organizational Psychology, 2,* 14–19.

Pearlman, K., & Barney, M. F. (2000). Selection for a changing workplace. In J. F. Kehoe (Ed.), *Managing selection in changing organizations* (pp. 3–72). San Francisco: Jossey-Bass.

Pearlman, K., & Sanchez, J. I. (2010). Work analysis. In J. L. Farr & N. T. Tippins (Eds.), *Handbook of employee selection* (pp. 73–98). New York: Routledge.

Pendry, L. F., Driscoll, D. M., & Field, S. C. T. (2007). Diversity training: Putting theory into practice. *Journal of Occupational and Organizational Psychology, 80,* 27–50.

Perrewé, P. L., & Spector, P. E. (2002). Personality research in the organizational sciences. In G. R. Ferris & J. J. Martocchio (Eds.), *Research in personnel and human resources management* (Vol. 21, pp. 1–63). Kidlington, UK: Elsevier.

Peterson, D. B. (2002). Management development: Coaching and mentoring programs. In K. Kraiger (Ed.), *Creating, implementing, and managing effective training and development* (pp. 160–191). San Francisco: Jossey-Bass.

Peterson, D. B. (2011). Executive coaching: A critical review and recommendations for advancing practice. In S. Zedeck (Ed.), *APA handbook of industrial and organizational psychology* (Vol. 2, pp. 527–566). Washington, DC: APA.

Peterson, N. G., & Jeanneret, P. R. (1997). Job analysis. In D. L. Whetzel & G. R. Wheaton (Eds.), *Applied measurement methods in industrial psychology* (pp. 13–50). Palo Alto, CA: Consulting Psychologists Press.

Peterson, N., & Sager, C. E. (2010). *The Dictionary of Occupational Titles* and the Occupational Information Network. In J. L. Farr & N. T. Tippins (Eds.), *Handbook of employee selection* (pp. 887–908). New York: Routledge.

Peterson, S. J., Galvin, B. M., & Lange, D. (2012). CEO servant leadership: Exploring executive characteristics and firm performance. *Personnel Psychology, 65,* 565–596.

Pfeffer, J. (2007). A modest proposal: How we might change the process and product of managerial research. *Academy of Management Journal, 50,* 1334–1345.

Pfeffer, J., & Veiga, J. F. (1999). Putting people first for organizational success. *Academy of Management Executive, 13,* 37–48.

Phillips, J. M., Gully, S. M., McCarthy, J. E., Castellano, W. G., & Kim, M. S. (2014). Recruiting global travelers: The role of global travel recruitment messages and individual differences in perceived fit, attraction, and job pursuit intentions. *Personnel Psychology, 67,* 153–201.

Phillips, J. M., Hollenbeck, J. R., & Ilgen, D. R. (1996). Prevalence and prediction of positive discrepancy creation: Examining a discrepancy between two self-regulation theories. *Journal of Applied Psychology, 81,* 498–511.

Phillips, J. S., & Lord, R. G. (1981). Causal attribution and prescriptions of leadership. *Organizational Behavior and Human Performance, 28,* 143–163.

Pierce, J. L., & Aguinis, H. (2013). The too-much-of-a-good-thing effect in management. *Journal of Management, 39,* 313–338.

Pierce, J. L., & Dunham, R. B. (1992). The 12-hour work day: A 48-hour, four-day week. *Academy of Management Journal, 35,* 1086–1098.

Pierce, J. L., Dunham, R. B., & Cummings, L. L. (1984). Sources of environmental structuring and participant responses. *Organizational Behavior and Human Performance, 33,* 214–242.

Pinder, C. C. (2008). *Work motivation in organizational behavior* (2nd ed.). New York: Psychology Press.

Pinto, B. (2011, October 6). Q-C Mart employee wins court decision over 'Guess who will be fired!!!' context. *ABC News.* Retrieved from http://abcnews.go.com/Business/ mart-employee-wins-court-decision-guess-wholl-fired/ story?id=14677100

Piotrkowski, C. S., & Carrubba, J. (1999). Child labor and exploitation. In J. Barling & E. K. Kelloway (Eds.), *Young workers: Varieties of experience* (pp. 129–157). Washington, DC: American Psychological Association.

Plowman, D. A., Baker, L. T., Beck, T. E., Kulkari, M., Solansky, S. T., & Travis, D. V. (2007). Radical change accidentally: The emergence and amplification of small change. *Academy of Management Journal, 50,* 515–543.

Ployhart, R. E. (2008). The measurement and analysis of motivation. In R. Kanfer, G. Chen, & R. D. Pritchard (Eds.), *Work motivation: Past, present, and future* (pp. 17–62). New York: Routledge.

Ployhart, R. E. (2012). Personnel selection: Ensuring sustainable organizational effectiveness through the acquisition of human capital. In S. W. J. Kozlowski (Ed.), *The Oxford handbook of organizational psychology* (Vol. 1, pp. 221–246). New York: Oxford University Press.

Ployhart, R. E. (2014). The study of phenomena that matter. In J. K. Ford, J. R. Hollenbeck, & A. M. Ryan (Eds.), *The nature of work* (pp. 259–275). Washington, DC: APA.

Ployhart, R. E., & MacKenzie, W. I. (2011). Situational judgment tests: A critical review and agenda for the future. In S. Zedeck (Ed.), *APA handbook of industrial and organizational psychology* (Vol. 2, pp. 237–252). Washington, DC: APA.

Ployhart, R. E., & Ryan, A. M. (1998). Applicants' reactions to the fairness of selection procedures: The effects of positive rule violations and time of measurement. *Journal of Applied Psychology, 83,* 3–16.

Ployhart, R. E., & Schneider, B. (2012). The social and organizational context of personnel selection. In N. Schmitt (Ed.), *The Oxford handbook of personnel assessment and selection* (pp. 48–67). New York: Oxford University Press.

Ployhart, R. E., Weekley, J. A., Holtz, B. C., & Kemp, C. (2003). Web-based and pencil-and-paper testing of applicants in a proctored setting: Are personality, biodata, and situational judgment tests comparable? *Personnel Psychology, 56,* 733–752.

Pocock, B. (2008). Equality at work. In P. Blyton, N. Bacon, J. Fiorito, & E. Heery (Eds.), *Industrial relations* (pp. 572–587). Thousand Oaks, CA: Sage.

Podlesny, J. A., & Truslow, C. M. (1993). Validity of an expanded-issue (Modified General Question) polygraph technique in a simulated distributed-crime-roles context. *Journal of Applied Psychology, 78,* 788–797.

Podsakoff, N. P., LePine, J. A., & LePine, M. A. (2007). Differential challenge stressor-hindrance stressor relationships with job attitudes, turnover intention, turnover, and withdrawal behavior: A meta-analysis. *Journal of Applied Psychology, 92,* 438–454.

Podsakoff, N. P., Whiting, S. W., Podsakoff, P. M., & Blume, B. D. (2009). Individual- and organizational-level consequences of organizational citizenship behaviors: A meta-analysis. *Journal of Applied Psychology, 94,* 122–141.

Podsakoff, P. M., MacKenzie, S. B., & Bommer, W. H. (1996). Meta-analysis of the relationship between Kerr and Jermier's substitutes for leadership and employee job attitudes, role perceptions, and performance. *Journal of Applied Psychology, 81,* 380–399.

Porah, N., & Porah, L. (2012). What are assessment centers and how can they enhance organizations? In D. J. Jackson, C. E. Lance, & B. J. Hoffman (Eds.), *The psychology of assessment centers* (pp. 3–24). New York: Routledge.

Porter, C. O., Hollenbeck, J. R., Ilgen, D. R., Ellis, A. P., West, B. J., & Moon, H. (2003). Backing up behaviors in teams: The role of personality and legitimacy of need. *Journal of Applied Psychology, 88,* 391–403.

Potosky, D., & Bobko, P. (2004). Selection testing via the internet: Practical considerations and exploratory empirical findings. *Personnel Psychology, 57,* 1003–1034.

Pratt, M. G., & Rafaeli, A. (1997). Organizational dress as a symbol of multilayered social identities. *Academy of Management Journal, 40,* 862–898.

Priem, R. L., & Nystrom, P. C. (2014). Exploring the dynamics of workgroup fracture: Common ground, trust-with-trepidation, and warranted distrust. *Journal of Management, 40,* 764–795.

Prieto, J. M. (1993). The team perspective in selection and assessment. In H. Schuler, J. L. Farr, & M. Smith (Eds.), *Personnel selection and assessment* (pp. 221–234). Hillsdale, NJ: Erlbaum.

Primoff, E. S., & Fine, S. A. (1988). A history of job analysis. In S. Gael (Ed.), *The job analysis handbook for business, industry, and government* (pp. 14–29). New York: Wiley.

Pritchard, R. D., Jones, S. D., Roth, P. L., Stuebing, K. K., & Ekeberg, S. E. (1988). Effects of group feedback, goal setting, and incentives on organizational productivity. *Journal of Applied Psychology, 73,* 337–358.

Pruitt, D. G. (1993). *Negotiation in social conflict.* Pacific Grove, CA: Brooks/Cole.

Pugh, S. D., Diefendorff, J. M., & Moran, C. M. (2013). Emotional labor: Organizational level influences, strategies, and outcomes. In A. A. Grandey, J. M. Diefendorff, & D. E. Rupp (Eds.), *Emotional labor in the 21st century* (pp. 199–221). New York: Routledge.

Pulakos, E. D. (1997). Ratings of job performance. In D. L. Whetzel & G. R. Wheaton (Eds.), *Applied measurement methods in industrial psychology* (pp. 291–318). Palo Alto, CA: Consulting Psychologists Press.

Pulakos, E. D. (2009). *Performance management: A new approach for driving business results.* West Sussex, UK: Wiley-Blackwell.

Pulakos, E. D., & O'Leary, R. S. (2011). Why is performance management broken? *Industrial and Organizational Psychology: Perspectives on Science and Practice, 4,* 146–164.

Pulakos, E. D., & Schmitt, N. (1995). Experience-based and structured interview questions: Studies of validity. *Personnel Psychology, 48,* 289–308.

Pulakos, E. D., Mueller-Hanson, R. A., & Nelson, J. K. (2012). Adaptive performance and trainability as criteria in selection research. In N. Schmitt (Ed.), *The Oxford handbook of personnel assessment and selection* (pp. 595–613). New York: Oxford University Press.

Purvanova, R. K. (2014). Face-to-face versus virtual teams: What have we really learned? *The Psychologist-Manager Journal, 17,* 2–29.

Putka, D. J., & Hoffman, B. J. (2013). Clarifying the contribution of assessee-, dimension-, exercise-, and assessor-related effects to reliable and unreliable variance in assessment center ratings. *Journal of Applied Psychology, 98,* 114–133.

Pyburn, K. M., Ployhart, R. E., & Kravitz, D. A. (2008). The diversity-validity dilemma: Overview and legal content. *Personnel Psychology, 61,* 143–151.

Quick, J. C., Murphy, L. R., Hurrell, J. J., & Orman, D. (1992). The value of work in the risk of distress and the power of prevention. In J. C. Quick, L. R. Murphy, & J. J. Hurrell (Eds.), *Stress and well-being at work* (pp. 3–13). Washington, DC: American Psychological Association.

Quiñones, M. A., Ford, J. K., & Teachout, M. S. (1995). The relationship between work experience and job performance: A conceptual and meta-analytic review. *Personnel Psychology, 48,* 485–509.

Ragins, B. R., & Sundstrom, E. (1989). Gender and power in organizations: A longitudinal perspective. *Psychological Bulletin, 105,* 51–88.

Ramsay, S., Troth, A., & Branch, S. (2011). Work-place bullying: A group processes framework. *Journal of Occupational and Organizational Psychology, 84,* 799–816.

Rapp, A. A., Bachrach, D. G., & Rapp, T. L. (2013). The influence of time management skill on the curvilinear relationship between organizational citizenship behavior and task performance. *Journal of Applied Psychology, 98,* 668–677.

Raver, J. L., Jensen, J. M., Lee, J., & O'Reilly, J. (2012). Destructive criticism revisited: Appraisals, task outcomes, and the moderating role of competitiveness. *Applied Psychology: An International Review, 61,* 177–203.

Raymark, P. H., Schmit, M. J., & Guion, R. M. (1997). Identifying potentially useful personality constructs for employee selection. *Personnel Psychology, 50,* 723–736.

Reb, J., Greguras, G. J., Luan, S., & Daniels, M. A. (2014). Performance appraisals as heuristic judgments under uncertainty. In S. Highhouse, R. S. Dalal, & E. Salas (Eds.), *Judgment and decision making at work* (pp. 13–36). New York: Routledge.

Ree, M. J., Earles, J. A., & Teachout, M. S. (1994). Predicting job performance: Not much more than *g. Journal of Applied Psychology, 79,* 518–524.

Reeve, C. L., & Hakel, M. D. (2002). Asking the right questions about *g. Human Performance, 15,* 47–74.

Reichman, W., & Berry, M. O. (2012). The evolution of industrial and organizational psychology. In S. C. Carr, M. MacLachlan, & A. Furnham (Eds.), *Humanitarian work psychology* (pp. 34–51). New York: Palgrave Macmillan.

Rennie, D. L. (2012). Qualitative research as methodological hermeneutics. *Psychological Methods, 17,* 385–398.

Reynolds, D. (2010). A primer on privacy: What every psychologist needs to know about data protection. *The Industrial-Organizational Psychologist, 48*(2), 27–32.

Reynolds, S. J. (2008). Moral attentiveness: Who pays attention to the moral aspects of life? *Journal of Applied Psychology, 93,* 1027–1041.

Rhodes, S. R., & Steers, R. M. (1990). *Managing employee absenteeism.* Reading, MA: Addison-Wesley.

Richards, J. (2012). What has the Internet ever done for employees? A review, map and research agenda. *Employee Relations, 34,* 22–43.

Richey, B., Bernardin, H. J., Tyler, C. L., & McKinney, N. (2001). The effect of arbitration program characteristics on applicants' intentions toward potential employees. *Journal of Applied Psychology, 86,* 1006–1013.

Ridley, M. (1999). *Genome: The autobiography of a species in 23 chapters.* New York: Harper Collins.

Riketta, M. (2002). Attitudinal organizational commitment and job performance: A meta-analysis. *Journal of Organizational Behavior, 23,* 257–266.

Riketta, M. (2008). The causal relation between job attitudes and performance: A meta-analysis of panel studies. *Journal of Applied Psychology, 93,* 472–481.

Roberson, L., Kulik, C. T., & Tan, R. Y. (2012). Effective diversity training. In S. W. J. Kozlowski (Ed.), *The Oxford handbook of organizational psychology* (Vol. 1, pp. 341–365). New York: Oxford University Press.

Roberson, Q. M. (2012). Managing diversity. In S. W. J. Kozlowski (Ed.), *The Oxford handbook of organizational psychology* (Vol. 2, pp. 1011–1033). New York: Oxford University Press.

Robinson, S. L., & Rousseau, D. M. (1994). Violating the psychological contract: Not the exception but the norm. *Journal of Organizational Behavior, 15,* 245–259.

Robinson, S. L., Kraatz, M. S., & Rousseau, D. M. (1994). Changing obligations and the psychology contract: A longitudinal study. *Academy of Management Journal, 37,* 137–152.

Roch, S. G., Woehr, D. J., Mishra, V., & Kieszczynska, U. (2012). Rater training revisited: An updated meta-analytic review of frame-of-reference training. *Journal of Occupational and Organizational Psychology, 85,* 370–395.

Rodell, J. B., & Judge, T. A. (2009). Can "good" stressors spark "bad" behaviors? The mediating role of emotions in links of challenge and hindrance stressors with citizenship and counterproductive behaviors. *Journal of Applied Psychology, 94,* 1438–1451.

Rogelberg, S. G., Luong, A., Sederburg, M. E., & Cristol, D. S. (2000). Employee attitude surveys: Examining the attitudes of noncompliant employees. *Journal of Applied Psychology, 85,* 284–293.

Ronen, S., & Primps, S. B. (1981). The compressed work week as organizational change: Behavioral and attitudinal outcomes. *Academy of Management Review, 6,* 61–74.

Rosen, H., & Stagner, R. (1980). Industrial/organizational psychology and unions: A viable relationship? *Professional Psychology, 11,* 477–483.

Rosen, S., & Tesser, A. (1970). On reluctance to communicate undesirable information: The MUM effect. *Sociometry, 33,* 253–263.

Rosenthal, R. (1991). *Meta-analytic procedures for social research* (2nd ed.). Newbury Park, CA: Sage.

Rosette, A. S., & Tost, L. P. (2010). Agentic women and communal leadership: How role prescriptions confer advantage to top women leaders. *Journal of Applied Psychology, 95,* 221–235.

Roth, P. L., & BeVier, C. A. (1998). Response rates in HRM/OB survey research: Norms and correlates, 1990–1994. *Journal of Management, 24,* 97–117.

Rotundo, M., & Spector, P. E. (2010). Counterproductive work behavior and withdrawal. In. J. L. Farr & N. T. Tippins (Eds.), *Handbook of employee selection* (pp. 489–512). New York: Routledge.

Rousseau, D. M. (1995). *Psychological contracts in organizations: Understanding written and unwritten agreements.* Thousand Oaks, CA: Sage.

Rousseau, D. M. (2011). The individual-organizational relationship: The psychological contract. In S. Zedeck (Ed.), *APA handbook of industrial and organizational psychology* (Vol. 3, pp. 191–220). Washington, DC: APA.

Rousseau, D. M., & Batt, R. (2007). Global competition's perfect storm: Why business and labor cannot solve their problems alone. *Academy of Management Perspectives, 21*(2), 16–23.

Rousseau, D. M., & House, R. J. (1994). Meso organizational behavior: Avoiding three fundamental biases. In

C. L. Cooper & D. M. Rousseau (Eds.), *Trends in organizational behavior* (Vol. 1, pp. 13–30). New York: Wiley.

Rousseau, D. M., & Parks, J. M. (1993). The contracts of individuals and organizations. In B. M. Staw & L. L. Cummings (Eds.), *Research in organizational behavior* (Vol. 15, pp. 1–43). Greenwich, CT: JAI.

Rousseau, D. M., & Schalk, R. (2000). Learning from cross-national perspectives on psychological contracts. In D. M. Rousseau & R. Schalk (Eds.), *Psychological contracts in employment: Cross-national perspectives* (pp. 283–304). Thousand Oaks, CA: Sage.

Rumsey, M. G. (2012). Military selection and classification in the United States. In J. H. Laurence & M. D. Matthews (Eds.), *The Oxford handbook of military psychology* (pp. 129–147). New York: Oxford University Press.

Rumsey, M. G. (2013). The elusive science of leadership. In M. G. Rumsey (Ed.), *The Oxford handbook of leadership* (pp. 455–466). New York: Oxford University Press.

Rupp, D. E., & Spencer, S. (2006). When customers lash out: The effects of customer interactional justice on emotional labor and the mediating role of discrete emotions. *Journal of Applied Psychology, 91,* 971–978.

Russell, J. S., & Goode, D. L. (1988). An analysis of managers' reactions to their own performance appraisal feedback. *Journal of Applied Psychology, 73,* 63–67.

Ryan, A. M., & Powers, C. (2012). Workplace diversity. In N. Schmitt (Ed.), *The Oxford handbook of personnel assessment and selection* (pp. 814–831). New York: Oxford University Press.

Ryan, R. M., & Deci, E. L. (2000). Self-determination theory and the facilitation of intrinsic motivation, social development, and well-being. *American Psychologist, 55,* 68–78.

Rynes, S., & Rosen, B. (1995). A field survey of factors affecting the adoption and perceived success of diversity training. *Personnel Psychology, 48,* 247–270.

Rynes, S. L. (2012). The research practice gap in I/O psychology and related fields: Challenges and potential solutions. In S. W. J. Kozlowski (Ed.), *The Oxford handbook of organizational psychology* (Vol. 1, pp. 409–452). New York: Oxford University Press.

Rynes, S. L., Brown, K. G., & Colbert, A. E. (2002). Seven common misconceptions about human resource practices: Research findings versus practitioner beliefs. *Academy of Management Executive, 16*(3), 92–103.

Sackett, P. R., & Laczo, R. M. (2003). Job and work analysis. In W. C. Borman, D. R. Ilgen, & R. J. Klimoski (Eds.), *Handbook of psychology* (Vol. 12): *Industrial and organizational psychology* (pp. 21–37). Hoboken, NJ: Wiley.

Sackett, P. R., & Wanek, J. E. (1996). New developments in the use of measures of honesty, integrity, conscientiousness, dependability, trustworthiness, and reliability for personnel selection. *Personnel Psychology, 49,* 787–829.

Sackett, P. R., Bonneman, M. J., & Connelly, B. S. (2008). High-stakes testing in higher education and employment. *American Psychologist, 63,* 215–227.

Sackett, P. R., Schmitt, N., Ellingson, J. E., & Kabin, M. B. (2001). High-stakes testing in employment, credentialing, and higher education: Prospects in a post-affirmative-action world. *American Psychologist, 56,* 302–318.

Salanova, M., Bakker, A. B., & Llorens, S. (2006). Flow at work: Evidence for an upward spiral of personal and organizational resources. *Journal of Happiness Studies, 7,* 1–22.

Salas, E., & Cannon-Bowers, J. A. (1997). Methods, tools, and strategies for team training. In M. A. Quiñones & A. Ehrenstein (Eds.), *Training for a rapidly changing workplace* (pp. 249–280). Washington, DC: American Psychological Association.

Salas, E., & Kozlowski, S. W. J. (2010). Learning, training, and development in organizations: Much progress and a peek over the horizon. In S. W. J. Kozlowski & E. Salas (Eds.), *Learning, training, and development in organizations* (pp. 461–476). New York: Routledge.

Salas, E., Burke, C. S., & Cannon-Bowers, J. A. (2002). What we know about designing and delivering team training: Tips and guidelines. In K. Kraiger (Ed.), *Creating, implementing, and managing effective training and development* (pp. 234–259). San Francisco: Jossey-Bass.

Salas, E., DeRouin, R. E., & Gade, P. A. (2007). The military's contribution to our science and practice: People, places, and findings. In L. L. Koppes (Ed.), *Historical perspectives in industrial and organizational psychology* (pp. 169–189). Mahwah, NJ: Erlbaum.

Salas, E., Priest, H. A., Stagl, K. C., Sims, D. E., & Burke, C. S. (2007). Work teams in organizations: A historical reflection and lessons learned. In L. L. Koppes (Ed.), *Historical perspectives in industrial and organizational psychology* (pp. 407–438). Mahwah, NJ: Erlbaum.

Salas, E., Stagl, K. C., & Burke, C. S. (2004). 25 years of team effectiveness in organizations: Research, themes, and emerging needs. In C. L. Cooper & I. T. Robertson (Eds.), *International review of industrial and organizational psychology* (Vol. 19, pp. 47–91). West Sussex: Wiley.

Salas, E., Weaver, S. J., & Shuffler, M. L. (2012). Learning, training, and development in organizations. In S. W. J. Kozlowski (Ed.), *The Oxford handbook of organizational psychology* (Vol. 1, pp. 330–372). New York: Oxford University Press.

Salgado, J. F. (1997). The five factor model of personality and job performance in the European Community. *Journal of Applied Psychology, 82,* 30–43.

Salgado, J. F. (1998). Sample size in validity studies of personnel selection. *Journal of Occupational & Organizational Psychology, 71,* 161–164.

Salgado, J. F. (2000). Personnel selection at the beginning of the new millennium. *International Journal of Selection and Assessment, 8,* 191–193.

Salgado, J. F., Anderson, N. R., & Hülsheger, U. R. (2010). Employee selection in Europe: Psychotechnics and the forgotten history of modern scientific employee selection. In J. L. Farr & N. T. Tippins (Eds.), *Handbook of employee selection* (pp. 921–941). New York: Routledge.

Salisbury, M. (2009). *iLearning.* San Francisco: Pfeiffer.

Salovey, P., & Mayer, J. D. (1990). Emotional intelligence. *Imagination, Cognition, and Personality, 9,* 185–211.

Sanchez, J. I. (2000). Adopting work analysis to a fast-paced and electronic business world. *International Journal of Selection and Assessment, 8,* 207–215.

Sanchez, J. I., & Levine, E. L. (2001). The analysis of work in the 20th and 21st centuries. In N. Anderson, D. S. Ones, H. K. Sinangil, & C. Viswesvaran (Eds.), *Handbook of industrial, work, and organizational psychology* (Vol. 1, pp. 71–89). London: Sage.

Sanchez, J. I., & Medkik, N. (2004). The effects of diversity awareness training on differential treatment. *Group & Organization Management, 29,* 517–536.

Sanchez-Runde, C. J., & Steers, R. M. (2003). Cultural influences in work motivation and performance. In L. W. Porter, G. A. Bigley, & R. M. Steers (Eds.), *Motivation and work behavior* (7th ed., pp. 357–398). Boston: McGraw-Hill Irwin.

Santuzzi, A. M., Waltz, P. R., Finkelstein, L. M., & Rupp, D. E. (2014). Invisible disabilities: Unique challenges for employees and organizations. *Industrial and Organizational Psychology, 7,* 204–219.

Savitz, A. W., & Weber, K. (2006). *The triple bottom line.* San Francisco: Jossey-Bass.

Schalk, K., & Rousseau, D. M. (2001). Psychological contracts in employment. In N. Anderson, D. S. Ones, H. K. Sinangil, & C. Viswesvaran (Eds.), *Handbook of industrial, work, and organizational psychology* (Vol. 2, pp. 133–142). London: Sage.

Schaufeli, W. B., Salanova, M., Gonzalez-Romá, V., & Bakker, A. B. (2002). The measurement of engagement and burnout: A confirmative analytic approach. *Journal of Happiness Studies, 3,* 71–92.

Schein, E. H. (1965). *Organizational psychology.* Englewood Cliffs, NJ: Prentice-Hall.

Schein, E. H. (1996). Culture: The missing concept in organizational studies. *Administrative Science Quarterly, 41,* 229–240.

Scherbaum, C. A., Goldstein, H. W., Yusko, K. P., Ryan, R., & Hanges, P. H. (2012). Intelligence 2.0: Reestablishing a research program on *g* in I-O psychology. *Industrial and Organizational Psychology, 5,* 128–148.

Schiavone, M. (2008). *Unions in crisis?* London: Praeger.

Schiemann, W. A. (2009). Aligning performance management with organizational strategy, values, and goals. In J. W. Smither & M. London (Eds.), *Performance management* (pp. 45–88). San Francisco: Jossey-Bass.

Schippmann, J. S. (1999). *Strategic job modeling: Working at the core of integrated human resources.* Mahwah, NJ: Erlbaum.

Schippmann, J. S., Ash, R. A., Battista, M., Carr, L., Eyde, L. D., Hesketh, B., Kehoe, J., Pearlman, K., Prien, E. P., & Sanchez, J. I. (2000). The practice of competency modeling. *Personnel Psychology, 53,* 703–740.

Schippmann, J. S., Prien, E. P., & Katz, J. A. (1990). Reliability and validity of in-basket performance measures. *Personnel Psychology, 43,* 837–859.

Schleicher, D. J., Hansen, S. D., & Fox, K. E. (2011). Job attitudes and work values. In S. Zedeck (Ed.), *APA handbook of industrial and organizational psychology* (Vol. 3, pp. 137–190). Washington, DC: APA.

Schleicher, D. J., Van Iddekinge, C. H., Morgeson, F. P., & Campion, M. R. (2010). If at first you don't succeed, try, try, again: Understanding race, age, and gender differences in retesting score improvement. *Journal of Applied Psychology, 95,* 603–617.

Schmidt, A. M., Beck, J. W., & Gillespie, J. Z. (2013). Motivation. In N. Schmitt, & S. Highhouse (Eds.), *Handbook of psychology* (Vol. 12): *Industrial and organizational psychology* (pp. 311–340). New York: John Wiley & Sons.

Schmidt, F. L., & Hunter, J. E. (1978). Moderator research and the law of small numbers. *Personnel Psychology, 31,* 215–232.

Schmidt, F. L., & Hunter, J. E. (1980). The future of criterion-related validity. *Personnel Psychology, 33,* 41–60.

Schmidt, F. L., & Hunter, J. E. (1981). Employment testing: Old theories and new research findings. *American Psychologist, 36,* 1128–1137.

Schmidt, F. L., & Hunter, J. E. (2001). Meta-analysis. In N. Anderson, D. S. Ones, H. K. Sinangil, & C. Viswesvaran (Eds.), *Handbook of industrial, work, and organizational psychology* (Vol. 1, pp. 51–70). London: Sage.

Schmidt, F. L., & Oh, I.-S. (2013). Methods for second order meta-analysis and illustrative applications. *Organizational Behavior and Human Decision Processes, 121,* 204–218.

Schminke, M., Ambrose, M. L., & Cropanzano, R. S. (2000). The effect of organizational structure on perceptions of procedural fairness. *Journal of Applied Psychology, 85,* 294–304.

Schmitt, N., & Landy, F. J. (1993). The concept of validity. In N. Schmitt & W. C. Borman (Eds.), *Personnel selection in organizations* (pp. 275–309). San Francisco: Jossey-Bass.

Schmitt, N., & Quinn, A. (2010). Reductions in measured subgroup mean differences: What is possible? In J. L. Outtz (Ed.), *Adverse impact: Implications for organizational staffing and high stakes selection* (pp. 425–452). New York: Routledge.

Schmitt, N., Arnold, J. D., & Neiminen, L. (2010). Validation strategies for primary studies. In J. L. Farr & N. T. Tippins (Eds.), *Handbook of employee selection* (pp. 51–71). New York: Routledge.

Schneider, B. (1987). The people make the place. *Personnel Psychology, 40,* 437–454.

Schneider, B. (1996). When individual differences aren't. In K. R. Murphy (Ed.), *Individual differences and behaviors in organizations* (pp. 548–572). San Francisco: Jossey-Bass.

Schneider, B., Ehrhart, M. G., & Macey, W. H. (2011). Perspectives on organizational climate and culture. In S. Zedeck (Ed.), *APA handbook of industrial and organizational psychology* (Vol. 1, pp. 373–414). Washington, DC: APA.

Schoenfeldt, L. F. (1999). From dust bowl empiricism to rational constructs in biographical data. *Human Resource Management Review, 9,* 147–167.

Schoorman, F. D., Mayer, R. C., & Davis, J. H. (2007). An integrative model of organizational trust: Past, present, and future. *Academy of Management Review, 35,* 344–354.

Schriesheim, C. A. (1978). Job satisfaction, attitudes toward unions, and voting in a union representation election. *Journal of Applied Psychology, 63,* 548–552.

Schuler, H. (1993). Social validity of selection situations: A concept and some empirical results. In H. Schuler, J. L. Farr, & M. Smith (Eds.), *Personnel selection and assessment* (pp. 11–26). Hillsdale, NJ: Erlbaum.

Schweitzer, M., Ordóñez, L. D., & Douma, B. (2004). The dark side of goal setting: The role of goals in motivating unethical behavior. *Academy of Management Journal, 47,* 422–432.

Scott, J. C., & Lezotte, D. V. (2012). Web-based assessments. In N. Schmitt (Ed.), *The Oxford handbook of personnel assessment and selection* (pp. 485–513). New York: Oxford University Press.

Scott, K. L., Restubog, S. L. D., & Zagenczyk, T. J. (2013). A social exchange-based model of antecedents of workplace exclusion. *Journal of Applied Psychology, 98,* 37–48.

Scott, W. D. (1903). *The theory of advertising*. Boston: Small, Maynard.

Scott, W. D. (1908). *The psychology of advertising*. New York: Arno Press.

Scott, W. D. (1911a). *Increasing human efficiency in business*. New York: Macmillan.

Scott, W. D. (1911b). *Influencing men in business*. New York: Ronald Press.

Scullen, S. E., Bergey, P. K., & Aiman-Smith, L. (2005). Forced distribution rating systems and the improvement of workplace potential: A baseline simulation. *Personnel Psychology, 58*, 1–32.

Scullen, S. W., Mount, M. K., & Goff, M. (2000). Understanding the latent structure of job performance ratings. *Journal of Applied Psychology, 85*, 956–970.

Seabright, M. A., Ambrose, M. L., & Schminke, M. (2010). Two images of workplace sabotage. In J. Greenberg (Ed.), *Insidious workplace behavior* (pp. 77–99). New York: Routledge.

Seligman, M. E., & Csikszentmihalyi, M. (2000). Positive psychology: An introduction. *American Psychologist, 55*, 5–14.

Senders, J. W., & Moray, N. P. (1991). *Human error: Cause, prediction, and reduction*. Hillsdale, NJ: Erlbaum.

Shadish, W. R. (2002). Revisiting field experimentation: Field notes for the future. *Psychological Methods, 7*, 3–18.

Shamir, B. (2013). Commentary: Leadership in context and context in leadership studies. In M. G. Rumsey (Ed.), *The Oxford handbook of leadership* (pp. 343–355). New York: Oxford University Press.

Shane, S. (2003). *A general theory of entrepreneurship*. Cheltenham, UK: Edward Elgar.

Sharf, J. C. (2011). Equal employment versus equal opportunity: A naked political agenda covered by a scientific fig leaf. *Industrial and Organizational Psychology, 4*, 537–539.

Sharf, J. C., & Jones, D. P. (2000). Employment risk management. In J. F. Kehoe (Ed.), *Managing selection in changing organizations* (pp. 271–318). San Francisco: Jossey-Bass.

Sheldon, O. J., Dunning, D., & Ames, D. R. (2014). Emotionally unskilled, unaware, and uninterested in learning more: Reactions to feedback about deficits in emotional intelligence. *Journal of Applied Psychology, 99*, 125–137.

Shen, W., Kiger, T. B., Davies, S. E., Rasch, R. L., Simon, K. M., & Ones, D. S. (2011). Samples in applied psychology: Over a decade of research in review. *Journal of Applied Psychology, 96*, 1055–1064.

Shockley, K. M., & Allen, T. D. (2012). Motives for flexible work arrangement use. *Community, Work & Family, 15*, 217–231.

Shockley, K. M., Ispas, D., Rossi, M. E., & Levine, E. L. (2012). A meta-analytic investigation of the relationship between state affect, discrete emotions, and job performance. *Human Performance, 25*, 377–411.

Shore, L. M., & Coyle-Shapiro, J. A-M. (2012). Perceived organizational cruelty: An expansion of the negative employee-organization relationship domain. In L. M. Shore, J. A-M. Coyle-Shapiro, & L. E. Tetrick (Eds.), *The employee-organization relationship* (pp. 139–168). New York: Routledge.

Shore, T. H., Shore, L. M., & Thornton, G. C. (1992). Construct validity of self- and peer evaluations of performance dimensions in an assessment center. *Journal of Applied Psychology, 77*, 42–54.

Shostak, A. B. (1964). Industrial psychology and the trade unions: A matter of mutual indifference. In G. Fisk (Ed.), *The frontiers of management psychology*. New York: Harper & Row.

Shuffler, M. L., Burke, C. S., Kramer, W. S., & Salas, E. (2013). Leading teams: Past, present, and future perspectives. In M. G. Rumsey (Ed.), *The Oxford handbook of leadership* (pp. 144–166). New York: Oxford University Press.

Silver, R. C. (2011). An introduction to "9/11: Ten years later." *American Psychologist, 66*, 427–428.

Silvester, J. (2008). The good, the bad, and the ugly: Politics and politicians at work. In G. P. Hodgkinson & J. L. Ford (Eds.), *International review of industrial and organizational psychology* (Vol. 23, pp. 107–148). Chichester, UK: Wiley-Blackwell.

Simons, T., & Roberson, Q. (2003). Why managers should care about fairness: The effects of aggregate justice perceptions on organizational outcomes. *Journal of Applied Psychology, 88*, 432–443.

Sitzmann, T., & Ely, K. (2010). Sometimes you need a reminder: The effects of prompting self-regulation on regulatory processes, learning, and attrition. *Journal of Applied Psychology, 95*, 132–144.

Sitzmann, T., Brown, K. G., Casper, W. I., Ely, K., & Zimmerman, R. D. (2008). A review and meta-analysis of the nomological network of trainee reactions. *Journal of Applied Psychology, 93*, 280–295.

Sitzmann, T., Brown, K. G., Ely, K., Kraiger, K., & Wisher, R. A. (2009). A cyclical model of motivational constructs in Web-based courses. *Military Psychology, 21*, 534–551.

Skarlicki, D. P., & Latham, G. P. (1996). Increasing citizenship behavior within a labor union: A test of organizational justice theory. *Journal of Applied Psychology, 81*, 161–169.

Skarlicki, D. P., & Latham, G. P. (1997). Leadership training in organizational justice to increase citizenship behavior within a labor union: A replication. *Personnel Psychology, 50,* 617–654.

Skarlicki, D. P., van Jaarsveld, D. D., & Walker, D. D. (2008). Getting even for customer mistreatment: The role of moral identity in the relationship between customer interpersonal injustice and employee sabotage. *Journal of Applied Psychology, 93,* 1335–1347.

Smart, B. (2005). *Topgrading: How leading companies win by hiring, coaching, and keeping the best people.* New York: Penguin.

Smith, C. S., Folkard, S., & Fuller, J. A. (2003). Shiftwork and working hours. In J. C. Quick & L. E. Tetrick (Eds.), *Handbook of organizational health psychology* (pp. 163–184). Washington, DC: American Psychological Association.

Smith, E. M., Ford, J. K., & Kozlowski, S. W. J. (1997). Building adaptive expertise: Implications for training design strategies. In M. A. Quiñones & A. Ehrenstein (Eds.), *Training for a rapidly changing workplace* (pp. 89–118). Washington, DC: American Psychological Association.

Smith, P. B., Fischer, R., & Sale, N. (2001). Cross-cultural industrial/organizational psychology. In C. L. Cooper & I. T. Robertson (Eds.), *International review of industrial and organizational psychology* (Vol. 16, pp. 147–193). West Sussex, England: Wiley.

Smith, P. C., Kendall, L., & Hulin, C. L. (1969). *The measurement of satisfaction in work and retirement.* Chicago: Rand McNally.

Smither, J. W. (2012). Performance management. In S. W. J. Kozlowski (Ed.), *The Oxford handbook of organizational psychology* (Vol. 1, pp. 285–329). New York, NY: Oxford University Press.

Society for Human Resource Management (2013). SHRM Survey Findings: Workplace Romance. Retrieved August 12, 2014, from http://www.shrm.org/research/surveyfindings/articles/pages/shrm-workplace-romance-findings.aspx

Society for Industrial and Organizational Psychology (2003). *Principles for the validation and use of personnel selection procedures* (4th ed.). Bowling Green, OH: Author.

Solinger, O. N., Van Olffen, W., & Roe, R. A. (2008). Beyond the three-component model of organizational commitment. *Journal of Applied Psychology, 93,* 70–83.

Sonenshein, S. (2012). Being a positive social change agent through issue selling. In K. Golden-Biddle & J. E. Dutton (Eds.), *Using a positive lens to explore social change and organizations* (pp. 49–69). New York: Routledge.

Sonnentag, S., & Frese, M. (2012). Dynamic performance. In S. W. J. Kozlowski (Ed.), *The Oxford handbook of organizational psychology* (Vol. 1, pp. 548–575). New York: Oxford University Press.

Sonnentag, S., & Frese, M. (2013). Stress in organizations. In N. Schmitt, & S. Highhouse (Eds.), *Handbook of psychology* (Vol. 12): *Industrial and organizational psychology* (pp. 560–592). New York: John Wiley & Sons.

Spector, P. E., & Fox, S. (2005). The stressor-emotion model of counterproductive work behavior. In S. Fox & P. E. Spector (Eds.), *Counterproductive work behavior: Investigations of actors and targets* (pp. 151–174). Washington, DC: American Psychological Association.

Spector, P. E., Allen, T. D., Poelmans, S. A., Lapierre, L. M., Cooper, C. L., O'Driscoll, M., Sanchez, J. I., Abarca, N., Alexandrova, M., Beham, B., Brough, P., Ferreiro, P., Fraile, G., Lu, C. Q., Lu, L., Moreno-Velazquez, I., Pagon, M., Pitariu, H., Salamatov, V., Shima, S., Simoni, A. S., Siu, O. L., & Widerszal-Bazyl, M. (2007). Cross-national differences in relationships of work demands, job satisfaction, and turnover intentions with work-family conflict. *Personnel Psychology, 60,* 805–835.

Speer, A. B., Christiansen, N. D., Goffin, R. D., & Goff, M. (2014). Situational bandwidth and the criterion-related validity of assessment center ratings: Is cross-exercise convergence always desirable? *Journal of Applied Psychology, 99,* 282–295.

Spence, J. R., & Keeping, L. (2011). Conscious rating distortion in performance appraisal: A review, commentary, and proposed framework for research. *Human Resource Management Review, 21,* 85–95.

Sperry, L. (2013). Executive coaching and leadership assessment: Past, present, and future. *Consulting Psychology Journal: Practice and Research, 65,* 284–288.

Spreitzer, G. M., Lam, C. F., & Fritz, C. (2010). Engagement and human thriving: Complementary perspectives on energy and connections to work. In A. B. Bakker & M. P. Leiter (Eds.), *Work engagement: A handbook of essential theory and research* (pp. 132–146). New York: Psychology Press.

Stagner, R., & Effal, B. (1982). Internal union dynamics during a strike: A quasi-experimental study. *Journal of Applied Psychology, 67,* 37–44.

Stahelski, A. J., Frost, D. E., & Patch, M. E. (1989). Use of socially dependent bases of power: French and Raven's theory applied to workgroup leadership. *Journal of Applied Psychology, 19,* 283–297.

Stahl, G. K., & Caligiuri, P. (2005). The effectiveness of expatriate coping strategies: The moderating role of cultural distance, position level, and time on the international assignment. *Journal of Applied Psychology, 90,* 603–615.

Stahl, M. J., & Harrell, A. M. (1981). Modeling effort decisions with behavioral decision theory: Toward an individual differences model of expectancy theory. *Organizational Behavior and Human Performance, 27,* 303–325.

Stanisavljevic, J., & Djuric, D. (2013). The application of programmed instruction in fulfilling the physiology course requirements. *Journal of Biological Education, 47,* 29–38.

Stanton, J. M. (1998). An empirical assessment of data collection using the Internet. *Personnel Psychology, 51,* 709–725.

Stanton, J. M. (2013). Data mining: A practical introduction for organizational researchers. In J. M. Cortina & R. S. Landis (Eds.), *Modern research methods for the study of behavior in organizations* (pp. 199–230). New York: Routledge.

Stanton, J. M., & Rogelberg, S. G. (2002). Beyond online surveys: Internet research opportunities for industrial-organizational psychology. In S. G. Rogelberg (Ed.), *Handbook of research methods in industrial and organizational psychology* (pp. 275–294). Malden, MA: Blackwell.

Starke, F. A., & Notz, W. W. (1981). Pre- and post-intervention effects of conventional versus final offer arbitration. *Academy of Management Journal, 24,* 832–850.

Steel, P. (2007). The nature of procrastination: A meta-analytic and theoretical review of quintessential self-regulatory failure. *Psychological Bulletin, 133,* 65–94.

Steel, P., & König, C. J. (2006). Integrating theories of motivation. *Academy of Management Review, 31,* 889–913.

Steele-Johnson, D., Osburn, H. G., & Pieper, K. F. (2000). A review and extension of current models of dynamic criteria. *International Journal of Selection and Assessment, 8,* 110–136.

Steelman, L., Levy, P., & Snell, A. F. (2004). The feedback environment scale (FES): Construct definition, measurement, and validation. *Education and Psychological Measurement, 64,* 165–184.

Steiner, D. D. (2012). Personnel selection across the globe. In N. Schmitt (Ed.), *The Oxford handbook of personnel assessment and selection* (pp. 740–767). New York: Oxford University Press.

Stern, P. C. (2011). Contributions of psychology to limiting climate change. *American Psychologist, 66,* 303–314.

Sternberg, R. J., & Horvath, J. A. (Eds.) (1999). *Tacit knowledge in professional practice.* Mahwah, NJ: Erlbaum.

Stone-Romero, E. F. (2011). Research strategies in industrial and organizational psychology: Nonexperimental, quasi-experimental, and randomized experimental research in special purpose and nonspecial purpose settings. In S. Zedeck (Ed.), *APA handbook of industrial and organizational psychology* (Vol. 1, pp. 37–72). Washington, DC: APA.

Streufert, S., Pogash, R. M., Roache, J., Gingrich, D., Landis, R., Severs, W., Lonardi, L., & Kantner, A. (1992). Effects of alcohol intoxication on risk taking, strategy, and error rate in visuomotor performance. *Journal of Applied Psychology, 77,* 515–524.

Strickler, L. J. (2000). Using just noticeable differences to interpret test scores. *Psychological Methods, 5,* 415–424.

Sturman, M. C. (2007). The past, present, and future of dynamic performance research. In J. J. Martocchio (Ed.), *Research in personnel and human resources management* (Vol. 26, pp. 49–110). Bingley, UK: Emerald Group Publishing, Ltd.

Suddaby, R., Hardy, C., & Huy, Q. N. (2011). Where are the new theories of organization? *Academy of Management Review, 36,* 236–246.

Sulsky, L. M., & Balzer, W. K. (1988). Meaning and measurement of performance rating accuracy: Some methodological and theoretical concerns. *Journal of Applied Psychology, 73,* 497–506.

Sulsky, L. M., & Day, D. V. (1992). Frame-of-reference training and cognitive categorization: An empirical investigation of rater memory issues. *Journal of Applied Psychology, 77,* 501–510.

Sung, S. Y., & Choi, J. N. (2014). Do organizations spend wisely on employees? Effects of training and development investments on learning and innovation in organizations. *Journal of Organizational Behavior, 35,* 393–412.

Surface, E. A. (2012). Training needs assessment: Aligning learning and capability with performance requirements and organizational objectives. In M. A. Wilson, W. Bennett, S. Gibson, & G. M. Alliger (Eds.), *The handbook of work analysis: The methods, systems, applications and science of work measurement in organizations* (pp. 439–464). New York: Routledge.

Sverke, M., & Kuruvilla, S. (1995). A new conceptualization of union commitment: Development and test of an integrated theory. *Journal of Organizational Behavior, 16,* 505–532.

Sverke, M., & Sjöberg, A. (1995). Union membership behavior: The influence of instrumental and value-based commitment. In L. E. Tetrick & J. Barling (Eds.), *Changing employment relations* (pp. 229–254). Washington, DC: American Psychological Association.

Sweet, S., & Meiksins, P. (2013). *Changing contours of work* (2nd ed.). Thousand Oaks, CA: Sage.

Swim, J. K., Stern, P. C. Doherty, T. J., Clayton, S., Reser, J. P., Weber, E. V., Gifford, R., & Howard, G. S. (2011). Psychology's contributions to understanding and addressing global climate change. *American Psychologist, 66,* 241–250.

Tannenbaum, S. I. (2002). A strategic view of organizational training and learning. In K. Kraiger (Ed.), *Cre-*

ating, implementing, and managing effective training and development (pp. 10–52). San Francisco: Jossey-Bass.

Tannenbaum, S. I., Beard, R. L., McNall, L. A., & Salas, E. (2010). Informal learning and development in organizations. In S. W. J. Kozlowski & E. Salas (Eds.), *Learning, training, and development in organizations* (pp. 303–332). New York: Routledge.

Tannenbaum, S. I., Mathieu, J. E., Salas, E., & Cohen, D. (2012). Teams are changing: Are research and practice evolving fast enough? *Industrial and Organizational Psychology: Perspectives on Science and Practice, 5*, 2–24.

Taras, V., Kirkman, B. L., & Steele, P. (2010). Examining the impact of *Culture's Consequences*: A three-decade meta-analytic review of Hofstede's cultural value dimensions. *Journal of Applied Psychology, 95*, 405–439.

Taylor, F. W. (1911). *The principles of scientific management.* New York: Harper.

Taylor, P. J., Russ-Eft, D. F., & Chen, D. W. (2005). A meta-analytic review of behavior modeling training. *Journal of Applied Psychology, 90*, 692–709.

Tehrani, N. (2012). Introduction to workplace bullying. In N. Tehrani (Ed.), *Workplace bullying: Symptoms and solutions* (pp. 1–17). New York: Routledge.

Tepas, D. I. (1993). Educational programmes for shiftworkers, their families, and prospective shiftworkers. *Ergonomics, 36,* 199–209.

Tepper, B. J. (2000). Consequences of abusive supervision. *Academy of Management Journal, 43*, 178–190.

Tepper, B. J., Duffy, M. K., Henle, C. A., & Lambert, L. S. (2006). Procedural injustice, victim precipitation, and abusive supervision. *Personnel Psychology, 59*, 101–123.

Tepper, B. J., Henle, C. A., Lambert, L. S., Giacalone, R. A., & Duffy, M. K. (2008). Abusive supervisors and subordinates' organization deviance. *Journal of Applied Psychology, 93*, 721–732.

Tesluk, P. E., & Jacobs, R. R. (1998). Toward an integrated model of work experience. *Personnel Psychology, 51,* 321–355.

Tetrick, L. E. (1995). Developing and maintaining union commitment: A theoretical framework. *Journal of Organizational Behavior, 16,* 583–595.

Tetrick, L. E., & Peiró, J. M. (2012). Occupational safety and health. In S. W. J. Kozlowski (Ed.), *The Oxford handbook of organizational psychology* (Vol. 2, pp. 1228–1244). New York: Oxford University Press.

Tetrick, L. E., Perrewé, P. L., & Griffin, M. (2010). Employee work-related health, stress, and safety. In J. L. Farr & N. T. Tippins (Eds.), *Handbook of employee selection* (pp. 531–550). New York: Routledge.

Tetrick, L. E., Shore, L. M., McClurg, L. N., & Vandenberg, R. J. (2007). A model of union participation: The

impact of perceived union support, union instrumentality, and union loyalty. *Journal of Applied Psychology, 92,* 820–828.

Tharenou, P. (1997). Managerial career advancement. In C. L. Cooper & I. T. Robertson (Eds.), *International review of industrial and organizational psychology* (Vol. 12, pp. 39–94). New York: Wiley.

Theeboom, T., Beersma, B., & van Vianen, A. E. M. (2013). Does coaching work? A meta-analysis on the effects of coaching on individual level outcomes in an organizational context. *Journal of Positive Psychology, 9*, 1–18.

Thompson, L. F., Surface, E. A., Martin, D. L., & Sanders, M. G. (2003). From paper to pixels: Moving personnel surveys to the Web. *Personnel Psychology, 56,* 197–227.

Thoroughgood, C. N., Padilla, A., Hunter, S. T., & Tate, B. W. (2012). The susceptible circle: A taxonomy of followers associated with destructive leadership. *The Leadership Quarterly, 23*, 897–917.

Tippins, N. T., Beaty, J., Drasgow, F., Gibson, W. M., Pearlman, K., Segall, D. O., & Shepard, W. (2006). Unproctored internet testing in employment settings. *Personnel Psychology, 59*, 189–225.

Tokar, D. M., Fisher, A. R., & Subich, L. M. (1998). Personality and vocational behavior: A selective review of the literature, 1993–1997. *Journal of Vocational Behavior, 53,* 115–153.

Tonidandel, S., Quiñones, M. A., & Adams, A. A. (2002). Computer-adaptive testing: The impact of test characteristics on perceived performance and test takers reactions. *Journal of Applied Psychology, 87,* 320–332.

Tornow, W. W. (1993). Perceptions or reality: Is multiperspective measurement a means or an end? *Human Resource Management, 32,* 221–230.

Tourangeau, R., & Yan, T. (2007). Sensitive questions in surveys. *Psychological Bulletin, 133,* 859–883.

Tracey, J. B., Tannenbaum, S. I., & Kavanagh, M. J. (1995). Applying trained skills on the job: The importance of the work environment. *Journal of Applied Psychology, 80,* 239–252.

Trice, H. M., & Beyer, J. M. (1993). *The cultures of work organizations.* Upper Saddle River, NJ: Prentice-Hall.

Trougakas, J. P., Jackson, C. L., & Beal, D. J. (2011). Service without a smile: Comparing the consequences of neutral and positive display rules. *Journal of Applied Psychology, 96,* 350–362.

Truxillo, D. M., & Bauer, T. N. (2011). Applicant reactions to organizations and selection systems. In S. Zedeck (Ed.), *APA handbook of industrial and organizational psychology* (Vol. 2, pp. 379–397). Washington, DC: APA.

Tuckman, B. W. (1965). Developmental sequences in small groups. *Psychological Bulletin, 63,* 384–399.

Tuckman, B. W., & Jensen, M. C. (1977). Stages of small-group development revisited. *Group and Organization Studies, 2,* 419–427.

Turner, M. E., & Horvitz, T. (2001). The dilemma of threat: Group effectiveness and ineffectiveness under adversity. In M. E. Turner (Ed.), *Groups at work* (pp. 445–470). Mahwah, NJ: Erlbaum.

Turnley, W. H., & Feldman, D. C. (2000). Re-examining the effects of psychological contract violations: Unmet expectations and job dissatisfaction as mediators. *Journal of Applied Psychology, 84,* 594–601.

Tyson, P. R., & Vaughn, R. A. (1987, April). Drug testing in the work place: Legal responsibilities. *Occupational Health and Safety,* 24–36.

U. S. Department of Labor (2006). *The Department of Labor's 2005 findings on the worst forms of child labor.* Washington, DC: Bureau of International Labor Affairs.

U. S. Department of Labor (2010). Mass layoff statistics. Bureau of Labor Statistics. *www.usdol.gov.* Accessed July 25, 2010.

U. S. Department of Labor (2014). *www.bls.gov/ooh/fastest-growing.htm.* Accessed January 16, 2014.

U. S. Safe Harbor Framework (2014). *www.export.gov/safe harbor.* Accessed January 12, 2014.

Uggerslev, K. L., & Sulsky, L. M. (2008).Using frame-of-reference training to understand the implications of rater idiosyncrasy for rating accuracy. *Journal of Applied Psychology, 93,* 711–719.

Ugrin, J. C., & Pearson, J. M. (2013). The effects of sanctions and stigmas on cyberloafing. *Computers in Human Behavior, 29,* 812–820.

Ullén, F., de Manzano, Ö., Almeida, R., Magnusson, P. K. E., Pedersen, N. L., Nakamura, J., Csikszentmihalyi, M., & Madison, G. (2012). Proneness for psychological flow in everyday life: Associations with personality and intelligence. *Personality and Individual Differences, 52,* 167–172.

United Nations Global Compact (2008). *United Nations Global Compact.* Retrieved September 15, 2010 from *http://www.unglobalcompact.org*

Vacharkulksemsuk, T., & Fredrickson, B. L. (2013). Looking back and glimpsing forward: The broaden-and-build theory of positive emotions as applied to organizations. In A. B. Bakker (Ed.), *Advances in positive organizational psychology,* (Vol. 1, pp. 45–60). Bingley, UK: Emerald.

Van Buren, M. (2001). *The 2001 ASTD state of the industry report.* Alexandria, VA: ASTD.

Van De Water, T. J. (1997). Psychology's entrepreneurs and the marketing of industrial psychology. *Journal of Applied Psychology, 82,* 486–499.

van der Rijt, J., van de Wiel, M. W. J., Van den Bossche, P., Segers, M. S. R., & Gijselaers, W. H. (2012). Contextual antecedents of informal feedback in the workplace. *Human Resource Development Quarterly, 23,* 233–257.

van Dyck, C., Frese, M., Baer, M., & Sonnentag, S. (2005). Organizational error management culture and its impact on performance: A two-study replication. *Journal of Applied Psychology, 90,* 1228–1240.

van Eerde, W. (2003). A meta-analytically derived nomological network of procrastination. *Personality and Individual Differences, 35,* 1410–1418.

van Eerde, W., & Thierry, H. (1996). Vroom's expectancy models and work-related criteria: A meta-analysis. *Journal of Applied Psychology, 81,* 575–586.

van Hooft, E. A., & Noordzij, G. (2009). The effects of goal orientation on job search and reemployment: A field experiment among unemployed job seekers. *Journal of Applied Psychology, 94,* 1581–1590.

Van Hoye, G., & Lievens, F. (2009). Tapping the grapevine: A closer look at word-of-mouth as a recruitment source. *Journal of Applied Psychology, 94,* 341–352.

Van Hoye, G., & Lootens, H. (2013). Coping with unemployment: Personality, role demands, and time structure. *Journal of Vocational Behavior, 82,* 85–95.

Van Iddekinge, C. H., Ferris, G. R., Perrewé, P. L., Perryman, A. A., Blass, F. R., & Heetderks, T. D. (2009). Effects of selection and training on unit-level performance over time: A latent growth modeling approach. *Journal of Applied Psychology, 94,* 829–843.

Van Iddekinge, C. H., Morgeson, F. P., Schleicher, D. J., & Campion, M. A. (2011). Can I retake it? Exploring subgroup differences and criterion-related validity in promotion retesting. *Journal of Applied Psychology, 96,* 941–955.

Van Iddekinge, C. H., Putka, D. J., & Campbell, J. P. (2011). Reconsidering vocational interests for personnel selection: The validity of an interest-based selection test in relation to job knowledge, job performance, and continuance intentions. *Journal of Applied Psychology, 96,* 13–33.

Van Iddekinge, C. H., Roth, P. L., Raymark, P. H., & Odle-Dusseau, H. N. (2013). The criterion-related validity of integrity tests: An updated meta-analysis. *Journal of Applied Psychology, 97,* 499–530.

van Jaarsveld, D., & Poster, W. R. (2013). Call centers: Emotional labor over the phone. In A. A. Grandey, J. M. Diefendorff, & D. E. Rupp (Eds.), *Emotional labor in the 21st century* (pp. 153–173). New York: Routledge.

Van Mierlo, H., & Kleingeld, A. (2010). Goals, strategies, and group performance: Some limits of goal setting in groups. *Small Group Research, 41,* 524–555.

Vancouver, J. B. (2005). The depth of history and explanation as benefit and bane for psychological content theories. *Journal of Applied Psychology, 90,* 38–52.

Vancouver, J. B., & Morrison, E. W. (1995). Feedback inquiry: The effect of source attributes and individual differences. *Organizational Behavior and Human Decision Processes, 62,* 276–285.

Vancouver, J. B., Weinhardt, J. M., & Schmidt, A. M. (2010). A formal, computational theory of multiple-goal pursuit: Integrating goal-choice and goal-striving processes. *Journal of Applied Psychology, 95,* 985–1008.

Vecchio, R. P. (2003). Entrepreneurship and leadership: Common trends and common threads. *Human Resources and Management Review, 13,* 303–327.

Verdi, B. (2000). Psychologists seek protection under the union label. *The Industrial-Organizational Psychologist, 38*(1), 31–35.

Vidyarthi, P. R., Erdogan, B., Anand, S., Liden, R. C., & Chaudhry, A. (2014). One member, two leaders: Extending leader-member exchange theory to a dual leadership context. *Journal of Applied Psychology, 99,* 468–483.

Vigoda-Gadot, E., & Drory, A. (2006). Preface. In E. Vigoda-Gadot & A. Drory (Eds.), *Handbook of organizational politics* (pp. *ix-xx*). Cheltenham, UK: Edward Elgar.

Vinchur, A. J., & Bryan, L. L. (2012). A history of personnel selection and assessment. In N. Schmitt (Ed.), *The Oxford handbook of personnel assessment and selection* (pp. 9–30). New York: Oxford University Press.

Vinchur, A. J., & Koppes, L. L. (2011). A historical survey of research and practice in industrial and organizational psychology. In S. Zedeck (Ed.), *APA handbook of industrial and organizational psychology* (Vol. 1, pp. 3–36). Washington, DC: APA.

Viswesvaran, C., & Schmidt, F. L. (1992). A meta-analytic comparison of the effectiveness of smoking cessation methods. *Journal of Applied Psychology, 77,* 554–566.

Viteles, M. S. (1932). *Industrial psychology.* New York: W. W. Norton.

Voydanoff, P. (2005). Social integration, work-family conflict and facilitation, and job and marital quality. *Journal of Marriage and Family, 67,* 666–679.

Vroom, V. H. (1964). *Work and motivation.* New York: Wiley.

Wagner, D. T., Barnes, C. M., Lim, V. K. G., & Ferris, D. L. (2012). Lost sleep and cyberloafing: Evidence from the laboratory and a Daylight Saving Time quasi-experiment. *Journal of Applied Psychology, 97,* 1068–1076.

Wagner, S. H. (2013). Leadership and responses to organizational crises. *Industrial and Organizational Psychology: Perspectives on Science and Practice, 6,* 140–144.

Wainer, H. (2000). *Computerized adaptive testing* (2nd ed.). Mahwah, NJ: Erlbaum.

Wallace, S. R. (1965). Criteria for what? *American Psychologist, 20,* 411–417.

Walumbwa, F. O., & Wernsing, T. (2013). From transactional and transformational to authentic leadership. In M. G. Rumsey (Ed.), *The Oxford handbook of leadership* (pp. 392–400). New York: Oxford University Press.

Walumbwa, F. O., Hartnell, C. A., & Oke, A. (2010). Servant leadership, procedural justice climate, service climate, employee attitudes, and organizational citizenship behavior: A cross-level investigation. *Journal of Applied Psychology, 95,* 517–529.

Wanberg, C. R. (1997). Antecedents and outcomes of coping behaviors among unemployed and re-employed individuals. *Journal of Applied Psychology, 82,* 731–744.

Wanberg, C. R., Brasburg, G., Van Hooft, E. A., & Samtani, A. (2012). Navigating the black hole: Explicating layers of job search context and adaptational responses. *Personnel Psychology, 65,* 887–926.

Wanberg, C. R., Welsh, E. T., & Hezlett, S. A. (2003). Mentoring research: A review and dynamic process model. In J. J. Martocchio & G. R. Ferris (Eds.), *Research in personnel and human resources management* (Vol. 22, pp. 39–124). Kidlington, UK: Elsevier.

Wanberg, C. R., Zhang, Z., & Diehn, E. W. (2010). Development of the Getting Ready for Your Next Job inventory for unemployed individuals. *Personnel Psychology, 63,* 439–478.

Wanberg, C. R., Zhu, J., Kanfer, R., & Zhang, Z. (2011). After the pink slip: Applying dynamic motivation frameworks to the job search experience. *Academy of Management Journal, 55,* 261–284.

Wang, D., Waldman, D. A., & Zhang, Z. (2014). A meta-analysis of shared leadership and team effectiveness. *Journal of Applied Psychology, 99,* 181–198.

Wang, M., Liu, S., Zhan, Y., & Shi, J. (2010). Daily work-family conflict and alcohol use: Testing the cross-level moderation effects of peer drinking norms and social support. *Journal of Applied Psychology, 95,* 377–386.

Wang, X. M. W., Wong, K. F. E., & Kwong, J. Y. Y. (2010). The roles of rater goals and rater performance levels in the distortion of performance ratings. *Journal of Applied Psychology, 95,* 546–561.

Warr, P. B. (2007). *Work, happiness, and unhappiness.* Mahwah, NJ: Erlbaum.

Warr, P. B., Allan, C., & Birdi, K. (1999). Predicting three levels of training outcome. *Journal of Occupational and Organizational Psychology, 72,* 351–375.

Warr, P. B., & Clapperton, G. (2010). *The joy of work? Jobs, happiness, and you.* New York: Routledge.

Wasserman, R. (2013). Ethical issues and guidelines for conducting data analysis in psychological research. *Ethics & Behavior, 23,* 3–15.

Weatherbee, T. G. (2010). Counterproductive use of technology at work: Information & communications technologies and cyberdeviancy. *Human Resource Management Review, 20,* 35–44.

Wee, S., Newman, D. A., & Joseph, D. L. (2014). More than *g*: Selection quality and adverse impact implications of considering second-stratum cognitive abilities. *Journal of Applied Psychology, 99,* 547–563.

Weekley, J. A., & Gier, J. A. (1989). Ceilings in the reliability and validity of performance ratings: The case of expert raters. *Academy of Management Journal, 32,* 213–222.

Weick, K. E. (2001). *Making sense of the organization.* Maldon, MA: Blackwell.

Weir, T. (2010). Developing leadership in global organizations. In K. Lundby (Ed.), *Going global* (pp. 203–230). San Francisco: Jossey-Bass.

Weiss, D. J., Dawis, R. V., England, G. W., & Lofquist, L. H. (1967). *Manual for the Minnesota Satisfaction Questionnaire.* Minneapolis: Industrial Relations Center, University of Minnesota.

Weiss, H. M. (1990). Learning theory and industrial and organizational psychology. In M. D. Dunnette & L. M. Hough (Eds.), *Handbook of industrial and organizational psychology* (2nd ed., Vol. 1, pp. 171–221). Palo Alto, CA: Consulting Psychologists Press.

Weiss, H. M. (2002). Antecedents of emotional experiences at work. *Motivation and Emotion, 26,* 1–2.

Werner, J. M., & Bolino, M. C. (1997). Explaining U.S. court of appeals decisions involving performance appraisal: Accuracy, fairness, and validation. *Personnel Psychology, 50,* 1–24.

West, M. A., & Lyubovnikova, J. (2012). Real teams or pseudo teams? The changing landscape needs a better map. *Industrial and Organizational Psychology: Perspectives on Science and Practice, 5,* 25–28.

Westman, M., Shadach, E., & Keinan, G. (2013). The crossover of positive and negative emotions: The role of state empathy. *International Journal of Stress Management, 20,* 116–133.

Wherry, R. J. (1957). The past and future of criterion evaluation. *Personnel Psychology, 10,* 1–5.

Whetten, D. A., & Cameron, K. S. (1991). *Developing management skills* (2nd ed.). New York: HarperCollins.

White, F. A., Charles, M. A., & Nelson, J. K. (2008). The role of persuasive arguments in changing affirmative action attitudes and expressed behavior in higher education. *Journal of Applied Psychology, 93,* 1271–1286.

Wiesen, J. P. (1999). *WTMA: Wiesen Test of Mechanical Aptitude* (PAR edition). Odessa, FL: Psychological Assessment Resources.

Wildman, J. L., Xavier, L. F., Tindall, M., & Salas, E. (2010). Best practices for training intercultural competence in global organizations. In K. Lundby (Ed.), *Going global* (pp. 256–300). San Francisco: Jossey-Bass.

Wille, B., De Fruyt, F., & De Clerq, B. (2013). Expanding and reconceptualizing aberrant personality at work: Validity and five-factor model of aberrant personality tendencies to predict career outcomes. *Personnel Psychology, 66,* 175–225.

Williams, C. R., & Livingstone, L. P. (1994). Another look at the relationship between performance and voluntary turnover. *Academy of Management Journal, 37,* 269–298.

Williams, J. (2010). *Reshaping the work-family debate: Why men and class matter.* Cambridge, MA: Harvard University Press.

Williams, K. M., & Crafts, J. L. (1997). Inductive job analysis. In D. L. Whetzel & G. R. Wheaton (Eds.), *Applied measurement methods in industrial psychology* (pp. 51–88). Palo Alto, CA: Consulting Psychologists Press.

Wilson, M.A. (2007). A history of job analysis. In L. L. Koppes (Ed.), *Historical perspectives in industrial and organizational psychology* (pp. 210–241). Mahwah, NJ: Erlbaum.

Winkler, S., Konig, C. J., & Kleinman, M. (2010). Single-attribute utility analysis may be futile, but this can't be the end of the story: Causal chain analysis as an alternative. *Personnel Psychology, 63,* 1041–1065.

Winters, M-F. (2014). From diversity to inclusion: An inclusion equation. In B. M. Ferdman & B. R. Deane (Eds.), *Diversity at work: The practice of inclusion* (pp. 205–228). San Francisco: Jossey-Bass.

Wong, K. F. E., & Kwong, J. Y. Y. (2007). Effects of rater goals on rating patterns: Evidence from an experimental field study. *Journal of Applied Psychology, 92,* 577–585.

World Health Organization (2007). Carcinogenicity of shift-work, painting, and fire-fighting. *The Lancet Oncology, 8,* 1065–1066.

Wu, J., & LeBreton, J. M. (2011). Reconsidering the dispositional basis of counterproductive work behavior: The role of aberrant personality. *Personnel Psychology, 64,* 593–626.

Wurtz, O. (2014). An empirical investigation of the effectiveness of pre-departure and in-country cross-cultural training. *International Journal of Human Resource Management, 25,* 2088–2101.

Yates, M. D. (2009). *Why unions matter* (2nd ed.). New York: Monthly Review Press.

Yeatts, D. E., & Hyten, C. (1998). *High-performing self-managed work teams.* Thousand Oaks, CA: Sage.

Yoo, T. Y., & Muchinsky, P. M. (1998). Utility estimates of job performance as related to the Data, People, and Things parameters of work. *Journal of Organizational Behavior, 19,* 353–370.

Yost, E. (1943). *American women of science.* New York: Stokes.

Youngblood, S. A., DeNisi, A. S., Molleston, J. L., & Mobley, W. H. (1984). The impact of work environment, instrumentality beliefs, perceived labor union image, and subjective norms on union voting intentions. *Academy of Management Journal, 17,* 576–590.

Yukl, G. (1994). *Leadership in organizations* (3rd ed.). Englewood Cliffs, NJ: Prentice Hall.

Yukl, G., Wall, S., & Lepsinger, R. (1990). Preliminary report on validation of the management practices survey. In K. E. Clark & M. B. Clark (Eds.), *Measures of leadership* (pp. 223–238). West Orange, NJ: Leadership Library of America.

Zaccaro, S. J., Heinen, B., & Shuffler, M. (2009). Team leadership and team effectiveness. In E. Salas, G. F. Goodwin, & C. S. Burke (Eds.), *Team effectiveness in complex organizations* (pp. 83–112). New York: Taylor & Francis.

Zaccaro, S. J., Kemp, C., & Bader, P. (2004). Leader traits and attributes. In J. Antonakis, R. Sternberg, & A. Ciancola (Eds.), *The nature of leadership* (pp. 101–124). Thousand Oaks, CA: Sage.

Zaccaro, S. J., Marks, M. A., & DeChurch, L. A. (2011). Multiteam systems: An introduction. In S. J. Zaccaro, M. A. Marks, & L. A. DeChurch (Eds.), *Multiteam systems: An organizational form for dynamic and complex environments* (pp. 3–32). New York: Taylor & Francis.

Zakon, R. H. (2004). *Hobbes' internet timeline* (v7.0). Retrieved February 10, 2004, from *http://www.zakon.org/robert/internet/timeline*

Zalesny, M. D. (1985). Comparison of economic and noneconomic factors in predicting faculty vote preference in a union representation election. *Journal of Applied Psychology, 70,* 243–256.

Zedeck, S. (1992). Introduction: Exploring the domain of work and family careers. In S. Zedeck (Ed.), *Work, families, and organizations* (pp. 1–32). San Francisco: Jossey-Bass.

Zedeck, S. (2010). Adverse impact: History and evolution. In J. L. Outtz (Ed.), *Adverse impact: Implications for organizational staffing and high stakes selection* (pp. 3–28). New York: Routledge.

Zedeck, S., & Cascio, W. F. (1982). Performance appraisal decisions as a function of rater training and purpose of the appraisal. *Journal of Applied Psychology, 67,* 752–758.

Zellers, K. L., & Tepper, B. J. (2003). Beyond social exchange: New directions for organizational citizenship behavior theory and research. In J. J. Martocchio & G. R. Ferris (Eds.), *Research in personnel and human resources management* (Vol. 22, pp. 395–424). Kidlington, UK: Elsevier.

Zhao, H., & Seibert, S. E. (2006). The big five personality dimensions and entrepreneurial status: A meta-analytic review. *Journal of Applied Psychology, 91,* 259–271.

Zhao, H., Wayne, S. J., Glibkowski, B. C., & Bravo, J. (2007). The impact of psychological contract breach on work-related outcomes: A meta-analysis. *Personnel Psychology, 60,* 647–680.

Zickar, M. J. (2001). Using personality inventories to identify thugs and agitators: Applied psychology's contribution to the war against labor. *Journal of Vocational Behavior, 59,* 149–164.

Zickar, M. J. (2003). Remembering Arthur Kornhauser: Industrial psychology's advocate of worker well-being. *Journal of Applied Psychology, 88,* 363–369.

Zickar, M. J., & Gibby, R. E. (2007). Four persistent themes throughout the history of I-O psychology in the United States. In L. L. Koppes (Ed.), *Historical perspectives in industrial and organizational psychology* (pp. 61–80). Mahwah, NJ: Erlbaum.

Zickar, M. J., & Kostek, J. A. (2013). History of personality testing within organizations. In N. D. Christiansen & R. P. Tett (Eds.), *Handbook of personality at work* (pp. 173–190). New York: Routledge.

Zieky, M. J. (2001). So much has changed: How the setting of cutscores has evolved since the 1980s. In G. J. Cizek (Ed.), *Setting performance standards: Concepts, methods, and perspectives* (pp. 19–52). Mahwah, NJ: Erlbaum.

Zimmerman, B. J. (1995). Self-efficacy and educational development. In A. Bandura (Ed.), *Self-efficacy in changing societies* (pp. 202–231). New York: Cambridge.

Author Index

Page numbers in *italics* indicate References section.

515

Subject Index

Page numbers in **bold** indicate where the entry is defined in the margin.